SCHOOL AND SOCIETY

Historical and Contemporary Perspectives

THIRD EDITION

Steven E. Tozer
University of Illinois, Chicago

Paul C. Violas
University of Illinois,
Urbana-Champaign

Guy Senese
Northern Arizona University

McGraw Hill

Boston, Massachusetts Burr Ridge, Illinois Dubuque, Iowa
Madison, Wisconsin New York, New York San Francisco, California St. Louis, Missouri

McGraw-Hill

A Division of The ***McGraw·Hill*** *Companies*

SCHOOL AND SOCIETY:

Historical and Contemporary Perspectives

Photo Credits appear on page 511, and on this page by reference.

This book was printed on acid-free paper.

2 3 4 5 6 7 8 9 0 DOW DOW 90 98

ISBN 0-07-065331-3

Editorial director: Jane Vaicunas
Sponsoring editor: Beth Kaufman
Editorial assistant: Adrienne D'Ambrosio
Marketing manager: Dan Loch
Project manager: Alisa Watson
Production supervisor: Karen Thigpen
Designer: Kiera Cunningham
Compositor: Carlisle Communications
Typeface: 10/12 Palatino
Printer: R.R. Donnelley & Sons Company

Library of Congress Cataloging-in-Publication Data

Tozer, Steven.
School and Society: historical and contemporary perspectives
Steven E. Tozer, Paul C. Violas, Guy Senese.—3rd ed.
p. cm.
Includes bibliographical references and index.
ISBN 0-07-065331-3 (alk. paper)
1. Educational sociology—United States. 2. Education—United States—History. I. Violas, Paul C. II. Senese, Guy III. Title
LC191.4.T69 1998
306.43'2'0973—dc21 97-29577

http://www.mhcollege.com

ABOUT THE AUTHORS

STEVEN E. TOZER is Professor of Education and chair of Policy Studies in the College of Education at the University of Illinois, Chicago, where he teaches preservice and graduate level courses in Social Foundations of Education. Prior to this he was on the faculty of the University of Illinois, Urbana-Champaign for 12 years, serving as the Head of the Department of Curriculum and Instruction from 1990 to 1994. He taught the preservice course in Social Foundations, for which he received the college and the campus awards for Excellence in Undergraduate Instruction.

Professor Tozer has been Chair of the Committee on Academic Standards and Accreditation for the American Education Studies Association and Chair of the Committee on Executive Affairs for the Philosophy of Education Society. He also served on the Board of Examiners for the National Council on Accreditation of Teacher Education. He has written for such journals as *Education Theory, Education Studies, Educational Foundations,* and *Teachers College Record* and is coauthor of two books on social foundations.

Professor Tozer completed his A.B. in German at Dartmouth College, his M.Ed. in Elementary and Early Childhood Education at Loyola University of Chicago, and his Ph.D. at the University of Illinois, Urbana-Champaign. He has taught at the early childhood, elementary, and secondary levels.

PAUL C. VIOLAS is Professor of History of Education in the College of Education at the University of Illinois, Urbana-Champaign. During the last decade, he has received the College of Education Award for Excellence in Undergraduate Teaching, the College Career Teaching Award, and the University's Luckman Award for Undergraduate Teaching. During the 1970s, with the aid of his graduate students, he designed the social foundations of education course on which this text is based. Currently, over 40 of his former advisees and graduate assistants are teaching at colleges and universities in the U.S. and Europe.

Professor Violas received his baccalaureate and master's degrees in history at the University of Rochester, where he later received his Ed.D. degree. He taught secondary school social studies for 6 years before later embarking on his career in higher education. In addition to teaching and lecturing assignments in England and Greece, he served for 6 years as Associate Dean of Graduate and Undergraduate programs at the College of Education, University of Illinois, Urbana-Champaign. He has been a regular contributor to such journals as *Education Theory, Teachers College Record, Harvard Education Review,* and *The History Teacher.* He is also the coauthor of *Roots of Crisis* and the author of *The Training of the Urban Working Class.*

GAETANO (GUY) SENESE is Associate Professor of Educational Leadership and Foundations at the Center for Excellence in Education at Northern Arizona University in Flagstaff. From 1988 to 1997, Professor Senese taught Philosophy of Education and Social Foundations of Education at Northern Illinois University. He received his Ph.D. in Education at the University of Illinois, Urbana-Champaign. His interests include social philosophy and education, the history of American education, critical theory in education, and Native American education. He taught school in Champaign, Illinois, and at the Rough Rock Demonstration School on the Navajo Reservation in Arizona.

Professor Senese has published in *Education Theory, Educational Foundations, Harvard Education Review,* and *Journal of Thought.* He is also the author of two books, one a study of Native American self-determination, and, most recently, *Simulation, Spectacle, and the Ironies of Educational Reform.* He is a past president of the Midwest History of Education Society.

CONTENTS IN BRIEF

CONTENTS

PREFACE

School and Society: Historical and Contemporary Perspectives, 3e is designed for courses in teacher education commonly labeled School and Society, Social Foundations of Education, History and Philosophy of Education, or simply Foundations of Education. Such courses may be offered at the introductory or more advanced levels in teacher education programs, at undergraduate or graduate levels. Normally, their purpose is to provide students with a broad, interdisciplinary examination of the school-society relationship in America and of the many issues imbedded in this relationship. More specifically, the intention is to help prepare teachers who are able to reflect critically on the social significance of their teaching practices as well as the institutional goals, policies and practices that surround and shape classroom practice. With this in mind, we built the following features into our text.

Historical-Contemporary Analysis Understanding contemporary educational processes, we believe, requires understanding their historical origins: how and why they first arose and then developed into their present forms. For this reason history plays a central role throughout this work. In Part 1, we analyze the relationships among the political economy, the prevailing ideology, and the educational practices of each major period in the development of American public education. For each period, we show how the intersection of these forces influenced one or more perennial issues in education that still confront us as we move into the 21st century. We try to show how a significant change in any one of these components (political-economic conditions, prevailing ideology, or educational practice) inevitably reflects or stimulates changes in the others. Students become familiar with these connections as they revisit them in different historical settings.

Whereas Part 1 examines perennial school-society issues in terms of their historical origins in American history, Part 2 provides a contemporary analysis of these same issues by discussing such questions as, What is the relationship between liberty and literacy? Is the professionalization of teaching good for education? What are the purposes of public education in a democratic society? Who should control the curriculum, and for what purposes? To what degree can schools promote social equality? What types of curriculum and teaching practices are most effective and most equitable? Thus each enduring issue receives a two-part, historical-contemporary examination. The result is a highly integrated text, in which each chapter in Part 1 has a matching chapter in Part 2.

Diversity-Equity Focus Today's educators must confront the complex question of how to provide an increasingly diverse school population with an education that is both equitable and of high quality. Consequently, we have made this issue a major focus of our text. In Part 1, Chapters 4, 5, 6, and 7 examine the histories of four educationally under-served groups in this country: the working class, women, African-Americans, and Native Americans. Then, in Part 2, Chapters 11, 12, and 13 analyze the educational status of these and other minority groups in contemporary America. The related themes of diversity and equity as seen in various forms (racial, ethnic, cultural, language, gender, and ability) constitute possibly the most important issue facing schools in the 21st century. Consequently, we have given it heavy emphasis.

Critical Thinking Skills Since good teachers must be able to think critically, we wanted to produce a text that actively promotes critical thinking skills within an educational context. Most foundations texts espouse this goal, but few accomplish it. To do so means (1) providing the basic conceptual tools needed for analytical inquiry, (2) demonstrating their use within the text, and (3) providing readers with opportunities to practice such analysis as they bring new understanding and past experiences to bear on primary source readings. Consequently, we have structured our text as follows. First, Chapter 1 presents six analytical concepts (social theory, political economy, schooling, training, education, and ideology) that we have found to be especially useful in understanding American public education. Next, we have systematically demonstrated their usefulness by organizing chapter discussions around them. Both the historical chapters in Part 1 and the contemporary chapters in Part 2 utilize these concepts. Finally, at the end of each chapter, we have provided original source readings that students are asked to critically evaluate using these terms. In short, each chapter models the analytical use of these terms, while end-of-chapter readings and questions provide an opportunity for their use. *In fact, it is our hope that reflective readers will use their own experiences and viewpoints to challenge the authors' analyses whenever there seems cause to do so.*

Text Integration Rather than producing a text of independent chapters on discrete topics in education, we have produced one that is highly integrated. We have already described two of the primary mechanisms used to accomplish this: (1) the use of perennial issues as a device for integrating the book's historical and contemporary parts and (2) the use of end-of-chapter readings as vehicles for applying (thereby mastering) the analytic terms. In addition, the analytic framework used throughout the text, especially the political-economic and ideological discussions, provide integrative threads rarely found in foundations texts. If, for example, the ideology sections found within chapters 2 through 15 are read together, they provide a minihistory of ideological thought from colonial times to the present.

Changes in This Edition The third edition of *School and Society* includes a number of significant changes. Chief among these are the following:

- Four new primary source readings have been included in this edition to engage students in critical reading of more current professional literature. The new primary source reading for Chapter 7 provides an opportunity for students to read contemporary Native American views on education appropriate to a people trying to preserve their cultural traditions while seeking to become proficient in the ways of the dominant culture. Chapter 10, on the profession of teaching, presents material from the influential policy report by the National Commission on Teaching and America's Future. Current research on bilingual education and English as a Second Language is included in the primary source reading for Chapter 13, about meeting the challenges of diversity in contemporary schools. Finally, Chapter 14 concludes with a 1997 state-by-state assessment of the quality of education in the U.S., prepared by the editors of *Education Week.*
- New chapter sections have been written for five chapters, most of these in response to suggestions made by students and faculty who use the text. In addition to updated data and minor revisions throughout the book, the five extensive new sections introduce substantially new material. The first is an original treatment of educator Emma Willard in Chapter 5, on the education of girls and women. Next, a section on the significance of technology has been written for Chapter 9, about liberty and literacy in contemporary culture. An entirely new discussion of legal and extralegal influences on schooling has been written for Chapter 10 by educational law specialist Julius Menacker. Chapter 12, on the nature of diversity in contemporary schools, has extended the sections on Asian American and Hispanic students. Finally, Chapter 14 on school reform has a new section on such current trends as school choice, technology, and parent involvement.
- ***Enhanced integration.*** We have continued to strengthen the integration of the two parts of the book (historical and contemporary) in

terms of their content coverage and their chapter titles and subheadings. Thus instructors have the option of teaching the chapters either in a conventional front-to-back sequence or as matched pairs in any sequence they wish.

Acknowledgments This book originated in Educational Policy Studies 201, a required undergraduate course in social foundations of education at the University of Illinois in Urbana-Champaign. The course was originally designed by Paul Violas and his graduate students in 1975 and was subsequently modified by Steve Tozer and his graduate teaching assistants from 1982 to 1990. Consequently, a great many doctoral students have contributed, over the years, to developing that course and the first two editions of this text.

We also gratefully acknowledge the important contributions to the third edition made by students and colleagues. We wish especially to thank Professors Mary Bay, Victoria Chou, Julius Menacker, Flora Rodriguez-Brown, Karen Sakash, and Connie Yowell, of the University of Illinois at Chicago; and UIC graduate students Alyson Boner and Margaret Klein.

Our most important partners in this effort have been those who wrote chapters for our first edition in their areas of expertise: James Anderson, Chapter 6; Steve Preskill, Chapter 8; Kal Alston, Chapter 10; and Robert Carson, Chapter 13. These faculty, all of whom once taught or currently are teaching at the University of Illinois at Urbana-Champaign, drafted a third of the original volume and gave it a depth of insight it would not otherwise have had. The chapters by Anderson and Preskill have remained virtually intact in this third edition, and the Alston and Carson chapters have been updated, as have all chapters in Part 2.

Steven E. Tozer
Paul C. Violas
Guy Senese

Introduction: Understanding School and Society

The public schools are perhaps the most familiar but the least understood institution in our society. Most Americans spend over twelve years of their lives attending public schools and later, as adults, confront a wide array of school-related issues. School board elections, school tax referendums, PTA meetings, and their own children's school experiences all require immediate personal attention.

Individuals and mass media often express concern about the overall quality of our society's public school system. Is it equipping our young to support themselves in a changing economy? Is it promoting an equitable society by educating all our students? Is it equipping them with the skills and attitudes needed to live in a society that is increasingly diverse and pluralistic? Is it teaching them to respect and protect an increasingly endangered environment? In short, how well does our nation's public school system serve the major needs of our society?

These are complicated questions open to competing interpretations, and not just any interpretation will do. Schools are complex institutions with varied and intricate relationships to their surrounding communities, and a great deal of scholarship has been conducted in an effort to understand these relationships. Explaining why children from some social and economic groups tend to perform better than others in schools, for example, may require reliance on a variety of historical, sociological, and theoretical arguments that most editorial writers and newspaper readers don't have at hand. Such explanations are not a part of commonsense knowledge, but they can and should be a part of a teacher's professional expertise.

The development of such professional levels of interpretation and understanding is a major purpose of this text. Achieving such understanding, however, requires that students engage not in "learning the text," but in actively inquiring into important questions about the purposes and consequences of education and schooling. To assist in this inquiry, this text uses a number of analytic concepts, or tools of inquiry.

TOOLS OF INQUIRY

These tools of inquiry are six analytic concepts: social theory, schooling, training, education, political economy, and ideology. Each of these will be examined, and then three will be arranged into an analytic framework. The final part of this chapter will provide two historical illustrations of the analytic framework in action, one dealing with education in European feudal society and the other dealing with education in classical Athens. The following chapters will then use this analytic framework to examine the evolution of American public schools (Part 1 of this textbook) and some of the most significant contemporary issues facing the public school system (Part 2).

Social Theory

The term "theory" is one of the most maligned among educationists. Frequently, educators in public schools and in colleges of education proclaim that they are interested in "practice," not "theory." Such announcements should make us pause to consider what the term "theory" means. It does not really have a complex meaning. Very simply, a theory is an interpretation and explanation of phenomena. A social theory is an attempt to make sense of and explain social phenomena. A theory attempts to answer the questions how and why. It is not something separate from "reality" and "practice"; rather, it attempts to explain reality and practice. Thus, to say that we are "not interested in theory" is to say that we are not interested in knowing how or why something occurs.

We might be interested, for example, in the rise in public school attendance during the past century. Why did increasing percentages of American children attend school for increasing lengths of time? One explanation (i.e., theory) is that the increase reflected the rise in democratic sentiment and greater potential for social mobility in the United States. An alternative theory emphasizes economic factors, such as the decreased dependence on child labor both on farms and in factories, accompanied by the need for adult workers with specialized skills (e.g., clerical training) and work force behaviors (e.g., punctuality).

These potentially conflicting theories raise an important question: How do we judge theories? Is it simply a matter of opinion or personal taste? If there were not adequate ways to evaluate theories, then those who assert that they are not interested in theory might be on sounder ground. Fortunately, there are criteria and procedures we can use to intelligently accept or reject a theory. First, we ask whether the theory is internally consistent. That is, are there contradictions within the theory itself? If so, the explanatory power of the theory is weakened. Second, how well does the theory account for the data (i.e., information) we have amassed about what we are trying to understand? Few theories, if any, will be able to account for all the data; nevertheless, the more data it can account for, the better the theory. Third, how well does a particular theory agree with other theories we have accepted that relate to what we are trying to understand? A theory that conflicts less with other theories is generally judged as more satisfactory.

A cautionary note to students: When we have subjected our theories to these evaluative procedures, we should not believe that we have achieved something called Truth. The notion that humans can achieve absolute, eternal truth is an ambitious goal that western civilization has long cherished. It found expression in fifth-century Athens with Plato, in the early Christian era with Augustine of Hippo, and in the 18th century with the Enlightenment philosophers. The evolution of 20th-century science has made us less optimistic about discovering absolute truth. This is especially so in the human sciences. When we argue that it is possible to judge theories, we are simply asserting that some theories explain social phenomena better than others, not that the ones we judge as better are absolutely true. Social theories will always need further refinement. What we seek are the best available explanations upon which to base our understanding and our most enlightened choices for social action.

Our theory-based explanations are not infallible, but neither are they "just an interpretation," if by that we mean that they are no better or worse than any other explanation. Our explanations may be strong or weak, more valid or less valid, depending on how well they stand up to critical investigation, that is, how thoroughly and consistently they explain the phenomena we are trying to understand. *Throughout this book, it is important to remember that you are reading neither "the absolute truth" nor "just another interpretation."* Instead, you are reading the best efforts of scholars who are trying to understand both the historical and the contemporary relationships between schooling and society. You should read these theoretical explanations critically, asking yourself if they do, in fact, help you to better understand your own experience with schools and the wider culture.

Schooling

Schooling is also a relatively simple concept, but one that is often confused with education. Schooling simply refers to the totality of experiences that occur within the institution called school, not all of which are educational. Schooling includes all the activities that take place within the curriculum of a school—that is, within courses and programs of study. It also includes the activities called "extracurricular," such as sports, clubs, school newspapers, and other activities not included within the formal curriculum. In addition, schooling involves teaching and learning not included in either curricular or extracurricular activities. This type of learning occurs in the school's "hidden curriculum" and is generally not spoken of as curriculum by school authorities. Such learning often occurs because of the way schools are structured: their organization, architecture, time management, teaching methods, and authority structures. In the "hidden curriculum," students learn powerful "lessons," for example, about punctuality, respect for and even fear of authority, time organization, and competition for limited rewards.[1]

Focusing on schooling as opposed to focusing more broadly on education can reveal the relation of the government to schooling. State governments provide for school buildings and establish length of school terms and teachers' qualifications. Those of us who have always believed that there was some special connection between public (i.e., state) schools and democracy should remember that for most of Western history this was not the case. Democratic Athens and republican Rome did not have state schools. For most of Western history, state schooling supported nondemocratic governments. The state schools of Sparta, the Roman empire, the German states during the Reformation, and until recently, 20th-century Soviet Russia all utilized state schooling for nondemocratic ends. All these state schools sacrificed individualism, creativity, and independent judgment in the interest of "citizenship."

Training

Training, like schooling, is often confused with education. Training may be described as a set of experiences provided to some organism (human or not) in an attempt to render its responses predictable according to the goals of the trainer. With the development of behavioral psychology in the 20th century, training techniques have become more sophisticated and have taken on the aura of science. The increased efficiency of training techniques has led many astute social observers to become somewhat pessimistic regarding the future of creative individualism. This pessimism can perhaps best be seen in the "anti-utopia" novels of this century, such as Aldous Huxley's *Brave New World* and George Orwell's *1984.* What these anti-utopian writers fear is the vast potential for social control and manipulation inherent in training techniques. The potential for indoctrination certainly should be of concern for all educators. However, this does not mean that all training is to be shunned. For example, when approaching a busy intersection, most motorists would hope that all other drivers approaching that intersection have been trained to automatically use their brakes when they see either a red or yellow traffic light. We all want that response to be predictable. Other examples of the value of training include memorizing the multiplication tables and all irregular verbs in Spanish. At a more ambitious level, we might refer to a musician's training in classical piano, or a doctor's medical training—both of which indicate preparation for specific roles. Training, then, has an important but specifically limited value in both schooling and education.

Education

Education is related to training but more difficult to explain. One of the more useful explanations was offered by Abraham Flexner in 1927:

> Between education and training there exists a vast distinction. Education is an intellectual and spiritual process. It has to do with opening the windows of the human mind and the human soul. It involves the effort to understand, to comprehend, to be sensitive to ideas, aspirations, and interests to which the individual might otherwise be indifferent. Not so with training. Training connotes improved ability to do something, without deepened understanding, widened sympathy, or heightened aspirations. One

> can train a brick layer to lay three hundred bricks instead of one hundred and fifty. One can train a stenographer to increase her speed and skill. . . . But one educates in the realm of thought, feeling, and intelligence. Occasionally, to be sure, training must precede education. One must be trained to read, before one can become educated in literature; one must be trained to add and multiply before one can be educated in the higher mathematics; one must be trained to use a fever thermometer, before one can be educated as a physician. But always training concerns itself with tools and devices, while education concerns itself with something that has intellectual or spiritual content and motive. Training is means; education is end.[2]

Although parts of Flexner's explanation of education conflict with our view (one can certainly talk about medical training to mean medical education, for example), he does identify significant differences between education and training. Education certainly involves some training. Moreover, it involves some of the processes that make communal living possible. But it is more. Education involves reason, the intellect, intuition, creativity. It is a process or set of experiences which allows humans to "create" themselves. The educated person's responses to a problematic situation will be based on trying to understand and make calculations about that situation, hypothesizing possible outcomes, and choosing among possible courses of action. Education builds on the successes and failures of ancestors, whereas training tends to reproduce the response(s) of the trainer. Education produces responses which the educator may not have even contemplated.

Because of these differences between training and education, we typically think of training as preparing a person for a specific social or economic role, while education seeks to prepare an individual for a wide range of roles. For example, we typically speak of a nurse's training, or a boxer's or a musician's training, emphasizing by

Training involves learning how to do something specific, such as how to operate a computer. Education involves learning how to think and create solutions and often incorporates specific training skills. The student here is composing a story, which requires prior training on the computer.

this term the skills and understandings needed for each specific role. To be educated, however, is to develop a wide range of human capacities that equip one to fill a variety of roles in one's culture: as a worker, a citizen, a parent, a person who relates ethically to others, a person who uses leisure in productive ways, and so on. Think about it: would you rather be trained or educated—or both?

Political Economy

Political economy is an old-fashioned concept that includes the social, cultural, economic, political, and demographic dimensions of a society. To study the political economy of a particular society is to examine how that society is organized—how its structures, processes, and physical and mental resources give it its character and distinctiveness. The school, like the family, the police force, and the banking industry, is one of the institutions that make up the political economy of American society. This book will focus on analyzing those aspects of the political economy which are of special relevance to American public schools. Crucial to the method of analysis is the assumption that when any part of the political economy experiences significant change, other parts of it are likely to be affected.

Ideology

Ideology, like education, is a frequently used concept that is difficult to define. Every society explains and justifies its social, political, and economic arrangements and its relations to the outside world in terms of what its members understand and value about the world. Members of one society might explain and justify their "free enterprise" system on the basis of beliefs in the importance of private property and individual freedom. Members of another society might justify their military dictatorship on the grounds that social order and control are more fundamental to human well-being than is equality or civil rights. In each case, those who are doing the explaining and justifying are revealing the underlying values that support their respective ideologies.

It may be useful to think of an ideology as an interpretive lens that a society looks through to organize its experiences. Although the notion of a "system of ideas" is no doubt too simplistic and too neat, it holds some value for understanding the term.

Ideology does not refer primarily to how individuals think; rather, it refers to the beliefs, value systems, and understandings of social groups. In this book, the term "ideology" will refer to the beliefs, values, and ways of understanding that guide policy formation in any society and that are *intended* to explain and justify the society's institutions and social arrangements—intended, because the ideas and values which explain and justify major social institutions may not be satisfactory to all members of society. The ideology which becomes dominant in a society is almost always articulated by those who derive the most power, goods, and prestige from the existing social organization. Generally, those who benefit most from the social arrangement are more satisfied with the "dominant" ideology than are group members who benefit less. Those who wield less power or are oppressed by society understandably are less satisfied by justifications of existing social arrangements. In many cases, such groups may embrace conflicting ideologies or variants of the dominant ideology. The result can be social unrest and even revolution. Colonial Americans of Benjamin Franklin's persuasion, for example, shared the same society, but not the same ideology, as loyalists to the king. Similarly, slaves and masters in the pre-Civil War South shared the same society, but usually not the same ideology.

Even in relatively stable societies in which social unrest does not approach revolution, it should not be assumed that the dominant ideology is fully endorsed by all social groups and economic classes. It is safe to assume that a society's dominant economic class can explain and justify the prevailing social arrangements according to the dominant ideology, but such explanations may not accurately reflect the views of people from less privileged economic classes. The police force in U.S. society, for example, may be understood by middle and upper classes as an institution that benevolently enforces the law and protects the rights and well-being of all members of society. People from less privileged economic classes, however, may have experienced the police as an organization that uses its special powers to harass and interfere with their lives in order to protect the advantages of wealth.

This does not mean that various segments of society necessarily develop entirely different ideologies; often they share important parts of the dominant ideology. The example does suggest, however, that all classes do not necessarily accept all parts of the ideology that the dominant class most fully articulates.

The history of the term "ideology" is marked by many different uses, but all fall more or less into two main categories: (1) ideology as "false belief," and (2) ideology as a universal condition that underlies all social understanding. Ideology as false belief is illustrated by the statement "Of course they don't understand freedom; they're blinded by their ideology." The underlying assumption here is that ideology is something that distorts "their" vision and prohibits understanding. Central to this notion is that ideology is something that "others," especially our opponents, have, while we are free of ideology and, consequently, are able to see things clearly. However, this is not the view of ideology used in this text.

The view employed here is that ideologies are embedded in all societies, that they facilitate the organization of a society's perceptions and understandings, and that it is important to recognize ideologies, both our own and others. To argue that ideologies are embedded in all societies is not to say that we cannot make judgments about ideologies or that the values of a given ideology are as "good" or as true as those of any other. We can, for example, use our own ideology to judge the dominant ideology of Nazi Germany as being morally corrupt. We need not hesitate to make moral judgments just because we recognize they are grounded in our own ideological framework. Without the values and beliefs that our own cultural history provides us, we would not be able to make moral judgments at all. Nevertheless, the beliefs and values of any culture should be critically examined for their internal consistency and for their consequences in practice.

Schooling plays an important role in teaching and legitimating a society's ideology. The ideology served by the public school is almost inevitably the dominant ideology of the surrounding society. This suggests both potential strengths and weaknesses in schooling. Whereas schooling may help people share in the life of their society, it may also help blind them to problems within it. Schooling prepares people to participate in a society's political economy and to share its dominant ideology, but by doing so, it may further disadvantage those from the less-advantaged groups while contributing to the already privileged position of the more powerful.

This ideological sharing need not be done in a mindless and uncritical manner that "indoctrinates" students into beliefs and values that might better be questioned. However, the danger is always there. At the heart of the democratic ideal is the belief that children will be afforded the opportunity to mature into independently thinking adults who can analyze and criticize their own society and its dominant ideology, who can recognize where its ways of thinking and ways of life are inadequate and in need of improvement. One of the aims of this book is to employ the above analytic concepts to help students develop just that kind of critical understanding.

ANALYTIC FRAMEWORK

The relationship between American society and its public schools can best be understood by examining the relationship among three of the six analytic terms: political economy, ideology, and schooling. The relationship is pictured schematically in Exhibit 1.1.

A basic premise of this analytic framework is that an ecological relationship exists among the three components. Any significant change or disturbance in one of them will set off a ripple effect through the others until some new state of equilibrium is achieved. Put another way, this framework shows how political economy (social conditions) and ideology influence each other and how both influence educational practice. It also shows how educational practice in turn influences a society's ideology and political economy. This is not to claim that each of these elements is equally powerful in bringing about changes in the others. It seems clear, for example, that changes in the political economy are more influential in causing

EXHIBIT 1.1 Analytic Framework

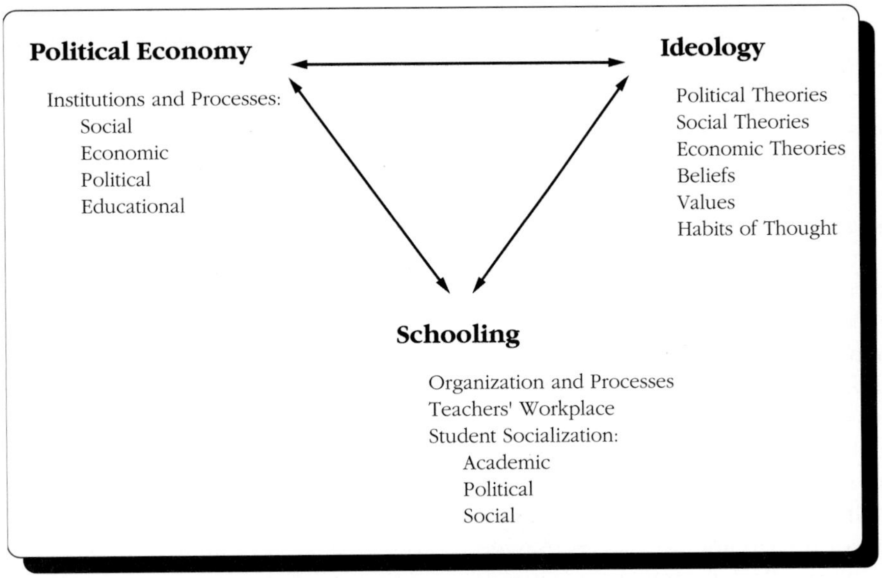

changes in the schools than vice versa. The important point here is that any one of these elements can be influenced by any one of the others.

The interactive relationship among political economy, ideology, and schooling becomes clearer when they are examined in different historical circumstances. Two different examples from very different societies, feudal Europe and classical Greece, underscore this point. Part 1 of this text will then apply the same analytical framework to each of the major historical periods of American education. Part 2 will apply it to some of the most perplexing issues facing today's schools.

APPLYING THE TERMS OF INQUIRY: TWO ILLUSTRATIONS

European Feudal Society and Education

Although feudalism took different forms in England, France, and Germany, some fundamental features existed throughout Europe. One such feature was the prevalence of rigid social hierarchies. The feudal social structure has often been likened to a pyramid in which a very few nobles and landholding clergy occupied the peak and the remainder of society filled the widening base below. The feudal economy was agrarian, and those few who owned the land ruled the serfs, who farmed the land and gave their crops as rent. The landholder's power over the serfs was absolute, unless it conflicted with the rule of nobility higher up in the hierarchy. At the very peak of this social order stood the king or queen, whose power was originally based on superior wealth and superior military force. The monarch protected his or her royal position through wealth and force, and the nobility protected their estates in the same way. Land, once granted by the monarch or acquired in battle, was passed down through family inheritance. Since there was no way a serf could acquire land, it is more accurate to say that the serfs belonged to the land they worked. Serfs simply inherited their families' status and their ties to some estate.

The feudal ideology that explained and justified this stratified political–economic order was characterized by a belief—held at least among the nobility—in the divine right of kings. In the 17th century, James I of England stated boldly that to dispute the word of a king was the same as disputing the word of God. He reasoned that kings ruled only at God's pleasure and that whatever a king did or declared was an act of God's will. The divine right of kings, therefore, constituted an explanation and justification for the absolute power of the ruler. This justification of power extended down through the dukes, counts, viscounts, and squires who ruled parcels of the king's land. The leading clergy, who themselves benefited from the extensive landholdings of the church, supported this feudal ideology.

In such a context, it is not surprising that the education of serfs differed entirely from the education of nobles and clergy at the top of the social order. The clergy was educated to read and write in order to interpret the Bible and other religious texts. Members of the nobility were educated in the refined manners and culture of the courtly aristocracy, a refinement that distinguished them from the masses of peasants throughout Europe. It has been argued that in language, values, and customs, more similarity existed among nobles from different parts of Europe than between nobles and serfs in their home regions. Serfs were not expected to read religious texts or to aspire to the cultural literacy of the courtly society. There were no economic reasons for serfs to become literate, for the barter system consisted of trading goods and services rather than calculating sums of money. Further, the nobles' accountants, not the serfs, determined the proportion of crops due to the landholding families. Similarly, the prevailing political processes required literacy for the ruling classes only, as serfs did not have a voice in the decisions affecting the feudal estates. The education of serfs was almost entirely vocational and consisted of on-the-job training to do the work of their mothers and fathers before them. Schools simply were not needed for such an education. Although numerous exceptions have been documented, this general pattern held true.

The nobles, by contrast, received formal tutoring in the homes of their parents and were occasionally sent away to schools run by famous tutors. In Italy, as early as the 1400s, male children of the nobility received instruction in Latin and Greek, rhetoric, and other "liberal studies" considered appropriate to men freed of labor for the pursuit of culture and leisure. Such educational differences between the courtly and servant classes helped to maintain the great gulf between them. Thus the hierarchical nature of feudal political economy and ideology was reflected in the hierarchy of education as well. Our theoretical perspective here is that any effort to understand feudal schooling would be enhanced by understanding that ideology and political economy.

Schooling and Culture in Classical Greece

To a great extent the courtly society of feudal Europe adopted its ideals of cultured refinement from classical Greek civilization of the fourth and fifth centuries B.C. Likewise, many contemporary educational debates can be profitably viewed through the Greek conceptions of reason, freedom, and citizenship and, especially, through the Greek contribution to the modern conception of democracy. Pluralistic democracy today continues to struggle with the status of groups who, because of class, gender, race, and ethnic prejudice, are systematically excluded from decision-making processes, just as similar groups were excluded from Athenian democracy. However, an understanding of Greek ideals in education first requires an understanding of the historical setting—the political economy and ideology—in which those ideals made sense.

The historical context from which classical educational ideals emerged is perhaps best illustrated by Athens. Although Athens was only one of many Greek city-states, it was the intellectual and creative heart of classical Greece, the home of both Plato and his teacher Socrates and the adopted home of Plato's student Aristotle, all of whose ideas have heavily influenced western educational thought.

Athenian Political Economy Athens was, first of all, a city-state: a political and geographical unit which included a central city and the surrounding villages and lands under its protection. During the fifth-century Golden Age of Athens, its population was 350,000 to 400,000 people, including citizens, slaves, metics (neither citizens nor slaves), and children. The foundation of the economy was agriculture, although there was also some limited trade, substantial handcrafting of goods for sale, and significant wealth achieved through victory in war. Most of the productive labor was done not by citizens but by metics and slaves.[3]

The most prominent Athenian social category was that of citizen. There were perhaps 50,000 to

70,000 citizens in Athens, less than one-fifth of the population, but they constituted the governing membership of the city-state. Citizens came from several social classes, ranging from the old Athenian aristocracy to peasants in remote Athenian villages. What these citizens had in common is that they were male, adult, and (with few exceptions) born in Athens. Unless they were very wealthy, they were expected to serve in the military, which the very wealthy supported through taxes rather than through combat.

Some citizens farmed, a few did craft work, and a very few pursued commerce, which was considered unseemly. All citizens owned property, sometimes in very small plots, sometimes in great tracts. The wealthiest of them did not labor on the land themselves, but had their slaves do the work. Leisure was considered very desirable since it brought an opportunity to cultivate the mind and character and to participate in the city's governance. Consequently, citizens avoided labor if they could afford to.

The most distinctive feature of citizenship was the opportunity to be a voting member of the Athenian general assembly and to serve on the legislative council. It was the business of the council—formally called the Council of Five Hundred because of the number of citizens who served on its various committees—to propose legislation to the assembly, which consisted of all citizens who wished to attend its meetings. Typically, about one citizen in eight attended the meetings of the assembly, at which time they could approve or reject the proposals of the Council of Five Hundred.

Membership on the council lasted only one year, and only two consecutive terms were permitted. Any citizen could run for council membership, but since the work and time required were considerable, the poorer citizens and those who lived far from the center of the city-state were not likely to serve. After candidates were identified, they were chosen by lottery rather than by election. Athenians considered it an important mark of their democratic way that they could trust any citizen, chosen by the luck of the draw, to serve in their legislative council.

It is probable that selection by lot came to an end shortly after Aristotle's death in 322 B.C., as the classical period drew to a close. During the time of his teacher, Plato, oligarchy (or government by the privileged few) had ruled briefly from 404 to 403 B.C. Therefore, it should not be assumed that the stable democratic processes that prevailed at the time of Plato's birth, in 429 B.C., continued unbroken throughout the Golden Age. Plato's career was a time of tension between the established aristocratic families of Athens and others who sought democracy. Although Aristotle's life spanned a more stable period of Greek democracy than Plato's, the rift between the wealthy few and the poorer common citizen remained.

Despite the achievements of the Athenians in establishing a more democratic way of life, the overwhelming majority of inhabitants were systematically excluded from citizenship. Among these were Athenian women, slaves, children, and metics. Women in Athens were not allowed to participate in public life, either socially or politically. The "proper" place for the wife of a citizen was in the household, where she could supervise domestic slaves, do household chores herself, and teach her daughters how to weave, tend garden, and so on. Women who were not wives or daughters of citizens were slaves or metics.

Despite major differences, the institution of slavery in Athens bears some similarity to the historical institution of slavery in the United States. Athenian slavery, like that in the southern United States, was chattel slavery, in which slaves were private property. This was not the case in Sparta, where slaves were state-owned. Also like U.S. slavery 2,000 years later, slavery in Athens was fundamental to the life of leisure that the upper-class citizen could expect to pursue. Without slavery, the economic and class systems could not have been what they were. This does not mean that only the wealthy owned slaves. As was later true of southern white farmers in the United States, poorer Athenians could sometimes afford one or two slaves, who might be required to labor in the house, in the field, in the shop, or in all three. Some slaves also managed farms and shops for their owners.

As was later true in the United States, the Greeks justified the institution of slavery on racist grounds. Non-Greeks were judged fit only to be slaves on the view that the Greeks were a separate and superior race of people. When Athenians defeated other Greeks in battle, men from opposing city-states were rarely made slaves, although the women and children might well be enslaved. Most slaves, however, came to Athens through a vigorous trade with eastern slave dealers.

Metics were a class of Athenian residents who were neither slaves nor citizens. They came freely to Athens from other lands and were allowed to pursue their lives, but were not granted the voting rights of citizenship. Some farmed, some became successful traders and bankers—occupations which were considered beneath the dignity of a citizen—and many became craftsmen. Some were allowed the privilege of going to battle for Athens if they were able to purchase armor, for each soldier supplied his own.

Metics worked side by side with slaves and citizens in a variety of occupations. Except for slaves, workers controlled the conditions of their labor, owning their tools, setting their own schedules, and setting the prices on finished products. Even massive projects, such as the building of the Parthenon, were contracted in small portions to individual teams of workers—citizens, slaves, and metics together—each man taking responsibility for his own piecework. On such civic projects, these craftsmen contracted individually with the city for their services, and were not employed by a large, wage-paying construction contractor, as is typically the case today. For one citizen to hire out his labor to another was, for the Athenian, a violation of his status as a free person.

The military, for which all male citizens were trained, was a significant feature of the Athenian political economy. First, of course, it protected the city-state against aggressive neighbors, such as Sparta. Second, it helped shape the classical conception of citizenship by replacing the great warrior heroes of Homer's time with multitudes of common men, who could win honor for themselves and their city. The army was supported by taxes paid by the Athenian wealthy as well as by the soldiers themselves, whose honor was to defend Athens.

Athenian Ideology To classical Athenians, the ideal life was one led in accord with Reason and Virtue. Through reason humans could perceive the true realities of the universe, and through virtue they could live in harmony with that universe. Athenians viewed the world not as a random tangle of hostile mysteries beyond human understanding, but as an orderly system governed by principles of nature that are discoverable through observation and logical reflection. They believed that humankind, particularly male Athenians, were distinctively equipped with the powers of reason that revealed the workings of the natural world. It was this rationality, they believed, that equipped common citizens to govern and be governed by turn in the Athenian democracy.

To live in accord with reason and with the virtues of Athenian culture, rather than according to arbitrary authority or in accord with momentary desires or inclinations, was, in the Athenian view, to live freely. Political democracy was important in order that each citizen might live as reason and virtue dictated—to live as one chose, and to choose wisely. Women, metics, and slaves were believed to be inferior in rational capacity, and thus their relative lack of freedom and political participation was justified by the dominant Athenian ideology.

Athenians believed that the road to virtue as well as to freedom was paved with reason. Virtue resided in acting justly, and justice was determined by reason. They believed that virtue resided in a harmony among the physical, emotional, and rational dimensions of each human being and that it was the rational dimension which must ultimately determine the proper harmony. Virtue also was to be found in moderation in all things, and the slogan "Nothing in excess" served as a guide for daily living. Athenians sought virtue in balancing the needs of the individual with the needs of society, balancing work with leisure, balancing cultivation of the mind and the body, and so on.

Athenian Schooling The schools of classical Athens clearly reflected the political–economic and ideological traits of Athenian society. Schools were available to all young male Athenians, for as citizenship was their birthright, so was the education needed for enlightened citizenship. Females and slaves did not attend schools, although they often received tutoring in order to conduct their affairs and to teach young males at home. Early schooling was not compulsory; it was simply assumed that all Athenian boys would attend in order to develop their minds and bodies for virtue and wisdom. Boys attended primary school from about age 6 to age 14, and the curriculum consisted of gymnastics, literature, and music. Those who could afford further schooling from private teachers—and those lucky enough to find teachers like Plato, who taught free of charge—went to secondary school from age 14 to age 18. There they continued their work in gymnastics, literature, and music, but also studied dialectic and philosophy as well. From age 18 to age 20, military training was compulsory for all Athenian males. The city-state's security, after all, depended on its ability to defend itself against enemy states.

The curriculum of gymnastics combined with music and literature was grounded partly in the Athenian respect for a balance of healthy mind and healthy body. It was grounded also in the view that rigorous gymnastics, including boxing and wrestling, contributed to the preparation for military service. The attention to music and literature was preparation for a life of wisdom, virtue, citizenship, and appreciation of the arts of leisure, such as poetry and drama. The school curriculum did not directly or specifically prepare Athenian youths for vocations or occupations. Plato himself noted that "technical instruction and all instruction which aimed only at money-making was vulgar and did not deserve the name education. True education aimed solely at virtue, making the child yearn to be a good citizen, skilled to rule and obey."[4]

Such a position is understandable in light of the Athenian regard for the leisurely pursuits of contemplation, politics, and appreciation of the arts. These leisurely aspirations are in turn understandable within the context of a society in which a privileged minority of citizens was able to rely upon a slave and noncitizen population to do the hard work of producing necessary goods. For Athenian citizens, the most important aspect of life was not material wealth but the development of wisdom and virtue. The school curriculum reflected these priorities in its concentration on activities of body and mind that would help develop the good man and citizen.

The case of classical Athens has been given extended treatment in order to introduce issues that will recur throughout the book. For example, the Athenian notion of democracy becomes subject to criticism when it is seen that the majority of Athenians were excluded from political decision making. This historical backdrop enables us to examine more clearly whether major segments of our own society have been, and continue to be, similarly excluded.

Further, Aristotle's notion that a democratic society seeks to provide the same basic education to all its citizens, so that all may be prepared to exercise rational judgment in ruling and being ruled, raises questions about whether our own society seeks to provide a similar education to all its citizens or whether, as in feudal Europe, different kinds of education are deemed suitable for different people according to their station in life. At issue too is the degree to which contemporary society embodies the Athenian faith that all citizens are endowed with sufficient rationality to be entrusted with public decision-making powers, and whether the primary goals of schooling include the greatest possible development of those powers for all citizens.

Finally, the Athenian notion that individual freedom should include self-governance in the workplace, not just periodic civic participation, raises questions about our limited view of what freedom means in contemporary society. Many other points of contact between Athenian and contemporary social and educational ideals exist. Several will emerge in subsequent chapters.

THE PLACE OF SOCIAL FOUNDATIONS IN TEACHER EDUCATION

Upon reading about schooling in feudal Europe or in classical Athens, you may well think, "That's all very interesting, but how is it going to make me a better teacher? Wouldn't it be better to spend this time studying methods that are successful in today's classrooms?"

While study and practice of teaching methods are a central part of strong teacher preparation, methods make sense only in particular social contexts and to achieve specific goals. These goals, for students and for the wider society, are not always agreed upon. In the last analysis, teachers must make decisions about goals and methods for themselves. How to educate teachers to make the best decisions on these matters has long been a topic of debate.

In the 1930s, for example, teacher educators at Teachers College, Columbia University, began developing a new program of study for school teachers and administrators called "social foundations of education." Rather than have teachers and administrators study such fields as philosophy of education, history of education, and sociology of education in isolation from one another, the scholars at Teachers College believed that school practitioners would benefit most if they integrated the study of all these fields around perennial school–society issues. Who should be educated? What knowledge and values should be taught? Who should control the curriculum and for what purposes? When, where, and how should education be delivered? To study such issues, they believed, required historical perspective, philosophical insights, and sociological knowledge. The problems to be understood, they reasoned, were multidimensional and did not fit neatly into any one of those disciplines. To study schooling required studying the social underpinnings (social foundations) of education, and they believed that the better teachers understood the larger society in which schools are embedded, the better they would understand the particular school problems they faced. The schools, in their view, were an important *expression* of the surrounding society—expressing its political and economic systems as well as its ideological commitments.

The authors of this text share this view. It is our conviction that teachers should have the best possible understanding of the relations between their schools and the larger society in which their schools are embedded. We think teachers need more than *training* in how to deliver a set curriculum or technique, though such training can be valuable. Teachers also need to be *educated* as critical thinkers who have the ability to diagnose unique and complicated situations and to create original solutions to these problems. Such professional education should take place in all components of a strong teacher education program. We believe that the purpose of studying social foundations of education is to equip teachers to make sense of classroom situations by understanding the larger social context that surrounds and shapes what goes on in their classrooms.

Study in the social foundations of education, then, provides background information about school–society relationships that helps teachers contextualize classroom events and thereby enables them to better understand and adjust their teaching practices. For example, unless you understand the effects that school culture can have on students from minority cultures in the United States, you may not be able to discriminate between a child with a learning disability and a child whose home culture differs so markedly from that of the school that he or she encounters academic and social adjustment problems. When is it fair to have different educational goals for different students, and when might different goals categorize students and lead to discriminatory practices on the part of teachers or other students?

The purpose of this book is, in part, to give you practice in thinking through such issues as these. By reflectively engaging such social and educational issues (including their historical origins), you will be developing as an educational thinker and decision maker, one whose ability to define and solve school problems is more highly developed than those of the everyday citizen who has not received such specialized education. Two examples illustrate these points.

The Meaning of Democracy in Educational Practice

One illustration of how teachers can apply social foundations knowledge to their teaching practice concerns the aims of teaching. Teachers typically accept the notion that a major goal of their teaching is to prepare citizens for life in a democratic society, and most teachers believe that their teaching contributes to achieving this goal. Yet college students preparing to teach are rarely given an opportunity to engage in a sustained study of what life in a democratic society really means or how to go about educating students for participation in such a society. To understand the meaning of democracy and to fit students for life in a democratic society require careful analysis. It is obvious, for example, that school systems in all cultures seek to fit people to their surrounding societies. It is not so obvious, however, that in a democratic society this fitting process should involve equipping people to think critically about the degree to which their own society is, in fact, democratic and to participate effectively in overcoming its undemocratic aspects. Thus, to prepare students for participation in a democratic society, a teacher may have to consider how well his or her own choice of teaching and management strategies fosters critical thinking and active political participation.

Similarly, the classical notion that the moral basis of democracy is not only fairness or even equality, but human development through participation in decision making, needs to be explored. Consideration of this point might lead a democratically oriented teacher toward a policy of greater student participation in problem solving and classroom decision making, in which students are encouraged to learn from their own mistakes. Whether a classroom is more student-centered or teacher-centered often stems from the teacher's belief concerning this basic issue.

Such sustained inquiry into democratic ideals might well lead prospective teachers to modify their teaching goals and, having done that, to identify classroom problems differently than before. For example, whereas an obedient and unquestioning classroom might have seemed desirable at one time, that same orderliness might seem alarming in a classroom focused on student development through shared decision making. One important goal of this book is to provide you with the opportunity to rethink what democracy means in practice and then to reevaluate your teaching goals and methods accordingly.

Education of Diverse Students

A second illustration concerns problems confronting teachers in multicultural classrooms. Teachers are increasingly called upon to teach students who are racially or ethnically different from themselves and to recognize that students of all races have the same academic potential. Yet new teachers' experiences seem at first to tell them otherwise. How can they avoid stereotyping certain groups as more or less academically able when they see first-hand significant differences in academic performance and attitudes toward school?

To understand and nurture the learning potential of *all* students, teachers need to understand the influences that culture and social class exert on both students and schools. The differences among the performance of different ethnic groups in this nation's schools have historical and sociolinguistic dimensions. In the case of African-American students, for example, teachers need to understand how schools have systematically discriminated against African-American children and to realize that black English vernacular is not indicative of impaired intellectual ability to learn standard English. They also need to understand that students from lower socioeconomic classes and lower-achieving ethnic groups tend to engage in resistant behaviors as they encounter a school environment that they sometimes experience as hostile. Well-informed teachers could then respond to those resistance strategies not so much as behavior problems but as intelligent yet counterproductive responses to school culture. Teachers who have studied the social contexts of schooling are able to view old school problems with new eyes and, as a result, to approach these problems with fresh ideas and open minds.

To summarize, prospective teachers need to recognize that problems in classroom learning are inevitably embedded in the broader social and cultural contexts that surround their schools and classrooms. Perceptions of gender differences, racial and ethnic attitudes, school organization and culture, social class differences, and prevailing ideologies are but some of the factors that teachers need to study in order to understand their workplace. Failure to understand these factors inevitably impairs their ability to interpret school and classroom events and consequently to construct meaningful solutions to perennial problems.

CONCLUDING REMARKS

Chapter 1 introduces the basic analytic vocabulary, or tools of inquiry, used throughout *School and Society*. These tools of inquiry include political economy, ideology, schooling, and social theory.

This chapter challenges the common view that good theory is impractical. Instead, it should be recognized that good social theory tries to identify and explain actual phenomena, including the phenomena of practice.

Political economy, ideology, and schooling comprise the three-part analytic framework used throughout this book. These terms should be understood in interaction with one another; each can influence the others. The concept "ideology" is a particularly difficult one. It is easy, but mistaken, to think of ideology only as consciously held views that can be stated as articles of belief, for example, the belief that "all men are created equal." It is important to recognize that behind statements of belief are many assumptions, values, and habits of thought that are less consciously held and that shape the meaning of "all men are created equal." An understanding of ideology helps us to understand what words mean for different actors in different historical settings.

This chapter presents brief sketches of feudal Europe and classical Athens to illustrate how schooling, political economy, and ideology are related to each other in particular cultural settings. Investigating how political economy and ideology underlie schooling in these cultures is an exercise in understanding the social foundations of education.

The chapter then addresses the question of how study in social foundations of education can help teachers in their classrooms. It is argued that study of social foundations provides background information about the social contexts of schooling that teachers need to understand the contexts and consequences of their own teaching practices. Because meaning depends on context, teachers need to understand the social context of schooling to better understand the meanings of student behaviors and other classroom events. Because different theoretical perspectives may lead to different understandings, students are urged to engage actively in this inquiry, and not simply to "learn the text." The authors, after all, are employing their own theoretical lenses as they try to understand the social contexts of education and schooling.

QUESTIONS FOR DISCUSSION AND EXAMINATION

1. In the example of feudal schooling, the hierarchy of feudal society was said to be reflected in the limiting of schooling to a privileged few. Some forms of higher education in U.S. society are also limited to a small portion of the population. To what degree does this reflect, and to what degree does it not reflect, a hierarchical social system in the United States? Explain.
2. Aristotle believed that in a democratic society all citizens ought to have the same basic education: one that would equip them to serve as legislators and to obey legislation intelligently. In a nondemocratic society, the basic education would differ among the population, for some would be equipped to rule, others to follow. Judging from your own experience in schools, which of Aristotle's models more resembles American schooling? Explain.
3. Given that the Athenian citizen was expected to participate directly (not just through representatives) in forming the laws of the city-state, but that this citizenship excluded women, slaves, and metics, was the Athenian view of democracy less restricted, or more restricted, than our contemporary view? Explain.
4. Aristotle argued that the primary purpose of education should be to develop human rationality. In your view, how does this compare with the primary purpose(s) of education in U.S. schools today? Defend your view.
5. Choose any single feature of schooling as you have experienced it—its organization, its rules, its processes, its curriculum content—and explain how that feature reflects elements of the ideology and political economy of the larger society.

NOTES

1. The term "hidden curriculum" is generally attributed to curriculum theorist Phillip W. Jackson, *Life In Classrooms* (New York: Holt, Rinehart & Winston, 1968).
2. Abraham Flexner, "The Gates of Excellence," *Journal of Adult Education*, January 1932, p. 5.
3. The material in this section relies heavily on Antony Andrews, *The Greeks* (New York: W. W. Norton, 1967).
4. Thomas L. Pangle, ed., *The Laws of Plato* (New York: Basic Books, 1980).

PART ONE

Educational Aims in Historical Perspective

Liberty and Literacy: The Jeffersonian Era

Our examination of American education begins with one of this nation's most enduringly important and controversial figures, Thomas Jefferson. In late 1996 and early 1997, two popular national magazines (*Atlantic Monthly* and *The New Republic*) featured major analyses of Jefferson's career, and the Public Broadcasting System aired a two-part documentary by filmmaker Ken Burns (best known for his documentaries on the history of baseball and the Civil War).[1] These were for popular audiences, not just historians. Why do Jefferson's social and educational ideals continue to intrigue people today?

Jefferson was arguably the single most prominent American liberal during the era of the revolution and the early republic. While his vocations were law and agriculture, he gained fame as a scientist, philosopher, statesman, and as a revolutionary recognized throughout the Western world. At age 33, he achieved immortality by authoring the American Declaration of Independence. Subsequently, he served as governor of Virginia, U.S. ambassador to France, the first American secretary of state, vice president, and president of the United States for two terms. His retirement activities included agricultural experiments and the founding of the University of Virginia. During Jefferson's entire adult life, he wrote about and worked for education. His educational thought was not simply another aspect of his many talents; it was an integral part of all his other work.

Yet while his greatness is praised, serious questions continue to be raised about Jefferson's ideas and practices. What was his commitment to the "self-evident" truth "that all men are created equal," which he proclaimed in the Declaration of Independence? Did he believe it applied to women, African-Americans, and Native Americans? How far did he follow his stated belief in intellectual freedom? What level of trust did he have in the "common man"? To what extent did his belief in the "natural aristocracy" conflict with democratic ideals, especially in his educational proposals? These kinds of questions should be kept in mind as we analyze Jefferson's ideas and work.

Jefferson's prominence as a spokesman for the prevailing ideology of his time and his dedication to education make him useful in understanding the problems and educational ideals of early liberalism in the United States. By examining the revolutionary era through the lens of Jefferson's thought, one can see the strengths and limitations of the ideology, political economy, and educational arrangements of a formative period in the evolution of American schooling.

Jefferson and his contemporaries debated social and educational problems with clarity and articulated their conclusions with a force seldom rivaled thereafter. This chapter first discusses the political economy of the Jeffersonian era, examining the geography, population, work culture, family structure, and governmental arrangements of the time. In examining these aspects of the society separately, one must remember that they influence one another in complex ways—only a few of which will be captured in the following descriptions.

POLITICAL ECONOMY OF THE JEFFERSONIAN ERA

Geography, Transportation, and Communication

Geographically, the new nation could be divided in several different ways. Most often it was thought to be separated into three regions: New England, the Middle Atlantic states, and the southern states. New England was mountainous, with rocky and relatively unproductive soil and harsh winters, but a rugged coast with fine harbors. As a result, New England became the center of fishing, shipping, and mercantile interests. During the three decades before the Civil War, it became the manufacturing center of the nation. The Middle Atlantic states were characterized by rich farmland, navigable rivers, and excellent ports. New York City and Philadelphia soon became the leading ports and largest cities of the nation. The major exports from these states were grains and livestock. The southern states were rich agricultural areas known first for their tobacco, rice, and indigo. After the invention of the cotton gin, in 1793, cotton increased in importance, and with it so did the "peculiar institution" of slavery.

A second conception of regional differences was to divide the country into port areas served by the coast and navigable rivers versus the interior areas. The port-served areas had better and cheaper transportation and more rapid communication. They tended to be easier places to live, more cosmopolitan, and more urban. It was in those areas that commerce and trade thrived. Often the inhabitants of the interior areas considered themselves at the economic mercy of these commercial centers. These divisions between port-served areas and the interior areas continued well into the twentieth century.

A third division, a concept which fired the imaginations of Americans in general and Jefferson in particular, was between the settled lands and the "frontier." This frontier was constantly moving west. First, the frontier was western Massachusetts; later, west of the Hudson River and the Appalachian mountains; and finally, west of the Mississippi River. As settlers pushed westward, forcibly removing the Native Americans from their ancestral lands, there was continuous conflict between the whites and the Native Americans, between the British settlers and the French, and finally, between the United States and whatever nation might stake a rival claim. The frontier played a significant role in the minds of Americans. What distinguished America from Europe in the imaginations of formerly land-starved Europeans was the magnificent promise of abundant land. The "West" would allow all ambitious Americans to be landowners. In reality, western lands were not that easy for the common person to acquire. Nevertheless, Jefferson and his contemporaries believed that landownership meant independence and freedom. The man who owned and farmed his land, it was thought, depended on no one for the livelihood of his family. Thus, Jefferson argued, the West would enable Americans to escape the fate of Europe, with its remnants of feudal distinction. He based his vision of free, independent yeoman farmers as the backbone of the new republic, in large part, upon the availability and promise of land to the west.

Thomas Jefferson was born in 1743, the son of a relatively prosperous landowner and farmer in western Virginia. What was to become the United States of America at that time consisted of several British colonies nestled along the Atlantic coast stretching from Massachusetts to Georgia. The western boundary was a line along the Appalachian Mountains. Most of the population lived along the coast or was concentrated next to navigable rivers inland. When Jefferson became President in 1800, the total free population of the United States was less than six million. Only New York City had more than 50,000 people, and only five other cities had over 10,000 people. About 94 percent of the population was classified as rural.[2]

Thomas Jefferson and many other colonial leaders felt that land ownership would encourage the attitude of independence and self-sufficiency needed in a democracy.

Over 90 percent of the working population were engaged in agriculture, with the remainder in shipping, commerce, the professions, and crafts. Except for some German and Dutch settlers in Pennsylvania and New York, the vast majority of the inhabitants were of British origin.

From our late 20th-century perspective of rapid transportation and instantaneous communications, it is difficult to conceptualize transit and communications during the years of revolution and the early republic. To do so, we must imagine a society without television, telephones, computers, photocopiers, telegraph, radio, tape recorders, automobiles, trains, or airplanes. Communication was by word-of-mouth, letter, or newspaper. All travel was propelled by humans, animals, river currents, or the wind. For example, in 1791 it took Jefferson 19 days to travel the 920 miles of roads and trails from New York to his home in Virginia.[3] With the introduction of steam-powered boats in the second decade of the nineteenth century, and the steam railroad in the third decade, travel time was greatly reduced. It was not until after the Civil War, however, that transportation and communication began to resemble those with which 20th-century Americans are familiar. The nature of transportation and communication in Jefferson's era ensured that speed, distance, and time were experienced in ways drastically different than they are today. Knowing this helps in some small part to explain some of Jefferson's political and educational ideas, especially his democratic localism—the belief that local communities should be self-governing, ruled as little as possible by authority from state or national governments.

The Family and Agrarian Society

Any analysis of work at the beginning of the nineteenth century must center on farming as a way of life. When Jefferson became President in 1800, agriculture was the source of income for over 90 percent of the population: slaves, free men and women, and indentured servants. There were important regional differences in agriculture. In the South, especially along the tidewater and navigable rivers, farms tended to be large estates worked by slaves and indentured servants, though small farms were plentiful too. In New England and the interior regions of both the South and the West, the farms were most often small. Family-worked subsistence farms rather than cash-crop farms were the norm, although indentured servitude was common here as well. Mechanized farming did not exist, so humans and animals supplied the requisite energy. Farming engaged the entire family and was a way of life as well as an occupation. Sons followed their fathers to the fields, and daughters helped their mothers in preserving food, spinning, weaving, and making clothing and candles. Values and vocations were learned by both sexes during daily life on the family farm. That farm life taught values and vocations was a social fact well understood by Jefferson as he worked out his educational proposals. The decline in farming during the 19th and 20th centuries and the resulting changes in the family would have been understood by Jefferson not only as an economic development, but as a moral, social, political, and educational crisis as well.

In addition to being the basic productive unit of the economy during the Jefferson era, the family remained the primary social unit, as it had been in colonial times. The family ruled the transmission of culture, values, and religion. It was therefore a major force in maintaining social order and continuity. The family was not, however, isolated or autonomous in these responsibilities.

Death was ever present in the early family. While the birth rate among American women was the highest in the contemporary European world and the average American wife would bear eight children, many women died in childbirth and infant mortality was also high.[4] One child in 10 died before reaching 6 months of age, and one in four did not reach age 22. For those who reached age 21, however, males would have an average life expectance of about 70 years and females approximately 63 years. The lower female expectancy resulted primarily from the fact that one in five adult females died from causes related to childbirth. One of every 30 births resulted in the mother's death.[5]

The family in Jefferson's time was patriarchal. The husband and father was expected to rule the family and provide wisdom and love as well as economic sustenance. Values exemplified by ideal males were hard work, duty, self-sufficiency, and temperance. The wife was expected to conform to the husband's wishes, and, in Jefferson's own words, her principal vocation was to bear children.[6] In New England and the Middle Atlantic states, the wife was valued for her utility, while the southern aristocratic ideal tended to portray the wife as an ornament. In only rare instances were women allowed to participate in the public or political arena. A woman's role was limited to her functions in the home as wife, mother, and producer of food and clothing. Children's education was primarily the responsibility of their parents, who were expected to teach values, manners, literacy, religion, and vocation. Discipline in the family was strict and often harsh.[7]

Early American Governance

During Jefferson's time the *community*, through its mores and together with court decisions and legislation, regulated and reinforced many of the activities of the family. Marriage was sanctioned by the community and was conceived as a contract designed to specify mutual responsibilities and rewards: regular and exclusive cohabitation;

peaceful living; division of economic roles; and heterosexual, exclusive sexual relations. The community also monitored the family in its child-rearing practices. If an individual family failed in its child-rearing responsibilities, the courts often intervened. When it was believed that many families were faltering, the colonial and, later, state legislatures intervened by introducing new institutions, such as town schools in colonial times and reform schools in the mid-19th century. Should such monitoring by the community and state be viewed as interference and an infringement on the rights and integrity of individuals, or was this community activity a legitimate reinforcement of familial values? The latter interpretation appears to have been most readily accepted by most Americans of the revolutionary era. While not autonomous or completely independent, the family was the basic social and economic unit of early America. This view was well reflected in local laws in colonial and state governance.

Jefferson lived under three different kinds of government. At his birth, the lands which were to become the original 13 United States were separate colonies under the authority of the British crown. Each had a colonial legislature more or less representative of the colonists, a British-appointed governor who exercised veto power, and final authority resident in the British crown. From the Revolution until 1789, there was a Confederation of States. In this arrangement, most of the power was reserved to the states' governments, which consisted of elected legislatures and an elected governor. In 1789 the present Constitution, which greatly increased authority for the national government, was adopted.

Although very dissimilar in particulars, there were certain important commonalities in all three forms of government. First and foremost, all three were based upon the assumption of the historic "rights of English-men" to have representation in their government. Precisely what this representation meant and how it would be effected was a matter of serious and continuing debate, yet some groups, such as women, African-Americans, and Native Americans, were consistently excluded from political influence. Second, each of these governmental arrangements assumed that male citizens' civil liberties could be infringed only for serious reasons of the state. Again, the specifications of the liberties and definitions of serious reasons were hotly contested. Third, it was assumed that education was important for white men and that the colonial and state governments each had ultimate authority in this area. Under each of these governments during Jefferson's time, this educational authority was most often delegated to the parents and local communities.

For Jefferson and his political allies, the most profound political fact, however, was the Revolution. The prerevolutionary era was seen as harboring remnants of feudalism. Special rights reserved for the aristocracy, close connection between church and state, the lack of intellectual freedom, restrictions on the civil and political rights of the common man, and the belief that only the "well born" could benefit from education were among the remnants of feudalism which Jefferson challenged. The Revolution symbolized a break from the old world and old regime. It initiated a "noble experiment" in self-government. Much of Jefferson's philosophical, political, and educational thought was directed toward ensuring the success of this experiment.

IDEOLOGY OF THE JEFFERSONIAN ERA

The preceding sketch of the political economy of Jefferson's time provides one of the two major societal contexts within which early American education must be understood. The second context is the ideology of the era. The men of Jefferson's time were roughly divided into two world views, liberal and conservative, although those terms differ markedly from their meanings today. Jefferson and his allies were classical liberals, while his opponents were conservatives. The conservatives were thus named because they wished to hold on to, or conserve, an older and established set of ideas and values inherited from European traditions. This conservative ideology bore the remnants of feudalism.

The Breakdown of Feudalism

Feudalism, as discussed in Chapter 1, was an economic, military, political, and religious system which developed in Europe during the centuries

In addition to serving two terms as President, Thomas Jefferson was the colonial era's most eloquent spokesperson for education and was the founder of the University of Virginia.

following the collapse of the Roman Empire. Although money was not absent, goods and services were generally bartered. A military class developed to provide protection in exchange for residence on the nobles' land and a portion of the peasant class's agricultural production. A religious class also developed which owned land through the church, provided spiritual solace, and exercised considerable political and economic power. Eventually these classes became somewhat fixed, and stations in life were assigned by heredity. The nobility and clergy were referred to as the "first estate" and the "second estate," respectively, and those who belonged to the land—the peasants—were the "third estate." Also discussed in Chapter 1 was that part of feudal ideology known as the "divine right" of the nobility. To resist the feudal order was to resist God's will. This theory was provided and assented to by the learned men of the court, the universities, and the church. It was not the first time, nor would it be the last, when the intellectuals would use their talents to justify the existing social, political, and economic order of the day.

This feudal system worked reasonably well until the beginning of the 18th century. It provided order and stability for a "closed" society. However, it could not easily accommodate new ideas, inventions, or trade. The beginning of the end came with the renaissances of the 12th and 14th centuries. Ideas from the Byzantine and Arab worlds stimulated European thinkers, who began to challenge the basic cosmology of the church. The ideas of men like Galileo, Copernicus, Kepler, and Newton shook the very foundations of feudal religious thought by challenging biblical and church accounts of the natural world with new scientific explanations. These challenges to church truths were grounded in a kind of authority new and different from religious revelation: scientific reason.

Intercourse with the Middle East included goods as well as ideas. Commerce produced the need for money, merchants, banks, craftsmen, and later, manufacturers. These tended to congregate in trading centers, which became cities. The people who lived in the cities and made a handsome living from trade became known as the *bourgeoisie,* from the original term, *bourg,* which was the fortress around which the cities developed.[8] They eventually developed into a very wealthy class, but with the same social and political status as the peasants—that is, they were members of the third estate. Additionally, the introduction of explosive powder from China paved the way for invention of firearms and rendered the feudal warrior, with his long training, heavy armor, and prestige, scarcely equal to the peasant soldier with a rifle or a cannon.

When these seeds of the feudal system's destruction were first sown, they went almost unnoticed, except as minor irritants. By the 15th century, however, feudalism was entering its decline, in some ways a victim of its own successful establishment of the nation-state under the authority of a king who ruled by "divine right." As the British and French kings established national control, they required larger standing armies which, along with other governmental functions now required at court, necessitated increased taxes. Although the path took somewhat different routes and schedules, eventually England in the 17th century and France in the 18th both experienced rebellions. The American Revolution can be seen as an extension or continuation of the unfinished English revolutions of the seventeenth century. In all cases, it was necessary to justify the action of rebellion against "God's appointed" ruler. By what right could common people challenge the centuries-old authority of the church and the monarch? This justification was part of the development of "liberalism." Major contributors to the development of liberalism were Milton and Locke in England; Voltaire, Montesquieu, Condorcet, and Rousseau in France; and Franklin, Jefferson, and Madison in the United States.

The Classical Roots of Liberal Ideology

One inevitably oversimplifies when attempting to summarize the major ideas of an ideology, since individuals always subscribe to an ideology in different degrees and with various nuances. Nevertheless, it is helpful for the student of education in Jeffersonian America to have a summary of what has come to be called the "classical" liberalism of that era to distinguish it from the "modern" liberalism that has descended from it in the 20th century. In addition, "classical" serves to associate this historic liberalism with the classical Athenian ideals upon which liberal enlightenment thought was based. One should remember, however, that the following ideas were not recited like a catechism, nor were they subjects of an oath of allegiance by classical liberals, who often conflicted with one another in how to apply these ideas in practice. Six ideas which were central or fundamental to classical liberalism will be examined: faith in reason, natural law, republican virtue, progress, nationalism, and freedom. Not only these ideas themselves, but the relations *among* these ideas, are central to an understanding of the classical liberal world view.

One shorthand way to think about the fundamental tenets of classical liberal ideology is to consider how the feudal commitment to hierarchy, in which one's worth was determined by one's place in society, was replaced by a commitment to individualism. Classical liberals embraced the right of individuals to control their economic destinies through *capitalism.* Rejecting a state religion, liberals argued for the individual's right to freedom of worship and the legal separation of church and state. Denying the "divine right of kings," liberals believed in the right of individuals to govern themselves through representative government, or *republicanism.* To the revolutionary American, classical liberal ideology took the institutional forms of capitalism and republicanism.

Faith in Reason These individualistic tendencies were justified in part by a fundamental tenet of liberalism, the belief in *reason.* The ruling classes of the feudal system had placed little faith in the human ability to reason. Indeed, basic to the religious underpinnings of the "old regime" was the notion that human reason was frail and incapable of guiding human action. Classical liberals, however, championed human reason as the best and most desirable guide in this world. They increasingly rejected tradition, custom, and dogmatic faith. Rather than believing that human reason had been mortally incapacitated by the taint of original sin, they viewed the mind as a "blank slate" upon which sensory perceptions from the environment could write any message. Humankind was capable of monumental intellectual feats, and the development and exercise of reason was the key to the future. This faith in human reason had been inspired by the startling advances in science during the previous centuries. Galileo, Copernicus, and above all, Isaac Newton represented what reason could accomplish. Jefferson said that "reason is the first born daughter of science." Jefferson's use of "daughter" here is ironic, because classical liberals placed little faith in the ability of females to reason as men could, and this prejudice was reflected in the relative exclusion of women from political life and even from formal education above the elementary level.

Natural Law If faith in human reason was the fundamental tenet of liberalism, its root metaphor was "the universe is a machine." The universe was often compared to a clock, at that time the most perfect machine, with its many interrelated parts operating in precise harmony. This metaphor, of course, flowed from liberals' belief in natural law. Although Sir Isaac Newton had many distinguished predecessors, the publication of his *Mathematical Principles of Natural Philosophy* in 1687 signaled a revolution in the way the Western world viewed nature. No longer would nature be mysterious and governed by divine whims or heavenly intercessions. In England, poet Alexander Pope wrote[9]

> Nature and Nature's laws
> Lay hid in night;
> God said, *Let* Newton *be!*
> And all was light.

Perhaps nature had been created by a divine intelligence, but this God created a perfect machine governed by precise mathematical laws. After creation, this God could return to rest and contemplate his perfectly ordered system. Equally important, men thought that through the use of reason they could discover these laws and comprehend the universe. Newton had already begun the task. And liberals were not long in discovering the notion that understanding yields control. Similarly, it did not take them long to generalize from the idea of natural law in the physical realm to the belief in *natural law* in the social arena. With the advent of Newtonian physics, science began to replace theology as the reliable guide to action—and the authority of reason increasingly challenged the authority of the church and monarchy.

Republican Virtue Classical liberals realized that human reason could be used for good or for ill, and they placed great store in another human capacity that was considered essential for the good life and the good society: *virtue* was an important part of their view of human nature. Historian John Miller has noted that during the revolutionary era "it was commonly believed that the republican form of government could not exist without 'virtue'—which signified, in the vocabulary of the eighteenth century Enlightenment, love of country, an austere style of living, probity, strict observance of the moral code and willingness to sacrifice private profit for the public good."[10] Classical liberals had great faith in the perfectibility of the individual, which was to be accomplished through virtue as well as reason. Virtue consisted largely in fulfilling one's duties to God and to nature. Meeting one's duties to God were understood as piety, which included worship, reading the Bible, and living a life of moral responsibility. The Protestant Reformation emphasized the duty to obey not the priesthood or an absolute king, but the dictates of individual conscience in a right relationship with God.

An important part of this conception of virtue was what is often referred to as the *work ethic.* Idleness, rather than money, was widely regarded as the root of all evil. Historian Louis B. Wright notes, "In the tradition of American life, few ideas have received greater prominence than the notion of dignity of labor and the virtue of diligent application to one's job, whatever it might be."[11] In the colonial and early American periods, respect for the virtue of work derived from the beginnings of the commercial class and was strengthened by the scarcity of labor and the opportunity for acquiring wealth through hard work. We see this reflected, for example, in Franklin's famous saying, "Early to bed, early to rise, makes a man healthy, wealthy, and wise."

While it might seem odd to us today that classical liberals were passionately committed to reason and natural law and at the same time emphasized virtue through piety and faith in God, there was no necessary contradiction in these commitments. Most classical liberals in the United States and England were Protestants. Not all Protestants, however, were classical liberals. Many of these liberals were deists, whose religious beliefs included the idea of God as the "first cause" in the universe but excluded most of the doctrine of Christianity.[12] Franklin, an ardent naturalist and scientist, spoke for many classical liberals when he said, "There is in all men something like a natural principle, which inclines them to *Devotion,* or the Worship of some unseen Power . . . ."[13] Knowledge of the world through science and of God through worship seemed to be a part of the natural scheme of things.

Also regarded as part of the natural scheme of things was the view that the womanly and manly virtues differed. Men's virtues were to be found largely in the public spheres of commerce and politics, while women's virtues were exercised in the home and hearth—the "private sphere." Women were thought virtuous if they did not speak in public gatherings, if they did not question public authorities on religion or law, and if they fulfilled the duties of child rearing and caring for the home. The socially valued virtues of women in early America were piety, purity, submissiveness, and domesticity.[14] Given that their responsibilities were limited to the home and hearth, women were educated for the private and not the public sphere.

Progress The fourth fundamental idea of liberalism was belief in *progress.* Historian Russell Nye writes, "If a majority of eighteenth century Americans agreed on one idea, it was probably the perfectibility of man and the prospect of his future progress." This was a secularization of the Augustinian and Protestant concepts of linear history: instead of a better life after death, liberal faith in progress promised improvement here on earth, generation after generation. The early-American physician Benjamin Rush wrote that he was "fully persuaded that it is possible to produce such a change in the moral character of man, as shall raise him to a resemblance of angels—nay more, to the likeness of God himself."[15] Through human reason and virtue, it was believed that both the human individual and the society could continually progress toward perfectibility. The belief in progress shows how interrelated these ideas were—free intellects developing their reason would continue to discover more about natural law, and with the resulting control over the physical universe and social relations, would constantly improve human life. Liberals assumed that men could discover what *ought* to be and that they would change the world accordingly. This was not only a justification but sometimes an injunction for revolution.

In feudal times the perfect society was thought to be the one which followed tradition, while classical liberals believed that society was progressive if it followed human reason, natural law, and the "natural rights" of individuals. When government violated those rights, wrote Jefferson, it was the duty of the people to overthrow it. Revolution, then, was an important classical liberal vehicle for progress. Imbedded in this idea was a commitment to *social meliorism* (the amelioration, or improvement, of imperfect social conditions) and humanitarianism. The liberal's method of meliorism was usually through environmental control and manipulation of institutions. At times such social intervention conflicted with the liberal's ideal of freedom from governmental control. Because of the history of strong and often oppressive government under feudalism, liberals were fearful of a strong government. Jefferson often expressed his belief that the best government was "that which governed least."

Jefferson's belief in the inevitability of progress without a strong central government was partly grounded in a strong faith in the benefits of *education.* It was through education that individuals would develop their reason and virtue. Education would facilitate the development of all that liberals held important. Enlightenment of the population was seen as essential for self-government. In a 1786 letter to George Wythe, Jefferson urged the establishment of education in the new republic in these words: "I think by far the most important bill in our whole code is that for the diffusion of knowledge among the people. No other sure foundation can be devised for the preservation of freedom and happiness," and he admonished his friend, "Preach, my dear sir, a crusade against ignorance: establish and improve the law for educating the common people."[16] The antithesis of virtue for the liberals was ignorance rather than sin, and the cure for ignorance was education. No one argued this case with more power, clarity, and elegance than Thomas Jefferson. While Jefferson, as we shall see, differed from many of his contemporaries in his belief that the state had a responsibility to provide schools for educating the children of the common man and woman, even the opponents of state-supported schooling regarded education as essential to a life well lived. Whether the poor could afford it or not, their education was for classical liberals a concern of the state.

Nationalism A fifth basic belief embedded in classical liberal ideology was the commitment to a nation-state. As European feudalism gave way to republican liberalism, a new spirit of *nationalism* emerged in changing European societies. Similarly, in the colonies, Americans increasingly saw themselves less as "American subjects of the King," in Franklin's words, and more as a people with a national mission. Even before the Revolutionary War, Patrick Henry proclaimed that "the distinctions between Virginians . . . and New Englanders are no more. All America is thrown into one mass. I am not a Virginian, but an American."[17] The emotions of the revolution, of course, heightened this nationalist allegiance, and citizens of the new nation began to forge a new identity. Americans saw themselves as blessed with unparalleled natural resources and a historical mission to differentiate themselves from the traditions and influences of the old country.

This emerging classical liberal nationalism was embodied in national policies in defense, in trade, and in acquisition of new land to the south and

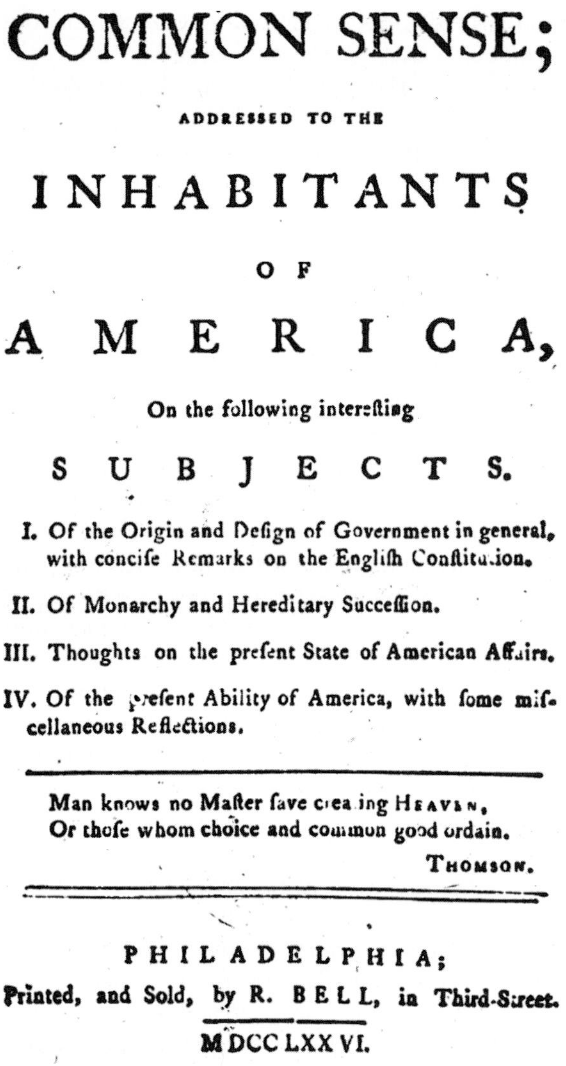
COMMON SENSE;

ADDRESSED TO THE

INHABITANTS

OF

AMERICA,

On the following intereſting

SUBJECTS.

I. Of the Origin and Deſign of Government in general, with conciſe Remarks on the Engliſh Conſtitution.

II. Of Monarchy and Hereditary Succeſſion.

III. Thoughts on the preſent State of American Affairs.

IV. Of the preſent Ability of America, with ſome miſcellaneous Reflections.

Man knows no Maſter ſave creating Heaven,
Or thoſe whom choice and common good ordain.
Thomson.

PHILADELPHIA;
Printed, and Sold, by R. BELL, in Third-Street.
MDCCLXXVI.

Thomas Paine, like Thomas Jefferson and other classical liberals, believed that when government violates human reason, virtue, and the human rights granted by nature, revolution is justifiable.

west, but it was still an infant nationalism compared to the nationalism of the modern industrial state. Despite Henry's brave sentiments, people felt strong allegiance to their home states and regions, and nationalism was often suspected as harboring a too ready acceptance of an unnecessarily strong federal government. As late as 1825, John Quincy Adams delivered an inaugural address that was considered a political disaster because it called for a powerful federal government. The young nation had struggled hard to rid itself of an oppressive central government in the form of the king, and tension still existed between a desire for national government and local self-determination. Classical liberals maintained an uneasy balance between these two liberal commitments to nationalism and freedom.

Freedom The classical liberal conception of *freedom*—the sixth fundamental belief in the ideology—was primarily what a 20th-century British philosopher, Isaiah Berlin, has called "negative freedom," that is, freedom from restraint or interference.[18] Four types of freedom were considered the basic rights of white males: intellectual, political, civil, and economic. Intellectual freedom was the most fundamental. Liberals argued that the intellect must be free from the chains of the state and the tethers of the church if reason was to comprehend and control the physical and social worlds. By the 18th century, the history of science was replete with examples of church and state thwarting scientific discovery by forcing allegiance to dogma (Galileo's persecution is perhaps the best-known illustration). Liberals believed that the future required an intellect free from external coercion. Similarly, political history had demonstrated the unacceptable consequences of political absolutism. British history, particularly, was interpreted by liberals as demonstrating progress away from unlimited royal authority and toward representative government. In the political realm, freedom meant freedom from the dictates of the monarchy or aristocracy. Liberals believed that the only way to ensure this was self-government, usually through some form of representative republic.

Closely associated with intellectual and political freedom was the liberals' advocacy of civic freedom, a notion often embodied in our current term "civil liberties." The distinction between political and civic freedom is at least as old as Aristotle, who distinguished between the freedom to participate in making the laws (political freedom) and the freedom to "live as one pleases" (civic freedom). This advocacy was for guarantees against the transgression of the limits of power and authority by even a representative government. It was usually manifested in demands for guarantees like the American Bill of Rights, which protected citizens from government interference in

EXHIBIT 2.1 **Fundamental Dimensions of Classical Liberalism: A Schematic Representation**

EMERGENCE FROM FEUDALISM

Feudal Ideology		*Classical Liberal Ideology*
State control of economy	→	Capitalism
State religion	→	Separation of church and state
Divine right of kings	→	Republicanism (representative government)

BASIC TENETS OF CLASSICAL LIBERALISM

Reason	Progress
Natural Law	Nationalism
Virtue	Freedom
	Economic
	Civil
	Political
	Intellectual

their right to speak as they saw fit, to assemble, to bear arms, to refuse the quartering of troops in their homes, and so on. The argument for economic freedom was informed by a long history of government control, appropriation, and taxation during the feudal era. The liberals tended to oppose most government action in the economic sphere. Their slogan, "Laissez-faire," literally "allow to act," was a demand for the protection of private property from government regulation. Imbedded in this idea of economic freedom was the belief, most clearly articulated by Adam Smith in *The Wealth of Nations,* that if left alone, the marketplace would self-regulate for the good of society. Historically, this economic principle of laissez-faire has provided government support for "free" enterprise capitalism with little accompanying government control. Conversely, it inhibited liberals from developing government policy to aid the poor.

Jefferson as Classical Liberal

This brief summary of classical liberal ideology suggests the lens through which Jefferson viewed the world and developed his ideas on education (see Exhibit 2.1). The Declaration of Independence, Jefferson's most famous written work, expressed the core of his ideology: "We hold these truths to be self-evident, that all men are created equal, that they are endowed by their Creator with certain unalienable Rights, that among these are Life, Liberty, and the Pursuit of Happiness." The effective establishment of life, liberty, and the pursuit of happiness were moral ends for Jefferson. Other issues, such as freedom of the press, ownership of property, and the form of government, were means to these ends.

Jefferson's substitution of "the Pursuit of Happiness" in the Declaration of Independence for John Locke's term "Property" in his *Second Treatise of Government* was deliberate. His attempt to correct Lafayette's draft of "rights" in the early stages of the French Revolution is explicit evidence of this. Lafayette had written that every man was born with rights which included "property and the care of his honor." Jefferson objected to both terms. He argued that property, like government, was only a *means* to human happiness and not a natural and unalienable right.[19] Further, his objection to excessive concentration of wealth as a cause of poverty and resulting decrease of happiness for the masses indicated his belief that property was only a means to happiness.

The conception of happiness which was central to Jefferson's philosophy was drawn in part from a conception of human nature that followed Aristotle (with whose work Jefferson was familiar) in believing that happiness was obtainable only if the rational part of one's nature governed the appetites and passions. Jefferson employed this Aristotelian model of the division in human nature, for example, in explaining why African-Americans and women, whom he understood to be governed more by appetites and passions than by reason, were less capable of self-governance than white men—and thus legitimately should submit to the reason of white men if they were to find happiness. In many ways, this conception of happiness governed Jefferson's life.[20]

Jefferson and Intellectual Freedom

Instrumental to the pursuit of happiness, for Jefferson, was intellectual freedom. Tradition, dogma, and coercion were antithetical to intellectual freedom. Jefferson considered his successful campaign against the union of church and state as one of his major victories for intellectual freedom and therefore an important contribution to human happiness. At the time of the revolution, most states had an established church, and these persisted until after the Civil War. The prohibition of established religion in the Bill of Rights was interpreted to apply only to the federal government and not the various state governments. As a result, state tax monies continued to be used to support the established church, and in some states nonmembers were barred from the exercise of certain civil rights, such as voting and holding public office. Moreover, the established church often had the authority to censor publication of books and condemn individuals for heresy.

Jefferson responded to this condition by designing the famous American "wall of separation" between church and state. In 1779, he wrote the Bill for Establishing Religious Freedom for the Virginia legislature. It was passed in 1786 and became the model for several subsequent state disestablishment laws. The bill contended that a man's religious beliefs were his own private affair and in no way should be infringed on by the state. It severed the connection between church and state. In it, Jefferson asserted the now famous justification for intellectual freedom and the determination of truth through the free competition of ideas: that "truth is great and will prevail if left to herself; that she is proper and sufficient antagonist to error, and has nothing to fear from conflict unless by human interposition disarmed of her natural weapons, free argument and debate; errors ceasing to be dangerous when it is permitted freely to contradict them."[21] His *Notes on the State of Virginia* angrily asserted the right of religious nonconformity: "Millions of innocent men, women and children, since the introduction of Christianity, have been burnt, tortured, fined, imprisoned; yet we have not advanced one inch toward uniformity. What has been the effect of coercion? To make one half the world fools, and the other half hypocrites."[22] And if uniformity could somehow be achieved, he believed, its results would stifle intellectual activity. Several years later, in 1815, Jefferson wrote to his friend P. H. Wendover: "Difference of opinion leads to inquiry, and inquiry to truth; and that, I am sure, is the ultimate and sincere object of us both."[23]

The issue which troubled Jefferson's conservative opponents was how to maintain social order. Like Jefferson, they sought a middle ground between the chaos of too little government and the tyranny of too much government. Unlike Jefferson, however, their primary concern was anarchy and chaos. Jefferson replied—in theory, although not always in practice—by relying on the free play of the human intellect and open debate. He resoundingly rejected coercion and force. His noted affinity for a free press stemmed from the same faith in a free intellect as the means to truth and human happiness. In a 1787 letter to his friend Edward Carington, he wrote, "Were it left to me to decide whether we should have a government without newspapers or newspapers without a government, I would not hesitate for a moment to prefer the latter." He went on with his important qualification: "But I should mean that every man shall receive these papers and be capable of reading them."[24] Newspapers, he believed, would be the instructor of the masses and the vehicle for debate. His ardor for them cooled considerably during his second administration as President, when partisan newspapers printed volumes of political gossip, half-truths, and outright lies. He even privately encouraged his political allies in Connecticut to bring suits against enemy papers.[25] He complained, "Nothing can now be believed which is seen in a newspaper." He modified his support for a free press, arguing that newspapers should be free to print the "truth."[26] On this issue, it should be remembered that a free press was not an end for Jefferson; rather, it was the means to bring information to citizens so that they could exercise intellectual freedom and come to the truth as part of their pursuit of happiness. Newspapers stood as a symbol for information: when they printed lies, Jefferson believed, they lost their usefulness.

One is left to wonder, however, why Jefferson thought that truth had lost its strength. Had he lost some of his earlier faith in the common man to follow free argument and debate? What is the justification for debate if only "the truth" is allowed a hearing? Are there special qualifications to be met before one is eligible to engage in an open debate between truth and error?

An 1825 letter Jefferson wrote to a friend and fellow trustee of the University of Virginia adds further sharpness to these questions. The letter was about Jefferson's plans for the upcoming meeting of the trustees. After stating the general principle that trustees should not interfere in the choice of texts by professors, Jefferson argued for an exception in regard to professors of government. He claimed that if the trustees were not watchful about what was taught in the subject of government, "heresies may be taught, of so interesting a character to our own state and to the United States, as to make it a duty in us to lay down the principles which are to be taught." He went on to assert that this was necessary because the trustees could not be certain of the political persuasion of future professors of government. Jefferson endorsed a resolution to this effect which he intended to offer at the trustees' meeting. He then requested, "I wish it kept to ourselves, because I have always found that the less such things are spoken of beforehand, the less obstruction is contrived to be thrown in their way."[27] Here Jefferson is not simply arguing to protect the common man from errors contained in newspapers; rather, that professors, university students, and his fellow trustees should be insulated from potential error. If one were to argue for selective admission to open debate between truth and error, who would be eligible if not professors, university students, and university trustees? In light of these examples, what are we to make of Jefferson's arguments for intellectual freedom?

Moreover, Jefferson and his contemporary liberals believed that "truth" could be discovered by man through the free exercise of intellect and reason. This was basic to their view of natural law and underpinned by Newtonian physics. This "truth," Jefferson believed, would be acknowledged by all rational men. Like other classical liberals, Jefferson believed that truth was not *created* by human inquiry and therefore subject to revision by further inquiry, but instead was a property of the natural world and therefore absolute and unchanging, waiting to be *discovered* by human inquiry. Once discovered, it followed for classical liberals, such truth should be taught—whether it was 2 + 2 = 4 or that republican government was the surest route to social justice and human happiness. Modern science, as we will see in Chapter 4, has become much more tentative about the origins and permanence of truth.

Jefferson, Democracy, and Education

A second major concern for Jefferson, then, was the establishment of the kind of government most likely to promote human happiness. Again, the Declaration of Independence can serve to summarize Jefferson's thought: "That to secure these rights [life, liberty and the pursuit of happiness], Governments are instituted among men, deriving their just powers from the consent of the governed. . . . " Eleven years later, in a letter to his closest political confidant, James Madison, he stated another of his political axioms: "I am not a friend of the very energetic government. It is always oppressive."[28] It is clear that Jefferson's political ideal would be a representative republic composed of educated, informed, and rational citizens. The government would have limited powers circumscribed by a constitution containing a declaration of rights reserved for the people. Daniel Boorstein has described Jefferson's aim as "a government too weak to aid the wolves yet strong enough to protect the sheep."[29]

Jefferson's arguments for a democratic republic as well as for education are based in his moral philosophy and are succinctly stated in a 1787 letter advising his young friend Peter Carr about his education. He noted that "man is destined for society." Therefore, the creator must have endowed us with a "moral sense of conscience" which "is as much a part of man as his leg or arm." Moral sense is innate in all humans, for Jefferson, "in a greater or less degree. It may be strengthened by exercise, as may any particular limb of the body."[30] This moral sense which equipped all men to participate in their own governance could be enhanced or debased according to environmental circumstances. Democracy was thus the most moral of governments for Jefferson, not only because it protected "inalienable rights," but also because it provided for the moral development of individuals. (This idea, that democracy is to be valued not because freedom is an end in itself, but because freedom through democratic participation allows people to develop their moral and rational capacities to the greatest extent possible, we will refer to as the "developmental" view of democracy.)

Innate moral sense or human conscience by itself was not sufficient to justify or sustain a democracy, according to Jefferson. It required the aid of an educated reason. Referring to the situation in the United States in 1820, Jefferson wrote, "I know of no safe depository of the ultimate powers of society but the people themselves; and if we think them not enlightened enough to exercise their control with a wholesome discretion, the remedy is not to take it from them, but to inform their discretion by education."[31] Four years later, he noted, "The qualifications for self-government are not innate. They are the result of habit and long training."[32] Jefferson remained remarkably constant in this belief. In a 1787 letter to James Madison, he had written, "above all things I hope the education of the common people will be attended to: convinced that on their good senses we may rely with the most security for the preservation of a due degree of liberty."[33]

This same letter indicated that in addition to an innate moral sense, sufficiently educated, an effective democratic citizenship required a particular kind of economic base. Then ambassador to France, Jefferson wrote, "I think our governments will remain virtuous for many centuries; as long as they are chiefly agricultural; and this will be as long as there shall be vacant lands in any part of America. When they get piled upon one another in large cities as in Europe they will become as corrupt as in Europe."[34] Agriculture was more to Jefferson than crops and income; it was a way of life which developed independence, perseverance, industry, self-sufficiency, and strength. These characteristics were essential to Jefferson for virtue and for human happiness. In his *Notes on the State of Virginia,* he referred to farmers as "the chosen people of God," and the "mobs of the great cities" as cancers sapping the strength of democratic governments.[35] His desire to guarantee an adequate supply of "vacant" land for agriculture led him as President to purchase the vast Louisiana Territory, even though this act expanded the power of the federal government—an expansion of power which Jefferson and other classical liberals generally opposed with vigor. The end he pursued in this act, however, was the pursuit of happiness, and thus to Jefferson more important, in principle, than keeping federal power limited.

Jefferson as Realist

The confluence of habit, long training, reason developed by education, innate conscience strengthened by exercise, and an agrarian economic base was a rare historical occurrence. In fact, Jefferson and many American liberals believed the "experiment" begun in 1776 was important because it was such a rare example to the world. The experiment had not been successful previously, in this view, because the necessary conditions had been lacking. Jefferson's realism led to the conclusion that political ideals required the appropriate time, place, and guidance for their fruition. This was clearly reflected in his statement, "What is practicable must often control what is pure theory, and the habits of the governed determine in a great measure what is practical."[36] The same sentiment surfaced in 1807 when he congratulated Tsar Alexander of Russia for his "herculean" efforts to bring freedom and happiness to "an unprepared people" by "dealing out good progressively as your people are prepared to receive."[37] Similarly, Jefferson analyzed the failure of the French Revolution: "It has failed in its first effort, because the mobs of the cities, the instrument used for its accomplishment, debased by ignorance, poverty and vice, could not be restrained to rational action." In the long term, however, Jefferson was optimistic even for Europe because "Science is progressive, and talents and enterprise on the alert."[38] With these reservations about the immediate and general applicability of free, representative democracy, Jefferson was not arguing that the principles of liberty were not objective and continuous, but rather that they should be applied with consideration for the conditions and development of the people. He labored, then, to improve the conditions and development of the population through democratic and educational institutions.

Jefferson's thought reflected a number of classical liberal rationalizations for Anglo-Saxon imperialism and the disfranchisement of women and nonwhites. Did Jefferson's "realism" contribute to the development of those rationalizations? How much despotism hides behind the argument that before democracy can be introduced the people must be "ready"? If it is the case that "readiness" is the prerequisite for freedom and democracy, what are the criteria to be used to determine readiness? Who is to be the judge? However we answer these questions and whatever judgments we make regarding Jefferson's realism, we should take into account his conviction that the foundation of liberty and democracy is the enlightenment of the masses. We might also do well to remember his argument that the economic independence of the common man was an important requisite for the exercise of democracy.

Government by a "Natural Aristocracy"

Even in the "noble experiment" which American liberals considered the beacon for all mankind, Jefferson did not intend for all free men to participate on an entirely equal basis. For 14 years, until both died on Independence Day in 1826, Jefferson and John Adams, who had been bitter political enemies from the early 1790s, carried on an extended correspondence. One of Jefferson's most interesting letters was written in the fall of 1813 and portrays his conception of the proper political aristocracy. He contrasts this "natural aristocracy" with an "artificial" or "pseudo-aristocracy." The "natural aristocracy" that Jefferson believed should govern was based on "virtue and talent," while the "artificial aristocracy" was based on birth and wealth. The previous, artificial aristocracy had been the target of the revolution. Because man had been created for society, Jefferson explained to Adams, it naturally followed that God would also provide for "virtue and wisdom" to manage society. He argued, "that form of government is best, which provides the most effectively for a pure selection of these natural *aristoi* into the office of government," and the most effective procedure was "to leave to the citizens the free election and separation of the *aristoi* from the *pseudo-aristoi,* of the wheat from the chaff."

Jefferson assured Adams that, in America, the common man usually "will elect the really good and wise." After lamenting the failure of the French Revolution, Jefferson concluded: "It suffices for us, if the moral and physical condition of our own citizens qualifies them to select the able and good for the direction of their government, with a recurrence of elections at such short periods as will enable them to displace an unfaithful servant, before the mischief he mediates may be irremediable."[39] Thus, while Jefferson was not so egalitarian as to think that any man might be an adequate legislator, he, more than most in his time, credited the common man with the capacity to choose his betters for the roles of governance. This capacity was based on the innate moral sense possessed by all humans and developed through exercise and enlightenment. The superior wisdom required to fulfill the responsibilities of the offices of government was also developed through exercise and enlightenment.

JEFFERSON'S PLAN FOR POPULAR EDUCATION

Education was not only crucial in Jefferson's political theory, it was also an important means for the pursuit of happiness, for he understood happiness to include the pursuit of knowledge. It should not be surprising that education commanded Jefferson's attention throughout his life. His public statements on education began when, in Virginia, he wrote the Bill for the More General Diffusion of Knowledge,[40] the Bill for Amending the Constitution of the College of William and Mary, and Substituting More Certain Revenues for Its Support,[41] and the Bill for Establishing a Public Library.[42] These three legislative proposals contained the core of his educational thought. Their contents were elaborated in his subsequent *Notes on the State of Virginia* and numerous private letters. After his administration, he authored a Bill for the Establishment of a System of Public Education[43] and the Report of the Commission Appointed to Fix the Site of the University of Virginia.

(It was referred to as the "Rockfish Gap Report" because it was at a tavern in Rockfish Gap, Virginia, on August 1, 1818, that the commissioners met to sign it.)[44]

There were four interrelated parts or tiers in Jefferson's proposed educational structure: elementary schools, grammar schools, the university, and life-long learning. Elementary and grammar school educations were outlined in his 1776 Bill for a More General Diffusion of Knowledge, his *Notes,* and the 1817 Bill for the Establishment of a System of Public Education. The elementary school was to be the foundation of the entire educational structure. Although both bills were defeated in the Virginia legislature, they provide us with important insights into Jefferson's conception of education.

Elementary School Districts

Jefferson proposed to divide the state into small districts, or "wards," of five to six square miles. These districts would serve a dual purpose. First, they would become the local unit of government. As he explained in a letter to John Adams, "My proposition had, for a further object, to impart to these wards those portions of self-government for which they are best qualified, by confiding to them the care of their poor, the roads, police, elections, the nominations of jurors, administrations of justice in small cases, elementary exercise of the militia; in short, to have made them little republics, with a warden at the head of each, for all those concerns which, being under their eye, they would better manage than the larger republics of the county or the State."[45] Thus, Jefferson not only would have decentralized governmental authority to local districts, which he believed could most effectively exercise power, but would have provided a laboratory for self-government. Additionally, this effort at decentralization of both civil and educational governance must be understood within the limitations of transportation and communication then available.

Second, each of the districts would establish an elementary school where "all free children, male and female," would be entitled to attend without cost for three years, or longer at their private expense. An overseer, responsible for approximately 10 schools, would be appointed by the alderman elected in the district. General governance of the elementary schools, including the hiring and dismissal of teachers, examination of students, and supervision of the curriculum, would have been in the care of the overseers.

The curriculum of Jefferson's elementary schools was uncluttered and wholly intellectual. "At every of these schools shall be taught reading, writing, and common arithmetic, and the books which shall be used therein for instructing the children to read shall be such as will at the same time make them acquainted with Graecian, Roman, English, and American history."[46] This 3-year curriculum would provide the extent of schooling for the mass of the population, certainly for the females, who would not go on to secondary or higher education. Jefferson conceived these elementary years as an education for life, providing the requisite skills for the daily life of the yeoman farmer and for the wife and mother of the household in the early American republic.

Common arithmetic would enable them to do the calculations to purchase goods, sell their surplus production, figure their taxes, and, in general, understand the relatively simple agrarian economy within which they labored. Writing would empower them to communicate with those at a distance. Reading was necessary to comprehend distant communications, newspapers, government announcements and laws and, most important, would enable graduates to continue their education throughout life through the medium of books. In *Notes on the State of Virginia,* Jefferson explained the emphasis on history in the 3-year curriculum, which would have provided the entire formal schooling for the common people:

> History, by appraising them of the past, will enable them to judge the future; it will avail them of the experience of other times and other nations; it will qualify them as judges of the actions and designs of men. . . . Every government degenerates when trusted to the rulers of the people alone. The people themselves therefore are its only safe depositories. And to render even them sage, their minds must be improved to a certain degree. This indeed is not all that is necessary, though it be essentially necessary.[47]

EXHIBIT 2.2 **Objectives for Elementary and University Education in Summary of the 1818 Rockfish Gap Report**

Elementary Education Is to Develop in Every Citizen	*University Education Is to Develop*
Information sufficient to transact business	Political leaders
Writing skills	Knowledge leading to political freedom
Calculation skills	Understandings to improve the economy
Reading skills	Reason, morals, virtue, and order
Improved morals	Understanding of science and math to promote the general health, security, and comfort
Understanding of duties	Habits of reflection and correct actions in students which render them examples of virtue to others and bring happiness to themselves
Knowledge of rights	
Ability to vote intelligently	
Ability to judge officeholders' conduct	
Ability to fulfill social relationships	

Source: Data from Roy Honeywell, *The Educational Work of Thomas Jefferson* (Cambridge, MA: Harvard University Press, 1931), p. 250.

History, then, would provide the masses with lessons to enable them to understand when their elected officials had mischief on their minds.

Each year the overseer of schools would choose from each elementary school "the boy of best genius in the school, of those whose parents are too poor to give them further education, and to send him forward to one of the grammar schools" at public expense.[48] After the first year at the grammar school, the scholarship boys would be examined and the bottom third dismissed. At the end of the second year, the best scholarship student in each grammar school would be chosen to continue and the remainder dismissed. As Jefferson put it in his *Notes on the State of Virginia,* "By this means twenty of the best geniuses will be raked annually from the rubbish, and instructed, at public expense, so far as the grammar schools go."[49]

In short, Jefferson had proposed three years of free elementary schooling, which he believed would function as a screen to identify future leaders from among the masses and equip the remainder to function effectively in the civic, economic, and private spheres of life. He expected this formal schooling to provide the basis for lifelong self-education among the population. Moreover, he understood that in America of the early 19th century, the school did not stand alone as the sole educating institution in society. Nevertheless, his goals were ambitious, so much so that the Virginia legislature did not approve the plan, either in 1779 or in 1817 (see Exhibit 2.2). One may pause to wonder how Jefferson might appraise the present condition of his "noble experiment."

Grammar Schools

The second tier of schools in Jefferson's proposals were called "grammar schools" in his 1779 bill and "district schools or colleges" in his 1817 bill. These schools should not be confused with the present-day American high school, for they were more like the European lyceum. They were to be boarding schools. Approximately 20 were to be established throughout the state at various locations in order to provide that no scholar would be required to travel more than one day's journey from home to school. Except for the 1779 provision for one scholarship student from each elementary school, scholars would be required to pay tuition, room, board, and other necessary expenses. Of the 20 scholarship boys who finished the grammar schools, half were to be chosen to receive a further scholarship to complete the university courses at public expense.

The grammar schools were seen as "preparatory to the entrance of students into the university." Because Jefferson believed that between the ages of 10 and 15 students were best suited to learn languages, and because languages were "an instrument for the attainment of science," languages were the center of grammar school. Greek, Latin, and English grammar, along with advanced arithmetic, geometry, navigation, and geography, were to be the basic subjects in the 6-year curriculum. Such a course of study, Jefferson asserted, would either fit the boy for entrance to the university or lay the foundation for the "various vocations of life needing more instruction than merely menial or praedial labor."[50]

It seems clear that Jefferson intended that local leaders would come from among those educated at the grammar school. Its graduates would provide leadership in business, transportation, surveying, the militia, and local government. He also expected that teachers for the elementary schools would be drawn from those who finished the grammar school curriculum, especially from the scholarship boys not chosen for university attendance.

University Education

Jefferson's conception of university education is displayed in a wide range of private letters and summarized in his Report of the Commission Appointed to Fix the Site of the University of Virginia.[51] His view of higher education differed considerably from the fashion of the day. He explicitly contrasted his university proposals with the popular academies of the early 19th century, which he called "petty academies." These he condemned in a letter to John Adams: "They commit their pupils to the theater of the world, with just taste enough for learning to be alienated from industrious pursuits, and not enough to do service in the ranks of science."[52]

He also rejected the Harvard model of a prescribed course of study. In a letter to George Ticknor, he stated, "We shall, on the contrary, allow them the uncontrolled choice in the lectures they shall choose to attend, and require elementary qualifications on and sufficient age .... Our institution will proceed on the principle ... of letting everyone come and listen to whatever he thinks may improve the condition of his mind."[53] Nevertheless, Jefferson modified free election somewhat in his Rockfish Gap Report. After stating that "every student shall be free to attend the schools of his choice, and not other than he chooses," the report added this qualification:

> But no diploma shall be given to anyone who has not passed an examination in the Latin language as shall have proved him able to read the highest classics in that language with ease, thorough understanding and just quality; and if he be also proficient in Greek, let that, too, be stated in his diploma. The intention being that the reputation of the University shall not be committed but to those who, to an eminence in some one or more of the sciences taught in it, and a proficiency in these languages which constitute the basis of a good education, and are indespensable to fill up the character of a well-educated man.[54]

This idea of relatively free election was based on the premise that all students would enter the university with a common basic education acquired in the grammar schools.[55] The University of Virginia was thus conceived as a place of professional and advanced scientific education rather than simply as a collegiate institution of general liberal studies, which was the model in American higher education of Jefferson's time.

The original plan for the university called for 10 professorships covering these areas of study: ancient language—Latin, Greek, and Hebrew; modern language—French, Spanish, Italian, German, and Anglo Saxon; pure mathematics; physico-mathematics; natural philosophy—chemistry and minerology; botany and zoology; medicine and anatomy; government; law; and ideology—grammar, ethics, rhetoric, belles lettres, and fine arts. It also provided space for private tuition in religion, gymnastics, military, manual arts, dancing, music, and drawing. Each student would specialize in one of the "sciences." Jefferson used the term "science" to refer to all branches or disciplines of knowledge.[56]

Jefferson was unrestrained in his goals for university education (see Exhibit 2.2) because he rejected "the discouraging persuasion that man is fixed, by the law of his nature, at a given point; that his improvement is a chimera, and the hope delusive of rendering ourselves wiser, happier or better than our forefathers were." On the contrary, he proclaimed that similar to the pruners' art of grafting, "Education in like manner, engrafts a new man on the native stock, and improves what in his nature was vicious and perverse into qualities of virtue and social worth."[57]

The university would provide the education for the natural *aristoi* for Jefferson's society. Its graduates would become the legislators, governors, and jurists who would provide governmental leadership. They would fill those vocations which would at a later time be called professions. Although he professed great distaste for Plato's *Republic* and once called it "unintelligible,"[58] Jefferson's educational plan remarkably resembled an improved and democratized form of the Athenian's proposals. In reality, Jefferson, like Plato in the *Republic*, proposed an educational state. The educational "system" was relatively simple because the political economy it was to serve was correspondingly uncomplicated. Both Jefferson's and Plato's proposed education would yield qualified leaders, order, stability, truth, and happiness. The important difference was that Jefferson's educational state was to be republican while Plato's—despite its promising title—was to be autocratic, ruled by a small cadre of philosopher-kings.

Jefferson's republic was to be based on what he called the natural aristocracy. Today we call such an arrangement a *meritocracy:* a social system in which positions of greatest influence and prestige are filled by those who "merit" them by demonstrated talent. He argued that education was a prerequisite for leadership. Is his argument convincing? Given that his proposals were defeated, it is worth speculating: *Would* his proposed educational system have provided the necessary education for leadership and for the masses? We might also ask whether in subsequent history the "people" have generally elected the "really good and wise." If not, is this because of a flaw in Jefferson's conception, or have we not fully developed his ideas? Perhaps most important, is the Jeffersonian meritocracy equivalent to democracy? If not, is it an adequate substitute for democracy? What kind of an educational system would be necessary for a democracy?

Self-Education

The elementary school, the grammar school, and the university were the first three tiers of Jefferson's educational structure. They did not, however, outweigh the fourth tier—lifelong self-instruction. Indeed, in important ways, the first three were but preparations for the fourth. Jefferson's passionate commitment to lifelong self-education was expressed in many of his private letters, in the construction of his own library, in his enthusiasm for newspapers, and in the Bill for Establishing a Public Library. In that bill, Jefferson proposed in 1779 that Virginia build a public library in Richmond and provide an annual allotment for the purchase of books, paintings, and statues.[59] His commitment to lifelong self-education was grounded in his conviction that the development of reason, the expansion of intellect, and inquiry into the mysteries of the universe were indeed fundamental to human happiness. In 1817, as he was preparing the Rockfish Gap Report for the Virginia legislature, he expressed in a letter to George Ticknor his fear that the legislature might not understand the "important truths, that knowledge is power, that knowledge is safety, and that knowledge is happiness." Nevertheless, he contended that persistence was necessary, for if "we fail in doing all the good we wish, we will do at least all we can. This is the law of duty in every society of free agents, where everyone has equal right to judge for himself."[60]

Most American educational theorists since Jefferson have agreed that a fundamental aim of all education is to prepare the student for lifelong learning. Again, a number of questions present themselves: To what extent has this goal been achieved? What are the factors which mitigate against its success? Why did Jefferson believe his proposed educational system would facilitate lifelong learning? What kind of lifelong learning would you expect from the graduates of each of Jefferson's three tiers of formal schooling? In each instance, would this learning be sufficient to enable the graduates to engage in Jefferson's ideal of the pursuit of happiness?

Educational Method and "Faculty Psychology"

Jefferson did not systematically address the question of educational methodology. Nevertheless, from his writings we may infer some of his predilections for how students should be confronted with educational materials. Jefferson urged the study of Latin and Greek in the grammar school because he believed that language acquisition was "chiefly a work of memory" and that the ages of

Jefferson, like most liberals of his day, believed in what would later be called faculty psychology, which held that disciplined study of the classics strengthened the "faculties" (memory, reason, creativity, etc.) of the mind.

10 to 15 were the best time for work requiring mostly memorization.[61] Moreover, he proposed the study of these languages because the literature they contained offered superb models of writing. His argument that mathematics "exercises our reason" and "stores the mind with Truths which are useful in the other branches of science" provides us with yet another insight into his understanding of pedagogy.[62] From these and other sources, we may conclude that Jefferson, like most classical liberals, held to what would later be called faculty psychology, which contended that the mind was made up of distinct "faculties." For Jefferson, the faculties of the mind included memory, reason, and imagination.[63] Like muscles, these faculties had to be exercised for development. Moreover, he conceived the mind as an empty vessel to be "filled" with useful facts. Faculty psychology held that developed faculties, with minds appropriately exercised and filled, could "transfer" this training and understanding to any situation in life—that is, the student would be able to generalize from school experience to life experience.

Common to those whose educational practice was based on faculty psychology was the preference for rote memorization in the early years, the study of models of excellent writing, the reading of literary classics, devotion to Latin and Greek as the basis for an educated man, and liberal doses of hard intellectual work. Jefferson's letters to his daughters and young acquaintances are filled with exhortations on diligent study and the development of habits of industry. This, to his daughter, is but one example: "Of all the cankers of human happiness, none erodes it with so silent, yet baneful a tooth, as indolence."[64] The following lament to John Adams in 1814 might well have been written as a response to the American university student of today:

> Our post-revolutionary youth are born under happier stars than you and I were. They acquire all learning in their mother's womb and bring it into the world ready-made. The information in books is no longer necessary; and all knowledge which is not innate, is in contempt, or neglected at least. . . . When sobered by experience, I hope our successors will turn their attention to education.[65]

One can probably safely infer that Jefferson's preferred educational methodologies would differ little from the preferences of those who embraced faculty psychology. Students under his tutelage would have labored hard at memorization, languages, mathematics, and literature. At an appropriate time, after they had mastered the "classical curriculum," they would specialize in a single branch or discipline of knowledge.

Jefferson's Views on Slavery, Native Americans, and Women

Jefferson was America's outstanding spokesman for the liberalism of his time, and perhaps of all time. His Declaration of Independence proclamations on human rights and human equality were borrowed by Lincoln for the first sentence of the Gettysburg address and a century later gave moral force to the Civil Rights and the women's equality movements in this country. Freedom, liberty, the rule of reason in human affairs, the unfettered pursuit of truth, the stimulation of scientific investigation, and the creation of political and educational structures for the support of those goals were his life's work. Nevertheless, we have seen that there are reasons to question some of Jefferson's ideas in these areas. Moreover, a serious study of Jefferson forces one to consider at least three additional problem areas: his actions and views on slavery, Native Americans, and women.

Slavery There can be little question that Jefferson's entire philosophy required the rejection of slavery. Indeed, Jefferson's first legislative act as a representative in the Virginia colonial assembly[66] was to offer a bill allowing the voluntary emancipation of slaves by their owners. In 1770, as a lawyer, he undertook the defense of a slave who sued for his freedom.[67] Most significantly, in his proposed draft of the Declaration of Independence Jefferson included the following about the British monarch:

> He has waged cruel war against human nature itself, violating its most sacred rights of life and liberty in persons of a distant people who never offended him, capturing and carrying them into slavery in another hemisphere, or to incur miserable death in their transportation hither. This piratical warfare, the opprobrium of INFIDEL powers, is the warfare of the CHRISTIAN king of Great Britain. Determined to keep open a market where MEN should be bought and sold, he has prostituted his negative for suppressing every legislative attempt to prohibit or restrain this execrable commerce.[68]

Although this section was struck by the full assembly, its inclusion by Jefferson and his emphasis of the word "MEN" are significant when one attempts to comprehend how slavery fits with Jefferson's social philosophy. It seems to indicate that philosophically Jefferson included African-Americans in the category of "men" and that they should be covered by all the provisions the Declaration makes for "men."

However, his writings about African-Americans provide an ambiguous judgment of the race. At times he seems to see African-Americans as inferior, at other times he calls them equal or superior to whites in some attributes, and at still other times he argues that their inequalities are due to the degradation of slavery and are remediable if they are placed in more favorable circumstances.[69] As a representative to the national Congress, he unsuccessfully proposed that the Northwest Ordinance prohibit slavery after 1800 in any states or territories created from the Northwest Territory. From that time until his death, however, Jefferson was remarkably quiet in public about his opposition to slavery. In private, Jefferson often condemned slavery. For example, in August 1825, he wrote in a private correspondence, "The abolition of the evil [slavery] is not impossible. It ought never to be despaired of. Every plan should be adapted, every experiment tried, which may do something towards the ultimate object."[70]

During his two terms as President, however, Jefferson did not actively support the abolition of slavery. Moreover, in none of his major legislative proposals on education did he include the education of slaves. This is most surprising, since those weaknesses he attributed to blacks were weaknesses which Jefferson believed could be improved through education. Jefferson's biographer, Dumas Malone, suggests that he may have remained silent on the slavery questions while President because he considered it a state rather than a federal issue.[71] This explanation, however, remains unconvincing, especially when one remembers Jefferson's willingness to expand federal power to purchase the Louisiana Territory. Such an expansion of power was justified by a higher end, he argued, and government was simply a means. Could the pursuit of open land for freehold farmers be more worthy than the elimination of human bondage? Was Jefferson practicing what he believed was political realism according to his own axiom: "No more good must be attempted than the nation can bear"?[72] If so, did this "realism" require that he continue to own slaves—at times as many as 200?[73] Is there a contradiction between "political realism" and moral leadership?

As historian Ronald Takaki points out, although Jefferson wrote in 1788 that "nobody [more] wishes to see an abolition of the [African slave] trade [and] of the condition of slavery; and certainly nobody will be more willing to encounter every sacrifice for that object," he continued to add slaves to his plantation while some 10,000 slaves were being freed by slave owners in Virginia alone in the 1780s.[74] Jefferson justified his slaveholding partly on economic grounds—he could not afford to free them until he paid off his debts (which he never succeeded in doing)—and partly on his belief that, unlike Native Americans, African-Americans did not have the natural intellectual endowment necessary for self-governance. Jefferson wrote in 1781:

> In general, their existence appears to participate more of sensation than reflection. . . . Comparing them by their faculties of memory, reason, and imagination, it appears to me that in memory they are equal to whites: in reason much inferior, as I think one could scarcely be found capable of tracing and comprehending the investigations of Euclid; and that in imagination they are dull, tasteless, and anomalous.[75]

Jefferson's beliefs about the racial inferiority of African-Americans led him to argue against intermarriage: Their "amalgamation with the other color produces a degradation to which no lover of his country, no lover of excellence in the human character can innocently consent."[76]

Native Americans As is often the case with racial and ethnic prejudice, Jefferson's racism regarding African-Americans took a different form where Native Americans were concerned. He believed that intermarriage between white people and Native Americans was acceptable because Native Americans in his view were equal to whites in natural endowment, but their culture was vastly inferior. He wrote in 1785, "I am safe in affirming that the proofs of genius given by the Indians of N. America, place them on a level with whites in the same uncultivated state. . . . I believe the Indian to be in body and mind equal to the white man. I have supposed the black man, in his present state, might not be so."[77] The consequence of this view for Jefferson was that Native Americans either had to be "civilized" into white culture or had to be driven west of the Mississippi. His economic priorities, as Takaki points out, influenced his views of both races: what the whites wanted from African-Americans was their labor, while what whites wanted from Native Americans was their land. If the latter agreed to cultivate the land as whites did, however, then they could stay—and Jefferson believed it was the province of whites to instruct the Native Americans in acquiring the necessities of European culture while abandoning their own. While U.S. President, he told the Potawatomies:

> We shall . . . see your people become disposed to cultivate the earth, to raise herds of the useful animals, and to spin and weave, for their food and clothing. These resources are certain: they will never disappoint you: while those of hunting may fail, and expose your women and children to the miseries of hunger and cold. We will with pleasure furnish you with implements for the most necessary arts, and with persons who may instruct you how to make and use them.[78]

Jefferson's stance toward forcing the Native Americans away from their own culture into the ways of European Americans, as we shall see in Chapter 7, is one that would become formal government policy in the 20th century.

Women If Jefferson was contradictory in his statements about African-Americans and inconsistent in his actions toward slavery, his views regarding women were clear, consistent, and regrettable. His conception of the female was as a wife, homemaker, bearer of children, and delight to her husband—period.[79] He was reportedly loving toward his wife and caring of his daughters, but he understood women to be the legal appendages to their husbands. When Jefferson stated, "All *men* are created equal . . . ," or made pronouncements regarding the rights and reason of man, his terms were always gender-specific.

In all his proposals for education, females were provided schooling only in the elementary school. The grammar schools and the university were exclusive male preserves. As important as he believed education was for the pursuit of happiness, and although he devoted the greater part of his adult life to thinking about the relationship between free men and education, in 1818, at age 75, Jefferson wrote, "A plan of female education has never been a subject of systematic contemplation with me. It has occupied my attention so far only as the education of my own daughters occasionally required." The education he provided for them was much as "might enable them, when they become mothers, to educate their own daughters, and even to direct the course for sons, should their fathers be lost, or incapable, or inattentive."[80] For Jefferson, the education of women should enable them to participate in such "amusements of life" as dancing, drawing, and music, and to assume their role in the "household economy."[81] It seems that Jefferson reflected too much the sentiments of George Saville, Marquis of Halifax, whose *Advice to a Daughter* saw 15 editions between 1688 and 1765, and too little those of Abigail Adams and Mary Wollstonecraft, both staunch defenders of women's rights during Jefferson's time. Like most other classical liberals, and just as the Greeks had done in Aristotle's time, Jefferson uncritically accepted the placement of women into the private or domestic sphere of the household and perceived no need to educate women for public participation in a democratic society in which citizenship was a male privilege.

Are the issues of slavery, domination of Native Americans, and women's rights simply anomalies in Jefferson's philosophy, or do they represent a deeper flaw in liberalism? Perhaps even the posing of such questions imposes unfair historical hindsight upon both Jefferson and classical liberalism. Jefferson's thought and actions in these issues were indeed an advance over his conservative opponents. Is that sufficient for one who is thought to be committed to democracy? Privileged white males, that is, Jefferson's natural aristocracy, have always been a tiny minority in American history. Did classical liberalism adequately provide for women, African-Americans, Native Americans, or nonprivileged white males—in other words, the non-*aristoi?* What becomes of Jefferson's democratic ideas if the large majority of the population are excluded from his most important goal, the pursuit of happiness? Are there possible corrections that could rescue Jefferson's philosophy? If not, what are our assessments of Jeffersonian democracy and of classical liberal ideology more generally?

CONCLUDING REMARKS

This chapter explored how the notions of political economy and ideology may be applied to an analysis of education and schooling during the 50-year period following the Revolutionary War. Agrarian rural life, the family, the limited form of republican government, and the relative homogeneity of local culture all influenced early educational processes both within and outside of schools. The exclusion of females, Native Americans, and African-Americans from formal schooling shows the contrast between the social–political roles of those groups and the roles of white males, particularly those with property.

From the standpoint of ideology, the breakdown of feudalism and the rise of classical liberalism in Europe and the United States were examined. The Greek origins of classical liberal thought were visible in American commitments to such ideals as human reason, natural law, virtue, progress, nationalism, and freedom. A commitment to education was seen as a means to these ideals. However, this should not suggest that classical liberals were uniformly committed to state-supported or state-controlled schooling, as illustrated in Thomas Jefferson's failure to win adequate support for a state system of schooling in Virginia.

Jefferson himself was presented as a prominent example of an early American whose thinking revealed a number of internal tensions in the tenets of classical liberalism. Like many others who shared his ideology, he professed belief in human freedom but supported slavery in his deeds, if not in his words. He argued for human equality but accepted uncritically the subordinate role of women in society. His prescriptions for schooling, which emphasized the development of the rational capacities of white males, reflected his biases with regard to race and gender; despite his plan for "raking the genius from the rubbish," his plans were still regarded as unnecessarily egalitarian by those of his contemporaries who voted against him. While other tensions among the various commitments of classical liberalism were also illustrated in Jefferson's thought, his emphasis on the interrelations between intellectual and political freedom and the education necessary for their realization is of particular interest—and might be said to remain a challenge to educators today.

Through Jefferson we can see that the meaning of such admirable ideals as freedom, democracy, and popular education must be understood within the context in which they are advocated. Commitment to popular education, for example, is diminished if it is meant to exclude a major portion of society. A commitment to democracy is similarly diminished if it means, in a particular political–economic and ideological context, the exclusion of most of the society from participation in the decisions that affect their lives. A commitment to individual freedom becomes problematic if, in the context of other commitments, cultural uniformity is sought. All of these meanings, and others, remain problematic as we move into subsequent chapters of this volume.

As we begin to think critically about the limitations of classical liberal ideology, we have a tendency to vilify, or at least to place at some distance from ourselves, an ideology that by today's standards had significant racist and sexist dimensions. This tendency to distance ourselves from the dominant ideology will also occur later when we critique modern liberal ideology. The danger of this tendency is that the dominant ideology of our culture, and its historical origins, become externalized as if we ourselves have not been importantly shaped by it. While we criticize the exclusionist tendencies of classical liberalism, we can also learn to identify and become more critical about how our own thinking has been conditioned by classical liberal commitments to such ideals as objective truth, private property, and a view of democracy that represents some portions of the population but not others.

PRIMARY SOURCE READING

The following selection was penned by a prominent classical liberal, the physician Benjamin Rush, who was one of Jefferson's revolutionary compatriots. Both Jefferson and Rush were signers of the Declaration of Independence, and both were influential with their countrymen. Each valued education highly and considered schooling to be an important building block for a free society.

This selection was written with regard to the education of youth in Rush's home state of Pennsylvania. Like Jefferson, he was eager to prepare citizens for a democratic, republican form of government, and like Jefferson, he looked toward the particular needs and character of his home state as well as the nation. Unlike Jefferson, however, Rush emphasized the religious character of education in his time. While Jefferson took pride in his bill for Religious Freedom, which said that every individual should be free to worship or not worship as "he" pleased, Rush felt that the fate of the republic rested in part upon Christian upbringing. Believing that "a Christian cannot fail of being a republican," Rush wanted schools to instill both Christianity and patriotism in young people, for he felt that the virtues of each were identical with the other. Like Jefferson, he appeared to believe that the state has no role in enforcing religious belief, yet it is clear that his proposed school system would have provided support for one religion and not others.

Other similarities and contrasts between Jefferson's and Rush's positions are also worth noting, and this you can do. Rush's classical liberal regard for private property, for education, for individual merit and virtue, for scientific reasoning, and for nationalism all come through clearly in his arguments, and these provide various bases for comparison. We present this selection by Rush because it underscores certain basic tenets of classical liberal ideology while simultaneously illustrating distinct points of departure within classical liberal thought on education and society. Every dimension of classical liberalism identified in this chapter can be found illustrated in Rush's arguments.

Both Jefferson and Rush attend to the role of the citizen, but Rush attends particularly to religious sources of individual virtue. He, like many classical liberal thinkers, could not think about the process of becoming more fully human—a primary function of education—without including religious development as part of that process. We will see that in subsequent generations such an assumption becomes increasingly problematic for educational leaders.

From *Essays on Education in the Early Republic* (Cambridge, MA: Harvard University Press, 1965), pp. 10–18.

THOUGHTS UPON THE MODE OF EDUCATION PROPER IN A REPUBLIC

Benjamin Rush

. . . I conceive the education of our youth in this country to be peculiarly necessary in Pennsylvania, while our citizens are composed of the natives of so many different kingdoms in Europe. Our schools of learning, by producing one general and uniform system of education, will render the mass of the people more homogeneous, and thereby fit them more easily for uniform and peaceable government.

I proceed in the next place, to enquire, what mode of education we shall adopt so as to secure to the state all the advantages that are to be derived from the proper instruction of youths, and here I beg leave to remark, that the only foundation for a useful education in a republic is to be laid in Religion. Without this there can be no virtue, and without virtue there can be no liberty, and liberty is the object and life of all republican governments.

Such is my veneration for every religion that reveals the attributes of the Deity, or a future state of rewards and punishments, that I had rather see the opinions of Confucius or Mahomed inculcated upon our youth, than see them grow up wholly devoid of a system of religious principles. But the religion I mean to recommend in this place, is that of the New Testament.

It is foreign to my purpose to hint at the arguments which establish the truth of the Christian revelation. My only business is to declare, that all its doctrines and precepts are calculated to promote the happiness of society, and the safety and well being of civil government. A Christian cannot fail of being a republican. The history of the creation of man, and of the relation of our species to each other by birth, which is recorded in the Old Testament, is the best refutation that can be given to the divine right of kings, and the strongest argument that can be used in favor of the original and natural equality of all mankind. A Christian, I say again, cannot fail of being a republican, for every precept of the Gospel inculcates those degrees of humility, self-denial, and brotherly kindness, which are directly opposed to the pride of monarchy and the pageantry of a court. A Christian cannot fail of being useful to the republic, for his religion teacheth him, that no man "liveth to himself." And lastly, a Christian cannot fail of being wholly inoffensive, for his religion teacheth him, in all things to do to others what he would wish, in like circumstances, they should do to him.

I am aware that I dissent from one of those paradoxical opinions with which modern times abound; and that it is improper to fill the minds of youth with religious prejudices of any kind, and that they should be left to choose their own principles, after they have arrived at an age in which they are capable of judging for themselves. Could we preserve the mind in childhood and youth a perfect blank, this plan of education would have more to recommend it; but this we know to be impossible. The human mind runs as naturally into principles as it does after facts. It submits with difficulty to those restraints or partial discoveries which are imposed upon it in the infancy of reason. Hence the impatience of children to be informed upon all subjects that relate to the invisible world. But I beg leave to ask, why should we pursue a different plan of education with respect to religion, from that which we pursue in teaching the arts and sciences? Do we leave our youth to acquire systems of geography, philosophy, or politics, till they have arrived at an age in which they are capable of judging for themselves? We do not. I claim no more then for religion, than for the other sciences, and I add further, that if our youth are disposed after they are of age to think for themselves, a knowledge of one system, will be the best means of conducting them in a free enquiry into other systems of religion, just as an acquaintance with one system of philosophy is the best introduction to the study of all the other systems in the world. . . .

Next to the duty which young men owe to their Creator, I wish to see a SUPREME REGARD TO THEIR COUNTRY, inculcated upon them. When the Duke of Sully became prime minister to Henry the IVth of France, the first thing he did, he tells us, "was to subdue and forget his own heart." The same duty is incumbent upon every citizen of a republic. Our country includes family, friends and property, and should be preferred to them all. Let our pupil be taught that he does not belong to himself, but that he is public property. Let him be taught to love his family, but let him be taught, at the same time, that he must forsake, and even forget them, when the welfare of his country requires it.

He must watch for the state, as if its liberties depended upon his vigilance alone, but he must do this in such a manner so not to defraud his creditors, or neglect his family. He must love private life, but he must decline no station, however public or responsible it may be, when called to it by the sufferages of his fellow citizens. He must love popularity, but he must despise it when set in competition with the dictates of his judgment, or the real interest of his country. He must love character, and have a due sense of injuries, but he must be taught to appeal only to the laws of the state, to defend the one, and punish the other. He must love family honor, but he must be taught that neither the rank nor antiquity of his ancestors, can command respect, without personal merit. He must avoid neutrality in all questions that divide the state, but he must shun the rage, and acrimony of party spirit. He must be taught to love his fellow creatures in every part of the world, but he must cherish with a more intense and peculiar affection, the citizens of Pennsylvania and of the United States.

I do not wish to see our youth educated with a single prejudice against any nation or country; but we impose a task upon human nature, repugnant alike to reason, revelation and the ordinary dimensions of the human heart, when we require him to embrace, with equal affection, the whole family of mankind. He must be taught to amass wealth, but it must be only to increase his power of contribution to the wants and demands of the state. He must be indulged occasionally in amusement, but he must be taught that study and business should be his principal pursuits in life. Above all he must love life, and endeavor to acquire as many of its conveniences as possible by industry and economy, but he must be taught that this life "is not his own," when the safety of his country require it. These are practicable lessons, and the history of the commonwealths of Greece and Rome show, that human nature, without the aids of Christianity, has attained these degrees of perfection.

While we inculcate these republican duties upon our pupil, we must not neglect, at the same time, to inspire him with republican principles. He must be taught that there can be no durable liberty but in a republic, and that government, like all other sciences, is of a progressive nature. The chains which have bound this science in Europe are happily unloosed in America. Here it is open to investigation and improvement. While philosophy has protected us by its discoveries from a thousand natural evils, government has unhappily followed with an unequal pace. It would be to dishonor human genius, only to name the many defects which still exist in the best systems of legislation. We daily see matter of a perishable nature rendered durable by certain chemical operations. In like manner, I conceive, that it is possible to combine power in such a way as not only to increase the happiness, but to promote the duration of republican forms of government far beyond the terms limited for them by history, or the common opinions of mankind.

To assist in rendering religious, moral and political instruction more effectual upon the minds of our youth, it will be necessary to subject their bodies to physical discipline. To obviate the inconveniences of their studious and sedentary mode of life, they should live upon a temperate diet, consisting chiefly of broths, milk and vegetables. The black broth of Sparta, and the barley broth of Scotland, have been alike celebrated for their beneficial effects upon the minds of young people. They should avoid tasting spiritous liquors. They should also be accustomed occasionally to work with their hands, in the intervals of study, and in the busy seasons of the year in the country. Moderate sleep, silence, occasional solitude and cleanliness, should be inculcated upon them, and the utmost advantage should be taken of a proper direction of those great principles in human conduct—sensibility, habit, imitations and association.

The influence of these physical causes will be powerful upon the intellects, as well as upon the principles and morals of young people.

To those who have studied human nature, it will not appear paradoxical to recommend, in this essay, a particular attention to vocal music. Its mechanical effects in civilizing the mind, and thereby preparing it for the influence of religion and government, have been so often felt and recorded, that it will be unnecessary to mention facts in favour of its usefulness, in order to excite a proper attention to it.

In the education of youth, let the authority of our masters be as *absolute* as possible. The government of schools like the government of private families should be *arbitrary,* that it may not be *severe.* By this mode of education, we prepare our youth for the subordination of laws and thereby qualify them for becoming good citizens of the republic. I am satisfied that the most useful citizens have been formed from those youth who have never known or felt their own wills till they were one and twenty years of age, and I have often thought that society owes a great deal of its order and happiness to the deficiencies of parental government being supplied by those habits of obedience and subordination which are contracted at schools.

I cannot help bearing a testimony, in this place, against the custom, which prevails in some parts of America, (but which is daily falling into disuse in Europe) of crowding boys together under one roof for the purpose of education. The practice is the gloomy remains of monkish ignorance, and is as unfavorable to the improvements of the mind in useful learning, as monastaries are to the spirit of religion. I grant this method of secluding boys from the intercourse of private families, has a tendency to make them scholars, but our business is to make them men, citizens and Christians. The vices of young people are generally learned from each other. The vices of adults seldom infect them. By separating them from each other, therefore, in their hours of relaxation from study, we secure their morals from a principal source of corruption, while we improve their manners, by subjecting them to those restraints which the difference of age and sex, naturally produce in private families. . . .

From observations that have been made it is plain, that I consider it is possible to convert men into republican machines. This must be done, if we expect them to perform their parts properly, in the great machine of the government of the state. That republic is sophisticated with monarchy or aristocracy that does not revolve upon the wills of the people, and these must be fitted to each other by means of education before they can be made to produce regularity and unison in government. . . .

QUESTIONS FOR DISCUSSION AND EXAMINATION

1. Jefferson believed that three years of literacy instruction in elementary school would be valuable in safeguarding the liberties of the population. Today this seems to be far too little schooling for so important a task. To what degree do the dimensions of political–economic life during Jefferson's time make his belief in the power of basic literacy plausible?
2. Jefferson's Bill for the More General Diffusion of Knowledge tried to establish state funding for schooling in Virginia, but it sought to protect local control of schools. To what degree is such a combination—state funding and local control of schools—consistent with various dimensions of the classical liberal conception of freedom?
3. In asserting that "the Christian cannot fail of being a Republican," did Benjamin Rush appear to be making a claim consistent with the several dimensions of classical liberal thought described in this chapter? Explain.
4. Was Rush's aspiration to "convert men to Republican machines" contradictory to classical liberal ideals of intellectual freedom? Further, was Rush's aim any different from Jefferson's in this regard? Explain your positions on both questions.,
5. Jefferson claimed that the Bill for the More General Diffusion of Knowledge would help locate the "natural aristocracy" of society: those with the virtue and talent to lead in a republican form of government. To what degree do you think his plan, if passed, would have adequately rewarded virtue and talent? What were the limitations of the plan in terms of social class, race, and gender?
6. In your experience, are today's schools successful in locating those students with the most "virtue and talent"? Do they successfully locate a natural aristocracy in today's society, or do "wealth, birth, or other accidental condition or circumstance," as Jefferson said, play a significant role? Explain.
7. This chapter raises the possibility that Jefferson's inadequate regard for women, Native Americans, and African-Americans in his educational thinking was rooted not just in his own personal prejudices, but in the liberal ideology of his time. Which dimensions of classical liberalism seem to have justified, to classical liberals, the subordination of women, African-Americans, and Native Americans? Explain.

NOTES

1. Recent popular-media treatments of Jefferson include: *Thomas Jefferson,* a film by Ken Burns. Public Broadcasting System, 1977; Sean Wilentz, "Life, Liberty, and the Pursuit of Thomas Jefferson," in *The New Republic,* March 10, 1997, pp. 32–42; and Conor Cruise O'Brien, "Thomas Jefferson: Radical and Racist," in *The Atlantic Monthly,* October 1996, pp. 53–74.
2. *Historical Statistics of U.S. Colonial Times to 1970,* Part 1, Bureau of the Census, 1975, pp. 11–12.
3. Dumas Malone, *Jefferson and His Time* (Boston: Little, Brown, 1948, 1951, 1962, 1963), vol. 2, p. 319.
4. Michael Gordon, ed., *The American Family in Social-Historical Perspective* (New York: St. Martin's Press, 1973), p. 350.
5. John Demos, *A Little Commonwealth* (New York: Oxford University Press, 1973), pp. 66, 131–32.
6. Dumas Malone, *Jefferson and His Time* (Boston: Little, Brown, 1951), pp. 397–405; Fawn Brodie, *Thomas Jefferson: An Intimate History* (New York: W. W. Norton, 1974), pp. 44–46.
7. Demos, pp. 82–107. See also Philip Gemer, *The Protestant Temperament.*
8. Henri Pierenne, *A History of Europe* (Garden City, NY: Doubleday.)
9. Alexander Pope (1730), "Intended for Sir Isaac Newton in Westminster Abbey," in Henry W. Boynton, *The Complete Poetical Works of Pope* (Cambridge, MA: Houghton Mifflin, 1931) p. 135 (emphasis original).
10. John Chester Miller, *The Wolf by the Ears: Thomas Jefferson and Slavery* (New York: The Free Press, 1977), p. 33.
11. Louis B. Wright, *The Cultural Life of the American Colonies* (New York, Harper Torchbooks, 1962), p. 23.
12. See G. H. Koch, *Religion of the American Enlightenment* (New York: Crowell, 1968), and H. M. Morris, *Deism in Eighteenth-Century America* (New York: Columbia University Press, 1934).
13. Benjamin Franklin, *Autobiography and Other Writings,* Russell B. Nye, ed. (Boston: Houghton Mifflin, 1958), pp. 163–64.
14. See, as an example, Nancy Cott, *The Bonds of Womanhood: "Woman's Sphere" in New England, 1780–1835* (New Haven: Yale University Press, 1977).
15. Both quotes from Russell B. Nye, *The Cultural Life of the New Nation* (New York: Harper Torchbooks, 1963), p. 29–30.
16. Julian P. Boyd, ed., *The Papers of Thomas Jefferson* (Princeton, NJ: Princeton University Press, 1950), vol. 10, pp. 244–45.
17. Patrick Henry, quoted in Russell B. Nye, *The Cultural Life of the New Nation: 1776–1830* (New York: Harper, 1960), pp. 38–39.
18. Isaiah Berlin, *Four Essays on Liberty* (New York: Oxford University Press, 1969).
19. Dumas Malone, vol. 2, pp. 222–23.

20. See Ronald Takaki, *Iron Cages: Race and Culture in 19th Century America* (Oxford: Oxford University Press), pp. 36–65. Also see Adrian Koch, *The Philosophy of Thomas Jefferson* (New York: Columbia University Press, 1943), chap. 1.
21. Boyd, *Papers of Jefferson,* vol. 2, pp. 545–47.
22. Quoted in Faun M. Brodie, *Thomas Jefferson: An Intimate Biography* (New York: Bantam Books, 1974), p. 194.
23. Andrew A. Lipscomb and A. E. Berg, eds., *The Writings of Thomas Jefferson* (Washington, DC: Thomas Jefferson Memorial Association, 1903), vol. 14, p. 284.
24. Boyd, *Papers of Jefferson,* vol. 2, p. 49.
25. Leonard W. Levy, *Jefferson and Civil Liberties: The Darker Side* (Cambridge, MA: Harvard University Press, 1963), chap. 3.
26. Malone, vol. 5, p. 388.
27. Henry A. Washington, ed., *The Writings of Thomas Jefferson* (New York: Riker and Thorne, 1854), vol. 7, pp. 397–99.
28. Boyd, *Papers of Jefferson,* vol. 123, p. 441.
29. Daniel Boorstein, *The Lost World of Thomas Jefferson* (Boston: Beacon Press, 1960), p. 190.
30. Boyd, *Papers of Jefferson,* vol. 12, pp. 14–19.
31. Letter to William C. Jarvis, September 28, 1820, in Paul L. Ford, ed., *The Writings of Thomas Jefferson* (New York: G. P. Putnam Sons, 1899), vol. 10, p. 161.
32. Letter to Edward Everett, March 27, 1824, in Lipscomb and Bergh, *Writings of Jefferson,* vol. 16, p. 22.
33. Boyd, *Papers of Jefferson,* vol. 12, p. 442.
34. Ibid.
35. *Notes on the State of Virginia,* in Saul K. Padover, ed., *The Complete Jefferson* (New York: Tudor Publishing Co., 1943), p. 687.
36. Koch, p. 130.
37. Quoted in Malone, vol. V, p. 444.
38. Letter to John Adams, 1813, in Ford, *Writings of Jefferson,* vol. 9, pp. 429–30.
39. Ford, *Writings of Jefferson,* vol. 9, pp. 424–30.
40. Boyd, *Papers of Jefferson,* vol. 2, pp. 526–33.
41. Ibid, pp. 535–43.
42. Ibid, pp. 544–45.
43. Roy Honeywell, *The Educational Work of Thomas Jefferson* (Cambridge, MA: Harvard University Press, 1931), pp. 233–45.
44. Ibid, pp. 245–60.
45. Ford, *Writings of Jefferson,* vol. 9, pp. 427–38.
46. Boyd, *Papers of Jefferson,* vol. 2, p. 528.
47. Ford, *Writings of Jefferson,* vol. 3, pp. 254–55.
48. *Notes on the State of Virginia,* in Ford, *Writings of Jefferson,* vol 3, p. 250.
49. Ibid.
50. "Report of the Commission," in Honeywell, pp. 248–60; "Notes" in Ford, vol. 3, pp. 250–55.
51. Honeywell, pp. 248–60.
52. Ford, *Writings of Jefferson,* vol. 9, p. 465.
53. Lipscomb and Bergh, *Writings of Jefferson,* vol. 15, p. 455.
54. Padover, p. 1108.
55. It was the case that each of the schools had required courses. Thus, while students had free election to choose their schools, they did not have free election among the courses.
56. Padover, p. 1100.
57. Honeywell, p. 252.
58. Letter to John Adams, Ford, *Writings of Jefferson,* vol. 9, p. 462.
59. Boyd, *Papers of Jefferson,* vol. 2, pp. 544–45.
60. Ford, *Writings of Jefferson,* vol. 10, p. 96.
61. "Notes," Ford, *Writings of Jefferson,* vol. 3, pp. 250–51.
62. Letter to Thomas Mann Randolph, Jr., in Boyd, *Papers of Jefferson,* vol. 10, p. 305.
63. Koch, chap. 9.
64. Boyd, *Papers of Jefferson,* vol. 11, p. 250.
65. Ford, *Writings of Jefferson,* vol. 9, p. 264.
66. For a more detailed analysis of Jefferson's views on slavery see John Chester Miller, *The Wolf by the Ears: Thomas Jefferson and Slavery* (New York: The Free Press, 1977).
67. Brodie, pp. 102–104.
68. Adrienne Koch and William Peden, *The Life and Selected Writings of Thomas Jefferson* (New York: Modern Library, 1944), p. 25.
69. Malone, vol. 1, p. 226; vol. 6, p. 542; Padover, pp. 661–66, Brodie, pp. 7, 42–48, 103–105, 195–99.
70. Quoted in John Chester Miller, p. 276.
71. Brodie, pp. 102–104.
72. Koch, p. 130.
73. Malone, vol. 1, p. 445.
74. Takaki, p. 43–44.
75. Ibid., p. 48.
76. Ibid., p. 50.
77. Ibid., p. 58.
78. Ibid., p. 56. The metaphor Jefferson chose in order to underscore his belief that agriculture was necessary for American democracy while commerce and especially manufacturing were detrimental to its health tells us as much about Jefferson's stereotypical mindset regarding women as it does about his belief in the potential evils of industry. He indicated that Americans must choose between three potential brides: Agriculture—the "pure damsel"; Commerce—the "vixen"; and Manufacturing—the "diseased harlot." (See Malone, vol. 2, p. 383).
79. Malone, vol. 3, chap. 8.
80. Letter to N. Burwell, in Padover, p. 1085.
81. Ibid., p. 1086.

School as a Public Institution: The Common-School Era

When Thomas Jefferson died, on Independence Day in 1825, his dream of a state-supported system of education was still unrealized, not only in Virginia but throughout the new nation. Nevertheless, the massive changes occurring in the political economy of New England would affect its educational efforts and provide the impetus for an educational system in Massachusetts which, by the Civil War, became the model for the nation.

From its founding, the Massachusetts Bay Colony had been known for its commitment to schooling. Soon after the ratification of the U.S. Constitution, in 1789, the state of Massachusetts renewed this commitment with the passage of a law requiring all towns having a population of 50 or more families to provide an elementary school for at least six months each year, and those having more than 199 families to provide a grammar school to teach classical languages. This law probably had little direct impact, as many towns were already in accordance and those which failed to comply were rarely called to task. In any case, at the turn of the 19th century only a small percentage of the school-age children attended schools, even in Boston.[1]

During the following three decades, education became a topic of increasing concern in Massachusetts as the number of elementary schools and school attendance both increased. By the 1830s most children in the state had access to elementary schooling. Locally controlled schools with voluntary attendance were almost universal. The conditions of these schools, however, were usually less than optimal. Most school buildings were poorly constructed, inadequately ventilated, and provided seats, desks, and lighting which were condemned by contemporary doctors. Moreover, schools were often located in the most undesirable sector of the town, in part because wealthier families hired private tutors for their children. Many of the teachers were barely literate; often they were hired because they would accept an inadequate salary. It was not unusual for a teacher to confront a large number of students ranging from 2 to 25 years of age, using whatever range of texts could be brought from home.[2] Educational historian Carl Kaestle's assessment of the state of American education at this time was especially applicable to Massachusetts: "America had schools, but, except in large cities, America did not have school systems."[3] It was within this educational context that the movement for educational reform began in the mid-1820s in Massachusetts. But the reform movement did not arise in a vacuum. Momentous economic, social, political, demographic, and intellectual developments impelled both the reformers and reform. These developments will be the focus of the first part of this chapter.

POLITICAL ECONOMY OF THE COMMON-SCHOOL ERA

Demographic Changes

The first demographic change was the massive flow of settlers from the coastal states into the interior territories, initially into the Ohio and Mississippi River valleys and subsequently the trans-Mississippi great plains and the Pacific coast. The territories of Kentucky, Tennessee, Ohio, Indiana, Illinois, and Michigan, for example, collectively grew from about 110,000 inhabitants in 1790 to almost 950,000 in 1810.[4] As there were definite overland and water routes from the settled to the "new" areas, groups of settlers from New England tended to congregate in specific locales, as did pioneers from other sections. These settlers tended to bring and retain many of their social, political, and religious values. This, in part, helped account for the establishment of familiar institutions in the territories. While the struggle over slavery in the territories may appear as the most important effect of this migration, there were other subtle but significant effects as well.

One such effect was the impact of westward migration on American nationalism. This migration stretched the population over a much larger expanse of territory. Long distances and resulting travel times loosened old ties of kinship, community, and national loyalty. It is important to remember that American nationalism was still in its infancy and relatively weak compared with loyalty to the various states. Consequently, a major concern of postrevolutionary intellectual leaders such as Benjamin Rush and Noah Webster had been to forge a unique and widespread sense of American identity or nationalism. Moreover, the War of 1812 and the subsequent controversy over slavery created heated sectional conflict, which further eroded nationalism and increased alarm among American nationalists. In this context of concern about the potential weakening of nationalism, the westward migration generated a felt need for increased patriotic impulses.

As if in response to this need, the three decades before the Civil War witnessed the development of such national symbols as the flag, patriotic songs, and cartoons such as Uncle Sam. The glorification of national heroes like George Washington also occurred at this time. Such patriotism led many to view the school as an obvious means of building a nationalistic spirit in the next generation.[5]

A second demographic development was immigration, especially by the Irish. Beginning with a trickle in the early 1820s, it increased to a tidal wave by 1850. Most of the Irish immigrants settled in the northeast, and especially in New England cities. The Irish presented a series of problems for New Englanders. They came to the United States because of economic privation in Ireland, and most were very poor. Moreover, many were uneducated and unskilled. What caused most concern, however, was their religion. Overwhelmingly, the Irish were Roman Catholic. To many native Protestants this was almost worse than atheism. Additionally, the Irish workers competed with native workers for jobs during times of economic distress, such as the recession of 1837. Thus the Irish were met with religious bigotry, economic and social prejudice, and occasionally mob violence. As their numbers increased, they huddled in segregated sections of the cities and became integrated into the economic system—especially in jobs that natives rejected, such as working in the factories, digging the canals, building the railroads, and constructing the urban sewers. Many of the natives worried about how these newcomers could fit into the nation. Once again, schooling seemed an obvious answer.

A third demographic feature of the era was urbanization. Between 1790 and 1810, the percentage of the population living in urban areas increased from 5.1 percent to 7.3 percent. Significantly, however, most of this increase occurred in the port cities of Boston, Baltimore, New York, and Philadelphia. The reason for this growth was the rapidly expanding maritime trade. Until the mid-1820s commerce remained the primary economic activity of American cities.[6] As we shall later see, a commerce-driven economy carries certain educational prerequisites. From 1830 to 1850 the percentage of urban dwellers in the U.S. population grew from 10 to 20 percent. At this time, however, urban growth was stimulated by industrialization, especially in cotton textiles.[7] This urban expansion was accompanied by a marked and growing gap between rich and poor, increased crime, a rise in the consumption of alcoholic beverages, and what the

The unprecedented flow of immigrants with different ethnic and religious backgrounds helped turn 19th-century schools into socialization factories where, it was hoped, "American" values could be instilled into a diverse population.

intellectual and religious leaders perceived as a general and dangerous lowering of morality. Many hoped that these problems caused by industrialization could be ameliorated by schooling.

Political Developments

The second category of change which stimulated educational reforms was political. The first third of the 19th century witnessed a major expansion in suffrage for white males. When the new federal Constitution went into effect, in 1789, fewer than one white male in seven was qualified to vote; by the election of Andrew Jackson, in 1828, four in seven were qualified. The major criterion for eligibility was property ownership. The expansion of the electorate gave increased power to the Jacksonian Democrats, who were the heirs to Jefferson's party. The New England upper classes, who had earlier supported the Federalist party, now supported the Whig party. They were generally alarmed at the political power of lower economic classes, whom they considered intellectually unready for the moral responsibilities of the vote. Further, the Irish Catholics were especially considered unready for representative government because of their perceived allegiance to the authority of a European Pope, rather than to independent self-government. One response by the largely urban, Protestant Whigs was to support education, which they believed would "inform" and thus "make safe" an otherwise ignorant electorate. The Whigs' conceptions of "inform" and "make safe" were, of course, grounded in their own view of what was right and good for society. "Right" and "good," as we shall soon see, were defined in accord with an ideology of Protestant, classical liberal values.

Economic Developments

Changes in demography and politics were significant factors in the school reform movement of the first half of the 19th century. Of equal, if not greater, importance were the changes in the economy of Massachusetts, where readily observable economic developments occurred in transportation. Through road building and improvement, then the digging of a vast system of canals, and finally the construction of a network of railroads, Massachusetts and the entire northeastern portion of the nation were soon connected by an impressive system for moving people, produce, and goods.

A perceptive observer would have seen another significant development during the first third of the century. This was the huge expansion of commerce centered in the great port cities, especially New York, Philadelphia, Boston, and Baltimore. Much of the rapid growth of these cities resulted from labor market demands as dockworkers, warehousemen, teamsters, and a variety of clerks were needed by the expanding mercantile establishments.[8] The educational needs of clerks, in particular, exceeded the mere literacy demanded by New England Calvinists for religious reading. To a large degree these needs were met by the academies, or private schools, and expanded public schooling in the urban areas. The growth of commerce also resulted in the amassing of large fortunes for some merchants and, at the other end of the economic scale, poverty for some workers, especially during slack seasons. Indeed, contemporary commentators noted with alarm the development of extremes of wealth and poverty.

The most complex and revolutionary economic change was the advent of industrialization. Initially subtle and almost unnoticed, industrial development did not begin in the cities. Rather, it began in the countryside as small-scale cottage industry in textiles and shoemaking. Generally, farmers and their wives practiced these crafts during slack time to supplement their farm livelihood. As demand for these products increased, the cottage industries underwent an evolution. Independent artisans producing and selling their goods directly to the public gradually lost their marketing freedom to enterprising merchants who not only organized the distribution of the finished good, but also attempted to organize production through a "putting-out" system, which placed the raw materials with the home artisans. The artisans, however, continued to control the production process; that is, they set the time, the place, the pace, and the quality of work, thus controlling the most important conditions of their own labor. The merchants had an economic stake in the productive process not only because they needed the finished products to satisfy their markets, but also because they had financed the raw materials. When the cottage artisans neglected shoemaking for financially more attractive pursuits, such as fishing and hunting, or were careless about the quality of their work, the merchants became convinced that the system of putting-out was inefficient and unsatisfactory. Eventually the production process was organized by manufacturers who concentrated the production in a central location. Thus, we see the beginning of factories in New England.

This development is described by Paul Faler, who notes that the central factor in the evolution of industry was the need to control the quality and quantity of production.[9] Integral to this control was the development of a set of values, or an industrial morality, in the producers. Historians E. P. Thompson and Herbert G. Gutman have explained how the development of an industrial morality was in reality the displacement of a traditional culture with a modern culture.[10] In a pre-industrial culture, values revolve around family, community, festivals, and seasons. Work, family life, and leisure are all integrated, and the transition from childhood to youth and, subsequently, to adulthood is blurred. In marked contrast, industrial morality or modern cultural commitments reflect a strict adherence to clock time and punctuality; continuous exclusive labor for a set number of hours in a setting sharply separated from family or leisure; enforced respect for rules, law, and authority; and a clear demarcation between childhood, youth, and adulthood.

Both the merchants who had organized the cottage industries and the entrepreneurs who developed factories felt the need to convert the workers from traditional to modern cultural commitments, that is, to instill an industrial morality. Economic rewards, reform movements such as temperance and religion, formal organizations like the Society for the Promotion of Industry, Frugality, and Temperance, and eventually schools were some of the means used to instill this industrial morality.[11]

The evolution from cottage to factory industry took place in Massachusetts during the first third of the nineteenth century. As factories became common during the 1830s, manufacturing displaced commerce as the principal economic activity of the state's cities. Several features of these early factories should be kept in mind. First, it was initially difficult to lure adult males into the factories. Many of the early establishments, especially textile mills, were run with women, children, and inmates of charitable institutions as laborers. Later, as Irish immigration increased, the immigrants replaced native-born females as factory workers. The native adult males appeared too incorrigibly committed to traditions of worker autonomy, and industrialists chose instead to focus their reform efforts on the next generation of workers. This focus ensured their attention to education and schooling. Second, as successive waves of immigrants came to the United States, it seemed necessary to enculturate them and their children to the appropriate values. This process continued well into the 20th century and was a factor in subsequent school reforms. Third, these early factories resembled post–Civil War factories primarily in employing workers for wages and requiring workers with an industrial morality. In terms of size, utilization of machine processes, and the complexity of technology, however, they were qualitatively different.

In Massachusetts during the 1830s, all of these political–economic factors provided the soil from which the school reforms grew. Demographic factors such as urbanization, immigration, and westward migration raised problems which many believed could be addressed by education. Likewise, the successive rise of commerce and then industrialization presented needs which schooling might fulfill. None of these changes in demography, politics, or economics occurred without conflict. The immigration of the Irish engendered overt opposition and sometimes physical violence as some natives resented the Catholic religion of the Irish and others resented their competition for jobs at or near the bottom of the economic structure. Importantly, each of these conflicts provided a powerful stimulus for school reform, for the schools were coming to be viewed by the business classes and Protestant reformers alike as institutions where common values could be developed as a basis for individual moral growth and social stability.

But these "common values" were not easily agreed upon. Shifts in Protestantism and in classical liberalism were sweeping Massachusetts, but they were vigorously resisted by Calvinists and Jeffersonian democrats. Political–economic changes were understood by leaders in Massachusetts within a shifting ideological framework, to which we now turn.

IDEOLOGY AND RELIGION

Throughout the 17th and most of the 18th centuries, Puritanism, with its Calvinist doctrines, held sway in New England. The Puritan God was an angry God who demanded strict justice with harsh punishment for sinners. Puritans believed all human history had been foreordained at creation and that only a few had been elected by God for salvation. While they required all believers to read the Bible and expected that personal as well as collective behavior might be a sign of election, no one could earn salvation through doing good works. Salvation was a gift from God for the select few. In an important sense, this was a faith with an aristocracy of the elect. The Puritans' theology had extensive ramifications for their definitions of human nature, the good society, the appropriate relationship of the individual to the social order, and discipline—in the home, society, and school.[12]

The defining religious characteristic of 19th century New England was the gradual but cumulative displacement of Puritanism by increasingly less harsh and more humane doctrines.[13] Immigration of non-Puritans helped dilute the strength of Puritan orthodoxy. More important was the impact of scientific discovery, which demythologized nature and replaced it with Enlightenment thought, which emphasized progress, human perfectibility, and reason. This change also occurred within Puritanism itself, as liberal ministers, such as Charles Chauncy, began chipping away at Calvinist dogma at the close of the 18th century. The center of gravity for religious thought in New England shifted from the Calvinist Congregational denomination to the more liberal Unitarian churches during the first three decades of the 19th century. Most influential in this shift was William Ellery Channing of Boston's Federal Street Congregation. Channing made a frontal assault on the basic dogma of Calvinism as he rejected the notion of human depravity and the absolute sovereignty of God. Instead, he proclaimed humans to be rational beings, capable of understanding God's works, and he asserted that God was a morally perfect being. From these positions Channing not only assailed Calvinism but built an alternative theology, a conception of human nature and of the good society that was both humane and in tune with Enlightenment thought. What Channing began was extended by other liberal ministers, such as Horace Bushnell, and the transcendentalists Ralph Waldo Emerson and Henry David Thoreau.

The result was a belief in a benevolent God who had created a rational universe and had endowed human nature with the rationality needed to develop an ever more perfect social order. The possibility of progress seemed to carry an injunction to New Englanders for reform. If God had given them the power for improvement, it seemed their duty to exercise it. The emphasis on the essential goodness of human nature and even the divinity of the human personality pushed the reform impulse in humanitarian directions.

The three decades prior to the Civil War were characterized by continuing efforts at such reforms. Model prisons were built with an emphasis on reforming the criminal rather than punishment and retribution. Hospitals for the mentally ill substituted the idea of illness and compassionate care for moral depravity and shame. New institutions for youthful offenders were developed, and their very name—reformatories—conveyed the new outlook. Temperance crusades were conducted to "rescue" over-indulgers. The women's suffrage movement received its first significant support during this era from those who believed that God had created even women with a rational capacity. The most militant and divisive reform movement was abolition. Not all abolitionists believed that African-Americans should be free because they were equal to whites, but those inspired by the new and liberal religious outlook believed that slavery should be abolished because Africans were God's creatures; this was sufficient to render involuntary servitude immoral.

The Calvinist position implied mass literacy because all believers were required to read the scriptures. The more liberal religious views of the nineteenth century, however, required more than mass literacy. The new views of human nature, progress, and a rational universe required mass education which would equip the young to understand the natural and social worlds in order to make rational responses to the challenges they would face in life. The safety, health, and progress of both individuals and society would depend, reformers believed, on the adequacy of these responses.

Consolidation of Classical Liberalism

During the common-school era the major development in ideology was the consolidation and spread of classical liberalism from the intellectual leaders to the general public. Among the primary components of classical liberalism, as discussed in Chapter 2, were a basic faith in human reason, in the enduring reality of Newton's conception of natural law, and in continuing progress; belief in the importance of education; a commitment to nationalism; and a belief in the value of republican virtue and in the centrality of freedom to the American condition. The principal vehicles for dissemination were politics, newspapers, and the churches. By the mid-1830s these ideas were commonly accepted across the United States. While the spread of classical liberalism from the intellectuals to the commoners was the defining characteristic of ideology from the 1820s to the mid–1840s, not all was static within that ideology. Already by the 1830s the forces of economic change were beginning to gather momentum, especially with the birth of the factory system and development of the railroads. Both would demand some degree of government assistance. Factory owners wanted protective tariffs. The railroads coveted financial aid and land grants. Moreover, the immigration of the Irish added a challenging dimension to the American social order. These developments would occasion some innovations in the prevailing ideology.

Subtle but significant ideological accommodations followed. The most important of these were in the beliefs about the role of government. Complete laissez-faire would not meet the new economic requirements, so government was asked to play a significant economic role. No longer was it sufficient for the government to stay out of economic affairs. At first the breach was slight, but it foreshadowed developments of the late 19th and early 20th century. Laissez-faire was amended to mean that government should stand on the sideline *except* when necessary for it to assist economic development. Such assistance would include protective tariffs to keep out foreign competition and financial aid to industries such as the railroads. Between the mid-1830s and the end of the 19th century, the federal government gave the railroad companies land equal in area to the state of Texas. The seed of the 20th-century welfare state had been sown; its earliest germination was welfare for the industrial class.

The demands for an increasingly active government in the economic area were accompanied by an increased willingness to allow the general growth of government power and centralization of authority. Again, this began slowly but increased over the succeeding decades. The concentration of state power over education, in the form of state school boards, was but one example of the decline of local self-government. Another was the passage of a compulsory school attendance law by Massachusetts in 1852. In part, this acceptance of increased state authority may have been stimulated by the fear of social disintegration engendered by Irish immigration.

Closely associated with the above ideological accommodations was a modification in the definition of freedom. Jefferson had argued for a "negative" freedom, that is, freedom from government interference in the individual's private life. However, leaders in the 1830s began to emphasize the responsibility of government to create the conditions for freedom through economic and educational intervention. This was a beginning step in the direction of the ideal of a "positive" freedom espoused in the 20th century by modern liberals, as we shall see in Chapter 4.

The third adjustment to classical liberal ideology occurred in the concept of rationality. Jefferson and other earlier classical liberals held that humans were capable of reason and should be approached on that basis. Horace Mann and other common-school reformers adopted the "new discipline" of love as a classroom methodology. This reflected a subtle but significant change in the idea of human rationality. The basis of the new discipline was manipulation of the child's nonrational psyche through the granting or withholding of affection. Rather than rely solely on a rational explanation of the rules and punishments for violation, Mann urged teachers to use affection to mold appropriate behaviors. This approach would later be amplified by modern liberals as they tried to shape children emotionally as well as rationally.

The debate between Mann and Orestes Brownson (see the Primary Source Reading) in large part concerned these redefinitions of classical liberalism. Brownson represented the older view, and Mann championed the modifications to that view. Brownson advocated local control of schools, attacked state normal schools, and attacked Mann's list of approved texts. All these moves reflected a Jeffersonian version of classical liberalism, while Mann's ideas signaled a newer view.

Horace Mann was perhaps the best example of a political leader whose policies and career embodied these ideological adjustments. He began his political career as a spokesperson for the industrial and railroad interests in the Massachusetts legislature. He also championed reforms such as temperance and the institutional care of the insane and of juvenile delinquents. Each of these reforms augured increased power for government and a shrinking of private freedoms. In totality, Mann was clearly a classical liberal. Nevertheless, he may be seen as a transitional figure bridging classical and new liberalism. In like measure, the era of the common school may also be seen as an era of transition to modern schooling.

HORACE MANN: AN EXEMPLAR OF REFORM

Early Life

Perhaps no individual more accurately represented through his family and personal biography the successive changes that altered the life and thought of Massachusetts than did Horace Mann. A direct descendant of William Mann, who came to the Bay Colony in 1633, his paternal ancestors included a graduate of Harvard College who became a Puritan minister and another who was a member of the Committee of Correspondence during the revolution. All had remained in Massachusetts, were Calvinists, and with the exception of one minister, had been farmers. Horace, born in 1796 at Franklin, Massachusetts, was the last child of Thomas Mann and Rebecca Stanley Mann.[14]

Thomas Mann raised his family on a farm that had been in the Mann family since 1709, when his grandfather, also named Thomas, purchased it. Horace's childhood resembled that of past generations of New Englanders. Subsistence farming provided nearly all life's necessities. Horace learned not only farming but traditional values while helping with the daily round of farm chores. The family was also a primary setting for literacy and religious training, with older siblings often helping parents introduce younger children to the mysteries of reading, ciphering, and dogma. Later in his life, after he suggested that he had been largely self-taught, his sister Lydia reminded Horace "Every day of your life when you were with your parents and sister you were at school and learning that which has been the foundation of your present learning."[15]

The church and the public school were twin institutions that reinforced the home in child rearing. Young Horace attended a crudely built, one-room district school where his home training in letters, numbers, morals, and religious dogma was supplemented and reinforced during a six- to eight-week session each year. Reverend Nathanael Emmons was pastor of the Congregational Church in Franklin, and through his powerful personal resolve, he labored to keep his flock faithful to Calvinist dogma during Mann's youth. Emmons's increasing difficulty with church members testified to the winds of change that were beginning to sweep even rural communities in the first decades of the eighteenth century.

Horace Mann, who was the first Secretary to the Massachusetts State Board of Education from 1837 to 1848, is best remembered as the primary champion of America's new common-school movement.

For young Horace, the break with Calvinism began the year after his father died, in 1809. It was occasioned by the tragic drowning of his brother Stephen, who had been swimming one Sunday while truant from church services. Reverend Emmons used the funeral as an opportunity to warn other youths of Franklin that such straying from God's commandments would as surely lead them to eternal damnation as it had Stephen. Previously, Emmons had used the death of his own son to issue a similar warning. His son had not experienced a conversion and thus, according to Emmons, was consigned to hell. These vivid examples were meant to encourage the young to greater religious commitment. If such "encouragement" had been effective before the turn of the century, it was becoming less effective thereafter. Young Horace joined a growing majority of his fellow New Englanders who could no longer abide the stern Calvinism of their fathers. Emmons's sermon ignited doubts in Calvinist dogma which would eventually lead Mann to Unitarianism.

The economic changes occurring in Massachusetts were also reflected in the Mann family. Shortly before Thomas Mann's death, the family, like other Franklin families, began to make straw braid, which they sold to manufacturers for use in making ladies' straw hats. Not only did this activity engage much of their free time, but it started the process which drew these rural families away from subsistence farming and into the cash economy. These same forces eventually drew Horace's older brother Stanley into manufacturing, first as a manager and later as part owner of a factory. When the latter endeavor failed, Stanley joined the multitude of New Englanders who sought their fortune in the "West."

Mann's Education

Mann's deeply felt responsibility to his widowed mother kept him working on the farm until 1816, when he left Franklin to enter Brown College in Providence. Except for the few years of elementary schooling and his home education, his preparation for entry into higher education consisted of tutelage during the winter of 1816 in classics under Samuel Barett and in mathematics under Reverend William Williams, the Baptist minister in Wrentham. The study with Williams required an eight-mile round-trip walk each day.

At Brown, after an interview with the president and two faculty members, Mann was admitted with sophomore standing. The first year he studied the required curriculum of Cicero, Caesar, Homer, geography, logic, public speaking, and geometry. Apparently most of the classes were based on memorization of texts and recitations to test the memory. Mann made a mark as a public speaker by engaging in extracurricular forensic activities, and as a scholar by graduating first in his class after attending for three years.

Between 1819 and 1822, Mann tutored at Brown and simultaneously studied law. After serving as an apprentice lawyer, he graduated from the Litchfield Law School and in 1823 was admitted to the Massachusetts bar in Dedham, where he began his practice as a lawyer. During the next 4 years Mann firmly established his reputation both as a lawyer and as an orator. His legal career reflected the importance of commerce in rural Massachusetts, as many of his clients were Boston mercantile firms that engaged Mann to collect debts owed by local farmers. The residents of Dedham recognized a rising legal talent when, in July 1826, they selected Mann to address their memorial service to honor the July 4th deaths of John Adams and Thomas Jefferson. This address firmly established his reputation as an orator and was probably influential in his subsequent election to the Massachusetts General Court (the state legislature) in 1827.

Mann's Political Career

Mann's career in the Massachusetts legislature continued until 1837, during which time he continued to reflect the changes in his society. His first legislative speech came during a debate on a petition of the First Religious Society of Blandford for incorporation. Mann opposed granting this Congregationalist group perpetual control over their endowment, resting his argument on the principle of religious freedom. The defeat of the petition strengthened the Unitarians in their struggle with the Congregationalists.

Mann's second speech was in favor of state support for the construction of a privately owned railroad. Here he displayed the reasoning which he would use to support the development of industry in Massachusetts: such development had as its main objective the public good rather than private gain. In the decade of the 1830s, as the railroads increasingly used public funding for private profit, his reasoning about the public good seemed less sustainable when applied to the railroads, for subsidies to the railroads benefited the rich more clearly than the public as a whole; nevertheless, he remained a staunch advocate of state support for them. During his initial support for the railroads in 1827, he demonstrated his clear understanding of the direction of economic development in the state as he provided statistics to support his contention that the state's future was not in agriculture but in commerce and manufacturing. As his biographer put it, "Mann placed himself squarely in favor of industrial development, improved transportation, and the growth of towns and cities."[16]

Mann's strong support for religious freedom was not the only indication that his legislative positions were influenced by the ideas of the Enlightenment. As a legislator he supported a number of humanitarian reforms, such as the overturn of the state's debtor laws, humane treatment of the insane, and the temperance movement.

Mann's concern for the treatment of the insane, who previously had been incarcerated in county and town jails, often in deplorable conditions, began developing in the late 1820s. In response to revelations about their plight, Mann delivered, in 1830, the first speech in the Massachusetts legislature supporting the construction and maintenance of a mental hospital by the state. His bill passed, and he was appointed one of three commissioners to oversee the construction and operation of the first state mental hospital in North America. Within 3 years, the Worcester State Lunatic Hospital received its first patients and a new era was begun in the treatment of the mentally ill.

Mann's support of the temperance movement followed a zigzag course. He first supported the conservative temperance groups, which advocated moral persuasion in favor of moderation. Later, he lent his support to the radical temperance groups, who pushed for legislation to enforce their views. While this shift certainly indicated a lessening of Mann's faith in the reasonableness of his fellows, it was nevertheless based on the Enlightenment belief that the state had the duty to protect social and economic harmony and the integrity of the electoral process. The presence of intemperate individuals, he believed, threatened this harmony and integrity. A reliance on the coercive power of the state to ensure social or individual benefits, even when it meant that individuals were to be controlled for their own good, was always implicit and often explicit in Enlightenment thought. Yet it also challenged the classical liberal distrust of government authority, a distrust expressed in the Jeffersonian dictum, "That government governs best which governs least."

The two major humanitarian reform movements which did not find Horace Mann in their ranks during the early 1830s were public education and abolition. His position on the abolition of slavery displayed the conflict between his moral beliefs, his economic and political commitments, and his sense of political reality. Mann considered slavery to be a moral abomination. As such he believed it required eventual eradication. The abolitionists, however, with their demands for the immediate end of slavery, seemed to him to be threatening not only the political stability of the republic but the very institution of private property. Moreover, he believed their demands and moral stridency only strengthened the slave states' resolve to defend their "peculiar" institution, thus delaying a peaceful resolution of the problem. The abolitionists' goals could be achieved, he felt, only by force of arms, and such a course would threaten the republic. Additionally, even if freedom could be peacefully won, it was not clear to Mann what could be done with the freed African-Americans.

As Jefferson once wrote, Mann thought that the African-American's future was not in America, but he was not sanguine about African recolonization. Interestingly, when it came to cases of individual African-Americans, Mann was egalitarian and sympathetic, often at great personal cost. In 1844, for example, he canceled his scheduled speech before the New Bedford Lyceum when he learned they restricted membership to whites. Three years later, when a black woman, Chloe Lee, was admitted to the State Normal School at West Newton and could not find accommodations among the townspeople, she was welcomed into the Mann home. It appears that especially during the years he was Secretary to the State Board of Education, his concern for preserving social harmony led him to silence his support for the abolitionist cause. Later, however, as a member of the U.S. House of Representatives, filling the seat of recently deceased John Quincy Adams, he delivered a memorable antislavery speech in opposition to the Compromise Bill of 1850, a speech which would nearly cost him his House seat in the next election and was a major factor in his defeat in the subsequent one.

While the abolitionists and slavery caused Mann considerable concern during his legislative career, educational questions had not been on his agenda. It was not until 1837 that his attention focused on public education. By then much of the groundwork for educational reform in Massachusetts had been already done by others. When Mann did enter the fray, however, he left a lasting mark on American education. The issue which directed Mann's interest to education was the dispersal of funds which had been allocated to the state by the federal government to compensate for the Massachusetts state militia service during the War of 1812. Mann supported the use of these monies for the state's common schools. Although he lost the fiscal battle, the legislature created a state board of education authorized to collect and disseminate information about schools to the local districts and the public at large. Much to the surprise of his contemporaries, Mann accepted the appointment as Secretary to the Board, a position he occupied from 1837 to 1848.

Mann resigned from the Secretary's post in 1848 and was elected in 1848 and 1850 to the U.S. House of Representatives from the Eighth Congressional District. During his four years in Congress, sectional issues surrounding the slavery question commanded most of his attention, and he gained national prominence for his antislavery position. His antislavery and temperance positions were the major factors in his defeat for reelection in 1852.

Soon after the electoral defeat, Mann accepted the presidency of the yet-to-be-established Antioch College in Ohio. In the last stage of his career he continued to reflect the mood of his times. He turned to higher education as the nation began to focus attention in that area. He moved west to Yellow Springs, Ohio, and thus became part of the great westward migration from the northeast. One of Mann's prime presidential concerns was the higher education of women. Shortly after the women's suffrage movement was launched, in July 1848 at Seneca Falls, New York, he was attempting to provide women with the same collegiate education as the male students received. To this end, he expanded the development begun earlier at Oberlin. Antioch College was open to men and women of all races, and no distinction was made for race or gender in curricular questions, although he was known to have some vocal reservations about absolute social equality among men and women. By the time he died, in 1859 at Yellow Springs, his life reflected nearly all the important intellectual, social, political, and economic developments of his time.

MANN AND THE COMMON SCHOOLS

Mann's most far-reaching contributions to education were made during the years he spent as secretary to the Massachusetts State Board of Education, 1837 to 1848. He had been at the pinnacle of his political career when he accepted Governor Everett's offer to quit the state senate and direct the state's efforts to reform public education. The importance he assigned to the task was evident when he wrote to a friend, "My lawbooks are for sale. My office is 'to let'! The bar is no longer my forum. My jurisdiction is changed. I have abandoned jurisprudence, and betaken myself to the larger sphere of mind and morals."[17] Although he had grown somewhat disillusioned with the possibility of voluntary reform in adults, his pessimism did not extend to the young. He explained his optimism saying, "Having found the present generation composed of materials almost unmalleable, I am transferring my efforts to the next. Men are cast iron; but children are wax. Strength expended upon the latter may be effectual, which will make no impression on the former."[18]

The Massachusetts State Board of Education held its first meeting on June 29, 1837, and formally elected Mann as its Secretary. The duties of the Board were closely circumscribed by the law which had created it; two of its duties were to present the legislature an annual abstract of the school reports received by its Secretary and to report to the legislature all its activities, its reflections on the condition of education in the state, and any recommendations it might have for improvement of that condition.[19] The Secretary's duties were similarly specifically prescribed: the Secretary "shall, under the direction of the board, collect information of the actual conditions and efficiency of the common schools and other means of popular education; and diffuse as widely as possible throughout every part of the Commonwealth, information of the most approved and successful methods of arranging the studies and conducting the education of the young, to the end that all children in this Commonwealth, who depend upon common schools for instruction, may have the best education which those schools can be made to impart."[20] While these duties were clearly prescribed, the means for effecting them were not. Moreover, the powers of the Board and its Secretary were limited to the collection and dissemination of information.

Regardless of their reform preferences, the only option open to Mann and the Board was to seek voluntary cooperation from local districts. To effect educational reform, Mann proceeded to demonstrate the power of information when systematically disseminated through an official government office. Initially, Mann's most effective device for conveying information to the people of the state was the county educational convention. During the first year he held an advertised meeting in every county of the state where he presented educational questions to the local citizens. A wide range of educational topics was discussed, including teaching methods, the most appropriate location of schools, school apparatus, texts, discipline, the duties of local school board members, attendance problems, finance, and European educational innovations. Mann took particular pains to ensure the attendance of local dignitaries who were known friends of education.

A second method of disseminating information was through the annual reports of the Board and the Secretary. These were sent to all district school boards as well as to the state legislature and the governor. Educational officials throughout the nation obtained copies of these reports, thus adding to the national influence of school reforms in Massachusetts. In addition, Mann established the semimonthly *Common School Journal* in 1839, which published articles and news items about education and was available to most teachers in the state.[21]

Among the wide variety of educational topics addressed by Mann during his tenure as Secretary, perhaps the most significant were school buildings, moral values, the example of Prussian education, discipline, teachers, and the economic value of education. The question of curriculum subject matter was not one of the most important issues for Mann, perhaps in part because the curriculum was mandated by the state legislation. He addressed this question only once, in his *Sixth Annual Report,* for the year 1842, where he noted that the law required instruction in "orthography, reading, writing, English grammar, geography and arithmetic." Mann further explained that these were "the minimum but not the maximum."[22] He then spent the remaining 110 pages presenting a detailed plan for studying physiology, a subject that he felt was wrongly neglected. Generally, however, when he dealt with curricular subjects, he approached the topic from the perspective of teaching methods rather than as subject matter. The six issues which the Secretary seemed to find most central to his reform efforts will now be examined.

School Buildings

Under the general heading of school buildings, Mann included a variety of items that involved the physical setting of schooling. One of his less acclaimed accomplishments, from which generations of school children benefited, was the vastly improved physical setting of school life. The idyllic "little red schoolhouses" nestled under giant oak trees beside babbling brooks and surrounded with green meadows were usually fictional creations of writers who romanticized the American educational past. Such scenes definitely did not describe the reality of most district schools in the late 1830s. Most were poorly constructed, offering little protection from the cold New England winters. Few had adequate windows or artificial means to provide sufficient light. Rare was the school large enough to accommodate its students. Many provided only backless benches, which were not only uncomfortable but dangerous. Frequently, schools were without the benefits of toilet facilities and water for drinking and washing. Many schools were located in unattractive, and sometimes unhealthful, sites apparently chosen because they were unsuitable for any other productive use.

The Secretary marshaled the power of "information" to combat these conditions. In the very first *Annual Report* the Board, under the subject of important topics, listed "the proper and commodious construction of school-houses." In the Secretary's section of the same report, he stated, "There are four cardinal topics. . . . First in order is the situation, construction and number of the school-houses."[23] The circular Mann sent to each county in 1837 to advertise his county educational conventions listed eleven questions "to direct attention to some leading considerations": the first was, "Is inconvenience or discomfort suffered from the construction or location of School Houses in your Town, and if so in what manner?"[24] The following year Mann praised the city of Salem's improvements in seating, ventilation, and reconstruction of their school as a carrot to tempt other districts to follow suit. Lest the recalcitrant miss the point, he warned,

> In many other places, improvements of the same kind have been made, though to a less extent, and in a part only of the houses. It would be a great mistake, however, to suppose, that nothing remains to be done in this important department of the system of public instruction. The cases mentioned are the slightest exceptions, compared with the generality of the neglect. . . . The children must continue to breathe poisonous air, and sit upon seats threatening structural derangement, until parents become satis-

> fied, that a little money may well be expended to secure to their offspring, the blessings of sound health, a good conformation, and a strong, quick-working mind.[25]

In his report 3 years later, Mann returned again to the question of school buildings as he expressed guarded optimism and satisfaction with the general progress around the state. He included, in the appendix, designs and descriptions of the new buildings at Springfield, Lowell, and Salem. He suggested that other districts might "select any one of them as a model, or they may attempt a combination which will be an improvement upon all. These and others erected during the past year, are ornaments to the respective places of their location, an honor to their inhabitants and a pledge of the elevated character of their posterity."[26] Moreover, the Secretary's annual publication of each town's rank in school expenditures caused some towns, like Palmer, "mortification" and others, such as Lowell, an occasion to boast.[27] It is not difficult to imagine the cumulative effect of this kind of publicized information.

Moral Values

At the core of Mann's effort to reform common schooling was his belief that the school must inculcate an appropriate set of moral values in the state's children. This belief was not entirely an innovation in Mann's time; schools in Massachusetts had traditionally been seen as institutions auxiliary to the home and the church in the inculcation of Puritan values in the young. What was new with Mann was the centrality of the school, the set of values to be inculcated, and the role of the state in determining and inculcating those values. Mann was particularly concerned with the apparent breakdown of moral consensus and the resulting conflict in his society. The religious struggle between the Calvinists and more liberal sects, the economic strife between rich and poor, the riots pitting Irish immigrants against native workers: all were evidence to Mann of a dangerous social disharmony which threatened the stability of society. The common school was to become the central institution to ameliorate this situation. It was necessary for all children to develop a commitment to a common core of values. But not just any core of values would suffice. The necessary values were those which later social scientists would call *modern* values—that is, values which would support and sustain industrial development.

Of course, it was not necessary for the Secretary personally to create these new values. Social thought rarely depends on one person consciously deciding what values are appropriate for an era. Rather, such ideas are generated from common experience with new socioeconomic conditions and subsequently appear as self-evident. By 1837 the appropriate values were self-evident to many in Massachusetts, particularly to those of Mann's background and social class. They were partially exhibited in the state law enumerating the duties of teachers. In his *First Report* Mann explained that the law required teachers "to impress on the minds of children and youth, committed to their care and instruction, the principles of piety, justice and a sacred regard to truth, love to their country, humanity and universal benevolence, sobriety, industry and frugality, chastity, moderation and temperance, and those other virtues which are the ornament of human society and the basis upon which a republican constitution is founded."[28]

Mann called these values the "common elements" of the common school. They would include the "great Christian truths" which he believed all rational men would agree upon. In one sense they were values based in religious belief, and as such they represented a pan-Protestant perspective which reinforced the liberal wing of New England Protestantism in direct opposition to the traditional Calvinism. This raised the opposition of a minority of Congregationalist ministers, who remained more committed to Calvinist dogma. The issue became galvanized when the State Board began the practice of recommending books which districts might purchase for school libraries. Led by Frederick Packard, the American Sunday School Union claimed, after some of their materials were rejected, that Mann was attempting to eliminate religion from the common schools.

It is significant that Mann received general support from Protestant ministers and even from an apparent majority of Congregationalist ministers.[29] Irish Catholics were later to object to the "common elements," especially when these were accompanied with the reading of the King James version of the Bible. They rightly saw the common school as positioned against Catholicism, and eventually they built a separate system of parochial schools. Thus, ironically, Mann's effort to unify society around commonly held values led to a competing private school system with potentially conflicting values. That the Catholic schools did not promote the divisive values that Mann feared from sectarian schooling is yet another irony which cannot be explored here.[30]

The predominance of Christian religious sentiment in New England blinded Mann and the constituents to an important implication of the "common elements" he believed should be taught in the common schools. The issue was raised, however, by the Englishman John Stuart Mill, one of the most prominent philosophers of the 19th century. In the late 1840s English public education was racked by religious conflict between Anglicans, various dissenting Protestant sects, and Catholics. In an attempt at compromise, educational reformers proposed a system of national education which would be "unsectarian" and which would adopt a "common elements" approach similar to Mann's. In a speech prepared in 1849, Mill fired withering salvos at the basic principles of this proposal, salvos which were equally applicable to Mann's program. Mill correctly noted that it was indeed religion which would be taught in the proposed public schools. And no matter how the final compromise among the competing Christian sects was effected, he argued, the resulting religion of the public school would be some variant of Christianity. And what would this result mean? Mill carefully pointed out to the proponents, "If you could carry all the sects with you by your compromise you would have effected nothing more but a compact among the more powerful bodies to cease fighting among themselves and join in trampling the weaker. You would have contrived a national education not for all, but for the believers in the New Testament. The Jew and the unbeliever would be excluded from it though they would not the less be required to pay for it. . . . Religious exclusion and inequality are as odious when practiced against minorities as majorities." Mill's conclusion was unambiguously stated: "Education provided by the public must be education for all, and to be education for all it must be purely secular education."[31] Mill's logic escaped most New Englanders, but not all. (Orestes Brownson was an exception, as the reading at the end of this chapter shows.)

In a way, Frederick Packard's criticism of Mann's common elements was probably correct. When Packard argued that Mann wanted to take religion out of the common school, he understood religion to mean Calvinism. Indeed, that and more was what Mann had in mind. Henceforth the public school would not contribute to the creation of Congregationalists, or Unitarians, or Baptists, or Methodists. Instead, it would attempt to create citizens committed to a secular faith whose moral values would play much the same role that doctrine had played in sectarian faith. In a figurative sense, the school would become the temple, the teacher the minister, and the school boards the temple elders. American schoolchildren would be taught a pan-Protestant brand of citizenship which would wed religion and nationalism in "one nation under God," as the Pledge of Allegiance would later put it. God, of course, was presumed to be the God of Protestantism. The principle was not new, for this idea had energized earlier Puritan education (and is reflected in the Benjamin Rush selection at the end of Chapter 2). What was new was the systemic government-supported scope of this approach. It would take a series of painful U.S. Supreme Court decisions in the mid-20th century to eliminate religious references and rituals in schools, thus rectifying the Protestant precedent set by Mann in Massachusetts.

Lessons from the Prussian School System

Soon after he turned his attention to educational questions, Mann began to read available commentaries on education. He was first introduced to Prussian schools by French educator Victor Cousins's popular report of their successes.[32] The Prussian system had been organized in the 1820s along a model recommended by Johann Fichte, the German philosopher, during the Napoleonic occupation of Prussia. Fichte's proposals, in his *Addresses to the German Nation,* were designed to develop Prussian nationalism and a nation strong enough to unite the German states for world leadership. By the mid-1830s the Prussian experiment had excited educators in western Europe and the United States.

The Prussians had developed a state-financed system which was free, universal, and compulsory through the elementary grades. The system was class-based and consisted of two separate tiers of schooling. The tier for the aristocratic class had three levels, beginning with the *vorschule.* This elementary school, responsible for preparing upper-class young for the *gymnasium,* was academically oriented. The *gymnasium* provided a classical education closely akin to American and English collegiate educations. Graduates of the *gymnasium* might continue their higher education in either the military academies, designed to produce the future officers of the Prussian military, or the universities. The university, as envisioned by Fichte and developed in nineteenth-century Germany, was primarily a research institution whose dual functions were to produce new knowledge and to educate the next generation of civic and religious leaders.

The tier for the common people, on the other hand, had two levels. The elementary *volkschule,* or people's school, was compulsory. Its goal was to develop patriotic citizens, and its motto was "God, Emperor, and Country." In addition to loyalty and obedience to authority, it taught basic literacy and numeracy. Most of the graduates of the *volkschule* went directly into the work force. A few continued their training in either the technical schools, which produced technicians and middle-range managers for the Prussian economy, or the normal schools, which trained teachers for the *volkschule.* The curricular emphasis in the normal schools was on how to teach, that is, methods. It was deemed not only unnecessary, but counterproductive, for *volkschule* teachers to have knowledge or understanding much beyond that necessary for the *volkschule.* Loyalty and obedience, not initiative or critical thinking, were the goals for the training of the common people. As Fichte had written on the education of the German child, "If you want to influence him at all, you must do more than merely talk to him. You must fashion him, and fashion him in such a way that he cannot will otherwise than you wish him to will."[33]

During the spring and summer of 1843, at his own expense, Mann traveled to Europe to examine its educational systems firsthand. He was relatively unimpressed with the quality of education in England and France. The Prussian schools, however, made a distinctly positive impression on him, and he devoted much of his 1843 *Annual Report* to enumerating its praises. Moreover, Mann continued to cite Prussian examples during the remainder of his tenure when he urged school reform. The Secretary was not completely oblivious to the dangers inherent in using institutions designed for an authoritarian society as models for a democracy, but he quickly dismissed these dangers as inconsequential. He argued that education was but a means which could be made to serve diametrically opposed ends. In summation, he said, "If Prussia can pervert the benign influences of education to the support of arbitrary power, we surely can use them for support and perpetuation of republican institutions."[34]

The Prussian *volkschule* evoked Mann's most enthusiastic responses. The idea of a free, state-financed and state-controlled universal and compulsory school which would affect all of the young was its most obvious attraction. He seemed to ignore the class separation into *volkschule* and *vorschule.* This is surprising, since he waged unending war against private schools for the wealthy in Massachusetts. These schools, he argued, would not only encourage class distinctions and thus class hatred, but would siphon off the interest and support of the best elements of society from the common schools to the private schools attended by their children.

His second observation about the *volkschule* was the joy of learning which it engendered among the students. The Secretary was fond of noting that during his extensive visits to the Prussian schools, he "never saw one child in tears."[35] This he claimed was due to the absence of corporal punishment and the superior methods of the teachers.

The superiority of Prussian teachers was not accidental, according to Mann. Rather, it was the direct result of their superior training. The Prussians had developed normal schools for the training of its *volkschule* teachers. In the normal schools the teachers were carefully schooled in pedagogy and the subjects taught in the *volkschule.* The apparent success of these institutions reinforced Mann's commitment to the state normal schools he had been struggling to secure in Massachusetts.

School Discipline

The problems surrounding discipline in the schools concerned Mann throughout his tenure as secretary. His approach to discipline reveals much about his educational beliefs and their relation to his broader social and political philosophies. He discussed disciplinary issues in several of his *Annual Reports* and speeches. One speech, "On School Punishments," first delivered in Boston in 1839, revised in 1845, and included in his *Lectures on Education* published in 1854, succinctly summarized his general position.

Mann began this speech with the assertion, "Punishment, when taken by itself, is always to be considered as an evil":[36] an evil, however, which may be used as a last resort, as a doctor uses poison to arrest a disease so that it may be treated. By punishment, Mann meant physical beatings or harsh words. Such treatment, he asserted, always caused fear in the child; "and fear is a most debasing, dementalizing passion."[37] He contended that fear corrupted not only the intellect but also the personality and morality of the child. Moreover, if the teacher is to control the moral, social, and intellectual development of the child, she must know the child, that is, she must have access to the child's inner self. But, "the moment a child's mind is strongly affected by fear, it flies instinctively away and hides itself in the deepest recesses it can find.... Instead of exhibiting to you his whole consciousness, he conceals from you as much as he can.... your communication with that child's heart is at an end."[38] In this discussion Mann exhibited insights into the nature of social psychology and the potential for manipulation of the psyche through affection, which was not generally understood until the end of his century. It would be left to the 20th-century progressive educational theorists (as discussed in Chapter 4) to further develop this approach to pedagogy—an approach which is both more humane and potentially more manipulative than a pedagogy of overt authoritarianism.

The common use of corporal punishment in New England had been inspired by Calvinist beliefs in the depravity of human nature, which led adults to think it necessary to "beat the devil out of children." In sharp contrast, Mann's conception of human nature was grounded in Enlightenment and Unitarian beliefs. He therefore saw the child as a rational being more appropriately approached through intelligence and love. The good teacher, "singularly gifted with talent and resources, and with the divine quality of love, ... can win the affection, and, by controlling the heart, can control the conduct of children...."[39] As a realist and a shrewd social observer, Mann understood that such an approach required two conditions: first, children who had been reared in homes where love, reason, and sound moral values predominated; and second, teachers who had been adequately prepared to understand the child, classroom management, and the subject matter. Neither of these conditions was universally present in Mann's Massachusetts. When teachers were not capable of more enlightened methods, or students were incorrigible because of bad home conditions, Mann believed punishment was the only alternative in order to "save" the young delinquents from a life of immorality, dissipation, or crime. The teacher, or parent, should always consider whether the evil to be cured was sufficiently greater than the evil of punishment. Mann went on to describe how and when, as a last resort, punishment should be used to prevent greater evils. He challenged teachers to constantly try to decrease their use of punishment, with the goal of eliminating it completely from the common school. Thus he effectively presented punishment as an acceptable alternative for those teachers who were not *yet* fully adequate but who, as they became more proficient in their profession, would obviously retreat less often to punishment. The good teacher would understand, according to the Secretary, that "a child may surrender to fear, without surrendering to principle. But it is the surrender to principle only which has any permanent value."[40]

In his *Eighth Annual Report,* Mann clearly indicated the relation between his ideas on discipline and his sociopolitical ideals. In the 1840s the number of schools which were closed before the

The Prussian School System in the Mid-19th Century

Popular Education	Aristocratic Education
Volkschule:	**Vorschule:**
1. Attendance was compulsory for all common children. 2. Curriculum: reading, writing, arithmetic, religion, and patriotism. 3. Objective: to develop students with literacy, loyalty, and obedience (motto: "God, Emperor, and Country"). 4. Teachers were normal-school graduates.	1. Students came from aristocratic families. 2. Curriculum: academic subjects. 3. Objective: to prepare students for the *gymnasium.* 4. Teachers were university or *gymnasium* graduates.
Technical Schools:	**Gymnasium:**
1. Students were drawn from the top ranks of the *Volkschule.* 2. Curricula: Various technological subjects (not science) designed to produce specialists in various specific technologies. 3. Objective: to produce the mid-rank managers and technicians. They were to transmit, not originate, orders, and were to provide stability for an in-place economic system. 4. Teachers were graduates of technical schools, generally after work experience.	1. Students came from the *vorschule.* 2. Curriculum: similar to a combination of grammar school and collegiate education in 19th-century America—i.e., a "classical curriculum" of Latin, literature, math, and some sciences. 3. Objective: to prepare students for universities, military academies, or upper levels of state and business bureaucracies. 4. Teachers were university graduates.
Normal Schools:	**Universities:**
1. Students were drawn from the top ranks of the *volkschule.* 2. Curriculum: heavily oriented toward methods courses and a few elementary content courses. How to teach was seen as more important than content. 3. Objective: to produce teachers for the *volkschule* who would develop loyal, patriotic, and efficient citizens. 4. Teachers were recruited from among graduates of normal schools after teaching experience.	1. Students came from the *vorschule* and the *gymnasium.* 2. Curricula: specialized research areas in the liberal arts, the sciences, math, engineering, and art. 3. Objective: to produce the intellectual leaders for the state and to produce "new knowledge." 4. Teachers were from the universities.
	Military Academies:
	1. Students came from the *gymnasium.* 2. Curricula: military strategy, tactics, and discipline. 3. Objective: to train future officers for the Prussian general staff. 4. Teachers were from the Prussian army general staff.

Note: This representation is idealized. Not all *volkschule* teachers, for example, were trained in normal schools; not all technical school teachers had technical school degrees.

One of Mann's most enduring legacies was to help replace the Calvinist view that children, being naturally depraved at birth, must have the "devil beaten out of them."

end of the term because teachers could not maintain the order necessary to conduct them was decreasing significantly, while the total number of schools was increasing. But this progress was not sufficient for Mann. He explained that one of the most important goals of schooling was "training our children in self-government." He proclaimed, "So tremendous, too, are the evils of anarchy and lawlessness, that a government by mere force, however arbitrary and cruel, has been held preferable to no-government. But self-government, self-control, a voluntary compliance with the laws of reason and duty, have been justly considered as the highest point of excellence attainable by a human being." He went on to argue that self-government required rational understanding of the rules and laws. This understanding could not come through fear inspired by punishment. Mann informed teachers that it was a teacher's duty to prevent "violations" of moral law, "by rectifying that state of mind out of which violations come. Nor is it enough that the law be obeyed. As far as possible, he is to see it is obeyed from right motives. As a moral act blind obedience is without value. As a moral act, also, obedience through fear is without value; not only so, but as soon as the fear is removed, the restrained impulses will break out and demand the arrears of indulgence as a long-delayed debt."[41] Mann left no room for doubt that he believed the implications of his notions of discipline and self-government extended beyond the school and childhood. He explicitly noted they have "extraordinary force, in view of our political institutions, founded as they are upon the great idea of the capacity of man for self-government."[42]

The Quality of Teachers

The importance of the teaching corps to Mann's educational reforms, while implicit in nearly all his work, was nowhere more explicit and obvious than in his discussions of school discipline. Both the Board and the Secretary noted their concern with the education and quality of the state's teachers in their *First Annual Report*,[43] and they continued to address the issue in each subsequent *Report* during Mann's 12-year tenure. Mann correctly understood that fundamental to the problems which he and others observed with common-school teachers was the inadequate preparation most teachers had received. Many teachers had not attended any institution of higher education. Some had graduated from, or at least attended, an academy or college, but for most of them teaching was a way station en route to a more attractive profession. While some academies had courses in pedagogy, there were few academies or colleges where one could find a full teacher-education program. In March of 1838 Edmund Dwight, a member of the original Board of Education, offered to provide $10,000 to help finance a state teachers' training institute, if the state legislature would appropriate a similar sum from state funds. By the end of the summer a bill appropriating the necessary funds had been hurried through the legislature and signed by Governor Everett.[44] A major new development in the history of American education was about to begin.

Normal Schools The first consideration involved the nature of teacher training. The response to this need by Mann and the Board defined teacher education for the subsequent century. The agenda they set resulted in both the best and the worst of what was to occur in American teacher education. Their fundamental principle was that common-school teachers needed special preparation to comprehend the nature of learners, the learning process, the subjects of the common-school curriculum, and how to teach. The last included organization of the curricular materials, classroom organization, and discipline, as well as pedagogic methods. These understandings, Mann argued, did not develop spontaneously and were not being adequately addressed in the available institutions of higher education, that is, the colleges and academies.

Rather than encouraging the incorporation of teacher education into existing institutions, Mann opted for new institutions which would be different and separate from the old. Moreover, the new normal schools were developed on the Prussian normal school model, where pedagogical methods not only were included in the curriculum, but dominated it. Additionally, he insisted that the "academic" portion of the curriculum be limited to the subjects taught in the common schools. The experiment began July 3, 1839, with the opening of the state normal school for women at Lexington, which was followed by the establishment of a coeducational normal school at Barre in September of the same year. By the end of his tenure Mann would see the opening of three additional normal schools in Massachusetts.

These schools would provide the nation with a model whose strength resided in the recognition of the need for special preparation for teachers. However, the model contained weaknesses which would plague teacher education to the present day. The isolation of teacher education from the rest of higher education and the accompanying denigration of academic subjects produced teachers whose subject-matter knowledge seemed confined to what was taught in elementary schools. This emphasis resulted in methods-trained teachers who knew how to teach but were less acquainted with what *should* be taught or *why*—matters they were not expected to decide upon anyway. In short, the normal-school approach was to train technicians, but not to educate scholars, and it might be argued that teacher education has yet to recover from this original deficit.

Teachers as Exemplars The lack of adequate preparation was not the only problem which Mann placed under the category of teacher quality. He was equally concerned that the teacher should be a model for students to emulate during their formative years. Like countless predecessors from Isocrates in Greece to Quintillian in Rome to De Feltre in Renaissance Italy, Mann emphasized the importance of the moral character of the teacher. In his *Fourth Annual Report* he admonished that local school committees "are sentinels stationed at the door of every schoolhouse in the State, to see that no teacher ever crosses its threshold, who is not clothed, from the crown of his head to the sole of his foot, in garments of virtue." He then noted strong concurrence from these committees: "as a single voice coming from a single heart—they urge, they insist, they demand, that the great axioms of a Christian morality shall be sedulously taught, and that the teachers shall themselves be patterns of the virtues, they are required to inculcate."[45] This notion of the teacher as a model of Protestant virtue led to an unprecedented invasion of the private lives of American teachers during Mann's time, a scrutiny that even today separates teachers from other professionals.

Feminization of Teaching The third aspect of Mann's concerns involved gender. During his tenure, the number and percentage of female teachers increased so dramatically that it is fair to say that by the end of the 1840s common-school teaching was viewed as a feminine occupation. This was a

Mann saw teaching as a nurturing process and, consequently, felt that women were more naturally fitted to the education of young children than were men, who supposedly were more driven by logic.

development Mann championed. In the 18th century, common-school teachers were almost universally males. Late in that century girls began to attend common schools during the summer terms, when the boys were in the fields helping with farm duties. At this time New England communities began to employ female teachers for the summer terms. Eventually, some females were employed to teach during the winter terms, especially when it was difficult to find male teachers and also because female teachers were much less expensive. Mann noted in the *First Annual Report* that the average wage of female teachers was about one-third that of male teachers. The average cost of a male teacher continued to be between two and one-half and three times that of a female teacher during his tenure.[46] While Mann cautioned that the differential was neither just nor wise, the repeated publication of the differential in his *Reports* may have had the effect of increasing the attractiveness of employing female teachers because of their lower salary.[47]

If the cost of female teachers was one factor in the feminization of teaching, a second impetus was Mann's arguments, which at least legitimated the trend and thus made it easier for school committees to justify hiring female teachers. He began his campaign for female teachers with a speech he delivered to the educational conventions of each county in the state during 1838. The Secretary forecast that the time was imminent when all would agree in "regarding female as superior to male teaching for the young children." After explaining the wastage of a "vast amount of female talent," Mann posed this rhetorical question:

> Is there not an obvious, constitutional difference of temperament between the sexes, indicative of a prearranged fitness and adaptation, and making known to us, as by a heaven-imparted sign, that woman, by her livelier sensibility and her quicker sympathies, is the forechosen guide and guardian of children of a tender age?[48]

In subsequent *Annual Reports,* he spelled out what he meant by temperament, fitness, sensibility, and sympathies. The basic contention was that a man was prone to be more rational than emotional or loving; thus male teachers would demand justice in retaliation for offenses. In contrast, the predominant female characteristic was affection rather than reason. Women would naturally love children rather than seek vengeance or justice for children's transgressions. This "natural" condition of women made them better equipped to be teachers, according to Mann, because their loving discipline would provide female teachers easier access to the inner psyche of the students.[49] The short- or intermediate-term effect of the acceptance of the Secretary's position was to open an important occupation to women. The long-term effect, however, was to reinforce the sexist belief that women were by nature not only fundamentally different from men but deficient in rational facilities.

Whatever the effect of Mann's campaign for female teachers, during his tenure as secretary the number of female teachers increased dramatically. Between 1837 and 1848 the increase of female teachers was 35 times as great as for males. Moreover, in each of the years from 1845 to 1848 the number of male teachers actually declined. By 1848 females accounted for 68 percent of all common-school teachers in Massachusetts.[50] The secretary reported Massachusetts as leading all states in the employment of female teachers, but predicted that as soon as other states provided normal schools to prepare women they would follow the Massachusetts example.[51] In this prediction he was correct. From this time on, one would speak of "schoolmarms" rather than "schoolmasters," and the pronoun *she* would be generally accurate when referring to teachers.

The Economic Value of Schooling[52]

During the 1840s Horace Mann developed a set of arguments which rallied the citizenry of the state to the banner of mass schooling. This was the first prominent American statement of what social scientists in the 20th century would name the "human capital theory" and for which they could claim originality.[53] The Secretary's arguments were persuasive because of the different messages they carried to various segments of his constituency. To the worker the message was: Send your children to school so they may become rich. Employers were advised that the common schools would provide them with workers who were not only more productive but also docile, easily managed, and unlikely to resort to strikes or violence. All segments of society could respond to the notion that schools would actually create wealth, thus relieving the plight of the poor without cost to the more affluent.

The *Fifth Annual Report* includes a major section devoted to the results of Mann's inquiry into "the effect of education upon the worldly fortunes or estates of men—its influence upon property, upon human comfort and competence, upon the outward, visible material interests or well-being of individuals and communities."[54] This he considered not the highest but, rather, the lowest of the beneficent influences of education. Nevertheless, he argued that material well-being was the prerequisite for the higher influences; moreover, if we take his rank-ordering at face value, it is ironic that his *economic* justification for schooling was to become the most enduring aspect of his educational thought. It continues to dominate educational discussion in the 20th century.

Mann's 1841 study centered on evidence solicited from "practical, sagacious and intelligent businessmen" who had employed large numbers of workers. The object was "to ascertain the difference in productive ability—where natural capacities have been equal—between the educated and the uneducated."[55] The results of this early version of survey research showed, according to the Secretary,

> a most astonishing superiority in productive power, on the part of the educated over the uneducated laborer. The hand is found to be another hand, when guided by an intelligent mind, processes are performed, not only more rapidly, but better, when facilities which have been exercised early in life, furnish their assistance. Individuals who, without the aid of knowledge, would have been condemned to perpetual inferiority of condition, and subjected to all the evils of want and poverty, rise to competence and independence, by the uplifting power of education . . . those who have been blessed with a good common school education, rise to a higher and higher point, in the kinds of labor performed, and also in the rate of wages paid, while the ignorant sink like dregs and are always found at the bottom.[56]

Secretary Mann included several specimen responses from businessmen in the *Report* to substantiate his conclusions on the productive consequences of education. A few excerpts from the letter of H. Barlett, Esq., a Lowell manufacturer who had employed between 400 and 900 persons during the previous 10 years, are instructive:

> I have no hesitation in affirming that I have found the best educated to be the most profitable help.... They make the best wages.... They have more order, and system; they not only keep their persons neater, but their machinery is in better condition....
>
> I have never considered mere knowledge, valuable as it is in itself to the laborer, as the only advantage derived from a good Common School education. I have uniformly found the better educated as a class possessing a higher and better state of morals, more orderly and respectful in their deportment, and more ready to comply with the wholesome and necessary regulations of the establishment, and in times of agitation, on account of some change in regulations or wages, I have always looked to the most intelligent, best educated and the most moral for support, and have seldom been disappointed....
>
> The owners of manufacturing property have a deep pecuniary interest in the education and morals of their help.[57]

In his farewell *Twelfth Annual Report,* the Secretary again returned to this theme in a section entitled "Intellectual Education as a Means of Removing Poverty and Securing Abundance."[58] He began with the claim that industrial and business operations had exposed Massachusetts "to the fatal extremes of wealth and poverty."[59] The specter of a European type of class division could best be avoided, according to Mann, by upgrading the lower orders through education. With the enormous confidence of the Enlightenment, he proclaimed that

> Education, then, beyond all other devices of human origin, is the great equalizer of the conditions of men—the balance wheel of the social machinery.... It does better than disarm the poor of their hostilities towards the rich; it prevents being poor.[60]

With a broadside aimed at revolutionary ideas, Mann argued his belief that the long-term economic benefits of education were far superior to short-term social upheaval designed to rectify perceived social inequities or injustices:

> The main idea set forth in the creeds of some political reformers, or revolutionizers, is, that some people are poor because others are rich. This idea supposes a fixed amount of property in the community, which, by fraud, or force, or arbitrary law is unequally divided among men; and the problem presented for solution is, how to transfer from those who are supposed to have too much, to those who feel and know that they have too little. At this point, both their theory and their expected reform stop. But the beneficent power of education would not be exhausted, even thought it should peaceably abolish all the miseries that spring from the coexistence, side by side, of enormous wealth and squalid want. It has a

Among other goals, 19th-century schools were expected to operate in a manner that would help produce diligent, obedient workers for the new industrial system.

> higher function. Beyond the power of diffusing old wealth, it has the prerogative of creating new ... education creates or develops new treasures not before possessed or dreamed of by any one.[61]

A few pages later Mann summarized these ideas in two sentences which have a familiar ring for anyone acquainted with the writings of subsequent human capital theorists or educators for whom economic justifications for education are paramount. The first: "For the creation of wealth then—for the existence of a wealthy people and a wealthy nation—intelligence is the grand condition."[62] And the second: "The greatest of all arts in political economy is, to change a consumer into a producer; and the next greatest is, to increase the producer's producing power;—an end to be directly attained, by increasing his intelligence."[63] Subsequently Mann provided several pages of examples showing how increased intelligence in artisan workers might result in their developing more ingenious labor-saving techniques, thus increasing the productive capacity of all workers intelligent enough to use the innovations.

Two aspects of Mann's contribution to the theory of human capital should be noted. First, his ideas must be placed within their ideological tradition. Mann wrote in the warm afterglow of the European Enlightenment and under the influence of classical liberal ideology. This tradition places ultimate faith in the human capacity to develop rational ability to solve all our problems. This belief reinforced a set of psychological concepts of long standing in western history which have become known as faculty psychology.

As described in Chapter 2, faculty psychology was built upon the notion that individuals learn best by vigorously exercising their mental faculties (e.g., memory, reason, precision) upon difficult learning tasks and the ideas of great thinkers. They would then be ready to apply, or "transfer," their strengthened mental faculties to other learning and to real problems.

Second, and somewhat contradictorily, Mann's businessperson–supporters failed to link a common-school education with the application of creative intelligence in workers. As Maris A. Vinovskis has shown, "Although each of the respondents to Mann's survey mentioned the ability of educated workers to work more efficiently than others, none of them emphasized the importance of the "inventiveness" which Mann stressed through the *Fifth Annual Report.* Instead, they tended to concentrate on the fact that these workers were able to follow directions better, were more punctual and reliable, and less likely to be unreasonable during periods of labor turmoil."[64] The traits emphasized by the industrialists were elements of what was then called "industrial morality" and is currently called "modern" (as opposed to "traditional") cultural commitments. While Mann was emphasizing the intellectual results of common schooling, his industrial supporters were emphasizing the enculturation of a value system amenable to industrialized factory life.

Opposition to Mann's Common-School Reforms

The Secretary's attempts to reform the common schools of Massachusetts did not go unchallenged. The opposition, inspired by different issues, came from three groups. The first conflict centered on Mann's efforts to make the common schools nondenominational. As we have seen, the conservative Calvinists led by Frederick A. Packard lost this battle in the early 1840s. The second, more parochial conflict resulted from the offense taken by the Boston schoolmasters to Mann's *Seventh Annual Report.* They believed that Mann's criticism of teaching methods, especially recitation and corporal punishment, had been directed at them. In response, they published *Remarks on the Seventh Annual Report of the Hon. Horace Mann,*[65] which challenged his pedagogic positions. After a war of words, the Boston schoolmasters attempted to rally the state's teachers against Mann by founding a state teachers' association, which they hoped would condemn Mann's policies. This tactic was generally unsuccessful, as Mann's supporters soon gained control of the organization.[66]

The third group in opposition to Mann's reforms was more broadly based and was concerned with the ideological and political implications of his approach. Mann was a member of the Whig party, which had created the state School Board and sponsored Mann's ideas in state government. The Democrats, led by Marcus Morton, had generally opposed his measures. A leading public spokesman for the Democratic position was Orestes Brownson, who had undergone a religious transformation similar to Mann's. Brownson moved from the Calvinism of his youth to Presbyterianism and then to Unitarianism by the early 1830s. In 1838 he became editor of a leading Democratic publication, the *Boston Quarterly Review,* and in this journal he launched his attacks on Mann's reforms. In an 1839 article, "Education of the People," Brownson lashed out at the state board for proposing a system which would be used for political domination of the people. He singled out the establishment of normal schools as particularly offensive. "The most we can hope from them is some little aid to teachers in the methods of teaching."[67] But more importantly, he argued, they were potentially dangerous to a free society. Based on the Prussian model, these normal schools, he believed, would produce conservative teachers who would in turn impart Whig values to the children of the state. Moreover, Brownson asserted, the Board was attempting to influence the books placed in the school libraries. The result of teachers' imparting Whig philosophy and controlling schoolbooks would be "to give Whiggism a self-perpetuating power."[68]

Underlying Brownson's opposition was his commitment to *democratic localism,* a belief that most governing and decision-making powers should be kept at the local level, in the hands of the people. He saw the common-school reforms as centralizing power at the state level, thus taking decisions out of popular control.[69] Two years later Brownson elaborated his critique of State Board–sanctioned books for school libraries: "We object also to the sanction of the Board, because it is an approach to a censorship of the press." Then, as if able to foresee the events of the 20th-century publishing world, he declared, "The publishers will not dare insert in their series a book not sanctioned by the Board, however valuable it may be in itself, or however acceptable it would be to a large number of school districts; and the author will not dare pour out his whole thought, but only such a portion of it as he has reason to believe the Board will not refuse to sanction."[70] Brownson's estimation of the Board of Education's goals for the common schools was summed up in the 1838 article when he claimed that

> In the view of this respectable Board, education is merely a branch of general police, the schoolmasters are only a better sort of constables. The Board would promote education, they would even make it universal, because they esteem it the most effectual means possible of checking pauperism and crime, and making the rich secure in their possessions. Education has, therefore, a certain utility which may be told in solid cash saved to the Commonwealth. This being the leading idea, the most comprehensive view which the Board seem to take of education, what more should be expected of their labors, than such modifications and improvements as will render it more efficient as an arm of general police?[71]

It is difficult to ascertain the effect which Brownson's attack had on the general populace of Massachusetts, but in the elections of 1839 the Democratic candidate for governor, Marcus Morton, won the statehouse after 12 previous unsuccessful attempts. In the spring of 1840 the legislature narrowly defeated a report of the Democratic-controlled Education Committee which condemned both the State Board of Education and the new normal schools. The vote was 245 to 182.[72] Although this vote did not end the attacks on Mann's reform efforts, by the mid-1840s he had prevailed over all opposition, and his reforms were well on the way to becoming institutionalized.

Accounting for the Success of the Common-School Reforms

Why were Mann's common-school reforms so successful? The answer is more complex than most historical accounts suggest. The first and perhaps the most important reason was that the Secretary was able to enlist the support of diverse elements in Massachusetts for his programs. One element of the supporting coalition was wealth. No reform movement in American history has had long-term success without forging an alliance with the money interests. Mann was successful, in part, because the mercantile, banking, and manufacturing interests were convinced that his common-school reforms would provide long-term benefits for them. Moreover, he seemed to convince many working people that the common school would provide better education than was previously available. Additionally, his suggestion that common-school education was the vehicle to up-

Comparison between Horace Mann and Orestes Brownson

Issue	Horace Mann	Orestes Brownson
Control of schools	State	Parents in local district
Religion in schools	State mandated	Local choice
Texts	From state-approved list	Local choice
Teacher training	State normal schools	Colleges and academies
Teacher certification	State	Local school boards
Purpose of certification	Moral, political, and economic	Moral and political
Agency to determine principles for schools to impart	State Board of Education	Local school boards
Political affiliation	Whig	Democrat

ward economic mobility was attractive to some less-than-affluent parents. Secondly, he gained the support of most of the religious (Protestant) communities because his "common elements," while not all that each group desired, did represent a compromise which was probably the most they could realistically expect. Finally, the common school and the slogans which carried its programs into the public discussion embodied the controlling classical liberal ideology of the age and thus successfully captured the popular imagination.

Horace Mann was the consummate educational salesman. He was not an innovator of educational, social, or cultural ideas; most of his proposals for educational reform were already current when he burst upon the educational scene. Onto existing educational practices and structures he grafted materials, ideas, and institutions borrowed from European (especially German) and American educators. The extent to which many of Mann's ideas were already conventional wisdom, although not yet institutionalized, in New England can be seen in the 1829 edition of *Hall's Lectures on School-Keeping.*[73] Samuel Read Hall was a New Englander, born a generation before Mann, who had devoted much of his life to education. He had been a schoolteacher and one of the early innovators of teacher education in private normal schools and academies. His 1829 *Lectures* was both a summation of his educational thought and one of the first American texts on how to teach. In it he discussed nearly every aspect of what Mann was later to incorporate into his reform efforts. Hall's discussion of the need for the special preparation of teachers, teaching methods, discipline, school facilities, the evils of private schools, and the teacher as moral model could have been substituted for Mann's discussions of these topics in his *Annual Report* or his *Lectures on Education,* and the reader would have hardly noticed the difference. That Horace Mann was not an innovator is not to his discredit. His significance was due to his ability to recognize the innovations of others, blend them into coherent programs for reform, and sell that reform package to an attentive audience by appealing to dominant ideological precepts under particular political–economic conditions. In this, he was successful to an historic degree.

Lessons from Horace Mann's Common-School Reforms

It seems that every item of Horace Mann's common-school reforms, with the possible exception of his campaign to improve the physical conditions of schools and school equipment, can be viewed as containing both positive and negative elements. Any fair evaluation of his efforts as well as any attempt to draw lessons from them must address both aspects. His insistence on the teaching of the "common elements" of the great Christian truths in order to inculcate a common set of moral values not only helped to stem the sectarian bickering among the major Protestant groups but provided the society with a potentially unifying value system to replace the outworn Calvinist doctrine. Did this contribution, however, outweigh the potential loss of a truly pluralistic society, where all individuals were more free to choose values compatible with their own cultural and class histories and characteristics? Did the Prussian model of universal state-supported and state-controlled education and improved pedagogic methods bring with it the antidemocratic impulses inherent in the despotic system of government it was designed to enhance? Mann's condemnation of punishment meant that henceforth the practitioners of child beating in schools would be on the defensive. But what would counter the potential dangers of psychological manipulation inherent in his "loving" pedagogy? Were Mann's contributions to the gains achieved by women in the teaching field adequate to offset the belief, made explicit in his arguments, that women are less rational than men? While the normal schools certainly represented a recognition that teachers needed education, was the pedagogically oriented education which they established as the norm for succeeding generations of teachers adequate? Mann's use of arguments asserting the economic value of schooling surely increased the popularity of schooling among nearly all segments of society. But should economic motives be the driving force behind education? Such questions require students of education to examine their own fundamental beliefs and values regarding human nature, the good society, and the appropriate relationship of the individual to that society—as well as their conception of the learning process and the teacher's role in that process. Such questions are inherent in all attempts to evaluate educational arguments, including those which dominated the common-school era of Horace Mann.

CONCLUDING REMARKS

This chapter has described a number of political–economic and ideological developments in early 19th-century Massachusetts which contrast with the preceding Jeffersonian era. Whereas late 18th-century Virginia was fundamentally slave and agrarian in its economy and of English Protestant descent in its free population, Massachusetts was beginning to feel the pressures of urbanization, industrialization, and the cultural conflict between its English and burgeoning Irish Catholic populations. While early-American Virginia, like most of the young nation, was preoccupied with the challenge of protecting the freedoms won by a revolutionary generation, the challenge facing Massachusetts in the 50-year period following Jefferson's death was to battle what Whig leaders perceived as the chaotic social disharmony brought about by urbanization, industrialization, and Irish immigration. In the context of these problems, plans for a state-funded and even state-controlled school system looked far more desirable than such proposals had looked to Jefferson's contemporaries, who rejected even state funding for common schooling, much less centralized state control.

In this later context, the work and ideas of Horace Mann illustrate the dominant ways of thinking about schooling and society in Massachusetts. A prominent social reformer even apart from his work in common schooling, Mann reflected the efforts of many of his Protestant Whig peers who engaged in such social-progress campaigns as abolition of slavery, the temperance movement, prison reform, mental health reform, women's suffrage, and provision of schooling for the poor. Like others of his era, Mann interpreted classical liberal ideology in accord with newly emerging social conditions. His liberal views of Protestantism, capitalism, and republicanism took a different shape than those commitments had taken for Jefferson in Virginia. For example, Mann (somewhat like Benjamin Rush in culturally diverse Pennsylvania) saw the schools as a primary vehicle for building support for republican and Protestant values in the population. Instead of advocating Jefferson's dictum, "That government governs best which governs least," Mann advocated a much more active role for government in solving social and economic problems that were not primary concerns for Jefferson.

Mann's penchant for a more active government and for a government-controlled school system which would address a wide range of social problems, together with his belief in the moral benefits of a proper education, led him to advocate a Prussian model of schooling derived from a thoroughly undemocratic European nation-state. This view stood in marked contrast, for example, with Jefferson's distrust of European educational traditions, which he had castigated as aristocratic and nondemocratic in temper. Some of Mann's contemporaries, including Orestes Brownson, were, like Jefferson, mistrustful of European models of education for American children. Mann, however, unlike Jefferson, was not driven by fear of tyranny but by fear of social disorder and moral decay. While Jefferson believed that revolution was a desirable and even necessary form of progress, Mann's classical liberal commitment to progress was limited to a belief in progress through moral and political consensus, the achievement of which he believed required a state system of schooling.

Mann advocated the establishment of normal schools to professionalize and standardize teaching in order to build moral consensus among the youth of Massachusetts. Mann's concerns for economy and for a "loving" pedagogy led him to work successfully toward the feminization of the teaching profession, a move which would bring into public service the nurturing capacities which Mann believed were "natural" to women in the private sphere of the family.

While Mann believed he was advocating education for religious and republican virtue, some of his contemporaries argued that he was instead instituting a system of schooling for social control. Whereas Mann believed that his well-educated, Protestant, Whig values were appropriate for all citizens, others argued that he was substituting Whig paternalism for the kind of democratic local control which Jefferson had insisted would ensure the involvement of all citizens in making decisions of public concern. This contrast, in the context of Massachusetts cities straining under the cultural conflicts between Irish Catholic immigrants and native-born Americans, raises difficult questions about the tensions between a common educational system in a culturally diverse society. Would Mann have been more democratic, for example, if he had advocated state funding but local control of schooling, so that Irish Catholics could take responsibility for deciding how their children would be educated? Or do the requirements of social order dictate that the majority should determine what is best for the minority? Partly at stake here is what was referred to in Chapter 2 as Jefferson's "development ideal of democracy": that is, that democracy is to be valued because genuine participation in decision-making is itself educational. Thus, the active participation of minority groups in the fundamental decisions affecting their lives is desirable for the educational effects it has upon those groups. Similarly, the classical liberal, "natural rights" argument would support the view that people have a right to be self-governing and not subjected to what John Stuart Mill in England called "the tyranny of the majority." Further, there is the matter of the contributions that various subcultures make to the wider culture and whether it therefore benefits the dominant culture to support and sustain such subcultures. Whether such commitments to cultural pluralism instead of cultural uniformity were a threat to the state was a matter of sharp disagreement in Massachusetts, but it was settled in favor of Horace Mann and his supporters.

PRIMARY SOURCE READING

Orestes Brownson was introduced in Chapter 3 as a member of the Democratic Party, a journalist, and a political and educational critic of Horace Mann. The following excerpt is a wide-ranging critique of Mann's political, religious, and educational aims for common schooling. Brownson further assails the wisdom of the normal-school effort which Mann successfully began in Massachusetts.

Part of Brownson's critique is grounded in a view of the educated person similar to Aristotle's notion of "the cultivation of human excellence for its own sake," an ideal that Brownson believes Mann is abandoning in favor of education for instrumental social ends. In making this argument, Brownson distinguishes between "special" and "general" education, a distinction borrowed from the Greeks and still important today as we debate the balance of specialized versus general liberal studies in the school or college curriculum. In considering what it means to be educated as a human being, Brownson attacks Mann's common-schooling approach to religious education as an abandonment of what gives religion its essential value to human life, and he argues that Mann's academically narrow and standardized teacher-education curriculum will only exacerbate this problem.

Brownson assails Mann's common-schooling ideas on other fronts as well, relying on Jeffersonian ideals of democratic localism in doing so.

DECENTRALIZATION: ALTERNATIVE TO BUREAUCRACY?

Orestes Brownson

We can hardly be expected at this late day, in this ancient commonwealth especially, to go into any labored argument in favor of popular education, either as a matter of right or as the only firm foundation of a free government. For ourselves, we hold that every child born into a community is born with as good a natural right to the best education that community can furnish, as he is to a share of the common air of heaven or the common light of the sun. We hold also that the community, which neglects to provide the best education it can for all its children, whether male or female, black or white, rich or poor, bond or free, forfeits its right to punish the offender. We hold, moreover, that a popular government unsupported by popular education is a baseless fabric.

But, while we bear our unequivocal testimony in favor of universal education and assert the duty of every community to provide the best education in its power for all its children, we are very far from regarding everything which passes, or may pass under the name of education, as something to be approved and never condemned. Education may be bad as well as good, a curse as well as a blessing; and in general its quality is a matter of even more importance than its quantity. Educated, in some sense, all our children are, and will be, whether we will it or not. Education, such as it is, is ever going on. Our children are educated in the streets, by the influence of their associates, in the fields and on the hillsides, by the influences of surrounding scenery and overshadowing skies, in the bosom of the family, by the love and gentleness or wrath and fretfulness of parents, by the passions or affections they see manifested, the conversations to which they listen, and above all by the general pursuits, habits, and moral tone of the community. In all these are schoolrooms and schoolmasters sending forth scholars educated for good or for evil or, what is more likely, for a little of both. The real question for us to ask is not, Shall our children be educated? but, To what end shall they be educated, and by what means? What is the kind of education needed, and how shall it be furnished?

As an individual I am something more than the farmer, the shoemaker, the blacksmith, the lawyer, the physician, or the clergyman. Back of my professional character there lies the man, that which I possess in common with all my species and which is the universal and permanent ground of my being as a man. This education must reach, call forth, and direct as well as my professional pur-

From "Second Annual Report of the Board of Education, Together with the Second Annual Report of the Secretary of the Board" (Boston, 1839), review in the *Boston Quarterly Review* 2 (October 1839) pp. 393–418.

suit. Individual education is divided then into general education and special—my education as a man and my education as a doctor, lawyer, minister, artisan, artist, agriculturalist, or merchant.

Special education appears to be that which we at present are most anxious to make provision for. Few people think of anything beyond it. The popular doctrine, we believe, is that we should be educated in special reference to what is to be our place in society and our pursuit in life. We think more of education as a means of fitting us for a livelihood than for anything else. The tendency has long been to sink the man in what are merely his accidents, to qualify him for a profession or pursuit, rather than to be a man. . . .

General education, which some may term the culture of the soul, which we choose to term the education of humanity, we regard as the first and most important branch of education. This is the education which fits us for our destiny, to attain our end as simple human beings. . . .

Man has a destiny, an end he should seek to gain, and religion is the answer to the question, What is this end, this destiny? According to the principles we have laid down then, education, to be complete, to be what it ought to be, must be religious. An education which is not religious is a solemn mockery. Those who would exclude religion from education are not yet in the condition to be teachers; long years yet do they need to remain in the primary school.

Man is also a social being and needs an education corresponding to his social nature. He is not a mere individual. He stands not alone . . . that deserves not the name of a social education which leaves untouched the problem of society, the destiny of the race. And the social education must needs vary precisely as vary our solutions of this problem. In Russia they solve this problem in their fashion. Society has there for its object the accomplishment of the will and the manifestation of the glory of the Autocrat. Hence, the Russian children are carefully taught, by authority, that they and all they may possess are his and that they must love him in their hearts and honor him as their God. In Austria the problem is solved much in the same way and so also in Prussia. Absolutism has its solution and educates accordingly. Liberalism has also its solution and its corresponding education. . . . If the aristocratic element be the true foundation of social order, then should our schools be under the control of the aristocracy, be aristocratic in their basis and superstructure, and be nurseries of the aristocratic principle. But, if the democratic element be the true basis of society, then should the social education give the democratic solution of the problem, create a love for democracy, and discountenance every aristocratic tendency. It should, also, not only accept the democratic element but disclose the means by which it may insure the victory and make all other social elements subordinate to itself. It must, then, touch the nature and organization of the state, determine the mission of government and the measures it must adopt in order to secure or advance the democracy. It rushes into the midst of politics, then, and decides on national banks and subtreasuries. An education which does not go thus far is incomplete and insufficient for our social wants.

Education, then, must be religious and social, or political. Neither religion nor politics can be excluded. Indeed, all education that is worth anything is either religious or political and fits us for discharging our duties either as simple human beings or as members of society. . . .

Assuming now the absolute necessity of religious and political education, and the worthlessness of every other kind of education, when taken alone, the great and the practical question becomes, How is this education to be provided? In what schools and under what schoolmasters?

We have looked into the reports before us, with the hope of finding an answer to this question, but here (as everywhere else in the world) we have been doomed to disappointment. . . . The normal schools, which the board proposes to establish, will do nothing to impart such an education as we contend for. The most we can hope from them is some little aid to teachers in the methods of teaching. Beyond improving the mechanism of education, they will be powerless or mischievous.

Schools for teachers require in their turn teachers, as well as any other class of schools. Who, then, are to be the teachers in these normal schools? What is to be taught in them? Religion and politics? What religion, what politics? These teachers must either have some religious and political faith, or none. If they have none, they are mere negations and therefore unfit to be entrusted with education of the educators of our children. If they have a religious and a political faith, they will have one which only a part of the community hold to be true. If the teachers in these schools are Unitarians, will Trinitarians accept their scholars as educators? Suppose they are Calvinists, will Universalists, Methodist, Unitarians, and Quakers be content to install their pupils as instructors in common schools?

But the board assure us Christianity shall be insisted on so far, and only so far, as it is common to all sects. This, if it means anything, means nothing at all. All who attempt to proceed on the principle here laid down will find their Christianity ending in nothingness. Much may be taught in general, but nothing in particular. No sect will be satisfied; all sects will be dissatisfied. For it is not enough that my children are not educated in a belief contrary to my own; I would have them educated to believe what I hold to be important truth; and I always hold that to be important truth, wherein I differ from others. . . .

If we come into politics, we encounter the same difficulty. What doctrines on the destiny of society will these normal schools inculcate? If any, in this commonwealth, at present, they must be Whig doctrines, for none but Whigs can be professors in these schools. . . . Establish, then, your Whig board of education; place on it a single Democrat, to save appearances; enable this board to establish normal schools and through them to educate this board to establish normal schools and through them to educate all the children of the commonwealth, authorize them to publish common-school libraries, to select all the books used in schools, and thus to determine all the doctrines which our children shall imbibe, and what will be the result? We have then given to some half a dozen Whigs the responsible office of forming the political faith and conscience of the whole community. . . .

The truth is, we have, in the establishment of this board of education, undertaken to imitate despotic Prussia, without considering the immense distance between the two countries. . . .

Let it be borne in mind that in Prussia the whole business of education is lodged in the hands of government. The government establishes the schools in which it prepares the teachers; it determines both the methods of teaching and the matters taught. It commissions all teachers and suffers no one to engage in teaching without authority from itself. Who sees not then that all the teachers will be the pliant tools of the government and that the whole tendency of the education given will be to make the Prussians obedient subjects of Frederic the king? Who sees not that education in Prussia is supported merely as the most efficient arm of the police and fostered merely for the purpose of keeping out revolutionary or, what is the same thing, liberal ideas?

A government system of education in Prussia is not inconsistent with the theory of Prussian society, for there all wisdom is supposed to be lodged in the government. But the thing is wholly inadmissible here not because the government may be in the hands of Whigs or Democrats, but because, according to our theory, the people are supposed to be wiser than the government. Here the people do not look to the government for light, for instruction, but the government looks to the people. The people give the law to the government. To entrust, then, the government with the power of determining the education which our children shall receive is entrusting our servant with the power to be our master. This fundamental difference between the two countries, we apprehend, has been overlooked by the board of education and its supporters. In a free government, there can be no teaching by authority, and all attempts to teach by authority are so many blows struck at its freedom. We may as well have a religion established by law, as a system of education, and have the government educate and appoint the pastors of our churches, as well as the instructors of our children. . . .

Introduce now a system of normal schools under the supervision of a government board of education. These schools must be governed by popular men, men of reputation, not men who have the good of the people at heart and are known only by their infidelity to popular interests, but men who are generally regarded as safe, in whom the mass of the active members of the community have confidence. But on what condition does a man come into this category of popular men? Simply on the condition that he represent, to a certain extent, the opinions now dominant. . . .

In order to be popular, one must uphold things as they are, disturb the world with no new views, and alarm no private interest by uttering the insurrectionary word, Reform. He must merely echo the sentiments and opinions he finds in vogue; and he who can echo these the loudest, the most distinctly, and in the most agreeable voice, is sure to be the most popular man—for a time. Men of this stamp do never trouble their age; they are never agitators, and there is no danger that they will stir up any popular commotion; they are the men to be on boards of education, professors in colleges, constables, mayors, members of legislative assemblies, presidents, and parish clerks. . . .

In consequence of this invariable law of Providence, the men who can be placed at the head of the normal schools, if established, will not be the men who represent the true idea of our institutions or who will prepare their pupils to come forth [as] educators of our children for the accomplishment of the real destiny of American society. They will teach them to respect and preserve what is, to caution them against the licentiousness of the people, the turbulence and brutality of the mob, the dangers of anarchy and even of liberty; but they will rarely seek to imbue them with a love of liberty, to admonish them to resist the first encroachments of tyranny, to stand fast in their freedom, and to feel always that it is nobler to die, nay, nobler to kill, than to live a slave. They will but echo the sentiments of that portion of the community on whom they are the more immediately dependent, and they will approve no reform, no step onward, till it has been already achieved in the soul of the community.

We confess, therefore, that we cannot look for much to meet the educational wants of the community, from the favorite measures of the Massachusetts Board of Education. In the view of this respectable board, education is merely a branch of general police, and schoolmasters are only a better sort of constables. The board would promote education, they would even make it universal, because they esteem it the most effectual means possible of checking pauperism and crime and making the rich secure in their possessions. Education has, therefore, a certain utility which may be told in solid cash saved to the commonwealth. This being the leading idea, the most comprehensive view which the board seem to take of education, what more should be expected from their labors except such modifications and improvements as will render it more efficient as an arm of general police? More, we confess, we do not look for from their exertions. The board is not composed of men likely to attempt more, and even if it were composed of other men, with far other and more elevated and comprehensive views, more could not be effected. Boards of trade may do something, but boards of education and boards of religion are worthy of our respect only in proportion to their imbecility. To educate a human being to be a man, to fulfill his destiny, to attain the end for which God made him, is not a matter which can, in the nature of things, come within the jurisdiction of a board, however judiciously it may be constituted.

Nevertheless, the board may, perhaps, do something. There is room to hope that it will do something to improve the construction of schoolhouses and to collect the material facts concerning the state of education as it now is; and, judging from the accompanying report of its accomplished secretary, it may also affect some progress in the methods of teaching our children to spell. This will be considerable and will deserve gratitude and reward. Nothing desirable in matters of education, beyond what relates to the finances of the schools, comes within the province of the legislature. More than this the legislature should not attempt; more than this the friends of education should not ask. Let the legislature provide ample funds for the support of as many schools as are needed for the best education possible of all the children of the community, and there let it stop. The selection of teachers, the choice of studies and of books to be read or studied, all that pertains to the methods of teaching and the matters to be taught or learned are best left to the school district. In these matters, the district should be paramount to the state. The evils we have alluded to are in some degree inseparable from all possible systems of education which are capable of being put into practice, but they will be best avoided by placing the individual school under the control of a community composed merely of the number of families having children to be educated in it.

For ourselves, we adopt the democratic principle in its fullest extent; but we believe that federalism—we use the word in its etymological sense—is the method by which its beneficial working is best to be secured. The individual state, as well as the Union, should be a confederacy of distinct communities. Our idea of the true form of a republican government for this country is, first, that the few material interests common to all parts of the whole country should be confided to a general congress composed of delegates from all the States; secondly, that the class of interests under these, common to the largest extent of territory, should be confided to a state congress, composed of delegates from counties; thirdly, the next more general class of interests under these should be confided to a county government composed of delegates from several townships or wards; fourthly, the next most general class to a township or ward government composed of delegates from the several districts of the town or ward; fifthly, the remaining interests which may be subjected to governmental action should be confided to all the citizens of the district, which should always be of size sufficient to maintain a grammar school: This is nothing but the actual idea of our government, freed from its exceptions and anomalies, and would require no new division to be introduced. Our legislature, in this commonwealth, is composed of delegates from corporations or communities, and we hope the hand of innovation will never succeed in giving it a different basis. . . .

Now, to the smallest of these divisions, corresponding to our present school districts, among other matters, we would confide the whole subject—with the exception heretofore made—of common-school education. This exception related to the finances; but we would make even this exception as narrow as possible. The more exclusively the whole matter of the school is brought under the control of the families specially interested in it, the more efficient will the school be. If the town manages part of it and the state a part of it, the district will be very likely to be remiss in managing its part, and so in fact no part, in the end, will be well managed. This results from a common principle: where responsibility is divided, there is always a greater or less want of fidelity in its discharge. Wherever there is a power to be exercised, there should always be a concentration of it in as few hands as possible; and, to counterbalance the centralizing tendency of this, the community should be so divided into subcommunities, that the power should in fact affect but a small number, and matters should be so arranged that this small number should be able to obtain speedy redress, if wronged.

At any rate, experience proves that when the powers of the school district were greater, and the interference of the state and the township were less than now, the common school was altogether better than it is at present. In this view of the case, we regard the board of education as an unwise establishment. It is a measure designed to reduce yet lower the powers and responsibilities of school districts, to deprive them of their rights, and to bring the whole matter of education under the control of one central government. In the district, we manage the school for our own children, but the board of education have no children in the district school. They are removed to a great distance from it by the fewness of their number and the populousness of the community for which they act, and they can never take the deep interest of parents in each individual school and, therefore, must want that which has thus far given to the common school its charm and its efficiency. To confide our common schools to the board is like taking the children from their parents, and entrusting them to strangers. . . .

. . . Government is not in this country, and cannot be, the educator of the people. In education, as in religion, we must rely mainly on the voluntary system. If this be an evil, it is an evil inseparable from our form of government. Government here must be restricted to material interests and forbidden to concern itself with what belongs to the spiritual culture of the community. It has no right of control over our opinions: literary, moral, political, philosophical, or religious. Its province is to reflect, not to lead, nor to create the general will. It, therefore, must not be installed the educator of the people. . . .

The real educators of the young are the grownup generation. The rising generation will always receive as good, as thorough an education, as the actual generation is prepared to give, and no better. The great work, then, which needs to be done in order to advance education, is to qualify the actual generation for imparting a more complete and finished education to its successor, that is to say, educate not the young, but the grownup generation. This educating of the grownup generation is what we mean by the *education of the people.* Society at large must be regarded as a vast normal school in which the whole active, doing, and driving generation of the day are pupils qualifying themselves to educate the young.

QUESTIONS FOR DISCUSSION AND EXAMINATION

1. It might be argued that Horace Mann's thinking about schooling and society is perfectly consistent with Jefferson's view, but that the differing political–economic contexts of late 18th-century Virginia and early 19th-century Massachusetts required different applications of Jeffersonian ideals. Assess that point of view, providing support from the text.

2. Were Orestes Brownson's ideas more consistent with Jefferson's view on the relations between education and republican forms of government than Horace Mann's? Defend your position.

3. Given the then-current view that religious instruction was an essential part of the formation of character, how satisfactory was Mann's common-school solution to the religious diversity of urban Massachusetts? Defend your view.

4. On the one hand, Mann's promotion of women into the teaching force might be regarded as a positive advance for women into the public sphere. On the other, it might be argued that Mann was reinforcing the subservience of women by limiting them to public-sphere nurturing roles in public institutions controlled by governing boards comprised entirely of men. In your view, was the feminization of teaching a positive advance for women, or more negative in its import?

5. To what degree do you believe that the current status of the teaching profession is traceable to such common-school origins as the feminization of teaching, the social role of schooling, and the development of normal schools? Defend your view.

6. If Mann's common-school successes came at the expense of such democratic ideals as local self-governance and cultural pluralism, to what degree were these compromises justified in your view? Defend your position.

NOTES

1. Stanley K. Schultz, *The Culture Factory* (New York: Oxford University Press, 1973), pp. 11, 23.
2. Carl F. Kaestle, *Pillars of the Republic* (New York: Hill & Wang, 1983), p. 62; Horace Mann, *First Annual Report* (Boston: Dutton & Wentworth, 1838), p. 32; *Second Annual Report* (Boston: Dutton & Wentworth, 1839), p. 38.
3. Kaestle, p. 62.
4. Calculated from Table 1 in Douglass C. North, *The Economy of the United States 1790–1860* (Englewood Cliffs, NJ: Prentice Hall, 1961), p. 35.
5. Freeman Butts and Lawrence Cremin, *A History of Education in American Culture* (New York: Henry Holt, 1953), pp. 157–60.
6. North, pp. 48–49.
7. Ibid, pp. 70–71; Kaestle, p. 63.
8. David Montgomery, "The Working Classes of the Pre-Industrial American City, 1780–1830," *Labor History* 9 (Winter 1968), 3–22.
9. Paul Faler, "Cultural Aspects of the Industrial Revolution: Lynn, Massachusetts, Shoemakers and Industrial Morality," *Labor History* 15, No. 3 (Summer 1974), 367–94.
10. E. P. Thompson, "Time, Work, Discipline, and Industrial Capitalism," *Past and Present,* No. 38 (December 1968), 56–97; Herbert G. Gutman, "Work, Culture, and Society in Industrializing America, 1815–1919," *American Historical Review* 78, No. 3 (June 1973), 531–88.
11. Faler, p. 368; Bruce Laurie, " 'Nothing on Compulsion': Life Styles of Philadelphia Artisans, 1820–1850," *Labor History* 15, No. 3 (Summer 1974), 337–66.
12. See Perry Miller, *The New England Mind: From Colony to Province* (Cambridge, MA: Harvard University Press, 1953); and *The New England Mind: The Seventeenth Century* (Cambridge, MA: Harvard University Press, 1954).
13. Irving H. Bartlett, *The American Mind in the Mid-Nineteenth Century* (New York: Thomas Y. Crowell, 1967), pp. 6–18.
14. Jonathan Messerli, *Horace Mann, A Biography* (New York: Alfred A. Knopf, 1972). This is the definitive biography and our source for biographical data; however, Messerli should not be held accountable for our interpretive use of the data he provides.
15. Quoted in ibid., p. 12.
16. Ibid., p. 107.
17. Quoted in Lawrence Cremin, ed., *The Republic and the School: Horace Mann on the Education of Free Men* (New York: Teachers College Press, 1957), p. 3.
18. Quoted in Messerli, p. 249.
19. Massachusetts State Board of Education and Secretary Horace Mann, *First Annual Report of the Board of Education Together with the First Annual Report of the Secretary of the Board* (Boston: Dutton & Wentworth, 1838), pp. 5–6. Hereafter referred to as *First Annual Report.*

20. Ibid., p. 21.
21. Mann, *Third Annual Report* (Boston: Dutton & Wentworth, 1840), p. 19.
22. *Sixth Annual Report* (Boston: Dutton & Wentworth, 1843), p. 51.
23. *First Annual Report* (Boston: Dutton & Wentworth, 1838), pp. 8, 26.
24. Ibid., p. 73.
25. *Second Annual Report* (Boston: Dutton & Wentworth, 1839), pp. 30–31.
26. Mann, *Fifth Annual Report* (Boston: Dutton & Wentworth, 1843), pp. 31–33, 121–35.
27. Carle Kaestle and Maris A. Vinovskis, *Education and Social Change in Nineteenth Century Massachusetts* (Cambridge, MA: Cambridge University Press, 1980), p. 196.
28. *First Annual Report,* p. 59.
29. For a full discussion see Raymond B. Culver, *Horace Mann and Religion in the Massachusetts Public Schools* (New Haven: Yale University Press, 1929). Also see *The Common School Controversy* (Boston: J. N. Bradley & Company, 1844), and *The Bible, The Rod, and Religion in Common Schools* (Boston: J. M. Whittmore, 1847).
30. See Robert Barger, "John Lancaster Spalding: Catholic Education and Social Emissary," unpublished, Ph.D. dissertation, University of Illinois at Champaign, 1976, chap. 4, pp. 78–100.
31. Harold J. Lasky, ed., *Autobiography of J. S. Mill with an Appendix of Hitherto Unpublished Speeches and a Preface by Harold J. Lasky* (London: Oxford University Press, 1924), pp. 327–29.
32. Messerli, p. 251.
33. George Armstrong Kelly, ed., *Johann Gottlieb Fichte, Addresses to the German Nation* (New York: Harper Torchbooks, 1968).
34. Mann, *Seventh Annual Report* (Boston: Dutton & Wentworth, 1844), p. 23.
35. Ibid., p. 133.
36. Horace Mann, *Lectures on Education* (Boston: Ide & Dutton, 1855), p. 304.
37. Ibid., p. 312.
38. Ibid., pp. 316–17.
39. Ibid., p. 308.
40. Ibid., p. 331.
41. Mann, *Eighth Annual Report* (Boston: Dutton & Wentworth, 1845), pp. 94–97.
42. Ibid., p. 94.
43. Pages 12, 26, 58–66.
44. Messerli, pp. 298–301.
45. Mann, *Fourth Annual Report* (Boston: Dutton & Wentworth, 1841), p. 59.
46. Mann, *First Annual Report,* p. 61; *Fourth Annual Report,* p. 10; *Sixth Annual Report,* p. 31; *Eleventh Annual Report* (Boston: Dutton & Wentworth, 1848), p. 26.
47. Mann, *Sixth Annual Report,* pp. 31–33; *Eleventh Annual Report,* pp. 26–27.
48. Horace Mann, *Lectures,* pp. vii, 72–73.
49. Mann, *Sixth Annual Report,* pp. 28–30; *Seventh Annual Report,* pp. 140–42; *Ninth Annual Report,* pp. 34–35; *Eleventh Annual Report,* pp. 26–27.
50. Mann, *Twelfth Annual Report,* calculated from table on p. 21.
51. Ibid., p. 22.
52. Substantial portions of this section were taken from Paul C. Violas, "Reflections on Theories of Human Capital, Skills Training and Vocational Education," *Education Theory* 31, No. 2 (Spring 1981), 137–51.
53. The ideas had first been articulated in England earlier in the 18th century by Robert Owen. Peter Drucker, T. W. Schwartz, and Burton A. Weisbrod are the 20th-century social scientists referred to. See Violas, pp. 137–39.
54. Mann, *Fifth Annual Report,* p. 81.
55. Ibid., p. 83.
56. Ibid., pp. 85–86.
57. Ibid., pp. 93–95.
58. Mann, *Twelfth Annual Report,* pp. 53–76.
59. Ibid., p. 58.
60. Ibid., p. 60.
61. Ibid.
62. Ibid., p. 67.
63. Ibid., p. 68.
64. Maris A. Vinovskis, "Horace Mann on the Economic Productivity of Education," *The New England Quarterly* 43, No. 4 (December 1970), p. 565.
65. (Boston, 1844).
66. Messerli, pp. 412–21.
67. Orestes Brownson, "Education of the People," *Boston Quarterly Review,* October 1838, p. 403.
68. Ibid., p. 406.
69. Ibid., p. 415.
70. Orestes Brownson, "The School Library," *Boston Quarterly Review,* April 1840, p. 229.
71. Brownson, "Education of the People," p. 412.
72. Messerli, p. 331.
73. Arthur D. Wright and George E. Gardner, eds., *Hall's Lectures on School-Keeping,* (Hanover, NH: Dartmouth Press, 1929). We are indebted to Professor Jeanne Connell for bringing this source to our attention.

Social Diversity and Differentiated Schooling: The Progressive Era

In 1918 a team led by researchers Abraham Flexner and Frank Bachman evaluated the school system of Gary, Indiana, an industrial city of 50,000 inhabitants located 27 miles southeast of Chicago. In their report, *The Gary Schools: A General Account*, Flexner and Bachman took pains to prepare readers for the fact that Gary's was no "traditional" school system, but rather a "progressive" system, and that traditional conceptions of the school would not be useful in understanding Gary's schools.[1] The student who comes to understand all the elements of the following excerpt from the Gary report will understand a great deal about progressive education in the United States of the early 20th century.

> The Gary schools can be properly understood only when they are viewed in the light of the general educational situation. For years, while the practice of education has in large part continued to follow traditional lines, the progressive literature of the subject has abounded in constructive suggestions of far-reaching significance. Social, political, and industrial changes have forced upon the school responsibilities formerly laid upon the home. Once the school had mainly to teach the elements of knowledge; now it is charged with the physical, mental, and social training of the child as well. To meet these needs, a changed and enriched curriculum, including, in addition to the common academic branches, community activities, facilities for recreation, shop work, [and] household arts, has been urged on the content side of school work; on the side of method and attitude, the transformation of school methods, discipline, and aims on the basis of modern psychology, ethics and social philosophy has been recommended for similar reasons.[2]

What did the authors mean, exactly, by "social, political, and industrial changes"? Or "physical, mental, and social training of the child"? Or "changed and enriched curriculum"? Or "modern psychology, ethics, and social philosophy"? Put differently, the authors might have said that one can understand the changes in the Gary schools only by understanding changes in the contemporary political economy and dominant ideology. Developing an informed and critical interpretation of these changes is a large part of the work of this chapter.

The 50-year period from the 1870s to the 1920s represented nothing short of a revolution in American schooling, with the most fundamental changes taking place in the 15 years on either side of 1900. Simply in terms of student enrollment, the changes were dramatic. In the 1889–90 school year, for example, the 358,000 students enrolled in public and private secondary schools represented

Note: A substantial portion of the primary research for this chapter was contributed by Frank Margonis and Stuart McAninch.

only 7 percent of all youth 14 to 17 years old (see Exhibit 4.1). By the 1919–20 school year, 2.5 million students were enrolled in secondary schools, and they represented 32 percent of their age group. (It would be only another 10 years before a majority of all 14- to 17-year-olds were enrolled in secondary school.) Further, of the relatively few students in secondary schools in 1889, just over half were enrolled in public schools. By 1919, however, 88 percent of all secondary school students were enrolled in public schools.

The number of students in secondary school had increased sixfold in those 30 years. This in itself would be enough to create an educational crisis, due to the explosion in requirements for buildings, teachers, teacher education programs, texts, and funds for all of these. But the changes that took place were not limited simply to quantitative increases. Fundamental changes were taking place in American life and in the American people, changes that challenged and altered the schools in fundamental ways. The first important changes that we shall examine are in the political economy of the 50-year period following 1870, specifically urbanization, immigration, industrialization, and centralization of decision-making power.

THE POLITICAL ECONOMY OF THE PROGRESSIVE ERA

Urbanization

Shortly after the Civil War, and through the end of the 19th century, the United States remained a predominantly agrarian society. In 1870, fewer than 10 million Americans, or only 26 percent of the population, lived in cities (communities of over 2,500 persons; see Exhibit 4.2). Not until about 1920 did over half the U.S. population live in cities. It was in this 50-year period, then, that the nation shifted demographically from being primarily rural to primarily urban in character. Between 1870 and 1920, as Exhibit 4.2 illustrates, the number of cities with population over half a million grew from 2 to 12.

The shift from rural to urban life, however, was not just a matter of numbers; it also involved matters of culture and the quality of life. As people came to the cities from rural areas in the United States and abroad, they encountered conditions few had ever imagined. Historians Dinnerstein and Reimers, in *Ethnic Americans,* provide some sense of the conditions under which urban dwellers lived in the larger cities at the turn of the century.

EXHIBIT 4.1 Development of a Modern Secondary School System, 1889–1940*

	TOTAL SECONDARY SCHOOL ENROLLMENT		*POPULATION 14–17 YEARS OF AGE*			
Year	*Number (000s)*	*Percentage Increase over 1889–90*	*Number (000s)*	*Percentage Increase over 1889–90*	*Number Enrolled per 100 Population 14–17 Years of Age*	*Percentage of Secondary School Enrollment in Public High Schools*
1889–90	358	—	5,355	—	7	57%
1899–1900	699	95%	6,152	15%	11	74
1909–10	1,115	211	7,220	35	15	82
1919–20	2,500	598	7,736	45	32	88
1929–30	4,811	1,244	9,341	75	51	91
1939–40	7,130	1,892	9,720	82	73	93

*For educational statistics from this period, secondary school and high school enrollment were still roughly synonymous. The seventh and eighth grades, now commonly included as part of secondary schooling, were still then considered to be elementary school grades for statistical purposes.

Source: Derived from *Biennial Survey of Education in the U.S., 1938–40* (Washington, D.C.: U.S. Office of Education, 1947), vol. 2, chap. 1, p. 12; and *Historical Statistics of the U.S., Colonial Times to 1970, Bicentennial Edition* (Washington, D.C.: U.S. Department of Commerce, Bureau of Census, 1975), pp. 368–69.

> Whole neighborhoods were filthy, foul-smelling, and overcrowded. In cities like Boston, New York, and Chicago houses adjoined stables, and offal, debris, and horse manure littered the streets. Piles of garbage in front of buildings or in narrow passageways between houses gave rise to stomach-turning odors and a large rat population. The population density was astronomical, some sections of Chicago, for example, having three times as many inhabitants as the most crowded portions of Tokyo and Calcutta. In 1901 a Polish neighborhood in the Windy City averaged 340 people per acre, and a three-block area housed 7,306 children! . . . One survey taker found that 1,231 Italians were living in 120 rooms in New York; another reporter could not find a single bathtub in a three-block area of tenements.[3]

The cities had other problems in addition to abject poverty, inadequate living quarters, and sanitation. As Jefferson had feared, urbanization brought an increase in crimes against persons and property, governmental corruption,[4] and, as we shall see, great strife between laborers and employers. All of these, together with a mistrust and misunderstanding of the burgeoning population of "new immigrants," did much to disrupt the American dream of peace, plenty, and harmony for all.

Immigration

The urbanization of late-nineteenth-century America could not have happened nearly so rapidly nor dramatically without massive immigration to swell the numbers of city dwellers. Just as significant as the great numbers of immigrants coming to the United States during this period were the national origins of these "new immigrants," as they were called by journalists of that time. Exhibit 4.3 illustrates a striking contrast in the "old" and "new" immigrants of the 19th century. In the 5-year period from 1866 through 1870, 98 percent of the 1.3 million Europeans who immigrated to the United States came from northern and western Europe and Germany. These settlers from England, Scotland, Wales, Ireland, Scandinavia, and Germany had left Europe largely during periods of economic depression and population growth in their homelands. European industrialization had decreased the number of people needed to work the farms at a time of economic boom in the United States.

As the industrial and agricultural revolutions spread eastward from Great Britain through Germany and into southern and eastern Europe, so did the origins of immigrants shift. By the 1906–1910 period, nearly 4.5 million immigrants were leaving their overcrowded conditions of scarcity for the United States, where jobs and land were reputed to be plentiful. Not only had the number of European immigrants more than tripled, but now only 22 percent were the "old" immigrants; the remainder were the new immigrants from southern and eastern Europe: Italy, Greece, Russia, Poland, Hungary, Bulgaria, Czechoslovakia, Lithuania, and other countries. Among these eastern Europeans were nearly two million Jews who fled persecution in Russia and elsewhere in hopes of finding religious, cultural, and economic freedom in the United States.

Open versus Restricted Immigration The dreams of the Jews, however, like the dreams of the new

EXHIBIT 4.2 The Nation Becomes Increasingly Urban

	1870	*1880*	*1890*	*1900*	*1910*	*1920*
Urban population (000s)	9,902	14,130	22,106	30,160	41,999	54,158
Rural population (000s)	28,656	36,026	40,841	45,835	49,973	51,553
Percentage of total U.S. population which is urban	26%	28%	35%	40%	46%	51%
Cities of over 500,000	2	4	4	6	8	12
Cities of 100,000–500,000	12	16	24	32	42	56
Cities of 25,000–100,000	38	57	96	122	178	219

Source: Historical Statistics of the U.S., Colonial Times to 1970, Bicentennial Edition (Washington, D.C.: U.S. Department of Commerce, Bureau of Census, 1975), pp. 11–12.

By the beginning of the 20th century, the Jeffersonian vision of a democracy built around independent yeoman farmers who shared a common culture was quickly being replaced. The new urban society was increasingly composed of immigrants with diverse cultural backgrounds.

immigrants in general, were only partially realized. There were greater opportunities in America than they had enjoyed in Europe, but they also encountered considerable prejudice from the "old" immigrants, who were by then the established Americans of the dominant culture. Just as English-origin, Protestant Bostonians had discriminated against Irish Catholic immigrants early in the 19th century, so did the established Americans regard the new immigrants with considerable disdain late in that century.

On the one hand, the United States had a traditional commitment to welcoming immigrants to the new world. In 1885, for example, a bill restricting the importation of contract laborers affirmed that open tradition by noting, "this bill in no measure seeks to restrict free immigration; such a proposition would be odious, and justly so, to the American people."[5] But 3 years earlier, in response to pressure from West Coast residents, Congress had passed the Chinese Exclusion Act of 1882, thus setting the precedent for limiting immigration of people from targeted countries. The anti-Chinese sentiment was overtly racist, as illustrated in an 1876 California legislative committee report which stated that "the Chinese are inferior to any race God ever made. . . . [They] have no souls to save, and if they have, they are not worth saving."[6]

Yet, in 1886, the Statue of Liberty was erected in New York Harbor as a symbol of freedom for immigrants, bearing an inscription that reads, in part,

> Give me your tired, your poor,
> Your huddled masses yearning to breathe free,
> The wretched refuse of your teeming shore,
> Send these, the homeless, tempest-tost to me;
> I lift my lamp beside the golden door![7]

Despite such assurances, prejudice against the new immigrants was inflamed by a kind of pseudoscientific racism that interpreted national differences as racial differences. Slavs, Jews, and Italians, for example, were thought to be of different racial "stock" than the Nordic peoples, who were

EXHIBIT 4.3 **Changing Patterns in American Immigration, 1886–1920**

Year	Total European Immigration to the U.S. (000s)	Percentage of Total European Immigration from Northwest Europe and Germany	NUMBER OF IMMIGRANTS (000s) Northwest Europe* and Germany	Southern Europe†	Central Europe‡	Eastern Europe§	Asia
1866–70	1,338	98	1,314	14	7	3	40
1871–75	1,462	94	1,368	37	33	24	66
1876–80	813	87	704	40	40	29	58
1881–85	2,508	86	2,154	121	149	84	60
1886–90	2,231	73	1,625	212	205	189	8
1891–95	2,073	55	1,143	314	277	339	24
1896–1900	1,477	34	501	390	315	271	52
1901–1905	3,646	26	939	1,051	944	712	116
1906–10	4,493	22	973	1,260	1,201	1,059	128
1911–15	3,801	21	790	1,138	890	983	124
1916–20	581	36	207	323	12	39	69

*Primarily includes immigrants from Great Britain, Ireland, and the Scandinavian countries.
†The vast majority of immigrants from this region during this period came from Italy.
‡Primarily includes immigrants from Austria-Hungary.
§Primarily includes immigrants from Russia, Poland, and Russian-controlled territories.
Derived from *Historical Statistics of the U.S., Colonial Times to 1970, Bicentennial Edition* (Washington, D.C.: U.S. Department of Commerce, Bureau of Census, 1975), pp. 105–9.

the established Americans. Since the publication of Charles Darwin's *Origin of Species* in 1859, bigots in the United States had created "scientific" arguments that some racial groups were more evolved than others, and American nativists argued that the nation had to decide whether it would be "peopled by British, German, and Scandinavian stock, historically free, energetic, progressive, or by Slav, Latin, and Asiatic races, historically downtrodden, atavistic, and stagnant."[8] The Nordic stock was characterized as tall and fair, while the new arrivals, especially those from Italy and Greece, were branded as shorter, darker, and low in intelligence. As early as 1894, the newly founded Immigration Restriction League led a campaign to restrict immigrants through the use of literacy tests, a device already found effective in limiting voter participation by African-Americans in the American South. It is noteworthy that the Ku Klux Klan, noted for its virulent attacks on southern black people, grew to a membership of over 4 million by the 1920s and worked to restrict the new immigration on the grounds of the immigrants' genetic inferiority.[9]

But it wasn't just crudely racist organizations such as the KKK that subscribed to eugenics theories and sought to control the gene pool of the American population. Prominent educators such as psychologist Edward L. Thorndike and University of Wisconsin President Charles Van Hise, leading sociologists such as E. A. Ross and Charles H. Cooley, and administrators of the Carnegie Institution of Washington (which took control of the independently established Eugenics Records Office in 1918) supported such efforts to "control the evolutionary progress of the race."[10] One popularizer of racist anthropology, Madison Grant, wrote in 1916 in his book *The Passing of the Great Race* that "the new immigration . . . contained a large number of the weak, the broken, and the mentally crippled of all races drawn from the lowest stratum of the Mediterranean basin and the Balkans, together with the hordes of the wretched, submerged populations of the Polish Ghettos."[11]

Such prejudice was exacerbated by public anxiety over the conditions of the cities in which the new immigrants lived, by worries about the impact of immigrants upon competition for jobs, and by the hostility toward foreigners fueled by World War I. By 1921 this antagonism finally resulted in Congress's establishing immigration restrictions based on nationality. This initial act was reinforced with even stronger national quotas in 1924 and 1929, and immigration from southern and eastern Europe was slashed dramatically after the 1920s. For many nationalities the annual quota was cut by 99 percent below the peak years of earlier immigration.[12]

Millions of new immigrants and their children were already part of the American social fabric, however, and the hostile and racist attitudes toward these new residents continued. In the large cities, a sizeable majority of the population consisted of immigrants or children born of immigrant parents. As Exhibit 4.4 indicates, in Chicago 78 percent of the total population had at least one foreign-born parent in 1910. The figure for New York was 79 percent; for Milwaukee, 78 percent; and for San Francisco, 68 percent. This meant, in addition, that the majority of factory workers and the majority of schoolchildren in the large cities were immigrants or children of immigrants. Established American civic and national leaders considered this predominance of foreign stock a significant problem for the workplace, for the schools, and for social order in general; and they would increasingly turn to the schools for solutions.

EXHIBIT 4.4 Ethnic Diversity in Five Selected Cities

	Chicago	*New York*	*Milwaukee*	*San Francisco*	*Atlanta*
TOTAL POPULATION (000s)					
	2185	4767	374	417	155
Foreign-born white	781	1928	111	131	4
Native white, foreign parentage	705	1445	135	107	4
Native white, mixed parentage	208	375	47	46	3
Black	44	92	1	2	52
Asian	2	6	0.1	15	0.1
PERCENTAGE OF TOTAL POPULATION					
At least one foreign-born parent (1910)	78	79	78	68	7
Foreign-born white:					
1900	35	37	31	30	3
1910	36	40	30	31	3
1920	30	35	24	28	2
Black:					
1910	2	2	0.3	0.5	34
1920	4	3	0.4	0.5	31

MAJOR IMMIGRANT GROUPS*

Chicago		New York		Milwaukee		San Francisco		Atlanta
Poland	(17)	Russia	(25)	Germany	(36)	Italy	(17)	NONE
Germany	(14)	Italy	(20)	Poland	(21)	Germany	(14)	
Russia	(13)	Ireland	(10)	Russia	(06)	Ireland	(13)	
Italy	(07)	Germany	(10)	Austria	(05)	England	(07)	
Sweden	(07)	Austria	(06)	Hungary	(05)	France	(05)	
Ireland	(07)	England	(04)			Canada	(05)	
Czechoslovakia	(07)	Hungary	(03)			Sweden	(04)	

* Percentage of total foreign-born population in 1920 in parentheses. Figures on major ethnic groups from 1920 rather than from 1910 were used because the 1920 census included separate figures for Polish, Czech, Slovak, and Hungarian immigrants, whereas the 1910 census included these figures in the figures for the nations which then controlled their homelands: Germany, Austria-Hungary, and Russia. The relative proportions of the various immigrant groups in 1920 are probably at least roughly comparable to those in 1910.

Source: Fourteenth Census of the U.S. Taken in the Year 1920 (Washington, D.C.: Government Printing Office, 1922), vol.3, pp. 109, 118, 222, 247, 261, 679, 691, 1,121, 1,131; *Thirteenth Census of the U.S. Taken in the Year 1910* (Washington, D.C.: Government Printing Office, 1913), vol. 2, pp. 162, 180, 400, 482, 504, and vol 3, pp. 216, 240, 1,078, 1,096.

Industrialization

Although the new immigrants found work in nearly all sectors of the labor market, skilled and unskilled, rural and urban, a great many of them found work in the mines, steel mills, factories, and slaughterhouses of industrial America. They often constituted the majority of laborers in such industries: immigrants constituted 16,000 of the 23,000 workers in the Homestead steel mill in Pennsylvania, for example, and immigrants and black migrants together were the majority of the meatpackers in the Swift and Armour plants in Chicago. Close to 60 percent of the industrial labor force in the years before World War I, reports labor historian David Brody, was foreign-born.[13]

Not only had the ethnic origins of the workers changed by this time, but the nature and organization of the work itself had been altered fundamentally by industrialization and industrial management. As Exhibit 4.5 indicates, the period from 1870 to 1920 marked a shift from a time when half of those employed worked on the farm to a time when slightly over a quarter did such work. At the same time, the proportion of manufacturing workers rose from 17 percent to 26 percent, nearly equaling the agricultural workers by 1920. In addition to those employed in manufacturing, the number of those working in mines multiplied sixfold, those employed in construction tripled, and those employed in transportation and other utilities increased sixfold. And as industry and production increased, so did business: the number of people employed in trade, finance, and real estate increased sixfold. By 1920, the modern age of business and industry had succeeded the age of agriculture.

From Artisan Craftsmanship to Monopoly Capital The number of manufacturing establishments more than doubled from 1860 to 1890, and the total production of manufactured goods increased at an even greater rate.[14] More significant than the overall growth of manufacturing was the change in how factories were organized. It is easy to believe that new inventions were fundamentally responsible for the industrial boom at the turn of the century. Economist Robert Reich, however, observes that it was not new inventions themselves, but the American knack for organizing them into mass-production techniques, that led to American leadership in the world of production. In the period from 1870 to 1920, says Reich, major

EXHIBIT 4.5 Changes in Patterns of Labor, 1870–1920

	1870	*1880*	*1890*	*1900*	*1910*	*1920*
Percentage of workers in agriculture	50%	50%	42%	37%	31%	27%
Percentage of workers in manufacturing	17%	18%	20%	22%	22%	26%

INDUSTRIAL DISTRIBUTION OF GAINFUL WORKERS (000s)

	1870	1880	1890	1900	1910	1920
Agriculture	6,430	8,610	9,990	10,710	11,340	11,120
Forestry and fisheries	60	95	180	210	250	280
Mining	200	310	480	760	1,050	1,230
Manufacturing and hand trades	2,250	3,170	4,750	6,340	8,230	10,880
Construction	750	830	1,440	1,660	2,300	2,170
Transportation and other public utilities	640	860	1,530	2,100	3,190	4,190
Trade	—	—	—	—	3,370	4,060
Finance and	830	1,220	1,990	2,760		
real estate	—	—	—	—	520	800
Educational service	190	330	510	650	900	1,170
Other professional service	140	190	350	500	770	1,080
Domestic service	940	1,080	1,520	1,740	2,150	1,700
Personal service	250	360	640	970	1,520	1,630
Government not elsewhere classified	100	140	190	300	540	920
Not allocated	140	195	170	370	600	380

Source: Adapted by Stuart McAninch from *Historical Statistics of the U.S., Colonial Times to 1970, Bicentennial Edition* (Washington, D.C.: U.S. Department of Commerce, Bureau of Census, 1975), p. 138.

new inventions (often based on discoveries made in Britain, which had an older industrial tradition) appeared in the United States about every 15 months, on average. Typewriters, telephones, phonographs, light bulbs, aluminum, vulcanized rubber, wireless radio, electric washing machines, airplanes, and many other technological developments came during this period.[15] Almost everything needed for mass production of manufactured goods seemed to be in place: abundant natural resources, cheap sources of energy, mass markets, and cheap, mobile labor. Transportation, too, was an asset: not only did a huge canal and lake system make transport of goods inexpensive, but the railroads had grown from 23 miles of track in 1830 to 208,000 miles of track in 1890. But none of these ingredients can in itself account for the remarkable growth in the factory system, argues Reich, without attention to how the organization of work itself was changed by those who owned and controlled the factory system.

Taylorization: Scientific Management and Skill Dilution As factories increased in size, factory owners sought new ways to increase worker efficiency, and one strategy was to increase the number of managers per worker on the shop floor. While the number of industrial workers increased only 50 percent in the 1890–1900 decade, the number of foremen increased 400 percent, from 90,000 to 360,000.[16] More importantly, a new "scientific" system of management was introduced into American industry—one which would increase production and worker dissatisfaction at the same time. The most famous proponent of scientific management of the workplace was Frederick Winslow Taylor.

Taylor, an upper-middle-class Philadelphia engineer, tried to apply the principles of engineering precision to the management of people and became a hero to the owners of production in doing so. His work began at Pennsylvania's Midvale Steel plant in the 1880s, where he did "efficiency studies" to try to determine where time, materials, and effort were being wasted in the men's work. His first internationally known paper on scientific management was delivered in 1895 (the same year, coincidentally, as Booker T. Washington's Atlanta Exposition address—see Chapter 6). After Taylor's presentation the notion of scientific management of the workplace became commonly known.

One of Taylor's main efforts was to break down each complex, skilled task into its component parts—simple moves that an unskilled person could be taught in a short time. This "de-skilling" development led to a need for fewer skilled workers, a greater number of unskilled workers, and a corresponding decrease in workers' wages and their power to decide upon the conditions of their labor. As long as workers were not highly skilled, they could be easily replaced. Although the deskilling of the American workplace had begun well before Taylor's innovations, his scientific management resulted in further de-skilling and was consciously aimed at control of knowledge and control of decision-making power. Historian David Brody describes Taylor's approach well:

> To his engineer's eye, the prevailing shop practice was a shocking violation of the industrial progressivism of the modern age. There was a traditional fund of practical knowledge that workers passed on to one another; they performed their tasks unsupervised and by "rule of thumb"; and, what was worse, they customarily worked at a slow pace that conformed to a group-approved norm. In short [said Taylor], "the shop was really run by the workmen, and not by the bosses." To remedy this retrogressive state, Taylor proposed two basic industrial reforms. The first would cut away the brain work inherent in what workers did and place it wholly in the hands of managers. . . . The second reform, essentially a function of the first, would deprive workers of the responsibilities they had normally exerted on the shop floor. [In Taylor's words] "Faster work can be assured . . . only through *enforced* standardization of methods, *enforced* adoption, of the best implements and working conditions, and *enforced* cooperation.
>
> . . . And the duty of enforcing . . . rests with the *management* alone."[17](Taylor's italics)

Taylor himself put his aims very clearly when he said that "All possible brain work should be removed from the shop and centered in the planning or laying-out department"; and further, "This task specifies not only what is to be done but how it is to be done and the exact time allowed for doing it."[18]

To illustrate the value of his approach, Taylor offered the account of his supervision of a Dutchman named Schmidt at the Bethlehem Steel mill in Pennsylvania. Taylor wrote that under the old system of management, Schmidt earned only $1.15 per day for loading 12.5 tons of pig iron. With proper scientific management, however, Schmidt's output increased almost fourfold. In Taylor's words:

> Schmidt started to work and all day long, and at regular intervals, was told by the man who stood over him with a watch, "now pick up a pig and walk. Now sit down and rest. Now walk—now rest," etc. He worked when he was told to work, and rested when he was told to rest, and at half-past five in the afternoon had his 47 1/2 tons loaded in the car.[19]

Taylor boasted that under scientific management, everyone benefits: goods can be produced more cheaply, workers receive higher wages, and total output increases. In Schmidt's case, noted Taylor, the laborer's wages rose from $1.15 daily to $1.85 daily, a 60 percent increase, while his production rose 400 percent.

But despite the prospect of wage increases for common laborers, Taylor encountered resistance directly from the workers themselves. As early as the 1880s, while working as a gang boss in a machine shop at Midvale Street, Taylor entered into a long battle with the machinists, who wanted to continue being paid by the piece rather than by the hour. Said Taylor,

> Now that was the beginning of a piecework fight that lasted for nearly three years, as I remember it—in which I was doing everything in my power to increase the output of the shop, while the men were absolutely determined that the output should not be increased. Anyone who has been through such a fight knows and dreads the meanness of it and the bitterness of it. I believe that if I had been an older man—a man of more experience—I should hardly have gone into such a fight as this—deliberately attempting to force the men to do something they did not propose to do.[20]

As we shall soon see, worker dissatisfaction did not end with one 3-year battle at one steel plant. It increased throughout the decades to follow, until the schools became one of the agencies to which anxious capitalists would turn in their battle for absolute control over the shop floor. The role of the schools in such a political-economic and ideologic struggle will be treated shortly.

Significance for Women and Office Work Before turning to further investigation of worker responses to industrialism and to scientific management in particular, one other important development needs attention: the significance of scientific management for the employment of women. While there is much to be said about the participation of women in the industrial workplace, about women in labor movements, and about legislation protecting women from long hours and injurious labor conditions, the aspect of women's labor in the progressive era, which is of most interest here, has directly to do with the increases in office work that were stimulated by scientific management.

As urbanization and industrialization increased in the 19th century, and as people left the countryside for the city, the home became less a place of production and more a place of consumption only. That is, whereas women on the farm were expected to help produce goods like foods and clothing for the family and for sale, city dwelling offered little in terms of resources for production. In order to supplement family income some family women, immigrants and rural migrants alike, boarded single men who were working in mills, factories, and meat-packing plants, and other women took in seasonal piecework of various kinds. Also, single women worked outside the home in a few different job categories. In fact, by 1900, 90 percent of all women working outside the home were working in just four different areas: domestic service (39 percent); manufacturing, particularly in the textile, clothing, and tobacco industries (25 percent); agriculture, especially among black women in the south (18 percent); and finally the professions, primarily in teaching and nursing (8 percent).[21]

The rise of business and industry, and particularly the rise of scientific management, brought great changes to this pattern of women's work. While the percentage of women in manufacturing held steady (as the actual numbers of women in manufacturing grew rapidly) and the proportion of agricultural women declined, office work emerged as the number one employer of working women by 1920. Prior to 1900, approximately 76 percent of clerks and secretaries were male, but with the growth of scientific management, these secretarial and clerical jobs were increasingly filled by women. By 1920, the four major job categories employing women had changed: office work (25.6 percent), manufacturing (23.8 percent), domestic service (18.2 percent), and agriculture (12.8 percent). Office positions were attractive to young women because they did not require a great deal of training and were therefore relatively easy to leave and to reenter, and they were considered more suitable for women than blue-collar industrial jobs. Further, these positions were considered dead-end jobs for men in that they did not lead to advancement and they paid very little, while for women these positions were considered to be opportunities to earn income outside the home.[22]

Such positions multiplied rapidly with the growth of scientific management after the 1890s because of the rise of the bureaucracy in business and industry. If all decision making and planning was to be taken away from workers on the shop floor, then elaborate systems of planning, monitoring, and reporting had to be established, systems that required a great deal of paperwork. Adding this layer of bureaucracy to the production process could be costly and inefficient unless it, too, was managed scientifically by having a low-paid, low-skilled corps of clerks who could follow directions and do the routine paperwork, such as record keeping, typing, and mailing, that would otherwise occupy their more highly paid decision-making superiors. Women were considered to be ideal candidates for such positions, in part because office employment would reduce the degree to which women competed with men for higher-paying industrial jobs.[23] The rise of women in office work, as will later be discussed, had significant impact upon the secondary-school curriculum provided for working-class girls.

Worker Responses to Industrial Management

Workers (including women) tried to fight against the new scientific management by forming unions in various kinds of labor, including office work.[24] But union organization was only one of the ways workers sought to protect their health, their incomes, and perhaps above all, their right to make decisions about the conditions of their own labor. In the late 19th century, workers fought against the industrial order in ways that cost many of them their jobs and in some cases their lives. What is important to recognize, however, is that workers did not fight against industrialization itself, but against the way in which the industrial workplace was organized and controlled by those who owned the factories.

One of the by-products of scientific management was bringing young women into office jobs previously occupied by men. Such jobs required little training, were relatively easy to leave and to reenter, and were considered more suitable for women than blue-collar industrial jobs.

The widespread and desperate rebellion of workers against scientific management can only be understood in the context of the history of manufacturing in America. As many historians have pointed out, the earliest manufacturers in America were artisans who, whether working with coal, wood, textiles, stone, or iron and steel, were highly skilled craftsmen and (particularly in colonial times) craftswomen whose skills had been painstakingly learned in lengthy apprenticeships with other craftspersons.[25] While the first American factory may be identified as a machine textile mill established in Pawtucket, Rhode Island, in 1791, the predominant forms of manufacture remained the craftsman's workshop until about 1870, by which time around 50 percent of all manufactured goods were produced in factories. By 1890, according to Raybeck, factories were producing 80 percent of all manufactured goods in the United States.[26]

The factory, in the modern sense, was characterized by large outlays of capital, concentration of many laborers in one location, use of mechanical instead of muscle power wherever possible, and use of machinery on the shop floor to replace workers having certain skills.[27] It would not necessarily be in the workers' interests to oppose any of these developments, if workers themselves were allowed a significant voice in how the work was organized. As David Brody notes, mechanization at the turn of the century did not in itself necessarily lower the skill levels of workers, because "new products sometimes generated a fresh demand for craft skills."[28] What did lower the skill levels of workers, and also lowered their autonomy and decision-making power as well as their social standing, was the owners' imposition of workplace management, particularly scientific management.

Since colonial times in America, skilled craftspersons were highly valued and well-rewarded members of their communities. Their skills were in short supply, and their earnings were relatively high. They owned their own tools, contracted their own jobs, decided upon their own hours, and set their own price on each piece produced. Simply put, they controlled the conditions of their own labor. This was true of most working males in the early American period, because the agrarian economy was such that 80 to 90 percent of free adult males were self-employed, either on farms, in trade, or in crafts. As late as the 1850s, Abraham Lincoln echoed a sentiment about freedom that was rooted in classical Athens: that a free man did not work for another man, except to earn enough to become self-employed. To be self-employed, whether in agriculture or industry, meant a great deal to workers of the 19th century, for they could exercise their intelligence as well as their skills, and their work reflected not just their skills, but their individuality, creativity, and intelligence. They could, and did, take great pride in planning their work and executing those plans. Increasingly, the management system alienated workers from those who ran it, and workers resented their loss of opportunities to exercise their skills and intelligence in their work. John Morrison, a 23-year-old machinist testifying before Congress during this period, recognized the deskilling developments in his own trade, and he recognized as well the loss of worker autonomy and the subsequent effects on the workers:

> The trade has been subdivided and those subdivisions have been again subdivided, so that a man never learns the machinist's trade now. . . . There is no system of apprenticeship, I may say, in the business. You simply go in and learn whatever branch you are put at, and you stay at that unless you are changed to another. . . . It has a very demoralizing effect on the mind throughout. . . . [the machinist] knows that he cannot leave that particular branch and go to any other; he has got no chance whatever to learn anything else because he is kept steadily and constantly at that particular thing, and of course his intellect must be narrowed by it. . . . In fact he becomes almost a part of the machinery.[29]

While the reduction of workers to being "almost a part of the machinery" was an indictment of the workplace from the worker's point of view, it was good for profits, from the capitalist's point of view. An observer described one female worker and her work: "One single precise motion each second, 3600 in one hour, and all exactly the same. The hands were swift, precise, intelligent. The face was stolid, vague and vacant." It is not surprising that her manager praised her as "one of the best workers we have. . . . She is a sure machine." Controlling people like machines instead of allowing them to make decisions, like people, led to widespread practices such as are reflected in this remark by a superintendent of Swift & Co.: "If you need to turn out a little more, you speed up the conveyor a little and the men speed up to keep pace."[30] Economist Robert Reich summarizes the experience of many workers:

> The organization was structured like the machine at its core, engineered to follow the sequence of steps specified by the settings on their controls. Scientific management made the large enterprise, and everyone who contributed to it, an extension of the high volume machine.[31]

Increasingly after 1870, the "large enterprise" of which Reich speaks was a corporate factory, not an artisan's shop. It was during this time that the old handicraft system, in which skilled craftspersons controlled the conditions of their own labor, gave way almost entirely to the new capitalist factory system, in which merchants who could capitalize the rising costs of factories brought men, machinery, materials, and management together under one roof. As the desire to make larger profits increased, capitalists formed partnerships and then corporations in which great amounts of capital could be raised from many stockholders. Between 1870 and 1900 the amount of capital invested per factory worker almost tripled, and the total capital invested in manufacturing increased even more.[32]

The move to corporate capitalism was intended to provide greater market share, even market control, for the capitalists, thus increasing their profits. But the capitalists' allegiance to profit and to the stockholders led to ever more authoritarian control of the workers in the effort to increase efficiency of production. The management movement had begun in the 1870s and 1880s, before Taylor's scientific management refinements, and worker resistance was already becoming strong by the 1880s. In the 5-year period from 1893 to 1898, surrounding the 1895 publication of Taylor's first paper on scientific management, over 7,000 strikes were reported against American companies. In the next 5 years, that number more than doubled, to 15,000.[33] But strikes were just one of the ways workers resisted the new industrial order of corporate capitalism.

Neither African-Americans arriving from rural America nor immigrants from predominantly rural portions of Europe, nor skilled craftsmen, nor women working outside the home for the first time were accustomed to the managed regimen of the factory system. For a variety of reasons, including subdivision of skills, low earnings, the authoritarian nature of the shop floor, the long hours and injurious practices, and other factors, workers resisted the new management system of corporate capitalism in organized ways. Some of these ways were initiated by workers themselves and challenged the very power of capital to determine and manage the organization of production: these organized forms of resistance included populism, socialism, and a militant trade unionism unfamiliar to most Americans today. Another form of resistance to the unbridled power of corporate capital, progressive reform, was not initiated by workers themselves and did not fundamentally challenge the power of capital to control the production processes. Each of these merits brief discussion.

Trade Unionism One form of organized worker resistance to the new industrial order was unionism. Today we are accustomed to thinking of unions as organizations which represent workers in a specific trade or occupation—miners, machinists, truck drivers, office workers, air traffic controllers, teachers, and so on—and which bargain on behalf of those people for higher wages, better benefits, and better working conditions—and conduct strikes if the bargaining process breaks down. This kind of union organization by specific trades, or *trade unionism*, had roots in trade organizations prior to the Civil War, although strikes before the war were few because most workers were self-employed. But unions late in the 19th century were not always organized by trades, and they did not necessarily accept wage bargaining as their primary task. Historian Norman Ware writes that "the reluctance of the labor movement to accept collective bargaining as its major function was due largely to the fact that this involved an acceptance of the wage system."[34] Again, it was not just low wages, but the organization of industry, to which workers objected.

After the Civil War, trade unions were extremely weak, especially when the nation was

The dehumanizing effects of scientific management and corporate capitalism led to a series of worker strikes in the late 19th century.

plunged into depression in the early 1870s. But the depression eventually led to a series of railroad workers' strikes, which culminated in a great national railway strike in 1877. Crowds of angry strikers stopped the railroads, stopped factory production in some cities, and became violent when fired upon by troops. In Pittsburgh, when the governor called in the militia to control the strikes, the militia joined the strikers. Six hundred more militia were called in, this time from Philadelphia, and they attempted to disperse the crowd by firing on them, resulting in the deaths of 26 people. The crowd then turned on the militia, trapping them in a railroad roundhouse, which was then set afire before the militia escaped. The crowd also burned 104 locomotives, over 2,000 railroad cars, and every railroad building they could find while the militia escaped from the city.

The Railway Strike of 1877 was the most extensive labor conflict of the 19th century, and it refocused public attention on labor and unions. The strike stimulated greater union membership, especially for the fledgling Knights of Labor, which rejected the trade union concept in favor of an organization which would unite all wage laborers, "the draughtsman, the time keeper, the clerk, the school teacher, the civil engineer, the editor, the reporter, or the worst paid, most abused and illy appreciated of all toilers—women," in an effort "to abolish the wage system."[35] The Knights were one of those organizations which, like the Populists and Socialists, challenged the power relations of capitalism. Membership in the Knights of Labor fluctuated, but by 1886 reached a peak of 729,000 members. In that year alone, strikes were conducted, by the Knights and by other labor unions, against 10,000 different establishments involving a half million workers. The "labor problem," as worker resistance to the organization of corporate capitalism was called, was widely regarded as the most pressing social problem of the era.

By 1892 the battle lines between labor and ownership were firmly drawn. In Chicago, the heart of the eight-hour-day movement, a bomb had killed or injured scores of people at a late-night workers rally that had been peaceful until the police, against orders from the mayor, attempted to disperse the assembly.[36] At the steel plant in Homestead, Pennsylvania, the Carnegie Steel Corporation hired an army of Pinkerton guards to put down a steelworkers' strike against wage cuts and other grievances. The armed Pinkerton troops numbered 32,000, more than the standing U.S. Army at the time, and the armed battles that followed their arrival killed some 70 people in all.

At Homestead, the state militia was brought in, but the strike only spread to other steel plants. Carnegie and the state militia responded by bringing in strikebreakers to work in the plant and by having the strike leaders arrested and charged with treason against the government. Although no strikers were found guilty, the tactic was successful at breaking down the strike after several months' struggle. When the mill was reopened, hiring preference was given to the least-skilled workers, who would work for less and were more controllable than the more highly skilled craftspersons. As a result, from 1892 to 1907 "daily earnings of highly skilled mill workers at Homestead shrank by one fifth, while their hours increased from eight to twelve."[37]

In this and other incidents, the industrial owners demonstrated that they would go to whatever lengths necessary to protect their control over the workplace and over the laborers themselves. Since the railroad strikes of 1877, state governments had increased the size of their militias and had begun building armories in cities in large part to be able to control labor resistance. Ownership had the wealth and power to define the issue in the press (also a profit-making enterprise) as "the labor problem" and to enlist the forces of the police and government to restore order when the problem became otherwise unmanageable.

Populism A second form of resistance to corporate capital industrialism had its roots in the ideology of agrarian localism that Jefferson considered to be the most fertile seedbed of democracy in America. *Populism* flourished in the 1890s primarily in the rural midwestern states, but it was not opposed to industrialism itself. Rather, it expressed opposition to the way in which industry was organized. Populists opposed the effects of industrial capitalism on costs of farm production, which were increasing, and upon prices for farm products, which were declining. They opposed in particular the growing legislative financial assistance to big business and industry, such as the millions of dollars' worth of land granted by the government to the railroad industry. Finally, populists strongly opposed the effects of management on workers, even before Taylor's scientific management movement matured. It was not just earnings, but the power to decide on the industrial organization that populists most disputed. One Nebraska newspaper called for the elimination of "monopolistic privileges and power," and a journal, the *Farmers Alliance,* called for the establishment instead of "an *industrial democracy* in which each citizen shall have an equal interest" (emphasis added).[38] In a speech in 1894, Kansas populist Frank Doster clarified the idea of industrial democracy by arguing that "the industrial system of a nation, like its political system, should be a government of and for and by the people alone."[39]

In order to achieve such an industrial democracy, rural populists worked with urban laborers to build a strong political base. One letter to the *Alliance* complained that "farmers and laborers are looked upon as a class but a little above the brutes; all we are fit for is to toil and support the whole business." And the *Alliance-Independent* editorialized that "in the condition of the labor market today, the laborer without an organization is at the mercy of the organized capital that knows no mercy." And a speaker at a meeting of the labor group Farmers Alliance in Nebraska proclaimed the populist position as follows: "Thus we see organized capital arrayed against the producers. . . . The irrepressible conflict between capital and labor is upon us."[40]

Space does not here allow treatment of the complex economic and political issues attending the rise and fall of populism as an organized movement and political party. The point here is simply to illustrate that workers had ways of understanding corporate capitalism that were very different from the ways in which capitalists understood their own enterprise, and that workers did seek to organize in the name of industrial democracy. In the 1892 election that brought Democrat Grover Cleveland to the White House, Populists peaked in their political power, winning six western states in the national elections, putting some 1,500 state legislators in office, and electing 15 U.S. Senators and Congressmen to office, a truly remarkable feat by today's standards. Soon thereafter, however, populism began to weaken as a political force. The party was divided by inner conflicts, and its positions were seen as too conservative by Socialist party leaders who might otherwise have supported populism. Further, support lagged among urban workers who were unaccustomed to traditions of agrarian democracy. And, too, Populist leaders believed that, in the absence of an adequate base of support for their more radical positions, at least some of their aims could be achieved by the progressive elements within the Democratic party. As historian Norman Pollack notes, third parties have historically not done well in the United States, and the Populist thrust was by the late 1890s absorbed and blunted by the Democratic party.[41]

Socialism A third major worker response to the new industrial order was socialism. The Socialist Labor party was founded in 1877 and developed an agenda that was in some ways very similar to that of the Populists.[42] The Socialists, however, regarded the Populists as too conservative and inadequately industrial-working-class in their ideology and origins. Further, the Socialists' base was primarily urban, not rural, and there was a certain amount of competition between Socialists and Populists for worker support.

A split within the Socialist Labor party in 1899 led to the founding of the Socialist party in 1901, and the party remained very strong, by today's standards, until 1919. The party grew throughout the first two decades of the 20th century, depending upon several different groups of workers for support. Among women, for example, a significant number of Protestants identified socialist values with Christian values because of their common concern for human equality, compassion for the poor, and sharing of goods, as opposed to the capitalist ethic of competition for limited wealth. Many feminists supported socialism because it stood for political and social equality for women, and immigrant women saw socialism as speaking for their interests against those of capital industrialists. Among African-Americans, socialism found support in both the North and the South for its stand on racial and class equality, and they, like workers more generally, found hope in the social advocacy of "industrial democracy"—the belief that workers should have power to shape the decisions that affect their labor.

In 1912, charismatic candidate Eugene Debs captured a remarkable 6 percent of the American presidential vote, and Socialists elected 79 mayors in 24 states. In all, Socialists won 1,200 political offices coast to coast in the 1912 election. By 1916, however, despite some success in local elections and the election of one Socialist congressman, the Socialist party had begun its decline. The Socialists could not find a compelling candidate to make up for the loss of the proven vote-getter Eugene Debs, and just as had happened with the Populists, the Democratic party took votes away from the Socialists by appearing to champion the working man. Even if the progressive reforms of the Democratic platform were pale in contrast to the Socialist platform, many Socialists supported Democratic candidates because the third party had little realistic chance of major success and the Democrats were regarded by Socialists as the lesser of two evils when compared with the Republicans, who had come to be identified with the interests of big business by the end of the 1880s.

Perhaps the most significant factor in the decline of socialism in America was the action of the federal government during and immediately after World War I. Using the War Powers Act, the federal government arrested several of the leaders of the socialist movement, confiscated the presses of socialist newspapers, and prohibited the sending of socialist materials through the U.S. mail. In 1918 Attorney General Palmer, during the infamous "Red Scare," had hundreds of socialists arrested and deported. These actions struck a blow from which American socialism never recovered.

Progressivism Insofar as militant trade unionism struggled for "workplace democracy," it resembled populism and socialism in its effort to challenge corporate power. However, the corporations had on their side not only armed forces, but also the support of the leadership of the two major political parties, which sought to address the labor problem *without* fundamentally challenging corporate power over production. As a response to industrialism, the *progressive* era (roughly the 1890s through the 1920s) saw government regulations over business and industry that sought to end the conflict between labor and ownership without altering the unequal power relations. As historian Gabriel Kolko has shown, it was this cooperation between business and government that lay at the heart of the progressive movement in the economy.[43] Kolko's important contribution to our understanding of the progressive era is captured in the title of his book, *The Triumph of Conservatism,* in which he argues that progressivism did not serve the interests of the laboring classes so much as it stabilized the economy and protected the power of ownership through government regulation.

History has tended to portray the progressive era as a triumph for the common person over the giant monopolies that emerged at the turn of the century. Kolko argues, however, that it was big business itself that ultimately succeeded in bringing about government regulation. It did so for several reasons. First, the "free market" system was so unstable that it led to countless business failures, severe economic depressions, and a seemingly unending string of worker revolts. Second, it made sense for business leaders to trust government officials to assist them because they shared the same social-class backgrounds and the same world views about what was good for society, and even shared close personal and professional ties. For example, Kolko cites President Grover Cleveland's past business partnership with financier J. P. Morgan's lawyer. And finally, the federal government had a good record of providing direct economic gain to big business in the form of land grants to the railroads, tariffs against imported goods, subsidies for corporations, and so on.

Further, contrary to the commonly held view that big monopolies were invincibly controlling the market, many if not most monopolies needed help desperately. As more and more businesses were bought up and merged into giant corporations, these enormous firms weakened in competitive power. Fewer than half the mergers in the era made a profit, and 40 percent failed altogether. As rapidly as new inventions were patented, small businesses were able to introduce innovations in production and marketing, while the monopolies could not so quickly change their giant operations to incorporate innovations. With high overhead costs and persistent difficulties in managing laborers, the big corporations failed to control the market. Even U.S. Steel, which resulted from merging 138 smaller steel companies, controlled only 60 percent of the market, and its stock declined from $55.00 per share in 1901 to $9.00 a share in 1904. By 1907 steel industry leaders began meeting with the Department of Justice and the Department of Commerce in efforts to reduce competition and protect monopoly investments by regulating the steel market.[44]

Major government regulation of the economy had been established earlier in the progressive period, and the presidencies of both Theodore Roosevelt and Woodrow Wilson were marked by a flurry of appointed regulatory commissions. These regulatory commissions, which were established by such legislation as the Interstate Commerce Commission Act (1887), the Sherman Anti-Trust Act (1890), the Federal Reserve Act (1913), the establishment of the Federal Trade Commission, and the Clayton Anti-Trust Act (both 1914), all put considerable power in the hands of officials who were not elected by the people—and therefore not directly accountable to them—but appointed by the executive branch in consultation with Congress and big business. The establishment of these regulatory commissions meant the centralization of economic and political power in the hands of the federal government such as had never been seen before, and this centralized power is one of the hallmarks of progressive reform at the federal, state, and local levels. We will soon see a progressive defense of this centralization model as we examine modern liberal ideology.

Progressive reform at the state level tended, in part, to follow the federal model of establishing appointive regulatory bodies to oversee commerce, politics, and labor relations. A different example of centralization of power at the state level is compulsory schooling legislation. Well into the progressive era, schooling was still largely a voluntary enterprise, and classical liberal presumptions about the limited right of the state to constrain individual choice about such matters prevailed. But in an effort to respond to humanitarian concerns about abusive employment of youth in mines and factories, to provide education for all youth, to "Americanize" immigrant youth, and in general to socialize youth to new political-economic conditions, all state governments had passed and begun enforcing compulsory attendance laws by 1918.[45] While more will be said about compulsory schooling later, it is mentioned here as an example of progressive centralization at the state level.

Progressive Urban Reform Of greater interest than state government is centralization at the city level, where, in Robert Wiebe's words, "The heart of Progressivism was the ambition of the new middle class to fulfill its destiny through bureaucratic means."[46] In Wiebe's view, progressive reform of city government amounted essentially to scientific management of the cities in ways that might be considered analogous to the scientific management of the worker in industry. This analysis challenges the traditional historical view that progressive urban reform was a victory for democracy, won by muckraking journalists, settlement-house social workers, educators, government officials, and other reformers who opposed harmful labor practices, slum conditions, and political corruption in city government.

The cities at the turn of the century were in many respects chaotic, particularly by the standards of the business and professional classes who lived there. Whether city life was more chaotic then than now might be a good question for historical debate, however, for the governmental corruption that the reformers despised was also a source of order and unity in the cities at the turn of the century. Journalists Lincoln Steffens and Lord James Bryce were among those who wrote articles attacking the "ward boss" system of machine politics.[47] The ward system promoted a kind of "you scratch my back, and I'll scratch yours" morality between the ward alderman and his constituency, most of whom were newly immigrated ethnics. As even the progressive social reformer Jane Addams had to admit, if the alderman brought business and city services to his ward, if he helped citizens out of problems with police and the courts, if he used his resources to distribute food during holidays, buy gifts at weddings and christenings and to outfit a local youth band, if he paid for funerals for poor immigrants so that they didn't have to be buried by the county, then his constituency would forgive his own obviously ill-gotten wealth and enthusiastically reelect him as well.[48] The ward system offered a way for immigrants to have a voice in the affairs of their neighborhood, even if that voice manipulated the law in doing so.

Not only did "honest graft" offend the moral sensibilities of the reformers, but the system of ward politics preserved ethnic identity and made possible the strength of such independent movements as socialism—both of which offended the established American, middle-class capitalist ideology shared by reformers, journalists, and the business community. This would in part explain why progressive reform in the cities was a decidedly middle-class and upper-class effort. Even if the middle class, made up largely of businessmen and professionals, was a small minority compared with the far greater numbers of blue-collar immigrants, it was a powerful minority. Historian Richard C. Wade characterizes progressive urban reform as "a movement of the periphery against the center," because the middle-class residential areas were located on the outer ring of the cities, while the source of the boss's strength was the inner city, where the new immigrants had settled.[49] Historian Samuel P. Hays expresses the source of the reform movement in stronger class terms, arguing that the reformers are more accurately described as upper-class than middle-class:

> The movement for reform in municipal government, therefore, constituted an attempt by upper-class, advanced professional and large business groups to take formal political power from the previously dominant lower and middle-class elements so that they might advance their own conceptions of desirable public policy. . . . Reformers, therefore, wished not simply to replace bad men with good; they proposed to change the occupational and class origins of decision-makers. Toward this end they sought innovations in the formal machinery of government which would concentrate political power by sharply centralizing the processes of decision-making.[50]

Centralization of Power and Expertise One effective way of centralizing power was to eliminate the ward system of balloting, creating instead a system in which city council representatives were elected at large from throughout the city. Any candidates with the wealth and stature to run a citywide campaign were usually backed by business and professional classes, and the class composition of city councils changed dramatically with the reform movements of the progressive era. Reformers claimed that the new citywide system was more democratic because it discouraged local ward corruption by eliminating ward bosses. But the immigrants, African-Americans, blue-collar workers, and small business-persons thereafter had a much-diminished voice in the affairs of the city government that ruled over their neighborhoods. The ideology of reform, together with the power of the professional classes to enact their agenda, resulted in a sweeping change in city governance in both large and small cities throughout the nation. Not until a landmark Supreme Court decision of 1986 did a neighborhood constituency—in this case, African-American voters in Springfield, Illinois—successfully challenge the at-large election system as unconstitutionally depriving citizens of representation in city government. The impact of that court decision on other city governments remains to be seen.[51]

If Hays and others are correct in viewing progressive urban reform as a victory of the professional and business class interests over the interests of the blue-collar and ethnic majority, there is another dimension to that victory as well: the victory of "expert" decision making over processes of public debate. The centralization process increased city governments' dependency on professional planners and administrators. These experts were hired by the cities to make decisions that would be scientifically planned for greater efficiency and reliability. In matters of urban planning, budgeting, and general administration, a cadre of accountants, engineers, administrative experts, and other professionals were called upon to make decisions that had formerly been made in heated council debates among ward aldermen. But those debates, it was charged, were often decided by corrupt politics resulting in personal gain to aldermen, and the reliance on experts would do away with such corruption and the waste and inefficiency that attended it.

Such reform was another example of how centralized power could be established to solve one set of problems—inefficiency and graft—while at the same time exacerbating another—the undemocratic concentration of power in the hands of a privileged minority of citizens. The principles of scientific management were not part of a commitment to democracy. They were instead part and parcel of what historian Raymond E. Callahan has called the "cult of efficiency." Many reformers believed that efficiency expert Frederick Taylor was correct in writing that principles of scientific management could be "applied with equal force to all social activities: the management of our homes; the management of our farms; the management of the business of our tradesmen, large and small; of our churches, our philanthropic institutions, our universities, and our governmental departments."[52] And clearly, one application of Taylor's principles of management would be the urban school systems.

Perhaps more than any other historian, David Tyack has shown that progressive reform in urban school governance followed the same pattern that Hays described in city government.[53] Tyack argues that city school reformers successfully eliminated neighborhood control over schools by replacing ward school boards with one central school board per city. This was more efficient in the sense that it allowed for greater coordination of budgetary and curriculum matters for the entire city. It allowed what Tyack calls "administrative progressives" to make important decisions affecting standards for teachers and administrators and to conduct schools along bureaucratic and hierarchical lines that had proved effective in business administration. Again, however, such centralization had its price. In this case, local ethnic communities were no longer allowed to play a significant role in making decisions about their own children's schools. One result was that neighborhood schools which had conducted classes in both English and a neighborhood immigrant language, such as Polish or Lithuanian, were no longer allowed to do so. Another result was that school decisions were no longer made by people from the same classes as people in the neighborhoods, but increasingly by members of the professional and business classes who now were elected to the central city school board. And finally, the voice of the common person was diminished in another way that was similar to what had happened to municipal government reform: decisions were being made not through public debate, but by administrative experts with formal training in areas of curriculum and pedagogy. Their claim to scientific knowledge, or "depoliticized expertise," appeared to legitimize their decision making, even if democratic processes of decision making were sacrificed.

The liberal reformers believed that these developments in urban and school government constituted important progress toward a more moral, more orderly, and more democratic society. An alternative interpretation, however, is that scientific management, which owners had imposed upon workers in industry at the beginning of the progressive period, had by the end of the era been extended to city government and school reform as well—and that democracy had been sacrificed in the process.

NEW LIBERAL IDEOLOGY

If it is even partly correct that the progressive movement in industry, in national, state, and local government, and in school governance resulted in the imposition of the will of the wealthy and educated few over the less educated and less powerful majority, the question arises, How could the progressive reformers have believed they were acting in the name of liberal democracy? The answer to this question must include an understanding of how the middle and upper classes changed in their view of what democracy itself meant in a complex, urban, industrial society divided by racial, ethnic, class, and gender allegiances. The old classical liberal understandings gave way to newer liberal beliefs and values which intellectuals at the time recognized as "new" or "modern" liberalism. The fundamental commitments to such classical liberal tenets as natural law, rationality, and freedom remained, but they were greatly modified to respond to new social and political conditions, as well as to new scientific understandings that followed Darwin's revolutionary contributions.

This chapter began with an excerpt from the Gary school report, which cautioned that in order to understand the progressive schools, one must take into account "modern psychology, ethics, and social philosophy" and their impact on educational thought. It is not just the changed political economy that must be understood, Flexner was saying in the Gary report, but the changes in liberal ideology as well.

Natural Law

One way to sketch very briefly the differences between the old Jeffersonian liberalism and the modern liberalism of the progressive era is to show how each of the components of classical liberalism was modified by new liberals. One can begin with the classical liberal belief that the world operated according to laws of nature, and that these laws could be known through science. The belief in natural law that was founded on the discoveries of Newton, Bacon, and other scientists was modified by the discoveries of Darwin. With the publication in 1859 of his *Origin of Species*, the universe was no longer seen as a fixed mechanism governed by the unchanging laws of nature. Rather, the universe was now understood as an organism, changing and evolving just as species of plants and animals in nature evolve. This in turn suggested that truth itself was not permanent and therefore could not be known with absolute certainty. What we believe to be true today, argued modern philosophers like William James and John Dewey, might be shown false tomorrow, as our ways of arriving at scientific truth are improved by new instruments and new methods.[54] That is, any truth is only as good as our methods of arriving at it, and our methods might improve with time. Since we can never be absolutely sure of even scientific truth, they said, the best we can have is a temporary agreement about what is true, based on our methods for verifying our claims. Dewey said the best we can do is to provide evidence and arguments to support our *assertions*, and thus instead of truth, only "warranted assertibility" is possible.

Scientific Rationality

Such a view had great significance for the modern liberal conception of human reason. Unlike Jefferson's faith in the common man's ability to arrive at reasonable ideas in the free marketplace of public debate, the modern liberal conception of truth required *scientific methods* for arriving at the most reasonable conclusions. Further, Darwin's research suggested to many intellectuals that not all races of humans were as fully evolved as others, and consequently some races were more capable of reason than others. The free marketplace of ideas was thus an unreliable way to arrive at rational conclusions; a reliance on experts was needed. The modern liberals still believed in reason as a route to progress, but they began to emphasize the importance of expert knowledge and scientific method as the way to achieve reason. Dewey, for example, as committed to democratic processes as he was, believed that scientific method was the "method of intelligence" itself. One effect of such thinking among many new liberals was to foster distrust of the thinking of the majority of common citizens in favor of reliance on experts as the arbiters of reason. Not all modern liberals were equally optimistic about the newly privileged position of experts in public affairs. Dewey, for example, argued that a society run by a class of experts would inevitably function to serve the interests of experts at the expense of the majority. The world had suffered more at the hands of experts, he wrote, than at the hands of the masses.[55]

From Virtue to Rational Ethics

The growing reliance on science as the embodiment of reason had great import for the modern conception of human morality. The classical liberal concept of "virtue," which was grounded in the absolute truth of religious teachings, gave way to a notion of civic morality which was more consistent with the nonpermanent truths of scientific rationality. That is, it was no longer taken for granted that what was moral and good was revealed for all time in religious texts. The Darwinian challenge to religious truth, together with the new faith in expert reason, suggested that the moral and the good must be determined with respect to what was reasonable in the context of particular social conditions. If social conditions changed, then what was moral might change also. Further, the best judges of what social conditions required of citizens, it was believed, were those experts who understood the situation best. Emphasis on the "virtuous person" was thus replaced by a view of the "good citizen," where what was "good" could be determined by debate among experts and might change over time. Further, if the social leadership could not trust the home, farm, and church to instill virtue in young people, then the public schools were an obvious choice as the institution to instill the civic morality of the 20th century. Whereas religious leaders have criticized this view as "secular, relativist morality," modern liberals believed it was a rational way to solve the problem of preserving an allegiance to moral life when the religious bases of morality were being challenged by scientific findings.

Progress

The modern liberal faith in expert rationality and in rationalist ethics provided the basis for modifying the classical liberal view of progress as well. For classical liberals, human progress was virtually inevitable and would eventually emerge from the temporary chaos of rebellions and revolutions. Jefferson, like others, believed that human reason would triumph over the basic tendencies of human nature and that rebellion against tyranny was sometimes the most rational way to achieve that progress. New liberals, however, influenced in part by Darwin's findings that species don't always survive and in part by the decline in public welfare brought about by urban crowding and poverty, industrial exploitation and strife, and other modern conditions that Jefferson had not foreseen, came to believe that progress was not necessarily inevitable. If progress was to be ensured, it would require human rationality of the scientific type. Thus, progressives again relied heavily on expert planning for a better society, and this helps explain their reliance on administrative experts rather than on citizen decision making in city and school governance. Democracy, they believed, was too risky a proposition in chaotic and

The progressive era saw the traditional liberal belief in the discovery of absolute truth via observation and reason give way to what Dewey called "warranted assertibility." This concept sees humans constantly amending their views of reality as scientific research allows us to probe ever deeper into nature.

threatening times; scientifically trained expertise held the most promising means to progress. In contrast to the classical liberalism that fueled the American and French revolutions, rebellion and revolution were considered by new liberals to be a failure of rational processes.

Nationalism

One other means to progress, for new liberals, was a greater emphasis on national identity. Classical liberals' allegiance to the nation had been tempered by the fear of a too-powerful national government (recall Jefferson's dictum, "That government governs best which governs least"). However, faced with worker alliances against ownership and with immigrant allegiance to ethnic origins, modern liberals viewed nationalism as a potentially unifying influence. Economic, political, and educational reform were increasingly justified "in the national interest," and it became taken for granted that some of the primary purposes of the school were national in scope.

Freedom

The growing emphasis on nationalism is particularly interesting in light of the classical Greek tradition which held that a too-strong government was the greatest enemy to freedom. In the progressive era, the national government was increasingly regarded not as an enemy to freedom, but as the only real route to freedom. The dominant conception of freedom in America's classical liberal era was earlier described as "negative freedom" to emphasize the idea that freedom was achieved by lack of interference from the government. Some have referred to the modern liberal conception of freedom as "positive freedom" to indicate the new liberal belief that the conditions for freedom require positive government action, rather than a noninterventionist, laissez-faire government. New liberals pointed out that a laissez-faire approach to freedom allowed the most powerful elements of society—like corporate owners—to prosper at the expense of the majority of citizens, and that people living in squalor could not exercise any freedoms worth having. Through government intervention, they believed, the freedoms of the least powerful could be protected. These new liberals could point, for example, to the 19th-century need for government intervention on behalf of slaves: a truly laissez-faire approach would have prohibited government from interfering with the power of slaveholders to earn a profit by enslaving others. In other instances, however, the case for government intervention was more difficult to support—as in government regulation to stabilize the economy and thus protect major corporations against the market forces that weakened them. Progressive-era conservatives such as sociologist William Graham Sumner argued that giving the government greater power to regulate society in the name of freedom achieved just the opposite, because a strong central government almost inevitably gave greater power

EXHIBIT 4.6 Comparison of Selected Components of Classical and Modern Liberalism

	Classical Liberals	*Modern Liberals*
Natural law	Newtonian mechanics Fixed truth	Darwinian biology Relative truth
Reason	Fundamental part of each human's nature	Defined by scientific method, experts, & organizations
Individualism	The rugged individual as the political ideal	The person only as a cell in social organism; the rugged individual seen as problematic
Progress	Inevitable: the result of natural law and reason	Possible: the result of scientific planning and management
Role of government	*Laissez-faire* as the route to individual freedom	Positive government: regulation to create conditions for freedom
Plasticity of human nature	Improvement of most people possible through education	Improvement limited by genetic endowment
Freedom	"Negative" freedom	"Positive" freedom

to the wealthy to use the government to manipulate the populace.

Sumner and his contemporary conservatives are often referred to as *social Darwinists* because they wanted individuals and institutions to survive difficult times on the merits of their own "fitness" to survive, rather than through government intervention to help them. The more dominant application of Darwin, however, held that society was one corporate organism, and that the misfortunes of some members had an inevitable impact on all members, like diseased cells in a corporate body. This way of thinking was used to justify the right and the responsibility of those in power to regulate society for the good of all.[56] Despite the arguments of Sumner and others, the progressive era saw greater and greater powers accrue to government in the name of a more free and democratic society. The days of laissez-faire, "negative" freedom were numbered.

Modern liberalism, then, was clearly an outgrowth of the classical liberalism of Jefferson's day, as Exhibit 4.6 suggests. The liberal democratic outlook continued, in altered form, to serve as a worldview which explained and justified the dominant political-economic institutions of the United States. As those institutions came under the pressures of urbanization, industrialization, and immigration, and as scientific knowledge changed with Darwin's findings, such classical liberal conceptions as absolute truth, human reason, progress, and even freedom itself underwent profound changes. These changes allowed modern liberals to justify, in the name of liberal democracy, centralization of power in the hands of governmental agencies and centralization of decision making in the hands of experts with professional training. Progress, they believed, demanded greater efficiency in public institutions, including the schools, and this greater efficiency could not be achieved through traditional policies of local governance. So powerful a hold did this revised liberal ideology have on the leadership of economic and political institutions that new liberalism became the central outlook of both major political parties—Democrat and Republican alike. Within each party, those who sought to preserve classical liberal perspectives and social policies became known as "conservatives," while those who embraced a stronger role for government in economic and social affairs were identified as "liberals." But the opportunities for alternative ideological positions—such as socialism, populism, or a labor-party position—to marshal any political power became increasingly scarce as new liberalism became more dominant.

New Psychology Before leaving discussion of the new liberal ideology, which Flexner and Bachman alluded to in explaining the Gary schools in light of "modern ethics and social philosophy," it is important to try to understand what they meant by "modern psychology" as well. Understanding any culture's approach to education requires understanding that culture's assumptions about the human mind and human learning, for there can be important relations between these ideas and schooling practices. If we assume that people learn best when they are under threat of physical punishment, for example, we might take a different approach to schooling than if we think people learn best when motivated by their own interest in subject matter. Similarly, while the educators of one era might assume that proficiency in Latin and Greek are indispensable to the educated mind, the educators of another era reject this assumption—because of a sharp change in how human learning is understood.

Chapters 2 and 3 briefly discussed the view of the human mind that dominated educational thought prior to the late 19th century—a view that had come to be called "faculty psychology" but which, in its basic principles, extended at least as far back into history as Plato. This view, which had influenced Thomas Jefferson, Horace Mann, and their contemporaries, portrayed the human mind as a collection of faculties which could be developed through rigorous exercise and which could be informed by the best thought and achievement that human culture had to offer.

On the one hand, faculty psychology led to a somewhat fixed and rigid approach to education and schooling. Students exercised what was thought to be one of the most important faculties, memory, by hour upon hour of rote memorization of texts. The texts themselves were those that were thought to be the highest achievements of western culture: passages from Homer, from Cicero, from the Bible, and from other "classics." And they were memorized in Latin and in Greek as well as English—not because translations were not available, but because the rigors of learning difficult languages would help strengthen the mind. Another reason was that students would develop a sense of style, rhythm, and grace by reading these works in the original, and these sensibilities would be applied by the students in other endeavors.

This notion of application, or "transfer" of learning from the classical curriculum to other learning, was central to faculty psychology. The classical curriculum was defended not primarily on the grounds that students would likely need such information in their daily lives, but that the strenuous rigors of studying traditional texts strengthened and informed the learner's mind for all of life's intellectual and ethical challenges. One learned, it was presumed, to develop one's ability to *think,* because the capacity for rationality set humans apart from all other creatures. This capacity for rationality was presumed to be essential to human freedom, for it was argued that one could be free only by obeying rationality, and not by obeying the dictates of others or the impulses of emotion.

While faculty psychology often led to schooling practices that were inflexible and even punitive for those who didn't bow to the fixed curriculum, it had an optimistic dimension: a high regard for the distinctiveness of human rationality and for the ability of each person to develop his or her rational capacities through intellectual exercise. In this regard, it might be argued that faculty psychology gave more credit to the power of reason than the "modern psychology" that replaced it during the progressive era.

Educational historian Clarence Karier has pointed out that what was known as "modern psychology" or "new psychology" during the progressive era was no single psychologic viewpoint, but a revised view of human nature that was influenced by several new approaches to psychology.[57] What these very different approaches had in common was that each of them claimed to be scientific; they all worked together to replace the more "unscientific" faculty psychology as the dominant conception of human mind and learning, and together they emphasized *nonrational* origins of human learning and behavior. Finally, these new psychologies, which still influence our ways of talking about the human mind and learning today, came to prominence during a critical period of change in schools and society, when together these new views would have significant influence on the conduct of schooling.

Karier draws attention, for example, to the *psychoanalytic* approach of Sigmund Freud (1856–1939) as one which emphasized the unconscious, and emotional, wellsprings of human thought and behavior. With a very different approach, G. Stanley Hall (1844–1924), the first man in the United States to receive a Ph.D. in psychology and the founder of the American Psychological Association, also provided support for attention to the emotional origins of human learning with his *primitivist* psychology, emphasizing biological stages of human development. Educators' growing awareness of the physiologic and emotional dimensions of learning was accompanied by the rise of *social psychology*, which was developed primarily by George Herbert Mead (1863–1949). Mead argued that human values, perception, identity, and behavior are all importantly shaped by social interactions, particularly those within the various groups of which a person is a member.

These various approaches to understanding the human mind did much to dispel the view that learning is exclusively, or even primarily, a rational and intellectual process. As they gained prominence, these views provided greater support for educating children and youth by emphasizing physiologic, emotional, and social dimensions of schooling. "Learning by doing" in the school workshop and home economics kitchen, in extracurricular clubs and other organizations in which groups of young people could be supervised by school personnel, and in school assemblies emphasizing patriotism and unity—all of these were progressive-era innovations which helped dramatically change the small schoolhouse to a physical plant with workshops, gymnasium, auditorium, and playground.

Easily the best-known educational psychologist of this time, as Karier points out, was Edward L. Thorndike (1874–1949). At Teachers College, Columbia University, Thorndike contributed much to the new changes in schooling. His contribution to modern psychology, referred to as *connectionism* for its emphasis on physiologic connections in the mind formed by stimulus-and-response processes, became the foundation of modern *behaviorism*, most associated in our time with B. F. Skinner (1904–1990). Thorndike based his theory of human learning on his studies of animal learning, challenging the old classical liberal view that the human mind is distinctively different from the animal mind. In fact, Thorndike specifically attacked faculty psychology and transfer-of-training assumptions, arguing that school subjects did not have general value for developing the mind but rather were valuable only for the specific information and skills they imparted. This argument proved influential in moving away from the classical curriculum of Latin and Greek toward a more "modern" curriculum of subjects directly applicable to the new industrial society. Thorndike's emphasis on learning as a physiologic, stimulus-response process helped provide support for the "learning by doing" of the vocational education movement, as well. Finally, Thorndike's view that intelligence was physiologic and therefore quantifiable made him a great apostle for the intelligence-testing movement, which helped educators to classify students into "superior" and "inferior" categories. Such classification, argued Thorndike, was important for educational efficiency and social progress. He wrote

> [I]n the long run, it has paid the "masses" to be ruled by intelligence. . . . What is true in science and government seems to hold good in general for manufacturing, trade, art, law, education, and religion. It seems entirely safe to predict that the world will get better treatment by trusting its fortunes to its 95- or 99-percentile intelligences than it would get by itself. The argument for democracy is not that it gives power to all men without distinction, but that it gives greater freedom for ability and character to attain power.[58]

For Thorndike, as for many other educators of his time, schools needed to be changed not only to reflect the changes in the population, in the workplace, and in social values, but also to reflect changes in how psychologists understood human learning. The emphasis on human beings as distinctively rational, in the image of God, gave way rapidly to an emphasis on human beings as physiologic, emotional, and social creatures who were not so very different from animals. The education of the "whole child," then, which both sought to recognize the complexity of the child and also categorized presumably different children for different kinds of learning, became a mixed legacy of the progressive era.

PROGRESSIVE EDUCATION

Progressive education is a simple term applied to a set of phenomena so complex that scholars continue to debate exactly what progressive education was. There is general agreement that the progressive movement in education started just before 1900 and had established its central innovations by 1920, although the Progressive Education Association (PEA) was founded only in 1919 and continued until the 1950s. There is also general agreement that progressive education constituted a response to urbanization, industrialization, and immigration, that it was articulated in terms of the emergent ideology we have termed new liberalism, and that it was shaped by new psychologic approaches which replaced faculty psychology. Finally, most writers would claim that progressive education rejected the traditional, classical curriculum and its methods of rote learning in favor of a child-centered curriculum that emphasized student interests and activities related to the larger society. But within those generalizations, progressive education varied greatly in conception and in implementation, and it is not always clear today what is meant by the term.

Educational historian Patricia Albjerg Graham argues that there were two different phases of progressive education: one phase roughly before America's involvement in World War I from 1913 to 1917, and the other following the war. Graham argues that the popular conception many people today hold about progressive education—that it was a permissive, experimental approach to schooling primarily for the children of the privileged—stems from the post–World War I innovations of a few highly publicized "progressive" schools.[59] The much more extensive phenomenon, according to Graham, was the progressive schooling prior to World War I, in which the "chief thrust of reforms was in the schools serving lower-class families," and in which "probably the most radical change . . . was the wide-scale introduction of vocational and technical courses."[60] Graham's division of progressive education into these two general periods, the first of which will be discussed in the next section, helps to locate an interesting irony. By the time the Progressive Education Association formed in 1919, the greatest work of the progressive movement had already been accomplished. After its formation, the PEA attended primarily to the "experimental school" kind of progressive education, the impact of which has been minimal compared to the pre-1920 innovations affecting the majority of American youth.

Two Strands of Progressivism: Developmental Democracy and Social Efficiency

The phase of progressive education to be examined here is the earliest and most important phase, that which dramatically transformed American schooling in less than three decades from the 1890s to the 1920s. As David Nasaw points out, beginning in the 1880s critics of the schools were already describing such problems as:[61]

- The failure of the traditional classical curriculum to interest and motivate students.
- High dropout rates at both elementary and secondary levels.
- Growing problems of juvenile delinquency and illiteracy among urban youth.
- Waste and inefficiency in school management practices in the neighborhood-controlled (especially immigrant-controlled) schools.
- Irrelevance of the traditional curriculum to the "real" needs of modern industrial society.

Under pressures from a business community unhappy with labor unrest, from muckraking journalists who wrote about waste and inefficiency in the schools, from social reformers concerned about the plight of youth in the cities, and from educators who argued that a new approach to educating "new students" was needed, a rough consensus emerged regarding the changes needed in schools. However, progressives differed sharply among themselves over the specifics of these changes. For example, progressive educators in general believed that it was important to replace the traditional classical curriculum with a "varied" curriculum that reflected the needs and interests of the children themselves. But within that general agreement came a sharp split between those who interpreted "needs and interests" to mean the specific concerns and motivations of each child and those who interpreted this phrase to mean "in the best interests of the child." In the first interpretation, the curriculum should respond to what each student finds interesting, while in the second interpretation, each child should be placed in the academic or vocational "track" for which his or her abilities are deemed most suited. These two interpretations of "replace classical curriculum with a varied curriculum" are distinctly different, but both are part of our inheritance from progressive education.

Differing interpretations also surround the conception of "progress." One conception of progress might be termed the *developmental-democracy* conception, in which it was believed that direct participation by all citizens in the decision-making processes of political and economic life, once begun, would develop individual and social capacities for problem solving through rational means. In this developmental view, grounded in the views of Thomas Jefferson and held by 20th-century educators Francis Parker and John Dewey, among others, school life should be organized very much like a democratic community, so that students could begin developing the understandings, dispositions, and intellectual skills necessary for mature participation in a participatory democracy in later life. In this developmental-democracy view of progress, then, school life would be democratic, and democratic life (both inside and outside the school) would be educational.

The *social-efficiency* view of progress, however, focused on achieving an orderly society in which political and economic institutions represented the interests of the governed through the application of the best principles of scientific knowledge and expertise. Social-efficiency progressives did not think of themselves as opposed to democracy. On the contrary, they believed that under modern urban conditions, schools could best prepare students for participation in a democratic society by identifying the "evident or probable destinies"[62] of different groups of students and educating them for these respective destinies. It would be just as inefficient, in this progressive view, to provide a college-preparatory curriculum to a child destined for factory work as it would be to provide a vocational shop curriculum to a college-bound student.

Several primary ideas in progressive education were subject to these competing interpretations. For the purposes of this chapter, five of these ideas may be identified as most important and most illustrative of how developmental-democracy progressives differed from social-efficiency progressives in their views of progress. Each of these assumptions is stated sufficiently loosely to allow for the competing interpretations of the era, but each is stated substantively enough to distinguish it from the traditional, classical-curriculum approach that had been assumed in the 19th century.

Progressive education assumes that

1. The traditional classical curriculum should be replaced by a varied curriculum based on the interests and needs of students.
2. Learning should be based on activities rather than on rote.
3. School aims, content, and processes should reflect social conditions.
4. A primary aim of schooling is to help solve social problems.

How each of these ideas was interpreted differently in the two contrasting strands of progressivism is the subject of the remainder of the chapter.

DEWEYAN DEVELOPMENTAL DEMOCRACY

Perhaps not very meaningful, but interesting nonetheless, is that John Dewey was born in 1859, a year which also marks Horace Mann's death and the publication of Darwin's *Origin of Species*. Certainly, something of the old order was passing and the new was beginning. Dewey would become

John Dewey, the most famous advocate of "progressive education," believed that children are by nature curious and active. Given meaningful tasks, they become active problem solvers seeking to carry out their own purposes.

one of the two or three most influential American philosophers of the 20th century, writing not just about education but about traditional philosophical questions such as the nature of reality, knowledge, and moral life. Although it is not known whether the Vermont town-meeting tradition of Dewey's childhood influenced his adult philosophy, Dewey would eventually articulate a democratic theory that would address the conditions of modern, urban, industrial life. As a professor at the University of Michigan, University of Vermont, University of Chicago, and later at Teachers College, Columbia University, Dewey developed an educational philosophy he believed to be consistent with his democratic theory. There are others who held Dewey's democratic approach to education during the progressive period, but Dewey is featured here because of his recognized importance to this major stream of progressive thought.

Following 18th-century philosopher Jean-Jacques Rousseau and 19th-century philosopher John Stuart Mill, Dewey believed that democracy was important not only because it stood for freedom and equality, but because of its educational consequences. To begin with, he recognized Jefferson's view that for a democracy to be successful, the people must be educated enough to recognize and express their own interests. But more important, Dewey believed, was the converse: *for education to be most successful, it is necessary that people participate in democratic forms of life.* That is, Dewey believed in a developmental argument for democracy which held that participation in democratic life is more educational for the population than participation in any other form of political life. He stated it best in *Reconstruction in Philosophy,* in which he argued that the democratic "test of all the institutions of adult life is their effect in furthering continued education. . . . Democracy has many meanings, but if it has moral meaning, it is found in resolving that the supreme test of all political institutions and industrial arrangements shall be the contribution they make to the all-around growth of every member of society."[63]

Dewey believed that the school could be a "laboratory for democracy" in which children developed the understandings, skills, and dispositions required for democratic life not only by reading about them in books, but by interacting democratically in their learning activities. His view of the child's nature was that while most children do not have a "distinctively intellectual interest" in learning out of books for the sake of learning itself, all children have a great capacity for intellectual development.[64] The schools as traditionally conducted, he believed, had failed to stimulate the intellectual capacities of most children, and they had failed to do so because they had not taken the nature of the child into account.

The Nature of the Child

Dewey believed that first, children are by nature actively social creatures; second, they are by nature constructive—they like making things; third, they are creatively expressive; and fourth, they are by nature curious and inquiring. Dewey argued that the traditional school not only failed to encourage but actively *penalized* the children for behaving in accord with these facets of their nature. The school required children not to interact with one another, to be passive receivers rather than actively and creatively constructive, to accept a fixed curriculum rather than to exercise their curiosity by following up on things of interest to them. In *Democracy and Education* Dewey remarked that children are prepared as if they were going to lead a life of slavery rather than a life as free individuals. Dewey reminded us in that volume and in others that Plato's definition of a slave was one who accepts as a guide to his own activities the purposes of another, while for Dewey *the mark of a free person was one who could frame and execute purposes of his or her own.*[65]

Dewey argued that the classroom could be an environment where children, working together in social activity, could frame and execute their own purposes. He urged that these activities should be selected by the students and teacher together on the basis of the students' interests, for when students are interested, he believed, they will pursue an activity for its own sake and will learn more readily. In the course of such student-chosen activities or projects, Dewey argued, the students would inevitably encounter obstacles and problems in reaching their own goals, and such problems should be solved by children working together under the teachers' guidance. Such cooperative problem solving would exercise the students' abilities to think critically about the causes and consequences of things they were interested in, and thus they would grow intellectually just by participating in their chosen projects. This growth would then lead to new interests, new choices of activities, new problems to overcome, and new growth in a cycle of learning driven by the ever-developing interests of the students. In this manner, Dewey believed, schools would respond to social problems by equipping students to become the sort of adults who could solve social problems for themselves.

For Dewey, the primary social problem of the time was not worker resistance to scientific management, nor poverty, nor ethnic conflict. His primary concern was that problems brought about by urbanization, immigration, and industrialization were being solved nondemocratically, by authoritarian methods which put some members of society in control of others. Dewey believed that the schools could be a part of, but not the whole, solution to this pervasive political, economic, and ideological problem.[66]

In the above brief sketch we can see how Dewey embodied three of the four main assumptions of progressive education: (1) replacement of the traditional curriculum with a varied, child-centered curriculum, (2) learning through activity, and (3) schooling as a response to social problems. The fourth dimension, that schools should reflect social realities, Dewey believed would be a function of the students' interests and the projects they would seek to pursue. Of Dewey's many books, the one most widely read during his lifetime, *The School and Society* (1899), argued that classrooms at the elementary level in particular should allow students to engage in activities based on occupations with which they were familiar. Such occupations would provide thematic unity to the students' constructive activities, their reading, their writing, and so on. The occupations would also provide connections to the world outside the classroom, so that classroom experiences would inform and enrich student experiences outside school and so that nonschool experiences could motivate, inform, and enrich classroom experiences as well.

Dewey cautioned, however, against using these activities to prepare students for specific occupations or vocations in the workplace. He insisted that such occupation-based projects "should never educate *for* vocations, but should always educate *through* vocations." Dewey believed that progressive teachers could use such activities to develop experiences in discussing, reading, writing, arithmetic, problem solving, and other intellectual pursuits in ways that would stimulate students' interests in these areas much better than did the traditional methods. And part of the basis of this interest would be that the classroom would visibly reflect the social environment, rather than be isolated from it.[67]

A Unique Meaning for Progressive Education

The meaning of "progressive" education, for Dewey, thus differed from the meaning as it was generally understood then—and as it is generally applied now. For most educators and observers during the progressive era, education was progressive because it was new and different from "traditional" education and because it was thought to result from and to contribute to social progress in general (see, for example, the opening paragraph of this chapter). For Dewey, however, the primary meaning of "progressive" education was that it marked an arrangement of student activities that grew progressively out of the student's interests and past experiences, leading to new experiences and new interests in a continuous and progressive cycle. For Dewey, education that did not grow organically from the student in this way was not progressive at all.[68]

Charles W. Eliot and Social Efficiency

Dewey's interpretation of society's needs, and of how education should meet them, was not the dominant nor the most influential view among progressive educators, if we are to judge by the claims of the social-efficiency progressives and by the actual school programs that took root during the progressive period. One of the most prominent educators of the time, Harvard president Charles W. Eliot, provides a good example of the social-efficiency stream of progressive thought, and through him the most important innovations of progressive education prior to 1920 can be examined. Although he was at one time an advocate of liberal education for all secondary-school youth, Eliot became an articulate spokesman for the replacement of traditional educational goals by four new educational objectives for the schools: social stability, employable skills, equal educational opportunity, and meritocracy.

Although Eliot had favored universal, liberal education at the secondary level through most of his career at Harvard, he recognized that his position applied to fewer than 10 percent of secondary-school children, because of high dropout rates. As the sheer numbers and ethnic diversity of high school students increased, Eliot became an advocate of vocational education. Eliot had distinct prejudices against those students not from "pure American stock," as he put it, and he was especially prejudiced against African-Americans and Indians. As Steve Preskill writes, "Frankly referring to blacks as savages, Eliot preached that they must learn the lessons of the six-day workweek and vigilant frugality before they could be accorded political and economic parity with whites." Eliot often lauded Booker T. Washington for his vocational approach to the education of African-American people, and he was a member of the national General Education Board, which just before the 1920s successfully instituted vocational education in schools for African-Americans throughout the South.[69]

Eliot's prejudices extended also to Southern- and Eastern-European immigrants, and he declared that new immigrants in New England presented "the same race problem to that part of the country that Negroes do to the South."[70] Reflecting the influence of Darwin on many intellectuals of his day, Eliot also endorsed a plan to discourage unmarried Southern and Eastern Europeans from immigrating to the United States, reasoning that married immigrants would present a lesser threat to the gene pool of the "pure American stock" of the nation.[71]

Apart from discouraging immigration from "objectionable" countries, national leaders such as Eliot increasingly turned toward education as a means of responding to the immigrants already here. To Eliot and other new liberals, the new immigrants were identified with a set of social problems which they believed schools might help solve. For example, the immigrants were a large part of the factory labor force that had been resisting scientific management of the workplace, and the resulting strife was a part of the larger disorder of the overcrowded cities. Further, the increasingly stratified industrial order demanded very different skills among workers, managers, and professionals. Two social and educational goals that became newly emphasized in progressive schools, then, were social stability and employable skills. It was believed that the differentiated curriculum, offering both academic and vocational courses of study, could achieve both of these goals. Further, it was believed that such a differentiated curriculum could contribute to democratic schooling and democratic institutions by achieving two additional aims: providing equal educational opportunity to all students and basing the democratic leadership of society on merit in school performance.

While none of these goals for schooling—social stability, employable skills, equal educational opportunity, and meritocracy—was entirely new to American society, they took on an unprecedented emphasis and distinctive character in the progressive period. Like most other educational leaders of his time, Eliot endorsed all of them. Although he differed from Dewey in his progressive vision, the differentiated curriculum, with its emphasis on vocational education, represented for Eliot an interpretation of progressivism that, like Dewey's, (1) abandoned the classical curriculum; (2) based learning on activities rather than on rote; (3) reflected social conditions in school aims, content, and processes; and (4) sought to help solve social problems. Yet these progressive characteristics, when put to the service of the four new aims of social stability, employable skills, equal educational opportunity, and meritocracy, helped shape progressive schooling in ways that were very different from Dewey's developmental-democracy approach.

Social Stability Born to one of Boston's wealthier families in 1834 (only 8 years after Jefferson's death and two years before Horace Mann assumed leadership of the Massachusetts Board of Education), Charles W. Eliot was tutored in the classics as a child and attended the Boston Latin School. After graduating from Harvard with a degree in chemistry at age 19 and later teaching there, Eliot subsequently studied in Europe before accepting the presidency of Harvard at age 35. It was at Harvard that his vision of the good society and the good school system took shape.

Given Eliot's unusually privileged background and Harvard's increasingly close ties with the business community of the nation, it is not surprising that Eliot was more supportive of business than of labor in the great strife between the two. Although he expressed considerable sympathy for the plight of workers and argued against excessive skill dilution and division of labor, Eliot attacked labor unions as a threat to individual freedom. In contrast, he identified the corporations as "really great reinforcements of public liberty," and he believed that one function of the schools should be to teach prospective workers a more accommodating and cooperative attitude toward management. Vocational education, thought Eliot, offered a particularly good way to address problems of labor unrest by adjusting students to the realities of the managed workplaces of business and industry.[72] Further, he believed that "governmental affairs must be conducted on the same principles on which successful private and corporate business is conducted," and that students should be taught to "respect and confide in the expert in every field of human activity."[73]

Other educators, too, emphasized the service schools could provide to social stability. A 1914 bulletin of the U.S. Bureau of Education declared, "The State maintains schools to render its citizenship homogeneous in spirit and purpose. The public schools exist primarily for the benefit of the State rather than for the benefit of the individual."[74] Stanford University's prominent progressive educator Ellwood P. Cubberley applauded this notion in 1919, claiming that not only vocational education, but such progressive innovations as night school, adult education, supervised playgrounds, and vocational guidance programs would serve the interests of the state by helping achieve a more stable society.[75]

Cubberley was correct in noticing the wide range of activities emerging as a part of the new progressive school. The one-room schoolhouse that taught the academic basics to those who voluntarily attended was rapidly being replaced by a more total institution, which represented, as Cubberley said, the "extension of education." Schooling was being extended from a voluntary to a compulsory institution, and therefore it was being extended from the privileged few to the mandatory many. The extended school was one which provided auditoriums for school assemblies, shops and kitchens for vocational education, and before- and after-school supervision of clubs and other extracurricular activities. Such activities were planned with the intention of preparing students to take their places in an urbanized, industrial order. In its extension from voluntary to compulsory, from the few to the many, from a unified to a differentiated curriculum, from traditional academic to new vocational subjects, and from classroom curriculum emphasizing intellectual learning to extracurricular activities emphasizing social learning, the progressive school reflected a consistent concern for social stability as a primary educational objective. But there were more objectives of equal importance.

Employable Skills One of these other objectives was that schools should prepare students with specific skills and attitudes for the workplace. Again, vocational education would play a major part in efforts to achieve this aim. Eliot, once a proponent of liberal education for all youth, was arguing by 1908 that modern American society was divided into four largely unchanging classes: (1) the small managing or leading class, (2) the commercial class devoted to buying and selling, (3) skilled artisans, and (4) "the rough workers." Failure to recognize these classes, argued Eliot, resulted in a system in which the "immense majority of our children do not receive from our school system an education which trains them for the vocation to which they are clearly destined."[76] He further argued before the National Education Association in 1910 that "serious modifications of the programs" in schools required teachers and administrators to accept their new "functions of guiding children into appropriate life work."[77]

By the time Eliot addressed the NEA, the nation's largest organization of educators, a sharp distinction had come to separate established hands-on learning activities from the new vocationalism. "Manual training" had begun growing in popularity in the 1880s, and it embraced hand-oriented learning as a way to enhance academic education for all students. The new "industrial education," however, focused on the development

goal

of workplace skills and attitudes considered appropriate for that majority of students who would one day be the industrial working class. The Primary Source Reading at the end of this chapter shows how the NEA Committee on the Place of Industries in Public Education came to reject manual training as too "abstract," while embracing industrial education for the "concrete social values" it would impart.

Eliot represents the predominant thinking of progressive educators who shifted their vision from a liberal education to a "manpower" model in which, as Ellwood Cubberley said, "Our schools are, in a sense, factories in which the raw materials are to be shaped and fashioned into products to meet the various demands of life. The specifications for manufacturing come from the demands of the 20th century civilization, and it is the business of the school to build its pupils to the specifications laid down."[78] Exhibit 4.7 illustrates the change in course offerings intended to teach employable skills in this manpower model.

EXHIBIT 4.7 **Enrollment of Public High School Students in Specified Subjects***

	SCHOOL YEAR ENDING				
	1900	*1910*	*1922*	*1934*	*1949*
	TOTAL ENROLLMENT (000s)				
	519	739	2,155	4,497	5,399
	PERCENTAGE ENROLLMENT BY SUBJECT				
General science	—	—	18.3	17.8	20.8
Biology	—	1.1	8.8	14.6	18.4
Chemistry	7.7	6.9	7.4	7.6	7.6
Physics	19.0	14.6	8.9	6.3	5.4
Physiology	27.4	9.5	5.1	1.8	1.0
Earth science	29.8	21.0	4.5	1.7	0.4
Algebra	56.3	56.9	40.2	30.4	26.8
General mathematics	—	—	12.4	7.4	13.1
Geometry	17.4	30.9	22.7	17.1	12.8
Trigonometry	1.9	1.9	1.5	1.3	2.0
Spanish	—	0.7	11.3	6.2	8.2
French	7.8	9.9	15.5	10.9	4.7
German	14.3	23.7	0.6	2.4	0.8
English	38.5	57.1	76.7	90.5	92.9
Latin	50.6	49.0	17.5	16.0	7.8
U.S. and English history	38.2†	55.0†	18.2	17.8	22.8
Civil and community government	21.7	15.6	19.3	16.4	8.0‡
Industrial subjects	—	—	13.7	21.0	26.6
Bookkeeping	—	—	12.6	9.9	8.7
Typewriting	—	—	13.1	16.7	22.5
Shorthand	—	—	8.9	9.0	7.8
Home economics	—	3.8	14.3	16.7	24.2
Agriculture	—	4.7	5.1	3.6	6.7
Physical education	—	—	5.7	50.7	69.4
Music	—	—	25.3	25.5	30.1
Art	—	—	14.7	8.7	9.0

*Covers enrollment in last 4 years of school
†Includes ancient history and medieval and modern history
‡Civil government only

Source: Adapted by Stuart McAninch from *Historical Statistics of the U.S., Colonial Times to 1970, Bicentennial Edition* (Washington D.C.: U.S. Department of Commerce, Bureau of Census, 1975), p. 377.

In 1900, about half a million students were enrolled in secondary schools, and their courses were overwhelmingly traditional "academic" subjects: Latin, English, algebra, geometry, physiology, earth science, physics, and history. Negligible percentages of students were enrolled in vocational subjects. By 1922, however, secondary school enrollment had quadrupled, while the percentage of students in most traditional academic subjects had declined markedly. Conversely, hundreds of thousands of students were now enrolled in the new vocational courses: industrial subjects, bookkeeping, typewriting, home economics, and agriculture, for example. Other subjects, such as music, art, and physical education, illustrate extension of the curriculum into areas that were neither clearly vocational nor academic, but were seen to have social value.

Before leaving Exhibit 4.7, note the predominance of new vocational subjects intended for female office-workers: bookkeeping, typewriting, shorthand, and home economics were from their inception heavily gender-typed. Likewise, vocational courses in industrial arts almost exclusively enrolled boys. Similar differences, though less pronounced, persisted in such academic subjects as advanced math and science. These differences led some psychologists and educators to challenge the value of coeducation itself, arguing that schools should provide separate curricula to "make boys more manly and girls more womanly."[79] As office work became increasingly a female occupation in the progressive era, business-occupations courses increased also. The published curriculum of the Beaumont, Texas, public schools illustrates the sentiment that home economics courses should be offered for women for different reasons.

> However inviting civic honors may appear to the suffragette, or vocational life may be to the breadwinning or to ambitious women, homemaking is the normal life activity of most womanly women. Our schools should accentuate this normal life for women by providing a course in Domestic Science. Thus our girls would have equal advantages with our boys in life training, as our boys for several years have had the advantage of a well-equipped and well-conducted manual training department.[80]

While such sentiment for keeping women in the home appeared to have greater support in southern schools than in the industrial North, both regions used the employment market to help justify the vocational curriculum. The San Antonio Board of Education in 1915 commissioned a survey which noted that "only nine of the boys leaving school each year, out of the thousand from all grades, will become lawyers. Only seven will become physicians. Only four will become teachers; an equal number clergymen. . . . The figures show clearly that the vocations for which training is needed by the large numbers are not professional. Into the professions only about five percent of the men go."[81] The president of the school board of Muncie, Indiana, put the matter more succinctly: "For a long time all boys were trained to be President. Then for a while we trained them all to be professional men. Now we are training boys to get jobs."[82]

While some vocational courses, particularly those in business classes for girls, provided training that would translate into immediately employable job-specific skills, the schools could not hope to provide adequate job-specific training in the many skills required by the workplace. Perhaps more important than specific skills, the schools sought to provide in their vocational courses proper *attitudes* for the workplace; or, as the Lewistown, Idaho, board of education stated it, "The senior high school is charged with developing a *spirit* of enthusiasm that will make every boy and girl who is prepared for the work eager to enter."[83]

One way in which this could be accomplished, it was believed, was by converting traditional academic subject matter into vocational "courses of study" or "tracks" that would not be limited to shop work and manual activities but would also include "vocational English," "vocational math," and so on. So presented, it was believed that students would see the relevance of their academic work to their vocational courses of study and would thus be more interested in them. The Deerfield, Illinois, public schools, for example, advertised their manual training course of study with the recognition that "the school does not teach an individual trade," but vocational students would achieve "a like-mindedness and a sympathy that cannot but help toward the preservation of American institutions."[84] By 1920, Eliot's call for "serious modifications of the programs" of American secondary schools was well under way, justified by the new progressive objective of schooling for employable skills.

Equal Educational Opportunity Since Jefferson's time, the view that education could be a source of social mobility for the lower economic classes was a part of the liberal faith of American society. Horace Mann had proclaimed that schools would be "the great equalizer" of social conditions, providing opportunity for all citizens to achieve their economic goals. And John Dewey in 1916 stated, "Only through education can equality of opportunity be anything more than a phrase."[85] It was not until the progressive era, in fact, that the term "equal educational opportunity" entered educational discourse. It became a newly explicit aim for progressives, in part because the differentiated curriculum had to be defended against charges that it was undemocratic, that it provided children from different backgrounds different and unequal educations. What progressive reformers meant by "equal educational opportunity" was not that students should receive the same educational experiences, as Aristotle had claimed would be appropriate for a democratic society, and as Mann had envisioned for the common schools. In fact, they meant just the opposite, as is illustrated in this 1908 explanation by the Boston superintendent of schools:

> Until very recently [the schools] have offered equal opportunity for all to receive *one kind* of education, but what will make them democratic is to provide opportunity for all to receive such education as will fit them *equally well* for their particular life work.[86]

That is, equal opportunity meant to this Boston educator that students would receive different kinds of education, but all students would have "equal opportunity" to receive the education appropriate to them.

This view of equal educational opportunity prevailed among the most influential progressive educators in part because it appeared to justify separating students into different curricula and preparing them for different occupational outcomes, both of which, while "socially efficient," seemed undemocratic on their face. The progressive interpretation of equal educational opportunity seemed to answer such charges and make the differentiated curriculum appear democratic. Furthermore, differentiation among students didn't need to wait until secondary school. "The teachers of the elementary schools ought to sort the pupils and sort them by their evident or probable destinies," said Charles Eliot in 1908. "We have learned that the best way in education is to find out what the line is in which the child can do best, and then to give him the happiness of achievement in that line. Here we come back to the best definition of democracy."[87] The "best definition of democracy," for Eliot, might more fairly be called "meritocracy."

Meritocracy Eliot argued that the schools could contribute to a more democratic society if, first, they taught students to "respect and confide in the expert in every field of human activity," and second, they helped locate and educate the most talented members of society for democratic leadership. "[An] important function of the public school in a democracy," he wrote, "is the discovery and development of the gift or capacity of each individual child. This discovery should be made at the earliest practicable age, and, once made, should always influence, and sometimes

EXHIBIT 4.8 **Progressive Educational Reform (1890s–1920s)**

Reformers	New objectives	Extension of schooling
Business community	Employable skills	From the few to many
Journalists	Social stability	From voluntary to compulsory
Social reformers	Equal educational opportunity	From unified curriculum to differentiated curriculum
New psychologists	Meritocracy	From academic curriculum only to extracurricular activities
Educators (e.g., Dewey, Eliot, Cubberley)		From local control to central administrative control

determine, the education of the individual. It is for the interest of society to make the most of every useful gift or faculty which any member may fortunately possess."[88] This, to Eliot, was democratic in that it provided equal opportunity for each student to be educated for his or her particular place in society. Since, as Eliot said, "There is no such thing as equality of gifts, or powers, or faculties, among either children or adults," such schooling would educate leaders and followers.

By 1919 Ellwood Cubberley would write that "a thoroughly democratic ladder has everywhere been provided" in the nation's schools. This ladder, according to the view of many progressives, was there for everyone, but only the most talented could be expected to climb it. Thus, the truly meritorious would rise to the top as a result of equal opportunity, completing the democratic argument. The result, wrote Cubberley, would clearly differentiate the leaders from the followers on the basis of merit:

> In our high schools and colleges the more promising of our youth must be trained for leadership and service to the State . . . along the lines of the highest and best of our national traditions in statesmanship, business, science, and government. In our common schools and in special schools those who labor must be trained for vocational efficiency, and given a sense of their responsibility for promoting the national welfare.[89]

The use of mass IQ testing beginning in the second decade of the century gave progressive educators a more "exact" and "scientific" way to assess the "evident and probable destinies," as Eliot had said, of children in schools. The differentiated curriculum and placement in vocational tracks could now be based on scientific measurement of student abilities. Developer of the Stanford-Binet test, Louis Terman wrote in 1923:

> Preliminary investigations indicate that an IQ below 70 rarely permits anything better than unskilled labor; that the range from 70 to 80 is preeminently that of semi-skilled labor, from 80 to 100 that of the skilled or ordinary clerical labor, from 100 to 110 or 115 that of the semi-professional pursuits; and that above all these are the grades of intelligence which permit one to enter the professions or the larger fields of business. . . . This information will be of great value in planning the education of a particular child and also in planning the differentiated curriculum here recommended.[90]

For Terman, E. L. Thorndike, and other advocates of the social-efficiency brand of progressive education, intelligence testing was a way to make the meritocratic aims of schooling more democratic. Students in the vocational programs were placed there not only for the social good, it was believed, but for their own good, because their talents best suited them to nonprofessional occupations.

CONCLUDING REMARKS

Educational reform movements take place in response to particular social conditions and are shaped by particular ideological commitments. This chapter has profiled the specific social and ideological conditions of the era in which the progressive education reform movement took place in the United States. In very general terms, the political-economic conditions included urbanization, immigration, industrialization, labor unrest, and the increasing centralization of decision making in business and government. Ideologically, the beginning of the 20th century was marked by a shift from the laissez-faire, limited-government commitments of classical liberalism toward a new liberalism marked by ever greater reliance on government and on scientific expertise to solve persistent social and economic problems. Older scientific conceptions of a fixed, mechanistic universe were replaced by a new conception of an evolving, organic universe. In the area of human learning, faculty psychology was rapidly replaced by new psychologies of the human mind and learning. It was in response to such new conditions and perceptions that the progressive education movement took place.

Who were these progressive educational reformers? What were their aims? And what were the consequences of their efforts? While these questions are answered at length throughout this chapter, Exhibit 4.8 on page 113 might help to organize some of the relevant information.

Students with a good understanding of this chapter should be able to explain the relations between the items in these three columns. Why, for example, did the business community take an interest in schooling objectives such as employable skills and social stability? What did equal educational opportunity in the second column have to do with any of the elements of extended schooling in the third column? Examining the relations among the interests of the various reforms, new objectives of schooling, and newly changed and extended schooling practices can help develop a good grasp of the progressive education movement.

It might seem odd, after detailing the differences between the progressive visions of John Dewey and Charles Eliot, to place them together in the above representation. If they were so different, how could they both have contributed toward the same general aims and outcomes of progressive education?

The chart is not intended to suggest that Dewey stands in the same relationship to the aims and outcomes of progressive education as do social-efficiency progressive educators such as Eliot and Cubberley. However, Dewey cannot be left out of the picture altogether, because he contributed much to the progressive movement, even if he later protested that the movement had strayed from the direction he sought. Although Dewey differed from Eliot and others on the aims and methods of progressive education, he gave great legitimacy to the central ideas that helped fuel the progressive movement: ideas such as the abandonment of the classical curriculum, the use of occupations in the classroom, notions of learning by doing, making schooling relevant to social conditions and solving social problems, and tailoring learning to the needs of the child. While these ideas may have meant one thing to Dewey and quite another to Eliot, all the ideas were new and radically different from the traditional approach to academic "book-learning." Although Dewey helped the educational community accept these new ideas, it was the social-efficiency variety of progressive education rather than Dewey's developmental-democracy variety that took root. The political-economic and ideological conditions of the time provided a more fertile seedbed for the social-efficiency approach to progressive education. In short, Dewey's own arguments for a new education helped nourish a form of schooling—complete with ability grouping of students, vocational education, and top-down decision making by administrative "experts"—that he would later harshly criticize.

PRIMARY SOURCE READING

The following report was written by a committee on industrial education for the National Education Association in 1910, well after the influence of both John Dewey and Charles Eliot had been first recognized. The committee's report was regarded as a major statement by leading educators on the status of vocational education.

This selection, like the Gary Schools Report excerpt on the first page of this chapter, can serve as a useful self-test of the student's knowledge and understanding of the Progressive Era (having completed the chapter, students are urged to return to that Gary Schools passage to test their ability to make sense of all *of it).*

This NEA report is valuable, too, because it is not the work of a philosopher, like Dewey, or a singular and prominent leader like Harvard President Eliot, but of members of the nation's largest educational association. It is important to see, in this report, how educators themselves (largely educational administrators) saw industrial education as necessary to meet the needs of the newly industrialized society. Here we see faculty psychology and its "general training" rejected in favor of more specific "preparation for a specific kind of life." Here we see democratic values portrayed as a "burden" to those who wish to differentiate education for different vocational futures, and we see how middle-grades education is embraced at a time when this differentiation should begin. The social-efficiency goals of employable skills, social stability, meritocracy, and equal educational opportunity are all evident in this one short piece. How might John Dewey have evaluated this statement?

REPORT OF THE COMMITTEE ON THE PLACE OF INDUSTRIES IN PUBLIC EDUCATION

National Education Association

The manual-training "movement" and its successor, the present vigorous industrial-education propaganda, have exercised for more than a quarter of a century a dominant influence in the educational thought of the United States. The early arguments for manual training and the later arguments for industrial education have a singular and significant resemblance. More vital motive for school work, better adaptation of the curriculum to the needs of the rank and file, reduction of school "mortality," and promotion of national industrial efficiency—these are among the more urgent reasons that have been advanced, thruout the entire period, for a more adequate attention to "handwork" as a supplement to, or substitute for, the traditional "headwork" of the schools.

With the abandonment of the theory of "general training" based upon the so-called "faculty psychology" the arguments for manual activities in the school, while retaining much of their original form and phraseology, have been given more specific application than was at first thought necessary. Not motor training, but specific motor abilities; not accuracy, judgment, and honesty, but keener appreciation of some of the most significant industrial processes; not preparation for life—any life—but preparation for a specific kind of life is now urged by those who are leading in the present demand for industrial education.

Notwithstanding the obvious similarity and direct connection between the early and later attitudes toward handwork and industrial activities, there is, then, a most important distinction between the two points of view. The earlier movement emphasized abstract psychological values; the later places the emphasis upon concrete social values. . . .

In the field of elementary education . . . the continuous and at times strenuous discussion of thirty years has not produced results commensurate with the importance attributed to manual training by its advocates. Notwithstanding much notable advance, due largely to the influence of manual training, toward a more intimate and vital connection between thinking and doing in the school, handwork in the school is still in the main abstract, isolated, impractical, and unsocial in character.

The industrial-education propaganda of the past decade has likewise, in a measure, failed to affect educational practice to the extent that public interest, professional and lay discussion, and legislative provisions might have justified one in

National Education Association, Report of the Committee on the Place of Industries in Public Education, 1910. Reprinted by permission of the publisher from Marvin Lazerson and W. Norton Grubb, *American Education and Vocationalism* (New York: Teachers College Press, 1974,): pp. 81–87.

expecting. There is doubtless a keener appreciation than ever before of the social need for industrial education; but there has been relatively little advance in the way of detailed working-out of curricula, organization, and procedure for industrial schools of various types. Within the last few years, however, the demand for industrial education has made itself felt even within the field commonly assumed heretofore to be the exclusive territory of elementary education: a few public intermediate schools and trade schools of a distinctly vocational type having come into being. The result of these experiments is being awaited with eager interest.

In the field of secondary education, there is even greater discrepancy between the promise of theory and the reality of practice. There are about one hundred and fifty schools of secondary grade in the country that are classified in the reports of the Commissioner of Education as manual and industrial training schools. Of this number, however, only one-half are reported as giving any attention to the manual arts. Thirty of these are public high schools; most of which devote from five to nine hours a week, and a very few as much as twelve hours a week; but fewer than half of them give as much as one-third of their time to such instruction. With two or three possible exceptions, none of these public high schools may be ranked as technical high schools according to the definition proposed in the present report—the distinctive industrial or vocational purpose being almost uniformly absent. . . .

Briefly summarized, the results of the committee's work may be stated as follows:

1. Industry, as a controlling factor in social progress, has for education a fundamental and permanent significance.
2. Educational standards, applicable in an age of handicraft, presumably need radical change in the present day of complex and highly specialized industrial development.
3. The social aim of education and the psychological needs of childhood alike require that industrial (manual-constructive) activities form an important part of school occupations.
   - **a.** In the elementary school, such occupations are necessary to provide concreteness of motive and meaning; to insure positive and lasting results for instruction; and to bring about a vital relation between life within the school and life outside.
   - **b.** In intermediate schools, industrial occupations are an important element in the wide range of experience necessary for the proper testing of children's aptitudes as a basis for subsequent choice of specific pursuits either in vocations or in higher schools.
   - **c.** In secondary schools, industrial occupations properly furnish the central and dominant factor in the education of those pupils who make final choice of an industrial vocation. Vocational purpose is the distinguishing mark of the "technical" high school as distinct from the "Manual Training" high school.
4. The differences among children as to aptitudes, interests, economic resources, and prospective careers furnish the basis for a rational as opposed to a merely formal distinction between elementary, secondary, and higher education. . . .

The present report assumes that a democratic community, by its very nature, must accept the obligation of providing every boy and girl with an educational opportunity that shall be not merely free, but enlightening; not merely compulsory, but compelling; not merely expansive, but vitalizing. A system of public education affording such opportunities is absolutely essential to the development of an intelligent, responsive, and efficient citizenship; and this, in turn, furnishes the most secure, if not the only, guarantee of a permanent and triumphant democracy. . . .

We have reached again from the standpoint of the study of the developing nature of the child the issue of specialized vocational training. It is evident that the general training of the earlier years of the elementary school should be what is deemed necessary to all and what introduces those who are to specialize in some form of industry to their work of specific preparation. We have not, however, as yet considered sufficiently the problem of the initial steps in differentiation or specialization. This problem is in our democratic system one among the most difficult and important that we face. It is a question whether the problem of determining what the vocation of the man shall be is not more difficult and exacting than that of preparing him for what has been chosen. The European systems of education, which have not been burdened to such an extent as our own with the ideals of a democracy, have found it easy to engraft vocational instruction upon an elementary system intended only for those destined by birth to some form of industry. In our boasted continuous ladder of schools, where the elementary school leads into the high school, and the high school into the college, the introduction of special training in industry has not been so simple. It means differentiation. It has seemed like cutting off from the children who took it the opportunity for such careers as were limited largely to those who had completed the higher course. We have felt that education shall give to all an equal chance to attain any distinction in life. Hence we have clung to a system associated with the training of leaders, even tho such a system may be poorly enough adapted to the education of anyone else.

. . . We may confine ourselves to the crying need for a system of education that shall provide training adequate, in the first place, to enable a fairly intelligent choice of a calling to be made and, in the second place, to prepare for whatever may be selected. We are fully alive to the need for the second of these advances. It is doubtful whether our educational leaders have been in general adequately impressed with the need for a system of school work the primary purpose of which should be to enable the pupil to find himself and the teacher to give to him intelligent advice on the matter.

From the point of view of the development of the child, the age at which this process of experimentation toward a calling should be definitely initiated corresponds fairly well with the beginning of the seventh school year. Its external symptom is the high rate of elimination from school at that time, and its internal sign is the unrest, the questioning of values, the beginnings of "storm and stress" that characterize the commencement of the age of independence, of adolescence. It would seem that at this time the secondary phase of education should begin.

. . . It is possible, however, to distinguish three well-marked functions of education, which might be assigned to elementary, secondary, and higher education, respectively, without much destructive readjustment of our present system. Elementary education concerns the essentials and the fundamentals. It is the education that precedes any attempt at differentiation. With the development of the child up into the age where such differentiation becomes necessary an epoch of experimentation sets in. The main purpose of the education of this period should be to afford an adequate basis of experience for the choice of a specialty and to guide the process of selection. Such education we may call secondary. When once it has been determined as well as is practically possible what the child should do, the time for higher education, that is, for the special preparation for a vocation, has appeared.

On this plan we should not have a system in which, while elementary education is supposed to be for all, secondary education is only for a few, and higher education for the very few; but each phase of the work would find representation in the education of all or most pupils. At the beginning of the seventh grade the work of experimentation might well begin. A large number of children have by this time demonstrated their unfitness for what might be called a professional career. For them the severer studies, involving the power of mind to grasp and utilize the abstract ideas and processes involved in mathematics, science, language, etc., are not profitable. They should be given experimental work along the line of industrial training supplemented by concrete cultural work in literature, civics, geography, and science, such as adapts them for the duties of citizenship and social life. We may tentatively suggest that two years of such work would put these children in the position of making an intelligent choice of a vocational school in which to complete their education.

At the beginning of the seventh school year those whose mental traits make it desirable might enter schools where the older type of secondary work is prominent. But we might expect that continually new revelations will be made in regard to the talents of such pupils, and that little by little those who are unable to do the work that leads to the higher professions will be selected out to enter vocational schools that prepare primarily for intermediate positions in industry, commerce, the civil service, etc.

QUESTIONS FOR DISCUSSION AND EXAMINATION

1. A central difference between the "social-efficiency" progressives and such "developmental-democracy" progressives as John Dewey was the way in which they conceived the notion of progressive education. Discuss that difference, and evaluate the degree to which one or the other concept, in your view, was a better response to the needs of American society in the decades following the turn of the century.
2. It seems that both the developmental-democracy and the social-efficiency approaches to progressive education abandoned the classical curriculum of the 19th century, in which the same academic subjects had been taught to all students, regardless of their economic or ethnic backgrounds. What argument might be made in favor of keeping that traditional approach, and how would you evaluate that argument? Take into account the major social changes occurring at the turn of the century.
3. In what respects did various strands of the "new psychology" emerging in the progressive era provide support for innovations in schooling, including differential curricula and extracurricular activities? Do you think these innovations were adequately justified by these new interpretations in psychology? Defend your position.
4. Charles Eliot and other social-efficiency liberals believed that they were serving the interests of democracy with their vision of progressive education. Explain their point of view according to their conception of democracy. Next, evaluate their educational and political points of view by using your definition of the educational requirements of democracy.
5. This chapter appears to be heavily biased against vocational education in favor of a more "academic" education for all young people. What justification does the chapter provide for its criticism of vocational education, and do you think this justification is adequate, given the historical circumstances of the progressive era? Defend your position.

NOTES

1. Abraham Flexner and Frank Bachman, *The Gary Schools: A General Account* (New York: General Education Board, 1919).
2. Ibid, p. 17.
3. Leonard Dinnerstein and David M. Reimers, *Ethnic Americans: A History of Immigration,* 3rd ed. (New York: Harper and Row, 1988), p. 54.
4. Paul C. Violas, *The Training of the Urban Working Class* (Chicago: Rand McNally, 1978), p. 2; for example, see Lincoln Steffens, *The Shame of the Cities* (New York: 1904). Also, for an introductory overview, see Bruce M. Stave, ed., *Urban Bosses, Machines, and Progressive Reformers* (Lexington, MA: D. C. Heath, 1972).
5. Barbara Kaye Greenleaf, *American Fever: The Story of American Immigration* (New York: Four Winds Press, 1970), p. 163.
6. Dinnerstein and Reimers, pp. 64–65.
7. From the sonnet by Emma Lazarus that appears on the Statue of Liberty.
8. Dinnerstein and Reimers, p. 71.
9. Ibid, p. 74.
10. Clarence J. Karier, "Testing for Order and Control in the Corporate Liberal State," in Clarence J. Karier, Paul C. Violas, and Joel Spring, *Roots of Crisis* (Chicago, Rand McNally, 1973), pp. 112–13. See also in that volume, Paul C. Violas, "Progressive Social Philosophy: Charles Horton Cooley and Edward Alsworth Ross," pp. 40–65.
11. Dinnerstein and Reimers, p. 76.
12. Ibid, pp. 76–77.
13. Ibid, pp. 50–51; James R. Barrett, *Work and Community in the Jungle* (Urbana: University of Illinois Press, 1987), p. 56; David Brody, "The American Worker in the Progressive Age," in *The Worker in Industrial America: Essays on the Twentieth Century Struggle* (London: Oxford University Press, 1980), p. 15.
14. Joseph G. Raybeck, *A History of American Labor* (New York: Free Press, 1966), p. 52.
15. Robert Reich, *The Next American Frontier* (New York: New York Times Books, 1983), pp. 26–27.
16. Ibid, p. 37.
17. Brody, "The American Worker in the Progressive Age," pp. 11–12.
18. Harry Braverman, *Labor and Monopoly Capital* (New York: Monthly Review Press, 1974), pp. 113, 118.
19. Ibid, p. 106.
20. Ibid, p. 94.
21. Alice Kessler-Harris, *Out of Work: A History of Wage-Earning Women in the United States* (New York: Oxford University Press, 1982).
22. Ibid.
23. Alice Kessler-Harris, "Where Are the Organized Women Workers?" in Linda K. Kerber and Jane De Hart Mathews, eds. *Women's America: Refocusing the Past* (New York: Oxford University Press, 1982) pp. 230–31.
24. Ibid.
25. Raybeck, *A History of American Labor,* pp. 3–53.
26. Ibid, p. 52.

27. Ibid, p. 49.
28. Brody, p. 6.
29. Leon Litwack, *The American Labor Movement* (New York: Simon and Schuster, 1962), p. 10.
30. Brody, pp. 6–7.
31. Reich, *The Next American Frontier,* p. 64.
32. Ibid, p. 30.
33. Ibid, p. 67.
34. Quoted in Jeremy Brecher, *Strike!* (Boston: South End Press, 1977), p. 29.
35. Brecher, p. 28.
36. Raybeck, pp. 167–68.
37. Brecher, pp. 55–63.
38. Norman Pollack, *The Populist Response to Industrial America* (Cambridge, MA: Harvard University Press, 1962), pp. 11–12.
39. Ibid, p. 18.
40. All three quotes, ibid, pp. 43–44.
41. Ibid, especially chaps. 5 and 6.
42. The material in this section is based largely on James Weinstein, *The Decline of Socialism in America* (New York: Monthly Review Press, 1967).
43. Gabriel Kolko, *The Triumph of Conservatism* (New York: The Free Press, 1963).
44. Ibid., p. 59ff.
45. Edward A. Krug, *The Shaping of the American High School: 1880–1929* (Madison: University of Wisconsin Press, 1969), pp. 266–67. Lawrence A. Cremin, *The Transformation of the School* (New York: Vintage Books), p. 127.
46. Robert Wiebe, *The Search for Order* (New York: Hill and Wang, 1967).
47. See, for example, Bruce M. Stave, *Urban Bosses, Machines, and Progressive Reformers* (Lexington, MA: D. C. Heath, 1972).
48. Ibid, pp. 11–14.
49. Ibid, p. xvii.
50. Quoted in ibid, pp. 127–129.
51. *Illinois Stage Journal Register,* July 30, 1986, p. 1.
52. Raymond E. Callahan, *Education and the Cult of Efficiency* (Chicago: University of Chicago Press, 1962), p. 43.
53. See, for example, David Tyack, *The One Best System* (Cambridge, MA: Harvard University Press, 1974); and David Tyack "City Schools: Centralization of Control at the Turn of the Century," in Jerome Karabel and A. H. Halsey, eds., *Power and Ideology in Education* (New York: Oxford University Press, 1977).
54. John Dewey, *Reconstruction in Philosophy* (Boston: Beacon Press, 1984); William James, *The Meaning of Truth* (Cambridge Massachusetts: Harvard University Press, 1975). See also R. J. Wilson, *Darwin and the American Intellectual* (Homewood, Ill: Dorsey Press, 1967).
55. John Dewey, *The Public and Its Problems* (Chicago: Swallow Press, 1929).
56. Paul C. Violas, "Progressive Social Philosophy: Charles Horton Cooley and Edward Alsworth Ross."
57. Clarence J. Karier, "Psychological Conceptions of Man and Society," in Karier, *The Individual, Society, and Education* (Urbana: University of Illinois Press, 1986), pp. 150–83.
58. Quoted in ibid, p. 174.
59. Patricia Albjerg Graham, *Progressive Education: From Arcady to Academe* (New York: Teachers College Press, 1967), p. 8.
60. Ibid, p. 2.
61. David Nasaw, *Schooled to Order* (Oxford: Oxford University Press, 1979).
62. Charles W. Eliot, "Equality of Educational Opportunity," in Marvin Lazerson and W. Norton Grubb, eds., *American Education and Vocationalism* (New York: Teachers College Press, 1974), p. 137. Originally published in 1908 by the National Society for the Promotion of Industrial Education, Bulletin No. 5.
63. Dewey, *Reconstruction in Philosophy,* p. 186. For a very recent, comprehensive intellectual biography of Dewey that supports this interpretation of his democratic theory, see Robert Westbrook, *John Dewey and American Democracy,* (Ithaca: Cornell University Press, 1991). For a more critical treatment of Dewey's notion of democracy, see Clarence J. Karier, "Liberalism and the Quest for Orderly Change," *History of Education Quarterly* 12 (Spring 1972), pp. 57–80.
64. John Dewey, *The Child and the Curriculum/The School and Society* (Chicago: University of Chicago Press, 1968). Originally published as separate volumes by the University of Chicago Press in 1902 and 1900, respectively.
65. John Dewey, *Democracy and Education* (New York: Macmillan, 1916), pp. 105–16.
66. John Dewey, "Education and Social Change," *The Social Frontier,* 3, No. 26 (May 1937), pp. 235–38.
67. John Dewey, *The School and Society.*
68. John Dewey, *Experience and Education* (New York: Macmillan 1938), pp. 88–89.
69. Stephen Preskill, "Educating for Democracy: Charles W. Eliot and the Differentiated Curriculum," *Educational Theory* 39, No. 4 (Fall 1989), pp. 353–54.
70. Ibid, p. 352.
71. Ibid, p. 353.
72. Ibid, pp. 354–55.

73. Charles W. Eliot, "The Function of Education in a Democratic Society," *Educational Reform* (New York: The Century Co., 1898), pp. 401–18.
74. Violas, *The Training of the Urban Working Class*, p. 23.
75. Ellwood P. Cubberley, *Public Education in the United States: A Study and Interpretation of American Educational History* (New York: Houghton Mifflin, 1919), p. 490.
76. Preskill, "Educating for Democracy," p. 356.
77. Ibid.
78. Quoted in Samuel Bowles and Herbert Gintis, *Schooling in Capitalist America* (New York: Basic Books, 1976), p. 199.
79. John L. Rury, "Vocationalism for Home and Work: Women's Education in the United States, 1880–1930," in B. Edward McClellan and William J. Reese, eds. *The Social History of American Education* (Urbana: University of Illinois Press, 1988), p. 250. Interestingly, in the 1980s and 1990s, coeducation has been questioned again, but for different reasons. It is argued by some that girls are disadvantaged in classes with boys, who receive disproportionate attention and who are socialized to be more confident and aggressive than girls in group settings.
80. *Course of Study 1910–1911* (Beaumont, TX: Beaumont Public Schools, 1910), p. 25.
81. J. F. Bobbitt, *The San Antonio Public School System: A Survey Conducted by J. F. Bobbitt* (San Antonio: San Antonio School Board, 1915), p. 20.
82. Robert S. Lynd and Helen Merrell Lynd, *Middletown* (New York: Harcourt, Brace Jovanovich, 1929), p. 194.
83. *Course of Study* (Lewiston, ID: Board of Education of Lewiston, 1914), p. 91.
84. *Yearbook of the Deerfield-Shields High School, 1912–1913* (Highland Park, IL: Highland Park Board of Education, 1912), p. 37.
85. Rena L. Vassar, *Social History of American Education, Vol. 2: 1860–Present* (Chicago: Rand McNally, 1965), p. 101.
86. Bowles and Gintis, *Schooling in Capitalist America*, p. 191.
87. Charles W. Eliot, "Equality of Educational Opportunity," in Lazerson and Grubb, eds., *American Education and Vocationalism*, p. 137.
88. Eliot, "The Function of Education in a Democratic Society."
89. Cubberley, *Public Education in the United States*, pp. 148, 151–52.
90. Clarence J. Karier, "Testing for Order and Control in the Corporate State," *Educational Theory* 11 (Spring 1971), pp. 159–80.

CHAPTER 5

Diversity And Equity: Schooling, Girls, and Women

Students may justifiably ask why it is necessary to devote a separate chapter of this text to the education of women. Shouldn't the history of educational thought and the evolution of schooling be examined in a unified, gender-free treatment? Until recently this was, in fact, the manner in which educational history was usually examined. Such examinations, however, ignore an important reality: namely, that the education of females in our culture, as in many cultures, has been importantly different, both in purpose and content, from the education of males. General statements about the history of education, then, may be misleading if they do not specifically attend to the experiences of girls as well as boys, women as well as men. While we have pointed out the significance of gender in specific instances in each chapter thus far, a more comprehensive treatment is needed to provide context for those instances. This chapter will provide an overview of the history of women's education to delineate the aspirations, limitations, and opportunities which American society held for one-half of its population through the first part of this century. These gender themes will be revisited repeatedly in Part 2 of the text, but this is the only chapter to attempt a comprehensive overview of the evolution of the education of girls and women in the United States.

Writing in the last decade of the 18th century, the Englishwoman Mary Wollstonecraft exposed her era's view of female education in observations such as the following:

> How grossly do they insult us who thus advise us to render ourselves gentile, domestic brutes! For instance, the winning softness so warmly, and frequently, recommended, that governs by obeying. . . . [A]ll writers who have written on the subject of female education and manners. . . have contributed to render women more artificial, weak characters, than they would otherwise have been, more useless members of society. . . . [M]y objection extends to the whole purport of those books, which tend, in my opinion, to degrade one half of the human species, and render women pleasing at the expense of every solid virtue.[1]

Unfortunately, Wollstonecraft's assessment remained true for over 100 years. During this period the primary goal of female education was to render women pleasing as wives and effective as mothers. The underlying assumptions behind this view were that women were fundamentally different from and inferior to men and consequently posed a danger to men. This assumption seems to have been tacitly accepted, apart from exceptions like Wollstonecraft, by both female and male proponents of women's education. Perhaps this is not as surprising as one might think. Even today, evidence of belief in fundamental differences between the sexes and the idea of inherent inferiority of women can be found in many dimensions of our culture, as we shall see.

IDEOLOGICAL ORIGINS IN EARLY CHRISTIANITY

In a country founded by religious dissenters, it is not surprising to find origins of basic ideological commitments in religious traditions. We have seen, for example, how such dimensions of classical liberalism as rationality and virtue were ascribed differently to men and to women by liberals in Jefferson's era. This bias had roots in Christianity.

The point of this discussion is *not* that institutional Christianity has historically justified the subordination of women more than other religions have. Nor do we suggest that Christianity is the primary cause of social and political biases against women. Rather, we are noticing that religious values contribute importantly to social ideology—and that the founding religious values and institutions of European America were Christian.

The idea of women's rational inferiority to men and their consequent need for a less rigorous education was supported by the Christian belief that Eve, who was presumed to be more sensual and less rational than Adam, was chosen for seduction by the serpent.

Early in the Christian era the tone for gender discussion was set by the apostle Paul in his instructions to Timothy regarding church organization. Paul said, "Let a woman learn in silence with all submission. For I do not allow a woman to teach, or go to exercise authority over men; but she is to keep quiet. For Adam was formed first, then Eve. And Adam was not deceived, but the woman was deceived and was in sin. Yet women will be saved by childbearing, if they continue in faith and love and holiness with modesty."[2] In this epistle Paul asserted the superiority of male over female because of Adam's prior creation and Eve's submission to the temptations of the serpent. It would take another four centuries before the full implications of Paul's assertion would become central to Christian gender considerations.

One of the most significant developments in western civilization's attitude toward gender occurred in the first part of the fifth century A.D. At that time, against the vigorous opposition of Pelagius and his followers, Augustine, Bishop of Hippo, successfully overturned previous Christian interpretations of Genesis 3.[3] Contrary to over four centuries of Christian teaching, Augustine held that the story of the Fall meant that the sin of Adam was transmitted from the first parents through sexual reproduction to all future humans, and because of that "original sin," subsequent humanity was incapable of exercising free will. This interpretation placed a heavy burden on Eve in particular and women in general. She was, in this tradition, the first one to succumb to the temptations of the serpent. Being created out of Adam's body, Eve was purportedly more prone to bodily or sexual passion and thus easier to seduce. In Augustine's words, the serpent had deceitful conversation with the woman—no doubt starting with the inferior of the human pair so as to arrive at the whole by stages, supposing that the man would not be so easily gullible.[4] Moreover, in this interpretation it was Eve who then persuaded Adam to join in her sin and thus condemned all future generations of humans. Historian Elaine Pagels succinctly summarizes the gender ramifications of Augustine's interpretation of Genesis 3:

> Although originally created equal to man in regard to her rational soul, woman's formation from Adam's rib established her as the "weaker part of the human couple." Being closely connected with bodily passion, woman, although created to be man's helper, became his temptress and led him into disaster. The Genesis account describes the result: God himself reinforced the husband's authority over his wife, placing divine sanction upon the social, legal, and economic machinery of male domination.[5]

Augustine's division of humankind into two inherently different kinds of beings contained all the necessary components for religiously justifying the subjugation of women and their inferior education for the next 15 centuries. Women were seen as complementary to, but different from, men. Properly fitted with men, women were the completing portion of humanity. They were seen as passionate and nurturing, while men were seen as rational and reserved. Women were prone to mercy, men to justice. Women were fitted for the domicile, men for work and public life. Men were to govern, women to obey. Because of their deficiency in rational capacity and their unstable emotional nature, women were to be subject to the more rational nature of their fathers, and later, their husbands.

GENDER AND EDUCATION IN COLONIAL AMERICA

It was this Augustinian legacy which formed the consciousness and guided the gender behavior of most colonial and 19th-century Americans.[6] At their best, white Americans were concerned with educating their sons to become productive workers, effective political agents, and independent rational actors. However, when they thought of education for their daughters, the concern was to prepare them as wives and mothers, not as independent, rational beings. As long as the home remained the primary economic unit in society, most of the girl's education could be obtained there, emulating her mother and obeying her father.

As described in Chapter 2, Americans began to develop schools for their sons early in the colonial era. Public elementary schools became common in New England, and a few colleges, such as Harvard, William and Mary, Yale, and Kings, were scattered among the colonies. Women were not admitted to the colleges and were only grudgingly admitted to the public elementary schools about the time of the Revolution. Most early school committees believed that the admission of girls to the common schools was "inconsistent with the design" of these schools.[7] Most girls who learned to read did so at home. Of course, such home schooling greatly disadvantaged some girls whose parents were illiterate or unwilling to teach them to read and write.

Early colonial school records are both scanty and obscure regarding the education of girls. Two historians, after searching the records of nearly 200 New England towns, could find only seven which had definitely voted to allow girls to attend the common schools before the 1770s.[8] Among the earliest were Dorchester, Massachusetts (1639), Hampton, New Hampshire (1649), Ipswich, Massachusetts (1669), and Wallingford, Connecticut (1678). Only in the last two towns is there any evidence that girls actually attended these schools before the revolutionary era. Generally, when girls were given permission to attend the common school, they were only allowed to do so when boys were absent. For example, London, Connecticut, allowed girls to receive instruction from 5:00 to 7:00 A.M. during the summer of 1774.[9] Two years later the town of Medford, Massachusetts, permitted girls to receive instruction from the schoolmaster two hours a day after the boys were dismissed. Later, in 1787, the Medford girls were admitted for instruction for one hour each morning and afternoon when the boys were not in attendance. Three years later the girls received instruction during the three summer months. Similar arrangements were common in other New England towns, such as Newburyport, Essex, and Salem, during the late colonial era. Not until 1834, two years before Horace Mann began his common schooling campaign in Massachusetts, were Medford boys and girls allowed to attend the common school together during the entire school year.[10]

In 1900 George Martin succinctly summarized the history of girls' education in the American colonies and the new nation:

During the Colonial era, most girls received their education in their homes either from literate parents or from private tutors. Such home education was limited to families where the parents could either afford tutors or were literate enough to do the job themselves.

> First, during the first one hundred and fifty years of colonial history girls did not attend the public schools, except in some of the smaller towns, and there only for a short time; second, about the time of the Revolution, the subject of the education of girls was widely agitated; third, against much opposition the experiment of sending girls to the master's school for a few hours in a day during a part of the year, but never in the same rooms or at the same times with the boys; fourth, this provision extended only to the English schools, no instruction being provided in Latin or even in the higher English branches; fifth, it was not until the present century [i.e., the nineteenth] was far advanced that girls and boys shared alike the advantages of the higher public schools.[11]

Martin's rather dismal picture of early female education has not been much improved by subsequent historical investigations. With rare exceptions girls were barred from public schooling from the 1630s to the eve of the Revolution. The exceptions occurred in religious communities that were not dominated by the Augustinian tradition. For example, the Quakers and Moravians, principally in Pennsylvania and the Carolinas, did provide elementary education for girls.[12] This 150-year exclusion of girls from American public schools was not the result of neglect or oversight, but rather the result of two factors. First, it was not considered necessary to educate girls in an agrarian and frontier society when only few people required education. Just as important, however, was the common belief that females were basically unsuited for intellectual activities. On April 13, 1645, John Winthrop, the governor of Massachusetts Bay Colony, wrote the following entry in his journal:

> Mr. Hopkins, the governor of Hartford upon Connecticut, came to Boston, and brought his wife with him (a godly young woman, and of special parts), who was fallen into a sad infirmity which had been growing upon her divers years, by occasion of her giving herself wholly to reading and writing, and had written many books. Her husband, being very loving and tender of her, was loath to grieve her; but he saw his error, when it was too late. For if she had attended her household affairs, and such things as belong to women, and not gone out of her way and calling to meddle in such things as are proper for men, whose minds are stronger, etc., she had kept her wits, and might have improved them usefully and honorably in the place God had set her.[13]

The historical record tells us that Governor Winthrop's view of women's appropriate place was clearly that of the majority. Nevertheless, in the face of considerable odds, some women were able to develop their intellectual interest during this 150-year era. The poetess Anne Bradstreet was taught by her father, Governor Dudley. Mercy Warren was tutored along with her brother by Rev. Jonathan Russell. Most remarkable of all, perhaps, was Phillis Wheatley, an African-American slave girl in Boston, who during the 1760s taught herself to read English and Latin and write poetry. Other colonial women of extraordinary intellectual attainment included Anne Hutchinson, Elizabeth Ferguson, Debora Logan, Susanna Wright, Hanna Means, and Mrs. Stockton.[14] For most colonial women, however, there was no formal education, only the hope of rudimentary literacy acquired in the home from a literate and willing parent. Consequently, most colonial women remained illiterate.

Private Schools

Those colonial women who did manage to acquire an education were overwhelmingly from affluent homes. Many of them were educated by tutors in the home. Others attended private female seminaries and academies. These private secondary institutions began to develop in the second quarter of the 18th century. Most were boarding schools. The Ursuline Convent for girls, established in New Orleans in 1727, was perhaps the earliest. Soon after, in 1742, the Bethlehem Female Seminary began educating girls in Pennsylvania. During the first half of the 19th century a large number of these female seminaries came into existence; the most respected were in Philadelphia, Pennsylvania; Salem, Massachusetts; Troy, New York; and Endicott Mills, New York.[15] Unfortunately, many of these female institutions were more interested in fitting girls for marriage than developing their minds. Much of the training focused on so-called polite accomplishments, such as dancing, music, drawing, and needlework.[16]

The social skills that dominated the formal education of colonial women flowed logically from contemporary opinion. Most colonial Americans believed that the only appropriate goal for a woman was matrimony. Typical of this attitude was the following poem, which appeared in 1805 in the *North Carolina Journal:*

> When first the nymph with in her breast
> Perceives the subtle flame,
> She feels a something break her rest,
> Yet knows not whence it came,
> A husband 'tis she wants.[17]

Jane Austen's *Pride and Prejudice* provides a most depressing account of the probable state of mind of many young women in this description of Charlotte Lucas just after she announced her engagement to Mr. Collins:

> The whole family . . . were properly overjoyed on the occasion. . . . [Her brothers] were relieved from their apprehension of Charlotte's dying an old maid. . . . Mr. Collins, to be sure, was neither amiable nor agreeable; his society was irksome and his attachment to her must be imaginary. But still he would be a husband. Without thinking highly of men or of matrimony, marriage had always been her object: it was the only honorable provision for well educated young women of small fortune, and, however uncertain of giving happiness, must be a pleasant preservation from want. This preservation she had now obtained; and at the age of twenty-seven, without ever having been handsome, she felt the good luck of it.[18]

If marriage was the approved goal for girls, it was understandable, perhaps, that a male-dominated society would try to fit women into the roles demanded by men. In early America, "a learned wife" was not sought after. A colonial poem often recommended to young women put this very clearly:

One did commend to me a wife both fair and young
That had French, Spanish, and Italian tongue.
I thanked him kindly and told him I loved none such,
For I thought one tongue for a wife too much,
What! love ye not the learned?
Yes, as my life,
A learned scholar, but not a learned wife.[19]

An interesting feature of this poem is its evidence of the belief that women were quite capable of intellectual development, but that it was not a feature men desired in them.

The Revolution and the Cult of Domesticity

Although the Revolution changed much in American society, it did not challenge most prevailing assumptions about the education of women. But independence brought considerable discussion about how a new nation could be forged, and this discussion would eventually bring about changes for the education of girls. As we saw in Chapter 2, the idea of using public schooling for building the nation was a major new concern.[20] Analysis of the requisite education for boys centered on (1) their future role as republican citizens, especially as informed voters, and (2) their role as economic agents, especially as producers. These considerations were not applied in the same way to girls, whose productive role would be limited to the family. It was their future role as wives and mothers which after the Revolution focused the discussion of appropriate female education. This nurturing role was to dominate thinking about girls' education until well into the 20th century.

By the 1820s many articles devoted to the "female role" appeared in educational journals, such as the *Annals of Education,* the *Common School Journal,* and the *American Journal of Education.* Additionally, there appeared numerous books, such as Coxe's *Claims of the Country on American Females,* Butler's *The American Lady,* and Todd's *The Daughter at School.* These authors argued that women's first responsibility was to provide for the comfort and solace of husbands, who faced an increasingly competitive and inhospitable economic world. Beyond this, they should attempt to improve the manners and morals of society by teaching and by example, and guide the development of the future generation during the early years of childhood.[21] Twentieth-century historians would name this shift in the understanding of the female role the "cult of domesticity."[22] It would provide a rationale for the formal education of increasing numbers of girls and young women of the new nation, rendering obsolete the colonial view that girls were simply not in need of schooling.

This cult of domesticity was first aimed at middle- and upper-class women, but in time its effects were felt in all but the lowest social classes. It was a double-edged sword. By considering homemaking and nurturing-teaching roles to be exclusively female, it encouraged the view that women should be educated. However, because of women's supposedly nurturing nature and the limits within which this nature was to be exercised, the education offered women was confined to the nurturing roles of wife, early educator, and moral exemplar.[23] It is fair to conclude that 19th-century Americans had not advanced much beyond Martin Luther's 16th-century admonition, "The world has need of educated men and women to the end that men may govern the country properly and women may bring up their children, care for their domestics, and direct the affairs of their households."[24]

Growing out of the combined cultural influences of sexist religious views, increasing capitalism, and the planning for nationhood, the cult of domesticity had a profound effect on female education. If women were to form morals and manners and provide initial education for children, they required some formal education. Consequently, most communities in the northeast slowly began admitting girls to the common schools during the first quarter of the 19th century. The effect of this increased educational opportunity can be seen in the greatly increased female literacy during this era.[25] As access to elementary schooling gradually became secured, proponents of female education then turned to higher education.

During the 19th century higher education was less well defined than it is presently. Any schooling beyond the common school was considered higher. The "ladder" system, with secondary schools serving as a prerequisite for collegiate training, was not established until late in the

The "Cult of Domesticity" dominated female education from the time of the revolution until well into the 20th century. It maintained that a woman's proper social role revolved around the home where she was to be (1) a proper wife (2) a nurturing mother and teacher of the young and (3) a moral exemplar to all. Recognition of the need for some formal education in order to carry out these responsibilities led to the establishment of many female academies and seminaries in the late 18th, 19th and 20th centuries.

century. Academies, seminaries, normal schools, the new public high schools, as well as colleges all offered what was considered higher education, and often they were seen as competing institutions. Women's access to these institutions, and the curricula women were to be afforded, constituted the major controversies concerning female education during the 19th century.

COMPETING IDEOLOGICAL PERSPECTIVES IN THE NINETEENTH CENTURY

Martha Maclear has shown that "three distinct currents of thought regarding the education of girls" emerged in the first half of the 19th century. The first current was that of the right wing, or conservatives, who wanted to maintain the status quo. The center, or liberals, while accepting the existing definitions of the appropriate female role, attempted to interpret those definitions in ways that would improve educational opportunities for women. Finally, radical, or left-wing, groups demanded both a new, expanded definition of female roles and the new education appropriate to the expanded opportunities they envisioned for women.[26] Both the conservative and liberal positions stood squarely within classical liberal ideology, with the liberals emphasizing progress through change and the conservatives emphasizing traditional notions of female virtue. The radical position, however, challenged both streams of classical liberal thinking on the education of women and their role in society. Yet it, too, relied on such classical liberal constructs as natural law, rationality, and freedom in opposing the ideological mainstream.

The Conservative and Liberal Positions

The conservative position was typified by William Johnson, Esq., in an 1845 edition of the *Literary Emporium.* He offered the timeworn male-centric advice: "Women's chief ambition is gratified by a single conquest: the scope of her happiness and usefulness is circumscribed by the domestic and social circle. Beyond this, her influence is only felt by its moral reflection on the hearts and lives of mankind. Nor is this the result of any system of education—it is a distinguishing circumstance in her existence—one which God never intended to be otherwise."[27]

The liberals similarly held that woman's destined role was exclusively as wife, mother, teacher of the young, and moral exemplar. Nevertheless, they argued that these roles required more and better education than was currently available for girls. No doubt America's growing trend toward a liberal Protestantism, exemplified by the transcendentalism of Emerson and the theology of Bushnell, made their arguments more palatable. This liberalizing trend deemphasized original sin and the evil side of human nature, lessening, in turn, the special sin of Eve and its resulting stain on all women. Leaders of the liberal wing included Benjamin Rush, Emma Willard, Horace Mann, Catherine Beecher, and Mary Lyon.[28]

Benjamin Rush provided the prototype program for female education in his "Thoughts on Female Education" at the beginning of the 19th century. He contended that women should be the stewards of their husband's wealth, homemakers, and child care givers. To fulfill these duties adequately, Rush proposed an education which included the English language, handwriting, arithmetic, bookkeeping, beginning astronomy, chemistry, natural philosophy, dancing, Christian religion, geography, and history. The last two subjects he recommended so "she might become an agreeable companion to a sensible man." Rush concluded his essay with the admonition to men that, "a weak and ignorant woman will always be governed with the greatest difficulty."[29]

Horace Mann, who championed women's higher education in normal schools, announced the limitations which the liberals would project for women in an 1838 article in the *Common School Journal.* In advocating women's special role in the "peaceful ministry" of teachers of the young, he said:

> And why should women, lured by false ambition to shine in courts or to mingle in the clashing tumult of men, ever disdain this sacred and peaceful ministry? Why, renouncing this serene and blessed sphere of duty, should she ever lift up her voice in the thronged marketplace of society, haggling and huckstering to barter away that divine and acknowledged superiority *in sentiment* which belongs to her own sex, to exhort confessions from the other of a mere equality *in reason?* Why, in self-abasement, should she ever strive to put off the sublime affections and the ever-bearing beauty of a seraph, that she may clothe a coarser, though it should be a stronger spirit, in the stalwart limbs and highness of a giant? . . . If the intellect of women, like that of a man, has the sharpness and the penetration of steel or iron, it must also be as cold and hard. No! but to breathe pure and exalted sentiments into young and tender hearts . . . to take the censers which Heaven gives and kindle the incense which Heaven loves . . . this is her high and holy mission.[30]

It was not only men like Rush and Mann who promoted women's education in order to make them more effective in their "female" roles. Many liberal women shared the prevailing view of their social role and resulting education. During the 1830s the noted educator Mrs. Phillips similarly noted, "To females geology is chiefly important, by its effect in enlarging their sphere of thought, rendering them more interesting as companions to men of science, and better capable of instructing the young."[31] Moreover, the female leaders of the liberals accepted the traditional role for women. Emma Willard's memorandum to Governor Clinton of New York, requesting that the state provide normal schools for women, argued for women's nurturing role on the basis of natural law: "That nature designed our sex for the care of children, she has made manifest, by mental as well as physical indications." Moreover, Willard concluded, not only would women teach better than men, but "they could afford to do it cheaper, and those men who would otherwise be engaged in this employment, might be at liberty to add to the wealth of the nation, by any of those thousand occupations, from which women are necessarily debarred."[32] Catherine Beecher, whose career as a proponent of women's education spanned most of the 19th century said, "Heaven had appointed one sex superior and to the other the subordinate station."[33] And throughout her career she maintained that all education for women must center on some phase of domestic training or teaching.

Emma Hart Willard (1787–1870) wrote a classic appeal on women's education to the public and the New York State legislature in 1819, then opened the academically ambitious Troy Female Seminary in 1821.

Frederick Douglas (1817–1895), born a slave in Maryland, became an author, orator, U.S. Minister to Haiti, abolitionist and defender of women's rights.

It might be argued that the liberals developed a pragmatic program that was intended to achieve all that was possible within the constraints of popular prejudice. And they did achieve notable advances for women's education during the century. Nevertheless, their writings seem to indicate an acceptance of the common assumptions regarding the inherent and fundamental division of the sexes which ultimately restricts the life possibilities for women. The belief that national, ethnic, cultural, economic, racial, or gender groups possess some inherent social, emotional, moral, or intellectual characteristic(s) has been endemic in American history. It is based on unwarranted and malevolent assumptions. Almost universally this belief has been used to justify political, economic, or educational exclusion, which in turn fosters subordination and repression. Such assumptions continue to hamper women's full development as equals rather than as subordinates to men.

The Radical Position

The idea that a political or ideological position is "radical" stems from that word's meaning "of or pertaining to the root." Radical thinking seeks to get to the root of a problem, and radical solutions thus require fundamental changes. While the liberals and the conservatives described by Maclear held similar views of women's role as wife, mother, teacher of the young, and moral exemplar, the radicals demanded a dramatically new vision of women's place in society: they demanded gender equality. The earliest expressions of these views were by such women as Frances Wright, Sarah M. Grimke, Margaret Fuller, and Ernestine Rose.[34] Grimke, writing in 1837, set the tone for the radical response to conservatives and liberals by constructing a different interpretation of the story of Adam and Eve:

> Adam's ready acquiescence with his wife's proposal, does not savor much of that superiority in *strength of mind* which is arrogated by man. . . . I ask no favors for my sex. I surrender not our claim to equality. All I ask of our brethren is, that they take their feet from off our necks and permit us to stand upright on that ground which God designed us to occupy. . . . All history attests that man has subjected woman to his will, used her as a means to promote his selfish gratification, to minister to his sensual pleasures, to be instrumental in promoting his comfort; but never has he desired to elevate her to that rank she was created to fill. He has done all he could to debase and enslave her mind; and now he looks triumphantly on the ruin he has wrought, and says, the being he has thus deeply injured is his inferior.[35]

The symbolic beginning of the radical women's movement can be located later, at the Seneca Falls Women's Rights Convention of 1848. As Gertrude Martin has shown, this was more than simply a demand for the vote; it envisioned the opening of higher education on an equal basis to women and subsequent equality in all occupations.[36] The radicals were led by Susan B. Anthony, Elizabeth Cady Stanton, Elizabeth and Emily Blackwell, Sojourner Truth, Victoria Woodhull, Matthew Vassar, and Wendell Phillips. They formed a public resistance, which continues in various forms to the present, against male privilege and dominance in such institutions as the ballot box, the professions, and collegiate education. The convention's Declaration of Sentiments and Resolutions in the second Primary Source Reading at the end of this chapter illustrates the thinking of the leadership of the Seneca Falls convention, particularly its conscious appeal to the classical liberal ideals of rationality, natural law, and freedom.

IDEOLOGY AND LIFE: EMMA WILLARD

It may be useful to move from the more general level of ideological analysis to the more specific level of biography. A brief examination of the life and work of Emma Willard may help us better understand 19th century conservative, liberal, and radical views regarding women. This biographical examination may also show that historical judgment is neither easy nor unambiguous. A cursory analysis of the ideological positions may suggest that the liberal position of Emma Willard was detrimental to women's education and their position in society. A closer examination, however, suggests that a more complex judgment is needed.

Emma Willard was born in 1787 in Berlin, Connecticut.[37] Her father, Samuel Hart, had been a Captain in the Revolutionary army. At the evening circle around the fireplace he shared with his family his great love for books, especially literature, history, political theory, and philosophy. As the 16th child, young Emma learned to participate in the evening discussions and acquired a lifelong love for learning. In many ways her early life was similar to her contemporary Horace Mann. Both were New Englanders and born to farm life. She, like Horace, also attended the district elementary school. When young Emma was 15, a new town academy opened at Worthington. She and her older sister Nancy entered it and studied for 2 years with Thomas Minter, a recent Yale graduate.[38]

Upon leaving the academy, Emma Hart began her teaching career. At age 17 she was employed to teach in Berlin's district summer school, and a year later in its winter session. This appointment to the winter session stands as strong testimony to the village's positive assessment of her teaching ability, for it was quite unusual for a woman to be allowed to teach during the winter session in district schools at this time. She soon had advanced from the village school to the Berlin Academy and from there to Westfield Academy and in 1807 to Middlebury. It was in Middlebury that she met Dr. John Willard, who had left medicine for politics. In 1809, although 28 years his junior, she married Dr. Willard and temporarily left teaching.

The next 4 years were important for Emma's intellectual development. She apparently spent considerable time studying her husband's medical books in an effort to become conversant with his medical interests. Lacking access to higher education institutions, it was common for 19th-century women intellectuals to educate themselves through the resources available to a father, brother, or husband. Emma Willard had the advantage of both a supportive father and husband. Additionally, Dr. Willard's nephew, John Willard, lived with them for a time while he attended Middlebury College. Emma and John spent considerable time discussing his college studies and she eagerly read his course texts. Without doubt, this exchange illuminated for Emma the world of learning from which she and nearly all other young women were excluded. The birth of her son, John Hart Willard, in 1810, introduced her also to the complexities of parenting. These activities would have lasting significance on her intellectual outlook.

A New Vision for Women's Education

By 1813 Dr. Willard's financial and political fortunes declined. In part to relieve her husband's financial woes, Emma returned to teaching, opening a boarding school for girls in their home. The following 5 years were instrumental in developing her educational ideas. Her school offered instruction more advanced than any then available in the United States for girls. In addition to the usual "refinements" of manners, she taught mathematics, geography, science, history, and languages. Because neighboring Middlebury College refused to allow her students to attend any of its courses, Emma was forced to teach all the courses in her school. This meant that she was not only required to train teachers but in some instances she needed to learn new subjects herself. This self-education in new subjects at an ever-increasing level of complexity became a hallmark of her teaching career. It reinforced her earlier belief that women were indeed capable of higher learning. Moreover, it led her to develop innovative teaching methods and materials. Soon her school had over 70 students, of which 40 were boarders.

It was during this time that Willard systematically began to collect her ideas on female education. The result was a thesis she titled "A Plan for Improving Female Education," which she eventually sent to Governor DeWitt Clinton of New York in 1818. She published it under the title "An Address to the Public: Particularly to the Members of the Legislature of New York, Proposing a Plan for Improving Female Education." The Plan quickly attracted much attention in the United States, although it stimulated little action. It even achieved international acclaim when the English educator, George Combe, published it in his *Phrenological Journal.*[39] Combe's phrenological theory would later be embraced by Horace Mann.

The primary purpose of the Plan was to convince the voters and legislators, i.e., males, to provide public funds for higher education of women. Toward this end Willard organized the Plan in four categories. The first deplored the existing state of female education. She pointed out that in most places opportunity for higher education did not exist for women. In the few places where it did, the schools were woefully inadequate. They were ill funded and therefore temporary institutions with insufficient physical facilities. Moreover these were "finishing" schools, which emphasized superficial social refinements and not intellectual attainments or sound moral qualities. Nowhere in the United States could young women receive an education even roughly equivalent to that offered in the abundant colleges for young men. Only when female schools received public funds could they be established on a permanent basis with resources to provide an adequate education.

The second aspect of Willard's Plan analyzed the principles that should regulate female education. Most importantly, she asserted: "Education should seek to bring its subjects to the perfection of their moral, intellectual and physical nature, that they may be of the greatest possible use to themselves and others. . . ."[40] A major error in existing female education, she argued, was that it sought to prepare females mainly to please men rather than to prepare them as humans. Willard quickly added, "I would not be understood to insinuate, that we are not, in particular situations, to yield to obedience to the other sex. Submission and obedience belong to every being in the universe, except the great Master of the whole. Nor is it a degrading peculiarity to our sex, to be under human authority. Whenever one class of human beings, derive from another the benefits of support and protection, they must pay its equivalent, obedience . . . Neither would I be understood to mean, that our sex should not seek to make themselves agreeable to the other. The errour complained of, is that of the taste of men, whatever it might happen to be has been made a standard for the formation of female character."[41] She went on to note that the education advocated for females was to be likened to that for males in its permanency and uniformity of operation, yet "adapted to the difference in character and duties" of females. To emphasize the difference between male and female higher education she made the distinction between male "colleges" and "female seminaries."

Thirdly, Willard outlined a "sketch of a female seminary." This seminary would be supported by public funds and include a building holding rooms for: student lodging, recitations, scientific apparatus, and a domestic department. It would provide instruction in four areas: religion and morals; literary (this included the usual collegiate intellectual subjects); domestic (probably the first call for home economics instruction in the United States); and ornamental (drawing, painting, penmanship, music, and grace of motion). This proposed instructional program was far superior to any then in existence for females in the United States.

The last section of the *Plan* was titled "Benefits of Female Seminaries." Willard rightly claimed that the proposed seminaries "would constitute a grade of public instruction superior to any yet known in the history of our sex."[42] The main benefits of this instruction would be felt in two areas: the common schools and the nation at large. The graduates of these seminaries would become teachers in the common schools where they would raise the level of instruction because of their specific training and Willard's belief "that nature designed for our sex the care of children." These seminary graduates "would be likely to teach children better than the other sex"; and, as we saw earlier, Willard had an economic argument. Not only could women teach at lower salaries than men, but men would increase productivity in male-dominated occupations because they would not be teaching.[43] Moreover, all seminary graduates would greatly lift the moral and cultural level of the nation and thus save it from the slide to barbarism and anarchy commonly predicted by its enemies. This national uplift would be accomplished, she believed, as these seminaries better suited their graduates to be mothers and wives of the nation's men. The female seminaries would regenerate the nation.

It is interesting how Emma Willard foreshadowed the arguments of Horace Mann for women teachers while representing views that 20th century historians later called the Cult of Domesticity, discussed earlier in this chapter. Women had a special role because of their supposed "natural" differences from men, in this domestic perspective. These differences included being more sensitive, empathetic, devoted to domestic duties and child rearing, and concerned with cultural affairs. These same qualities, which uniquely fitted women as teachers, wives, and mothers, according to her argument, "necessarily debarred" women from other occupations. While the exponents of the Cult of Domesticity mirrored many of Willard's ideas, they generally neglected to include her strong belief that women were equally capable with men to rationally understand academic subjects. This was a difference of considerable importance.

The Troy Female Seminary

After the positive reception of her Plan by Governor Clinton and the legislature, Willard was confident enough that the State of New York would fund her proposed seminary to move her school in 1819 from Middlebury, Vermont, to Waterford, New York. This confidence, however, was to prove misplaced. Repeatedly, the all-male legislature refused to appropriate funds for female seminaries. The Waterford school managed with precarious finances for 2 years. Then the city of Troy offered municipal backing for a female seminary. Willard accepted the offer and in 1821 relocated her school for the last time; it became the Troy Female Seminary.

For the next 17 years Willard continue to expand her experiment in female education in the relatively safe haven of the Troy Female Seminary.[44] The early years were greatly eased by the role of Dr. Willard, who acted as school doctor, financial director, and sympathetic supporter of his wife. His death in 1825 was not only a severe personal loss, but it added a considerable workload to the already overextended head mistress as she assumed the financial management of the growing institution.

Willard made significant curricular contributions to 19th-century education. This was a time when most people considered females incapable of serious academic study. Fashionable opinion considered algebra or history beyond the capacity of the female mind, and physiology probably dangerous to it. Respectable authorities believed that if such study did not cripple the weaker female mind, then certainly it would misshape it to an "unfeminine" mold. In the face of such attitudes, Willard broadened the curriculum at the Troy Female Seminary and was in the forefront of allowing "electives." The required subjects included the Bible, composition, elocution, drawing, and physical education. Among the electives were modern foreign languages (including French, German, Italian, and Spanish), Latin, astronomy, algebra, geometry, trigonometry, geography, history, literature, logic, physiology, and other natural sciences. Not only did she pioneer in adding these subjects to female instruction, but because she was self-taught in most of them, she understood the difficulties of comprehending each subject. This understanding was partially responsible for her innovative instructional methods. Far in advance of most of the 19th-century colleagues, she developed teaching techniques and learning materials that facilitated student involvement and critical analysis rather than rote memorization. While at Troy Seminary, Willard wrote five major geography and history textbooks.[45] The geography texts became especially popular and earned considerable royalties.[46] They were widely used in female seminaries and in secondary schools for males, as well.

The preparation of teachers at the Troy Seminary eventually became its most famous function. It occurred, however, almost accidentally. Early in the history of the Seminary, Willard received requests for admission from girls who could not afford the tuition or board. Her response was to provide for what she called "teacher scholars." These girls were provided tuition, board, and, in some cases, clothing. In return, they promised to repay the expense after they graduated and were employed as teachers. It was estimated that Willard loaned approximately $75,000 to students during her tenure at Troy.[47] Not all of the teachers from Troy had been teacher scholars, but this device provided many young women an avenue to an education and a profession. Willard was particularly proud of her role in teacher training: "I continued to educate and send forth teachers, until two hundred had gone from the Troy Seminary before one was educated in any public normal school in the United States." She called her school the nation's "first normal school".[48] Troy Female Seminary became so well-known for teacher training that Willard's signature on a letter of recommendation was often a guarantee of employment. It may have functioned as the first teacher certification in the country. Anne Firor Scott estimated that over 1,000 teachers may have been prepared at Troy Seminary by 1863.[49]

Willard's influence on these teachers did not cease once they left the Seminary. In 1837, the year Horace Mann assumed leadership of the Massachusetts schools, she organized the Emma Willard Association for the Mutual Improvement of Female Teachers. Its purpose was to retain contact through letters and publications with former students in the teaching profession. The communications contained suggestions on a wide range of topics from pedagogy and textbooks to healthy exercise and sound psychologic habits.[50] These suggestions seemed to reinforce the lessons Willard taught at the Seminary. In 1898 a group of Troy Seminary alumnae gathered testimony from former students. Over 3,500 of the 12,000 students who had spent time at the Seminary between its founding and 1871 responded. From these responses Professor Anne Firor Scott has constructed a convincing portrait of the influence of Willard on her students.[51] This portrait suggests that she provided them with a model of female independence fueled by intellectual competence and fiscal independence. Her students were expected to learn subjects previously thought to be "beyond" female comprehension. They were taught self-reliance, to prepare for self-support, and that the "women's sphere" included the professional work of teaching.

This brings us back to the questions at the beginning of this section: how do we evaluate the effect of Emma Willard on the history of women? She seemed to champion the ideal of a "women's sphere," which was to be separate from the male sphere. Her belief in the "special" qualities of women led her to argue for women's place as mothers and teachers, but these qualities "necessarily debarred" women from other occupations and roles. The patriarchal family and women's domestic role seemed very dear to her. She admonished her students for even secretly debating the politics of the 1828 election and never fully embraced the idea of suffrage for women.[52] All of this would seem to bode ill for improving women's position in society. Phillida Bunkle, without specific reference to Willard, has described this set of ideas as "a sexual ideology," which was an "antifeminist system of belief [that] dominated the perception of women in the nineteenth century."[53] And yet, there is more to say about Willard's beliefs and achievements.

Her Troy Female Seminary educated over 12,000 women and inspired over 200 schools to follow its example. Willard provided a role model for her students and others, exemplifying a self-confident woman who was a successful administrator, author of respected texts, skilled teacher, and independent thinker. Moreover, she cultivated those same qualities in her students. Professor Scott pointedly noted, "nowhere else in the country in the 1820s were young women told that they could learn any academic subject, including those hitherto reserved to men, and that they should prepare themselves for self-support and not seek marriage as an end in itself."[54] With this observation Scott has uncovered the most significant contribution of Emma Willard to the education of American women. No doubt, Willard did not inspire a "feminist" revolution, but her work provided an ideal of educated women, and a critical mass of such women, who would eventually contribute to such a revolution.

HIGHER EDUCATION FOR WOMEN

Academies

The first inroads for female higher education were thus made in the academies. Although the first American academy was Franklin's Academy, established in 1751 in Philadelphia, the "age of the academy" was from 1820 to 1870. The academy was a curious institution. Sometimes it was a church foundation; at other times it was a private venture supported by public subscription or, in some instances, by public tax monies. Thus, it was usually a semipublic school. Its curriculum was so varied that it competed both with the Latin grammar schools and with the colleges. Moreover, it generally offered "practical" subjects, such as surveying, pedagogy, and bookkeeping.[55] As a new institution, it was not bound to tradition like the colleges and Latin grammar schools. One prominent tradition that it increasingly violated in the 19th century was the exclusion of women. In fact, some academies were founded exclusively for women, including the Moravian's Friends Academy at Salem, North Carolina, in 1802; and the academies at Pittsfield, Massachusetts, in 1807; Derry, New Hampshire, in 1823; and Ipswich, Massachusetts, in 1828. Others were coeducational, like Bradford Academy (1803) and Friends Academy (1812) at New Bedford, Massachusetts. The most famous, and probably the most rigorous, were Emma Willard's Troy Female Seminary and Mary Lyon's Mt. Holyoke Seminary.[56] At a time when women were barred from colleges and when public high schools were just beginning, the academies offered women the best opportunities for education beyond the elementary level.

The academy, however, had at least three fundamental problems with respect to women's education. First, academy attendance was restricted to those who could pay the tuition. Second, the academies reflected the early-19th-century bias against educating girls and boys together, and even many of the coeducational academies educated the girls in separate buildings or separate rooms. In 1852 the trustees of Rome Free Academy in New York were forced to resign due to the angry reaction against their proposal to admit girls to the same classes with boys. Eventually the new trustees enacted a program of "coordinate education" with a female department of the academy in a separate building.[57] Third, the girls' curriculum was usually different from that of the boys, reflecting the reality that "separate" did not mean "equal" in educational resources or goals. In many academies the curriculum continued to focus on "ladylike" subjects.[58] Even the Mt. Holyoke curriculum emphasized teaching and domestic pursuits rather than the classical curriculum considered fundamental for the liberal education of young men.

Normal Schools

The opening of elementary school teaching to women and the subsequent development of normal schools to train those teachers demonstrate both strengths and weaknesses in the liberal posi-

The symbolic beginning of the radical women's movement can be traced to the Seneca Falls Women's Rights Convention of 1848 where women like Susan B. Anthony (left), and Elizabeth Cady Stanton began to demand gender equality in such institutions as the ballot box, the professions, and higher education.

tion on female education. On the positive side, liberals such as Horace Mann, Henry Barnard, Dewitt Clinton, Emma Willard, Catherine Beecher, and Mary Lyon successfully opened higher education to women during the first half of the 19th century by establishing both private and state-supported normal schools. Samuel Hall's private normal school at Concord, New Hampshire (founded in 1823), was a pioneering example. Horace Mann's efforts to establish state normal schools in Massachusetts were decisive in the drive for trained elementary school teachers in America. A consummate rhetorician, he successfully employed an image of women as inherently nurturing and thus better common-school teachers than men. This public image substantially promoted female attendance at the normal schools, thus opening to tens of thousands of 19th-century American women education beyond the elementary level as well as respectable employment. The primary alternatives for young women at the time were factory work and domestic work in other people's homes.

While this public image of women as natural teachers due to their special nurturing qualities did open some doors to higher education and employment, it also helped keep other doors closed. Most professions, such as law, medicine, and commerce, together with virtually all branches of government, were thought to require such "manly" characteristics as logical reasoning abilities, stern discipline, and a sense of justice based on rationality rather than on such dispositions as compassion and mercy. Therefore, while women were welcomed to teaching and to the normal schools, the very rationale which justified their entrance into those arenas helped block their entrance into other areas of higher education and into the professions. Outside the home and the elementary school, a "motherly" disposition was not a desired quality. Women's struggle for admission to secondary and collegiate education was thus won, but at a price.

High Schools

The English classical school, soon renamed the high school, began in the second decade of the 19th century as an "effort to create for youth a public institution which would do without cost what the academy had done for a fee."[59] In 1821 Boston opened its English Classical School for boys. Five years later the Boston school committee opened a similar school for girls, directed by Ebenezer Bailey. The girls' school was so successful that it apparently could accommodate only about a quarter of those desiring admittance. However, the committee closed the school after 3 years, and Boston was without a public high school for girls until 1852, when the Girls' High School was opened as part of its Normal School.[60] Concurrently, George Emerson operated a private English classical school for girls in Boston, whose long waiting list for admission was further evidence that Boston's females desired education beyond the common school.[61] The first public high school for girls opened in Worcester, Massachusetts, in 1824. It was followed by others in New York City, in 1826; North Glastonbury, Connecticut, in 1828; East Hartford, Connecticut, in 1828; Buffalo, New York, in 1828; and Rochester, New York, in 1838. The first coeducational public high school opened in Lowell, Massachusetts, in 1841. This example was followed in the 1840s in New Hampshire, Connecticut, and Vermont.[62] These new high schools clearly extended the educational horizons for females. The Worcester school committee noted that it hoped to "provide an education for girls comparable to that provided for boys in the Latin Grammar School and the English School."[63]

Care should be exercised against an overly favorable evaluation of these developments. First, the justification for girls' high school education almost always followed traditional gender-biased lines. The Salem, Massachusetts, school committee discussed girls' education in the 1840s, saying

> It is a matter of complaint in our city, and seemingly just, that girls have too much intellectual and too little home education. . . . Boys need, strictly speaking, a more intellectual education than girls, since the latter are destined for duties in the home, while the main province of the former, as men, is ever abroad, in the complications of business, requiring the rigid analysis and calculation happily spared to the wife and mother.[64]

The address by John T. Irving at the opening of New York's high school for females is typical. He noted that girls must be educated in order to ensure their "domestic happiness," to make them more "fit companions for their husbands," and for their role as mothers. He pointed out that "such a judicious selection has been made both of study and employment for the pupils as is suited to their sex, and will prepare them for presiding with skill and prudence in those domestic stations, for which Providence has designed them." Irving left no doubt regarding the nature of these "divinely" appointed female stations:

> It would be a great mistake if we were to consider female education as calculated merely to render ladies useful and agreeable companions in domestic life. That is undoubtedly one important object. But it has a higher and nobler purpose: the best and most durable lessons, and the most happy direction which the youthful mind receives, is from the mother. It is her task to inspire her sons with the earliest love of knowledge, to teach them the precepts of religion, the charities of life, the miseries of vice, and to lead them into the paths of a just and honourable ambition.[65]

In short, female education was still captive to the benefit it would bring to males—husbands and sons. Women were seen as destined exclusively for marriage and motherhood, with a few entering teaching before marriage. Like most visions which divide humanity into subordinate and dominating groups, this vision was rather myopic. By 1845 over 75,000 women were working in the textile industries in the United States. In 1837 women were engaged in over 100 different occupations. Women were listed as employers in many manufacturing and business concerns in the 1840s. By 1880 almost 15 percent of females aged 10 or older were gainfully employed, while fewer than 60 percent of women were married.[66] Clearly the assumption that *all* women were "destined for duties of the home" while only men were to encounter the "complications of business" was less warranted by facts than by the wishful imagination of contemporary commentators.

A second cautionary note regards the limited impact of secondary education in the 19th century. By 1872 the number of girls attending high school outnumbered boys by 43,794 to 37,978, but this figure represents less than 4 percent of the total number of girls aged 15 to 18. By 1890 female graduates of public high schools outnumbered males by nearly three to two, but the figures represent less than 10 percent of the total high-school-aged population in the United States at that time.[67] Finally, during the 19th century high school attendance was generally limited to the most affluent.

Colleges

A fourth battlefield for female advancement in higher education was the American college. In 1836 six young women interviewed President Quincy in his office at Harvard. When one of them demanded to know whether there was any reason they could not be admitted with their brothers, Quincy's answer was simple, direct, and representative of the contemporary male opinion: "Oh yes, my dear, we never allow girls at Harvard. You know the place for girls is at home."[68] This answer was unacceptable to radical proponents of female education, who had already begun to work for female collegiate education. Their early struggle faced huge odds. For example, when the LeRoy Female Seminary in New York applied to the state legislature in 1851 for a charter as a women's college, it was turned down simply because of precedent: there were no colleges for women.[69] During the 1860s the state's regents appointed a commission to study charters for female colleges. It did so not because the regents were favorably disposed to the idea but in order to respond to those "who would demolish all distinctions, political, educational and social between the sexes, ignoring alike the providence of God and the common sense of mankind."[70] The argument was grounded in classical liberal thought: the same Creator who endowed men with inalienable rights had ordained that men and women should occupy distinctly different spheres in society.

Nevertheless, substantial progress was already being made. The Georgia legislature chartered the Georgia Female College at Macon in 1836.[71] Antioch and Oberlin colleges in Ohio became coeducational during the 1840s, admitting women and men of color, as well. During the fourth and fifth decades of the century, four female colleges were opened in Ohio, three in Pennsylvania, one in Tennessee, and one in Illinois.[72] Before 1870 eleven colleges in New England and New York admitted women. In New York State the following colleges were chartered to admit females: Ingham University in 1842, Genesee College in 1851, Central College in 1851, Elmira College in 1855, St. Lawrence in 1856, Alfred University in 1858, Vassar in 1861, and Rutgers Female College in 1867. In Massachusetts several institutions were similarly chartered: Boston University in 1869, Wellesley in 1875, and Smith in 1875. With the exception of Vassar and Boston University, all of the institutions that began admitting women before 1870 were plagued with similar problems: insufficient endowments, inability to overcome the weight of traditional opposition to female higher education, and lack of sufficient social and educational vision.[73]

A major breakthrough for female collegiate education was the establishment of Vassar College, at Poughkeepsie, New York, in 1861. Founded by Matthew Vassar with an endowment of half a million dollars, Vassar began with a sound financial foundation. Moreover, its founder started from the premise that women were equal to men, and he demonstrated that liberal ideology could be used to justify equal rights for women: "It occurred to me that woman, having received from her Creator the same intellectual constitution as man, has the same right as man to intellectual culture and development."[74] Thus, from the outset, Vassar intended to provide women with collegiate educations equal to those provided in the best male colleges—and it had the financial resources to do so.

Matthew Vassar understood that quality would be expensive and was willing to charge high tuition for superior education. He argued, "to court public patronage by catering to cheap or low prices of instruction is to my mind ridiculous. . . . I go for the best means, cost what they may, and corresponding prices for tuition in return. . . . I am therefore giving the daughters of the public the very best means of education and make them pay for it."[75]

This attitude was reflected in Vassar's program. While other female colleges often taught "geography of Heaven," for example, at Vassar Maria Mitchell used the second largest telescope in America to teach astronomy. Vassar's library had seven times the holdings of Elmira College and was nearly equal to the library at Columbia. Vassar's salary budget for instructors was one of the largest in the nation, and its male instructors' salaries compared favorably with those at Harvard and Yale. The entrance requirements and curriculum at Vassar were equal to those of the best male colleges.[76] The inevitable result was that Vassar provided an education for women that was at least equal to that of the best male institutions. Indeed, in 1870, after visiting Vassar's classes, Harvard's president Eliot remarked, "the boys at Harvard did not recite so well in German, French or Latin or even in mathematics as did the girls at Vassar."[77] Perhaps most significant was that Vassar provided an obvious counterexample to the time-honored belief in female inferiority.

WOMEN AND VOCATIONAL EDUCATION

The Vassar example did not produce a revolution in American attitudes toward gender and education. As described in Chapter 4, the two decades surrounding the turn of the 20th century found Americans' attention focused on an array of other problems: major new immigration from southern and eastern Europe, urbanization, the demands of the new industrial enterprises, and the disquieting social and economic disturbances resulting from these phenomena. Not surprisingly, Americans turned to the schools to alleviate these difficulties. Educators and social commentators soon become enamored of the idea that vocational training would make schools more responsive to social and economic conditions. Soon the demand for vocationalism became a roar that drowned out most other considerations in educational policy making. With respect to gender, most of the vocational training discussion assumed that girls should be trained for traditional women's activities, while boys should be trained for men's occupations. Girls' vocational training was generally confined to domestic science and commercial education.

Domestic Science Training

Without exception, the literature on vocational training for girls emphasized the woman's natural role as wife and homemaker.[78] A leading educator, John D. Philbrick, while analyzing city school systems for the U.S. Commissioner of Education in 1885, set the tone for the era when he stated, "no girl can be considered properly educated who cannot sew."[79] The chairperson of the woman's branch of the Farmer's Institute of North Carolina, Mrs. W. N. Hutt, put it a bit more bluntly when she informed the 1910 National Education Association convention that, regardless of what other vocation a woman might temporarily adopt, "She will, with it all, wake up some fine morning and find herself in some man's kitchen, and woe be unto her if she has not the knowledge with which to cook his breakfast."[80] A year earlier, in New York City, the city schools' director of cooking, Mary E. Williams, emphatically delineated women's "natural vocation." She argued that every girl should study domestic science because once a woman heard the "God-given call of her mate," she would desert all other vocations to assume the "position of the highest responsibility and the holiest duties of human life, those of homemaking and motherhood; upon which the progress of civilization and of human society depend."[81]

There was an ethnic and class bias in the campaign for domestic science. In the North these programs were specifically aimed at the daughters of immigrants and the working class, and in the South, at African-Americans. Middle-class educators were convinced that these children came from homes which could offer no lessons on adequate diet, food preparation, home management, or family life. Properly trained in the school's domestic science classes, educators thought that girls would regenerate working-class homes and provide "stability" for America's industrial workers. New York City's superintendent of schools argued in 1910 that homemaking courses "have been a factor

The vocational education movement of the late 19th and early 20th centuries continued to pattern its female curriculum around the old domestic science pursuits such as sewing, cooking, hospitality, and keeping the family accounts.

during the past years in helping to solve the economic questions of the nation."[82] Describing the impact of domestic science courses in Chicago's schools, the principal of Spry School said, "The evening meal of the factory hand may be made more tempting than the lunch counter, and the clothing of the family, as well as the arrangement and tidiness of the living room at home may be as attractive as the gilded home of vice. Domestic science may become the unsuspected, and yet not the least efficient, enemy of the saloon."[83]

Indeed, Chicago led the rush to implement domestic science training for girls in the middle grades. Almost three-fourths of Chicago's seventh- and eighth-grade girls were enrolled in household arts courses in 1900.[84] Ten years later, approximately half of New York City's girls of the seventh and eighth grades were in similar programs, and the superintendent announced that all high school girls would be required to receive domestic instruction.[85] By 1928, 30 percent of all female high school students in the United States were enrolled in domestic science courses.

Domestic science programs aimed at more than merely teaching girls to cook, sew, and order a household. They were sophisticated efforts at shaping reality for students. The method can be seen in the National Education Association's 1910 "Report of the Subcommittee on the Industrial and Technical Education in the Secondary Schools." In the section devoted to industrial training for girls, the report described programs at Boston's Girls' High School of Practical Arts and at Cleveland's Technical High School. The principal of the Boston school noted that a major aspect of the girl's mathematics course involved solutions to simple problems like the maintenance of household accounts. He continued, "Our academic work, as well as the drawing, correlates with the shop. Descriptions of various processes, with materials in hand, are required as lessons in good English. The chemistry deals with questions of food, clothing, and shelter. The aim of these courses is to set before the girl the highest ideals of home life; to train her in all that pertains to practical housekeeping." The description of the industrial training department in Cleveland's Technical High School reveals a similar orientation. Domestic science topics were assigned in English classes, chemistry revolved around food preparation, and mathematics was devoted to adding household accounts and dividing cooking recipes. "In short, all technical subjects involving homemaking are taken as the basis of the course for girls, and the rest of the studies are grouped around these."[86]

In 1910 the National Education Association held that one important aim of girls' vocational education was to "train work in *distinctly feminine* occupations."[87] In 1906 the Massachusetts Commission on Industrial and Technical Training recommended that if a woman was obliged to work (outside of the home), vocational education should "fit her so that she can and will enter those industries which are most closely allied to the home."[88] Secretarial practice, bookkeeping, and general office work were often seen as the office equivalent of the wife. Women in these positions were expected to do the routine and "housekeeping" chores of the office.

Commercial Education

As industry and business became increasingly bureaucratized and Taylorized at the turn of the century, the amount of paperwork greatly increased as instructions and reports were sent along the growing chain of managerial command. An efficient, technically trained, and cheap clerical workforce was required to process, send, store, and retrieve this mountain of paper. Women fitting this description were available in significant numbers, so clerical work would quickly shift from a male occupation to become considered as women's work. Public secondary schools quickly stepped forward to satisfy the desires of industry. As historian John Rury reports, "Commercial education was among the fastest growing areas of study in high schools across the country in this period. . . . Commercial education became an important aspect of female high school education in the opening decades of the twentieth century, and represents one of the earliest examples of the manner in which women's education responded to changes in the labor market."[89] The fact that clerical work was designed to mirror the supposed female qualities was reflected in business educators' assessment of the appropriate kind of training needed by their students. Again Rury is instructive:

> [Business educators commented] repeatedly on the different career patterns men and women followed in business, and some argued that distinctive male and female curricula ought to be established to accommodate such differences. A survey of sixty-six high school principals in 1917 found that nearly two-thirds believed that businessmen wanted training for men and women to differ. Boys, it was felt, required preparation for careers in administration and management, while women needed training for relatively short-term employment as secretaries and typists. Consequently, men ought to be given a broader education commensurate with the responsibilities they were expected to assume, while the technical details of office procedure were considered sufficient for women, whose working careers were generally short. Surveys of the occupational status of men and women in business confirmed the accuracy of these expectations. One of the best known such surveys found in Cleveland that "regardless of the position in which boys and girls started in life, boys worked into administrative positions," while women remained secretaries or clerks until they left the office to get married.[90]

Rury points out that although few commercial education programs were actually sex-segregated, the commercial courses generally became women's education because "women were entering these courses more rapidly than their male counterparts." Commercial education was largely female because the labor market sought women for low-paying clerical positions.[91]

Most of the evidence suggests that like domestic science, commercial education was not only sex-segregated but also class-biased. It was primarily a curriculum for women and especially for the daughters of less affluent families. Timothy Crimmins's study of Atlanta's Girls' High School is an excellent case in point. Girls' High School was opened in 1872. Its composition reflected both the caste and the class system in contemporary Atlanta. African-Americans were excluded; 29.9 percent of the students were from the upper class, and 61.3 percent were from middle-class families. None were from lowest-class families.[92] Given this social class composition, what curriculum might we expect to find—classical or vocational? The curriculum included Latin, French, mathematics, physical science, composition, English literature, and philosophy.[93] By 1896 enrollment had doubled, the percentage from upper-class families had declined, and the percentage from the lower-middle and lower classes had increased substantially. The student body still had no girls from the lowest-class white families.[94] As the social composition of the school changed, however, so too did its curriculum. In 1889 a commercial curriculum was added, which allowed girls to "substitute typing, bookkeeping, and stenography for Latin, algebra, and philosophy." This curriculum "led directly to employment as secretaries, stenographers, and typists in the city's burgeoning bureaucracies."[95] The social class composition of the two curricula is enlightening: all of the upper-class students and 224 of the 297 middle-class students were in the literary curriculum. All of the girls in the commercial curriculum came from middle- and lower-class families.[96]

CONCLUDING REMARKS

We have examined how a particular religious interpretation of humanity and Augustine's division of humankind into two inherently different kinds of beings helped form an intellectual justification for the subordination of women for 15 centuries. This Augustinian legacy helped shape classical liberalism itself, so most Americans of the colonial and post-Revolution eras did not see contradictions between an ideology of progress and freedom and the subjugation of women. Early Americans were concerned with educating their sons to become productive workers, effective political agents, and independent rational actors, but they appeared to be much less concerned about their daughters' education. When they thought of education for their daughters, the concern was to prepare them as wives and mothers, not as independent and rational beings.

This chapter illustrates how a major political economic change, accompanied by a tension within classical liberal ideology, led to changes in the nature and purpose of women's education, while the underlying assumptions about the subordinate position of women were not radically altered. The political-economic change was the American Revolution, which stimulated discussion about how a new nation could be forged and how public schooling could be used for nation building. The ideological tension was created by the dominant view that women were entitled to education but that they were, nevertheless, inferior to men. The resulting developments in schooling were the increasing enrollment of girls in public schools, on the one hand, and on the other hand, the strengthening of the belief that women are naturally destined for domestic roles and that schooling should prepare girls for those adult roles. Given the relatively few employment opportunities for women, the "cult of domesticity" would be transformed in the Progressive era to a curriculum of "domestic sciences," a new vocational solution to the problem of what kind of schooling girls should receive. During this transition the teaching profession came to be seen as an extension of the domestic role and thus an appropriate occupation for women.

The chapter also examined how women's education has reflected ideological differences regarding the role of women in society. Conservative and liberal streams of classical liberalism included those who wanted to keep the status quo and those who wanted to introduce a modest change in the status and education of women in society. Those who advocated a radical departure from mainstream classical liberalism nevertheless sought to extend classical liberal ideals of freedom and equality fully to women. The project of gender equity, which was set in motion in the 19th century by Susan B. Anthony, Elizabeth Cady Stanton, Elizabeth and Emily Blackwell, and others, continues to divide opinion on social and educational policy today. Part 2 of this textbook will illustrate how gender equity in contemporary American society is still an unfinished project.

PRIMARY SOURCE READING

Elizabeth Cady Stanton and Lucretia Mott, both of whom were deeply influenced by the antislavery movement, organized the Seneca Falls conference in July 1848 to bring men and women together to consider the subordinate role of women in the United States. The two organizers, together with others, drew up this declaration using the Declaration of Independence as a model. At the conference, attended by some 300 persons and chaired by Lucretia Mott's husband, James, 11 resolutions were passed unanimously, and the 12th was narrowly passed after a stirring speech from the floor by Frederick Douglass. The language of Jeffersonian liberalism would come to be used by women and African-Americans to extend the meaning of equality before the law for the next 150 years, right up to our own time.

The Declaration is presented here so students may see the political-economic conditions that were foremost in the minds of women's rights advocates in mid-19th century; consider the ideological tensions in classical liberalism, the ideology that justified the oppression of women and yet provided the conceptual underpinning of this Declaration; and finally, examine the various educational issues implicit in these sentiments and resolutions.

DECLARATION OF SENTIMENTS AND RESOLUTIONS

When, in the course of human events, it becomes necessary for one portion of the family of man to assume among the people of the earth a position different from that which they have hitherto occupied, but one to which the laws of nature and of nature's God entitle them, a decent respect to the opinion of mankind requires that they should declare the causes that impel them to such a course.

We hold these truths to be self-evident: that all men and women are created equal; that they are endowed by their Creator with certain inalienable rights; that among these are life, liberty, and the pursuit of happiness; that to secure these rights governments are instituted, deriving their just powers from the consent of the governed. Whenever any form of government becomes destructive of these ends, it is the right of those who suffer from it to refuse allegiance to it, and to insist upon the institution of a new government, laying its foundation on such principles, and organizing its powers in such form, as to them shall seem most likely to effect their safety and happiness. Prudence, indeed, will dictate that governments long established should not be changed for light and transient causes; and accordingly all experience hath shown that mankind are more disposed to suffer, while evils are sufferable, than to right themselves by abolishing the forms to which they were accustomed. But when a long train of abuses and usurpations, pursuing invariably the same object evinces a design to reduce them under absolute despotism, it is their duty to throw off such government, and to provide new guards for their future security. Such has been the patient sufferance of the women under this government, and such is now the necessity which constrains them to demand the equal station to which they are entitled.

The history of mankind is a history of repeated injuries and usurpations on the part of man toward woman, having in direct object the establishment of an absolute tyranny over her. To prove this, let facts be submitted to a candid world.

He has never permitted her to exercise her inalienable right to the elective franchise.

He has compelled her to submit to laws, in the formation of which she had no voice.

He has withheld from her rights which are given to the most ignorant and degraded men—both natives and foreigners.

Having deprived her of this first right of a citizen, the elective franchise, thereby leaving her without representation in the halls of legislation, he has oppressed her on all sides.

He has made her, if married, in the eye of the law, civilly dead.

He has taken from her all right in property, even to the wages she earns.

He has made her, morally, an irresponsible being, as she can commit many crimes with impu-

Source: Miriam Schneir, ed., *Feminism, the Essential Historical Writings* (New York: Vintage), 1972, pp. 76–82.

nity, provided they be done in the presence of her husband. In the covenant of marriage, she is compelled to promise obedience to her husband, he becoming, to all intents and purposes, her master—the law giving him power to deprive her of her liberty, and to administer chastisement.

He has so framed the laws of divorce, as to what shall be the proper causes, and in case of separation, to whom the guardianship of the children shall be given, as to be wholly regardless of the happiness of women—the law, in all cases, going upon a false supposition of the supremacy of man, and giving all power into his hands.

After depriving her of all rights as a married woman, if single, and the owner of property, he has taxed her to support a government which recognizes her only when her property can be made profitable to it.

He has monopolized nearly all the profitable employments, and from those she is permitted to follow, she receives but a scanty remuneration. He closes against her all the avenues to wealth and distinction which he considers most honorable to himself. As a teacher of theology, medicine, or law, she is not known.

He has denied her the facilities for obtaining a thorough education, all colleges being closed against her.

He allows her in Church, as well as State, but a subordinate position, claiming Apostolic authority for her exclusion from the ministry, and, with some exceptions, from any public participation in the affairs of the Church.

He has created a false public sentiment by giving to the world a different code of morals for men and women, by which moral delinquencies which exclude women from society, are not only tolerated, but deemed of little account in man.

He has usurped the prerogative of Jehovah himself, claiming it as his right to assign for her a sphere of action, when that belongs to her conscience and to her God.

He has endeavored, in every way that he could, to destroy her confidence in her own powers, to lessen her self-respect, and to make her willing to lead a dependent and abject life.

Now, in view of this entire disfranchisement of one-half the people of this country, their social and religious degradation—in view of the unjust laws above mentioned, and because women do feel themselves aggrieved, oppressed, and fraudulently deprived of their most sacred rights, we insist that they have immediate admission to all the rights and privileges which belong to them as citizens of the United States.

In entering upon the great work before us, we anticipate no small amount of misconception, misrepresentation, and ridicule; but we shall use every instrumentality within our power to effect our object. We shall employ agents, circulate tracts, petition the State and National legislatures, and endeavor to enlist the pulpit and the press in our behalf. We hope this Convention will be followed by a series of Conventions embracing every part of the country.

Resolutions

WHEREAS, The great perception of nature is conceded to be, that "man shall pursue his own true and substantial happiness." Blackstone in his Commentaries remarks, that this law of Nature being coeval with mankind, and dictated by God himself, is of course superior in obligation to any other. It is binding over all the globe, in all countries and at all times; no human laws are of any validity if contrary to this, and such of them as are valid, derive all their force, and all their validity, and all their authority, mediately and immediately, from this original; therefore,

Resolved, That such laws as conflict, in any way, with the true and substantial happiness of woman, are contrary to the great precept of nature and of no validity, for this is "superior in obligation to any other."

Resolved, That all laws which prevent woman from occupying such a station in society as her conscience shall dictate, or which place her in a position inferior to that of man, are contrary to the great precept of nature, and therefore of no force or authority.

Resolved, That woman is man's equal—was intended to be so by the Creator, and the highest good of the race demands that she should be recognized as such.

Resolved, That the women of this country ought to be enlightened in regard to the laws under which they live, that they may no longer publish their degradation by declaring themselves satisfied with their present position, nor their ignorance, by asserting that they have all the rights they want.

Resolved, That inasmuch as man, while claiming for himself intellectual superiority, does accord to woman moral superiority, it is preeminently his duty to encourage her to speak and teach, as she has an opportunity, in all religious assemblies.

Resolved, That the same amount of virtue, delicacy, and refinement of behavior that is required of woman in the social state, should also be required of man, and the same transgressions should be visited with equal severity on both man and woman.

Resolved, That the objection of indelicacy and impropriety, which is so often brought against woman when she addresses a public audience, comes with a very ill-grace from those who encourage, by their attendance, her appearance on the stage, in the concert, or in feats of the circus.

Resolved, That woman has too long rested satisfied in the circumscribed limits which corrupt customs and a perverted application of the Scriptures have marked out for her, and that it is time she should move in the enlarged sphere which her great Creator has assigned her.

Resolved, That it is the duty of the women of this country to secure to themselves their sacred right to the elective franchise.

Resolved, That the equality of human rights results necessarily from the fact of the identity of the race in capabilities and responsibilities.

Resolved, therefore, That, being invested by the Creator with the same capabilities, and the same consciousness of responsibility for their exercise, it is demonstrably the right and duty of woman, equally with man, to promote every righteous cause by every righteous means; and especially in regard to the great subjects of morals and religion, it is self-evidently her right to participate with her brother in teaching them, both in private and in public, by writing and by speaking, by any instrumentalities proper to be used, and in any assemblies proper to be held; and this being a self-evident truth growing out of the divinely implanted principles of human nature, any custom or authority adverse to it, whether modern or wearing the hoary sanction of antiquity, is to be regarded as a self-evident falsehood, and at war with mankind.

[At the last session Lucretia Mott offered and spoke to the following resolution:]

Resolved, That the speedy success of our cause depends upon the zealous and untiring efforts of both men and women, for the overthrow of the monopoly of the pulpit, and for the securing to woman an equal participation with men in the various trades, professions, and commerce.

PRIMARY SOURCE READING

This article was written by journalist Mary Leal Harkness for a popular, well-educated audience in 1914. It illustrates a number of the issues raised in this chapter: a criticism of the prevailing view that a woman's place is in the home or in a limited number of "female" roles outside the home; the role of schooling in supporting these limited life options for women; the various ideological justifications for the subordinate place of women in society; and so on. Harkness's piece cannot be dismissed simply as just another tirade against the subordinate roles of women. She is thoughtful about the value of those creative dimensions of gendered domestic experience, such as cooking or sewing, that she finds rewarding. However, she strongly criticizes relegating any such experience to boys or girls alone. Moreover, she calls into question the entire progressive notion of using schools for vocational preparation, whether for girls or for boys, as a "wasting of children's time."

THE EDUCATION OF THE GIRL

By Mary Leal Harkness

I do not know why an utterance on that subject in yesterday morning's paper stirred me up more than similar ones which I am constantly seeing in print. Perhaps it was because the utterer was

Excerpted from Mary Leal Harkness, "The Education of the Girl," *Atlantic Monthly: A Magazine of Literature, Science, Art and Politics,* 113, (1914), pp. 324–30. Karen Graves suggested this article.

advertised as an "authority" on "vocational education," for his words did not differ essentially from the current platitude. "The problem of girls education is simple," he said in effect, "since what you have to do is merely to train them to be home-keepers; to teach them the details of the management of the house and the care of children, and not to despise domestic duties."

. . . But why, I beg to ask, does everyone know that the vocation which is sure to delight every girl and in which she is sure to succeed (always provided, of course, that she is given the proper "practical" training in her school-days) is housekeeping and the rearing of children, when even the cocksure vocationalist has to admit that he cannot always foretell with absolute certainty whether a boy of fourteen was made to be a carpenter or an engineer, a farmer or a Methodist preacher? In our outward configuration of form and feature we women confessedly differ as greatly from one another as do men. Why this assumption that in the inward configuration of character, taste, and talent we are all made upon one pattern? I must say that the perpetual declaration on the "woman's page" of modern periodicals that "every woman should know how to cook a meal, and make her own clothes, and feed a baby" fills me with scorn unutterable. But then for that matter the mere fact of a "woman's page" fills me with scorn. Why not a "man's page," with a miscellany of twaddle, labeled as exclusively, adapted to the masculine intellect? The idea that literature is properly created male and female is no less absurd than the idea that there is one education of the man and another of the woman. And it is no more essential to the progress of the universe that every woman should be taught to cook than that every man should be taught to milk a cow.

I do not propose to enter into any discussion of the possible mental superiority of either sex over the other (although I cannot resist quoting in an "aside" the recent remark to me of a teacher of distinguished judgment and long experience: "the fact is, girls are much better students than boys"), but only to maintain this: that girls show as much diversity of taste in intellectual work as boys, that their aptitude for work purely intellectual is as great, and that, therefore, whatever variation is made in the present plan of their education, it should not be based upon the narrow foundation of preconceived ideas of differences inherent in sex. I do not believe that anything necessarily "becomes a woman" more than a man, except as our superstition has made it seem to do so.

Yet, as a matter of fact, superstition begins to hamper a girl's education almost at the very beginning, and one of the first forms which it takes is "consideration for her health." Consideration for the health of a child of either sex is more than laudable, if it be intelligently exercised; but I really cannot see why our daughters deserve more of such consideration than our sons. And the typical consideration for the health of the little girl and the young maiden is not infused with a striking degree of intelligence, as is evidenced by the very small amount of intelligence with which we invariably credit the girl herself. For absolutely the only kind of activity which we ever conceive to be injurious to her is mental activity.

One might perhaps agree to the reiterated parental excuse for half-educated daughters that "nothing can compensate a girl for the loss of her health," if parents would explain how they think that anything can compensate a boy for the loss of his. But they take that risk quite blithely, and send him to college. Personally I have never seen any evidence that the risk for either sex is more than a phantom, and I believe that it is yet to be proved that the study of books has ever in itself been responsible for the breaking down in health of any human being. Many foolish things done in connection with the study of books have contributed to the occasional failure in health of students, but there is, I firmly believe, no reason but prejudiced superstition for the unanimity with which the fond mamma and the family physician fix the cause of the break-down in the books, and never in the numerous and usually obvious other activities. And in the spasms of commiseration for the unfortunates whose "health has been ruined by hard study" nobody has taken the trouble to notice the by-no-means infrequent cases of young persons, and girls especially, of really delicate health, who have stuck to their studies, but with a reasonable determination not to try to stick to ten or a dozen other side issues at the same time, and have come out of college, not physical wrecks, but stronger than when they went in. And who shall say with what greater capacity for enjoying life than those who have devoted the principal energy of their adolescence to the conservation of their health—frequently with no marked success?

So far as the normal child is concerned, his—and her—brain is naturally as active as his body, and it is not "crowding," nor yet "overstimulation," to give that active and acquisitive brain material worth while to work with. Therefore, the pathetic picture which has been painted recently in certain periodicals of the lean and nervous little overworked school-girl may be classed, I think, among the works of creative art rather than among photographs taken from life. Such pictures, as Art, may rank very high, but do not deserve great commendation as a contribution to the science of education. I am not saying that there are not many abominations practiced in our schools, especially of primary and secondary grade; but they are not in the direction of overeducation.

The thing against which I pray to see a mighty popular protest is the wasting of children's time, and the dissipation of all their innate powers of concentration, through the great number of studies of minor (not to use a less complimentary adjective) educational value, which is now one of the serious evils in our schools. And I think that this evil is bearing rather more heavily upon the girls than upon the boys . . .

But my objection to the whole movement to "redirect" the education of girls is not that many very good things are not put into the redirected curriculum, but that its whole direction is wrong. I cannot say that it is not a good thing for *some* women to know how to cook and sew *well*, for it is indeed both good and necessary to civilized life. I cannot say that some of the subjects introduced into a good domestic-science course are not educative and truly scientific, because I should be saying what is not true. But I do believe that the idea at the basis of it all is fundamentally false. For the idea is this: that one-half of the human race should be "educated" for one single occupation, while the multitudinous other occupations of civilized life should all be loaded upon the other half. The absurd inequality of the division should alone be enough to condemn it. The wonder is that the men do not complain of being overloaded with so disproportionate a share of the burden. I dare say it is their chivalry which makes them bear it so bravely.

This statement of the division is not inconsistent with my complaint that women try to do too many things. They do, but they are all things which are supposed to be included in some way or other within their "proper sphere," the maintenance of the home. Sometimes I grow so weary of The Home that if I did not love my own I could really wish that there were no such thing upon this terrestrial ball. I do love my own home, but I protest that the primary reason is not because my mother is a good cook, although she is, notably. Even as I write these words I thrill with the thought of my near return to her strawberry shortcakes. But I know other homes where there is also strawberry shortcake of a high order, in which I yet think that even filial devotion would have a hard task to make me feel much contentment. I might say the same of the various things that make my home attractive to look upon. Yet the course of study which would graduate "homemakers" is based upon the principle that "home" consists primarily of these things. I am aware that its makers would include certain studies supposed to contribute to "culture," but even where these are well taught, they are still, in my opinion, rendered largely ineffectual by the false motive for study inculcated from the beginning, which makes them all, for women, only side-issues.

I cannot see that girls were created essentially to be "home-keepers" any more than boys. Men and women, so far as they choose to marry, are to make a home together, and any system of education which so plans the division of labor between them that the woman shall "make" and stay in a place for which the man pays and to which he returns once in twenty-four hours, is wrong for at least two good reasons. It trains to two such different conceptions of responsibility that true companionship and community of interest is diminished, and often almost destroyed; and it so magnifies a specialized manual training for the woman that it places her at the end in the artisan class, and not in the educated. If a woman so trained knows how to care for the minds of her children as well as she knows how to feed and dress and physic and spank them, she owes it to the grace of Heaven and not to her "vocational" education "for motherhood." But I do not believe that girls should be "educated to be mothers" at all, in the absurdly narrow sense in which such education is now conceived.

Every form of special instruction as a preparation for parenthood that can be necessary for a girl is necessary for a boy also. For what does it profit a woman or her offspring to have kept herself strong and clean, to have learned the laws of sex-hygiene and reproduction, or of care of the child, if the father of the child has failed to do the same?

But I cannot see how the world can have gone so mad as it has over the idea that *the birth of the child*, and its few subsequent months of existence, constitute the epochal point, the climax, as it were, in the life of any married pair. Surely, it is a very narrow view of life which fails to see how much is to be done in the world besides rearing children. It is true that society does perhaps in a way recognize this, but it seems to wish all active doing relegated to the men, while the woman's contribution is confined to "influence" exerted while nursing a numerous progeny through the diseases of infancy in a happy and perfectly sanitary home. It is time for a more general recognition that such "feminine influence," like honesty, *laudatur et alget.* The average woman only influences her husband or children to anything good through her brains and character, and the degree of power to express either brains or character depends mainly upon education. It sounds well to proclaim the mothering of the world as woman's greatest profession, her truest glory; but it would be well also to consider that such "mothering" as is mostly done—and will be, so long as women are taught to prepare only for its physical demands, its purely material services—is never going to be either great or glorious. An education which can give the greatest intellectual strength, the completest mental sanity, and so the broadest outlook upon life, is the need and the right of girls and boys alike.

But surely it cannot be said that their need is met alike unless the likeness in their education extends also to the ideal of the use that is to be made of it after school-days are past. If the colleges in which women are taught have failed at all in accomplishing their full possibility, it has been in the comparatively small degree to which they have succeeded in removing even from the minds of the young women themselves the hoary idea that, after all, the principal thing to be expected of the higher education of women is still the diffusion of an exceptionally exalted type of the aforementioned "influence." It does seem rather a small return for years of collegiate effort that the best that can be said of them is that a woman's mental attainments have proved a great assistance to her husband's career as a Cabinet officer. I cannot think that we shall have what wholly deserves to be called an educated womanhood until we have dissipated the idea, still so prevalent even among women themselves, that a woman needs to have a definite occupation only until she marries, or if she fails to marry. That "a woman must choose between marriage and a career" is the most detestable of all the woman platitudes in the entire collection, because, while most of these platitudes are merely stupid, this one is wholly vicious. It has been so incessantly reiterated, to the accompaniment of much shallow sentimentalizing on the sacredness of home and mother, that the public has never been allowed a quiet moment to reflect on its injustice, and to realize how possible, and therefore imperative, is its removal along with other ancient injustices.

As I have urged in a previous article, the recently born and phenomenally growing department of education which styles itself variously Domestic Science, Household Economy, and I believe one or two other impressive things, might be the pioneer in this great work of justice, if it would. So far as that educational movement adds to woman's ability to become a good citizen by leading her to an intelligent interest in the civic problems of housing, feeding, teaching, and amusing not alone her immediate family group, but a whole community, it does more in the right direction. But the very women who are themselves making a successful profession of teaching this group of subjects (thanks mainly to their having received the sort of education they now deprecate for women in general) apparently claim for them no greater mission for the average young woman than ability to guard her husband from ptomaine poison in his ice-cream, or to make gowns and shirt-waists well enough so that she can earn a living, "if she ever has to work."

Shall we never cease to hear that contemptible reason for a girl's education? An age in which women have proved themselves possessors of intellects might naturally be expected to recognize as a province of their education the ability to discover some particular intellectual bent whose training and development for life-long use are not contingent upon matrimony and the financial condition of two men—their fathers and their husbands respectively. It is held rather reprehensible to say it, but I do not see why every girl has not as good a right as every boy to dream of fame, and to be put in the way of reaching fame. If ninety-nine percent of the girls fail of even the smallest title to fame, just as ninety-nine percent of the boys do, yet the level of their lives must inevitably be raised by the education and the educational ideals which we should provide for them all for the sake of the hundredth girl. The supreme ideal which I hope that our schools may some day inspire is that every girl should discover something, whether of fame-bringing probabilities or not, which will seem to be worthy of being a life-work.

In nearly every present plan for the education of girls there lurks the same fatal weakness; girls are not made to realize as boys are that they are being educated for a business which must last as long as life lasts; that they are to feel an interest in it and grow in it,—to develop it, if possible; they are not taught that a definite purposeful share in the outside world's work is a privilege not a misfortune. My own theory is that the only way in which such a state of feminine mind can be made general is by broadening woman's education on the purely intellectual side; but of course I am open to conviction that the result can be better attained by "scientific" bread-making,—even to the exclusion of Latin and Greek.

QUESTIONS FOR DISCUSSION AND EXAMINATION

1. This chapter tries to show that fifth-century Augustinian thought was one significant point of origin for the subordinate role and status of women in our national history. Do you believe that any of Augustine's views on women and men continue to influence the educational experiences of girls and women today? Specifically, how or how not? Defend your view.
2. Clearly, the education of girls and women has progressed toward greater parity with the education of males since the time of the early republic. The progressive era was one time during which new opportunities for girls developed most markedly, but it is clear that many of these opportunities were gender-typed. On balance, did the progressive era result in greater or less educational parity for girls?
3. The Seneca Falls Declaration of Rights and Sentiments is presented as a prominent illustration of a "radical" point of view on the role of women in society. Making clear what you mean by "radical," discuss whether any of the perspectives reflected in that document would be considered radical by most citizens today. Give examples and evidence to support your view.
4. If the Seneca Falls Declaration was purposely based on classical liberalism, which was the dominant ideology of the time, how could the document be considered radical and extreme in its views? Explain.
5. The article by Mary Leal Harkness was written about 70 years after the Seneca Falls Declaration, and the dominant ideology had shifted from classical liberalism to modern liberalism. To what degree is this shift evident in Harkness's article, and to what degree does it continue to show its roots more directly in classical liberalism? Defend your view with illustrations from the article.

NOTES

1. Mary Wollstonecraft, "A Vindication of the Rights of Woman," in Miriam Schneir, ed., *Feminism: The Essential Historical Writings* (New York: Vintage, 1972), pp. 6–7.
2. Timothy 2:9–15.
3. Elaine Pagels, *Adam, Eve, and the Serpent* (New York: Random House, 1988), chap. 6.
4. Augustine, *City of God* (New York: Penguin Books, 1984), XIV:12, p. 570.
5. Pagels, p. 114.
6. It still so informs many contemporary Americans. See, for example, treatments of gender inequity in Shirley Brice Heath and Milbrey W. McLaughlin, eds., *Identity and Inner-City Youth: Beyond Ethnicity and Gender* (New York: Teachers College Press, 1993); and Lois Weis and Michelle Fine, *Beyond Silenced Voices: Class, Race, and Gender in U.S. Schools* (SUNY Press, 1993).
7. Thomas Woody, *A History of Women's Education in the United States*, Vol. 1 (New York: Science Press, 1929), p. 92.
8. Ibid., p. 142.

9. Carl F. Kaestle, *Pillars of the Republic: Common Schools and American Society 1780–1860* (New York: Hill and Wang, 1983), p. 28.
10. Ibid. pp. 142–46.
11. George Martin, "Early Education of Girls in Massachusetts," *Education* 20 (1899), p. 326.
12. Woody, pp. 94, 179, 197, 202, 216, 225, 271, 330–33, 339.
13. John Winthrop, "Journal," in Perry Miller, ed., *The American Puritans* (Garden City, NY: Anchor Books, 1956), pp. 44–5.
14. Woody, pp. 106–7, 128–35.
15. Ibid., pp. 108–10.
16. Ibid., pp. 108, 217–19, 230.
17. Ibid., p. 241.
18. Quoted in Martha Maclear, *A History of the Education of Girls in New York and New England 1800–1870* (Washington, DC: Howard University Press, 1926), p. 6.
19. Woody, p. 93.
20. See, for example, Benjamin Rush, "Thoughts on Female Education," in Frederick Roudolph, ed., *Essays on Education in the Early Republic* (Cambridge, MA: Harvard University Press, 1965), pp. 25–41.
21. Woody, pp. 97–104.
22. Nancy Cott, *The Bonds of Womanhood* (New Haven, CT: Yale University Press, 1977).
23. Kaestle, p. 84.
24. Quoted in Elwood P. Cubberly, *The History of Education* (Boston: Houghton Mifflin, 1920), p. 313.
25. Kaestle, p. 28.
26. Maclear, p. 12–26.
27. Quoted in ibid., p. 12.
28. Ibid., pp. 14–23.
29. Rush, pp. 29, 39.
30. *Common School Journal* 2 (1838), p. 100.
31. Quoted in Woody, p. 318.
32. Quoted in Woody, p. 311.
33. Quoted in Maclear, p. 18.
34. See Miriam Schneir, ed., *Feminism: The Essential Historical Writings* (New York: Vintage Books), 1972.
35. Sarah M. Grimke, "Letter," in Schneir, p. 38.
36. Gertrude Martin, "The Education of Women and Sex Equality," *Annals of the American Academy of Political and Social Science,* November 1914, p. 41.
37. See: John Lord, *Mrs. Emma Willard* (New York, 1873); Alma Lutz, *Emma Willard Pioneer Educator of American Women* (Boston, 1964); Mrs. A. W. Fairbanks (ed.), *Mrs. Emma Willard and Her Pupils or Fifty Years of the Troy Female Seminary 1822-1872* (New York, 1898); Henry Fowler, "Educational Services of Mrs. Emma Willard." *American Journal of Education,* Vol. 6, 1859, p. 123–68; Willystine Goodsell, *Pioneers of Women's Education in the United States* (New York, 1931); Anne Firor Scott, "The Ever Widening Circle: The Diffusion of Feminist Values from the Troy Female Seminary, 1822-1870," *History of Education Quarterly,* Spring 1979, vol. 19, pp. 3–27.
38. Fowler, p. 128.
39. Lutz, p. 29; Fowler, p. 144.
40. Quoted in Goodsell, p. 54. This work includes a reprint of the *Plan,* pp. 45–81.
41. Quoted in Goodsell, p. 57.
42. Quoted in Goodsell, p. 71.
43. Quoted in Goodsell, p. 72.
44. Although Willard retired from the principalship of the Troy Female Seminary in 1838, she continued to influence not only the Seminary but American educational thought until her death in 1870.
45. See: Goodsell, p. 85; Lutz, pp. 40, 93, 97, 113.
46. Fowler, p. 152.
47. Lutz, p. 47.
48. Lutz, pp. 47–48.
49. Scott, p. 17.
50. Lutz, p. 98; Emma Willard, "Letter Addressed as a Circular to the Members of the Willard Association for the Mutual Improvement of Female Teachers," Troy, 1838.
51. Scott, p. 5; Although Mrs. Willard relinquished the principalship of the Seminary to her daughter-in-law in 1838, she returned to live at the Seminary in 1844 and continued to exercise personal influence on the students until her death in 1870. Lutz, pp. 108–10.
52. Lutz, pp. 49, 115–23.
53. Phillida Bunkle, "Sentimental Womanhood and Domestic Education, 1830-1870," *History of Education Quarterly,* Spring 1974, Vol. 14, p. 13.
54. Scott, p. 8.
55. For a fuller description of the academies, see Theodore R. Sizer, ed., *The Age of the Academies.* Classics in Education, no. 22 (New York: Teachers College, Columbia University, 1964).
56. Woody, pp. 341–63; Maclear, pp. 39–46.
57. Maclear, p. 40.
58. Ibid., p. 41.
59. Woody, p. 519.
60. Ibid., pp. 519–21, 528.
61. Maclear, p. 46.
62. Woody, pp. 519–24; Maclear, pp. 56–60.
63. Quoted in Woody, p. 525.
64. Quoted in Kaestle, p. 86.
65. Quoted in Woody, pp. 527–28.
66. Woody, pp. 105–106.
67. Ibid., pp. 396, 546.
68. Quoted in Maclear, p. 11.
69. Maclear, p. 69.

70. Ibid., p. 69.
71. Woody, Vol. 2, p. 140.
72. Ibid., pp. 140–47.
73. Maclear, pp. 68–78.
74. Quoted in Maclear, p. 80.
75. Quoted in Maclear, p. 80.
76. Maclear, pp. 80–88.
77. Quoted in Maclear, p. 82.
78. See, for example, *Report on Vocational Training* (Chicago: City Club of Chicago, 1912), p. 16.
79. John D. Philbrick, "City School Systems in the United States," Bureau of Education, *Circulars of Information* (Washington, DC: Government Printing Office, 1885), p. 89.
80. W. N. Hutt, "The Education of Women for Homemaking," *NEA Addresses and Proceedings* (Washington, DC: National Education Association, 1910), p. 513.
81. *New York Annual Report,* 1909, p. 531.
82. *New York Annual Report,* 1910. p. 259.
83. Henry S. Tibbets, "The Progress and Aims of Domestic Science in the Public Schools of Chicago," *NEA Addresses and Proceedings* (Washington, DC: National Education Association, 1901), p. 259.
84. Tibbets, "Progress and Aims of Domestic Science," p. 258.
85. *New York Annual Report,* 1910, p. 131.
86. Both quotations from "Report of the Subcommittee on Industrial and Technical Education in the Secondary Schools," *Report of the Committee on the Place of Industries in Public Education to the National Council of Education* (Washington, DC: National Education Association, 1910), pp. 112, 113.
87. Report of the Subcommittee on Industrial and Technical Education, p. 11.
88. *Report of the Commission on Industrial and Education,* (Boston, 1906), p. 18.
89. John L. Rury, "Vocationalism for Home and Work: Women's Education in the United States, 1880–1930," in B. Edward McClellan and W. J. Reese, eds., *The Social History of American Education* (Urbana: University of Illinois Press, 1988).
90. Ibid., p. 245.
91. Ibid., p. 246.
92. Timothy J. Crimmins, "The Crystal Staircase: A Study of the Effects of Caste and Class on Secondary Education in Late 19th Century Atlanta, Georgia," *Urban Education* 8, no.4 (January 1974), pp. 401–21.
93. Ibid., p. 413.
94. Ibid., p. 416.
95. Ibid., p. 415.
96. Ibid., pp. 417–18.

Diversity and Equity: Schooling and African-Americans

After the common-school movement began in the Northeast, it spread rapidly throughout the rest of the United States. State governments began to pass schooling legislation before the Civil War, and by the 1870s thousands of children were attending schools in the North and South. While state school legislation moved more rapidly in the North, one of the most significant developments of this postwar period was the increasing number of African-American children attending school in the South. In fact, as early as the 1870s, in parts of the South, black children were attending school in proportionately higher numbers than white children. However, the educational history of African-Americans in the postwar South presented cause for concern as well as for celebration.

POLITICAL-ECONOMIC DIMENSIONS OF RECONSTRUCTION AND REDEMPTION[1]

On New Year's day in 1863, in the midst of the Civil War, President Abraham Lincoln issued the Emancipation Proclamation announcing the end of slavery for all states in rebellion against the Union. It was not until several months after the war ended in the spring of 1865, however, that Congress passed the Thirteenth Amendment to the Constitution, which freed 4 million slaves, 3½ million of them in the South. By that time, Congress had already created the Freedmen's Bureau as part of the effort to "reconstruct" the southern political economy. The South needed to be reconstructed not only because it had been ravaged by war, but also because the new economic, political, and social order would not, for the first time in over 200 years, include slavery at its center.

The Reconstruction period was marked by radical changes and resulting tensions throughout the South. In 1866 the Fourteenth Amendment was passed by Congress, giving full citizenship to former slaves upon its ratification in 1868. Even before that ratification, however, the Ku Klux Klan was founded by southern white people, in part to keep African-Americans from voting. And just as quickly, southern state governments set up "Black Codes," which segregated African-Americans from whites and prohibited black people from exercising their newfound freedoms. At the same time, many southern whites resisted racial equality with violence. Riots in Memphis and New Orleans resulted in the murders of several black people and brought increased national attention to Reconstruction conflicts.

In 1867 the North increased its influence in the South with the first Reconstruction Act, which gave Congress greater control over the Southern political economy. Northern soldiers occupied the South in an effort to establish a new order, and southern resentments grew. By the end of 1870, all ten ex-"rebel" states had been readmitted to the Union, and the Fifteenth Amendment established the right to vote for all African-American males. The result: black men constituted the majority of voters in five southern states and supported the majority party in the other five. Clearly, the South was being reconstructed with elements it had never known before.

One such mark of the new South was the construction of a number of institutions for the higher education of African-Americans. Many of the colleges and universities that are known today as historically black colleges were founded in the Reconstruction period, usually by missionary aid societies and other Protestant church groups. They include Howard University, in Washington, D.C.; Fisk University, in Nashville; Atlanta University; Hampton Institute, in Virginia; Talladega College, in Alabama; and many others. That African-Americans had a strong desire for education at all levels became clear immediately following the war, and their schooling efforts during Reconstruction were remarkably successful.

Reconstruction also meant dramatic change in the political life of black southerners. Hundreds of African-American politicians sought and won local, state, and U.S. congressional offices. During the first 15 years following the Civil War, two black U.S. Senators were elected from the South. This was double the number of black senators elected over the next 100 years. That fact alone raises the question: why did the gains initiated in the Reconstruction period fail to develop as they should have? The answer lies in what happened following the withdrawal of federal troops from the South in 1877. That point marks the end of the Reconstruction era and the beginning of what white southerners referred to as the "period of redemption." At that point, white southerners were left to "redeem" the South by restoring almost total white domination over political and economic life.

Redemption

Throughout Reconstruction, the Ku Klux Klan and southern "rifle clubs" had continued to fan the flames of white hostility toward black people. Hundreds of African-Americans were lynched by gangs of white racists during Reconstruction, and the northern military presence was often ineffectual. At the same time, the North became less and less committed to reconstructive efforts in the South as northern economic problems deepened. The major depression of 1873 focused northern attention on its own recovery, and the South became a less urgent concern for President Grant and northern lawmakers. Finally, in a political compromise in 1877, southern white support enabled Rutherford B. Hayes to assume the presidency in exchange for removal of federal troops from the South, and the Reconstruction era effectively came to an end.

The South moved swiftly to "redeem" itself from northern influence. As C. Vann Woodward indicated in *Origins of the New South,* most powerful white southerners saw Reconstruction as an interruption in the working-out of the place of free African-Americans in the South.[2] As Woodward points out, despite the considerable educational and political gains black people had made during Reconstruction, their economic gains were meager. In 1900, only 1 out of every 100 African-Americans in 33 predominantly black Georgia counties owned land; only 1 black out of 100 in 17 black Mississippi counties owned land; 1 out of 20 in 12 other black Mississippi counties owned land; and so on throughout the South. What this meant was that black people, the overwhelming majority of whom were still engaged in agriculture, were working white men's land, with white men's mules and plows, and they were required to give up a share of their crop as rent. By 1900, 75 percent of black farmers in the South were sharecroppers or tenant farmers, working for subsistence only.[3]

During this time the southern redemption movement attacked the civil and political rights granted by the Fourteenth and Fifteenth Amendments and enforced during Reconstruction. Following the end of Reconstruction in 1877 and into the 1890s, local white supremacy laws were passed to prohibit black people from using public facilities, such as parks, buildings, cemeteries, railroad cars, rest rooms, and so on. "Pig laws" were passed, which imposed harsh, multiyear prison terms for minor crimes (such as stealing a pig) if they were committed by black people. At the same time, "convict lease" programs were implemented so that white southern industrialists, lumber companies, and mine owners could lease chained convicts from the state and put them to work essentially for free. The death rate on these chain gangs was even higher than the death rate for slaves on the prewar plantations.

In 1890 Mississippi used a constitutional convention to establish literacy and poll-tax requirements that deprived most black people of the vote, and 11 other states followed the "Mississippi Plan" in the next 20 years. In Louisiana, for example, the number of black voters was cut from 130,000 to 1,300 in a 6-year period. States were further encouraged to follow the Mississippi example when the United States Supreme Court upheld the Mississippi Plan as constitutional in 1898. Two years before, the Supreme Court had upheld the "separate but equal" laws that segregated African-Americans from whites in public places, even though it was clear that these "Jim Crow" laws were being used to create a caste system that institutionalized the inferior status of African-Americans in southern social, political, and economic life.[4] The redemption period successfully destroyed most of the advances made by African-Americans during Reconstruction.

At the very time when white America was hailing Booker T. Washington's efforts to improve the lot of African-Americans through a combination of hard work and education, most black southerners were losing the political and educational gains made during the Reconstruction era.

RECONSTRUCTION, REDEMPTION, AND AFRICAN-AMERICAN SCHOOLING

This period of intense oppression of southern black citizens included economic privation, violation of civil and political rights, and racially motivated lynchings that numbered in the thousands. In this atmosphere, an educator from Alabama's Tuskegee Institute became the most prominent African-American leader of his time. In part, Booker T. Washington achieved this leadership position by announcing, before a national audience at the Atlanta Exposition in 1895, that it was acceptable for black people to remain separate from whites in social and political matters, but that black people could help themselves economically by being more industrious and thrifty—and by obtaining the kind of education that would equip them for manual labor in the southern economy. Rather than calling for African-Americans to directly confront their segregated and oppressed social and political status, Washington told his black listeners, "Cast down your buckets where you are!" They would thus take their places as laborers and tradesmen, thereby earning the respect of whites in the South. The "Atlanta compromise" speech was a message that southern white leaders and northern industrialists were delighted to hear.

Washington's accession to power and recognition was crowned in 1901 by dinner at the White House with President Theodore Roosevelt and his family. From his base at Tuskegee he gradually built what became known as the "Tuskegee machine," and from 1901 to 1915 he was in the heyday of his career. Yet "what was for Washington personally the best of times was for most blacks the worst," writes Louis Harlan, "the most discouraging period since the freeing of the slaves."[5]

Indeed, as Washington's rise to power was crowned in 1901, white Alabama Democrats convened to crown their political supremacy over African-Americans. The state's legislature authorized a constitutional convention for May 1901. The convention was so permeated with racially extremist convictions that former governor William C.

Oates felt compelled to comment on the change in white politicians' opinions regarding the status of black people. He was appalled by the shift in racial hatred since Reconstruction, when black people were enfranchised and competing for political office. "Why, sir, the sentiment is altogether different now, when the Negro is doing no harm, why, people want to kill him and wipe him from the face of the earth." These were the times that historian Rayford Logan called the nadir of African-American history.

The most virulent "anti-Negro" speakers at the 1901 Alabama constitutional convention were the Democrats from the black belt or from counties bordering on the black belt.[6] The black belt representatives successfully presented a resolution on education that brought the new state constitution into harmony with the 1890 House Bill 504, which allowed township trustees to fund white schools at a higher level than black schools. The black belt representatives substituted the phrase "just and equitable" for the corresponding phrase in the constitution of 1875, which required that all funds be appointed "for the equal benefit of all the children." During the convention the black belt delegates indicated what they meant by justice and equity. One delegate said, "There is no necessity for paying a teacher for a colored school the same amount you pay to white school teachers, because you can get them at much less salary. Under the present laws of Alabama, if the law is carried out, the colored pupil gets the same amount of money per capita as the white pupil, and that is not justice."

In this atmosphere of racial animosity, the state's constitution was changed to permit local school officers to control apportionments and discriminate against black schoolchildren. The concept of "just and equitable" expressed at this convention stood in marked contrast to the freedmen's politics that had endorsed educational and political equality regardless of race. To the extent that Booker T. Washington aligned himself with the black belt planters, he joined the most antidemocratic forces of his era.[7] But in order to assess Washington's approach to schooling for African-Americans in the South, it is first necessary to examine those schools in the Reconstruction and redemption periods.

Schooling in the Black Belt

Few values and aspirations were more firmly rooted in the freedmen's culture than education. Their crusade for universal schooling was perhaps the most striking illustration of their postwar campaign for self-improvement. Their idea of universal public schooling, regardless of race or class, was a conception of education and democracy unprecedented in southern history. The prewar constitutions and laws of the Confederate states denied literacy and formal schooling to black people and paid little attention to public education at all. South Carolina's constitution made no mention of education. Alabama, Arkansas, and Florida had brief general clauses about encouraging the means of education and about using the proceeds of federal land grants to support schools. A clause in the Georgia constitution of 1777 about schools was omitted in later revisions, though provision was made in 1798 for promoting "seminaries of learning." Mississippi and North Carolina alluded to the value of learning in their constitutions but made no specifications about state schools. Virginia used a "capitation" (or per capita) tax for use of white primary schools. Louisiana and Texas went somewhat further than the others, providing for superintendents, a school fund, and state school systems, but hedging the language regarding the implementation of public systems of education. For example, Louisiana's constitution of 1852 stated that the legislature might abolish the superintendent's office, while in Texas the legislature was to establish a school system "as early as practicable."[8]

These haphazard and halting constitutional provisions for education in the antebellum South were transformed into elaborate legal frameworks for universal public schooling in the Reconstruction era. The freed men and women helped set in motion customs, laws, and political movements that fundamentally altered the definition of public education. They formed the core of the political vanguard that inserted universal public education into the Reconstruction constitutions of the former Confederate states. The constitutional provisions for public schooling shifted from vague clauses to decisive *shall* declarations and highly specific requirements.[9]

EXHIBIT 6.1 **Percentage of School-Age Population Enrolled in School by Race in Selected Alabama Counties: 1877, 1887, 1897, and 1915**

	1877		1887		1897		1915	
County	Black	White	Black	White	Black	White	Black	White
Autauga	37.5	25.4	37.1	48.9	40.5	69.4	39.6	70.3
Barbour	35.3	53.9	54.5	54.0	51.4	60.0	35.3	71.6
Bullock	21.8	28.5	39.6	44.6	39.7	72.0	43.6	80.1
Butler	29.4	26.5	54.4	45.5	54.1	64.4	43.3	66.3
Chambers	25.8	25.0	67.0	60.8	78.5	70.8	31.8	80.2
Choctaw	35.2	27.7	59.0	55.2	70.9	86.1	55.3	84.4
Clarke	47.5	42.4	53.1	48.1	80.9	52.8	41.8	73.5
Dallas	28.7	26.3	37.2	44.4	40.3	26.8	37.4	72.2
Greene	27.8	32.0	45.6	41.6	47.5	48.1	51.8	93.1
Hale	24.6	25.4	42.5	50.5	40.1	68.5	51.9	69.2
Lee	45.6	38.5	57.0	40.3	47.4	53.4	42.5	71.8
Lowndes	30.5	36.4	36.8	41.0	24.7	68.1	38.2	72.2
Macon	41.0	36.4	58.4	37.4	49.5	59.6	61.4	69.4
Marengo	20.3	24.0	36.6	54.9	44.2	66.7	32.5	78.4
Monroe	71.3	64.1	97.3	63.4	52.3	65.4	47.4	80.6
Montgomery	14.5	19.3	34.2	26.6	44.0	73.5	36.6	68.9
Perry	32.3	29.9	32.5	39.6	26.1	59.6	43.1	68.5
Pickens	48.9	62.3	59.1	67.0	68.9	63.9	72.1	80.9
Russell	30.5	37.5	65.4	65.8	65.9	47.2	43.9	71.8
Sumter	32.5	32.3	55.9	52.0	46.6	69.9	29.7	73.0
Wilcox	27.7	32.2	50.1	55.5	37.3	71.4	19.6	78.9

Sources: Report of Superintendent of Education for the State of Alabama, 1878, with Tabular Statistics of 1876–7 (Montgomery: Barrett and Brown, 1879), pp. xlix–lvi; *Thirty-third Annual Report of the Superintendent of Education of Alabama, 1887* (Montgomery: W.D. Brown, 1888), pp. 99–116; *Report of Superintendent of Education of Alabama, 1898* (Montgomery: Brown Printing Company, 1898), pp. 268–70, 327–28; *Annual Report of the Department of Education of the State of Alabama, 1915* (Montgomery: The Brown Printing Company, 1915), pp. 110–16.

Events in Alabama paralleled regional developments. In 1867, Alabama freedmen coalesced with other Republicans to enact constitutional laws that provided ample sources of public education revenue for the schools, discouraged private contributions to finance public education, promised equal opportunities regardless of race or class, and did not mandate racially separate schools, though the state constitution did leave the decision entirely to the discretion of the state board of education. Still, so far as the black belt freedmen were concerned, the constitution of 1868 provided virtually every promise of equal opportunities. Further, their rights were ensured in part by the presence of Peyton Finley, an African-American citizen from the black belt, on the state board of education. He pressed constantly for an equal division of the public school fund among African-Americans and whites.[10]

Educational opportunities were not always equal, but black people's political participation and the racial equality established in Alabama's Reconstruction constitution enabled them to make gains in public schooling between 1868 and the reestablishment of planter dominance in the late 1870s. For instance, in 1877, in 11 of the 21 Alabama black belt counties, the percentage of black children of school age enrolled in school exceeded the percentage of white children enrolled (see Exhibit 6.1). For the black belt as a whole, the average length of public school terms for black children was longer than that for white children, though the average length of white school terms in 11 of the counties exceeded that for black children (see Exhibit 6.2). The average monthly pay for black teachers in 1877 exceeded that for white teachers in 18 of the 21 black belt counties (see Exhibit 6.3). As long as the state funding of

EXHIBIT 6.2 Average Length of Public Schools in Days by Race in Selected Alabama Counties: 1877, 1887, 1897, and 1915

	1877		1887		1897		1915	
County	Black	White	Black	White	Black	White	Black	White
Autauga	86	60	89	61	63	63	93	140
Barbour	74	81	85	71	68	62	91	148
Bullock	71	69	106	70	63	64	86	163
Butler	105	67	82	65	72	60	84	122
Chambers	78	87	131	120	60	60	91	156
Choctaw	64	80	65	65	60	64	56	120
Clarke	74	72	82	72	65	80	72	110
Dallas	92	74	75	60	68	70	108	172
Greene	93	122	106	74	86	85	94	158
Hale	79	57	80	64	78	79	102	115
Lee	81	94	95	71	60	60	89	156
Lowndes	78	98	83	60	72	92	91	142
Macon	79	80	70	60	78	79	101	158
Marengo	71	63	95	70	78	71	93	126
Monroe	125	87	59	63	70	65	65	120
Montgomery	100	88	100	97	72	80	121	174
Perry	88	79	96	72	77	79	109	152
Pickens	68	84	60	60	60	75	80	108
Russell	76	81	83	71	62	64	80	152
Sumter	80	91	79	79	70	81	86	152
Wilcox	99	102	78	60	60	66	81	151
Total averages	84	82	86	71	69	71	89	143

Sources: Report of Superintendent of Education for the State of Alabama, 1878, with Tabular Statistics of 1876–7 (Montgomery: Barrett and Brown, 1879), pp. xlix–lvi; *Thirty-third Annual Report of the Superintendent of Education of Alabama, 1887* (Montgomery: W.D. Brown, 1888), pp. 99–116; *Report of Superintendent of Education of Alabama, 1898* (Montgomery: Brown Printing Company, 1898), pp. 268–70, 327–28; *Annual Report of the Department of Education of the State of Alabama, 1915* (Montgomery: Brown Printing Company, 1915), pp. 110–16.

Alabama's black belt remained nearly equal between the races, or even if the school fund was divided according to the poll tax and real estate taxes paid by the two races, black communities, given their quest for education, could continue to foster the expansion and improvement of public schools. But this was all to change with the end of Reconstruction.

The seeds for the destruction of educational advancement in black communities were planted in 1875, the year the redeemers—white Democrats—began to regain control of Alabama's black belt. In Macon County, for example, in 1875 the county's two state representatives, both black Republicans, were charged with and convicted of felonies—adultery and grand larceny—by the newly elected circuit judge, James Edward Cobb. They were sentenced by Cobb to chain gangs. Cobb, a Democrat and former Confederate colonel, had been captured at Gettysburg and spent the remainder of the war in Union prisons. He charged the district's white Republican state senator with perjury, but the senator avoided prosecution by resigning office. Throughout Alabama's black belt in 1875, freedmen were driven from political office and either disfranchised or controlled firmly by white Democrats. Consequently, the state's constitution of 1875, reflecting the reestablishment of planter political supremacy, severely restricted the amount of money available for public schools.[11]

The constitution framed by the black belt redeemers in 1875 legally required racial segregation in schools. It also altered the governance of public education in ways that placed it permanently in white hands. However, there was no wholesale demolition of the structures that the former slaves and their Republican allies had created. Most importantly, the legal framework of school finance in

EXHIBIT 6.3 Average Monthly Pay of Teachers by Race in Selected Alabama Counties: 1877, 1887, 1897, and 1915

	1877		1887		1897		1915	
County	Black	White	Black	White	Black	White	Black	White
Autauga	$34.36	$37.13	$22.08	$26.50	$19.51	$29.80	$24.78	$47.93
Barbour	23.50	13.50	29.30	23.33	18.99	24.93	27.54	55.72
Bullock	28.46	16.65	27.50	20.00	30.50	35.50	25.57	60.48
Butler	24.50	17.50	26.04	25.56	16.24	24.20	25.54	55.30
Chambers	18.00	18.75	31.57	38.00	27.30	27.30	30.87	49.76
Choctaw	26.70	23.00	25.93	22.95	18.60	20.00	22.12	52.58
Clarke	20.18	17.00	22.33	24.75	16.15	19.85	30.65	64.23
Dallas	17.80	12.50	34.33	17.00	28.00	27.00	22.93	71.73
Greene	32.77	13.50	29.22	19.30	18.16	17.65	24.29	55.89
Hale	31.00	16.00	36.86	19.53	21.33	30.65	25.68	63.55
Lee	19.41	14.57	20.75	18.00	18.52	26.45	32.93	62.28
Lowndes	29.00	22.00	29.47	26.44	25.00	50.00	27.84	74.58
Macon	15.00	18.00	20.00	20.00	15.06	20.20	28.87	56.65
Marengo	35.05	27.28	34.50	25.18	19.29	27.90	22.48	68.66
Monroe	25.00	22.58	19.93	21.77	10.01	15.50	30.52	49.27
Montgomery	27.60	18.06	22.00	30.00	21.11	30.05	31.52	78.96
Perry	27.96	17.35	32.39	20.57	11.70	15.79	26.08	53.65
Pickens	32.00	19.31	14.00	16.00	16.00	21.00	20.75	50.22
Russell	20.12	12.60	31.00	36.95	17.51	28.13	29.26	70.71
Sumter	30.07	21.80	27.75	27.07	19.25	34.93	26.46	66.68
Wilcox	22.44	13.76	25.60	16.30	14.30	31.98	19.88	62.63

Sources: Report of Superintendent of Education for the State of Alabama, 1878, with Tabular Statistics of 1876–7 (Montgomery: Barrett and Brown, 1879), pp. xlix–lvi; *Thirty-third Annual Report of the Superintendent of Education of Alabama, 1887* (Montgomery: W.D. Brown, 1888), pp. 99–116; *Report of Superintendent of Education of Alabama, 1898* (Montgomery: Brown Printing Company, 1898), pp. 268–70, 327–28; *Annual Report of the Department of Education of the State of Alabama, 1915* (Montgomery: Brown Printing Company, 1915), pp. 110–16.

the 1875 constitution was strictly on a per capita child basis and for the equal benefit of each race, thus leaving no discretion to any official to discriminate for or against either racial group. Reconstruction had nearly ended in the black belt in 1875, and the redeemers were committed to retrenchment in public education. But two key factors protected the continued development of education in the black communities. First, black people could still vote, and the redeemers knew that as long as they sought to win black votes it was politically dangerous to tamper excessively with black public education. Second, black public education was protected in part because of the legal safeguards for equal funding that the freedmen had inserted in the state constitution of 1868 and which remained a part of the 1875 constitution.[12]

Hence, even during a decade of redeemer government in Alabama's black belt from 1877 to 1887, black education continued to prosper. In 1887, as in 1877, the percentage of school-age black children enrolled in school exceeded the percentage of white children enrolled in 11 of the 21 counties (see Exhibit 6.1). With respect to length of school terms, in 20 of 21 counties in 1887, the black school terms were longer than or equal to the white school terms (see Exhibit 6.2).

Moreover, racial disparities in the average length of school terms had increased considerably in favor of black children since 1877—from 84 to 86 days for black pupils and from 82 to 71 days for white pupils. This represented significant improvement of educational conditions in black communities between 1877 and 1887. Conditions for whites declined as black students took advantage of schooling opportunities that whites did not have. These included schools supported by churches, the Freedmen's Bureau, and local black citizens. Only in a few instances did whites move toward parity. The average monthly pay of black teachers in 1887 exceeded the average monthly pay of white teachers in 13 counties, but blacks had earned more than whites in 18 counties in 1877 (see Exhibit 6.3). Hence, as we shall see, Booker T. Washington entered the black belt in 1881 in the midst of an era of advancement in black education dating back to the Reconstruction constitution of 1868.

Approximately 10 years after Washington's arrival, black education fell on hard times. In 1890, State Superintendent of Education Solomon Palmer, in his annual report, introduced his discussion of major problems confronting public education by declaring that Alabama had to increase school revenues in order to keep pace with other states and meet the growing demand of its school population. He then proceeded to review the complaints against the way in which the school funds were apportioned and spent. The two principal complaints were first, that blacks in the black belt counties received nearly all of the area's school funds while paying virtually no taxes; and second, that black pupils were not mentally advanced to the point where they needed as much education as white pupils, and therefore did not need as much money for their education. Palmer's response was to place public school funds in the hands of local white school authorities to be spent at their discretion.

In 1890, Palmer's plan was introduced in the Alabama legislature as House Bill 504. It passed in the House and Senate in February of 1891. The new law required the state superintendent to apportion the public school fund according to the school-age population, but authorized township trustees to apportion funds as they deemed "just and equitable." This law effectively relieved the superintendent of education of the responsibility for apportioning the school fund between the races, and it was used to get around the state's constitutional provision requiring that the school fund be apportioned on a per capita basis and for the equal benefit of both races.[13]

No political faction in Alabama was more in favor of this new plan than the white Democrats of the black belt counties. Representative Smith of Russell County thought it was the best bill ever introduced in the Alabama legislature, and he declared that the author of the bill "deserved a vote of thanks from the white people of the state." The superintendent of schools of Wilcox County, where in 1891 above 85 percent of the school-age population was black, welcomed the new law by proclaiming that "Wilcox never had such a boom on schools. The new law has stimulated the whites so that neighborhoods where no schools existed for years, are now building houses and organizing schools." It was clear both to black people and to whites that this law assigned state funds to white county officials to allocate as they chose. The result in black belt counties was to permit school officers to pour money into white schools and to give tiny sums to the black schools. Ironically, the black belt Democrats favored a "color-blind" distribution of the school fund over creating a racially distinct tax base and apportionment because the former would permit them to take an even larger share of the tax base.[14]

The day following the passage of House Bill 504, a "colored convention" convened in Montgomery, the state's capital. The general purpose of the convention was to "discuss subjects which would benefit the Negro race in Alabama." A pressing concern was the newly passed school-fund apportionment law. In the evening session of the convention, Booker T. Washington spoke against the law. His speech was described by a reporter for the Montgomery *Advertiser* as a "bitter" indictment of the Alabama legislature for authorizing school officers to bypass the 1875 constitutional provision for equal apportionment of the already meager school funds. Ironically, only 3 years earlier, Washington had said, "The rate at which prejudice is dying out is so rapid as to justify the conclusion that the Negro will in a quarter of a century enjoy in Alabama every right that he now enjoys in Pennsylvania." He had spoken too soon. Black Alabamians were about to enter the era from 1890 to 1910, referred to by Benjamin Brawley as the "vale of tears." With the new school-funding statute in place, the campaign to shortchange black education had an open field.[15]

After 1890, the Democrats in black belt counties seized the school funds of the disfranchised black citizens. Consequently, the general enrollment and school terms of black children and the average pay of black teachers came to a standstill, and in many cases actually decreased, while educational condi-

African-American commitment to education was so strong that 10 years after the end of Reconstruction, attendance at black schools was still higher than at most white schools.

tions among whites began to improve sharply (see Exhibits 6.1, 6.2, and 6.3). In vital respects, black education in the black belt counties, which had advanced steadily from 1867 to 1887, declined significantly from 1887 to 1897. In ten counties, the percentage of school-age black children enrolled in school was lower than in 1887. In 17 counties, the black school terms were shorter than they had been in 1887, and the average monthly pay of black teachers had decreased in 19 of the 21 counties between 1887 and 1897. Hence, two years following Washington's "Atlanta Compromise" address, the speech that catapulted him into national prominence as educational statesman of black America, the postwar struggle for education in Alabama's black communities had reached its nadir.

This period of retrogression must have been difficult and peculiar for Washington. In general, as Louis Harlan has written, "Washington allied himself with the southern planters and businessmen against the poorer class of whites." The legal, political, and extralegal movements to crush the development of black education were led by some of the same allies, the white planter Democratic coalition from the black belt counties.[16]

As Louis Harlan has documented in his classic study, *Separate and Unequal,* the campaign by local and state governments to improve public schools in the South from 1901 to 1915 was aimed at white people, and it sharply increased the disparities between the schools the two races attended. In short, law and government had been used successfully to recreate inequality.

White public education steadily gained ground on black public education. In 1915, in every black belt county the percentage of school-age white children enrolled in school exceeded that of black schoolchildren (see Exhibit 6.1). This was not the case in 1877, 1887, or 1897. Moreover, in 14 counties in 1915, the percentage of school-age black children enrolled in school had fallen below the 1897 rates (see Exhibit 6.1). Thus, relative to white enrollments and relative to their own position in 1897, black school enrollments declined significantly during the apex of Washington's career. Similarly, in 1915, the length of white school terms and the average monthly pay of white teachers exceeded those for blacks, usually by significant margins, in every black belt county. In all but four counties in 1915, the average monthly pay of white teachers doubled that of black teachers (see

Exhibit 6.3). This was a drastic turnaround from 1877, when the average monthly pay of black teachers exceeded that of white teachers in 19 of the 21 black belt counties. Finally, the percentage of black teachers decreased, generally sharply, in 19 of the 21 black belt counties (Exhibit 6.4). After 1890 and until Washington's death in 1915, African-Americans' conception of community advancement turned inward. Assuming a defensive posture, they concentrated on strengthening their institutions and surviving in the face of an undemocratic and unjust social order, since they no longer had political clout. Their educational advancement during the Washington era depended heavily on private sacrifices. In 1915, approximately 60 percent of the schoolhouses for black children in Alabama's black belt were privately owned (Exhibit 6.5). A large amount of money was contributed by blacks to public education over and above that paid as taxes. It was through such traditions and customs of self-sacrifice that black communities kept afloat a fragmented and feeble school system during the "vale of tears."[17]

BOOKER T. WASHINGTON'S CAREER

While appraising Booker T. Washington's influence on public education for blacks in Alabama, African-American reformer and historian Horace Mann Bond wrote that "the historian of educational events may find in the life of the builder of Tuskegee Institute perhaps the most illuminating point of departure from which to evaluate the times and the social and economic forces in which he was involved." Bond cautioned us not to make two grave errors. First, we should not attribute momentous social and economic changes to Washington's heroic leadership. Second, we should not judge his greatness by immediate quantitative and institutional results. After all, said Bond, Booker T. Washington had become a legend, and "who shall deny the importance of legends, as social forces, in affecting the course of human history?" The continuing interest in Washington and his era gives at least some credence to Bond's observations.[18]

There is also much validity to Bond's suggestion that Washington's life is an "illuminating point of departure" from which to examine a most critical historical moment in the development of African-American education, the period from Reconstruction to the great migration of southern African-Americans to the urban North from 1914 to 1930. Born a slave in 1856, he was already of school age when the former slaves mobilized to create in the South a system of universal public education. Washington, a part of this movement himself, described most vividly their struggle for education: "Few people who were not right in the midst of the scenes can form any exact idea of the intense desire which the people of my race showed for education. It was a whole race trying to go to school. Few were too young, and none too old, to make the attempt to learn." As a schoolboy, he worked at a salt furnace from four to nine in the morning before attending day school, and later, he worked in the morning and attended school for a few hours every afternoon. In 1872, at age 16 and crudely educated, he went off to the Hampton Normal and Agricultural Institute in Hampton, Virginia. He was one of hundreds of young African-Americans who flocked to the normal schools and colleges in search of an education that would enable them to lead their people effectively.[19]

Washington started working as a teacher in 1875 and in 1879 became a teacher and assistant at Hampton Institute. In 1881, he went to Tuskegee and began his life's work. By this time Reconstruction had collapsed, and his career as educational statesman was launched in a fundamentally different political context from the one in which he attended elementary and normal school. The South became a one-party region under the control of a reactionary ruling elite that sought to contain the freedmen's progressive campaign for democracy and universal schooling. In this context, Washington rose to great heights as educational and political statesman for African-Americans everywhere. Again, we are reminded, as historian Louis R. Harlan has written, "Washington's rise coincided with a setback of his race."[20]

With Bond's cautions kept in mind, great social and political changes will not be attributed to Washington's influence here, nor will his contribution be evaluated in terms of institutional results. Nonetheless, it should be borne in mind that one of Washington's important claims and a central

EXHIBIT 6.4

Black Percentage of School-Age Population, Schools, and Teachers in Selected Alabama Counties: 1877, 1887, 1897, and 1915

	1877			1887			1897			1915		
County	Percent of school-age population	Percent of schools	Percent of teachers	Percent of school-age population	Percent of schools	Percent of teachers	Percent of school-age population	Percent of schools	Percent of teachers	Percent of school-age population	Percent of schools	Percent of teachers
Autauga	44.8	40.3	40.4	63.6	53.3	57.7	65.2	49.2	49.2	61.2	43.7	35.1
Barbour	53.4	37.0	37.0	60.1	48.1	48.0	63.6	41.9	43.4	65.4	39.6	34.0
Bullock	69.8	50.0	49.0	74.7	54.9	52.2	80.5	54.7	54.7	87.8	60.2	47.8
Butler	41.7	18.7	18.5	45.4	37.5	35.0	48.1	38.8	43.5	58.2	39.0	33.8
Chambers	43.1	25.6	25.6	45.4	33.6	33.6	52.7	42.1	42.1	56.5	38.0	27.0
Choctaw	50.1	45.8	45.8	53.8	47.2	38.8	51.4	42.7	43.3	63.4	37.1	33.0
Clarke	53.4	38.4	38.5	56.9	52.3	60.0	53.1	41.5	41.5	59.5	38.7	34.8
Dallas	84.1	63.8	63.8	88.0	76.4	74.7	90.3	74.1	74.1	85.2	68.8	55.4
Greene	80.8	64.7	64.7	86.1	72.0	70.3	86.4	60.2	60.2	88.1	63.4	63.4
Hale	77.5	69.4	69.4	83.4	65.9	63.0	85.8	63.6	63.1	81.5	57.6	53.2
Lee	48.4	46.3	46.3	49.3	46.3	46.3	63.5	52.6	51.6	65.1	42.1	35.8
Lowndes	80.0	68.5	68.5	86.5	75.5	75.5	90.9	63.5	63.5	90.9	62.4	58.5
Macon	57.7	53.9	53.9	65.3	57.1	57.1	74.1	62.8	61.4	85.9	37.2	61.3
Marengo	73.9	48.4	48.4	76.0	58.4	58.0	76.9	50.0	50.0	74.4	39.5	33.5
Monroe	47.4	29.7	29.7	54.1	57.9	43.0	55.7	40.4	40.4	58.2	38.7	33.0
Montgomery	72.9	57.4	57.4	73.0	69.6	69.6	85.3	64.5	63.6	75.8	60.6	45.4
Perry	73.5	47.3	47.3	76.0	58.3	58.8	79.5	51.0	50.5	83.1	55.0	32.3
Pickens	49.1	32.9	32.9	55.3	47.0	41.8	55.1	44.0	37.9	53.5	40.3	36.9
Russell	66.5	61.9	61.9	71.5	54.7	54.7	73.0	64.6	64.6	83.9	61.1	50.0
Sumter	70.9	60.6	60.6	75.9	68.3	62.1	80.9	64.2	60.2	84.6	53.6	40.2
Wilcox	75.6	61.7	61.7	77.3	57.9	57.9	79.3	50.0	50.0	83.8	33.3	40.0.

Sources: Report of Superintendent of Education for the State of Alabama, 1878, with Tabular Statistics of 1876–7 (Montgomery: Barrett and Brown, 1879), pp. xlix–lvi; *Thirty-third Annual Report of the Superintendent of Education of Alabama, 1887* (Montgomery: W.D. Brown, 1888), pp. 99–116; *Report of Superintendent of Education of Alabama, 1898* (Montgomery: Brown Printing Company, 1898), pp. 268–70, 327–8; *Annual Report of the Department of Education of the State of Alabama, 1915* (Montgomery: Brown Printing Company, 1915), pp. 110–16.

EXHIBIT 6.5 Number and Percentage of Schoolhouses by Race and Ownership in Selected Alabama Counties

	Schoolhouses for black children				Schoolhouses for white children			
County	Public	Private	% Public	% Private	Public	Private	% Public	% Private
Autauga	4	26	13.4	86.6	30	10	75.0	25.0
Barbour	19	23	45.2	54.8	55	10	84.6	15.4
Bullock	17	30	36.2	63.8	24	9	72.7	27.3
Butler	30	17	63.8	36.2	63	8	87.5	12.5
Chambers	31	4	88.6	11.4	56	1	98.2	1.8
Choctaw	36	0	100.0	0	53	8	86.9	13.1
Clarke	31	21	59.6	40.4	74	9	89.2	10.8
Dallas	9	90	9.1	90.9	26	19	57.7	42.3
Greene	33	26	66.0	44.0	27	2	93.1	6.9
Hale	5	51	9.0	91.0	25	17	59.5	40.5
Lee	30	9	77.0	23.0	42	3	93.3	6.7
Lowndes	18	40	30.0	70.0	20	15	57.1	42.9
Macon	45	6	88.2	11.8	24	8	75.0	25.0
Marengo	8	37	17.8	82.2	49	20	71.0	29.0
Monroe	26	20	56.5	43.5	53	20	72.6	27.4
Montgomery	18	77	18.9	81.1	44	18	71.0	29.0
Perry	5	46	9.8	90.2	33	12	73.3	26.7
Pickens	31	19	62.0	38.0	65	9	87.8	12.2
Russell	14	30	31.8	68.2	27	2	93.1	6.9
Sumter	3	34	8.1	91.9	22	10	68.8	31.2
Wilcox	13	14	48.1	51.9	32	22	59.3	40.7
Totals	426	630	40.3	59.7	844	232	78.4	21.6

Source: Annual Report of the Department of Education of the State of Alabama for the Scholastic Year Ending September 30, 1915 (Montgomery: Brown Printing Company, 1915), pp. 110–16.

part of his legacy was the belief that despite political compromises, he had a favorable impact on the advancement of public education in black communities. In *Up From Slavery,* Washington wrote about teachers in Alabama's black belt, where schools were in session only three to five months out of the year, and how he and his graduates worked to improve these conditions. He spoke frequently of Tuskegee graduates who were "showing the people how to extend the school term to 4, 5, and even 7 months." In 1911, he claimed that as a result of the Tuskegee program there existed in Macon County "a model public school system, supported in part by the county board of education, and in part by the contributions of the people themselves."[21]

Undoubtedly, Washington was a ceaseless propagandist for education. On speaking platforms, through periodicals, and in the white and black press, he lost no opportunity to plead for the advancement of public education. Indeed, the chief benefit that Washington intended black people to receive from the "Atlanta Compromise" speech was the chance to attain an education that would fit them for useful employment. The central concern of this chapter is with what actually happened to black public education during Washington's career, particularly in Alabama's black belt, where he became the chief spokesperson for that struggle.

Washington and Schooling in the Black Belt

In the summer of 1881, Washington went to Macon County, Alabama, to become principal of the newly created black state normal school in the town of Tuskegee. This was a place in the deep South—the black belt—where he had never been before, but where his people had struggled for generations to forge and nurture a culture that placed a high premium on literacy and formal schooling.

The "Tuskegee story" of Washington's era runs counter to the parallel development of black education. The story is symbolized by a statue on Tuskegee's campus portraying Washington as "lifting the veil of ignorance from the Negro race." This particular legacy holds that there is plenty of room for debate over Washington's methods, but none over his results. He demonstrated that against overwhelming odds he could turn a dilapidated shanty and a run-down church in rural Alabama into the most famous black institution of learning of its time. Over the years, schools and colleges (normal schools) founded and taught by Tuskegee alumni sprang up throughout the rural South, helping downtrodden African-Americans to improve and expand their local school systems by finding a common ground of understanding with powerful white politicians. This pragmatic philosophy, which propelled Washington into national fame and power, is believed to have worked at the local level to systematically improve public educational opportunities in black communities. Thus, despite the setbacks in politics, civil rights, and human rights that occurred during the age of Washington, his disciples were credited with steadily building an infrastructure of practical education that protected black students from the worst tendencies of southern racism. Some even suggest that Washington's pragmatic approach, his emphasis on the work ethic, traditional morality, and industrial education, "may well have saved Negro education from total destruction." It is maintained that Washington's promises to keep the Negro in "his place" and to educate him to be a more efficient laborer "reconciled many whites to the idea of Negro education."[22]

Whatever grain of truth may be contained in the above version of the Tuskegee story, it is largely mythology. The age of Booker T. Washington was characterized by the worst treatment of black public education by state and local school officers since the end of slavery. Indeed, Washington's generation was sandwiched between two important progressive eras in southern black public education: (1) the two decades (1877–97) following Reconstruction and (2) the two decades (1915–35) following Washington's death. Both progressive eras were sustained by grass-roots movements in black communities designed to challenge rather than cooperate with southern white authorities.

It is revealing that the post-Washington school campaigns were precipitated mainly by ordinary black men and women who defied one of his sacred principles: "Cast down your bucket where you are." Washington urged African Americans to remain in the South and find common ground with white planters and businessmen. But many African Americans were willing to tolerate only one generation of state-enforced illiteracy. Hence, in 1915, black southerners en masse picked up their "buckets" and headed northward in search of better economic and educational opportunities. Just as the freedmen had used political power to foster universal schooling during the Reconstruction era, black workers during the post-Washington era used the withdrawal of their labor power as a powerful form of protest against intolerable economic and social conditions. Many black families remained in the South, however.

What they did in the two decades following his death was monumental. Their defiance of southern white authority, coupled with a grassroots campaign for universal schooling, radically altered the educational opportunities for black schoolchildren. The proportion of southern black children aged 5 to 14 enrolled in school increased from 36 percent in 1900 to 78 percent by 1935, and the corresponding rate for whites went from 55 percent in 1900 to 79 percent in 1935. Younger black children, whose rates of enrollment were significantly lower than those of younger whites in 1900, had reached parity by 1935. Black high school enrollment increased from 3 percent of the high-school–age black population in 1910 to 18 percent in 1935, and the white high school enrollment increased from 10 percent to 54 percent. There was far from parity at the secondary level, but the overall improvements in black elementary and secondary schooling represented significant improvement since the age of Washington. Undoubtedly, Booker T. Washington would have been proud of the educational achievements of his successors, particularly of rural black people. It was an educational awakening of the same kind as the freedmen's school campaigns which he recalled with such pride. It was also a kind that he never witnessed during his career as educational statesman of black America.[23]

Washington had tried in his own passive style to halt the Democrats' dismantling of the black public school system. He urged white school reformers, especially northern white philanthropists who worked in the South, to take a strong stand on behalf of state support for black rural schools. He arranged in 1909 for the publication and dissemination of a pamphlet by Charles Coon, a white county school superintendent in North Carolina, showing that more tax money was paid by black North Carolinians than was allocated to their schools. Washington was propagandizing against the southern white claim that white taxpayers were paying for black public schools, especially in black belt counties. He had hoped that such efforts would generate a greater spirit of fairness toward black public schools.

In several ways Washington sought to expose the gross racial inequality in southern public education. For example, in 1909 he sent the members of the Southern Education Board evidence that in Lowndes County, Alabama, $20 per capita went to white schoolchildren and $0.67 per capita to black schoolchildren. Lowndes was located in Alabama's black belt, just two counties west of Macon. However, there was virtually nothing that Washington could do through letters and propaganda to slow the decline of black public education. In earlier times, particularly from 1868 to 1890, black communities were able to check assaults on their public school systems through political clout and legal safeguards. Ironically, it was Washington who made the observation in 1902 that "not one of his students had ever broke into jail or Congress." Now, in order to protect the reform movement that he cherished the most—the advancement of education in black communities—he found himself needing the very political involvement he had once discouraged. Without political clout, Washington could only stand by and observe quietly, as he did in 1909, that the advancement of white education "is being made at the expense of Negro education, that is, the money is actually being taken from the colored people and given to white schools."[24]

Historians have tended to see Washington's accommodationist style of leadership as appropriate to the context of its time, that is, as a pragmatic response to the racial injustices of the late 19th and early 20th centuries. They maintain that, given the basic inhumanity of the era, it is hard to see how Washington could have preached a radically different philosophy in his time and place. However, other leaders of the same era did in fact articulate a radically different philosophy, including W. E. B. Du Bois, William Monroe Taylor, Ida B. Wells-Barnett, and John Hope, to name only a few.

What is perplexing and interesting about Washington's era is the manner in which African-American leaders of similar social experiences developed such varied understandings of, and solutions to, the problem of racial oppression. This had much to do with their different perceptions of social reality and the political meanings they derived from their perceptions. One of the essential qualities of an effective leader is the ability to raise the consciousness of his or her people from the personal to the social. Common men and women experience an oppressive social system in a thousand personal and seemingly disconnected ways. It is a leader's challenge to help the masses see their oppression as flowing from a common social source and to help them identify their oppressors. The quality of leadership is determined in large part by the ideological cohesion that leaders provide for their followers, which in turn stems directly from the leaders' own perceptions of their social environment. Put another way, Washington, Du Bois, and other leaders held different perceptions of the causes of racial oppression and these different perceptions in turn led them to put forward different proposals for liberation. The remainder of this chapter will first examine Washington's perceptions of the so-called race problem during his times and then contrast his views with those of W.E.B. Du Bois.

AN IDEOLOGY OF AFRICAN-AMERICAN INFERIORITY

Early in his career, Washington was forced to examine his perceptions of racial conflict and to formulate a coherent explanation of racial inequality in America. As he put it, "One of the first questions that I had to answer for myself after beginning my work at Tuskegee was how I was to deal with public opinion on the race question." For an answer to this question he resorted not to the social perceptions—folklore and slave-community perceptions of race and slavery—implicit in

African-American traditions, nor to his day-to-day experiences in an oppressive system of racial subordination, but to the precepts and lessons he had learned at Hampton Institute under the tutelage of Samuel Chapman Armstrong, a white Union officer in the Civil War who worked for the Freedmen's Bureau in the South. The hallmarks of Washington's leadership, his conservative social philosophy, his accommodation with white supremacy and racial segregation, and his romantic belief in industrial education and skilled labor as a means to overcome all racial and class discrimination were well developed in the 1870s and early 1880s. What Washington learned as a student at Hampton Institute from 1872 to 1875 and as a postgraduate from 1879 to 1881 were perceptions of race development, politics, economics, and education that tended to rationalize historical and contemporary oppression while offering hope in the distant future.[25]

According to historian Louis R. Harlan, Washington found in Armstrong "the great white father for whom he had long been searching." Since Washington knew that his own father was white but was never certain of his father's identity, it is plausible that he longed for this father figure. What is more certain, however, is that Washington was overwhelmed by Armstrong and began to model his own conduct and thought on Armstrong's. In his autobiography, *Up From Slavery,* Washington said of Armstrong, "I shall always remember that the first time I went into his presence he made the impression upon me of being a perfect man; I was made to feel that there was something about him that was superhuman." He described Armstrong as "the most perfect specimen of man, physically, mentally and spiritually" that he had ever seen, and he considered the best part of his education to have been the privilege of being permitted to look upon General Armstrong each day. Washington had the opportunity of observing Armstrong closely, for throughout his 3 years at Hampton he was janitor in the academic building, close to the general and the other white teachers.[26]

A Liberal Justification for Racial Oppression: Darwinian Evolution

One of the first and more enduring lessons Washington learned from Armstrong was the meaning of race, its significance throughout human history, and its bearing upon relationships between European Americans and African-Americans. Armstrong sincerely believed that race was the key to understanding morality, industry, thrift, responsibility, ambition, and the overall social worth of human beings. He believed that the human race was appropriately divided into the white and darker races. The white races were civilized, superior because they had centuries of Christian moral development, hard work, self-government, and material prosperity. The darker races, including Indians, Polynesians (Armstrong was a child of missionaries in Hawaii), and Africans were weak in Christian morality, lacked industrious habits, and were incapable of self-government and political leadership. As Armstrong put it, "The [American] white race has had three centuries of experience in organizing the forces about him, political, social, and physical. The Negro has had three centuries of experience in general demoralization and behind that, paganism."[27]

This theory of racial evolution was grounded in metaphors derived from Darwin's theory of biological evolution, which swept the European-American intellectual world and fed the roots of new liberal ideology. The main purpose of race-evolution theory was to provide a rational explanation of the unequal distribution of wealth and political power among racial groups. The Hampton faculty taught black students that the subordinate position of their race in the South, even in places where they were the overwhelming majority, was not the result of oppression but of the natural process of moral and cultural evolution. In other words, black people had only evolved to a cultural stage that was 2,000 years behind that of white people, and their inferior position in society therefore represented the natural order of social evolution. The darker races were likened to children, who must crawl before they can walk, must be trained before they can be educated. For it was only after the backward races put away childish things, stilled their dark laughter, and subordinated their emotional nature to rational self-discipline that they would be ready to vote, hold political office, and enjoy the rights and privileges of first-class citizenship.

Washington learned this lesson well while attending Hampton and internalized it as a lens through which he perceived and interpreted questions of race development, political inequality, and civil rights. As he said in 1900 before the General Conference of the African Methodist Episcopal Church, "My friends, the white man is three thousand years ahead of us, and this fact we might as well face now as well as later, and at one stage of his development, either in Europe or America, he has gone through every stage of development that I now advocate for our race." Instead of regarding the difficulties of his race as the result of arbitrary and unjust oppression, Washington interpreted them as the natural difficulties which almost every race had been compelled to overcome in its upward climb from uncivilized life. He cautioned white people not to overlook the fact "that geographically and physically the semi-barbarous Negro race has been thrown right down in the center of the highest civilization that the world knows anything about." The black race lagged behind the white race not because of slavery and racism but because a semibarbarous race naturally could not keep pace with a highly civilized race.

While Washington did not condone the enslavement of African people, he maintained constantly that during slavery African-Americans' exposure to a highly civilized race gave them advantages over other uncivilized races. As he put it,

> The Indian refused to submit to bondage and to learn the white man's ways. The result is that the greater portion of the American Indians have disappeared, the greater portion of those who remain are not civilized. The Negro, wiser and more enduring than the Indian, patiently endured slavery; and contact with the white man has given him a civilization vastly superior to that of the Indian.[28]

Although this viewpoint did not condone slavery, it did portray it as a school where the allegedly uncivilized Africans received a jump start on the road to civilized life by imitating the best they found in white culture. "The Indian and the Negro met on the American continent for the first time at Jamestown, in 1619," said Washington. "Both were in the darkest barbarism." Two hundred and fifty years later the "Negro race" had learned "to wear clothes, to live in a home, to work with a high degree of regularity and system, and a few had learned to work with a high degree of skill." Not only this, the African race had learned a fair knowledge of American culture, "and changed from a pagan into a Christian race." Thus, in Washington's mind slavery was a blessing in disguise since it gave "pagan" Africans the opportunity to have contact with highly civilized Europeans. This conception of history and progress as racial evolution led Washington to conclude that racial inequality was merely the natural order of evolutionary laws, which in turn would lead to equality as the darker, semibarbarous races became more civilized.[29]

Would Charles Darwin, the scientist, have condoned the philosophy of social Darwinism, which was used to justify social oppression through a theory of racial evolution?

Avoiding the Issue of Political Power

Directly and closely related to this perception of racial evolution was the question of whether the freedmen should vote and pursue political office, since such rights and privileges were reserved for the fully civilized. In Armstrong's view, the "colored people" should "let politics severely alone." African-American voters, he maintained, were "dangerous to the country in proportion to their numbers." His desire to disfranchise the freedmen followed logically from his premise that the freed men and women were not civilized and therefore incapable of self-government. Washington also internalized this view of black participation in the body politic. Although he was opposed to depriving black men of the legal right of franchise, like Armstrong, he advised that it was a mistake for them to enter actively into politics. Washington went beyond urging black people not to vote or run for political office; he also counseled them not to speak out against racial injustices. Race prejudice, he believed, was something to be lived through, not talked down.

In 1888, one of Tuskegee's employees, George M. Lovejoy, wrote a letter to a Mississippi black newspaper protesting the effort of a white mob in Tuskegee to take a black man from the county jail. The local white newspaper, the Tuskegee *News*, asked if it were the purpose of Tuskegee Institute to breed hatred of the white race and warned Lovejoy to leave town. Washington sent a card to the Tuskegee *News* bearing this message: "It has always been and is now the policy of the Normal School to remain free from politics and the discussion of race questions that tend to stir up strife between the races, and whenever this policy is violated it is done without the approbation of those in charge of the school." Thus, Washington publicly advised the general black population to abstain from voting, running for political office, or speaking out against racial injustices.

This directive, however, was not a blanket condemnation of political activity by all African-Americans. The white registrars in his Alabama county gave him a special invitation to come in and awarded him a lifetime voting certificate, which he framed and hung in his home. Washington voted and urged a few selected African-Americans to do likewise, but both publicly and privately he favored restrictions that would prevent the propertyless and illiterate of both races from voting.[30]

During Washington's career as head of Tuskegee Institute, Macon County's black population increased from 74 percent of the county's population in 1880 to 85 percent of the total in 1910. The position he took encouraged the disfranchisement of the masses of black voters. Meanwhile, the state constitution protected the white vote with various loopholes. The result was that the small white minority maintained exclusive control of the county's political system during Washington's era, a control that continued until after the passage of the Voting Rights Act of 1965. Washington's major complaint was that the whites in power did not apply the voting restrictions equally to both races. Nevertheless, as state after state placed property and educational restrictions on voting, he refused to take a public stand against ratification of the undemocratic constitutions. He sincerely believed in the disfranchisement of the propertyless, the illiterate, and "backward" races, and therefore found it difficult to fight publicly against restrictions on popular voting even when such restrictions were more racially qualified than he preferred. Indeed, to Washington, the worsening position of African-Americans since emancipation seemed to result from the reaction of white voters against black participation in the body politic. He did not object to educational or property tests because he believed that citizenship rights were to be secured by education, property, and character, not by constitutional guarantees. Black people, he insisted, needed moral training, education, and property before they would be ready to vote and hold political office.[31]

A Liberal Faith: Social Progress through the Marketplace

The most critical dimension of Washington's perceptions of his social environment was his belief that hard labor and the accumulation of property were the keys to resolving all social problems. Although this component of his social perceptions diverged from reality to a breathtaking degree, in order to understand it, it is necessary to see how Washington viewed his world and posed solutions based on those perceptions. The gospel of thrift, industry, and property ownership had been instilled in Washington during his student years at Hampton Institute. Armstrong taught that southern white opposition to black participation in politics did not exist in the arenas of education and economics. He insisted that "there was no power and little disposition on the part of leading white conservatives to prevent the colored people from acquiring wealth and education." He argued further that "competition in the North" held back skilled African-American workers "more than prejudice at the South." Southern black mechanics, according to Armstrong, had "a fair field." He was very careful to point out that it was only in the South that black people had practically a fair field in the commercial world and in the world of skilled labor.[32]

Washington, like Armstrong, made sharp distinctions between what did and could happen in the economic world versus what did and could happen in the social and political worlds. "Man may discriminate," said Washington, "but the economic laws of trade and commerce cannot discriminate." He thought that economic life and all men's economic actions were controlled by natural laws, which men defied at their peril. These perfect laws disallowed anything so irrational as race prejudice. "When an individual produces what the world wants," Washington believed, "the world does not stop long to inquire what is the color of the skin of the producer." This perception distorted the fact that, in reality, the South was very conscious of skin color, especially in the realm of economics. The region had just emerged from two and one-half centuries of slavery, a system of economic exploitation based exclusively on race. Washington saw slavery differently and interpreted it in a manner consistent with his perception of the natural laws of economics. In his view,

> Under God, as bad as slavery was, it prepared the way for the solving of this [race] problem by this [business] method. The two hundred and fifty years of slavery taught the Southern white man to do business with the Negro. If a Southern white man wanted a house built he consulted a Negro mechanic about the building of that house; if he wanted a suit of clothes made, he consulted a Negro tailor. And, thus, in a limited sense, every large plantation in the South during slavery was, in measure, an industrial school.[33]

Since emancipation, perceived Washington, "The Negro in the South has not only found a practically free field in the commercial world, but in the world of skilled labor." He often told black southerners that "when one comes to business pure and simple, stripped of all ideas of sentiment, the Negro is given almost as good an opportunity to rise as is given to the white man." To Washington it followed, as the night the day, that the South was a place where African-Americans had equal opportunity to succeed in the labor market and commercial world. "Whenever the Negro has lost ground industrially in the South," said Washington in 1898, "it is not because there is prejudice against him as a skilled laborer on the part of the Native Southern white man, for the Southern white man generally prefers to do business with the Negro as a mechanic rather than with a white one."[34]

What was particularly peculiar about this article of faith was Washington's belief that racially neutral laws of labor and commerce existed in the South, the land of slavery and peasantry, but not in the North, the land of capitalism and free labor. In almost every speech or essay where he extolled equal economic opportunity for black southerners, he was quick to point out that race prejudice was a key barrier to black economic progress in the North. The following story, which he told to a Brooklyn, New York, audience in 1896, is typical of Washington's perception of economic opportunities for black people in the North:

> Not long ago a mother, a black mother, who lived in one of your Northern states, had heard it whispered around in her community for years that the Negro was lazy, shiftless, and would not work. So when her boy grew to sufficient size, at considerable expense and great self-sacrifice, she had her boy thoroughly taught the machinist's trade. A job was secured in a neighboring shop. . . . What Happened? . . . Every one of the twenty white men threw down his tools and deliberately walked out, swearing that he would not give a black man an opportunity to earn an honest living. Another shop was tried, with the same results, and still another and the same.[35]

Booker T. Washington believed in the racial neutrality of the marketplace, and that if African-Americans achieved economic success, political and social gains would automatically follow.

In such instances Washington did not ignore the fact that racism was present in the labor markets and contradicted his notion that the natural laws of labor and commerce precluded race prejudice. "Hundreds of Negroes in the North become criminals who would become strong and useful men if they were not discriminated against as bread winners," observed Washington in 1900. But this was the North; he saw the South as the exact opposite. Throughout his career he held to the belief that race prejudice and discrimination did not influence occupational and commercial opportunities in the South.[36]

Although this perception of economic reality had virtually no basis in fact, Washington held to it unswervingly, in part because it was most critical to his proposals for solving the problem of racial oppression. "There is almost no prejudice against the Negro in the South in matters of business, so far as the native whites are concerned, and here is the entering wedge for the solution of the race problem," said Washington in 1898. Economic development and its foundation, industrial education, were viewed by Washington as the entering wedge for solving the race problem because he believed strongly that material prosperity was the real basis of civil and political equality. "In proportion as the ignorant secure education, property and character," he said in 1898, "they will be given the right of citizenship." This social perception and its inherent resolution shifted the question of citizenship from rights guaranteed by federal and state constitutional law to a reward granted for material success.

Washington argued that whenever black southerners demonstrated the virtues of good businessmen by getting property, good jobs, nice houses, and bank accounts, white southerners would give black people the ballot and other perquisites of full citizenship without a qualm. Consequently, he did not believe in political means toward liberation and equality, thinking that political action was at best a waste of time and at worst the cause of white backlash. "We have spent time and money in political conventions, making idle political speeches, that could have been better spent in becoming leading real estate dealers and leading carpenters and truck gardeners, and thus have laid an imperial foundation on which we could have stood and demanded our rights," he proclaimed in 1898. He said that it was right that all the privileges guaranteed to blacks by the U.S. Constitution be sacredly guarded. But the "mere fiat of law," he cautioned, "could not make a dependent man an independent man" or "make one race respect another." "One race respects another in proportion as it contributes to the markets of the world," he contended. Washington alleged that "almost without exception, whether in the North or in the South, wherever I have seen a Negro who was succeeding in business, who was a taxpayer, a man who possessed intelligence and high moral character, that man was treated with respect by the people of both races." Hence, respect and first-class citizenship would come to blacks in proportion to their accumulation of property, education, and good jobs. In reality, from Reconstruction to 1915, black people were acquiring significantly more property and education as they were being stripped of basic civil and political rights. As Washington perceived his social world, he stood reality on its head, believing that the accumulation of property and education would lead to respect and first-class citizenship precisely at the moment when the exact opposite was unfolding.[37]

The Washington Solution

Perhaps because he accommodated so easily to the southern system of racial inequality, Washington romanticized the region's economic life as providing a firm foundation for emancipation from racial oppression. Acquiescence in racial segregation was one of the prices he believed he had to pay for peace with white southerners. He also counseled black people to stay away from politics and not to agitate for civil rights. Another concession was a rather sweeping abandonment of the First Amendment guarantee of free speech. It was his policy to refrain from discussions of controversial race-relations questions, and he forbade his faculty and students from speaking out against racial injustice. In his imagined world of southern economics no law could push individuals forward if they were worthless and no law could hold them back if they were worthy. Thus his solutions for

In 1897 Du Bois accepted a faculty position at Atlanta University, where he and his graduate students began authoring what would become a series of 18 volumes on African-American life. He was at this time primarily a scholar, and he had little interest in political activism. "By 1905," he wrote, "I was still a teacher at Atlanta University and was in my imagination a scientist, and neither a leader nor an agitator; I had much admiration for Mr. Washington and Tuskegee."[43] Despite that admiration, Du Bois was also critical of Washington. In his early Atlanta years, Du Bois came to see that when he did disagree with the black leader's beliefs, such disagreements were considered to be an attack on Washington and were interpreted by Washington's followers as therefore hostile to black people in general. This stifling of criticism, perhaps more than any other facet of Washington's organization, aroused Du Bois's ire. As Du Bois records in his *Autobiography,* the "Tuskegee machine" was able to use white financial backing to buy up black-owned newspapers that criticized Washington's leadership. In 1903, in *The Souls of Black Folk,* Du Bois took Washington to task for stifling the "earnest criticism" which Du Bois believed was the "soul of democracy."[44]

A second major problem for Du Bois was the unabated oppression of black southerners. From his college days at Fisk until 1900, over 2,000 African-Americans had been lynched. Black citizens were taken out of their homes by white gangs and executed in front of their families. Others were taken out of jails and hanged without trial. Washington preferred not to talk about such racist violence, and in fact avoided discussing discrimination and prejudice in his public life whenever possible. Du Bois, however, like a number of other black leaders in the South, soon came to believe that racist whites were only too happy to see the energies of the only powerful black leader in the nation directed toward vocational education.

As a direct result of a 1908 racially motivated street riot in Springfield, Illinois, which involved the lynching of two black men, the National Negro Committee was formed in New York. Du Bois was one of the featured speakers at the inaugural meeting, and he chaired the committee that nominated its first governing body. Two years later, the committee became the National Association for the Advancement of Colored People, and Du Bois was invited to be its director of publications and research. At the NAACP, he founded and edited *Crisis,* a magazine to educate black and white people alike to the realities of racism. The magazine, which published such information as running totals of racist lynchings, reached a remarkable circulation of 100,000 by 1918. Not surprisingly, the Tuskegee machine opposed the formation of the NAACP. And not surprisingly, Du Bois used the pages of *Crisis* to criticize Washington in return. "To discuss the Negro question in 1910 was to discuss Booker T. Washington," Du Bois later wrote in his autobiography.[45] For example, after Washington had presented a series of speeches in England "along his usual conciliatory lines," Du Bois wrote the following to a British and European audience:

> Mr. Washington . . . is a distinguished American and has a perfect right to his opinions. But we are compelled to point out that Mr. Washington's large financial responsibilities have made him dependent on the rich charitable public and that, for this reason, he has for years been compelled to tell, not the whole truth, but that part of it which certain powerful interests in America wish to appear as the whole truth.

The "whole truth," for Du Bois, included attention to the institutionalization of racism and racist oppression in the United States: not just in the South, but in the North as well. Du Bois believed that Washington's failure to confront and emphasize that racism—institutionalized in the nation's laws, in its educational system, in political life, and in economic practices—was tacit acceptance of the oppression of African-Americans. Washington's route to assimilation of African-Americans into mainstream American life was through acquiescence, charged Du Bois, who argued that assimilation should be obtained through self-assertion instead. Where Washington advocated that black people should make the best of a bad situation by acquiring vocational education and earning a living, Du Bois called for organized public protest, legal action against racist institutions, and higher education for blacks. It was a source of great pain to Du Bois that Washington's approach to assimilation was as influential as it was, while his own emphasis on civil rights, political rights, and higher education was not implemented until the civil rights movement of the 1950s and 1960s. Du Bois lived until 1963, long enough to see some of his ideas influence civil rights legislation and higher education for African-Americans. In fact, when news of Du Bois's death reached the leadership of a massive civil rights march on Washington, D.C., on August 28, 1963, NAACP Executive Secretary Roy Wilkins told the assembled throng, "It is incontrovertible that at the dawn of the twentieth century, his was the voice calling you to gather here today in this cause."[46] It is that voice that we let speak for itself at some length in the chapter-end reading from *Souls of Black Folk,* 1903.

CONCLUDING REMARKS

We have examined how a major political-economic change, coupled with a fundamental ideological tension, led to dramatic new developments in schooling. The political-economic change was the emancipation of African-Americans from slavery, the ideological tension was created by the dominant view that black people were entitled to education but that they were nevertheless inferior to white people, and the dramatic new developments in schooling were the widespread establishment of schools for African-Americans on the one hand and, on the other, the emergence of a new vocational "solution" to the problem of what kind of schooling black people should receive.

Entering the 20th century, not only the South but the entire United States was undergoing basic changes in its political economy and its dominant ideology. Not surprisingly, the conflict of educational ideas between Booker T. Washington and W. E. B. Du Bois reflected similar conflicts among educational thinkers throughout the nation. Nationally prominent St. Louis educator William Torrey Harris spoke for many when he observed that Washington's approach to the education of black people was of "so universal a character that it applies to the downtrodden of all races, without reference to color."[47]

As Chapter 4 also illustrated, educating "the downtrodden" became a primary concern for educators almost exactly a hundred years ago. If Booker T. Washington's approach was controversial for African-Americans in the South, it was to become just as controversial for the education of poor and immigrant children throughout the nation. The differences between Washington and Du Bois can be viewed in terms of several basic controversies regarding the education of American youth in general—black or white, Italian or Swedish, male or female. Five of these issues, which would remain central issues throughout the revolution in American schooling in the early 20th century, are as follows:

1. *Education for social stability:* If schools take as one of their primary missions the education of children for a *stable* society, what becomes of developing in children the intellectual and critical capacities necessary for a *free* society? In general, do education for social stability and education for freedom mean the same thing?
2. *Education for employable skills:* If schooling is intended primarily to develop employable skills among students, might this not result in most students being educated at a level well below their highest intellectual capacities, which include the ability to think analytically and critically in the various disciplines of the humanities, social sciences, mathematics, and science? In general, does education for employable skills tend to conflict with education for intellectual development?
3. *Schooling for social reform:* If schools are assigned the task of responding to deep social problems such as racial discrimination, civil rights, or conflicts between labor and management, might this not result in failure to address those and other social problems in more direct and more effective ways—such as legislation for basic changes in civil rights or in the workplace? In general, does schooling for social reform take attention away from the more fundamental and achievable educational goal of education for individual human development?
4. *Education for group differences:* If differences among people (like skin color, gender, or economic class) are considered so important that different kinds of education should be provided for children of those different groups, might this not result in the most valuable—and valued—kinds of education being reserved largely for those who are already most privileged? In

general, which is better—education for group and individual differences, or education for what people have in common?

5. *Education for whose interests?* If people in positions of economic power decide that schools should serve the interests of industry and the economic order, might this not fail to serve the interests of (in Du Bois's words) "those most nearly touched" by schooling—the students themselves? In general, will serving the interests of the economically and politically powerful also serve the interests of the majority of young people?

Each of these questions represents a fundamental area of disagreement between Washington and Du Bois and, as Chapter 4 demonstrated, each one also represents fundamental disagreements about how, and for what purposes, young people were to be educated in the United States at the turn of the 20th century.

Perhaps the most interesting summary of the basic differences between Booker T. Washington and W. E. B. Du Bois is contained in the following poem by Dudley Randall. The student who can readily provide an interpretation of each of its stanzas is likely to have a good grasp of several major issues in this chapter.

Booker T. and W. E. B.

***by Dudley Randall*[48]**

"It seems to me," said Booker T.,
"It shows a mighty lot of cheek
To study chemistry and Greek
When Mister Charlie needs a hand
To hoe the cotton on his land,
And when Miss Ann looks for a cook,
Why stick your nose inside a book?"

"I don't agree," said W. E. B.
"If I should have the drive to seek
Knowledge of chemistry or Greek,
I'll do it. Charles and Miss can look
Another place for hand or cook.
Some men rejoice in skill of hand,
And some in cultivating land,
But there are others who maintain
The right to cultivate the brain."

"It seems to me," said Booker T.,
"That all you folks have missed the boat
Who shout about the right to vote,
And spend vain days and sleepless nights
In uproar over civil rights.
Just keep your mouths shut, do not grouse,
But work, and save, and buy a house."

"I don't agree," said W. E. B.,
"For what can property avail
If dignity and justice fail?
Unless you help to make the laws,
They'll steal your house with trumped-up clause.
A rope's as tight, a fire as hot,
No matter how much cash you've got.
Speak soft, and try your little plan,
But as for me, I'll be a man."

"It seems to me," said Booker T.—

"I don't agree,"
said W. E. B.

PRIMARY SOURCE READING

Below is the full text of Booker T. Washington's Atlanta Exposition Address as he recorded it in his autobiography, Up From Slavery. *It is presented here so students may critically and appreciatively examine Washington's own analysis of the social, economic, and educational prospects for blacks in the South at that time. This speech was controversial in its own time, and its significance in educational and African-American history is debatable today. While white leaders and many black citizens sympathetic to Washington's position applauded the address, others criticized Washington for failing to challenge the racist ideology and social structure that were responsible for the oppression of blacks in the United States. This speech represents the very kind of thinking that W. E. B. Du Bois would later criticize, as represented in the second primary source reading at the end of the chapter. Students should read both selections carefully and critically, keeping in mind the historical context of the differences between the two black leaders.*

ATLANTA EXPOSITION ADDRESS OF 1895

Booker T. Washington

One-third of the population of the South is of the Negro race. No enterprise seeking the material, civil, or moral welfare of this section can disregard this element of our population and reach the highest success. I but convey to you, Mr. President and Directors, the sentiment of the masses of my race, when I say that in no way have the value and manhood of the American Negro been more fittingly and generously recognized than by the managers of this magnificent Exposition at every stage of its progress. It is a recognition that will do more to cement the friendship of the two races than any occurrence since the dawn of our freedom.

Not only this, but the opportunity, here afforded will awaken among us a new era of industrial progress. Ignorant and inexperienced, it is not strange that in the first years of our new life we began at the top instead of at the bottom; that a seat in Congress or the state legislature was more sought than real estate or industrial skill; that the political convention of stump speaking had more attractions than starting a dairy farm or truck garden.

A ship lost at sea for many days suddenly sighted a friendly vessel. From the mast of the unfortunate vessel was seen a signal, "Water, water; we die of thirst!" The answer from the friendly vessel at once came back, "Cast down your bucket where you are." A second time the signal, "Water, water; send us water!" ran up from the distressed vessel, and was answered, "Cast down your bucket where you are." And a third and fourth signal for water was answered, "Cast down your bucket where you are." The captain of the distressed vessel, at last heeding the injunction, cast down his bucket, and it came up full of fresh, sparkling water from the mouth of the Amazon River. To those of my race who depend on bettering their condition in a foreign land or who underestimate the importance of cultivating friendly relations with the Southern white man, who is their next-door neighbour, I would say: "Cast down your bucket where you are"—cast it down in making friends in every manly way of the people of all races by whom we are surrounded.

Cast it down in agriculture, mechanics, in commerce, in domestic service, and in the professions. And in this connection it is well to bear in mind that whatever other sins the South may be called to bear, when it comes to business, pure and simple, it is in the South that the Negro is given a man's chance in the commercial world, and in nothing is this Exposition more eloquent than in emphasizing this chance. Our greatest danger is that in the great leap from slavery to freedom we may overlook the fact that the masses of us are to live by the productions of our hands, and fail to keep in mind that we shall prosper in proportion as we learn to dignify and glorify common labour and put brains and skill into the common occupations of life; shall prosper in proportion as we learn to draw the line between the superficial and the substantial, the ornamental gewgaws of life and the useful. No race can prosper till it learns that there is as much dignity in tilling a field as in writing a poem. It is at the bottom of life we must begin, and not at the top. Nor should we permit our grievances to overshadow our opportunities.

To those of the white race who look to the incoming of those of foreign birth and strange tongue and habits for the prosperity of the South, were I permitted I would repeat what I say to my own race, "Cast down your bucket where you are." Cast it down among the eight millions of Negroes whose habits you know, whose fidelity and love you have tested in days when to have proved treacherous meant the ruin of your firesides. Cast down your bucket among these people who have, without strikes and labour wars, tilled your fields, cleared your forests, builded your railroads and cities, and brought forth treasures from the bowels of the earth, and helped make possible this magnificent representation of the progress of the South. Casting down your bucket among my people, helping and encouraging them as you are doing on these grounds, and to education of head, hand, and heart, you will find that they will buy your surplus land, make blossom the waste places in your fields, and run your factories. While doing this, you can be sure in the future, as in the past, that you and your families will be surrounded by the most patient, faithful, law-abiding, and unresentful people that the world has seen. As we have proved our loyalty to you in the past, in nursing your children, watching by the sickbed of your mothers and fathers, and often following them with tear-dimmed eyes to their graves, so in the future, in our humble way, we shall stand by you with a devotion that no foreigner can approach, ready to lay down our lives, if need be, in defence of yours, interlacing our industrial, commercial, civil, and religious life with yours in a way that shall make the interests of both races one. In all things that are purely social we can be as separate as the fingers, yet one as the hand in all things essential to mutual progress.

There is no defence or security for any of us except in the highest intelligence and development of all. If anywhere there are efforts tending to curtail the fullest growth of the Negro, let these efforts be turned into stimulating, encouraging, and making him the most useful and intelligent citizen. Effort or means so invested will pay a thousand percent interest. These efforts will be twice blessed—"blessing him that gives and him that takes."

> There is no escape through law of man or God from the inevitable:—
>
> The laws of changeless justice bind
> Oppressor with oppressed;
> And close as sin and suffering joined
> We march to fate abreast.

Nearly sixteen millions of hands will aid you in pulling the load upward, or they will pull against the load downward. We shall constitute one-third and more of the ignorance and crime of the South, or one-third its intelligence and progress; we shall contribute one-third to the business and industrial prosperity of the South, or we shall prove a veritable body of death, stagnating, depressing regarding every effort to advance the body politic.

Gentlemen of the Exposition, as we present to you our humble effort at an exhibition of our progress, you must not expect overmuch. Starting thirty years ago with ownership here and there in a few quilts and pumpkins and chickens (gathered from miscellaneous sources), remember the path that has led from these to the inventions and production of agricultural implements, buggies, steam-engines, newspapers, books, statuary, carving, paintings, the management of drug-stores and banks, has not been trodden without contact with thorns and thistles. While we take pride in what we exhibit as a result of our independent efforts, we do not for a moment forget that our part in this exhibit would fall far short of your expectations but for the constant help that has come to our educational life, not only from the Southern states but especially from Northern philanthropists, who have made their gifts a constant stream of blessing and encouragement.

The wisest among my race understand that the agitations of questions of social equality is the extremest folly, and that progress in the enjoyment of all the privileges that will come to us must be the result of severe and constant struggle rather than of artificial forcing. No race that has anything to contribute to the markets of the world is long in any degree ostracized. It is important and right that all privileges of the law be ours, but it is vastly more important that we be prepared for the exercises of these privileges. The opportunity to earn a dollar in a factory just now is worth infinitely more than the opportunity to spend a dollar in an opera-house.

In conclusion, may I repeat that nothing in thirty years has given us more hope and encouragement, and drawn us so near to you of the white race, as this opportunity offered by the Exposition; and here bending, as it were over the altar that represents the results of the struggles of your race and mine, both starting practically empty-handed three decades ago. I pledge that in your effort to work out the great and intricate problem which God has laid at the doors of the South, you shall have at all times the patient, sympathetic help of my race; only let this be constantly in mind, that, while from representations in these buildings of the product of field, of forest, of mine, of factory, letters, and art, much good will come, yet far above and beyond material benefits will be that higher good, that let us pray God, will come, in a blotting out of sectional differences and racial animosities and suspicions, in a determination to administer absolute justice, in a willing obedience among all classes to the mandates of law. This, then, coupled with our material prosperity, will bring into our beloved South a new heaven and a new earth.

PRIMARY SOURCE READING

OF MR. BOOKER T. WASHINGTON AND OTHERS

W. E. B. Du Bois

From birth till death enslaved; in word, in deed, unmanned!
. . . .
Hereditary bondsmen! Know ye not
Who would be free themselves must strike the blow?

Byron

From *The Souls of Black Folk*, reprinted in John Hope Franklin, ed., *Three Negro Classics* (New York: Avon Books, 1965), pp. 242–52.

Easily the most striking thing in the history of the American Negro since 1876 is the ascendancy of Booker T. Washington. It began at the time when war memories and ideals were rapidly passing; a day of astonishing commercial development was dawning; a sense of doubt and hesitation overtook the freedmen's sons,—then it was that his leading began. Mr. Washington came, with a single definite programme, at the psychological moment when the nation was a little ashamed of having bestowed so much sentiment on Negroes, and was concentrating its energies on Dollars. His programme of industrial education, conciliation of the South, and submission and silence as to civil and political rights, was not wholly original; the Free Negroes from 1830 up to war-time had striven to build industrial schools, and the American Missionary Association had from the first taught various trades; and Price and others had sought a way of honorable alliance with the best of the Southerners. But Mr. Washington first indissolubly linked these things; he put enthusiasm, unlimited energy, and perfect faith into this programme, and changed it from a by-path into a veritable Way of Life. And the tale of the methods by which he did this is a fascinating study of human life.

It startled the nation to hear a Negro advocating such a programme after many decades of bitter complaint; it startled and won the applause of the South, it interested and won the admiration of the North; and after a confused murmur of protest, it silenced if it did not convert the Negroes themselves.

To gain the sympathy and cooperation of the various elements compromising the white South was Mr. Washington's first task; and this, at the time Tuskegee was founded, seemed, for a black man, well-nigh impossible. And yet ten years later it was done in the word[s] spoken at Atlanta. "In all things purely social we can be as separate as the five fingers, and yet one as the hand in all things essential to mutual progress." This "Atlanta Compromise" is by all odds the most notable thing in Mr. Washington's career. The South interpreted it in different ways: the radicals received it as a complete surrender of the demand for civil and political equality; the conservatives, as a generously conceived working basis for mutual understanding. So both approved it, and today its author is certainly the most distinguished Southerner since Jefferson Davis, and the one with the largest personal following.

Next to the achievement comes Mr. Washington's work in gaining place and consideration in the North. Others less shrewd and tactful had formerly essayed to sit on these two stools and had fallen between them; but as Mr. Washington knew the heart of the South from birth and training, so by singular insight he intuitively grasped the spirit of the age which was dominating the North. And so thoroughly did he learn the speech and thought of triumphant commercialism, and the ideals of material prosperity, that the picture of a lone black boy poring over a French grammar amid the weeds and dirt of a neglected home soon seemed to him the acme of absurdities. One wonders what Socrates and St. Francis of Assisi would say to this.

And yet this very singleness of vision and thorough oneness with his age is a mark of the successful man. It is as though Nature must needs make men narrow in order to give them force. So Mr. Washington's cult has gained unquestioning followers, his work has wonderfully prospered, his friends are legion, and his enemies are confounded. Today he stands as the one recognized spokesman of his ten million fellows, and one of the most notable figures in a nation of seventy millions. One hesitates, therefore, to criticize a life which, beginning with so little has done so much. And yet the time is come when one may speak in all sincerity and utter courtesy of the mistakes and shortcomings of Mr. Washington's career, as well as of his triumphs, without being thought captious or envious, and without forgetting that it is easier to do ill than well in the world.

The criticism that has hitherto met Mr. Washington has not always been of this broad character. In the South especially has he had to walk warily to avoid the harshest judgements,—and naturally so, for he is dealing with the one subject of deepest sensitiveness to that section. Twice—once when at the Chicago celebration of the Spanish-American war, he alluded to the color-prejudice that is "eating away the vitals of the South," and once when he dined with President Roosevelt—has the resulting southern criticism been violent enough to threaten his popularity. In the North the feeling has several times forced itself into words, that Mr. Washington's counsels of submission overlooked certain elements of true manhood, and that his education program was unnecessarily narrow. Usually, however, such criticism has not found open expression, although, too, the spiritual sons of the Abolitionists have not been prepared to acknowledge that the schools founded before Tuskegee, by men of broad ideals and self-sacrificing spirit, were wholly failures or worthy of ridicule. While, then, criticism has not failed to follow Mr. Washington, yet the prevailing public opinion of the land has been but too willing to deliver the solution of a wearisome problem into his hands, and say, "If that is all you and your race ask, take it."

Among his own people, however, Mr. Washington has encountered the strongest and most lasting opposition, amounting at times to bitterness, and even today continuing strong and insistent even though largely silenced in outward expression by the public opinion of the nation. Some of this opposition is, of course, mere envy; the disappointment of displaced demagogues and the spite of narrow minds. But aside from this, there is among educated and thoughtful colored men in all parts of the land a feeling of deep regret, sorrow, and apprehension at the wide currency and ascendancy which some of Mr. Washington's theories have gained. These same men admire his sincerity of purpose, and are willing to forgive much to honest endeavor which is doing something worth the doing. They cooperate with Mr. Washington as far as they conscientiously can; and, indeed, it is no ordinary tribute to this man's tact and power that, steering as he must between so many diverse interests and opinions, he so largely retains the respect of all.

But the hushing of the criticism of honest opponents is a dangerous thing. It leads some of the best of the critics to unfortunate silence and paralysis of effort, and others to burst into speech so passionately and intemperately as to lose listeners. Honest and earnest criticism from those whose interests are most nearly touched,—criticism of writers by readers, of government by those governed, of leaders by those led,—this is the soul of democracy and the safeguard of modern society. If the best of the American Negroes receive by outer pressure a leader whom they had not recognized before, manifestly there is here a certain palpable gain. Yet there is also irreparable loss,—a loss of that peculiarly valuable education which a group receives when by search and criticism it finds and commissions its own leaders. The way in which this is done is at once the most elementary and the nicest problem of social growth. History is but the record of such group leadership; and yet how infinitely changeful is its type and character. And of all types and kinds, what can be more instructive than the leadership of a group within a group—that curious double movement where real progress may be negative and actual advance be relative retrogression. All this is the social student's inspiration and despair.

Now in the past the American Negro has had instructive experience in the choosing of group leaders, founding thus a peculiar dynasty which in the light of present conditions is worth while studying. When sticks and stones and beasts form the sole environment of a people, their attitude is largely one of determined opposition to and conquest of natural forces. But when to earth and brute is added an environment of men and ideas, then the attitude of the imprisoned group may take three main forms,—a feeling of revolt and revenge; an attempt to adjust all thought and action to the will of the greater group; or, finally, a determined effort at self-realization and self-development despite environing opinion. The influence of all of these attitudes at various times can be traced in the history of the American Negro, and in the evolution of his successive leaders.

Before 1750, while the fire of African freedom still burned in the veins of the slaves, there was in all leadership or attempted leadership but the one motive of revolt and revenge,—typified in the terrible Maroons, the Danish blacks, and Cato of Stono, and veiling all the Americans in fear of insurrection. The liberalizing tendencies of the latter half of the eighteenth century brought, along with kindlier relations between black and white, thoughts of ultimate adjustment and assimilation. Such aspiration was especially voiced in the earnest songs of Phyllis, in the martyrdom of Attucks, the fighting Salem and Poor, the intellectual accomplishments of Banneker and Derham, and the political demands of the Cuffes.

Stern financial and social stress after the war cooled much of the previous humanitarian ardor. The disappointment and impatience of the Negroes at the persistence of slavery and serfdom voiced itself in two movements. The slaves in the South, aroused undoubtedly by vague rumors of the Haitian revolt, made three fierce attempts at insurrection,—in 1800 under Gabriel in Virginia, in 1822 under Vesey in Carolina, and in 1831 again in Virginia under the terrible Nat Turner. In the Free States, on the other hand, a new and curious attempt at self-development was made. In Philadelphia and New York color prescription led to a withdrawal of Negro communicants from white churches and formation of a peculiar socioreligious institution among the Negroes known as the African Church,—an organization still living and controlling in its various branches over a million of men.

Walker's wild appeal against the trend of the times showed how the world was changing after the coming of the cotton-gin. By 1830 slavery seemed hopelessly fastened on the South, and the slaves thoroughly cowed into submission. The free Negroes of the North, inspired by the mulatto immigrants from the West Indies, began to change the basis of their demands; they recognized the slavery of slaves, but insisted that they themselves were freemen, and sought assimilation and amalgamation with the nation on the same terms with other men. Thus Forten and Purvis of Philadelphia, Shad of Wilmington, DuBois of New Haven, Barbadoes of Boston, and others, strove singly and together as men, they said, not as slaves; as "people of color," not as "Negroes." The trend of the times, however, refused them recognition save in individual and exceptional cases, considered them as one with all the despised blacks, and they soon found themselves striving to keep even the rights they formerly had of voting and working and moving as freemen. Schemers of migration and colonization arose among them; but these they refused to entertain, and they eventually turned to the Abolition movement as a final refuge.

Here, led by Remond, Nell, Wells-Brown, and Douglass, a new period of self-assertion and self-development dawned. To be sure, ultimate freedom and assimilation was the ideal before the leaders, but the assertion of the manhood rights of the Negro by himself was the main reliance, and John Brown's raid was the extreme of its logic. After the war and emancipation, the great form of

Frederick Douglass, the greatest of American Negro leaders, still led the host. Self-Assertion, especially in political lines, was the main programme, and behind Douglass came Elliot, Bruce, and Langston, and the Reconstruction politicians, and, less conspicuous but of greater social significance Alexander Crummell and Bishop Daniel Payne.

Then came the Revolution of 1876, the suppression of the Negro votes, the changing and shifting of ideals, and the seeking of new lights in the great night. Douglass, in his old age, still bravely stood for the ideals of his early manhood,—ultimate assimilation through self-assertion and on no other terms. For a time Price arose as a new leader, destined, it seemed, not to give up, but to re-state the old ideals in a form less repugnant to the white South. But he passed away in his prime. Then came the new leader. Nearly all the former ones had become leaders by the silent suffrage of their fellows, had sought to lead their own people alone, and were usually, save Douglass, little known outside their race. But Booker T. Washington arose as essentially the leader not of one race but of two,—a compromiser between the South, the North, and the Negro. Naturally the Negroes resented, at first bitterly, signs of compromise which surrendered their civil and political rights, even though this was to be exchanged for larger chances of economic development. The rich and dominating North, however, was not only weary of the race problem, but was investing largely in Southern enterprises, and welcomed any method of peaceful cooperation. Thus, by national opinion, the Negroes began to recognize Mr. Washington's leadership; and the voice of criticism was hushed.

Mr. Washington represents in Negro thought the old attitude of adjustment and submission—but adjustment at such a peculiar time as to make his programme unique. This is an age of unusual economic development, and Mr. Washington's programme naturally takes an economic cast, becoming a gospel of Work and Money to such an extent as apparently almost completely to overshadow the higher aims of life. Moreover, this is an age when the more advanced races are coming in closer contact with the less developed races, and the race-feeling is therefore intensified; and Mr. Washington's programme practically accepts the alleged inferiority of the Negro races. Again, in our own land, the reaction from the sentiment of war time has given impetus to race-prejudice against Negroes, and Mr. Washington withdraws many of the high demands of Negroes as men and American citizens. In other periods of intensified prejudice all the Negro's tendency to self-assertion has been called forth; at this period a policy of submission is advocated. In the history of nearly all other races and peoples the doctrine preached at such crises has been that manly self-respect is worth more than lands and houses, and that a people who voluntarily surrender such respect, or cease striving for it, are not worth civilizing. In answer to this, it has been claimed that the Negro can survive only through submission. Mr. Washington distinctly asks that black people give up, at least for the present, three things,—

First, political power,

Second, insistence on civil rights,

Third, higher education of Negro youth,—

and concentrate all their energies on industrial education, the accumulation of wealth, and the conciliation of the South. This policy has been courageously and insistently advocated for over fifteen years, and has been triumphant for perhaps ten years. As a result of this tender of the palm-branch, what has been the return? In these years there have occurred:

1. The disfranchisement of the Negro.
2. The legal creation of a distinct status of civil inferiority for the Negro.
3. The steady withdrawal of aid from institutions for the higher training of the Negro.

These movements are not, to be sure, direct results of Mr. Washington's teachings; but his propaganda has, without a shadow of doubt, helped their speedier accomplishment. The question then comes: Is it possible, and probable, that nine millions of men can make effective progress in economic lines if they are deprived of political rights, made a servile caste, and allowed only the most meagre chance for developing their exceptional men? If history and reason give any distinct answer to these questions, it is an emphatic *No.* And Mr. Washington thus faces the triple paradox of his career:

1. He is striving nobly to make Negro artisans businessmen and property-owners; but it is utterly impossible, under modern competitive methods, for workingmen and property-owners to defend their rights and exist without the right of suffrage.
2. He insists on thrift and self-respect, but at the same time counsels a silent submission to civic inferiority such as is bound to sap the manhood of any race in the long run.
3. He advocates common-school and industrial training, and depreciates institutions of higher learning; but neither the Negro common-schools, nor Tuskegee itself, could remain open a day were it not for teachers trained in Negro colleges, or trained by their graduates.

This triple paradox in Mr. Washington's position is the object of criticism by two classes of colored Americans. One class is spiritually descended from Toussaint the Savior, through Gabriel, Vesey, and Turner, and they represent the attitude of revolt and revenge; they hate the white South blindly and distrust the white race generally, and so far as they agree on definite action, think that the Negro's only hope lies in emigration beyond the borders of the United States. And yet, by the irony of fate, nothing has more effectually made this programme seem hopeless than the recent course of the United States toward weaker and darker peoples in the West Indies, Hawaii, and the Philippines,—for where in the world may we go and be safe from lying and brute force?

The other class of Negroes who cannot agree with Mr. Washington has hitherto said little aloud. They deprecate the sight of scattered counsels, of internal disagreement; and especially they dislike making their just criticism of a useful and earnest man an excuse for a general discharge of venom from small-minded opponents. Nevertheless, the questions involved are so fundamental and serious that it is difficult to see how men like the Grimkes, Kelly Miller, J.W.E. Bowen, and other representatives of this group, can much longer be silent. Such men feel in conscience bound to ask of this nation three things:

1. The right to vote.
2. Civil equality.
3. The education of youth according to ability.

They acknowledge Mr. Washington's invaluable service in counselling patience and courtesy in such demands; they do not ask that ignorant black men vote when ignorant whites are debarred, or that any reasonable restrictions in the suffrage should not be applied; they know that the low social level of the mass of the race is responsible for much discrimination against it, but they also know, and the nation knows, that relentless color-prejudice is more often a cause than a result of the Negro's degradation; they seek the abatement of this relic of barbarism, and not its systematic encouragement and pampering by all agencies of social power from the Associated Press to the Church of Christ. They advocate, with Mr. Washington, a broad system of Negro common schools supplemented by thorough industrial training; but they are surprised that a man of Mr. Washington's insight cannot see that no such educational system ever has rested or can rest on any other basis than that of the well-equipped college and university, and they insist that there is a demand for a few such institutions throughout the South to train the best of the Negro youth as teachers, professional men, and leaders.

This group of men honor Mr. Washington for his attitude of conciliation toward the white South; they accept the "Atlanta Compromise" in its broadest interpretation; they recognize, with him, many signs of promise, many men of high purpose and fair judgment, in this section; they know that no easy task has been laid upon a region already tottering under heavy burdens. But, nevertheless, they insist that the way to truth and right lies in straightforward honesty, not in indiscriminate flattery; in praising those of the South who do well and criticizing uncompromisingly those who do ill; in taking advantage of the opportunities at hand and urging their fellows to do the same, but at the same time in remembering that only a first adherence to their higher ideals and aspirations will ever keep those ideals within the realm of possibility. They do not expect that the free right to vote, to enjoy civic rights, and to be educated, will come in a moment; they do not expect to see the bias and prejudices of years disappear at the blast of a trumpet; but they are absolutely certain that the way for a people to gain their reasonable rights is not by voluntarily throwing them away and insisting that they do not want them; that the way for a people to gain respect is not by continually belittling and ridiculing themselves; that, on the contrary, Negroes must insist continually, in season and out of season, that voting is necessary to modern manhood, that color discrimination is barbarism, and that black boys need education as well as white boys.

In failing thus to state plainly and unequivocally the legitimate demands of their people, even at the cost of opposing an honored leader, the thinking classes of American Negroes would shirk a heavy responsibility,—a responsibility to themselves, a responsibility to the struggling masses, a responsibility to the darker races of men whose future depends so largely on this American experiment, but especially a responsibility to this nation,—this common Fatherland. It is wrong to encourage a man or a people in evil-doing; it is wrong to aid and abet a national crime simply because it is unpopular not to do so. The growing spirit of kindliness and reconciliation between the North and South after the frightful difference of a generation ago ought to be a source of deep congratulation to all, and especially to those whose mistreatment caused the war; but if that reconciliation is to be marked by the industrial slavery and civic death of those same black men, with permanent legislation into a position of inferiority, then those black men, if they are really men, are called upon by every consideration of patriotism and loyalty to oppose such a course by all civilized methods, even though such opposition involves disagreement with Mr. Booker T. Washington. We have no right to sit silently by while the inevitable seeds are grown for a harvest of disaster to our children, black and white.

First, it is the duty of black men to judge the South discriminatingly. The present generation of Southerners are not responsible for the past, and they should not be blindly hated or blamed for it. Furthermore, to no class is the indiscriminate endorsement of the recent course of the South toward Negroes more nauseating than to the best thought of the South. The South is not "solid"; it is a land in the ferment of social change, wherein forces of all kinds are fighting for supremacy; and to praise the ill the South is to-day perpetrating is just as wrong as to condemn the good. Discriminating and broad-minded criticism is what the South needs,—needs it for the sake of her own white sons and daughters, and for the insurance of robust, healthy mental and moral development.

To-day even the attitude of the Southern whites towards the blacks is not, as so many assume, in all cases the same; the ignorant Southerner hates the Negro, the workingmen fear his competition, the moneymakers wish to use him as a laborer, some of the educated see a menace in his upward development, while others—usually the sons of the masters—wish to help him to rise. National opinion has enabled this last class to maintain the Negro common schools, and to protect the Negro partially in property, life, and limb. Through the pressure of the moneymakers, the Negro is in danger of being reduced to semi-slavery, especially in the country districts; the workingmen and those of the educated who fear the Negro, have united to disfranchise him, and some have urged his deportation; while the passions of the ignorant are easily aroused to lynch and abuse any black man. To praise this intricate whirl of thought and prejudice is nonsense; to inveigh indiscriminately against "the South" is unjust; but to use the same breath in praising Governor Aycock, exposing Senator Morgan, arguing with Mr. Thomas Nelson Page, and denouncing Senator Ben Tillman, is not only sane, but the imperative duty of thinking black men.

It would be unjust to Mr. Washington not to acknowledge that in several instances he has opposed movements in the South which were unjust to the Negro; he sent memorials to the Louisiana and Alabama constitutional conventions, he has spoken against lynching, and in other ways has openly or silently set his influence against sinister schemes and unfortunate happenings. Notwithstanding this, it is equally true to assert that on the whole the distinct impression left by Mr. Washington's propaganda is, first, that the South is justified in its present attitude toward the Negro because of the Negro's degradation; secondly, that the prime cause of the Negro's failure to rise more quickly is his wrong education in the past; and, thirdly, that his future rise depends primarily on his own efforts. Each of these propositions is a dangerous half-truth. The supplementary truths must never be lost sight of: first, slavery and race-prejudice are potent if not sufficient causes of the Negro's position; second, industrial and common-school training were necessarily slow in planting because they had to await the black teachers trained by higher institutions,—it being extremely doubtful if any essentially different development was possible, and certainly a Tuskegee was unthinkable before 1880; and, third, while it is a great truth to say that the Negro must strive and strive mightily to help himself, it is equally true that unless his striving be not simply seconded, but rather aroused and encouraged, by the initiative of the richer and wiser environing group, he cannot hope for great success.

In his failure to realize and impress this last point, Mr. Washington is especially to be criticised. His doctrine has tended to make the whites, North and South, shift the burden of the Negro problem to the Negro's shoulders and stand aside as critical and rather pessimistic spectators; when in fact the burden belongs to the nation, and the hands of none of us are clean if we bend not our energies to righting these great wrongs.

The South ought to be led, by candid and honest criticism, to assert her better self and do her full duty to the race she has cruelly wronged and is still wronging. The North—her co-partner in guilt—cannot salve her conscience by plastering it with gold. We cannot settle this problem by diplomacy and suaveness, by "policy" alone. If worse comes to worst, can the moral fibre of the country survive the slow throttling and murder of nine millions of men?

The black men of America have a duty to perform, a duty stern and delicate,—a forward movement to oppose a part of the work of their greatest leader. So far as Mr. Washington preaches Thrift, Patience, and Industrial Training for the masses, we must hold up his hands and strive with him, rejoicing in his honors and glorying in the strength of this Joshua called of God and of man to lead the headless host. But so far as Mr. Washington apologizes for injustice, North or South, does not rightly value the privilege and duty of voting, belittles the emasculating efforts of caste distinctions, and opposes the higher training and ambition of our brighter minds,—so far as he, the South, or the Nation, does this,—we must unceasingly and firmly oppose them. By every civilized and peaceful method we must strive for the rights which the world accords to men, clinging unwaveringly to those great words which the sons of the Fathers would fain forget: "We hold these truths to be self-evident: That all men are created equal; that they are endowed by their Creator with certain unalienable rights; that among these are life, liberty, and the pursuit of happiness."

QUESTIONS FOR DISCUSSION AND EXAMINATION

1. Some students familiar with Du Bois's criticism of Washington have defended Washington's approach as a "practical" solution that sought to accomplish what could be done for black people under the conditions of that particular place and time. Yet Du Bois believed that Washington fundamentally misinterpreted those conditions, and that given the political-economic and ideological realities of the period, the Washingtonian solution was truly impractical as a route to black advancement. Which leader had the stronger position, in your view, and why?
2. Du Bois relied on Washington's autobiography in writing that "the picture of a lone black boy pouring over a French grammar amid the weeds and dirt of a neglected home soon seemed to him the acme of absurdities" (see Primary Source Reading). Why, in your view, did Washington see this image as so absurd, and why did Du Bois see Washington's view as so wrong in this instance? Which position do you believe is stronger, and why?
3. In your Primary Source Reading, Du Bois wrote, "Honest and earnest criticism from those whose interests are most nearly touched,—criticism of writers by readers, of government by those governed, of leaders by those led,—this is the soul of democracy and the safeguard of modern society. If the best of the American Negroes receive by outer pressure a leader whom they had not recognized before, manifestly there is here a certain palpable gain. Yet there is also irreparable loss,—a loss of that peculiarly valuable education which a group receives when by search and criticism it finds and commissions its own leaders." To what degree do you find this statement consistent or inconsistent with Thomas Jefferson's views on intellectual freedom and the developmental value of democracy? Support your position.
4. Du Bois also wrote, "When to earth and brute is added an environment of men and ideas, then the attitude of the imprisoned group may take three main forms,—a feeling of revolt and revenge; an attempt to adjust all thought and action to the will of the greater group; or, finally, a determined effort at self-realization and self-development despite environing opinion." However Du Bois might characterize

Washington, how would *you* place Washington's vocational-education approach with respect to the three responses proposed by Du Bois? To what degree does Washington's approach fit one or more of those descriptions? Explain.

5. Du Bois identifies the following "dangerous half-truths": "The distinct impression left by Mr. Washington's propaganda is, first, that the South is justified in its present attitude toward the Negro because of the Negro's degradation; secondly, that the prime cause of the Negro's failure to rise more quickly is his wrong education in the past; and, thirdly, that his future rise depends primarily on his own efforts. Each of these propositions is a dangerous half-truth." To what degree do you agree that each of those propositions is partly true but partly false, and why would it be "dangerous" to overlook the falseness you identify in each? Defend your view.

NOTES

1. For a thorough treatment of the Reconstruction period, see Eric Foner, *Reconstruction: America's Unfinished Revolution, 1863–1877* (New York: Harper and Row, 1988). See also Kenneth M. Stampp, *The Era of Reconstuction, 1865–1877* (New York: Vintage Books, 1965).
2. C. Vann Woodward, "From *Origins of the New South,*" excerpted in Foner, p. 241ff.
3. Ibid., pp. 241–42.
4. C. Vann Woodward, *The Strange Career of Jim Crow* (New York: Oxford University Press, 1955). Woodward notes that while the origin of the term "Jim Crow" is lost in obscurity, a song and dance named "Jim Crow," written by Thomas D. Rice in 1832, apparently is the source of the term as applied to white supremacy practices in the South. By 1890, Woodward notes, the term was being used in its adjective form.
5. Louis R. Harlan, *Booker T. Washington: The Wizard of Tuskegee, 1901–1915* (New York: Oxford University Press, 1983), p. viii.
6. The black belt was the geopolitical area in America in which blacks constituted a majority of the population, and the area in which they demonstrated the greatest political, economic, and cultural solidarity during the life and career of Washington. This area embraced a group of counties in eastern Virginia and North Carolina; a belt of counties extending from the South Carolina coast through South Carolina, central Georgia, and Alabama; and a detached area embracing a portion of the lower Mississippi River Valley. Tuskegee Institute was located in Alabama's black belt, which extended from the west central to the southeastern portion of the state where Macon County is located. This portion of Alabama's black belt contained, in 1910, twenty-one counties, all with majority black populations, ranging from a low of 51.7 percent in Pickens County to a high of 88.2 percent in Lowndes County. Alabama's and the South's black belt populations showed remarkably little change from emancipation to the end of Washington's career in 1915. It was in this context that Washington emerged as the educational statesman of black America and sought to apply the Hampton doctrines of economic interdependence, racial separation, and industrial education.
7. Delegates to Alabama's constitutional convention quoted in Horace Mann Bond, *Negro Education in Alabama: A Study in Cotton and Steel* (New York: Atheneum, 1939), 1969 ed., pp. 167–68, 181–82, 192. While the term "freedmen" has a regrettable masculine bias, it is an important historical designation, enshrined by Congress in the Freedmen's Bureau, for ex-slaves.
8. Foner, *Reconstruction: America's Unfinished Revolution,* p. 96; David Tyack, Thomas James, and Aaron Benavot, *Law and the Shaping of Public Education 1785–1954* (Madison: University of Wisconsin Press, 1987), p. 144.
9. Tyack, James, and Benavot, p. 144.
10. Bond, *Negro Education in Alabama,* pp. 148–49, 156.
11. Robert J. Norrell, *Reaping the Whirlwind: The Civil Rights Movement in Tuskegee* (New York: Alfred A. Knopf, 1985), 1986 Vintage Books ed., pp. 10–11; Bond, p. 135; and Jonathan M. Wiener, *Social Origins of the New South: Alabama, 1860–1885* (Baton Rouge: Louisiana State University Press, 1978), pp. 93–111.
12. Bond, pp. 148–49, 156.
13. Ibid., pp. 156, 160.
14. Ibid., p. 161.
15. Ibid., p. 157; Louis R. Harlan, Pete Daniel, Stuart B. Kaufman, Raymond W. Smock, and William M. Welty, *The Booker T. Washington Papers,* (Urbana: University of Illinois Press, 1972), Vol. 2, p. 443; and Benjamin G. Brawley, *A Social History of the American Negro* (New York: MacMillan, 1921).
16. Louis R. Harlan, *Booker T. Washington: The Making of a Black Leader 1856–1901* (New York: Oxford University Press, 1972), 1975 paperback ed., in Preface.
17. James D. Anderson, *The Education of Blacks in the South, 1860–1935* (Chapel Hill: University of North Carolina Press, 1988), pp. 148–50.
18. Bond, pp. 224–25.
19. Booker T. Washington, quoted in Anderson, *The Education of Blacks in the South,* p. 5.

20. Louis R. Harlan, *Booker T. Washington 1856–1901,* pp. 35–36, 44, 228.
21. Booker T. Washington, quoted in Bond, p. 218, 220–25; Booker T. Washington, *My Larger Education: Being Chapters from My Experience* (Garden City, New York: Doubleday, Page, 1911), p. 305.
22. Raymond Wolters, *The New Negro on Campus: Black College Rebellions of the 1920s* (Princeton: Princeton University Press, 1975), p. 7.
23. Anderson, pp. 178–85; Robert A. Margo, *Disenfranchisement, School Finance, and the Economics of Segregated Schools in the United States South, 1890–1910* (New York: Garland Publishing, 1985), pp. 6, 16, 24–25, 110–11.
24. Quoted in Louis R. Harlan, *Separate and Unequal: Public School Campaigns and Racism in the Southern Seaboard States 1901–1915,* 1958 (Reprint. New York: Atheneum, 1968), and Harlan, *Booker T. Washington: The Wizard of Tuskegee, 1901–1915,* pp. 162, 192–93.
25. Booker T. Washington, "The Successful Training of the Negro," *World's Work* 6 (August 1903), pp. 3731–51.
26. Louis R. Harlan, "Booker T. Washington in Biographical Perspective," *American Historical Review,* October 1970, p. 1589; Harlan, *Booker T. Washington: The Making of a Black Leader, 1856–1901,* p. 58.
27. Booker T. Washington, quoted in Anderson, *The Education of Blacks in the South,* p. 39.
28. Harlan, *Booker T. Washington: The Making of a Black Leader, 1856–1901,* p. 61.
29. Anderson, *The Education of Blacks in the South,* pp. 51–52; Booker T. Washington and W. E. Burghardt Du Bois, *The Negro in the South: His Economic Progress in Relation to His Moral and Religious Development* (New York: Citadel Press, 1970; also published in 1907 in London by Moring Ltd.), pp. 14, 26, 74.
30. Anderson, *The Education of Blacks in the South,* pp. 37, 52; Harlan, "Booker T. Washington in Biographical Perspective," p. 1594; Raymond W. Smock, ed., *Booker T. Washington in Perspective: Essays of Louis R. Harlan* (Jackson: University Press of Mississippi, 1988), p. 113.
31. Anderson, *The Education of Blacks in the South,* p. 44.
32. Ibid.
33. Smock, *Booker T. Washington in Perspective,* p. 104; quoted in James D. Anderson, *Education for Servitude: The Social Purpose of Schooling in the Black South,* Ph.D. Dissertation, University of Illinois, 1973, p. 175; Washington and Du Bois, *The Negro in the South,* p. 28; quoted in Anderson, *The Education of Blacks in the South,* p. 44; Harlan, *The Booker T. Washington Papers,* Vol. 4, p. 369.
34. Harlan, *The Booker T. Washington Papers,* Vol. 4, p. 220; Louis R. Harlan and Raymond W. Smock, eds., *The Booker T. Washington Papers* (Urbana: University of Illinois Press, 1976), Vol. 5, p. 617.
35. Harlan, *The Booker T. Washington Papers,* Vol. 4, pp. 197–98, 369–72, 383; Smock, *Booker T. Washington in Perspective,* p. 105.
36. Harlan, *Booker T. Washington in Biographical Perspective,* pp. 1593–94.
37. Smock, *Booker T. Washington in Perspective,* p. 106.
38. Anderson, *The Education of Blacks in the South,* Chap. 2.
39. Ibid.
40. Ibid., p. 75.
41. John Hope Franklin, *Three Negro Classics* (New York: Avon Books, 1965), p. xii. See also the recent and acclaimed biography by David L. Lewis, *W. E. B. Du Bois 1868–1919: Biography of a Race* (New York: Holt, 1993).
42. W. E. B. Du Bois, *The Autobiography of W. E. B. Du Bois* (New York: International Publishers, 1968), p. 83.
43. Ibid., p. 236.
44. Ibid., pp. 237–39; also see selection at end of chapter.
45. Du Bois, *Autobiography,* p. 262.
46. Lewis, *W. E. B. Du Bois 1868–1919,* p. 2.
47. Quoted in Merle Curti, *The Social Ideas of American Educators* (New York: Charles Scribner's Sons, 1935), p. 309.
48. Margaret Danner and Dudley Randall, *Poem Counterpoem* (Detroit: Broadside Press, 1966), p. 8.

Diversity and Equity: Schooling and American Indians

On the west side of the Mississippi River, in St. Louis, Missouri, there stands a metal arch that towers over the riverfront and dominates the city skyline. It is meant to symbolize St. Louis as the historic gateway to the West, the jumping-off point for the parties of migrants, trappers, and adventurers once bound for the western frontiers. The arch stands as an imposing symbol of American progress, portraying the dominance of man over nature in the cold logic of stainless steel. Yet it represents not the beginning of westward expansion, but rather its end.

By the time St. Louis was firmly established as the gateway to the West, the West had already been won. By the mid-19th century, European Americans had established their dominance over the continent with settlements extending from coast to coast. Questions of Anglo-American sovereignty in the Southwest and North had been resolved. Aboriginal American resistance was contained, and the relation of white to Native America was moving from trade, to war, to management. Schooling of the American Indian child would play an important role in this transition. [Note: Following the example set by Native-American writers themselves, this chapter uses the terms "Native American," "American Indian," and "Indian" interchangeably. The primary-source readings by American Indians at the end of this chapter illustrate the use of all three terms.]

Any consideration of European-American efforts to educate American Indians must take into account pluralist versus assimilationist visions of Native-American life in the United States. In general, a regard for pluralism represents a recognition that the strength of a society depends in part on the extent to which cultural differences are honored for their vital contribution to healthy diversity. *Pluralism,* thus conceived, means valuing and maintaining cultural and linguistic differences within a society. It is also a yardstick of tolerance, a virtue inherent in the democratic belief that diversity of belief and outlook ultimately contribute to, rather than detract from, social and political life.

The concept of *assimilation* has come to mean that process by which diverse cultures—immigrant, racial, ethnic, and linguistic minorities—alter their customs, habits, and languages so as to allow absorption into a *dominant culture.* It can also be argued that assimilation produces a variety of effects on the dominant culture, both positive and negative. Assimilation into the dominant European-American culture has meant radical change for most minority groups involved. When W. E. B. Dubois called for assimilation for African-Americans only through "self-assertion" and not "acquiescence," he was favoring a form of cultural pluralism. For Native Americans in particular, as anthropologist Alexander Lesser has said, assimilation has a "crucial finality," since they have no other homeland but America to look to for cultural identification and regeneration.

Native-American cultures were forged in a land which has subsequently been transformed from its original state. Yet, despite great changes in the larger society, Native Americans have not forfeited their right to pursue a tribal life and culture which are distinct from the dominant American culture. The explicit Native-American right to a distinct culture, protected by treaties, by a special governmental relationship, and by the maintenance of tribal homelands, has ensured that assimilation can never have the same meaning for Indian people as it has for other minority groups.

In this chapter we will be dealing with the impact of the new liberal ideology (described at length in Chapter 4) on the development of a unique pluralist vision for Native Americans in the United States. We will explore the impact of this developing ideology by examining the work of several crucial figures who shaped Indian education reform in the 20th century, particularly W. Carson Ryan, John Collier, and Willard W. Beatty. These individuals, more than any others, believed that the techniques of social-scientific rationality could be used to solve the problems of Indian America. For them, relations between Indians and whites could be organized according to sophisticated social-science knowledge. Theirs was a vision of assimilation with elements of democratic participation, but it was to be carefully controlled participation, coordinated with "scientific" administration of Indian affairs. Although these men wished to alleviate the marginal living conditions that confronted the Indian populace, the programs and policies they developed offered Indian citizens only limited involvement in shaping their own social institutions.

In this clash between Native-American and European-American value systems in the first half of the 20th century, education was seen as an important tool for achieving the distinctive kind of assimilation planned for Indians by new liberal reformers.

The American Indian relationship to formal schooling is a complex one that cannot be generalized. The expansion of efforts to bring formal schooling to Native Americans coincides with general expansion of schooling in the early 20th century. As such, the emerging and changing nature of progressivism greatly affected Native Americans. Although many Indians during the progressive era were living in rural areas, the character of schooling was greatly influenced by the industrial education movement. Likewise, the Americanization efforts directed toward immigrants in the growing urban environment took an ironic twist in schooling for Native Americans. Curricular standardization, character education, and Protestant humanism each affected Indian boarding and mission school efforts, as did the increasing effort to make compulsory public school a reality. The nearly successful genocide of the "Indian Wars" made way for more sophisticated efforts at "cultural adjustment."

Beginning with the early 20th century, administrative progressivism and managerial control were exemplified by the growth and influence of the Bureau of Indian Affairs and the institutionalization of tribal governments under the Indian Reorganization Act. Cultural and political research under the auspices of the Bureau of Ethnology illustrate the faith of that time that scientific experts could rationalize tribal culture and adjustment.

Part of the complexity of Indian education is due to the ambiguous and paradoxical nature of Native people's citizenship, sovereignty, and ongoing resistance to assimilation. Native Americans, like African-Americans, have always been aware of the benefits of education. They seem often to have resisted schooling, however, as an institution that could much damage the traditional spiritual and historic knowledge without which tribal survival was at risk or in some sense meaningless. Like African-Americans, Indian leaders often used whatever educational means they could glean: self-education, the military, boarding schools, the home. All could be used to better their communities and to wage legal and political battles. Understanding the complex relationships between American Indians and European-American schooling requires historical perspective and a recognition that, for most of their thousands of years of civilization, Indians have lived independent of white efforts to educate them.

POLITICAL-ECONOMIC FOUNDATIONS OF INDIAN SCHOOLING

It is impossible to sum up in a few pages the state of Native Americans prior to their transition from sovereignty to quasi-dependence. There are several reasons for this. Native-American tribes are molded together in the minds of most non-Indians as simply "Indians," the "first Americans." Even those of us who have been educated about and attempt to acknowledge tribal differences often do not fully understand the depth of these differences—linguistic, cultural, and environmental. Indeed, it is impossible to envision a single "state" of Native Americans without grossly oversimplifying. Rather, each group of Indian people reveals itself as a unique and complex cultural adaptation within the North American environment. It is also difficult to understand pre-Columbian Indian life because most of our firsthand knowledge, apart from archeological knowledge and Indian oral tradition, comes from European accounts of encounters that changed the lives of everyone on the continent.

A World before "Progress"

First, it is helpful to consider a sketch of one Native-American group's freedom in a world before "progress." The northeastern Indians were the "red men" of the European imagination. Covered with a red-pigmented grease to protect from cold in the winter and insects in the summer, these were the tribes first encountered by the English and French during colonial times. From approximately 4500 B.C. through A.D. 1200, these peoples developed in the woodlands of the East as hunters who would gradually employ planned agriculture as part of their subsistence.

Eastern Canada and the western Great Lakes area were populated primarily by speakers of the Algonquian language family, and the eastern Great Lakes and north Atlantic regions were populated largely by the Iroquoian peoples. These were the peoples with whom Europeans began commerce in the East. All later European-Indian relations in the East were conditioned by these early encounters. Algonquian groups included the Cree in Quebec, the Beothuk, Micmac, Passamaquoddy, Penobscot, Massachuset, Naragansett, Pequot, and Mohegan. In the eastern Great Lakes and upstate New York lived the powerful Iroquoian confederation, the speakers of Senecan, Onandagan, and Cayugan dialects, and the Mohawk and Oneida. Whereas the Puritans had engaged in early wars of extermination against the loosely organized Algonquians, they struck an alliance with the Iroquois, who were organized by representative government.

The Iroquois lived in "towns"—two acres of cleared ground surrounded by a palisade of logs. Iroquois societies were matrilineal, ownership and possession of property being controlled by the women of the band. They hunted, fished, and grew crops of corn, squash, and beans, which surrounded the towns. Indians lived in a complex symbiosis with their environment. Deer were harvested from "parks," which were shared by towns; the combination of hunting, trade, and agriculture provided the requirements for material prosperity in the temperate eastern forests. This pattern of coexistence with nature contrasted sharply with the capitalistic organization of the Europeans, who quickly began to subdue nature and turn its resources to the generation of profit through intensive agriculture and machine production.

Coexistence with neighboring tribes became an important method of survival for the Iroquois. The league of Iroquois nations was a confederation of five Iroquois groups formed to encourage cooperation rather than competition and warfare. This organization served as part of the model for the confederation of American states during the early development of the republic. Indeed, Indian people had a viable social and political existence for millennia prior to European contact. They lived rich lives, in harmony with a demanding environment and, more often than not, with neighboring tribes. They provided for their own needs, cared for their sick, and educated their young in tribal knowledge, values, and skills. This life, lived close to the environmental requirements of the continent, would be permanently altered by European settlement.

War and European-imported disease hastened the decline of aboriginal peoples in the Northeast during the colonial period. Although the exact population of North American Indians before the arrival of whites can never be known for certain, it appears that by the 1890s the number of American Indians in the United States had been reduced from about 1.5 million to roughly 250,000. A pattern of encroachment and war had become typical of European-Indian contact during the westward expansion of the 18th century. Indians were becoming less important in the East as a source of trade, and European Americans saw them as a physical impediment to expansion and progress.

While war and disease were accelerating Indian change and dissolution, Indians were constantly being encouraged to assimilate into European Christian culture. Throughout the 18th and 19th centuries, as Indians died, were removed, or were pushed into smaller areas of habitation, Europeans actively attempted to colonize both their lands and the minds of their young people.

The story of this colonization is told best through the study of formal Indian schooling. Yet this schooling must be understood in light of the unique nature of the relationship between the U.S. government and the tribes, a relationship which was forged through a series of treaties. Though their provisions have often been under attack, these treaties provide the basis for establishing a semi-sovereign Native-American "polis" within the federal system. It is in the context of the development of this semi-sovereignty that Native-American education must be analyzed, as the treaties provide for educational services to be provided to American Indians.[1]

Treaties and the "Trust Relationship"

As Indian resistance slowly gave way in the late 19th century, a lengthy treaty process unfolded between tribes and the federal government. These treaties stipulated that Indian people would agree to cease hostilities in exchange for safe title to specific areas of land. These exchanges often included agreements that the federal government would provide food and sometimes clothing and shelter during the transition to the new land. In addition, educational provisions, such as government boarding schools for Indian children, frequently were part of the agreement. Reasons for the provision of education are to be found in the special *trust* status established. Indeed, the first important key to understanding Indian social life in America and to Indians' relationship with the dominant society is to grasp how the concept of trust affected this relationship.

Four hundred years of treaties between tribes and the colonial and U.S. federal governments formed the basis of the *trust,* which is a distinctive use of the word that refers to the special relationship of mutual agreement between Indian nations and the United States, the "trustee" for protecting Indian rights. These treaties are legal agreements between sovereign, self-determined nations. After the Revolutionary War, the sovereign status of the tribes was reaffirmed first in the Articles of Confederation and later in the U.S. Constitution. In the early 1830s Supreme Court Chief Justice John Marshall further reaffirmed the tribes' sovereignty in *Cherokee Nation* v. *Georgia* and *Worcester* v. *Georgia.* These rulings limited the power of states to treat with and impose their laws on tribes within their boundaries. The Court ruled that traditionally the Cherokee tribe was a "distinct political society . . . capable of managing its own affairs and governing itself." While the tribes were not foreign nations, they were "domestic, dependent nations," and accordingly were to be protected by the federal government, not by states. Indian property, resources, and political rights are, by agreement, also protected in this trust relationship.

The unique and special status of tribal people has thus come to be during a long history of established precedent in the form of legal treaties, constitutional provisions, and High Court action. Both the sovereignty of the tribes and the federal government's responsibility to act as a kind of administrative trustee to protect Indian resources and to provide Indians' education are included in this history. However, the relation between Indian sovereignty and this trusteeship is a complicated and contested issue. Much of the debate on the status of Indian social policy has revolved around such questions as the following: To what extent can sovereigns remain under the protection of another sovereign? Are there any legal or moral grounds for ending the trust relationship, or should it remain in force in perpetuity? Even today, such questions remain unresolved and divisive.

Because the parties in this relation have historically had conflicting ideological perspectives, the guaranteed provision of education has been a particularly problematic dimension of the trust relationship. Whose version of education should be provided? And who decides? As we shall see, in the 1930s and 1940s these questions were not decided by Native Americans, but rather for them.

IDEOLOGY

John L. O'Sullivan's often-quoted term "manifest destiny" describes a popular American justification for subduing all native cultures on the continent. European Americans would see the domination of North American soil not simply as an opportunity, but as a manifest, God-given duty. This growing American nationalism resulted in an inevitable clash of ideological perspectives: pan-Christianity versus tribal religion, capitalism versus communal property and labor, republicanism and representative democracy versus consensual decision making.

Formal Indian education began as an attempt by Euro-American missionaries and government officials to lessen these differences by training the Indian in the standards and expectations of the dominant culture. Material progress could not be halted by recalcitrant aboriginals, nor would responsible Christians ignore the spiritual "needs" which they perceived in Native Americans. Consequently, Indian education became defined as training for roles in non-Indian America, roles which would require teaching Indians new ways of viewing the world.

During the 19th century, when Indian schooling was being established, European Americans were deeply influenced by the belief that their culture was the definition of civilization. American Indian societies were viewed as savage, for they sought not to master but rather to coexist with the natural environment. Indeed, they defined civilization quite differently from European Americans. The earth, they reasoned, could not be mastered, and such effort was to tempt fate. Thus, for them, to be civilized was to live in harmony with, not to subdue, the environment. In contrast, European Americans understood the world as a great chain of dominance, with man second only to God in a hierarchy of creation. For Native America, when God was conceptualized at all, God and nature were seen as one.

To European Americans, man was a rational animal who could reasonably take for granted the following cultural values: accumulation of goods, profit as a motive for labor, the primacy of the independent self, Christian morality and virtue, and the hostility of nature. These are just a few of the European-American values which are not typically represented in American Indian civilizations. Yet, these were the values that U.S. educators hoped to instill in Indian Americans through schooling.

Traditional Knowledge versus Science and Progress

Some observers would claim that the central tenet of both classical liberalism and new liberalism is the idea of progress. Here, too, the Native American outlook differs sharply from the European American. For the liberal, to value progress is to seek social and technological change and to be dissatisfied with the status quo. For a traditionally oriented society, however, the truths handed down by ancestors are the most important truths of all, and society is healthy when it embodies ancestral values and ways of life. In short, social and technological change are considered threatening and undesirable in traditional societies. Moreover, the new liberals' particular brand of "scientific" decision making and planning by centralized authorities contrasted still more sharply with the Native-American belief in tribal autonomy and prescientific decision-making processes. As late as 1933, Chief Luther Standing Bear wrote in his autobiography:

> True, the white man brought great change. But the varied fruits of his civilization, though highly colored and inviting, are sickening and deadening. And if it be the part of civilization to maim, rob, and thwart, then what is progress?
>
> I am going to venture that the man who sat on the ground in his tipi meditating on life and its meaning, accepting the kinship of all creatures, and acknowledging unity with the universe of things, was infusing into his being the true essence of civilization.[2]

Native Americans considered themselves a part of nature and sought to live in harmony with their environment, while European Americans, who understood the world as a great chain of dominance, sought to master nature.

It is not too strong to claim that Native-American values, spirituality, and mode of life were a direct challenge to the ideological assumptions of European culture. European notions of private property conflicted with the tribal and familial interdependence of Indian people. Most tribal groups possessed no strong concept of private property and little concept of land ownership, beyond customary use. European domesticity and agriculture contrasted with the variety of subsistence methods used by Native Americans, none of which depended on mercantile exchange. European ideas of capital gain and accumulation clashed with the tribes' marginal or subsistence economies. The writing culture clashed with oral cultures, especially since among tribal peoples promises were spoken rather than written.

Seeing this, European-American leaders attempted to acculturate the Indians into the value system of European America. Literacy, domesticity, Christianity, agriculture, the dignity of labor, personal wealth, hygiene, manners—these standards became the first line of attack in the effort to eliminate the tribal Indian presence. If the Indian couldn't be eliminated, then "Indianness" could be. Education thus became the primary ingredient in the federal government's policy of Indian assimilation following the great Indian Wars of the 19th century. The effort began in mission schools, continued in federal boarding schools established through the Bureau of Indian Affairs (B.I.A.), and finally included state public schools in the 20th century. To this day, the web of institutions delivering education to Indian people remains divided among private, federal, and state institutions as well as a few tribally and community-controlled contract schools. Yet, despite more than one hundred years of experimentation, Indian education remains an institution that is only marginally successful in its attempt to heal the persistent wounds of illiteracy, poverty, and cultural division which it was purportedly designed to heal.

SCHOOLING THE NATIVE AMERICAN

Indian people have for centuries been characterized by white America as a "problem"—the uncivilized force standing in the way of progress and westward expansion. European-American attempts to educate Native America were intended to be part of a civil solution to a problem which had long been pursued by violent means. Both formal schooling and the general social education of Indian people are separate but intertwined efforts to socialize Indians to the dominant European-American culture. The term *social educa-*

tion, as used here, includes agricultural and industrial policy, as well as formal schooling. As such, social education of Native Americans was a broad-based governmental effort using a variety of public policy mechanisms, including schools, to socialize the Indians to the "requirements" of modern American society.

Between 1866 and 1887 the push to expand schooling was affecting Native Americans, but not to the degree expected. In 1878, 137 schools were serving Indian children and the school population was only 3,500. By 1887 there were 231 schools serving 10,000 children out of a total Indian population of 400,000. Such a small fraction is a reminder of the extent to which Native-American families resisted formal education and its assimilative approach.

Social Education, from Land Allotment to Boarding Schools

In 1886 Congress passed the Dawes Allotment Act. Its purpose was to distribute tribal lands to individual tribesmembers who could demonstrate their "blood quantum" Indian heritage and a minimal competency in farming and animal husbandry. This legislation, it was argued, would encourage Indian people to become functioning members of a domestic, agricultural society in a primarily capitalist economy. However, it enticed many impoverished Indians to sell their holdings and thus liquidate the "problem" of communally held land in a European-American culture committed to the ownership of private property. Whereas allotment was intended to change Indian notions of communal property, the policy would reduce tribal lands by 100 million acres between 1886 and 1933, after which the policy was suspended for the next two decades.

The allotment policy was intended to teach Indians the habits and practices of the yeoman farmer. At the same time, the federal government was providing formal education for Indian children at boarding schools with the intention of hastening their assimilation into mainstream American society and values. During the late 18th and 19th centuries, the federal government had funded a number of Indian schools, most of which were run by missionaries. After 1880, a large number of off-reservation, federal boarding schools were opened. By the turn of the century, 25 were in operation. Increasingly during this time, Indians were also educated in on-reservation boarding schools and in public schools, both of which were less expensive than schools located far from the reservation.

The policy of allotment contributed to the breakup of tribal Indian lands and therefore to the breakup of tribal unity and identity. Boarding education also contributed to tribal breakups by assimilating young Indians into non-Indian culture. The boarding school environment began to draw many critics during the early part of the 20th century.

Criticism of the Boarding School

European-American reformers and opinion leaders soon joined the Native-American tribes themselves in voicing opposition to land-allotment and boarding-school policies which were contributing to the rapid destitution rather than the assimilation of Native Americans. These critics objected to both the barbarism of living and working conditions in the schools and to the fact that boarding education, in seeking rapid assimilation, actually fostered resistance and rebellion to the dominant culture. Indians returning from the schools would go "back to the blanket," unwilling or unable to adapt to the civilization for which they supposedly had been trained. Assimilation was considered synonymous with progress, and no effort was spared in pursuing this end. Values integral to land allotment—veneration of private property, individual competition, domesticity, toil, and European standards of beauty, dress, and "hygiene"—were all a part of the boarding school environment. In 1887, the Indian Rights Association, one of the most influential Indian support groups, had celebrated the Dawes Act as a great advance toward the association's "general policy of gradually making the Indian in all respects as the white man."[3] Yet it was the general failure—moral and practical—of the radical assimilation policy which spurred the next generation of reformers to criticize and change Indian social education policy.

Francis E. Leupp was one of the first government voices to be critical of the off-reservation

Indian boarding schools were established to assimilate young Indians into the dominant European-American values: veneration of private property, individual competition, domesticity, toil, and European standards of dress and hygiene.

boarding school. In 1905, Leupp became commissioner of Indian Affairs, the chief administrator of the Bureau of Indian Affairs. His criticism of allotments and boarding education presaged later developments, for he attacked not the intention of assimilation but the method by which it proceeded. Leupp, believed that the allotment of lands to Indians to make farmers out of hunters was an error. "A people reared to war or the chase," he wrote, "could not be turned into farmers or laborers overnight."[4] He supported the use of reservation day schools so that civilization could be brought to the Indian instead of bringing the Indian to civilization.

During Leupp's tenure, policymakers were beginning to see the failures of the allotment policy and of the boarding school in more graphic detail. Helen Hunt Jackson's popular *Century of Dishonor* reminded educated readers of the injustice, immorality, violence, and maladministration perpetrated by the Bureau of Indian Affairs. It had become clear that some allotted lands were both unsuited for agriculture and too small for rangeland. It was believed that some Indians were not gaining "competence" to handle their allotments and were selling out or "misusing" their land.

The generation which followed Leupp believed that scientific administration and rational management, rather than rapid assimilation, were the answer to the "Indian problem." The goal for the next generation of reform was, in the words of modern liberals, "to make scientifically rational" the assimilation process. They sought to fit education to varying abilities and conditions, all in the service of an eventually more "efficient" assimilation.

Scientific Management and Educational Reform

As early as 1866, Commissioner of Indian Affairs Dennis Cooley made an extensive survey of Indian education. The government survey was an example of numerous efforts under the emerging progressive impulse to study, with the help of the rational eye of the social scientist, those conditions germane to the administration of Indian affairs. Cooley characterized Indian education as "the only means of saving any considerable portion of the Indian race from the life and death of the heathen."[5]

Progressive social study and management is well illustrated in the 18-month study of the U.S. Indian service carried out by the Brookings Institution's Institute for Government Research under the direction of Lewis Merriam in 1926. Issued in 1928, titled the "Problem of Indian Administration," the so-called Merriam Report concluded that reform of the Indian service must not be a simple overhaul of Bureau management. Instead, the report recommended revising the B.I.A. policy of cultural assimilation through boarding school education and land allotment. Representing the progressive management approach of its time, the study argued that more, not less, government administration would be required to effect policy change and maintenance.[6]

The Merriam Report stated that education was the most fundamental concern of the Bureau. Through education, the Indian could begin to understand better the demands of modern culture and technology. This concern had been implicit throughout the history of federal Indian education policy, but starting with Merriam, reformers began to apply pressure for a different approach. The report concluded that it was important, in light of the most modern anthropological and social science, that Indians retain their cultural wisdom; or at least that a benevolent policy of noninterference be instituted. If the Indian school was not directed to teach Indian culture, it was also directed not to interfere with tribal life and ways. Through the influence of anthropologists and the new cultural science, antitribal, pro-Anglo indoctrination in the schools began to fall into disfavor with the Bureau, in principle if not always in practice.

Indian culture thus became a value previously unrecognized by the B.I.A. administration. Since Leupp's tenure, tens of thousands of acres of Indian land had been sold off, and there had been significant Indian combat participation in World War I. Partly as a result of these assimilationist steps, Indians had won citizenship, while they retained their special trust-protected status. Throughout the 1920s muckraking journalists had pressured Congress to examine the condition of Indian America, especially conditions prevailing in the Indian boarding schools. The Merriam Report, significantly, criticized the boarding schools for failing to assimilate Indian children. Citing a number of deficiencies in the Indian service, it declared that the new generation of Indian service administrators would spearhead redoubled efforts in social education, aided by the new human sciences of anthropology, psychology, and sociology, together with new administrative expertise and efficiency. Indians would progress, it was argued, only if the most sophisticated management techniques and educational practices were employed. This new generation of solutions to the "Indian problem" would be crafted not by old soldiers or civil servants but by progressive educators and administrators.

"Progressive" Indian Education: Early Years

The education section of the 1928 Merriam Report was prepared under the direction of W. Carson Ryan, a Swarthmore College professor of education. Ryan was committed to the new concepts of progressive education. As past president of the Progressive Education Association and a specialist in vocational education, he believed that education should be fitted to the "needs" of the individual—that is, geared to "reasonable" expectations with respect to their position in society and potential in the work force.

Education, for Ryan, was a process of adjustment to the dominant economic and social factors facing the individual. Ryan wanted a complete readjustment of the B.I.A. education forces. As he would later write, "a mere three Rs type of education is sufficiently absurd anywhere, but nowhere more so than among the Pueblos (Indians) where life itself provides genuinely the elements that many progressive schools can only reproduce artificially."[7] The Merriam Report urged reform of a coercive, mismanaged, haphazard assimilationist social and educational policy—and Ryan was joined by other social reformers in this position.

Yet, when we study their arguments and methods, what we see is not an attack on how assimilation resulted in the dissolution of Indian societies, but, like Francis Leupp's criticisms from two decades earlier, an attack on the methods by which the dissolution was to be carried out.

As Chapter 4 detailed, progressive education reflected emerging interest in such areas as democratic-participatory education based on the needs and interests of students, activity-based learning, the union between work and learning, and the incorporation of prevailing social conditions as a fundamental part of education. Yet, as progressivism worked its way into Indian policy, a number of contradictions arose. Democratization of schools conflicted with the fact that all Indian schooling was planned and administered in the B.I.A. hierarchy. Indian control of education was not intended by the Bureau, for despite the long Indian tradition of consensual decision making, it was supposed that Indians lacked the rationality for a democratic educational decision. (It would not be until the 1960s that the first Indian boards of education would be formed in the Indian contract schools, and they would be of limited autonomy.) Activity-based learning reflecting the world of work, intended to adjust Indians to their social reality, would increasingly alienate them from schooling and from higher education. All too often, their progressive schooling experience centered on training in arts and crafts, wood shop, and shed building.

Progressive educators and social scientists advocated responding to the interests and needs of Indian children. They tried to strengthen Indian cultures, and they lamented the destruction of Indian language and habits. They encouraged cultural development and began the first programs of Indian bilingual education. Yet, from the beginning, cross-cultural education and bilingual education, as well as new arts and crafts programs, were instituted not as a means of strengthening Indian cultures for their own sake, but as motivational tools to encourage the willing acquisition of English and the acceptance of schooling, and also as a cure for the ever-present "problem" of Indian recalcitrance and apathy. Progressive educators such as Ryan encouraged these innovations as a practical way to prepare the Indian for a prideful place in the world of work. Yet, this pride was supposed to well up in the breast of a marginally employed or unemployed laborer, engaged in short-term, low-status assembly work, agricultural piecework, or the production of arts and crafts for the profit of white traders and middlemen. Anything more ambitious was not seen by progressive educators as part of the "available" Indian reality.

The Influence of John Collier

During the progressive era, described in Chapter 4, the administration of the Indian service came under the influence of individuals who saw the developing social sciences as a key to successful management in the Bureau of Indian Affairs. A principal figure in this development was John Collier, a social reformer who would come to have the greatest impact on the Indian service of any person in this century. During his tenure as commissioner of Indian Affairs, between the early 1930s and 1945, Collier's policies would have a wide-ranging effect on Indian education. Collier was confident that solutions to Indian problems could be found through the application of human sciences such as psychology, sociology, and anthropology. Throughout the 1930s and into the 1940s, Collier and the Indian Bureau employed social scientists in social and educational planning. From thinkers like Dewey and George H. Meade, who believed that a community of shared interests was central to modern progress and democracy, Collier derived his commitment to the resurgence of "community." Group identity and community feelings were central to emerging theories that indigenous people would progress and thrive only if they retained their cultural, communal selfhood. The rapid destruction of Indian community consciousness, whether by land allotment or boarding school regimentation and culture blindness, represented to Collier a form of social failure.

Working with social scientists from the Bureau of American Ethnology, Collier developed a focus on cross-cultural education which appeared to repudiate a century-long effort to assimilate the Indian child, and which reviled the concept of manifest destiny by acknowledging the value of Indian culture. Indeed, Collier worked to bring an end to allotments and to establish Indian tribal government through the Indian Reorganization Act (I.R.A.) of 1934. This law was the most dramatic change in Indian affairs since the Dawes Act. Elected tribal corporations were formed, apparently intended to speak for the people in the tribe. These councils, while eventually answerable to the Bureau of Indian Affairs, served as administrative centers with whom the government and the B.I.A. could engage in the development of reservation America.

Yet, accompanying all these developments were counterthemes. On the one hand were changes announcing the presence of a pluralist approach, exalting Indian culture and purportedly renouncing assimilation and paternalism. On the other were growing arguments among educators that new forms of schooling, closer to the "needs" of the Indian child, would soften the psychologic effects of an ongoing policy of assimilation and absorption. Acknowledging Indian culture, it was thought, would make Indians less likely to resist the inevitable changes before them. Willing participation would replace apathy and defiance.

Collier's Early Career

No one had more to do with the beginning of this subtle shift in attitude than Collier. While it is not the central purpose of this discussion to follow the career of any one reformer or administrator in the Indian Service, it is useful to understand the growth of Collier's social philosophy and life, because he became the main architect of a new age in Indian affairs. Collier's early, more radical commitment to cultural pluralism gradually changed to a belief in scientifically, bureaucratically managed pluralism. At the roots of Collier's approach to American Indian social policy we will find the roots of new liberal schooling policy for Indians—schooling for assimilation to white society.

To understand Collier's social (and aesthetic) vision, it is important to identify his intellectual models. Collier was born to a well-to-do, politically prominent Atlanta family. His father, a progressive businessman, believed in the importance of cooperation between industry and government. The elder Collier eventually became mayor of Atlanta, and before that had organized the Cotton States International Exposition, where Booker T. Washington, in his famous "Atlanta Compromise" speech, extolled the virtues of the black South as a great potential engine of labor.

John Collier attended Columbia University in 1902, but it was his friendship with a New York tutor whom he had met earlier in Atlanta which most influenced the course of his life. Lucy Crozier introduced Collier to the ideas of Nietzsche, the symbolist poets, and the work of new liberal sociologist Lester Frank Ward. Collier's studies with Crozier and in particular the ideas of Ward were to shape his belief in planned social change and the application of "social intelligence" (guided by social science) to the solution of human problems.

In 1904, for example, Collier and others tried to convince the railroad companies to transport trainloads of unemployed northern immigrants to Appalachian regions, where the mixture of northerners and southerners would revitalize the biological and cultural character of both racial "stocks."[8] After this venture failed, Collier became deeply involved in the New York settlement house movement. Here he joined with others in trying to use forums and lectures to address the "problems of social unrest and assist in the peaceful, democratic evolution of our society."[9] He believed that settlement house social centers could teach low-income and immigrant children such virtues as "citizenship, ethics, social good will, play, and aesthetics."[10] Interestingly, he believed that the new technology of motion pictures could prove to be a useful tool in this effort.

Collier's interest in motion pictures led to his leadership of the first movement to censor movies in the United States, from 1908 to 1914. As General Secretary of the National Board of Censorship of Motion Pictures, he worked at "assisting" film producers to upgrade the educational, moral, and artistic content of their films. His belief that the arts could rehabilitate and harmonize social life would eventually play a role in his social-management approach to Native-American culture.[11]

While in New York, Collier became a part of the famous salon of wealthy New York socialite Mabel Dodge, who hosted radicals and progressives, such as Lincoln Steffens, Walter Lippman, John Reed, Emma Goldman, and William "Big Bill" Haywood, each of whom would leave a mark on history. The intellectuals and activists who gathered at the Dodge salon tended to place more faith in writing and the arts than in worker revolution, though they believed that America was on the verge of a "cooperative commonwealth that would be socialist, not capitalist, in its economy."[12] Dodge had a special interest in American Indians, and she eventually persuaded Collier, who had been involved in a failed community-organizing effort in California, to visit the Pueblo people in Taos, New Mexico.[13]

Collier was so struck by what he found among the Pueblos that he stayed in New Mexico from 1920 through 1930. He came to believe that the Pueblos' communal lifestyle nurtured human personality and potential in a manner that had been lost to Western culture, and that European Americans were a continuing threat to the Indian ways of life. "The deep cause of our world agony," he wrote, "is that we have lost passion and reverence for human personality and for the web of life and the earth which the American Indians have tended as a central, sacred fire since the Stone Age."[14]

In 1922, Collier had opportunity to put his beliefs into action. He joined with the Pueblos in fighting a U.S. Congressional bill that would not only transfer tribal land to white squatters but would also place the internal government of the Pueblo "city states" under jurisdiction of the U.S. district court. Since Pueblo internal affairs were guided almost solely by religious traditions, this bill would have created a legal basis for government control of Indian religious practices. The first all-Pueblo tribal council since 1680 was convened to discuss the bill, and Collier and a few other whites were invited. Together, they denounced the bill in the newspapers and helped bring about its defeat.[15]

This victory helped shape Collier's career as an Indian advocate and government policy reformer. He next joined with a number of other white new liberals to form the Indian Defense Association, which he served as executive director. Mixing aesthetic values with a pragmatic economic and social agenda, Collier sought to support the revitalization of Indian culture, community ideals, traditional manufacture, and tribal ownership of land.[16]

During the years that Collier worked with the Indian Defense Association, there was little evidence of any great change in Bureau policy toward Indian tribal solidarity. The Bureau reported in 1925 that the future well-being of the Indian lay in the ability to adapt, that Native people would have to absorb European civilization with school or without it.[17] As late as 1932, one year before Collier's appointment to the office of commissioner of Indian Affairs, the secretary of the interior reported the Interior Department's aim to terminate the relationship between Indian people and the federal government.[18] The Interior Department leadership must have felt acute economic pressure, both from the expense of Indian welfare and education and from its knowledge of the yet-unexploited resources of Indian lands. The call for Indian independence was in part a move intended to release the government from the financial obligations of the so-called Indian problem. John Collier, however, was soon to become commissioner of Indian Affairs, and the Interior Department's intentions would be thwarted.

Collier as Commissioner of Indian Affairs

President Franklin Roosevelt, on the strength of interior secretary Harold Ickes's recommendation, appointed Collier commissioner of Indian Affairs

John Collier, Commissioner of Indian Affairs from 1933 to 1945, sought to exalt Native-American culture and renounce earlier policies of forced assimilation. However, his policy of "managed liberalism" also had as its long-term goal to bring Indians willingly into the mainstream of American culture.

in 1933.[19] The fact that Ickes got Collier this appointment testifies to his influence in the New Deal administration. Ickes had established his reputation as a trustbuster in Chicago after the war and was also regarded as "a man deeply concerned with friendless groups such as Indians."[20] He was also an early member of the Indian Defense Association.

At the time of his appointment as commissioner, Collier had been influential in Indian affairs for 10 years. His crusade on behalf of the Indians resulted in strong feelings for and against him, and his appointment was unilaterally praised by neither white people nor Indians. Nevertheless, the strong support of Ickes made possible Collier's lasting influence on Bureau policy.

Beginning in 1933, Collier began the attempt to realize his dream of resurgent Indian community. With the help of Ickes, he began an effort to dismantle the remaining boarding schools. Indians would now attend public schools in increasing numbers, as Collier began the groundwork for a progressive social policy.[21] His efforts provide a good example of the centralized social planning which was characteristic of the New Deal. He attempted to weld his unified philosophy of Indian cultural values to a firm base of New Deal social reconstruction. However, the uniformity of his dream did not take into account the diversity of the Indian people. Native Americans, always a people of great social and cultural diversity, had become even more fragmented due to the effects of poverty, social disintegration, and assimilation.

In 1933, Collier helped institute school programs which he hoped might foster Indian racial heritage and identity. Arts and crafts were encouraged, and the day school was praised as the vehicle which would provide a center for Indian community growth.[22] There were other examples of such social-engineering programs, and the Interior Department reported applause for the effectiveness of such "practical" programs as the Indian Arts and Crafts Board.[23]

Just as the indigenous art became a means of boosting Indian self-sufficiency, so Indian language became a new touchstone for the social progressives. Bilingual-bicultural educational programs were proposed as a way to effect a recovery in Indian self-awareness and to increase educational success. Tribal language deterioration was a fact that Collier's administration did not ignore.[24] Yet the new bilingual emphasis, like other appeals for cultural renaissance, was not presented as an argument for Native life in itself, but instead as a vehicle to more rapid acquisition of English. This educational policy, like land reform, was developed so that Indians might become "bilingual, literate, yet proud of their racial heritage, completely self-supporting," that is, self-supporting in an English-language, industrial economy.[25] At its best, it might be argued, Collier's administration supported a model of pluralism that did not seek to erase Indian culture and identity, but instead sought to educate a people for participation in two cultures. At its worst, these policies saw Indian culture only as a necessary step to assimilated membership in the dominant white culture. The result, however, was a new affirmation of Indian cultural tradition.

In 1934, for example, at the beginning of Collier's "Indian New Deal," Secretary Ickes reported that through 50 years of "individualization," Indians had been robbed of economic initiative by the breakdown of their spirit. Thus, an effort to boost morale would benefit Indian economic independence and rehabilitation. To do this, Indian policy would now focus on spiritual regeneration. This effort implied a new recognition of the beauty and worth of tribal cultural forms. Schools soon began to recognize Indian religions as a legitimate expression of Indian culture. The rhetoric in the Department of Interior reports stated a policy of noninterference with tribal religious practice, where only a few years before, the Bureau had termed Indian rites pagan and "pornographic."

Collier genuinely respected traditional Indian values of democratic and equitable land use.[26] Largely because of his experience with Pueblo life, he believed that a renewal of Indian sovereignty, of tribal hegemony, would be the beginning of recovery for all Indian societies. He believed that the basic goal of any community is growth through democratic self-governance. In a climate of recovery politics, this appeal to democracy, to constitutional rights, and for a program of economic rebirth, proved highly persuasive to an administration ready for social experiment.

Collier and the Bureau cooperated with the University of Chicago Committee on Human Development in a series of thorough "case studies" of individual Indian nations. Appealing to principles of progressive social science rather than to Indian self-determination, this "action anthropology" was, for Collier, "a case in scientific exploration, wherein a practical problem of broad shape . . . became translated into a scientific problem."[27] Collier's reason for supporting detailed culture study is clearly indicated in his foreword to one of those same culture studies, *The Hopi Way,* which is excerpted at the end of this chapter. That statement reflects his emphasis on social management through scientific, progressive thought, and it prefigures the prominent place which the principles of progressive education were to play in the Education Division of the B.I.A. Collier asks:

> Does one seek to influence an individual or group? Let him discover what is central to the being of that individual or group. Let his effort at influence be near to, and not deviate sharply from, the line of force which is central to the being of the individual or group. Thus may he influence profoundly and helpfully. Remember that deep and central preoccupations, devotions and views of life can be helped to apply themselves to new practical ends. Here is the secret of efficient and democratic administration.[28]

Collier went on to say how Indian policy had moved more centrally to "things Indian," promoting greater response than ever before from Indians themselves. "There is hardly any limit," he writes, "to the energy, the good-will and the happiness which will meet us from within the Indian—if only we will work with him at his own centers."[29] Progress on the "Indian question" could now be scientifically managed. What was required was, first, scientific study of the Indian culture, and second, application of progressive education principles for enlisting Indian children into willing participation in assimilationist education.

Collier left an ambiguous legacy of tribalism that would foster some of the best and worst influences on future Indian sovereignty and the trust relationship. Indian people therefore responded to Collier's social engineering and administrative progressivism in very different ways. The several nations of the Iroquois, for example, showed conflicting Indian responses to Collier's efforts. The Eastern Iroquois were largely opposed to Collier's paternalism and heavy-handedness, and Seneca leader Alice Jamison waged a fierce campaign to blunt the liberal reforms of the Indian Reorganization Act. She charged that such changes, while rationalizing the tribal government relationship, would ultimately compromise the Iroquois league sovereign status as a nation.[30] Yet, while the majority of Iroquois fought the Indian Reorganization Act and its pluralist progressivism, the Oneida Iroquois near Green Bay, Wisconsin, still look favorably on the New Deal Writer's Project, which funded the Oneida Language and Folklore project for the reservation. Through Bureau anthropologists' efforts, the rapidly disappearing stories, language, and customs of the Oneida were revitalized and tribesmembers were put to work recreating lost crafts. In part, the memory of these early successes laid the groundwork for the legitimization of culturally sensitive curricula in Indian controlled schools today.

At the same time, the ambiguity of Collier's legacy can be seen in his support of the Indian education efforts of Willard Walcott Beatty, Collier's director of the Education Division of the Bureau of Indian Affairs. Just as close examination of Collier's career sheds light on how modern liberalism translated into progressive social policy toward American Indians, so does Beatty's career illuminate the distinct presence of progressive education in the European-American education of Native Americans.

Willard Walcott Beatty: Progressive Education for Native Americans

Collier retained his social emphasis in the Education Division of the B.I.A. through his association with and support of W. Carson Ryan and Willard Walcott Beatty. Both were presidents of the Progressive Education Society and frequent contributors to the journal *Progressive Education,* and throughout their careers both closely associated themselves with the theories of educational progressivism. Whereas both Ryan and Beatty served Collier as directors of the Education Division, Beatty was Collier's personal appointee and brought a vigorous, almost messianic approach to Indian education administration.

Before coming to the Bureau, Beatty had championed progressivism in the Bronxville School in New York and as an elementary school principal in Skokie, Illinois. He received his widest recognition, however, as architect of the "Winnetka technique," which consisted of progressive education principles he applied as superintendent of the Winnetka, Illinois, schools, located ten miles north of Chicago. He served as president of the Progressive Education Association from 1933 until 1937, at which point Collier appointed him director of the Bureau. *Time* magazine pronounced Beatty the "tribal leader" of progressive education in the United States.

Beatty was an indefatigable writer, constantly expressing his views on the the direction of Indian education policy in the pages of *Indian Education,* an official B.I.A. newsletter. Indeed, most of the articles in the newsletter—which focused on educational philosophy issues relating to Indian Service workers, administrators, and teachers—were authored by Beatty himself.

Compared to the boarding school, assimilationist approach, the progressive orientation of student-centered, activity-based learning within Indian communities seemed to be a clear step forward for Native Americans. Since federal Indian policy was moving away from assimilation and toward pluralism, educational policy was encouraged to follow. Yet, some questions must be raised about these efforts. In one article,"Education for What?" Beatty reflected on the proper approach to Indian education. Although he consistently appealed to the principles of the dynamic connection between work and learning, he nevertheless seemed to regard the labor status of the educated Indian as fixed. "The world," he wrote, "will always need its hewers of wood and drawers of water. . . The time will never come when all can make a living as lawyers, doctors, teachers, bankers, or stockbrokers. The assumption that education is the stepping stone from work with the hands to work with the brain is fundamentally fallacious; we need educated and intelligent hand workers, for within any conceivable period of time there will be many more of them, than all the rest of mankind put together."[31] Like the social-efficiency progressives described in Chapter 4, Beatty's focus on "employable skills" assumed that higher academic skills were not appropriate to the employment prospects of the population he was trying to help.

Although Beatty continued to champion education for the laboring classes, citing the positive effect it would have in a democracy, he wanted to establish an education which would deal "honestly" with the Indian. According to Beatty, Indian males were limited to such works as bricklaying, auto mechanics, carpentry, and plumbing, while females were capable only of teaching or of doing stenography, beauty culture, or housework for white people. In an article entitled "All Labor Is Honorable" he counseled, "Let us at least try to be honest with ourselves and our children. Let us get away from sentimental escapes from reality and realize that more than 50 percent of the employed whites in this country make their living, and are glad to do so, from some of the types of labor we've been guiding Indian children away from as 'beneath them.' All honest labor is honorable. Indian young people must be taught to do the things that will make them self-sufficient, which, in many instances, will provide them with subsistence but little ready money. . ." He continued, "If this much can be accomplished and Indians freed from their present dependence upon charity and direct relief, they will have been placed on a plane of economic equality with half their fellow white citizens and more than half the population of Europe."[32] The similarities to the educational philosophy of Booker T. Washington are striking.

Beatty would argue that Indian people could be profitably educated to increase their already "tempermental" inclination to manual labor. He would put forth as evidence certain social-scientific experiments which argued that people can be encouraged to accept and even enjoy a work environment which had been regarded as low-status, disagreeable drudgery. Such acceptance was to be accomplished not by fundamental changes in the nature of production, but instead by fundamental changes in worker attitudes toward toil.

Beatty cited the success of the Hawthorne experiments as evidence that progressive principles could increase all kinds of work output, whether job or school related. The Hawthorne effect was a phenomenon discovered in a study of how lighting adjustments made at a Western Electric assembly plant near Chicago would affect the workers.

Native-American education policy focused on industrial education, since European-Americans considered a liberal education inappropriate for Indian males.

The "efficiency experts" who conducted the study measured the effect of light adjustments on productivity and discovered that no lighting adjustment was as effective in increasing production as was the attention workers were receiving during the study itself. Beatty remarked that it was crucial to make workers "feel important," since in this way workers "found stability, a place where they belonged and work whose purpose they could clearly see. And so they worked faster and better than they ever had in their lives."[33]

The scientific study of human labor thus was intended to change not the actual repetitive drudgery of the tasks themselves, but how workers felt about such tasks. The object was to encourage positive attitudes without altering the relationship of labor to production; by altering the workers' attitudes, management could offer the illusion of control and thus increase cooperation and production. An interesting and influential spin-off of these principles can be seen in some characteristics of progressive school practice. One of the chief methods of applying these principles to education was to foster the illusion that students had a hand in the design of instruction, just as workers were given the feeling they had control over conditions of their labor. In this way, progressive schooling effectively prepared students for the progressive factory.

Reacting to the aforementioned Merriam Report, which had objected to harsh labor conditions in the boarding schools, Beatty said that while it was appropriate that children should help with the cost of school upkeep, industrial work in the school would now be more "educational" and more closely fitted to the world of work. No longer would students labor with no purpose beyond their own upkeep in school laundries or printshops; instead, they would learn skills which could be generalized to the world of work. "The schools cannot train for all occupations," he wrote, "but they can aid the boy or girl in acquiring those types of skills that are common to many occupations."[34] The object was to develop "good work habits and attitudes" as much as it was to learn a "vocation" or receive an education. Efforts to teach Indian language and culture—often hailed as a method of preserving basic tribal values and encouraging a pluralist Indian presence—were in fact used as a technique of the kind suggested by the Hawthorne experiment, to discourage apathy and encourage willing Indian participation in the "normal transition" to assimilation.

Along similar lines, Beatty also encouraged the production of bilingual materials for students.

However, linguistic pluralism was never the goal, only a feeling of pluralism. In *Language, A Foundation Tool,* he wrote, "In 1934 when John Collier declared that an Indian has as much right to his native language as anyone, the decision was greeted with doubt and scorn. Older teachers in the service predicted that the already difficult problem of teaching English to their charges would be made more difficult. Naturally, this was not borne out by the facts. With the removal of the ban has come the beginning of that increased pride in race and culture which is necessary for worthy achievement. And for the moment, what is equally important, *an increased desire to learn English* . . . Psychologically we have won a great advantage in the schooling of Indians."[35]

Later, he attacked the problems posed by Indian consciousness, perceptions, and worldview, as expressed in both language and behavior. Those who worked among the various tribes had noted for many years that the tribal worldview, whether conditioned by language or culture, was very different from the European-American worldview. Indian peoples, for instance, often possessed a very different concept of duration, or time-sense. In *Education for Cultural Change,* Beatty referred to "the Great God Time," to which, in his view, all of the white world bowed. He encouraged the Indians to do the same, to join this worship and become accustomed to "our clockwork civilization." For Beatty, therefore, a greater understanding of Indian cultural consciousness was valuable primarily as a means of *eliminating,* rather than fostering, traditional tribal perceptions. Under Beatty's direction, education for Indians in the new progressive climate varied from earlier attempts to assimilate Indian children only in form, not in function. While the new progressive methods differed from the old boarding school approach, the ultimate goals of assimilation remained fundamentally the same.

Schooling and Assimilation of the Indian Child

Throughout the 1930s and 1940s many Indian boarding schools were closed in favor of public schools. Viewed by reformers as a needlessly harsh method of assimilation, the boarding schools, like land allotment, not only were a domestic moral embarrassment, but were inconsistent with the new climate of efficient, scientific human management. Public and day schools would replace the boarding schools to a greater degree than ever. In support of these new schools Beatty wrote, "Watching the whites about them who surround themselves with material comforts, far beyond anything ever evolved with Indian culture, it is natural for the Indian to ask himself wherein the white man differs from the red man that enables him to produce this disparity in material well being. If the Indian expressed his inquiry to the average white man, he is likely to be told that education has produced these differences in status—and what is more natural than for the Indian to assume that if he can secure an education identical with that of the white man, he can at once achieve the same material well being." School was to be the main vehicle for assimilation, Beatty wrote, although "a more rapid means by which to accomplish this same goal would be to marry off all the Indians to non-Indians, so that the children of mixed marriages would actively live with aspects of non-Indian culture. As we will continue to have full bloods with us for many generations, the school must serve as the culture spreading medium."[36]

After World War II, Beatty continued to apply progressive principles to the schooling of Indian children. The rhetoric of the principles cannot be allowed to obscure their purpose, however. To repeat, indigenous culture and language study was not undertaken primarily in recognition of their innate legitimacy, but as a psychologic technique to improve morale and to increase the willingness of Indians to learn English. Similarly, neither democratic participation in the creation of instruction nor hands-on activities were supported by the progressives in recognition of the intrinsic legitimacy of such activities. Rather, they were seen as a way of overcoming the Indians' apathy and resistance toward unfamiliar labor, both at school and at work. Like Booker T. Washington's Tuskegee students, Indians would receive an education appropriate to their status as marginal laborers suited primarily to repetitive handwork. The integration of work with schooling was a tacit admission that, for reasons of race and "temperament," Indians were considered permanent members of the laboring classes.

Beatty's progressive vision helped shape the direction of Indian education for decades, during which time the influence of progressivism on Indian education had its greatest impact due to increasing federal administration of Indian society. Meanwhile, John Collier had professed his faith in Indian cultures as part of a cure for the ills of industrial materialism and the ethical decline of western society. But while the progressive efforts he inspired and supported increased the educational emphasis on Indian language and culture and provided a school setting more in tune with the realities of Indian life, his pluralist vision and his recognition of Indian social and political sovereignty served, ironically, to further assimilationist goals. It also led Indians into the special status of marginal laborers reserved for America's marginal peoples. Education would be carefully designed to accomplish both goals, as progressive administrators used new liberal principles of social science efficiently to manage manifest destiny.

AFTERWORD: THE CASE OF THE NAVAJO

The European education of the Indian represents part of the shift from war to peace policy, from genocide to assimilation. European settlers first justified the conquest of tribal peoples by highlighting their savagery, their lack of humanity. Education of Indians was pursued in the belief that savagery could be turned to a useful purpose. Through conquest and assimilation, the Indian people of the East were changed forever, in accommodation to the forces of European expansion. Today the tribes of the Northeast are found in small pockets in the large cities and on several small scattered reservations. Though their numbers are small, the voice that remains—as heard, for example, through such publications as the Mohawk "Akwasasne Notes"—is strong in its identity and tribal solidarity. Its presence is a testament to survival despite crushing opposition, and witness to the resurgence of the Native-American voice in recent years.

The largest Indian territories today are found in the reservations west of the Mississippi, beyond the St. Louis Arch, in the Dakotas, the Northwest, the former "Indian territories" in Oklahoma, and especially in the Southwest—New Mexico and Arizona. Although many Indian people have moved to large urban centers, the reservations comprise the great population of landed Indian peoples. The largest tribal enrollment and largest reservation is an area covering parts of Arizona, New Mexico, and Utah—the Navajo Reservation. "Navajoland" is larger than the state of West Virginia and is home to approximately 240,000 people. It is a varied land of great beauty and extensive natural resources. Whereas the Eastern Algonquin and Iroquois were the original Indians of the Euro-American imagination, the Navajo, if only because of their large numbers and the size of their homeland, represent an important part of contemporary Native-American reality.

The Navajo have rich social, cultural, and religious traditions. Despite centuries of pressure to assimilate, they, as much as any tribal people in the U.S., have managed to retain much of their language and culture. This persistence is a testimony to their adaptability as well as to their isolation. However, life for the Navajo people today is fraught with complications, pressures, and poverty. Having largely preserved their tribal and familial identity, they deal daily with the contradictions of extensive resource exploitation and unrelenting poverty, television and third-world mortality rates, high technology and low employment. In 1975, a landmark study by the U.S. Commission of Civil Rights reported that Navajo per capita personal income was $900 per year, compared to the U.S. average of $3,921. Navajo unemployment was 60 percent; the U.S. average was 6 percent. Infant mortality was more than double that of the general population. Average number of school years was 5, compared with 12 for the general population. The most recent figures show that these disparities continue to widen.

In 1950, the gap between personal income for the U.S. population and Navajo's was around $900. By 1972, that gap had grown to $3,021. Yet, that period witnessed an unprecedented growth in the "development" of Navajo mineral, natural, and tourism resources.[37] This development takes a neo-colonial form, in which most of the dollars generated on the reservation are not spent there; most of the jobs in resource development are not Navajo jobs. Sixty-seven percent of the dollars made on the reservation is spent outside Navajo country; only 13 percent is spent inside, the remainder includes taxes [12%], savings [3%], and "other" [5%].[38]

Indian education has always been a response to the perceived ill-preparedness of Indian people to fit into Euro-American society. Indian education is the history of efforts to create the "competent" Indian, the civil Indian—to civilize the primitive, so that when properly trained he would assimilate smoothly into American economic and social life, but on a level suited to his marginal status.

If the struggle is difficult for the largest tribe, one with semi-sovereign title to some of America's richest natural, mineral, recreational and historic resources, consider the difficulties faced by those Native Americans living in urban environs, or those living on the marginal lands they have retained as homeland remnants or "inherited" by exile during the removals of the 19th century. Today there are over a million Native Americans and roughly half, living on nearly 300 tribal lands, cling to their homelands, many struggling to revive traditional languages, values, and traditions that define them as persons and that were seldom counted by non-Indian educators as available cultural capital to be fostered in any form of formal education.

For the urban dweller, or landless rural tribal member, sovereignty is guarded by the concept of treaty rights and aboriginal title. Hunger for Indian material and human capital has coincided with efforts to erode legal and moral concepts of aboriginal title and "trust," which give meaning to sovereignty. The dominant models of Indian formal schooling and social education have been efforts to either force or wean the Indian culturally, socially, and physically away from the land. Yet the lands and the special relationship between the federal government and the tribes were part of treaty rights gained in exchange for peace. Non-Indians seeking to understand Native Americans must not forget that Indian people are not immigrants. They continue to struggle to maintain their treaty rights and through them, their lands, unique cultures, and religions. For the Navajo, as well as for all other Native-American people, that struggle is waged often in spite of, rather than as a consequence of, their exposure to schooling and other powerful forms of social education.

Education is often understood to refer to socialization training for positions in the dominant culture and employment market, and one argument given in favor of that interpretation is that education thus conceived would solve the staggering poverty suffered by generations of native peoples. Yet, the Navajo people, along with many other tribes, have struggled at the local and tribal level with the problem of balancing educational and economic growth with continued cultural and spiritual integrity.

During the post-World War II period, increasing activism on the part of Indian people culminated in an era of community and tribal sovereignty. The Self-Determination and Education Assistance Act of 1975 (SDEA) was one part of that movement. In the mid-1960s American Indian education again conducted an experiment in biculturalism. The Rough Rock Demonstration School in Arizona began as an experiment in local community control of all significant aspects of schooling. Located near the center of the Navajo reservation, in one of its most isolated and tradition-oriented locations, Rough Rock became the symbol for a generation of schools, numbering more than 95 of the total 185 B.I.A. funded schools, which operate on grants and contracts from the federal government. But lurking beneath the promise of Indian community control lay the threat that such control must satisfy traditional, dominant-culture standards of "competence." Failure in this regard will seem to justify the federal government's transfer of contract schools from local to state control, thereby abrogating the federal treaty trust responsibility. Currently, in many areas the ability of schools to provide needed supplies and funds comes from the ability of tribal gambling casinos to offset the shortfall. Whether this is a healthy and positive source of social capital remains a controversial topic all over Indian Country.

CONCLUDING REMARKS

The provision of public schooling for Native Americans in the first half of the 20th century raised unique questions about the role and governance of education in a pluralist society. In particular, can public schooling in a modern, materialist, capitalist society serve the well-being of cultures whose worldviews are in important ways antithetical to those of European Americans? More generally, can a national agenda for public education in a multicultural society serve the well-being of all subcultures within that society? Who should determine what that "well-being" consists of—the members of the subcultures, or the government appointees of the dominant culture? Or is there some process by which bicultural values can be served?

A significant point of overlap, and yet also of conflict, between liberal democratic ideology and Indian perspectives had been the desire of Native Americans to determine their own destinies. One test of the majority culture's commitment to democratic ideals might be its support for the right of Native-American people to establish and control their own schools. However, it was not until 1975 that the Self-Determination and Education Assistance Act was created to embody that principle. Yet, with the economic base of Native-American culture destroyed by European-American aggression, it would be difficult for Indians to achieve self-sufficient self-governance—particularly by European-American standards. Thus, what appears to be the dominant culture's granting of independent status to a dependent subculture could actually serve further to debilitate the subculture as the newly independent status forgoes the protections previously afforded by the trust relationship.

Even when it seemed to espouse pluralism, educational policy toward Native Americans in the early 20th century effectively embodied notions of managed cultural change, assimilation, termination of the trust relationship, and eventual elimination of traditional native cultures and values. The relationship between the dominant culture and Native Americans thus raises profoundly disturbing questions concerning the relationship between democracy and education in American society—and particularly about the place of cultural diversity in liberal democratic educational policy.

PRIMARY SOURCE READING

A major theme of this chapter has been the degree to which American Indians have been free to fashion their own institutions—economic, educational, and political—in 20th-century society. John Collier, as commissioner of Indian Affairs, was one of the more enlightened European Americans to affect U.S. policy toward the Indians, but even his version of Indian democracy was grounded in progressive liberal ideals foreign to Indians. Collier's emphasis on scientific expertise and the use of specialists for solving Indian problems was not ultimately embraced by the tribal peoples, who simply wanted the resources and the authority to establish their independence and self-governance.

The difference in viewpoints is partly represented in the difference between an "assimilationist" policy toward Indians and a "pluralist" policy. Contrary to Collier's ultimately assimilationist aims, a pluralist policy seeks to allow groups to sustain their own cultures in harmony with one another. A pluralist view is illustrated in the accompanying selections from the writing of American Indians, written well after Collier left the commissionership of the Bureau of Indian Affairs. These excerpts affirm a desire to nurture Indian culture in modern society. Preceding those excerpts is a selection from Collier's foreword to Laura Thompson and Alice Joseph's The Hopi Way.

THE HOPI WAY (1944)

John Collier, Commissioner of Indian Affairs

Now, to pass straight into Indian Service and its aims and perplexities. Indian Service in the United States deals in total ways with whole societies. It does this for ill or for good. Through generations that look gray and cold now in retrospect, Indian Service pursued one and another special and discreet aim: to Christianize Indians, to substitute the individual for the societal Indian, to make Indians into land individualists, to obliterate Indian superstition, to make go-getters of Indians. And policy was dominated by preconceptions as to the nature of Indian society. I cite two of these, from annual reports of Indian Commissioners in the 80's of the last century. The second quotation, dated 1886, reflects a usual view as to the types of emotion evoked in Indians by their own societies.

"To assist in the great work of redeeming these benighted children of nature from the darkness of their superstition and ignorance . . ."

"When they (Indian young people) return to their homes at night, and on Saturdays and Sundays, and are among their old surroundings, they relapse more or less into their former moral and mental stupor."

The presumption was one of administrative omnipotence. What was willed by authority, and put into action by authority—that was the thing which would be. The obscure complexes of personality and of group influence and ancient, present physical environment were ignored; good intention was deemed to be enough, without the need to measure results; and the law of the multiplication of effects was taken into account not at all. It followed, that not even the sense of reality of the Indian Service men and women out on the ground among the Indians was used in the making of headquarters policy. But I move into the immediate past, and the present.

. . . Change, at varying speeds, inhabits all of Indian life; change, at varying speeds, inhabits each group, each personality of the Indians. Is there any way to understand more surely, to predict more reliably, to act with knowledge more precise, so that we can know, genuinely, what worth our Indian effort has and how it may be made significantly more realistic, and so that our good (which we presume) may not become the enemy of a better?

The answer, if indeed there were one, must rest, it seemed to us, in the use of not one but many techniques of observation and measurement *integratively.* Our hypothesis—a truism, which yet leads to discovery when deeply meditated—was that the web of life and the world-field operate beneath as well as above the conscious threshold. And that the group and the individual are dynamically inseparable. And that the past, in the web of life and in the unconsciousness, is far more potent than can easily be known. And that trends

---

From Collier's foreword to Laura Thompson and Alice Joseph's *The Hopi Way* (Chicago: University of Chicago Press, 1944).

of action and tensions of the body-soul are stubborn and imperious in men, though men may not know this fact at the conscious level.

From this hypothesis, there followed the method which we sought to have applied. Social history and the social present must be studied in relation to each other. The group structure, the group imperatives must be known, and the individual must be known as that personality-formation where the group forces clash and build (but not the group forces alone). Mind and performance in the individual must be measured, and through depth-psychology techniques, the types and trends of the individual unconsciousness must be explored. Bodily health must be examined. The physical environment, past as well as present, must be brought clearly, concretely into the picture. And finally, administration, in its subdivisions and as a whole, must be viewed afresh in the light of all of this data—data previously interrelated, so far as possible, within itself.

Into contact with the specialists—anthropologists, psychologists, physicians, and students of administration—the workers of Indian Service and, ideally, the Indians themselves, should be brought; and in the event, it has proved that important parts of the project have been done by the lay members (White and Indian) of Indian Service.

With this object in view—the scientific evaluation of Indian Service, and scientific planning—and under the sway of the hypothesis stated, and by the correlative or integrative use of the methods implied, the several monographs of this series have been produced. Supplements dealing with administrative application will be presented at dates soon after the publication of each of the volumes, and it is hoped that there will be a final volume devoted to principles of Indian administration treated as a special case of universal democratic administration, and another devoted to the utilization of the whole body of the material for its light upon the science of society.

I have stated a view of life (and in so far, the view is merely my own), and an intended goal of investigation, and intended use of methods. None is likely to realize as acutely as those who have given themselves to the present enterprise, how incomplete is the accomplishment. If it should prove to have carried forward by one critical fraction of a degree (in the vast arc which will be explored through centuries) the integrative use of the special sciences in the knowing of man and the helpful control of his destiny, this result will have been enough. Certainly into our problem of Indian Service the enterprise has cast many beams of light that reach far. Areas immanently important, never clearly brought into the light before, are now in a clear and growing light. Will we administrators, who include all the field forces of Indian Service, use the light?

In a recent issue of INDIANS AT WORK, I wrote, and my thought took form from a reading of some of the materials of the present and the forthcoming monographs:

"Does one seek to influence an individual or a group? Let him discover what is central to the being of that individual or group. Let his effort at influence be near to, and not deviate sharply from, the line of force of that which is central to the being of the individual or group. Thus, he may influence profoundly and helpfully. Remember that deep and central preoccupations, devotions and views of life can be helped to apply themselves to new practical ends. Here is the secret of efficient and democratic administration. Indian policies in the last ten or twelve years have come much nearer to the things central in the Indian's being than they came in previous decades. Hence the marked increase in the social energy of Indians, and their great and persevering response to the various practical programs. But we need to keep on trying, with greater, not with diminishing, energy, and we need to press ever inward toward discovery of those attitudes, hopes, fears, and patterns of functioning, and trends of the inner drive, which are central to the Indians. There is hardly any limit to the energy, the good-will, and the happiness which will meet us from within the Indian—if only we work with him at his own centers."

PRIMARY SOURCE READING

Indians have seldom been asked what they want, nor have programs allegedly designed for their benefit often been developed through their participation. Indian initiative was so long repressed that it is only recently that they have rediscovered this own voice. The first effective national organization of Indians was the National Congress of American Indians, organized in 1944. Many large tribes, however, such as the Navajo, do not participate in it. The Indian cause has also been supported by white-initiated organizations, such as the Indian Rights Association (organized by Quakers in 1882) and the Association on American Indian Affairs (since 1923).

The following are excerpts first from Dillon Platero, and second from Ethelou Yazzie, Navajo educators who were the second and third directors of the demonstration schools at Rough Rock. Platero's statement was drawn from a paper he prepared in 1973 entitled: "Community Control-Historical Perspectives and Current Efforts, Both Public and Private." Yazzie's comments were drawn from testimony she gave at Yellowknife, Northwest Territories, Canada, in 1976. These are followed by a discussion of a stipulated Native-American curriculum and governance plan outlined by Patricia Locke, past president of the National Indian Education Association, who is affiliated with the White Earth Chippewa (Mississippi Band) and the Standing Rock Sioux-Hunkpapa Tribe.

These three statements, by different American Indian educational leaders, represent a view that differs significantly from the view represented in the John Collier piece—and Collier was one of the more enlightened liberal educators of his era. The Collier piece was written in the 1940s, and each of the selections below was written in the 1970s, but the differences are greater than the passage of three decades; they are differences in worldview.

STATEMENTS BY THREE AMERICAN INDIAN EDUCATORS

I. Dillon Platero, second Director, Rough Rock Demonstration School

"Today a major and fundamental shift in Indian education is taking place. This new direction and emphasis has been selected and directed by the Indian People themselves: it is Indian control over Indian education . . .

"This principle of local control is characteristic of a democracy which is predicated upon reflecting the value and dignity of each individual and places on local communities major responsibilities for developing and molding an educational system uniquely tailored to the peculiar needs of each community.

"It needs to be noted that this local responsibility and local control over education does not mean complete local financing of that education. While the principle of community control is recognized, it has rarely or never meant that community resources are the only, or even the major, source of education funds . . .

"It is necessary to distinguish between involvement and control. It is equally important to understand that control often comes in parts, or pieces. Involvement was a treasured objective in Indian education during the 1930s. During that period of time many 'community schools' were created and many provided for participation and involvement in the operation of schools on the part of parents and community residents. Parents were encouraged to visit schools, special adult programs were developed and community improvement activities centered around the school . . .

"This was, and is, good. The parents felt the school filled an important need in the life of the community which exceeded merely the education of children.

"Yet this was not control! Control ultimately and finally consists of hiring, firing, setting priorities, allocating funds and approving the curriculum. Forty years ago we had participation and involvement without control: today we are obtaining control and must consciously work toward community participation . . .

"While elsewhere in this great nation the principle of local control over education is accepted, it has been the exception rather than the rule in Indian education . . .

". . . The only viable option is that of community (Indian) control over Indian education. The obstacles which exist in realizing this objective can and will be overcome. There is no other acceptable alternative. Indian and non-Indian people must unite so that community (Indian) control over Indian education is a reality rather than a dream and so that Indian people enjoy the right to be wrong: the right to be right."

II. Ethelou Yazzie, third Director, Rough Rock Demonstration School

"One of society's purposes in requiring the formal education of its children is to use its power and its ability to transmit, preserve, and examine a society's

Both selections from Robert A. Roessel, Jr., *Navaho Education and Action* (Rough Rock Curriculum Center, Rough Rock, Arizona, 1977), pp. 138–40.

history, language, religion and philosophy. This power was totally reversed in the education provided for the Navajo and other Native Americans. The purpose of that system was to *erase* Navajo history, language, religion and philosophy, and to replace it with the dominant culture of the Western European by means of an extensive and intensive resocialization process.

"Through education, the dominant establishment tried to exert full control over the Navajo young. Navajo children were forcibly taken from their parents and families as early as seven years of age, and kept at distant boarding schools for ten months out of twelve. This severing of the young from their Indian backgrounds was supposed to make resocialization and cultural domination easier—and it was done through a show of power.

"Cultural shock was inevitable. Disorientation and frustration occurred. To many children and parents the conflicting values were simply not acceptable. Other students, not knowing who to believe, resisted both sets of values. These students were then in a 'no man's land' with little self-esteem, identity, or values to guide them. Even Indian teachers had difficulty teaching these students . . .

"Failure to introduce varying languages and cultures in a positive light discourages the growing child's receptivity and his willingness not to pre-judge others and their cultures. Cultural domination has no place in education.

"A Bicultural system respects both cultures and works with *all* segments of the community to the support of each. The family and the educational system need to work together as one with *all* parents knowing and caring about what goes on in the classroom. Neither group should be allowed to undermine the other, but must work together consciously to complement each other throughout the educational process . . .

"Community members, if they are willing to assume the effort that it takes, can control their own schools, as does Rough Rock, right now. And in doing so, they transform more than an educational program. The involvement of the community in the school has ramifications far beyond the educational realm."

III. PATRICIA LOCKE, FORMER PRESIDENT, NATIONAL INDIAN EDUCATION ASSOCIATION

AN IDEAL SCHOOL SYSTEM FOR AMERICAN INDIANS: A THEORETICAL CONSTRUCT

We are forced to adapt to the educational systems of the immigrant culture only because they are so numerous, insistent and all-pervasive. It would be ideal if Indian people could live, learn and die in the contexts of our cultures as they would have evolved, but we cannot. We have been forced to compromise educationally, to seem to adapt to some of the dominant society's mores in our educational patterns, because the prevailing educational hierarchy is so sure of its infallibility. And they impose laws and customs to make us conform.

We suffer in the name of education from their nursery schools, Head Start programs, secular and religious boarding schools, public day schools with formal hours and foreign curricula, non-Indian foster parent programs, vocational schools and other foreign post-secondary systems. Finally, there is the absurdity of "Golden Years" programs where our elders learn to plan for their retirement and funerals.

A listing of simple causes and effects of this educational system would illustrate the damage being done to tribal people:

Nursery schools include deprivation of family nurturing and interruption of the organic learning process. Head Start programs increase deprivation of the extended family influence, freeing the mother to enter the work force and causing marital disfunction. Secular boarding schools cause total deprivation of the family nurturing process; alienation from tribal language and culture occur. The same is true of religious boarding schools with the addition that the child is indoctrinated with alien myths and legends and becomes increasingly mutant as concepts of sin, hell and paganism are reinforced.

Non-Indian foster parents' boarding programs means the child loses his family and tribal con-

From Thomas Thompson, ed., *The Schooling of Native America.* (Washington, DC: American Association of Colleges for Teacher Education, 1978), pp. 120–31.

tacts. Parents are bereaved as the child assumes a non-Indian identity and is lost as a contributing tribal member. At vocational schools the student accepts the Christian work ethic: he learns individualism, mercantilism, and acquisitiveness. Post-secondary school systems create continued alienation from the tribal environment. They impose useless curricula that impede the students' contribution to tribal support systems. Probable assimilation into the dominant society occurs if the student survives foreign counseling services. Finally gradual assumption of alien rhetoric and life styles takes place. "Golden Years" Programs involve the acceptance of the concept of "the generation gap." Elders are lost as teachers; apathy, senility, and death occur in isolation.

Education for American Indian tribal people must be related to the tribes' cosmologies, and integrated into the past and future of the particular tribe. A traditional Indian does not think of a career for self-fulfillment. He thinks of personal attainment only to serve tribal goals. Career satisfaction is often only a by-product of the degree of effectiveness reached in serving short and long range tribal goals.

The child normally begins learning at birth in an organic way. It is important to emphasize this intrinsic and non-formal learning procedure because it is a life-long process. The individual's uncles, aunts, grandparents and the respected elders of the tribe are the nurturers and teachers along with the parents. The function of tribal members as teachers, administrators, counselors, policy-makers and curriculum developers of the young Indian should be an integral part of the entire process of education.

A CONCEPTION OF THE IDEAL ADMINISTRATION AND TEACHING FACULTY

School administrators, supportive staff, teachers and teacher's aides will be tribal members. When this is not possible, personnel may be recruited from other tribes. Non-Indian persons will sometimes be recruited, especially from the Asian community where religion and life-styles are closer to American Indian Mores. For instance, it would be preferable to have English taught by an Asian teacher, since semantic understandings and interpretations would not be so diametrically opposed to Indian cosmologies.

Dillon Platero, head of the Navajo's Rough Rock Demonstration School at Chinle, Arizona, emphasized the disparity between Indian and non-Indian educational systems. He speculated that of both Indian and non-Indian graduates of this country's Schools of Education who become involved in Rough Rock's teacher training program, only thirty percent are retrainable. He further stated that a minimum of two and one-half years is required in the retraining and learning process.

Another controversial statement made at a national Indian education meeting was the effect that *no* college and university graduates should be allowed to teach Indian children. They should be used as consultants only. The obvious alternative would be to establish Indian Education Programs for Indian Teachers of Indian Children. This idea will be discussed later under the model for post-secondary education.

A vital and necessary part of the faculty would be respected persons of the tribe. They would receive remuneration commensurate with other teachers. The status of these older persons has traditionally been eminent. They are the repositories of oral literature and knowledge. They would serve a double function as guidance counselors, and would provide natural motivation by transmitting essential human knowledge for the continuance of tribal support systems.

The school board may wish to hire non-Indian custodians and janitors.

It is important that the child learns dual cultures and multi-cultures from the fourth grade onward. He must learn well the behavior of people from other cultures if he is to help his people survive. He will learn the values and behavior expectations of other cultures *as skills, not as values.* He may be chosen early by his tribe to pursue a non-Indian college education or a technological education in order to help the tribe survive. If he is to become an attorney or a physician, he will have to learn the necessary academic skills. But great care should be taken so that the student does not walk a path that will cause him to fall over the brink into complete acculturation and assimilation.

High schools will be located on the reservations. Policy will be mandated by the tribe's Education Committee, by elected representatives from the reservation districts or chapters, or by the tribe's Department of Education. All school personnel should be Indian except for individuals who teach foreign languages and white studies.

It is important that decisions be made about the individual students' direction of study for ensuing years. The Tribal Council will have determined short and long range goals—with help from consultants of the American Indian Tribes Research Institute (see below)—and will have made a human resource inventory. The tribe will know which areas of skill it is deficient in, and can pinpoint these needs to the secondary student so that he may prepare himself in these directions in keeping with specific tribal customs and ceremonies. Non-Indian holidays will not be observed. Classes will be open and students will not be grouped by age levels, but by aptitude and interest. Teacher discussions with parents and the student will take the place of a formal grading system. School attendance will not be mandatory. Beginning at eleven or twelve years, the student will participate in the tribe's "school on wheels." Groups of ten to twelve students will travel to nearby and selected distant reservations and off-reservation Indian communities, for "field work" in learning about other tribal people, and for the purpose of exchanging cultural programs with their peers. College students, who are members of the tribes to be visited, will "conduct" these traveling classes. Not only will the student learn about and come to appreciate the richness and diversity of the tribes, but this understanding will help him to overcome latent tribal antagonisms that still persist. The groundwork will have been laid for improved *transtribal* communications and unity. Arrangements will be made so that the college student receives a stipend and course credit for the teaching experience.

The "traveling school" mechanism will also be integral to the secondary school system. Secondary school age youth will not be required to attend all White Studies courses unless it has been mutually determined that the individual will relate to external governments in later life for the benefit of the tribe.

Dual record systems will have to be maintained at the Tribal Council's Computer Center or one of the Regional Computer Centers so that the Indian student will not be *penalized* if he must leave the reservation and transfer to a non-Indian school. A report card with grades in such acceptable courses as American history, English, geography, spelling, social studies, home economics, reading and arithmetic will be maintained and made available for the transferring student.

Sample secondary curricula in Indian Studies and White Studies might be:

Indian Studies

Tribal Government Systems
Indian Reorganization Act Tribes
Terminated Tribes
Non-Federally Recognized Tribes
Tribes of Mexico
Tribes of Central America
Tribes of South America
Tribes of Canada
Modern Indian Religions
Ancient Indian Religions
American Indian History
American Indian Pre-Law
American Indian Medicine
Minority and Ethnic-Minority Relations
Land Reform
Comparative Minority Rhetoric
Introduction to American Indian Business Administration
American Indian Arts
American Indian Law and Order
Ecology
American Indian Literature and Poetry
Indian Communications Systems
Grantsmanship
Regional Languages and Dialects

White Studies

State Governments
The U.S. Constitution
The Congress

Federal Agencies, Bureaus, and Departments, i.e.:
Department of the Interior
(Bureau of Land Management,
Bureau of Indian Affairs)
Department of Labor
Army Corps of Engineers
Department of Commerce
Department of Health, Education and Welfare
Comparative Religions
Christianity, Buddhism,
Taoism, Hinduism
English Literature
Spanish Conversation
Caucasian Sociology
Black Sociology
Caucasian Law and Order Systems
European History
History of the Mexican Conquest
History of the U.S. Conquest
History of the Canadian Conquest
Caucasian Psychology
Caucasian Concepts of Real Estate
European Philosophy
Caucasian Art History
Caucasian Diseases
Caucasian Communications Systems
Computer Science
Mathematics
Economics
Caucasian Nutrition

QUESTIONS FOR DISCUSSION AND EXAMINATION

1. The history of the American "melting pot" idea suggests that all minority cultures share basically the same problem: how to fit into the larger dominant culture of the United States. Yet each minority group is different, with a different history and different needs. What particular issues associated with the development of a system of public education for Native Americans are different from those experienced by other American minorities? Rely on your own experience as well as the material from this chapter in developing your response.
2. In Chapter 4, various objectives and practices of progressive education were presented in the context of an urbanizing, industrializing, and heavily immigrant society. To what degree are progressive education aims and practices relevant to the changes in schooling developed for Native Americans in the 20th century? Explain.
3. American Indian educational reform during the first half of the 20th century might be characterized as partly pluralist and partly assimilationist in nature. How would you describe and assess the character of the pluralism embodied in Indian schooling reform? In explaining your position, explain also the degree to which those reforms appear to you to be consistent with democratic ideals—and why.
4. The point of view informing this chapter suggests a strong connection between U.S. reform of American Indian education and the elimination of native culture and values. If Indians could have controlled their own educational destinies on a continent won in battle by Europeans, how could they have pursued an educational policy any different from that imposed by the United States? In developing your response, consider differences in ideology between the dominant European-American culture and the various Indian cultures; political-economic constraints; and the Primary Source Readings as well as the chapter material itself.

NOTES

1. Brian Dippie, *The Vanishing American: White Attitudes and U.S. Indian Policy* (Middletown, Conn.: Wesleyan University Press, 1982). See also Virgil Vogel, ed., *This Country Was Ours: A Documentary History of the American Indian* (New York: Harper and Row, 1972); Francis Jennings, *The Invasion of America: Indians, Colonialism and the Cant of Conquest* (Chapel Hill: University of North Carolina Press, 1975); and Alice B. Kehoe, *North American Indians: A Comprehensive Account* (Englewood Cliffs, NJ: Prentice Hall, 1981), pp. 224–44. Also, see Francis P. Prucha, ed., *Documents of U.S. Indian Policy* (Lincoln: University of Nebraska Press, 1975).
2. Quoted in Howard Zinn, *A People's History of the United States* (New York: Harper and Row, 1980), p. 515.
3. Dippie, *The Vanishing American,* p. 181.
4. Ibid.
5. Prucha, *Documents of U.S. Indian Policy,* p. 688.
6. See Lawrence Kelly, "John Collier and the Indian New Deal: An Assessment," in Janet Smith and Robert M. Kvasnicka, eds., *Indian-White Relations: A Persistent Paradox* (Washington, DC: Howard University Press, 1976).

7. W. C. Ryan and R. K. Brandt, "Indian Education Today," *Progressive Education* 9, No. 2 (February 1932), p. 81.
8. See Lawrence C. Kelly, *The Assault on Assimilation: John Collier and the Origins of Indian Policy Reform* (Albuquerque: University of New Mexico Press, 1983).
9. Ibid., p. 24.
10. Ibid., p. 36.
11. Ibid., p. 29.
12. R. Lawrence Moore, "Directions of Thought in Progressive America," in Lewis L. Gould, ed., *The Progressive Era* (Syracuse: Syracuse University Press, 1974).
13. Lawrence C. Kelly, *The Navajo Indians and Federal Indian Policy, 1900–1935* (Tucson: University of Arizona Press, 1968). Also see Emily Hahn, *Mabel: A Biography of Mabel Dodge Luhan* (Boston: Houghton Mifflin, 1977).
14. See John Collier, *Indians of the Americas: The Long Hope* (New York: New American Library, 1947).
15. Ibid.
16. Kenneth R. Philp, *John Collier's Crusade for Indian Reform, 1920–1954* (Tucson: University of Arizona Press, 1977).
17. Reports of the Secretary of the Interior (Washington, DC: U.S. Government Printing Office, 1925, 1932).
18. Ibid. (1932).
19. See Arthur Schlesinger, Jr., *The Coming of the New Deal* (Boston: Houghton Mifflin, 1959).
20. Ibid.
21. M. K. Sniffen, ed., *Indian Truth* (Philadelphia: Indian Rights Association, May 1933), p. 1.
22. Department of the Interior, 1933.
23. Department of the Interior, 1935.
24. See Thomas Weaver, ed., *Indians of Arizona: A Contemporary Perspective* (Tucson: University of Arizona Press, 1974).
25. Oliver LaFarge, ed., *The Changing Indian* (Norman: University of Oklahoma Press, 1942).
26. Ibid.
27. See Laura Thompson, *Personality and Government* (Mexico City: Educaciones Del Instituto Indigenista Interamericano, 1951), Foreword by J. Collier, p. xiii.
28. Laura Thompson and Alice Joseph, *The Hopi Way* (Chicago: University of Chicago Press, 1944), Foreword by J. Collier.
29. Ibid., p. 9.
30. Laurence M. Hauptman, *The Iroquois and the New Deal* (Syracuse: Syracuse University Press, 1981); Francis Paul Prucha, *The Great Father: The U.S. Government and the American Indians* (Lincoln: University of Nebraska Press, 1984), Vol. 2.
31. Willard W. Beatty, *Education for Action: Selected Articles from Indian Education 1936–1943* (Washington, DC: U.S. Indian Service, 1944), p. 11.
32. Ibid., p. 17.
33. Ibid., p. 24.
34. Willard W. Beatty, *Education for Cultural Change: Selected Articles from Indian Education 1944–51* (Washington, DC: U.S. Indian Service, 1953).
35. Beatty, *Education for Action,* p. 147.
36. Beatty, *Education for Cultural Change,* p. 238.
37. U.S. Commission on Civil Rights, *The Navajo Nation: An American Colony,* p. 41.
38. Ibid, p. 264.

National School Reform: The Early Cold War Era

By Stephen Preskill

By the turn of the century most American children attended school, public or parochial. Most, however, proceeded only as far as the eighth grade. Very few young people went on to high school and even fewer graduated. The public high school did not become a mass institution until the 1930s. Even after World War II, educators continued to tinker with the high school's structure and curriculum as new populations of students sought to enter its doors and as policymakers increasingly looked to it for answers to society's problems. This period of American educational history, extending from the 1930s to the 1960s, not only witnessed the institutionalization of the public high school, but also saw policymakers forge an inextricable connection between educational quality and national security. Fervently committed to the notion that the schools could be used effectively to fight the cold war, James B. Conant became one of the chief architects of the public high school during this era. As educational philosopher James E. McClellan wrote in 1968, "If a foreign visitor to these benighted shores were required to take his views about the policies governing American education from one, and only one man . . . there could be only one sensible choice. . . If any man spoke for and to American educational policy (granted that in a most important sense no man does or can)—that man would be James Bryant Conant."[1]

As the president of Harvard University from 1933 to 1953 and later as a public school investigator and reformer, Conant took advantage of an unprecedented opportunity to influence educational policy. For over thirty years, Conant promoted his meritocratic vision, stressing the selective function of schooling and the advancement of the talented youngster. Through his judicious use of powerful contacts and skillful appeal to public opinion, Conant's ideas appeared frequently in the popular press, often setting the agenda for educational debate.

Conant's initial interest in public schools grew out of efforts to attract to Harvard highly able students from all social classes. Within 10 years, he had become one of America's most notable advocates of school reform by arguing that a reconstructed educational system could lead to a better society. Put simply, Conant favored an educational system from kindergarten through college that would sort students according to their ability, challenge the academically able, and specifically prepare all others for useful places in society. Only then, he maintained, would the best and the brightest secure society's most responsible and powerful positions, with the less able pledging their political and moral support. Furthermore, Conant's ideal educational system would effectively combat what he regarded as threats to the social order—whether those threats were fascism in the 30s, communism in the 40s and 50s, or domestic unrest in the 60s.

POLITICAL ECONOMY AND IDEOLOGY OF THE EARLY COLD WAR ERA

By the 1920s, the American economy had become the envy of the world. Americans appeared to have more food to eat, better clothes to wear, and more things with which to amuse themselves than any other people on earth. Big business raked in huge profits, corporate offices scoured the globe for new markets to exploit, and American stockholders were consumed in a prolonged frenzy of stock speculation and get-rich-quick schemes. But abundance for some overshadowed the hardships of others. In the 1920s, agriculture reached a new low from which it did not recover for two decades. Poverty increased in urban areas, and starvation prevailed in many pockets of the South. The New Deal legislation that would later empower labor unions had not yet been passed, and many members of the working classes toiled for long hours with little hope of advancement or job security. With racism continuing unabated, black people suffered severely in the midst of this economic boom. Almost universally denied a decent standard of living, most black people eked out an existence as tenant farmers in the southern countryside or in the most menial and lowest-paid jobs northern cities had to offer.[2]

With the collapse of the stock market in 1929 and the onset of the worst depression in American history, these disparities of wealth and poverty became even more glaring. Industrial output fell precipitously, and over one-fourth of the adult population lost their jobs. While the working classes and oppressed minorities fared poorly, the great depression also victimized many others who were unaccustomed to such hard times. Even those who held on to their jobs saw their wages slashed and their standard of living drastically reduced. The stock market crash also impoverished a few wealthy Americans who had sunk their fortunes in high-priced securities, but others benefited by taking advantage of the depression's greatly deflated prices. Although Franklin Delano Roosevelt's New Deal temporarily reduced unemployment and raised some hopes, in general government failed to blunt significantly the depression's devastating impact.[3]

In Europe, economic ruin increased acceptance of radical ideas from both right- and left-wing sources. In Italy, Germany, and Spain, fascist dictators flourished, while other countries established communist parties. In the United States, both of these ideologies had vocal supporters, though neither became dominant. Some prophesied capitalism's demise, while others counted on institutions like the public school to help rescue free enterprise. In general, ideological extremes were readily tolerated until post-World War II "red-baiting" brought dire consequences to those Americans who had supported radical causes in the thirties.[4]

Most observers agree that U.S. mobilization for World War II ended the great depression. The war forced the application of Keynesian principles of deficit spending that Roosevelt's New Deal had never fully employed. Furthermore, the demand for soldiers abroad and defense plant workers at home almost immediately erased unemployment. Indeed, with the government footing the bill, it appeared that anybody who wanted to work could work, and any business that wanted to make money could do so. As a consequence of war mobilization, the United States again entered an era of enormous economic growth, with multinational corporations enjoying huge profits with the tax-based support of the federal government.[5]

U.S. Fear of Soviet Communism

Following the end of World War II, in 1945, the new prosperity, the pent-up demand of the war years, and the increasingly sophisticated advertising techniques of large corporations combined to launch a consumer buying binge that appeared to know few bounds. A boom in low-cost single-family housing fueled further demand for family cars and the latest household appliances. Despite a brief period of inflation, the demand for consumer goods continued without letup. Although unemployment mounted, it never exceeded 7 percent in the 1950s, and Americans showed little sympathy for the poor or the dispossessed in the form of popular press attention to poverty or in government legislation.

Yet, the health of the war-fueled economy depended upon a continued buildup of the military arsenal that the United States government had amassed to wage its two-front war during World War II. Only the challenge of a powerful new military foe would provide the United States with a justification for further augmenting its already massive store of armaments, and the Soviet Union presented the United States with the perfect adversary. Although in 1945 they were still 4 years away from developing the atomic bomb, the fully mobilized Soviets were intent on using their military might to occupy eastern Europe as a buffer against further foreign attack. The United States government feared that unless the Soviet Union's relentless march into Europe and Asia was halted, communism would spread around the globe. The threat of Soviet expansion and the accompanying instability it would bring particularly disturbed those American multinational companies that had extended their operations to dozens of countries abroad. They argued that Soviet insurgents would create a political climate antithetical to economic growth, and that this in turn would threaten American well-being. Fearing the political and economic consequences of communist expansion, American government officials devised two key policies to slow the Soviet juggernaut.[6]

Under *containment,* the first of the two policies, the United States declared its intention of taking whatever economic and military means were necessary to stop the spread of communism. When President Harry S. Truman declared in 1947, "I believe that it must be the policy of the United States to support free people who are resisting attempted subjugations by armed minorities or by outside pressures," he was opening the door to United States involvement in other nations' affairs throughout the world.[7] Massive humanitarian aid to Greece and Turkey in 1947 under the Truman Doctrine became one manifestation of the policy of containment. Marshaling United Nations support for U.S. intervention in Korea in 1950 served as another. In that same year, United States support for French aid to the South Vietnamese in their civil war with North Vietnam set in motion a series of events ultimately leading to the U.S. war with Vietnam.

With the second policy, known simply as the *doctrine of first use,* the United States declared its prerogative to initiate nuclear bombing whenever enemy forces, whether nuclear or conventional, threatened American military installations. These policies required the United States to stockpile thousands of nuclear weapons at great cost to American taxpayers. But they also permitted the United States to continue reaping the benefits of a wartime economy without the added burden of waging a major war. The enormous growth of what President Eisenhower later called the "military-industrial complex" served as another tangible result of America's first-use and containment policies.[8]

Fear of Soviet communism reached nearly hysterical levels in the late 40s and early 50s. The House Committee on Un-American Activities, Senator Joseph McCarthy, and such organizations as the John Birch Society all accused government agencies of harboring communists. Hearings were held and blacklists were compiled to rid the United States of "reds" and "pinkos." A cloud of fear and dread overshadowed almost every institution in American life. Schools were no exception; teachers were increasingly required to take loyalty oaths and to forswear any involvement in the Communist party.[9]

Although fears of communist infiltration lessened considerably after the mid-1950s, for the next two decades American foreign policy continued to be based on the ideological split between the two superpowers and on the premise that the Soviets were intent on spreading communism around the globe. It should not be ignored that the United States leaders had their own expansionist plans. Truman had declared in 1947, "The whole world should adopt the American system. . . . The American system can survive in America only if it becomes a world system." Believing that "at the present moment in world history every nation must choose between alternative ways of life," Truman assumed that any leftist insurrection was the work of Soviet expansionism, and that the "American way of life" of representative democracy and corporate capitalism was therefore threatened by revolutions in small nations throughout the globe.[10]

Protests against the Vietnam War in the late 1960s and early 1970s would later question the foundation of these assumptions, and for a few years during and after Vietnam, few educators or policy analysts stressed the link between national security and educational quality. But, as will be discussed in Chapter 14, the *Nation at Risk* report in 1983 employed language that again stirred the emotions of erstwhile cold warriors, warning Americans everywhere that our failure to teach math and science adequately was tantamount to unilateral disarmament.

In addition to the Soviet threat, the issue of race discrimination confronted Americans in the post-World War II era. Since emancipation, African-Americans had been systematically deprived of life, liberty, and the pursuit of happiness. After the war, slow steps were taken toward the elimination of segregation. President Truman desegregated the armed forces, and the United States Supreme Court declared segregated schools inherently unequal in the *Brown* v. *Board of Education* decision in 1954. Also, the increasing number of novelists, playwrights, and filmmakers who focused on the theme of racial prejudice brought new attention to this most central of American problems. Still, resistance to these changes in both the South and the North affirmed the deep and historical roots of racial discrimination. In some cases, parents of children from predominantly white schools literally battled black people and government authorities to forestall the integration of their schools. Zoning ordinances were devised to keep African-Americans out of white neighborhoods, and major banks ordered the redlining of black business districts, which set down burdensome guidelines for the granting of loans to black merchants.

Largely because of the civil rights movement of the 1950s and 1960s (about which more will be said in part 2 of this volume), face-to-face discrimination against African-Americans diminished and affirmative-action initiatives helped to foster a new class of black professionals and entrepreneurs. Yet backlashes against these advances and the persistence of a faceless institutional racism contributed to the continuing hardships of urban poverty. Public officials called on the schools to halt the vicious cycle of poverty that plagued many black families, but the schools' inadequacies were a reflection of society's unwillingness or inability to commit the resources necessary to address this problem effectively.[11]

New Liberal Ideology in the Cold War Era

The beliefs and values shared by leaders of American economic, political, and military institutions after World War II were a clear extension of progressive-era new liberalism. Although domestic and international conditions had changed, these changes had not challenged the fundamental commitments of corporate liberalism (explained in Chapter 4). The progressive era had replaced classical liberal faith in human reason by faith in scientific methods, for example, and in the post-World War II era the triumphs and perils of scientific advancement dominated the thinking of American policy analysts. With the advent of nuclear weapons, the potential costs of war had never been so great. The growing complexities of modern science and modern statecraft therefore further enhanced the position of the highly trained expert, while appearing to dwarf the role of the ordinary citizen. The exigencies of modern life, with its emphasis on specialized knowledge, interdependence, and cooperation, more than ever seemed to overwhelm the individual.

Progress continued to be central to 20th-century liberal ideology, and progress was considered achievable primarily through science and technology. It was technological superiority, in the form of the atomic bomb, that had defeated the Japanese in war. Technology seemed also to contribute to a rapidly rising standard of living as new uses for plastics, home appliances, and various medical breakthroughs (such as immunizations from childhood illnesses) won a great deal of public attention. As progress itself seemed to be the product of various kinds of expertise, the ideological linkage between expert, centralized decision making and public well-being grew stronger.

Similarly, the assembly lines and increasingly sophisticated technology of American industry further concentrated workplace decision making among a few elite managers and engineers. The emergence of large labor unions ushered in an age

Centralized management by "experts," begun during the progressive era, became even more entrenched during the 1950s as science and technology seemed to move decision making ever farther from the realm of the ordinary citizen.

of increased job security and better wages and benefits, but the centralized decision making established during the progressive era became further intensified. Another trend begun in the 19th century contributed to such centralized management: farm work became increasingly scarce. Whereas in 1920, 27 percent of the working population worked on the farm, by 1960 only 6 percent of the working population worked on the farm. Although only a hundred years before that time, Abraham Lincoln had extolled the importance of being self-employed, that ideal was effectively eliminated as an option for some 90 percent of all workers. Nearly everyone was managed by someone else.

These developments were reflected in the conduct of political affairs and in attitudes toward the common person. Democracy had come to be regarded as a form of government that was properly administered by experts with only the perfunctory consent of the governed. The so-called common man was characterized as too selfish, uninformed, and conformist to be capable of the rigors of governing in a complex age. Following the notion of the bell-shaped curve, leaders from all walks of life assumed that only a few individuals had superior intellects and that the welfare of the United States depended on locating these superior minds and placing them in positions of authority. The prevailing view of liberty was in a sense what George Santayana had called "provisional freedom," one that somehow always led back to orthodoxy—an orthodoxy that embraced the virtues of American military and economic dominance, meritocracy, and social stability.[12]

This "provisional freedom" that emerged from the postwar period was increasingly tied to nationalism. For classical liberals, a strong central government was feared as a potential enemy to individual freedom. Conversely, in the progressive era, modern liberals posited a strong central government as the only real route to freedom, for only "big government" was strong enough to regulate monopolies, big banking, labor exploitation, poverty, and other internal threats to the freedom of the common person. The two world wars, however, seemed to establish that the greatest threats to the freedom of the American citizen were not from within, but were from abroad—first fascism and later Soviet communism. Freedom became increasingly identified with "our" way of life, and "theirs" was unfree. Socialism, which had enjoyed a period of popularity in the United States earlier in the century, was increasingly characterized as a "foreign" system of thought, totalitarian, and anti-American. "Free-market capitalism" was opposed to "state-controlled economies" in public discourse, even though capitalism in the United States had long since ceased to be free-market. However, the identification of the United States with freedom itself, politically and economically, stifled critical discourse about our own social system. The enemy to freedom was not viewed as our own "military-industrial complex," despite the warnings of President Dwight Eisenhower in 1961. Rather, the enemy to freedom was the Soviet threat, a threat which was kept alive in the public mind through ongoing cold-war rhetoric amidst a series of international military involvements on the part of the United States.

It was extremely difficult for the common citizen to question the actions of the United States military-industrial complex in the cold-war era. A massive increase in U.S. intelligence operations after World War II gave increased credibility to the notion that the government knew what it was doing, even if the people did not, and ("for security reasons") could not, know. Thus, to enjoy the freedoms of the United States, it seemed necessary to leave the decision making to others, rather than participate in that decision making. Some, such as James B. Conant, argued that this was entirely consistent with Jefferson's democratic ideal, in which the talented would rise to the top and the people could be counted on to elect the "truly good and wise."

JAMES BRYANT CONANT

James B. Conant's modest origins hardly suggested a future as one of America's most respected educators. Born in 1893, Conant was reared in a plain, middle-class home in Dorchester, Massachusetts. He struggled through his first few years in school, blossoming as a scholar only upon encountering the challenges of the prestigious Roxbury Latin School. After distinguishing himself at Roxbury in the physical sciences, he went on to Harvard, where he completed the requirements for an A.B. degree in 3 years. He stayed on at Harvard to take his Ph.D. in organic and physical chemistry in 1916.

After completing his doctorate at the age of 23, Conant eagerly accepted a post as instructor of organic chemistry in the Harvard chemistry department. Despite a successful first year, the United States entry into World War I stalled Conant's plans for advancement. Thinking he could

Classical versus New Liberal Conceptions of Freedom

Classical liberal	New liberal
1. Negative freedom: freedom from government restraint.	1. Positive freedom: government responsibility to act in public interest.
2. Government must stay out of individuals' lives, except where safety of society is at stake.	2. Government may intervene in individuals' lives to promote their happiness and well-being.
3. The individual is free to pursue own interests.	3. Individuals' activities are always interconnected with those of others.
4. Faith in individual to act with rational self-interest.	4. Faith in decisions of experts to decide the interests of society and individuals.
Examples	**Examples**
a. State may provide schools but not require attendance.	a. Compulsory attendance is considered to be in the public interest.
b. Education for individual freedom.	b. Education for social responsibility.
c. The state should not mandate personal behavior, unless that behavior threatens others or public safety.	c. The state may require the individual to wear seat belts or motorcycle helmets both to protect the individual and to protect public interests.

James Bryant Conant's far-reaching influence on the American high school is still plainly apparent today—for better and for worse.

best serve his country in the Chemical Warfare Service, Conant quickly rose to the head of a division that would develop an improved method for producing mustard gas. Although he regarded the poison gas research as a highly unattractive task, he considered it essential to the war effort. He also expressed no misgivings about the morality of this work, saying years later that he did not see "why tearing a man's guts out by a high-explosive shell is to be preferred to maiming by attacking his lungs or skin."[13]

At war's end, Conant enthusiastically resumed his academic career, plunging into a series of significant research projects. Within a decade he had gained a national reputation for his chemical research and had achieved the rank of full professor. Fellow chemists from around the world hailed Conant's investigations into the structure of chlorophyll, and Harvard rewarded him with an endowed chair in chemistry in 1929. For his distinguished scholarly achievements, Conant also received Columbia University's Charles F. Chandler Medal and the William H. Nichols Medal of the American Chemical Society. In 1931, Harvard named him the head of its chemistry division.

Conant's meteoric rise reached its zenith 2 years later, in the depths of the great depression, when he agreed to assume the responsibilities of Harvard's presidency. A vocal critic of the Harvard presidency of Abbot Lawrence Lowell, Conant attributed the perceived decline in the quality of the Harvard faculty to Lowell's preference for scholars with broad liberal arts backgrounds but little specialized knowledge. Conant, on the other hand, agreed that breadth was desirable but also resoundingly affirmed that great universities must recruit researchers of the first rank who were acknowledged experts in their fields of specialization. Conant also regretted Lowell's marked aversion to students from racial and ethnic minorities, stressing what he regarded as Harvard's mission to educate the best and the brightest students, regardless of their social or economic backgrounds.

Leading periodicals lauded Harvard's decision to pass the presidential mantle from Lowell to Conant. They acclaimed Conant's scholarly accomplishments and expressed particular satisfaction with the fact that Conant did not belong to the elite circle of Boston Brahmins. The editors of *The Nation* dissented, noting that Conant's record lacked evidence of a broad social consciousness. His affiliations with large corporations, such as DuPont, indicated to *The Nation* that Conant might be "of that category of technicians for whom the captains of industry loom as great men, wisely entrusted with the destinies of our social order."[14]

The early years of Conant's presidency were marked by his decision to upgrade the faculty and bring a broader range of students to Harvard. He sought first to clear the faculty ranks of what he regarded as dead weight, while hiring and promoting those professors who had made important scholarly contributions to their fields. Some praised this new "up or out" policy, as it came to be called, but others attacked it as unfairly subordinating good teaching to the promotion of research. Conant maintained that the university gave equal consideration to both teaching and research in making faculty promotions, and that "up or out" was a painful but effective way to enhance faculty quality.

Standardized Testing and Student Selection

Seeking to tear down some of the geographic and financial barriers that had traditionally limited Harvard's enrollment to students from the elite public and private schools of the Northeast, Conant proposed a National Scholarship Program. This program would identify able young scholars and make it feasible for them to attend Harvard. But Conant believed the program was doomed to fail unless a reliable and valid measure of academic aptitude could be found to ensure objectivity in determining scholarship eligibility. After much deliberation and consultation with his assistant deans, Henry Chauncey and Wilbur Bender, Conant settled on the Scholastic Aptitude Test. Assistant deans Bender and Chauncey favored the SAT for the efficiency with which the multiple-choice test could be administered and evaluated. Perhaps they were also impressed with the test developer's description of the exam as a series of progressively more difficult questions, each with its own unambiguous solution and increasingly tempting "traps."

By the mid-1930s, Harvard had adopted the SAT, finding it a very satisfactory device for selecting promising scholars. Owing to this success, Harvard employed the SAT as a standard by which all undergraduate applicants would be measured. As Conant himself said: "The record seems to show that Harvard's interest in the use of objective tests for selecting national scholars was an important factor in promoting the use of the tests for general admission purposes. My own interest in the new type of examinations certainly was aroused by the report of Bender and Chauncey and its outcome. Eventually it would lead to my playing a part in the establishment of the Educational Testing Service."[15]

Indeed, as Conant recalled it, his enthusiasm for the SAT represented an "almost naive faith" in standardized tests. He came to believe that exams such as the SAT offered a nearly foolproof method for ascertaining academic promise. He also thought that the testing movement provided a solution to some of the problems of public school instruction. With the help of testing, he maintained, a child's inherent abilities could be determined as early as age 12 and appropriate instruction then prescribed. Despite minor shifts in his point of view, for three decades Conant remained one of the most vigorous supporters of testing, vocational guidance, and the selective function of schooling.

Throughout the 1930s, Conant traveled extensively to convince Harvard alumni and the general public of the need for national scholarships and standardized testing. Frequently, he referred to himself as an "educational Calvinist." By this Conant meant that most students were "predestined" to exhibit certain set capacities early in their school careers which were "highly resistant to change by external agencies." Moreover, as Conant saw it, a "strict educational Calvinist" was primarily concerned with sorting and classifying students according to their aptitude as measured by tests.[16]

Conant's view of the education process suited him well for his leading role in the creation of the Educational Testing Service. In the 1930s, the College Entrance Examination Board, the American Council on Education, and the Carnegie Corporation all provided colleges and universities with a variety of standardized tests for making admissions decisions. Advocates of testing, such as Conant and Henry Chauncey, thought that consolidating the testing divisions of these three agencies would strengthen the testing movement and give new impetus to the SAT as a leading admissions criterion. After many years of debate, the three divisions merged in 1947 to form the Educational Testing Service. As a member of its first board of trustees, Conant played a crucial role in the formation of ETS, stating in his memoirs, "The establishment of ETS was part of an educational revolution in which I am proud to have played a part." With the appointment of Henry Chauncey, Conant's former assistant dean, to the presidency of ETS, Conant boasted that he set Mr. Chauncey up in business. He also could have boasted that with the establishment of the Educational Testing Service, America had moved one step closer to Conant's vision of the meritocratic society.[17]

The college success of World War II veterans, many of whom had poor educational backgrounds, helped discredit the notion of Conant and others that the bill's nonselective nature would lead to massive academic failures.

Who Merits a College Education?

Like many other Americans, Conant feared the long-term consequences of the great depression. The hard times dampened the traditional optimism of Americans, engendering skepticism of the value of free enterprise and democracy. Some found fascism and communism appealing, while others wanted to expand significantly the role of government in economic planning. Many Americans looked to Germany, Italy, and Japan for alternative roads back to prosperity. Developments abroad intensified Conant's sensitivity to the fragility of democracy and led to a redoubling of his commitment to capitalism and free enterprise. He concluded that the depression and totalitarianism jeopardized what he regarded as the very backbone of democracy—social mobility.

Redistributing wealth or achieving equality of condition would not resolve this crisis. But school reform could help to forestall permanent class stratification. Scholarships and accelerated classes would encourage the intellectually gifted, while vocational education would meet the needs of the less academically able. Conant counted on Harvard and other elite institutions to awaken the rank-and-file teachers to the new demands of modern society and to work with him to foster a new sense of community in the schools. Separate schools for the gifted and dull, although advantageous in some ways, would in the long run only contribute to further divisiveness and a continued retreat from Conant's ideal of social mobility. Echoing Charles Eliot's fears and hopes, Conant wrote in 1940, "In short, a horde of heterogeneous students has descended on our secondary schools, and on our ability to handle all types intelligently depends in large measure the future of this country."[18]

In the dark days before World War II, Conant advanced the view that by giving recognition to the best students and by helping the rest of the students to find their educational niche, the schools would be promoting social stability and thus greatly enhancing national security. He feared, however, that in practice schools were not doing enough to discourage the "marginal" high school students from pursuing a college education. In 1940, with 11 percent of high school students going on to college, Conant called them the wrong 11 percent and far more than American colleges could effectively teach without lowering standards. In addition to the problem of standards, Conant was concerned that an excessively large population of college students might cause disruptions in the social order. With social stability, not the intellectual fulfillment of each student, as his first priority, Conant warned: "I doubt if society can make a graver mistake than to provide advanced higher education of a specialized nature for men and women who are unable subsequently to use this training. Quite apart from economic considerations the existence of any large number of highly educated individuals whose ambitions have been frustrated is unhealthy for any nation."[19]

Near the end of World War II, the GI Bill of Rights provided full college scholarships to all veterans regardless of their academic "aptitudes." As a group, veterans had worse academic records and lower SAT scores than the average college student. Prior to the passage of this bill, Conant had lobbied vigorously for granting college subsidies only to a select group of veterans who had demonstrated high intellectual capacity. Given Conant's view that college should maintain a high level of selectivity, failure to win support for his version of the bill must have been a bitter defeat. Like his presidential counterpart at the University of Chicago, Robert Hutchins, Conant feared that the influx of nontraditional students would lead to a lowering of academic standards. Years later, he complained that the passage of the GI Bill of Rights indicated America's unwillingness to accept the selective principle of education, which he regarded as essential in a free and fluid society.

Conant did not address the fact that his and Hutchins's fears of lowered standards had proved unwarranted. The GI Bill became one of the greatest academic successes in American history. Over 2 million veterans took advantage of the opportunity to attend college during the 7 years the program was offered, and almost one-fourth of these probably would have never attended college at all without the bill's subsidies. Most impressive of all, more veterans distinguished themselves in academically rigorous courses than nonveterans. Veterans earned better grades than nonveterans, and contrary to Hutchins's predictions, they enrolled in liberal arts courses in far greater numbers than nonveterans. Although Congress passed the GI Bill partly to forestall massive postwar unemployment, the results of the bill showed that mature students, even from nonacademic backgrounds, could flourish in an academic atmosphere.[20]

School Reform Reports and Social Stratification

In 1945, with World War II coming to a close and concerns about the postwar era becoming increasingly acute, a spate of reports appeared on the future needs of American education. Three of the most widely read and discussed of these documents were Harvard University's *General Education in a Free Society,* the Educational Policy Commission's *Education for All American Youth,* and a sociological study, *Who Shall Be Educated?* The Harvard report set forth lucidly and eloquently the theory and philosophy of general education. In searching for an overall logic or unity to secondary school instruction, the authors emphasized the goals of effective thinking and clear communication of thought. Moreover, the authors of this report affirmed that the great majority of high school students would benefit from a challenging course of study largely derived from the liberal arts.

The goals of the Harvard report stood in stark contrast to the objectives of the Educational Policy Commission's *Education for All American Youth* and Lloyd Warner, Robert Havighurst, and Martin Loeb's *Who Shall Be Educated?* The EPC, with its life-adjustment orientation, asserted that only the 15 or 20 percent of students going on to college should be encouraged to take a full complement of academic subjects. The less able students, the EPC explained, would focus on three practical goals during their 4 years of high school: vocational efficiency, civic competence, and personal development. Largely agreeing with the EPC, Warner, Havighurst, and Loeb argued that schools should be used to increase the degree of social mobility only moderately. To try to do more than this, the authors maintained, would be to encourage more students to rise to the top of the social pyramid than could be accommodated by the status system. The authors thus called for a secondary school that would differentiate students according to measured ability, and that would use an experienced staff of guidance counselors to carry out a sorting function closely corresponding to society's vocational needs.

As the initiator of the Harvard report, a member of the commission that had produced *All American Youth,* and an admirer of *Who Shall Be Educated?,* James Conant sought to offer a picture of American education that would draw liberally on all three documents. He got his chance when Columbia University invited him to deliver the prestigious Julius and Rose Sachs Lectures in November of 1945. In the three lectures, which he collectively titled *Public Education and the Structure of American Society,* Conant focused on what he regarded as the necessary relation between education and equality of opportunity. Although education had the potential to foster a high degree of social fluidity and to reduce emphasis on class distinctions and hereditary privilege, he lamented that in the first decades of the 20th century education had tended to increase stratification in the United States. Without progress toward greater social mobility, Conant feared that more discontented Americans would endeavor to foment social change through violent action. He thus concluded that "the chances of a nonrevolutionary development of our nation in the next fifty years seem to me to be determined largely by our educational system."

As Conant saw it, if Americans would accept his vision of the ideal democracy, then the potential violence and disruption of the postwar years could be averted. First, Conant maintained, Americans must acknowledge the important place of the well-trained, meritorious expert in every important field. Second, they must reject advancement through hereditary privilege and embrace a fluid social structure that would allow talented people from any social class to rise to positions of importance and responsibility. And third, all types of labor must be regarded as equal, with no position being accorded more social status than any other. Once these values were accepted, Conant observed, students would no longer feel compelled to attend college to reap the rewards of high status. Higher education, then, would be attractive only to those who genuinely merit it and require it in their eventual occupations. Public schools would play a crucial role in this process by sorting students according to their ability, and guidance counselors would assume the important job of selecting students for college preparatory courses. In response to those who feared that guidance counselors might use their positions of authority to coerce students, Conant stated that school personnel could be counted on to employ "the democratic method of enlightenment and persuasion."[21]

Education in a Divided World

Three years later, with tensions between the United States and the Soviet Union steadily increasing, Conant expanded the Sachs Lectures into a book titled *Education in a Divided World.* In this book, Conant argued that by promoting greater cultural and social unity, the American public schools could serve as the first bulwark of defense against the Soviets. As Conant saw it, the United States would prevail in the protracted struggle between the two superpowers if American students learned to recognize and condemn the defects of the Soviet system, while absorbing "the historic goals of our unique society."

In one section of *Education in a Divided World,* Conant attempted to demonstrate the superiority of American ideology by contrasting Soviet and American attitudes toward the individual in society. Whereas the United States regards the individual as sacrosanct, Conant offered, the Soviets subordinate the individual's welfare to the demands of the state. Yet, as we have seen, Conant himself had consistently treated the individual as a means to the end of greater cultural, social, and political unity. Ironically, Conant employed quotations from Arthur Koestler's novel *Darkness at Noon* to heighten this contrast. Yet, as educational philosopher James McClellan had pointed out, Conant did not fully explore the implications of Koestler's work. A major theme in *Darkness at Noon* is that even more important than making a choice of values or demonstrating the superiority of one ideology over another is the necessity of keeping responsible discourse and inquiry going. Conant, however, appeared willing to sacrifice the pursuit of knowledge and mutual understanding to the pursuit of American dominance.[22]

Conant's contribution to a 1951 pamphlet called *Education and National Security* extended the theme of how educators could help the United States to compete more effectively with the Soviet Union. While the school must impart certain moral and spiritual values, its overriding purposes involved supplying the armed forces with adequate personnel and with training people to meet the nation's critical needs. While they condoned the study of history and critical thought, the authors also praised instructors for teaching their charges to accept and support American foreign-policy engagements, such as the "police action" that then raged in Korea. The authors also wrote approvingly that teachers determine "how readily the young recruit adapts himself to military life, how the industrial employee learns his assigned operation, and with what speed and accuracy the new stenographer transcribes her notes."[23]

In his last year before leaving Harvard in 1953 to be United States high commissioner to Germany, Conant published *Education and Liberty*. Based on a series of lectures delivered at the University of Virginia, this book again affirmed Conant's faith in American public schools. It also showed his growing mastery of the complexities of educational systems in Australia, New Zealand, Scotland, and England. Conant's recent investigations of Australian and New Zealand schools (made possible by a grant from the Carnegie Corporation) and his increasingly broad knowledge of British educational history considerably sharpened his ability to draw parallels between these school systems and public education in the United States. Although he noted the effectiveness of these nations in educating talented youngsters, Conant's comparative study amounted to a celebration of both the diversity and the democratic unity of American public education.

For the first time in his major writings, Conant stressed the unique function of the American comprehensive high school. By mixing students of vastly different backgrounds and abilities in the same school, he observed, the comprehensive high school minimized class distinctions and avoided many of the social cleavages that characterized the other societies he investigated. Whereas schools in most other countries were highly centralized and run by the state, local communities administered American schools, greatly increasing educational diversity and the opportunity for experimentation. Conant conceded that inferior schools tended to emerge under America's decentralized system, and that some of these schools were poorly equipped to prepare the academically talented for college. In general, however, he acclaimed the American comprehensive high school for its role in nourishing democratic unity.

Although Soviet communism largely remained a tacit backdrop to *Education and Liberty*, at one point Conant articulated the chief assumption of his educational proposals. "If the field of Waterloo was won on the playing fields of Eton, it may well be that the ideological struggle with Communism in the next fifty years will be won on playing fields of the public high schools of the United States. That this may be so is the fervent hope of all of us who are working to support and improve these characteristic American institutions."[24]

As Conant left Harvard, he continued to reflect on the role of the American comprehensive high school. In *Education and Liberty* he had accumulated and presented more firsthand knowledge of Australian and New Zealand schools than he had of American schools. By closely studying test results and directly observing selected American high schools, Conant particularly hoped to demonstrate that comprehensive secondary schools educated the academically talented as thoroughly as European-style homogeneous secondary schools. This objective would serve as the initial basis for Conant's investigation of the American high school, a task he would undertake after serving his country for 4 years in Germany.

School Reform in the Postwar Era

In the postwar years, educational debate in the United States centered on the value of schooling for "life adjustment." In 1945, Charles Prosser, one of the early boosters of vocational education, declared that schools had failed to educate the majority of high school youth for the demands of modern life. Claiming that most students had spurned the traditional academic curriculum or had rejected vocational education, Prosser argued that these students needed instruction in the practical arts of home and family life and civic competence. Although the life-adjustment curriculum would not omit science, math, and the humanities, these courses would stress hands-on experience and focus on contemporary problems. As one life-adjustment document put it, "citizenship training must concentrate on understanding the present, not studying the past."[25]

Although life-adjustment educators intended to make schooling more relevant and "functional," many of the courses that appeared in school districts around the country in the half-decade after the war appeared to reflect a powerful anti-intellectual bias. In some school districts, entire instructional units were devoted to the etiquette of dating, including discussion of such questions as

One of Conant's major victories was helping establish the Educational Testing Service, which was responsible for developing the Scholastic Aptitude Test (SAT).

"Do girls want to 'pet'?" and "Should you go in with a girl after a date (to raid the ice box)?" As educational historian Diane Ravitch has pointed out, time and again one could find evidence of school instruction during this period that taught "children what kind of behavior was socially acceptable and how to adjust to group expectations."[26]

Beginning in 1949 and continuing for about a decade, a torrent of articles and books appeared that censured the public schools for lowering standards and in general miseducating American youth. Almost all these observers of the educational scene agreed that progressive reforms and especially life adjustment had sadly diminished the importance of academic achievement. By stressing personality development and meeting each student's individual needs, the critics argued, the schools were neglecting the traditional intellectual subjects and were thus failing to impart mental and moral discipline.

Of all the critics, perhaps the most interesting and perceptive were former urban school board member Mortimer Smith and noted professional historian Arthur Bestor. Both adamantly maintained that the primary purpose of schooling should be intellectual training. And both men tenaciously clung to the belief that even the most ordinary student could profit from a rigorously intellectual course of study. While conceding the importance of serving a student's needs, interests, and abilities, Smith insisted that to develop well-roundedness, all students should be required to work at things for which they might not have talent. Bestor affirmed the importance of giving all students a solid liberal arts education, regardless of how deficient their family or cultural background might appear to be. As Bestor saw it, the school could have no more important function than to overcome educational handicaps, thereby achieving its true democratic mission of meeting the fundamental need of all people for intellectual enrichment.

In 1956, Smith, Bestor, and colleagues of theirs formed the Council for Basic Education. The CBE's commitment to making intellectual training the highest priority of the public schools was as strong as its opposition to the differentiation of students by ability. The CBE's original statement of purpose declared "that only by the maintenance of high academic standards can the ideal of democratic education be realized—the ideal of offering to all the children of all the people of the United States not merely an opportunity to attend school, but the privilege of receiving there the soundest education that is offered any place in the world."[27]

Another critic of life adjustment education, admiral Hyman Rickover, took a different view. For Rickover, a naval engineer and nuclear submarine designer, technical and scientific education for a small, talented elite took precedence over all other kinds of schooling. As a naval admiral and stalwart cold-warrior, Rickover asserted that "education is America's first line of defense" in effectively competing with the Soviet Union. Although Rickover spoke of educating all children well, he focused attention on the 15 or 20 percent whom he regarded as academically talented. The future mathematicians, physicists, and linguists, he believed, must be trained in homogeneous, European-style secondary schools, where academic standards would be maintained and sentimental attachments to the slow child would not impede the main task at hand. Rickover not only rejected mixed-ability classes, but he also regarded the comprehensive high school as an unfortunate vestige of a less complicated era. Rickover envisioned a school system that would identify talented students at an early age and enroll them in accelerated educational programs. In the long run, he argued, this highly selective process would enhance American freedom by helping the United States to keep pace with the Soviets. Rickover's envisioned school system might slight the majority of students, but as Rickover reminded his readers, "The future belongs to the best educated nation. Let it be ours."[28]

After the Soviets launched *Sputnik* in 1957, alarming the American news media into popularizing the view that our schools had failed to teach science and math to an entire generation of students, Rickover's elitist perspective sparked new interest. In response to spreading fears that the United States was losing the cold war because of its intellectually feeble school system, Congress passed the National Defense Education Act of 1958. With strong endorsement from President Eisenhower, this legislation allocated millions of dollars for upgrading the teaching of science and math and improving procedures for identifying and educating gifted students. The hearings that led up to this legislation and the general concern regarding Russian technological superiority launched a new round of attacks against the public schools.

In the midst of this continuing debate, in the late winter of 1959, James B. Conant released his first study of secondary schools, *The American High School Today.* Conant asserted that the comprehensive high school, by educating academic and vocational students under the same roof, contributed to democratic unity, while also doing an adequate job of preparing both populations for their respective post-high school destinations. Most important to school people, who had grown tired of defending themselves against an unremitting barrage of educational criticism, Conant appeared to accept the educational status quo with only minor modifications. Indeed, Conant's skillful manipulation of public opinion ensured *The American High School Today* wide and favorable exposure, which tended to defuse subsequent educational criticism. How Conant accomplished this feat requires us to examine closely some of the events that led up to the publication of *The American High School Today.*

The Great Talent Hunt

Between 1953 and 1957, while Conant served as high commissioner to Germany, John Gardner, the president of the Carnegie Corporation, and Henry Chauncey, the head of the Educational Testing Service since 1947, indicated in their annual reports that their thinking about the education of the academically talented closely paralleled Conant's. At ETS, which had quickly become the most powerful institution for sorting young people in American society, Chauncey referred year after year to the role standardized tests were increasingly playing in identifying scientific and technical talent. He feared Soviet technological superiority, but suggested that testing and guidance could become America's "secret weapon," by making "our education system fit the needs of youth better than the Russian system meets the needs of Russian youth."[29]

Although less concerned with the Soviets, John Gardner also emphasized the importance of educating talented youth. In his first annual report for the Carnegie Corporation, Gardner showed that he put great faith in IQ tests. He stated that a student receiving an IQ score between 108 and 115 would barely qualify for admission to a 4-year college and that an IQ below 108 just about eliminated a student's chance to compete effectively in college. Increasingly, Conant frequently referred to an IQ of 115 as an appropriate cutoff for identifying the academically talented.

In 1956, Gardner entitled his second annual report "The Great Talent Hunt." He described at length the important new role that the gifted must play in American society and the special obligation of educators to challenge these students and develop their talents. In subsequent reports, Gardner continued to stress the education of the talented, but also tried to make a case for counseling students away from college who he believed were not suited for it. In his book *Excellence,* which appeared shortly before the first Conant report, Gardner wrote that the educational system must work effectively as a "sorting-out process." As Gardner put it, "The Schools are the golden avenue of opportunity for able youngsters; but by the same token they are the arena in which less able youngsters discover their limitations." Thus, in the late 1950s, Gardner was advancing the same themes that Conant had been voicing since the late 1930s: identifying and promoting the talented while discouraging the rest of the students from enrolling in college preparatory programs.[30]

In December 1956, Conant proposed to Gardner that the Carnegie Corporation finance his investigation of the education of talented youth in comprehensive high schools. Although he sought to ascertain whether a school containing college-bound and non-college-bound students could educate both populations effectively, he was chiefly interested in the academically talented. Could the comprehensive high school identify and develop students with IQs of 115 or better and provide them with solid instruction in a foreign language, mathematics through calculus, physics and chemistry, English literature and language, and several years of history? If this important task could be accomplished in a school also attended by less able students, the comprehensive high school would be realizing its crucial mission: the identification and development of the most academically talented and the social integration of both college-bound and non-college-bound students.

On May 16, 1957, the board of trustees of the Carnegie Corporation announced that it was approving the appropriation of $350,000 to the Educational Testing Service for the administration of the study of the American high school by James B. Conant. By that time the objectives for the study had been clarified, the staff had been hired, the schools to be studied had been identified and contacted, and even a tentative schedule of school visits had been worked out.

Between September 1957 and July 1958, Conant conducted the first phase of his study. During this period, Conant and an associate visited over 50 comprehensive high schools in 18 states, filing a detailed report after each visitation. According to Conant, these schools all had a "high degree of comprehensiveness"—that is, with more than half the students enrolled in vocational programs and with a significant minority taking college preparatory classes. Conant and his staff deemed a comprehensive high school satisfactory if it gave "a good general education for *all* the pupils as future citizens of a democracy, provide[d] elective programs for the majority to develop useful skills, and educate[d] adequately those with a talent for handling advanced academic subjects—particularly foreign languages and advanced mathematics."[31]

At the conclusion of his investigations, Conant reported that eight schools were successfully fulfilling his objectives for the comprehensive high school. Although reluctant to make sweeping generalizations about the condition of public secondary education in the United States, Conant admitted that "no radical alteration in the basic pattern of American education is necessary in order to improve public high schools." By so uncritically accepting the educational status quo, Conant ensured a favorable reception for his report. While Conant did offer 21 recommendations for improving public high schools, as historian Raymond Callahan has said, "Any superintendent who could say he was adopting Conant's recommendations, or better yet, that his school system had already been following them for years, was almost impregnable." Consequently, shortly after the publication of *The American High School Today,* Conant achieved wide renown as America's premier educational statesman. To express their gratitude formally, the American Association of School Administrators presented Conant with a specially inscribed award:

> Thomas Jefferson, more than any other man, convinced the new nation that education is essential to a free people. Horace Mann, more than any other man, convinced the expanding nation that public schools supported by all and open to all must be established if the nation was to achieve its destiny. A century later, with the people frightened, the nation threatened, free institutions held in doubt, and the public schools under severe criticism, James Bryant Conant, more than any other man, by his logic, keen analysis, patriotic sacrifice, and courageous vision rekindled the nation's flame of faith in free men's basic human values and rebuilt confidence in the public schools of America.[32]

Although the upbeat message Conant communicated to public educators partly explained the favorable reception his first report enjoyed, a skillfully engineered media blitz also greatly increased its chances for success. Both Conant and the Carnegie Corporation/ETS conglomerate maintained important ties to leading book publishers, newspapers, and magazines that helped to keep Conant's name constantly before the public eye. Furthermore, the publicity campaign for *The American High School Today* was planned meticulously. The campaign organizers designated themselves the "joint chiefs"; they called the Carnegie Corporation offices the "control center," and often wrote of the best way to deploy their forces. To sustain media coverage over a period of months, the "joint chiefs" built a news release structure that ensured the appearance of a continuing stream of newspaper and magazine articles about Conant and his study. As the "joint chiefs" put it, they wanted to treat the publication of *The American High School Today* as a news story, not a literary event that might put them at the mercy of unfriendly book reviewers. With McGraw-Hill lined up to publish the Conant reports, a key pillar of the envisioned release structure was intact. One of McGraw-Hill's initial advertisements indicated their willingness to promote Conant's study forcefully. In boldface letters, it read

> "THE CONANT REPORT—A BOOK THAT WILL AROUSE NATIONAL ATTENTION AND MAKE EDUCATIONAL HISTORY."[33]

Careful timing also helped Conant to attract attention with *The American High School Today.* After spending his first year personally investigating secondary schools, Conant had planned to take another full year talking to school boards and getting their reactions to his findings and tentative recommendations. Conant curtailed these visits in order to hurry the report's release. As Conant and his advisers knew, by January 1959 the public was ready for an affirmative and constructive study on public education. Conant consciously wrote the report to give the public exactly what they wanted.

Conant praised the comprehensive high school and condemned radical solutions. But two major concerns tempered his upbeat message. First, the small high school (with a graduating class of fewer than 100 students) would have to be eliminated. According to Conant, it was expensive and inefficient to maintain good academic and vocational programs for so few students. Since the small schools rarely bore the necessary costs willingly, inferior education was the usual result. Second, Conant believed that too many schools, both large and small, were not sufficiently challenging the academically talented. Too many boys were neglecting courses in the humanities in favor of science and mathematics, and too many able girls were avoiding science, math, and foreign languages. Conant particularly lamented the dearth of 4-year foreign language programs in the high schools he visited. In addition to believing that foreign language study exposes the future scientist or engineer to another culture, Conant stressed that "our grim competition with the Soviet Union in the newly developing countries calls for people who can pick up a language quickly and match their Russian counterparts who realize the importance of linguistic competence."[34]

Even before *The American High School Today* had become a best-seller, positioning him as the nation's number-one educational expert, Conant wrote a confidential memo to his staff that took the public schools to task for failing to challenge the academically talented. In the memo, he admitted that he presented his findings more positively than he would have had he not been writing in reaction to a negative and tense atmosphere of debate. He confided that the vast majority of the schools he visited were badly neglecting the education of the most gifted students. Conant particularly blamed the educational establishment in state universities for graduating so many teachers who tended to give the same amount of attention to all of their students, regardless of their academic aptitude.[35]

In *The American High School Today,* Conant did not reveal his underlying reasons for vigorously promoting the training of the best students. Although his earlier writings showed that concerns about the Soviet threat had spurred his school reform efforts, school people unfamiliar with these ideas had to consult a lesser-known companion volume to understand the full thrust of Conant's educational message. Titled *The Child, the Parent, and the State,* this book represented in a sense the social and philosophical underpinnings of *The American High School Today*. Throughout this work, Conant maintained that the divided world he had described 10 years earlier still prevailed, and that the schools had the same responsibility to take up the challenge of halting the spread of Soviet communism. Conant believed Americans had adjusted too easily to living in a "divided world" and had failed to take seriously the role of the schools in effectively competing with the Soviets. If Americans conceded the gravity of the rivalry between the United States and the Soviet Union, Conant argued, then they too would actively work to eliminate the small, inefficient high school, increase foreign language study, and in general see to it that talented youth developed their abilities as fully as possible. After all, Conant warned, these future scientists, engineers, and professionals would prove to be invaluable weapons in the technological race with the Soviets.

Conant rejected Admiral Rickover's proposal that Americans support separate schools for the academically talented. He believed that the public high school should enroll students preparing for vocations along with those preparing for college, but his rationale was largely social, not educational. First and foremost, this arrangement would foster greater democratic feeling. It would forge closer relationships among future professional people, craftspersons, engineers, and labor leaders and in turn help to promote "not only equality of opportunity but equality of esteem in all forms of labor." Conant wavered on the direct benefits of vocational education, however. At times he thought it could effectively prepare students for particular vocations. At one point, he compared vocational education to the advanced placement program, because, like the gifted college preparatory student, the able vocational student should be in a position to assume the responsibilities of a second-year apprentice in many skilled trades. But more often and more realistically, Conant referred to vocational education as a "motivating force" that would keep the potential dropout in school, where he would learn the vocational habits and citizenship responsibilities demanded by modern American society.[36]

Slums and Subversives

Conant's continuing interest in the comprehensive high school as a source of social cohesion led him eventually to investigate the segregated urban and elite suburban high schools of the Northeast and Midwest. The schools Conant visited, which formed the basis for his next book, *Slums and Suburbs,* were the very antithesis of the comprehensive high school. At one extreme, the urban schools in low-income and poverty neighborhoods stressed vocational education and direct preparation of students for the workplace. At the other extreme, the wealthy suburban schools educated almost all of their students for college. Conant particularly regretted the tendency of suburban parents to push their children into college preparatory courses regardless of their academic ability. Wider use of guidance services and standardized test scores would encourage more students to enter vocational programs, Conant thought, and increase the comprehensiveness of these elite schools. When it came to the impoverished urban schools, however, as historian Clarence Karier has said, Conant's "sense of ideal community gave way to what he judged was practically possible." Thus, in considering ways to improve urban schools, Conant rejected both racial integration and expansion of academic offerings as impracticable and unnecessary.[37]

Few readers of *Slums and Suburbs* were aware that the threat of Soviet communism again played a key role in arousing Conant's sympathy for the plight of urban schoolchildren. Though he mentioned this threat in only one paragraph of the book, Conant had not lost his talent for dramatically drawing parallels between America's social problems and the waging of the cold war. He wrote: "I do not have to remind the reader that the fate of freedom in the world hangs very much in balance ... Communism feeds upon discontented, frustrated, unemployed people ... These young people are my chief concern, especially when they are pocketed together in large numbers within the confines of the big city slums. What can words like 'freedom,' 'liberty,' and 'equality of opportunity' mean to these young people? With what kind of zeal and dedication can we expect them to withstand the relentless pressures of communism? How well prepared are they to face the struggle that shows no sign of abating?"[38]

Conant believed that the struggle to win the hearts and minds of urban youth depended upon the effectiveness of vocational education programs. He cited a number of examples of how vocational education in predominantly black high schools had fostered stability and other desirable social behaviors. Dunbar Vocational High School in Chicago provided a paradigm. While the school tailored its curriculum to meet the students' vocational needs, the academic program also had successfully prepared a handful of students for college, though this was clearly not the school's primary purpose. In fact, students at Dunbar could not remain in the academic program without successfully completing all shop classes. One cannot help wonder how many more students would have gone on to college from Dunbar, or simply enjoyed new intellectual challenges, had academic courses been stressed as much as vocational ones. Conant approved of some academic courses for minority students and actually claimed they should constitute at least half of the curriculum. But the entire tone of the "Slums" section of *Slums and Suburbs*—with hardly a reference to the education of the academically talented—had a decidedly pro-vocational cast.

Conant's advocacy of a system of vocational education for slum schools followed logically from the rest of his educational philosophy. If most black students scored poorly on IQ and SAT tests and other accepted measures of academic aptitude, and if students performing below the expected levels of excellence (IQ below 115) were to be counseled away from academic courses, then guidance counselors would be encouraging most African-American students to concentrate on vocational studies. Somehow, the thought that the schools themselves might be contributing to the "social dynamite" in the cities never occurred to Conant; he just studied the data and offered his recommendations accordingly. He did not seem to understand, as historian Henry Perkinson has pointed out, that "instead of enhancing and fulfilling his expectations of determining his own destiny, this educational 'equality of opportunity' simply corroborated the black child's feelings of powerlessness." By condoning vocationally oriented education for most urban black youth, Conant was harking back to the theory of "Negro education" promulgated by Booker T. Washington, which called for a direct line between the educational experiences of youth and their probable employment opportunities.[39]

A bitter irony resides in Conant's vocationalist thinking for students who didn't meet his definition of "academically talented," a definition that excluded all but a few urban African-American students. The irony is that in 1954, the U.S. Supreme Court had just ruled that segregation of the races in public schooling is unconstitutional. This ruling, *Brown* v. *the Board of Education,* overturned the Supreme Court ruling of 1896, *Plessy* v. *Ferguson,* which had made "separate but equal" the law of the land shortly after Booker T. Washington had delivered his Atlanta "Cast down your buckets" address. While the *Brown* decision made school segregation illegal, Conant's policies had the consequence of segregating black students from white students in the college preparatory and advanced placement classes that Conant so vigorously endorsed. While separate vocational schools for African-Americans would no longer be legal after 1954, a more insidious kind of segregation would come to be seen as normal in comprehensive high schools throughout the latter half of the 20th century.

As the 1960s wore on, Conant's fears of the communist bogey gave way to new fears of social unrest. The "social dynamite" that he had observed in America's cities began exploding in the middle sixties. Conflagrations in almost every major city alerted the nation that urban blacks were fed up with second-class treatment. On college campuses, students staged numerous protests against the Vietnam War and authoritarian educational practices. Conant especially feared these developments. He thought that the emergence of the new left posed the latest threat to a stable American democracy. He also became increasingly convinced that the colleges' willingness to accommodate larger and more diverse populations of students had strengthened the position of radical elements on campus. In response to these campus disruptions, Conant became an active promoter of the junior college movement. Not only would the junior colleges accommodate some of those dissatisfied and presumably, for Conant, less talented students who fueled the fires of the protest movement, they would satisfy the educational ambitions of "marginal" students. Moreover, the junior colleges would meet technical training needs rarely addressed in high schools and would appear to enhance equal opportunity without sacrificing meritocratic principles and the high standards of the 4-year college.[40]

Whatever success the junior colleges might have had in "cooling out" the discontented and defusing the explosive atmosphere on some college campuses, Conant was dismayed that his school reforms had not opened the door to a better world. He applauded the new attention that teachers were giving the academically talented as a result of his efforts, but he regretted the new round of attacks that the schools were once again forced to endure. This time the attacks came from the left, with most critics inveighing against the rigid structure and "mindlessness" that characterized public schools. Nevertheless, Conant adamantly maintained that a properly conceived educational system could help to bring about his version of the ideal society. Yet it remained a very unimaginative vision, with an education system designed to help most people seek satisfaction in mind-numbing employment or in occasional exercise of the vote. Despite his constant references to democracy, Conant sought a government run by experts with only limited participation by the masses. The education system he had worked for throughout his career would make an important contribution to shaping what the nation's citizens would come to take for granted about how high schools should serve the social order.

CONCLUDING REMARKS

James B. Conant used his Harvard pulpit to preach the gospel of meritocracy, striving to make the university and the public school adhere to the principles of selectivity and excellence as he understood them. Conant repeatedly warned that the school must first prepare talented youth for strategically necessary scientific, professional, and technological occupations. Only secondarily should the school train the rest of the students for occupational roles that played less significant support roles in advancing the national interest.

Despite his enduring interest in public education, Conant's first allegiance was to college and university training. Only at the college level did the immense investments in the education of young people begin to pay dividends in the production of urgently needed engineers and scientists. It followed that if the lower schools were to serve the more essential colleges, university leaders had to exert considerable influence upon the public secondary schools. Believing that the strength of higher education depended upon the sorting efficiency of the elementary and secondary schools, Conant and his university allies pioneered the SAT, advanced placement, and the academic inventory (a survey of advanced courses available to "talented" students in each school) to differentiate more sharply the bright from the dull and the gifted from the average. Accordingly, these reforms increased the schools' ability to funnel qualified students into colleges to meet more directly the technological and strategic needs of the nation. Not surprisingly, Conant and his other university counterparts gave only the most superficial consideration to the education of the non-college-bound student.

When Conant did attend to the problem of educating those students whom he regarded as less able, his solution was vocational education. Instead of seeking to produce self-educating and self-cultivating men and women, he favored an education that would psychologically prepare students for a future occupation, thus ensuring a smooth transition from school to work. He opposed giving all students a liberal education, for even if they could profit from such an education, he reasoned, they could not possibly find jobs commensurate with their educational experiences. And knowing the unchallenging nature of most modern work, Conant feared that the resulting frustration would disrupt the social order. Of course, vocational education carried the additional virtue of keeping potential troublemakers in school. At least they would be off the street, perhaps picking up some useful skill, while absorbing the responsibilities of citizenship in a pluralistic society. In general, Conant's fears of instability and his belief that most people were incapable of deriving benefit from rigorous teaching and learning impelled him to renounce liberal education for all but a small minority.

The progressive education goals examined in Chapter 4, including social stability, employable skills, meritocracy, and equal educational opportunity, continued to shape school reform in the post-World War II era. The Conant-era reforms did not establish new directions for schooling, but rather consolidated old gains in the social-efficiency approach. Two dimensions of the social-efficiency approach which had been disputed during the progressive era emerged from the Conant era as virtually taken for granted by most American educators and by the public at large. First, it became a settled assumption that schooling should take as its first priority not that "all-around growth of every individual," as Dewey had put it, but instead the "national interest," where that interest was defined by those in leadership positions. School curriculum became increasingly and explicitly decided by what was best for society, rather than what was best for each child. Second, the assumption followed that the way for schools to protect national interests in a cold-war world was by selecting and preparing students for their vocational futures in an expert-led society. As a result of Conant's years of efforts, the role and function of the American comprehensive high school became increasingly defined by those assumptions.

Educators will remember the 1980s as the decade of reform that the *Nation at Risk* report launched. This report lamented the miseducation of American children, of whom the majority had taken few courses in science, mathematics, or a foreign language. While a variety of educational officials scrambled to assign blame and provide explanations, few of them assessed this situation historically. Yet the historical record is that reformers such as Conant used enormous power to fashion the current structure of American public education. The result of this structure, with IQ testing, tracking, and the differentiated curriculum at its base, has been that the vast majority of students eschew the most academically challenging subjects in favor of courses deemed more appropriate to their skill levels and their presumed vocational futures. Although Conant and other reformers claimed to weigh the best interests of all students, in effect they shifted the focus of educational concern from realizing the all-around growth of each schoolchild to promoting political, economic, and social stability. Consequently, only a small group of ostensibly "talented" students have been provided with the sort of intellectual challenge that might otherwise be the birthright of every American youth.

PRIMARY SOURCE READING

The following selection presents a view of the aims of education in contrast to James B. Conant's position that the conditions of the cold-war world should influence how different people should be educated, and to what purposes. Columbia University English professor and poet Mark Van Doren argued instead that education ought not prepare people for any particular kind of society or political system, but should treat people "as ends in themselves." In Van Doren's view, the only proper aim of education was to develop the intellectual and personal capacities of each person to the greatest degree possible, after which society would be well taken care of by such well-educated people. If this selection seems particularly difficult to read, the student might consider whether it is Van Doren's prose or the relative unfamiliarity of his ideas that causes one to stop frequently to review the course of the argument.

Van Doren's essay was first published in 1943, during World War II, and then republished in his book, Liberal Education, *in 1959—the same year that Conant published* The American High School Today. *Van Doren's use of masculine pronouns was typical of the time.*

Excerpts from "Education for All"

Mark Van Doren

Education is for all, and there can be no compromise with the proposition. "Just as in his mother's womb each man receives his full complement of limbs—hands, feet, tongue, etc.—although all men are not to be artificers, runners, scribes, or orators; so at school all men should be taught whatever concerns man, though in after life some things will be of more use to one man, others to another." Thus Comenius, the title page of whose *Great Didactic* promised that it would set forth "The whole art of teaching all things to all men"—to "the entire youth of both sexes, none excepted."[1] It was a noble vision, and it has never been realized. We teach our entire youth, but we do not teach them enough.

What was once for a few must now be for the many. There is no escape from this—least of all through the sacrifices of quality to quantity. The necessity is not to produce a handful of masters; it is to produce as many masters as possible, even though this be millions. An ancient sentence about liberal education says it is the education worthy of a free man, and the converse is equally ancient; the free man is one who is worthy of a liberal education. Both sentences remain true, the only difficulty being to know how many men are capable of freedom. The capacity was once a favor bestowed by fortune; the gentleman was a rare fellow whose father was rich or famous. It is also, however, a capacity which nature bestows, and nature is prodigal. Liberal education in the modern world must aim at the generosity of nature, must work to make the aristocrat, the man of grace, the person, as numerous as fate allows. No society can succeed henceforth unless its last citizen is as free to become a prince and a philosopher as his powers permit. The greatest number of these is none too many for democracy nor is the expense of producing them exorbitant. "A new degree of intellectual power," said Emerson, "is cheap at any price," and this is true no less for a country than for one of its citizens. In proportion as the theory is clear it will not confound itself with notions that the education of men, as distinguished from the training of animals, is something for a class—say a leisure class. The only slaves in our society ought to be its machines. There is a myth that machines have minds and so are educable, but no man will admit this. "We Americans," says Alexander Meiklejohn, "are determined that there shall not be in our society two kinds of people. We will not have two kinds of schools—one for gentlemen and ladies, the other for workers and servants. We believe that every man and woman should be governed. All the members of our society must have both

Excerpt from Mark Van Doren, *Liberal Education* (New York: Beacon Press, 1959), pp. 28–42. First published in 1943 by Henry Holt and Company.

[1]John Amos Comenius was a Czech educational reformer, born in Moravia. He lived from 1592 to 1670.

liberal and vocational education. There shall be one set, and only one set, of schools for all people. The first postulate of a democracy is equality of education. The gospel of Comenius is still true." In proportion as our theory is clear it will agree with the foregoing.

What, then, of the fact that education when liberal, when occupied with human discipline, is arduous beyond all other known pursuits? Sufficient wisdom sometimes seems almost esoteric, an accomplishment of genius which the mass is bound to find unintelligible, no surface difference appearing between the subtlety of the philosopher and the caprice of the tyrant. Socrates supposed that philosophers would be useless only in a democracy, where he assumed they would not be heard. It is a question once more of the few and the many. And the answer is never that all men will be the best men. The sensible desire is simply that all men should be as good as possible. The higher the average the safer the state. But the pyramid will have symmetry only if the same attempt is made with every person: to produce in him the utmost of his humanity, on the assumption that this is what he possesses in common with every other person.

A democracy that is interested in its future will give each of its members as much liberal education as he can take, nor will it let him elect to miss that much because he is in a hurry to become something less than a man. It is obvious that all must not be less than they are; and a democracy must be prepared to give the entire quantity of itself that can be taken.

"A state which dwarfs its men in order that they may be more docile instruments in its hands even for beneficial purposes will find that with small men no great thing can really be accomplished." The warning of John Stuart Mill has lost no force. The good state wants great democrats; and gets them by teaching the love of truth; and teaches that by teaching the importance of thinking well. It does not achieve its end by pretense or coercion, or by a conspiracy to confuse the attempt with the deed. "There is no such thing," says Albert Jay Nock, "as democratic manners; manners are either bad or good."[2] So with anything else that is human. There is no such thing as democratic morals and ideas. Morals are either bad or good; ideas are either shallow or profound. Democracy's business is with morals as such, and with the deepest ideas available to its citizens.

Democracy cannot survive a loss of faith that the best man will make the best citizen. It certainly cannot afford to educate men for citizenship, for efficiency, or for use. Its only authority is reason, just as its only strength is criticism. It will not distinguish between its own good and the happiness of its members. It will study how to distribute well the things that are good for men, but it will study with equal care the goods of men, which incidentally make more sense in the singular: the good of man. The citizen will never forgive a society, democratic or otherwise, which taught him to do what time has shown to be wrong or silly. He can never blame a society which encouraged him to be all that he could be. If the teaching was good, he has no one else to blame. Democracy does not provide alibis.

The circle of the relation between the state and the individual, a circle which is drawn when we say that each depends upon the other for its good, can be broken only if we distinguish between the individual and the person. The individual has no relation to anything except the state or society of which he is a member, and to which he is a relative. But the person is not a member. He is the body of himself, and such is always to be understood as an end, not a means. As a ruler, he has first ordered his own soul. As the ruled, he likewise orders his soul. And this is something which he is unique among creatures in knowing how to do, even though he may never do it perfectly. The good state—democracy—will let him try, on the theory that good citizenship will follow naturally from even moderate success; though it will let him try anyway. For without autonomy he cannot find the center in himself from which in fact emanate the very generosity and lawfulness, the respect for others that is a form of respect for himself, necessary to the operation of society at all. Society may command fear and obedience; it cannot force love or friendship, which are irreducibly personal, and developed in places to which politics as most conceive it has no access. Yet they are the foundation of good politics, which in this sense must be

---

[2]Professor Albert Jay Nock was a humanist professor at Columbia University early in the twentieth century.

personal to succeed greatly. Democracy wants millions of one-man revolutions, if only because the result might be a nation of persons worth organizing. Norman Foerster has suggested that "the individual, while learning to live wisely, becomes progressively more fit to be lived with."[3] He supports the remarks with a line from Aeschylus: "The wise have much in common with one another." The only common good is that which is common to good men.

The powers of the person are what education wishes to perfect. To aim at anything less is to belittle men; to fasten somewhere on their exterior a crank which accident or tyrants can twist to set machinery going. The person is not machinery which others can run. His mind has its own laws, which are the laws of thought itself. A congressman recently recommended that American youth be "taught how to think internationally." It would be still better to teach them how to think. Democracy depends for its life upon the chance that every man will take all the judgments he can. When he falls short of that he gives the government another name. He is no longer at home in the republic of the mind, where, since thought is free and only merit makes one eminent, he is less than a slave.

The state is doubtless superior to the individual on many counts. But when the question is one of good or bad, right or wrong, true or false, democracy must appeal to insight, imagination, and judgment; and these are personal things—things, that is, of man rather than society. By personal, it should be clear, the eccentric is not signified. Insight into what? Imagination about what? Judgment concerning what? Not, surely, the accidents of individual belief, but the essentials of the human situation. The individual, thinking about these, becomes personal in the grand dimension. The trivial dimension is something with which we happen to be more familiar, but this should not discourage us from using the word, which has a long and important history. To be personal in the trivial dimension means that in politics we cultivate little areas of freedom where we can live in isolation from the wilderness of compulsion. We have secrets; we lead the buried life. The large area of human freedom is a better place to breathe in. It is a general area, and in it some of our license is lost. But it is the only region where personality is finally possible. For the paradox once more emerges: an individual, thinking the best thoughts of which he is capable, and mastering the human discipline without jealousy for his own rule, becomes more of himself than he was before. "Certain men," wrote Plato in one of his letters, "ought to surpass other men more than the other men surpass children." If that is a definition of aristocracy, the definition of democracy would be a condition in which all men surpass themselves, putting behind them childish things.

Democracy when it is secure will not deny its inferiority to persons. The superiority of its persons is its only strength. To say as much is to say that democracy lives dangerously. For humanity is dangerous, and is not to be controlled by committees of men. But the danger from its freedom—from a program which asks it what it can be rather than tells it what to do—is less than the blind risk that is run when the program is to mislead and miseducate it; or, what amounts to the same thing, to educate it partially. No risk is as real as that. There is danger anyway, as all teachers of pupils and parents of children know. Good teachers, parents, and states, however, will prefer the high danger to the low.

"The question, 'What is a good education?'" says Mortimer Adler in a summary that must be borrowed here, "can be answered in two ways: either in terms of what is good for men at any time and place because they are men, or in terms of what is good for men considered only as members of a particular social or political order. The best society is the one in which the two answers are the same."[4] That best society, doubtless, is still to exist on earth. But when it completely exists, perhaps at the end of history, its name will be democracy. And all of its citizens will be educated persons.

---

[3]Professor Norman Foerster was a humanist professor at the University of Iowa early in the twentieth century.

[4]Mortimer Adler is a University of Chicago philosopher, educator, and, most recently, author of *The Paideia Proposal,* a humanist educational approach for school-age pupils.

QUESTIONS FOR DISCUSSION AND EXAMINATION

1. It might be argued that James B. Conant's major educational initiatives were entirely consistent with progressive-era educational reforms and that he deepened and extended those reforms. To what degree is such a conclusion warranted by the material presented in Chapters 4 and 8?
2. This chapter suggests a significant connection between standardized testing in schools and what might be called cold-war ideology. What connection is being suggested—and do you believe this is a valid association to make? Explain.
3. What are Conant's ideological and political-economic justifications for the system of tracking or ability grouping? Are these justifications consistent with what John Dewey (in Chapter 4) called the "moral meaning" of democracy, namely, that all social institutions should contribute to the "all-around growth of every member of society"? Defend your view.
4. To what degree does your high school experience reflect the educational vision Conant expressed for the "comprehensive American high school"? Did such a school serve your educational and long-term interests well? Did it serve the interests of all students, from all social and ethnic backgrounds, equally well? Explain your position on each of these three issues.
5. To what degree does the educational position argued by Van Doren constitute a criticism of vocational education as recommended by Conant? Do you consider this criticism valid? Explain.
6. Although Van Doren wrote well after the progressive revolution in American schooling, it could be argued that his educational view is significantly grounded in both Aristotelian and Jeffersonian educational ideals. Evaluate that assertion, and evaluate also the degree to which Van Doren's viewpoint is responsive to your assessment of the needs of modern society.
7. In your view, which educational thinker—Van Doren or Conant—offers an educational vision that is more likely to serve the needs of all members of a diverse society such as our own: male and female, rich and poor, European-American, Hispanic-American, African-American, Asian-American, and other groups?

NOTES

1. James McClellan, *Toward an Effective Critique of American Education* (Philadelphia: J. B. Lippincott, 1968), p. 59.
2. Bernard Bailyn et al., *The Great Republic* (Lexington, MA: D. C. Heath, 1981), pp. 767–72; William Leuchtenberg, *The Perils of Prosperity, 1914–32* (Chicago: University of Chicago Press, 1958), chap. 10; Frederick Lewis Allen, *Only Yesterday* (New York: Harper and Row, 1931), chap. 12.
3. Bailyn et al., pp. 779–83, 798–802; David Tyack, Robert Lowe, and Elisabeth Hansot, *Public Schools in Hard Times* (Cambridge, MA: Harvard University Press), pp. 6–27.
4. Tyack et al., 13–26, 59–76.
5. Peter Carroll and David Noble, *The Free and the Unfree* (London: Penguin Press, 1977), pp. 348–49.
6. Ibid.; William Appleman Williams, *The Tragedy of American Diplomacy* (New York: Dell Publishing, 1959), pp. 268–76; and Stephen Ambrose, *Rise to Globalism* (London: Penguin Books, 1980), chap. 5.
7. Harry Truman, quoted in Stephen E. Ambrose, "From Korea to Vietnam: The Failure of a Policy Rooted in Fear," in Blanche Wiesen Cook, Alice Kessler Harris, and Ronald Radosh, eds., *Past Imperfect: Alternative Essays in American History* (New York: Alfred A. Knopf, 1973), Vol. 2, p. 205.
8. McGeorge Bundy, Morton H. Halperin, et al., "Back from the Brink," *Atlantic Monthly,* August 1986, pp. 35–41.
9. Ambrose, "From Korea to Vietnam," p. 204.
10. Eric Goldman, *The Crucial Decade* (New York: Vintage Books, 1960), chap. 6.
11. See Harvard Sitkoff, *The Struggle for Black Equality* (New York: Hill and Wang, 1981); John Hope Franklin, *From Slavery to Freedom,* 3rd ed. (New York: Vintage Books, 1969), chaps. 30 and 31; Meyer Weinberg, *A Chance to Learn* (Cambridge, England: Cambridge University Press, 1977), chaps. 2 and 3.
12. Harry Braverman, *Labor and Monopoly Capital* (New York: Monthly Review Press, 1974), chaps. 5 and 6; David Noble, *America by Design* (New York: Oxford University Press, 1977), chap. 7; David Riesman, *The Lonely Crowd* (New Haven: Yale University Press, 1961), chaps. 6 and 7; Joel Spring, *The Sorting Machine* (New York: Longman, 1976), chap. 6; George Santayana, *Character and Opinion in the United States* (New York: W. W. Norton, 1934), p. 11.
13. James B. Conant, *My Several Lives* (New York: Harper and Row, 1970), p. 49.
14. *The Nation,* May 24, 1933, p. 571.
15. Conant, *My Several Lives,* p. 134.
16. Examples of the use of the Calvinist metaphor include the following: Conant, *Vital Speeches of the Day,* July 15, 1936, p. 638; Feb. 1, 1937, p. 254; *Harvard Annual Report, 1936–37,* pp. 14–15.
17. Conant, *My Several Lives,* pp. 428–32.

18. Conant, *Education for a Classless Society* (Cambridge, MA: Harvard University Press, 1940), pp. 1–18.
19. Ibid., pp. 33–35. Also see Thomas Grissom, "Education and the Cold War: James B. Conant," in Clarence Karier, Paul Violas, and Joel Spring, *Roots of Crisis* (Chicago: Rand McNally, 1973). Later Conant also wrote that "From frustrated individuals with long education and considerable intelligence society has much to fear. From such people come the leaders of antidemocratic movements." Conant, *Ladies Home Journal,* June 1948, p. 107.
20. James B. Conant, *Thomas Jefferson and the Development of American Public Education* (Charlottesville: University of Virginia Press, 1979), pp. 173–82.
21. Conant, *Public Education and the Structure of American Society* (New York: Teachers College Press, 1945), pp. 2–41. Also see Conant, "Selection and Guidance in the Secondary School," *Harvard Educational Review,* Winter 1948, pp. 61–75.
22. Conant, *Education in a Divided World* (Cambridge, MA: Harvard University Press, 1948), pp. viii–ix, 233, 35–37, 104–5; James McClellan, *Toward an Effective Critique of American Education,* p. 104.
23. Educational Policies Commission and the American Council on Education, *Education and National Security* (December 1951), pp. 12, 15, 27–28, 38, 45.
24. Conant, *Education and Liberty* (Cambridge, MA: Harvard University Press, 1953), p. 62.
25. Lawrence Cremin, *The Transformation of the School* (New York: Vintage Books, 1961), pp. 334–38; Harold Alberty et al., *Let's Look at the Attacks on the Schools* (Columbus: Ohio State University, 1951), pp. 3–4.
26. Diane Ravitch, *The Troubled Crusade* (New York: Basic Books, 1983), p. 68.
27. Mortimer Smith, *And Madly Teach* (Chicago: Henry Regnery, 1949), pp. 10, 22–23, 37, 43; Arthur Bestor, *Educational Wastelands* (Champaign: University of Illinois Press, 1953), pp. 36–37, 79–80; *The Case for Basic Education,* James D. Koerner, ed. (Boston: Atlantic Monthly Press, 1959), p. v.
28. Hyman G. Rickover, *Education and Freedom* (New York: E. P. Dutton, 1959), p. 38.
29. Henry Chauncey, *Annual Report of the Educational Testing Service, 1957–58* (Princeton: Educational Testing Service), p. 28. For evidence of how ETS works as a sorting machine, see Allan Nairn, *The Reign of ETS* (Washington, D.C.: Ralph Nader Report on the Educational Testing Service, 1980).
30. John Gardner, *Annual Report of the Carnegie Corporation of New York, 1956* (New York: Carnegie Corporation of New York, 1957), p. 25; John Gardner, *Excellence* (New York: Harper and Row, 1961), p. 66.
31. Conant, *The American High School Today* (New York: McGraw-Hill, 1959), p. 15.
32. Ibid., pp. 22, 40; Raymond Calahan, *Education and the Cult of Efficiency* (Chicago: University of Chicago Press, 1962), p. viii; Conant Personal Papers, Box 3, Folder 40, Harvard University Archives.
33. "Report on Dissemination Campaign," March 25, 1959; Tentative Plan for Dissemination Campaign for the Publication of *The American High School Today,* October 28, 1958, both in Conant Personal Papers, Box 2, Folder 34, Harvard University Archives.
34. Conant, *The American High School Today,* pp. 37–38, 40; Conant, *The Child, the Parent, and the State* (New York: McGraw-Hill, 1959), pp. 36–39, 42.
35. Robert Hampel, *The Late Little Citadel* (New York: Houghton Mifflin, 1986), pp. 68–70.
36. Conant, *The Child, the Parent, and the State,* pp. 32–35, 43–44, 191–92.
37. Conant, *Slums and Suburbs* (New York: McGraw-Hill, 1961), pp. 31, 96–98, 115, 131–33; Clarence Karier, *Man, Society, and Education* (Glenview, IL.: Scott, Foresman, 1967), p. 254.
38. Conant, *Slums and Suburbs,* p. 34.
39. Henry Perkinson, *200 Years of American Educational Thought* (New York: Longman, 1976), pp. 255–56.
40. Conant, *The Comprehensive High School* (New York: McGraw-Hill, 1967), pp. 74–79; Conant, *My Several Lives,* pp. 640–46.

PART TWO

Educational Aims in Contemporary Society

Liberty and Literacy Today: Contemporary Perspectives

Arlette I. Willis, contributing author

Chapter 2 described Thomas Jefferson's faith in the ability of an educated populace to safeguard its liberties. In particular, Jefferson believed that the skills of reading and writing would equip people to stay informed about social, economic, and political events and thereby help them recognize and protect their interests. Popular literacy was for Jefferson and other classical liberals one of the cornerstones of a free society.

At the same time, Jefferson's view of literacy reveals serious limitations in his social and political thought. Like his contemporaries, for example, he limited nonwhites' access to literacy. His Bill for the More General Diffusion of Knowledge provided for literacy for white children, but not children of African-American or Native American descent. Jefferson's classical liberal assumptions about the inherent superiority of whites undergirded his views about literacy and political participation.

The issue of literacy has periodically attracted national attention since Jefferson's time, but perhaps never so dramatically as it has in the past 10 years. Network television, popular magazines, and education journals have treated illiteracy rates as a national scandal, and much fingerpointing has been done in an effort to locate the blame.

The issue of literacy, when reflectively considered, tells us a great deal about school and society in the United States today. This chapter focuses on literacy as a way to illuminate the relationships between schooling, political economy, and ideology in contemporary culture. First, as a fundamental objective of education, the study of literacy helps us understand particular features of schooling—for example, how schools serve some groups in society more successfully than others. Second, because literacy is affected not only by schools but by social processes and institutions outside the schools, the study of literacy illuminates important details of the political economy of today's society. Social context must always be examined when judging the successes and failures of our schools. Finally, the study of literacy helps us recognize the competing ideologies within our own society. Different opinions prevail regarding why literacy is important, and these different views are often grounded in differing ideological perspectives.

A BRIEF HISTORICAL PERSPECTIVE

It is difficult to compare literacy rates in contemporary society with literacy rates in earlier times. First of all, there is lack of agreement about how to define literacy. Second, in the 18th and 19th centuries there were no widespread, systematic studies of literacy such as exist today. Available studies of early American literacy are generally based on the ability of individuals to sign their names on legal documents such as wills. By that standard, illiteracy was near zero for males in some New England communities by 1800, and it is near zero throughout the country today. The ability to produce a signature, however, leaves unanswered fundamental questions about someone's ability to read and write. It really isn't clear how much literacy existed in the Jeffersonian and common-school eras discussed in Part 1. Further, these studies of crude literacy, known as signature literacy, have led some researchers to conclude that the literacy rate of white males exceeded that of white females and was nearly universal in New England and the middle-Atlantic and southern regions in the 1800s. The self-reports of adults to the U.S. Census Bureau in 1850, however, indicate that white male and female signature rates were nearly equal.[1]

Still, some things do seem clear about literacy in the last two centuries, and they are instructive. It appears certain, for example, that people from upper social classes were more literate than those from lower social classes. Wealthier people had access to more forms of education—including schools, tutoring, and parental instruction—than did poorer people. Gender, too, was an obstacle to literacy. Because formal schooling and participation in public and commercial life were considered important primarily for men, women of the past two centuries had lower literacy rates than men.[2] Ironically, however, mothers and women in "dame schools" provided the earliest literacy instruction that most children received.

Race, too, affected the chances of acquiring literacy. Prior to the Civil War, in most southern states it was illegal for a slave to learn to read and write, for it was widely believed that a literate slave would not make an obedient slave. Despite such laws, many African-Americans learned by individual or group efforts to acquire literacy, including secret lessons held in privately funded schools housed in churches. In addition, schools were established for African-Americans as early as 1770 in Philadelphia, 1787 in New York, and 1792 in Baltimore. Nonetheless, it is estimated that in 1865, 90 percent of African-Americans, slave or free, were illiterate.[3] After emancipation, political and economic discrimination together with educational segregation created new obstacles to literacy among the black population.

The Native Americans offer a special case worthy of mention. Many Native American nations resisted white values, customs, and ways. However, members of the Cherokee nation sought to emulate whites by adapting themselves to white ways. They formed a governing body, schools, and a newspaper and owned African slaves. Chief Sequoya developed a syllabary for the Cherokee language. Many people were taught to read, and children attended schools where they learned to read and write Cherokee. On February 21, 1828, their first newspaper, *The Cherokee Phoenix*, written in Cherokee and English, was published. Like the newspapers printed for whites, the Cherokee viewed their newspaper as a source of information about events important to them.[4]

Literacy rates also varied by region in 18th- and 19th-century America. New England, with its more urban demography and commercial base, tended to emphasize schooling and literacy more than the South, which was more rural and almost feudal in its social order. With fewer schools, inhabitants of the western frontier were also less literate, in general, than people of the Northeast. It should be remembered, however, that many pre-20th-century Americans learned to read and write outside of schools, especially at home.

Local community ordinances, however, could make schooling a public, not simply a personal, issue. The Massachusetts Education Act of 1789 allowed for the equal education of males and females. In addition, the law did not prevent the use of public funds to educate African-Americans. Historian Stanley Schultz reports that in Boston at the beginning of the 19th century, few African-American children attended school. Schultz attributed the low attendance patterns to poor economic conditions and overt acts of prejudice experienced by African-American children in schools. In 1798, African-American parents petitioned the school board for separate schools for their children. The request was initially rejected, and then later accepted, by the school board. By the 1820s, however, African-American parents, frustrated by the poor quality of teaching in the segregated schools, began to request that schools be reintegrated. In 1855, the Governor of Massachusetts signed into law an act preventing communities from denying access to school on the basis of race or religious belief.[5]

LITERACY AS A SOCIAL CONSTRUCTION

Past and present literacy rates are not only affected by differences in social class, race, gender, and region; they are also closely tied to social need. To be illiterate in today's culture is to be significantly handicapped in the conduct of everyday affairs, to be so regarded, and to be relegated to the "margins" of mainstream life. This was not so true in earlier centuries, when the everyday requirements for literacy were less demanding. In that predominantly agrarian society, literacy was not so essential to employment and the conduct of daily affairs. In fact, an illiterate person could be a respected and productive member of the rural community.[6] Most people could not vote anyway, for example, and thus were not in that way disadvantaged by illiteracy. Although Jefferson and others considered literacy necessary to the conduct of republican government, it is important to note that in 1800, women, people of African descent, and Native Americans had no voice in government, and only a small minority consisting of white, male property owners was eligible to vote. Nor did religious life depend absolutely on literacy. Bible reading was considered essential in Protestant culture and was therefore an inducement to literacy, but people could participate in religious life without reading. Thus being illiterate in the 18th century, and throughout much of the 19th, did not necessarily mean being handicapped in the pursuit of well-being and full participation in society. The socioeconomic marginality of the illiterate is largely a 20th-century phenomenon, though the valuing of literacy is deeply rooted in western culture.

Nevertheless, all marginalized groups in U.S. history, e.g., African, Asian, Native, and Mexican and their descendants, have desired access to literacy. They have *valued* literacy and education. The history of each group in the United States reveals that they desired to educate themselves, often in the hope of economic and social advancement. Parents did not want to see their children

What counts as adequate literacy is very much dependent on social context. One might be counted as "literate" but not have sufficient literacy skills to succeed in this college economics class, for example.

experience the servitude they had endured. Employers, landowners, or overseers, however, had limited interest in educating the children of workers. They wanted to maintain a cheap source of labor and feared an educated work force. Unlike slaveholders who denied African slaves any access to literacy, however, most employers allowed limited access to literacy. Usually this meant allowing children to be educated up to the sixth or eighth grade. The emphasis in schooling was often on the development of a "good" worker and on vocational training.

What counts as adequate literacy for management might not be adequate from the worker's perspective, and what is adequate literacy in one social setting may not be adequate in another, depending on the function we wish literacy to serve in a given context. For these reasons, among others, the study of literacy has shifted away from simple or "conventional" literacy (reading and writing) to "functional" literacy—that is, the reading and writing skills necessary for functioning in contemporary culture.

FOUR CONTEMPORARY PERSPECTIVES ON LITERACY

Both functional and conventional literacy are limited concepts that fail to capture some important dimensions of literacy. Conventional literacy might tell us whether someone can read a newspaper story, for example, but not whether he or she comprehends the information. Again, a functionally literate person understands the significance of events reported in the daily newspaper—for Jefferson, one of the more important functions of literacy. It is not enough, from this perspective, to be able to read the newspaper; citizens should also be so well informed about their cultural context that the information they encounter makes sense. Such an understanding of the various dimensions of culture may be thought of as *cultural* literacy, and this term is frequently used today.

A final perspective on literacy seeks to go beyond conventional, functional, and cultural views. According to this perspective, people could be literate in all the above ways but still fail to live up to the Jeffersonian ideal of being able to recognize and resist abuses of power by the government and by the wealthy. What is needed is a form of literacy that will empower people to criticize and to emancipate themselves from oppressive social or economic conditions. This view may be considered *critical* or *emancipatory* literacy.

These four different perspectives on literacy—*conventional literacy, functional literacy, cultural literacy,* and *critical literacy*—each express different understandings of schooling, political economy, and ideology. The following sections examine these differences and how each perspective contributes to our understanding of school and society.

Conventional Literacy

Probably the simplest definition of literacy is that which appears in most dictionaries: "the ability to read and write." It is this simple form of literacy that most citizens of the United States have in mind when we think about ourselves as a highly literate nation. After all, virtually the entire population of this country has attended school, where reading and writing are taught in the earliest grades.

This is exactly the reasoning employed by the U.S. Bureau of the Census, which found in the 1980 census, for example, that 99.5 percent of U.S. adults are literate.[7] The Census Bureau defined literacy as "the ability to read and write a simple message in any language." The literacy rate was determined by asking people what grade level they had completed in school, and, for those who completed fewer than five grades, whether they could read. Nearly all the respondents claimed either to have finished the fifth grade or to be able to read anyway. Thus the Census Bureau concluded that only 0.5 percent of the nation's adults are illiterate.

As linguist Shirley Brice Heath notes, many scholars and policymakers have challenged the Census Bureau's findings and its simple definition of literacy.[8] First, its findings are highly suspect because they rely heavily upon written questionnaires and telephone interviews. The former method is very ineffective for reaching the illiterate and the latter method ineffective for reaching the poor, among whom illiteracy is most common.

More damaging to the Census Bureau's findings, however, is its definition of literacy. In the view of Heath and other critics of the conventional literacy perspective, even if people respond that they are able to read and write—the conventional notion of literacy—the most important questions remain unanswered. One unanswered question, for example, is *what* 99.5 percent of U.S adults are able to read and write. If, for example, they can read and write their own names, they can legitimately answer the Census Bureau in the affirmative. This standard, after all, had been used to judge the literacy rates of Americans in the 18th and 19th centuries. But we do not know what level of literacy is reflected in the Census Bureau's data.

Another question not addressed is whether the respondents can read and write in English. For many recent immigrants, particularly adults without access to U.S. education programs, literacy in their own language does not translate into literacy in English. Participation in the economic and political life of an English-speaking society may be as limited for such people as for those who are illiterate in any language. This being so, a further question is raised about defining literacy as the ability to read and write. Of major concern to Heath are "the social meanings of literacy."[9] The ability to read and write in Spanish but not in English, for example, significantly restricts one's options in contemporary American society. Nevertheless, a person so restricted is as literate as the readers of this book, according to the Census Bureau perspective. Similarly, a person who can barely decipher street signs in order to get to work is literate according to the conventional perspective. For a prospective employer or a college admissions committee, such social differences in the meaning of literacy are crucial. Yet these differences are masked by the conventional perspective, which places 99.5 percent of adults in the United States in the same category: literate.

In reality, argues Jonathan Kozol, even by the conventional literacy standard, "well above ten million adult residents of the United States are absolute or nearly absolute illiterates." Despite our government's desire to compare well with other nations in literacy rates, Kozol continues, these ten million "would be judged illiterate by any standard and in any social system."[10] The Census Bureau's approach to literacy obscures such a perspective.

Conventional Literacy: Whose Interests Are Served? The conventional literacy perspective serves some ends better than others. For example, if we want to emphasize the educational progress of the United States in the past two centuries, we could point to a higher literacy rate today than existed in Jefferson's time, taking all regions and income levels into account. That is, compared with a time when many young women and nearly all African descendants and American Indians were excluded from schooling by custom or by law, it is likely that a higher percentage of today's Americans at least know how to sign their names and recognize a few words. Such an observation appears to emphasize the successes of modern schooling rather than the failures.

The conventional literacy perspective is also useful to those who would argue against the need for funding adult education, particularly adult literacy education today. When a literacy rate of 99.5 percent is cited, the need for literacy and adult education programs seems less than urgent. Such a conception of literacy allows us to overlook or to minimize the barely literate condition of many poverty-level adults, whether domestic whites, recent immigrants, or domestic ethnic minorities. If there are indeed several million such adults in our society, our social and educational system is serving some segments of the population very poorly, and significant remedial steps might well be in order. Those who wish to minimize such social programs naturally prefer the government's definition of literacy, while those who would expand social programs prefer a richer, more complex definition that is better able to differentiate among people's literacy skills.

The conventional literacy perspective does not focus on the vast differences in literacy that prevail among different population groups in the United States. African-Americans, Latinos, Asian Americans, Native Americans, recent immigrants from Europe and elsewhere, and the poor of all ethnic backgrounds call attention to the fact that some population groups in our society are much more literate than others and that these differences greatly influence their lives. By claiming that virtually everyone in society is literate, we obscure important questions about levels of literacy among the various groups in our society and what this means in terms of social benefits and costs. In sum, the conventional literacy perspective appears to emphasize social and educational progress and to obscure the social and educational inequalities that other conceptions of literacy might reveal.

Functional Literacy

Shifting definitions of literacy have helped to obscure accurate literacy rates. In addition, the age of adulthood is often defined differently in different surveys of adult literacy. Historically, the early U.S. Census reports consisted of self-reports of white male adults who responded to questions regarding their ability to read and write. Later, white female adults were allowed to offer self-reports. More recent surveys of adult literacy include self-reports of English and non-English speakers, who respond to similar questions of the ability to read or write without clarifying in which language they are literate. The latest report of adult literacy, offered in 1993 by the National Center for Education Statistics, redefined literacy beyond reading and writing; asked participants to complete tasks; defined an adult as someone 16 years of age or older; and scored responses in a range of literacy achievement. The definition of literacy used in the survey is illustrative of the shifting concerns about literacy. In the report, literacy is defined as "using printed and written information to function in society, to achieve one's goals, and to develop one's knowledge and potential."[11] This report, the National Adult Literacy Survey (NALS), provides recent data on 26,000 adults and will be referred to at several points in this chapter.

One well-known early effort to investigate functional literacy was conducted in the mid-1970s at the University of Texas using an index called the adult performance level (APL).[12] The APL project tested how well adults could function in 65 tasks requiring literacy skills in everyday life. From 20 to 60 percent of those tested failed to perform successfully at tasks such as writing a check that a bank would process, addressing an envelope adequately, figuring the difference in price between a new and a used appliance, making change for a purchase, matching personal qualifications to a written job application, and determining whether a paycheck was correct. The APL researchers concluded that 30 million people are "functionally incompetent" and that another 54 million "just get by." Author Jonathan Kozol, in his recent book, *Illiterate America,* argues that approximately 60 million people cannot read well enough to understand the antidote instructions on a bottle of kitchen lye, the instructions on a federal income tax return, or the questions on a life insurance form. He writes that these 60 million people are "illiterate in terms of U.S. print media at the present time." In other words, one-third of the adult population is functionally illiterate. The more recent NALS findings suggest that Kozol's figures may somewhat overstate functional illiteracy in the nation today, but that 40 to 44 million adults function at the lowest of five levels of literacy identified.[13]

The origin of the term *functional literacy* tells something important about its nature. The term was first used by the U.S. Army during World War II to mean "the capability to understand written instructions necessary for conducting basic military functions and tasks . . . a fifth-grade reading level." Rather than using a fixed definition of literacy such as the ability to read and write, the Army recognized that literacy needed a definition that was adjustable to particular contexts. If a recruit could read and write, but not well enough to function in the context of the written materials provided by the Army, then that recruit was judged functionally illiterate.[14]

Because functional literacy is conceived with respect to particular social contexts, being functionally literate may differ greatly in different societies. This makes functional literacy difficult to define with precision. The United Nations suggested the following definition in 1971: "A person is literate when he has acquired the essential knowledge and skills which enable him to engage in all those activities in which literacy is required for effective functioning in his group or community."[15] The Literacy Volunteers of America, Inc., also invokes the notion of "effective functioning" in its definition of functional literacy:

> Functional literacy relates to the ability of an individual to use reading, writing, and computational skills in everyday life situations. For example, a functionally illiterate adult is unable to fill out an application, read a medicine bottle [or] newspaper, locate a telephone number in a directory, use a bus schedule or do quality comparison shopping. In short, when confronted with printed materials, such people cannot function effectively.[16]

Such definitions, although leaving open what it means to "function effectively," do help raise important questions about society and education. For example, the functional literacy perspective shows how social groups differ in literacy rates, something the conventional literacy perspective obscures. The APL study, for example, suggested that now, just as in Jefferson's time, gender affects the chances of being literate: About 23 percent of women over the age of 18 were identified as functionally illiterate, compared with 17 percent of men. The more recent NALS data, however, did not confirm these gender differences, except in quantitative literacy activities.[17]

Perhaps more disturbing are the differences in literacy among different ethnic groups. The APL study indicated that 16 percent of white people, 44 percent of black people, and 56 percent of Latinos over the age of 18 are functionally illiterate. Although the illiteracy rate among minority youth is lower than that among adults, it is still scandalous. The President's Commission on Excellence in Education estimates illiteracy among minority youth to be as high as 40 percent, whereas the figure for school-age youth in general is only 13 percent. Jonathan Kozol reported 1985 figures suggesting that 50 percent of all African-American 17-year-olds would be functionally illiterate by 1990 unless the trend was somehow reversed.[18] Definitive data are not yet available on youth literacy in the 90s, and Kozol's bleak prediction has not been verified thus far. The National Assessment of Educational Progress, however, issued a 1992 report, based on a nationally representative sample, which described increases in literacy and improvement in reading for students aged 9 and 17 since their 1971 report. They also reported little change in performance for students in a middle group, 13-year-olds.

Data on social class and literacy levels are difficult to obtain, but it is significant that both the poverty and illiteracy rates for African-Americans and Latinos are much higher than for the white population. This trend is reflected in *The Reading Report Card,* which indicates that fewer than one out of five "disadvantaged urban" high school seniors can read at the 12th-grade level and that only one out of four can read as high as the 7th-grade level.[19] As poor as these literacy levels are, they are much worse for the urban youth who have already dropped out of school—and the dropout rate for many inner-city schools exceeds 50 percent. Among "urban advantaged" high school seniors, by contrast, about 50 percent are reading at the 12th-grade level and only 7 percent are reading as low as the 7th-grade level. The incidence of functional illiteracy in the latter group is near zero. About 40 percent of adults with incomes under $5,000 are functionally illiterate, in contrast to 8 percent of adults with incomes over $15,000. The 1993 NALS reported that over 40 percent of all adults in the lowest literacy levels "were living in poverty, compared with only 4 to 8 percent of those in the two highest proficiency levels." Consequently, it is safe to say that social class and literacy acquisition go hand in hand.[20]

Limitations of the Functional Literacy Perspective The value of the functional literacy perspective is that it shows how our society educates (in terms of literacy, at least) different social groups to different degrees. There are, however, limits to this approach. Despite his own use of the functional perspective to illustrate the severe problems of illiteracy in the United States, Jonathan Kozol argues against the term *functional.* He writes, "If there is a single word we would do well to wipe away from the vocabulary of a literate society, it is the invidious modifier 'functional.' It is a bad word, chosen by technicians but unfortunately accepted without protest by the humanistic scholar and the pedagogic world alike."[21] Kozol's basic objection to the functional literacy perspective is that it denotes, as a goal, "the competence to function at the lowest levels of mechanical performance," instead of indicating a more ambitious conception of literacy. Certainly Jefferson, for example, did not have only minimum competence in mind when he described the connections between literacy and a free society.

Indeed the functional literacy perspective tends to frame desirable functions in very mechanical ways. The APL study, for example, emphasized the importance of effective functioning in five spheres of understanding and activity: consumer, occupational, health, government and law, and community resources. Nowhere is it indicated that "effective functioning" might include the ability to think critically and creatively about changes in such arenas. Instead the emphasis is on becoming competent in the basic skills these arenas require.

Educator Colin Lankshear and others have added to Kozol's criticism of the functional literacy perspective. A second limitation on this perspective, according to Lankshear, is its tendency to blame the victims of social inequality for illiteracy. The emphasis tends to fall on the personal deficiency of the illiterate person. Consequently, the concept of functional illiteracy, in practice, tends to initiate illiterate people into a powerful series of assumptions:

(i) The problem is within me. If I cannot get a job, or the job I want, it's because of something about me rather than something about the world (such as a shrinking or shifting labor market, or an economic crisis);

(ii) If others do better than I do, that is because they are better than I am. If I want to do as well, then I have to improve. The "game" or "race" itself is proper, legitimate, beyond question. I'm just not a sufficiently skilled or competitive "player";

(iii) To get better I will have to have my faults diagnosed and be taught how to improve. Others have this knowledge. It is not for me to determine the problem or the cure.[22]

In sum, says Lankshear, the functional literacy perspective leads people to see the illiterate person as someone who must be improved by others. This view, Lankshear argues, is "an initiation into passivity." It also implies that the illiterate person need only be trained to the minimum work levels that industry needs. Who does this benefit most, the learner or industry? Lankshear asks.

This limitation of the functional perspective becomes apparent in popular news articles on illiteracy that portray illiteracy as a threat to institutions—"The Scourge of Adult Illiteracy," as *The New York Times* put it.[23]

Popular news stories warn that illiteracy is so high that soon "there won't be enough people equipped to handle complex new technology," and that "these functional illiterates exact a high national price" in terms of the costs of welfare and unemployment compensation. Or, as Barbara Bush, wife of former President George Bush, argued, "Most people don't know we spend 6.6 billion dollars a year to keep 750,000 illiterates in jail. I'm trying to remind people that there's a direct correlation between crime and illiteracy, between illiteracy and unemployment."[24] These comments emphasize that functional illiteracy is dysfunctional for society. It is a "social disease that affects us all," proclaims an advertisement by Gulf & Western Corporation. To help people become functionally literate, from this perspective, is to indicate how they can help institutions to function better. Educator Neil Postman notes in this connection that "some minimal reading skill is necessary if you are to be a 'good citizen,' but 'good citizen' here means one who can follow the instructions of those who govern him."[25]

The New York Times.
LATE CITY EDITION
NEW YORK, SATURDAY, JUNE 17, 1933. TWO CENTS
PRESIDENT STARTS RECOVERY PROGRAM, SIGNS BANK, RAIL AND INDUSTRY BILLS; WHEAT GROWERS WILL GET $150,000,000
REICH ASKS RETURN OF AFRICAN LANDS AT LONDON PARLEY
COMMON COLD LAID TO 2 AGENTS UNITED
KIDNAPPERS SEIZE ST. PAUL BREWER
AIDS FARMERS THIS YEAR
Powers Granted to the President
ROOSEVELT HAILS GOAL
WIDE WORK SPREAD ASKED BY JOHNSON
TREASURY TO ORDER $25,000,000 WORK
Roosevelt Takes Special Train for Boston To Embark on Vacation Voyage 'Down East'

To what degree does "functional literacy" help one to make adequate interpretations of headlines from a 1930s New York Times? What might "cultural literacy" bring to bear? "Critical literacy"?

In general, critics of the functional literacy perspective decry what they see as an overemphasis on the mechanical skills of reading and writing necessary to conform to the requirements of modern institutions. They would prefer to see the meaning of literacy expanded to include the conceptual sophistication necessary to understand and critically evaluate those institutions. To be able only to meet the objectives of functional literacy as articulated by the APL team, writes Lankshear, "is precisely to be inducted into the values of a competitive capitalist consumer society."[26]

Lankshear does not mean that educators should avoid vocational preparation for contemporary society. He merely wishes to caution against limiting the perspective of literacy to a mechanical and conformist one that ignores the critical capacities that Jefferson, for example, so highly valued.

Functional literacy, as popularly understood, seems to emphasize the mechanics of reading and writing rather than their value to a life lived richly and freely. Functional literacy would seem to emphasize the ability to read a newspaper rather than to understand all the historical, political, and cultural references made therein. Such a perspective seems to limit literacy to functioning within existing institutions rather than enabling people to become active participants in shaping institutions for human ends.

Two other perspectives on literacy have been developed in an effort to overcome the limitations of the functional perspective. The more conservative of the two has become known as cultural literacy, while the more radical of the two may be regarded as critical or emancipatory literacy.

Cultural Literacy

Recognizing the limitations of the functional literacy perspective, scholars such as De Castell, Luke, and MacLennan have called for a conception of literacy that takes into account particular cultural contexts and "the broader literacy needs for social and political practice, as determined by the needs of any truly participatory democracy."[27] Perhaps the most prominent effort to describe a conception of literacy consistent with the cultural context and democratic ideals of U.S. schools is E. D. Hirsch, Jr.'s best-selling 1987 book *Cultural Literacy*. Hirsch deplores any conception of literacy that reflects only a technical "skills orientation" to reading. In a related article written for educators, Hirsch argues that language cannot be disentangled from the cultural knowledge and understandings that give language meaning. Thus, "if one believes in literacy, one must also believe in *cultural* literacy."[28] Hirsch claims that his conception of cultural literacy goes beyond the technical reading of functional literacy to embrace the democratic ideals of Thomas Jefferson and Martin Luther King. His critics, of course, disagree.[29]

Hirsch argues (as educational philosopher Harry S. Broudy has argued for many years) that the writers of newspapers, books, magazines, and other scripted material assume certain background knowledge shared by readers.[30] Being able to read words on paper is only "the tip of the iceberg" of real literacy for Hirsch, because true literacy depends on *understanding* those words, and such understanding depends on a great deal of background knowledge of cultural institutions and values. To illustrate Hirsch's point, consider the knowledge a person would need in order to make sense of the following headlines from the front page of *The New York Times* on May 4, 1997:

- New York City Celebrates a Century of Uneasy Unity
- Zairian President is Ready to Quit, U.S. Diplomats Say
- Separatists End Texas Standoff as 5 Surrender
- Crews are Scarce to Put Up Towers for New Digital TV
- Deletion of Word in Welfare Bill Opens Foster Care to Big Business

To make sense of these headlines, a person must have more than the technical skill of decoding text. Some background knowledge, or contextual knowledge, is needed. To be able to interpret these headlines meaningfully, and to make sense of the stories beneath them, an individual would have to understand something about the history of urban consolidation and centralization; U.S. relations with political leadership in Africa; the history of Texas's independence from the United States; new television technology; and why government aid to nonprofit (the word deleted from the bill) social service agencies is a very different policy from government aid to social service agencies run for a profit. The authors of the articles themselves do not explain all these things, but instead assume a great deal of background knowledge in the reader. Writers are justified in assuming such background knowledge, says Hirsch, for it is part of the culture of literate people in our society—and it is this literature culture that makes communication effective.

Education for cultural literacy, then, is not merely a matter of teaching people to read and write. Hirsch is one among many who argue that education must provide people with a basic knowledge foundation to give meaning to the words they read. This basic information should include historical names and events, geographical places, authors and works from national and world literature, patriotic songs, nursery rhymes, and much more—all of which in Hirsch's terms are a part of readers' "intellectual baggage."

as a set of skills for merely functioning in existing society, or as a way to become "culturally literate," but rather as a means to understand, express, and change the social relations that favor some people at the expense of others. Giroux, Kozol, Shor, and others recognize that those who are unable to read and write are easily victimized by a society that values reading and writing so highly. But learning to read and write will not in itself prevent such victimization. For critical literacy to exist, there must be a combination of critical understandings and actions together with the ability to use the language tools of the dominant culture. A critical consciousness, while of primary importance, is not enough; it must be accompanied by reading and writing skills, which have the potential to enhance personal and social liberation. Donaldo Macedo writes that the radical educator "will enable students to become literate in their culture as well as in the codes of the dominant classes." Freire elaborates on this point using the illustration of black students in U.S. schools:

> The successful usage of the students' cultural universe requires respect and legitimation of students' discourse, that is, their own linguistic codes, which are different but never inferior . . . In the case of black Americans, for example, educators must respect black English . . . The legitimation of black English as an educational tool does not, however, preclude the need to acquire proficiency in the linguistic code of the dominant group.[49]

A tension clearly exists here. What balance should the critical perspective seek between criticism of the dominant culture on the one hand and learning its "linguistic code" on the other? Such tension is inherent, from the critical literacy perspective, in learning both to "read the world" critically and to "read the word," which may be uncritical and biased. Without the critical reading of the unequal power relations that structure society, however, literacy does not realize its essential value of liberating the literate—at least in the critical literacy perspective. Contemporary curriculum theorist Cameron McCarthy is among those who argue that teachers can effectively engage students in examining how knowledge is produced and sustained in U.S. schools and the wider cultures and that such an investigation will necessarily have to consider relations of power in the wider culture.[50]

In the educational reform movement of the 1980s, a great many different "literacies" were advocated: functional literacy, computer literacy, civic literacy, aesthetic literacy, and so on. Each use of the term *literacy* focuses on a different realm of learning that its advocates wish to designate is as fundamental to education as the three Rs. Using the word *literacy* seems to accomplish this. As a result, the term is often used to mean that which the one using it believes should be learned. Thus, the meaning of the term becomes altered in ways that serve different social and educational aims.

From this perspective, one can see what kind of education is being promoted by the advocates of each kind of literacy treated in this chapter. Those who advocate functional literacy want people to function in society's existing social and economic roles; those who promote cultural literacy want a greater understanding of the established culture; those who advocate critical literacy focus on empowering people to criticize and change political and economic oppression. There are no advocates of conventional literacy as an educational goal because it is so minimal. Are all these perspectives on literacy equally good and valuable? Now that we have examined how they fit into different educational orientations, how can we use them?

The usefulness of the various perspectives on literacy depends on the goal we have in mind. For example, if we want to provide evidence of the successes of the U.S. social and educational systems, the conventional literacy perspective is the most useful and valuable, because it indicates that illiteracy has been virtually eliminated in the United States. Yet we have seen that this perspective obscures the way illiteracy and power are distributed among the various social groups in this country.

If our goal is to measure people's ability to function at a minimum level within existing social and economic institutions, the functional literacy perspective will seem most valuable. However, we have seen that this perspective tends to settle for a minimum-skill view of literacy that does not attend to higher-order thinking and that may promote passivity in the learner. Further, there is reason to question this view because it seems to locate the source of illiteracy primarily in individuals themselves rather than in the larger social order—a social order that seems systematically to allocate illiteracy to some socioeconomic groups but not to others.

If the goal is to promote familiarity with the traditional knowledge base of our culture, then the cultural literacy perspective would seem to be appropriate. But here again, questions must be raised. Cultural literacy appears to value traditional knowledge that has historically minimized attention to African-Americans, Hispanics, women, and working-class people. Further, the cultural literacy view seems to encourage a passive learning of random, unintegrated knowledge, rather than an ability to think critically and deeply about the relationships within that body of knowledge. Finally, the content and processes of such learning have historically been very ineffective for educating the lower socioeconomic groups of U.S. society. Consequently, if the cultural literacy perspective is to be of benefit, it might be regarded as a necessary but not sufficient insight into the reality that those who succeed in the dominant culture have a working knowledge of the "cultural capital" of that culture.

Finally, if the goal is to emphasize the relationship between literacy and empowerment, the critical literacy perspective seems most valuable. It begins with the notion that power is unequally and undemocratically distributed in contemporary society; it emphasizes that those in power define *their* knowledge as the most worthwhile; it recognizes that traditional definitions of literacy serve the interests of those who have the greatest wealth and power, not those who have the least; and it asserts that literacy should help those with the least power to understand these relationships and act to change them. Paulo Freire has long practiced such an approach to literacy in Brazil and elsewhere, but the practice of critical literacy in the United States lags behind the theory.

We can evaluate the different literacy perspectives, then, by reference to various goals. It is therefore important to evaluate these perspectives carefully. How might different components of each one serve the interests of urban schoolchildren? An urban teacher or school that embraces a functional literacy perspective may be largely satisfied if all students can read at the sixth-grade level when they graduate from high school, for such students will be able to function in society. But the teacher who embraces cultural literacy might ask, "What understandings do such students have of western civilization, of U.S. economic, social, and political institutions? Enough to participate as citizens and voters, or only enough to choose the best buy at the supermarket?" And the teacher of critical literacy could ask, "And what if students *did* have such knowledge of historical and contemporary institutions? Whose interests would such knowledge serve: their own interests in becoming equal participants in political life or the interests of those who benefit from leaving political power and participation unequal?" Different perspectives on literacy reflect different educational aims.

It is instructive at this point to reflect upon Thomas Jefferson's view of the importance of literacy in the United States (see Chapter 2). Clearly Jefferson thought literacy was important for the everyday reading and writing, buying and selling functions that people had to do at that time. He also valued literacy for the cultural understanding it made possible; he advocated the teaching of history, for example, in the elementary grades. And Jefferson clearly prized the cultural achievements of civilized humanity; he valued reading the works considered classics for the pleasure of learning and enjoyment of literature.

But Jefferson was not satisfied with a literacy that was restricted to everyday functioning and cultural appreciation, though he valued these. He argued that literacy was necessary for political power and freedom, and particularly necessary for guarding against undemocratic abuses of power. In proclaiming that "knowledge is power," Jefferson was recognizing a relationship between knowledge and power that the critical literacy theorists of today have elaborated upon and extended. Unlike the critical theorists, however, Jefferson was content to allow members of the nonmajority culture to be excluded from the benefits of literacy and the benefits of power. Nor was he sensitive to the potential of a genuine cultural pluralism that honored the cultures of people of color. According to historian Ronald Takaki, "Jefferson had envisioned . . . a nation of racially homogeneous people covering the entire continent."[51]

Jefferson recognized that literacy is in part minimum reading, writing, and computational skills, and he thought that these skills could be taught to most students in 3 years of elementary instruction. He did not think, however, that it was enough to employ such skills mechanically; he did not settle for a conception of learning that overlooked the relationship between literacy and liberty. Similarly, both the cultural literacy perspective and the critical literacy perspective claim to preserve an indispensable relationship between liberty and literacy, yet they do so in different ways. The cultural literacy perspective emphasizes traditions of representative government and participation in established institutions. The critical literacy perspective asserts that these institutions are themselves constituted undemocratically, and that only by developing a critical perspective on power and knowledge can literacy serve the goal of political and economic liberty for all citizens, not just the privileged classes.

Jefferson believed he had articulated a conception of literacy that, for his own time, was consistent with democratic ideals. There is one question we may ask of each perspective on literacy examined in this chapter: "To what degree is it consistent with democratic ideals in our own time and place?" It is a question we may rightfully ask of any educational approach in our society, and one that recurs in various forms throughout the remainder of this text.

HEGEMONY THEORY: LITERACY AND IDEOLOGY[52]

While Thomas Jefferson believed that popular literacy could ensure the democratic distribution of power, the 20th century has witnessed power flowing into business and government in ways that he could not have foreseen. Especially since World War II, the complex relationship between corporate power and the mass media requires a reexamination of the relations between liberty and literacy in the United States today.

In 1961, two events revealed contrasting assessments of power in the United States: the publication of Robert Dahl's *Who Governs?* and President Dwight Eisenhower's farewell address to the nation.[53] Dahl's book was a major contribution to the pluralist school that dominated political science in this country during the 1950s. Pluralists argued that, despite being governed by a very small group of decision makers, modern societies are consistent with democratic ideals so long as the governing groups represent competing political interests and are accountable by election to the general population. That this normative account of democracy described political conditions in the United States was virtually an article of faith in the pluralist camp, and *Who Governs?* was intended to provide empirical data to bolster that faith.

It came as some surprise, then, that President Eisenhower would warn the nation in 1961 of "the potential for the disastrous rise of misplaced power" of a "military-industrial complex" under which "public policy itself could become the captive of a scientific technological elite."[54] Whereas Dahl's work strengthened our traditional view of political power, Eisenhower's speech echoed the leftist critique of power that C. Wright Mills had advanced 5 years earlier in *The Power Elite*.[55] In Mills's analysis, which the pluralists took pains to reject, the important power in the United States was concentrated in the hands of an elitist group made up of those in leadership positions in government, the military, and the corporate establishment. For Mills, this elite was neither open to competition from other interests nor significantly accountable to the citizenry. Eisenhower was warning the nation, in effect, that Mills was closer to the truth than the pluralists cared to admit.

To what degree is the exercise of power in contemporary society "open"? In *Who's Running America?*, first published in 1976 and then revised during the Carter and Reagan administrations, Thomas Dye agrees with Mills that power resides not primarily in individuals, but in institutions.[56] Dye's approach provides a concrete look at the most powerful positions in three major sectors of American society: corporate, public interest, and government. By identifying the most powerful positions in each of the top 100 industrial corporations, the top 50 utilities, communications, and transportation companies, the top 50 banks, the top 50 insurance companies, and the top 15 investment firms, Dye finds that 4,325 positions carry extraordinary influence in the corporate sector. In the public interest sector, he identifies 2,705 positions in the mass media, in education, in philanthropic foundations, in the most prestigious law firms, and in civic and cultural organizations. In the government sector, Dye identifies the most

President Dwight D. Eisenhower along with social analysts such as C. Wright Mills and Thomas Dye have warned of an undemocratic power elite that controls the major institutions of this country.

influential committee positions in Congress, the most powerful positions in the legislative and executive branches, and the key positions in the military for a total of 284 government positions. The total from these three sectors is 7,314 positions that, according to Dye, wield the major decision-making power in the most influential institutions in political and economic life.

The influence of these institutions and of those who run them is remarkable in Dye's account. The positions in Dye's list control, for example, over half the nation's industrial assets, over half the utilities, banking, and transportation assets, over two-thirds of the nation's insurance assets, over half the endowed assets in the nation's private colleges and universities, one-third of the nation's daily newspaper circulation, and over nine-tenths of broadcast news. In addition, these positions dominate the legal field and investments and securities, all the major standing committees in the House and Senate, the Supreme Court, and the four branches of the military. These are the positions occupied by those whom Mills called "the power elite" and whom Prewitt and Stone have more recently called "the ruling elite."

In *Power and Powerlessness,* John Gaventa found that his efforts to study the power relations in an Appalachian community required asking "not why rebellion occurs in a 'democracy' but why, in the face of massive inequalities, it does not."[57] It is tempting to ask similarly of U.S. society in general: If power relations are as undemocratic as elite theorists describe, why do citizens not only accept it, but continue to think of the social order as democratic? Answering this question raises issues that are fundamentally educational in character.

If the concentration of power has been accurately portrayed by elite theorists, what are the educational consequences? First, it is necessary to miseducate a population in important ways for people to perceive a nondemocratic society as democratic, thereby sustaining unequal power relations. Second, the processes of participating in such a society are not as educational as Jefferson, Dewey, and others would have us believe. Each of these points will be treated in turn.

The theory that best contributes to our understanding of how society miseducates in order to sustain nondemocratic power relations is that of ideological hegemony. The term "hegemony" refers to unequal power relationships between two or more cultures, ideologies, socioeconomic groups, and so on. Since there is no single, definitive account of ideological hegemony theory, it is regarded as one of the most suspect collections of concepts in the social sciences. Some formulations are better than others, however, and the intent of this section is to provide a coherent account of the available literature. T. Jackson Lear's essay on cultural hegemony is an exemplary discussion, and parts of this account rely on his treatment.[58]

The first thing to note about hegemony theory is that, like all theories, it is an effort to explain selected facts. These general facts appear to be most relevant in contemporary society: The United States is made up of many individuals and groups with different and often conflicting interests; the social order benefits some groups far more than others, in terms of health, wealth, access to positions of power, and freedom to pursue personal interests. Despite conflicting interests and differing benefits, U.S. society is a very orderly one, with stable economic, government, and social institutions and a class structure that has not appreciably changed throughout the 20th century. This stable social order is maintained not at gunpoint or through threat of force, but through the cooperation of its citizenry. Hegemony theorists seek to explain the basis of this cooperation as the foundation of the social world itself.

A first attempt to explain hegemonic social order might be expressed this way: A small minority of U.S. citizens control the political and economic institutions that shape the civic beliefs, values, and behavior of most of the population. In contrast to traditional democratic theory, which holds that the social order is based on public consensus, ideological hegemony argues that the social, political, and economic institutions of this society serve a relatively small group at the expense of the majority of citizens. Hegemony theory can be summarized in four general propositions, each of which requires further development:

1. Institutional elites who share common economic and political interests control the dominant political and economic institutions of the United States.
2. Though they may disagree on particular policies or strategies, these institutional elites share a common world view, or ideology, which reflects and justifies the organization of dominant institutions.
3. Through such institutions as the government, the workplace, the school, and the mass media, the general populace is socialized into accepting these ruling ideas.
4. Although ruling ideas do not reflect the experience of all social classes, they serve to limit discussion and debate, to prevent the formation of alternative social explanations, and to promote a general acceptance of the status quo.

It is not possible to document all the ways in which various social institutions structure experience to legitimize the dominant ideology, but we can examine two institutions that have particularly concerned hegemony theorists: the popular media and the schools. These two institutions are particularly important to hegemony theorists because they explicitly communicate ideological perspectives to the general population. It is valuable in this regard to recall Jefferson's high regard for both newspapers and schools as pillars of a democratic society. Jefferson's faith in a free marketplace of ideas led him to claim that newspapers were even more important to democracy than government. Cultural hegemony theorists argue that we now have reason to doubt the effectiveness of both the news media and the schools in preserving democratic understandings and lifestyles.

Mass Media and Cultural Hegemony

The news media report a great many negatives about American society, but these criticisms nearly always stay within clearly acceptable bounds. For example, even though criticisms often address problems faced by American institutions, they do not address problems in the institutions themselves. The media may criticize how the game is being played but it never questions the rules of the game itself. A few detailed examples can illustrate this point.

Reports on the domestic economy of the United States often point out unemployment, job layoffs, welfare cuts, and the flight of corporations to third-world nations. This is presented as bad news, but the American public is given no way of understanding how such bad news is an inevitable outcome of the structure of corporate capitalism itself. A structural critique would examine how unemployment is built into our capitalist system and how it benefits capitalists by keeping workers in competition with one another for scarce jobs. Such a critique could show how the interests of corporate owners makes it rational for them to sometimes act against the interests of the workers—for example, by investing their profits in the less expensive work forces of foreign countries rather than in industries that would benefit workers in the United States.

Similarly, with respect to foreign policy, Americans are often treated to the supposedly bad news that developing countries are turning to socialism and communism, are told that this is a threat to the national interest of the United States, and are informed that the United States must intervene in the affairs of these nations with military force if necessary. What the public does not hear is what constitutes our national interest in these developing nations. History has shown that we can tolerate deep differences in ideology with our business partners in the third world. In fact, we have come under much international criticism for our support of tyrannical regimes that violate human rights as an ongoing part of their domestic policy. Ideological differences are claimed to threaten our national interest primarily when developing nations will not give U.S. corporations a free rein in developing the natural resources and labor markets of those nations for the profit of U.S. corporations.

Given our present economic structure, the interests of labor are dependent upon the interests of capitalists, and the interests of capitalists are best met, as they themselves proclaim, by developing third-world labor markets. Thus what is represented as our national interest is largely determined by the interests of corporate directors who readily abandon the American worker for cheap foreign labor and who support a foreign policy that ultimately relies on the American worker to die in foreign battles to protect the interests of capitalists. This perspective, which has been developed by a number of scholars in the United States and abroad, is typically not made available to the American public through the news media.[59] News corporations in America are, after all, capitalist institutions; their interests would be threatened if they alienated advertisers who depend upon current American foreign policy for their profits. Further, representatives of U.S. multinational corporations serve as directors of major U.S. news corporations.

When Thomas Jefferson argued that daily newspapers were so essential to democratic life that he would rather see a society without government than a society without newspapers, he had no way of knowing that multinational corporations would one day control the public's exposure to the media. The most extensive treatment of this relatively recent development is *The Media Monopoly,* written by Ben H. Bagdikian, a Pulitzer Prize-winning journalist and professor of journalism at the University of California, Berkeley. Bagdikian writes:

> At the end of World War II . . . 80 percent of the daily newspapers in the United States were independently owned, but by 1989 the proportion was reversed, with 80 percent owned by corporate chains. In 1981 twenty corporations controlled most of the business of the country's 11,000 magazines, but only seven years later that number had shrunk to three corporations.[60]

For Jefferson, the notion of a "free marketplace of ideas" was predicated on a diverse array of privately owned newspapers and pamphlets with competitive points of view. Each citizen would be free to accept or reject those publications on the basis of how well his or her own interests were reflected. In a controlled marketplace of ideas, however, such choice has largely evaporated. Bagdikian notes that "in order to have the power of rejection, the public needs real choices and choice is inoperative where there is monopoly, which is the case in 98 percent of the daily newspaper business, or market dominance of the few, which is the case with television and most other mass media"[61]

It is not only newspapers and magazines that have fallen into such concentrated ownership. Bagdikian notes that this pattern has permeated all the mass media. For example:

> There are fourteen dominant companies that have half or more of the daily newspaper business (seven years ago there were twenty), three in magazines (seven years ago there were twenty), three in television (seven years ago there were three), six in book publishing (seven years ago there were eleven), and four in motion picture production (seven years ago there were four).[62]

Astoundingly, only 17 companies receive half or more of all revenue from media sources, including recording, cable, and videocassettes. What is so dangerous about such concentration of ownership, for Bagdikian, is that it severely restricts the range of viewpoints that can be found in public debate. Those who control the decision making in these corporations rose to their positions in part because they embrace business values that influence the ideological content of the media. When dealing with the dominant profit orientation of the United States, the media serve as a vehicle for one point of view largely to the exclusion of others.

> Today, the chief executive officers of the twenty-three corporations that control most of what Americans read and see can fit into an ordinary living room. Almost without exception they are economic conservatives. They can, if they wish, use control of their newspapers, broadcast stations, magazines, books, and movies to promote their own corporate values to the exclusion of others. When their corporate interests are at stake—in taxes, regulation, and antitrust action—they use that power in their selection of news, and in the private lobbying power peculiar to those who control the media image—or nonimage—of politicians.[63]

Bagdikian's analysis of the importance of daily newspapers to democratic life is very similar to Jefferson's. He believes that only local papers can be expected to present any kind of in-depth account of issues confronting citizens in their local communities, where the most direct democratic participation can take place. Yet most local communities, even urban areas, don't even have a local paper. Bagdikian writes: "No national paper or broadcast station can report adequately the issues and candidates in every one of the 65,000 local voting districts. Only locally based journalism can do it, and if it does not, voters become captives of the only alternative information, paid political propaganda, or have no information at all."[64] He continues by noting that the number of U.S. newspapers declined at the same time that the number of urban communities increased: "In 1920 there were 2,722 urban places and 2,400 daily papers in the country. By 1980 there were 8,765 urban places and only 1,745 dailies. Today more than 7,000 American cities have no daily paper of their own."[65]

In 1930 there were 132 newspapers sold daily per 100 households in the United States. By 1965, the number was reduced to 111 papers per 100 households, and in 1986 the number had declined to 72.[66] Bagdikian reports that the 1982 edition of the *World Press Encyclopedia* ranked the United States 20th in papers sold per person, with only 272 daily papers sold per 1,000 population. This compares, for example, with 572 sold per 1,000 people in Sweden, 526 in Japan, 472 in East Germany, and 447 in Luxembourg, to cite the top four. UNESCO's 1990 *Statistical Yearbook* shows that by 1990 the United States had fallen still farther behind the leading nations.[67]

Of course, the pervasiveness of television has contributed to the decline of newspaper circulation in the United States, but this is not encouraging news. Ownership of television stations, even when cable TV is taken into account, is more concentrated than ownership of newspapers, and the intellectual and critical content of TV programs is less than that of newspapers. Bagdikian notes that "the three networks still have more than two-thirds of the audience." And again, the ideological content of television is predictably conservative. For example, General Electric, owner of RCA and the National Broadcasting Company, is the 10th largest U.S. corporation and a major defense contractor. It could hardly be expected that such a corporation would present points of view that would vary significantly from the dominant ideology.[68] Jefferson's "free marketplace of ideas" becomes difficult to find in such a media climate.

Reporters themselves tend to operate in a closed circle that ignores ideological perspectives that would enable them to understand the hegemony process itself. One Gallup poll showed that print and broadcast journalists receive the bulk of their information on domestic and foreign policy from other journalists in mainstream news media that represent the dominant corporate-government ideology. From 60 to 90 percent of media journalists read *Newsweek, Time,* local daily papers, and *The Wall Street Journal,* but only 3 percent of broadcast journalists and 7 percent of print journalists read the reputable leftist weekly *The Nation.* It is notable that of the 28 publications listed by journalists as their media sources of information, only *The Nation* can be considered leftist in orientation, unless *Rolling Stone* magazine fits the leftist description as well.[69]

There is much more that could be written—and has been written—about the ways in which the communications media have institutionalized violations of a free marketplace of ideas. And the news media perhaps make up a smaller part of that picture than do the entertainment media. Todd Gitlin is one of several writers who have described the ways in which television programming, apparently designed for entertainment, reinforces rather than questions the dominant ideology.[70]

Further, it can be argued that it is not just the messages on television that affect people's ability to think about their culture. The technology itself may have an impact on our ability to develop the literacy skills to read deeply and critically. A U.S. government study, for example, showed that:

> Students who watched 3 or fewer hours of television a day showed higher levels of reading proficiency than those who watched 6 or more hours each day. In 1994, 57 percent of 4th-graders and 59 percent of 8th-graders watched 3 or fewer hours daily, while 75 percent of 12th graders did so.[71]

While it might be marginally encouraging that most (barely) fourth graders watched television three hours or less a day, the percent of U.S. 13-year-olds who watch 5 or more hours of TV per day was 20, as compared to 5 percent in France, 7 percent in Switzerland, 10 percent in Taiwan, and 11 percent in Korea. Interestingly, the same percentage of adults in the U.S., in a 1994 international reading assessment of adult literacy, scored at the lowest level of text reading, and nearly 24 percent fell into the lowest level of comprehending documents.[72] But the role of communications technologies in society's literacy development is complex and difficult to analyze, especially given the rapid pace of change. Nowhere is this more vivid than in the recent developments in personal computers and the Internet.

Communications Technologies: from Jefferson's "Free Marketplace of Ideas" to the "Information Marketplace"

Michael Dertouzos, Director of the MIT Lab for Computer Science, just published (1997) a critically acclaimed book about the future of technology and society in the U.S. and in the world, *What Will Be: How the New World of Information Will Change Our Lives.* In this volume, Dertouzos compares the current information technology revolution with the industrial revolution in England and the technology revolution of the early 20th century: "The Industrial Revolution began in England when the steam engine was invented in the middle of the eighteenth century.... Technical change had largely stopped by the end of the nineteenth century when a new wave of innovations appeared: the internal combustion engine, electricity, synthetic chemicals, the automobile ... Both revolutions had dark sides as well as bright." The author goes on to assert that the current "Information Revolution will trigger a similarly sweeping transformation," which he calls "The Information Marketplace." In 1980 he wrote this about the information marketplace:

> By Information Marketplace I mean the collection of people, computers, communications, software, and services that will be engaged in the intraorganizational and interpersonal information transactions of the future. These transactions will involve the processing and communication of information under the same economic motives that drive today's traditional marketplace for material goods and services. The Information Marketplace already exists in embryonic form. Expect it to grow at a rapid rate and to affect us as importantly as have the products and processes of the industrial revolution.[73]

It would appear that Dertouzos's vision, announced in 1980, is rapidly coming into view for the rest of us. Keeping track of the growth of computer technology in society is difficult to do with any accuracy, but various studies were reported recently by *Internet World* magazine, suggesting the magnitude of change in the following data:

- The Internet doubled in size from 6.6 million hosts in mid–1995 to 12.6 million hosts in mid-1996.
- While it is not clear how many people are using the Internet, studies suggest from 9 million to 27 million consistent users in the United States.
- Thirty-eight percent of U.S. adults have a computer of some sort in their home, and 24 percent of them have a modem.
- A WWW survey conducted in April 1996 showed that U.S. users represent 73 percent of Web users worldwide, with Europeans next at 11 percent.

- Average age of U.S. Internet users seems to be about 33 years, with women's share of users at about 31.5 percent, representing an increase of 2.2 percent over the past year.
- The average income of users remains very high—$59,000, compared to the 1994 U.S. average individual income of $20,690.[74]

In addition to these data on the growth of the use of computers and the Internet in society in general, recent data (February 1997) from the U.S. Department of Education include:

- Sixty-five percent of U.S. public schools had access to the Internet in fall 1996—a gain of 15 percentage points for each of the last 2 consecutive years.
- Urban fringe (or suburban) schools reported higher rates of Internet access than schools in rural locales or towns.
- Public schools with high levels of students in poverty were less likely to be connected to the Internet. Internet access was available in about half (53 percent) of schools in which 71 percent or more students were eligible for the free or reduced lunch programs and 58 percent of those in which 31 to 70 percent were eligible.[75]

Given this dramatic growth in the availability of computers and the Internet in schools and homes, we can expect to see many studies being conducted with titles similar to this one by Ronald D. Owston: "The World Wide Web: A Technology to Enhance Teaching and Learning?" In this 1997 study, Owston asks, Does the Web increase access to education? Does it promote improved learning? Does it contain the costs of education? He finds that "a promising case exists for the Web in all three areas. The case is rooted largely in how educators are actually using the Web today."[76] Owston's study illustrates the great potential of the Web, but it also shows that this potential is not always tapped.

This should not surprise us. Recall Dertouzos's claim that each revolution in technology has a bright and a dark side, and notice that in the data presented above, it is clear that some segments of society—those with greater economic resources—have greater access to new technologies in homes and schools. Dertouzos believes this is a matter of great concern, given the political economy of the United States and the influence of capitalism on the market economies of the world:

> With the productivity gains made possible by all the information and information tools at their disposal, the rich nations and rich people of the world will improve and expand their economic goods and services, thereby getting richer. As they get richer they will leverage the Information Marketplace even further, thereby experiencing exponentially escalating economic growth. The poor nations and poor people, by contrast, can't even get started. . . . The painful conclusion is that, *left to its own devices, the Information Marketplace will increase the gap between rich and poor countries and between rich and poor people.*[77]

Later, Dertouzos argues: "We must help ensure that with respect to this critical gap the Information Marketplace is not 'left to its own devices.' " This resolution, however, is far from easy to attain. If public or governmental intervention is being advocated, the spectre of Orwell's Big Brother is immediately raised: do we want a strong central government to control powerful information technologies? If the Government does not take a role, however, is it not inevitable that the haves will move further ahead of the have-nots in information, power, and wealth?

Dertouzos recognizes that the political economy of capitalism will play a major role in the nature and distribution of technology resources. He writes that market forces will coerce national policies in some directions and not others:

> Already, the world is moving with giant strides in the quest for massive economic growth. The Information Marketplace is a central factor in this growth and can even be regarded as the largest potential market in the world. A nation that seeks economic growth in the global economy has no choice but to join in. Most of the control over the machinery of the Information Marketplace will be exerted by the industrially wealthy nations, which are democratic nations as well . . . By its very definition, this control distributed in the hands of the bulk of the people who will use the Information Marketplace runs counter to centralized control by Big Brother. . . . [N]o self-respecting dictator would want it.[78]

It could be argued, however, that Dertouzos is missing a central point about how ideological hegemony works. Domination of power and of ideas does not require a dictator, as we have seen. It requires instead much more subtle, but more powerful forces of control of information technologies—the kind of control that government-assisted capitalism has structured into the culture of the United States. It is this recognition, in part, that led Bob Ingle, President of Knight-Ridder News Media, to remark about Microsoft President Bill Gates's assurances that Microsoft had no intention of intruding on newspapers' turf, "Hell no, I don't buy it . . . What are they after? They're after share of mind and advertising revenues."[79]

In schools, the inequalities that will undoubtedly remain a part of the information revolution are something for all educators to be aware of and to address. While Owston appears optimistic about the computer and the Web as learning tools, Michael Apple notes that not only do schools differ in the access they provide to the Web, but *the way computers are used* differs for different schools and different groups of children. He cites studies to support the following claims:

> There is evidence of class, race, and gender based differences in computer use. In middle-class schools, for example, the number of computers is considerably more than in working class or inner-city schools populated by children of color. The ratio of computers to children is also much higher. This in itself is an unfortunate finding. However, something else must be added here. These more economically advantaged schools not only have more contact hours and more technical and teacher support, but the very manner in which the computer is used is often different than what would generally be found in schools in less advantaged areas. Programming skills, generalizability, a sense of the multitudinous things one can do with computers both within and across academic areas, these tend to be stressed more (though simple drill and practice uses are still widespread even here). Compare this to the rote, mechanistic, and relatively low level uses that tend to dominate the working class school. These differences are not unimportant, for they signify a ratification of class divisions.[80]

Apple's point is not that computers should be resisted, but that, as with all technologies, we must ask, how can this technology be applied in a way that serves all children equally well? As Dertouzos warns, technology has harmful as well as helpful potentials. The computer and the web will not *necessarily* serve democratic values well, though in the hands of the right teacher in the right setting, a tool for deep learning, and deep literacy, can be made available to all children regardless of socioeconomic status.

Schooling and Cultural Hegemony

A number of researchers have investigated ways in which schooling socializes students into an authoritarian and unequal social order that claims allegiance to freedom and equality. So examined, the school can be seen as a status quo institution that reinforces dominant values and ideologies and teaches uncritical acceptance of the existing social order. Ideological hegemony theory suggests that it is not consent, but compliance, that is fostered in the schools, and that both the organization and the curriculum of schools are responsible for this compliance. This analysis suggests that, while schools may serve democratic ideals by contributing to a functional and culturally literate citizenry, they also obstruct democratic tendencies by socializing students to be uncritical followers in a social order where major decisions are made by an elite few. In short, schools do not practice critical literacy.

Jean Anyon has provided perhaps the most concise accounts of these hegemonic processes in schooling.[81] Three examples that are relevant here are (1) the hierarchical distribution of power in the schools, (2) the nature of student work, (3) and social stratification within the school structure. First, students quickly learn that the school is an institution in which unequal power relations prevail. They must obey not only the authority of the teacher's knowledge but institutionalized authority in the form of school rules as well. Teachers have authority over students because of the rules of the school. In turn, teachers themselves must obey the rules of the school and the authority of the principal, who in the students' eyes is the root authority, the court of final jurisdiction that governs both the teachers' and the students' behavior. Teachers frequently admit to students that they themselves do not approve of a certain rule, but that they must enforce it because of the requirements of the institution. Grading students is an example. Teachers often tell students that they dislike having to give grades, that it does more harm than good, but that they have no choice in the matter. The message delivered to students is that the hierarchical authority of the institution may not necessarily make sense, but it cannot be questioned. This contributes to students' disposition to obey institutional authority—to comply with the social order of the school—even if they have deep disagreements with it. It is just the way things are, and "we all have to live with it." It is not the value of consent that is being fostered here, but compliance despite dissent. The result is that compliance itself becomes a value.

Second, the nature of school determines the nature of work within the school. Work—and only work—is compulsory. At school, we work not because it is intrinsically interesting and satisfying, but because it is assigned. We learn to take for granted that play may be cooperative (the idea of teamwork is emphasized in sports and extracurricular activities); but work, despite the increase in cooperative learning activities in recent years, is individualistic and competitive. There are scarce rewards available, and the nature of schoolwork is to compete for those scarce rewards. Further, we learn in schools that our successes and failures are due to our individual talents and achievements, not to faults in the school. Winners are credited with their successes; losers are blamed for their failures. Anyon cites a study in which 102 lower-track fifth-grade students were asked why they were in the low track, and two-thirds of them replied "because I am too dumb" or "because I can't think good"—or some other response that located their failures in themselves.[82] This personalization of school failure eventually helps legitimize the unequal distribution of goods in contemporary society. Inequalities of reward are understood in terms of personal failures or successes in school and in the workplace, not in terms of a structure that guarantees—like a grading curve—winners and losers.[83]

A third example of Anyon's analysis of schooling is the stratification of students. Students are grouped in a variety of ways: by skill level, by IQ score, by age, by classroom behavior, and so on. Such groupings can produce very different kinds of education and very different opportunities for success. Students learn to take these inequalities as natural: Different income groups and different races occupy different tracks both in and out of school. That black, Hispanic, and poor white families should occupy the bottom of the social order does not seem surprising to people who long ago came to accept this in their school experience. Justification for such a state of affairs rests in the view that people deserve what they get because of their performance levels in the competitive school system. An acceptance of institutionalized inequality in schools becomes an acceptance of institutionalized inequality in the workplace and in society in general: It may not be good, but "it is the way things are."

Hegemonic theory also focuses on the content of school curriculum material. Students are socialized into the existing political-economic system, not just by practicing it in schools but by having it portrayed in their texts as desirable and legitimate. Texts routinely praise our economic and political system and routinely criticize other systems. Likewise, texts rarely criticize our system. The first kind of political socialization is sometimes referred to by hegemony theorists as positive inculcation; the second is referred to as selective omission. These can be illustrated by statements from social studies textbooks.

An example of positive inculcation is the praise of the free market system that routinely appears in social studies textbooks, the corresponding claim that the U.S. free market economy is democratic, and the delegitimation of alternative political-economic systems. Such claims are in some measure misleading: There is no free market economy in the United States, and if there were it would not necessarily be democratic. Slavery and some of the most antidemocratic abuses of immigrants, women, and children occurred in a historical period when our economy was *much less* regulated by government than it now is. Similarly, trumpeting the U.S. political-economic system over the systems of other nations obscures important truths. As Derek Bok recently showed, citizens in the U.S. lag behind the citizens of most other industrialized nations in the majority of measures of quality of life.[84]

It is not merely beliefs based on mistaken or carefully selected facts that schools inculcate, however; it is general attitudes of patriotism and reverence for authority, no matter how antidemocratic that authority might be. After the Watergate episode raised questions about the presidency in 1972 and 1973, one of the most widely used government texts proclaimed, "The Presidency is more than executive responsibility. It is an inspiring symbol of all that is highest in American ideals and purposes. No one could think of it except in terms of solemn consecration."[85] This is neither history nor social studies, of course, but rather a clear attempt to instill a particular attitude in young people, regardless of what is factual.

At the same time that our system of capitalist democracy and its founders are praised, a number of important details of American social history are selectively omitted. One of these is the role of conflict in producing progressive social change. Anyon's study of high school social studies texts reveals that positive social changes in civil rights, the resolution of the Vietnam War, labor unions, and the women's movement are presented as triumphs of the legal system and of processes of discussion and bargaining. The role of disruptive protests that often involved violent repression by the police and military is ignored. The message explicitly communicated in these texts is that consensus, rather than power or conflict, is what makes history and leads to progress. The effectiveness of protest and militant collective action is selectively omitted.

A related example is omission from history texts of the success of the Socialist party early in the 20th century. If portrayed at all, it is most often portrayed negatively, as an insignificant movement on the part of an irresponsible few.[86]

As Michael Apple points out, a fundamental linkage exists between the overt and implicit messages in school texts and the economics of textbook publishing itself. Some states regulate the political content of their texts, and publishers cannot afford to ignore those guidelines if they want to sell books.[87] Texas, for example, is the second-largest textbook market in the nation, spending upward of $50 million a year on schoolbooks. Any textbook used in Texas schools must "promote citizenship and the understanding of the free enterprise system, emphasize patriotism and respect for recognized authority," according to the State Board of Education guidelines. A commission of private citizens oversees the Texas purchase each year to make sure that the guidelines are rigidly observed. Consequently, textbook publishers have tailored the content of the books they sell throughout the nation in order not to offend Texan sensibilities. Other states, too, use approval processes that publishers ignore only at risk of market failure.[88]

Given such ideological and economic constraints, it is not surprising to find gross misrepresentations of reality in school texts. In a 1980s middle-school social studies text called *American Neighbors,* the bulk of the relations between the United States and Latin America were described in entirely friendly terms, dwelling mainly on economic aid to our southern neighbors. When conflict was addressed, it was flatly misrepresented, as in the following passage:

> Several times, when some of the Latin American governments were too weak to keep order at home, the U.S. sent armed troops into the countries. Sometimes the troops went in to collect debts that one nation owed to other nations. At other times they went in to bring order and keep the peace. Then . . . the U.S. began to realize that it should be more friendly to its southern neighbors. It sent no more troops into their countries, and it began to show respect for their governments.[89]

The truth, as Chomsky has documented, is that the United States successfully carried out a policy of destabilization among left-leaning Latin American nations for the past 45 years of the Cold War. Our admitted policy of trying to overthrow the Nicaraguan government throughout the early 1980s was nothing new.[90] Young people—or their parents, for that matter—trying to understand that policy would have a very difficult time resolving the contradictions between what they are taught in schools and what continues to take place in Latin America today, with Cuba as the most recent example. As long as the press remains friendly to administration efforts, the contradictions scarcely arise. Still, signs of a less than virtuous foreign policy occasionally surface, as when U.S. policy is condemned by the World Court, as happened during the Nicaraguan civil war in the 1980s. The content of school texts simply does not equip citizens to make sense of such a news story.

Just as schools strengthen the prevailing cultural hegemony through both their processes and their academic content, so society as a whole strengthens the prevailing cultural hegemony through the decision-making processes of most workplaces and through the ideology that underlies and controls the media. The decision-making processes of the great majority of workplaces, for example, are characterized by authoritarian, hierarchical structures in which workers do not participate in major decisions that affect their working lives. On the one hand, this hierarchy is legitimized by claims of talent and training on the part of superiors and by the need for efficiency in decision making. On the other hand, the resulting forms of work life are decidedly nondemocratic. This nonparticipatory experience in the workplace contrasts markedly with the prevailing political rhetoric that U.S. society is democratic. This conflict between the nondemocratic relations of daily experience and the culture's proclamations of democracy is rarely analyzed and evaluated in popular discourse. Instead, people live with the contradictions, generally not recognizing them as such. Antonio Gramsci argued this position some 50 years ago, saying that the working person in a capitalist society tends to be paralyzed into passivity and inactivity by this basic contradiction between democratic political rhetoric and the daily experience of nondemocratic forms of life.[91] Gramsci's account perhaps goes a long way toward answering Gaventa's question cited earlier: "not why rebellion occurs in a 'democracy' but why, in the face of massive inequalities, it does not."

If correct, the hegemony theorists' analysis has many implications for education, two of which are fundamental. First, it appears that society is educating in deeply contradictory ways. On the one hand, citizens are taught in the schools and through the media that they live in a democratic society. On the other hand, they are taught through daily experience not to expect participation in fundamental decisions affecting their lives. Finally, they are not educated by either school or society to examine and question such contradictions between rhetoric and reality. Instead, citizens learn from an early age to tolerate the contradictions if they see them at all. It requires nothing less than indoctrination to convince people in a hegemonic, nondemocratic society that democracy is working well. If the hegemonic theorists are correct in arguing that American education contains a stiff dose of indoctrination, then we should not be surprised that the most literate classes are the most convinced.[92]

Second, cultural hegemony theory points out a more subtle form of popular miseducation, which Peter Bachrach contrasts to the "developmental" view of democracy.[93] This view holds that democratic forms of life place upon citizens demands that are themselves uniquely educative. As Jefferson believed in the 18th century, and John Dewey in the 20th, there is no democratic justification for a ruling class that monopolizes decision making, no matter what its credentials and expertise. A democracy stripped of significant, systematic participation by people in the fundamental decisions affecting their lives is not democracy at all, and it therefore fails to educate the populace through political participation. Democratic decision makers continue to learn about the world around them in order to make their decisions; they learn from the consequences of their decisions and go on. Those who do not participate in the decision-making process are not required to learn, and if hegemony theorists are correct, the already large educational gap between the powerful and powerless grows greater.

CONCLUDING REMARKS

As this chapter illustrates, the literal and political significance of "literacy" has changed as society has changed. Although one who could read and write a bit was considered literate in Jefferson's era, such rudimentary literacy skills do not necessarily qualify one as literate in our own time. To some extent, the definition of literacy has changed with society. The various dimensions of literacy in contemporary life are coined in such terms as *functional literacy, cultural literacy,* and *critical literacy,* all of which differ from the conventional notion of literacy as the simple ability to read and write. While there is no universal agreement on the meanings of these coined terms, each points to a different way in which literacy is embedded in social contexts and is relative to a particular society and its conditions.

The concept of *functional literacy,* for example, is grounded in a view of the degree of literacy that people need to function well or independently in a world pervaded by the written word. In this respect, functional literacy in one time and place may differ from another. A question arises regarding what it is to function well or independently. Are the skills of reading and writing, however fluently, enough to interpret written text well? Or are some kinds of background knowledge also important in the uses of functional literacy?

Such a question lies at the foundation of the notion of *cultural literacy,* which proposes that fluent reading and writing skills are not adequate for interpreting written text. Embedded in all such text are cultural meanings, and the reader's understanding of those meanings will influence the interpretation of the text. One task of education, in this view, is not just to teach functional literacy skills, but to teach the background knowledge necessary to interpret written text in its cultural context. Thus, knowledge of history, literature, politics, science, and other dimensions of human experience is necessary to make sense of written text. As the background knowledge differs, so will the reader's interpretation of the text differ.

Advocates of *critical literacy,* however, argue that any adequate conception of literacy should include a conceptual connection to human liberty. They assert that it is important for citizens to develop the knowledge, skills, and dispositions to reflect critically upon their experiences and upon the power relations within their daily lives. They further argue that functional or even cultural literacy is a tool that can be used to liberate or to dominate; if literacy is to be liberating, people need to be educated to think carefully about power. The reading selection at the end of this chapter presents an example of how two teachers engage their students in critically "reading" the world around them and in using literacy skills to do so.

The power of functional and cultural literacy to dominate a population's ways of understanding the world is illustrated by the concept of *ideological hegemony,* sometimes referred to as *cultural hegemony.* Consideration of the decision-making processes of modern capitalist culture suggests that while Jefferson may have been correct that a society cannot be ignorant and free, neither is an education a guarantee of freedom. The popular press and other news and entertainment media, together with the schools, can inculcate ways of thinking and valuing in a population that leave gross concentrations of economic and political power in the hands of a very small minority while a society proudly proclaims itself democratic. Nor is there strong reason to believe, at this time, that new communications technologies will seriously challenge the concentrations of wealth and power in the hands of a few.

We are left to wonder what Jefferson would think of the role that today's schools play in the process of developing self-governing citizens. It would appear that our schools—and the kind of literacy they develop—play at least some role in helping students accept that participatory self-government is no longer a realistic goal in modern society.

PRIMARY SOURCE READING

William Bigelow, a secondary school teacher in Portland, Oregon, believes that public schooling in the United States serves social and economic class interests unequally, and that one justifiable response for the educator is to help equip students to understand and critique the society in which they live. This article portrays students and teachers engaging in the kind of structured dialogue that Bigelow says is essential to the critical pedagogy he employs. The article is included as an example of two teachers' efforts (Bigelow works collaboratively with colleague Linda Christensen) to engage their students in critical literacy as a means of achieving skills in reading and writing as well as cultural understanding. Following Paulo Freire, Bigelow engages his classes in reading "students' lives as classroom text."

INSIDE THE CLASSROOM: SOCIAL VISION AND CRITICAL PEDAGOGY

William Bigelow

There is a quotation from Paulo Freire that I like; he writes that teachers should attempt to "live part of their dreams within their educational space."[1] The implication is that teaching should be partisan. I agree. As a teacher I want to be an agent of transformation, with my classroom as a center of equality and democracy—an ongoing, if small, critique of the repressive social relations of the larger society. That does not mean holding a plebiscite on every homework assignment, or pretending I do not have any expertise, but I hope my classroom can become part of a protracted argument for the viability of a critical and participatory democracy.

I think this vision of teaching flies in the face of what has been and continues to be the primary function of public schooling in the United States: to reproduce a class society, where the benefits and sufferings are shared incredibly unequally. As much as possible I refuse to play my part in that process. This is easier said than done. How *can* classroom teachers move decisively away from a model of teaching that merely reproduces and legitimates inequality? I think Freire is on the right track when he calls for a "dialogical education."[2] To me, this is not just a plea for more classroom conversation. In my construction, a dialogical classroom means inviting students to critique the larger society through sharing their lives. As a teacher I help students locate their experiences socially; I involve students in probing the social factors that make and limit who they are and I try to help them reflect on who they *could* be.

Students' Lives as Classroom Text

In my Literature in U.S. History course, which I co-teach in Portland, Oregon, with Linda Christensen, we use historical concepts as points of departure to explore themes in students' lives and then, in turn, use students' lives to explore history and our society today. Earlier this year, for instance, we studied the Cherokee Indian Removal through role play. Students portrayed the Indians, plantation owners, bankers, and the Andrew Jackson administration and saw the forces that combined to push the Cherokees west of the Mississippi against their will. Following a discussion of how and why this happened, Linda and I asked students to write about a time when they had their rights violated. We asked students to write from inside these experiences and to recapture how they felt and what, if anything, they did about the injustice.

Seated in a circle, students shared their stories with one another in a "read-around" format. (To fracture the student/teacher dichotomy a bit, Linda and I also complete each assignment and take our turns reading.) Before we began, we suggested they listen for what we call the "collec-

---

Reprinted by permission of the publisher from Tozer, Steven, Anderson, Thomas H., and Armbruster, Bonnie B., *Foundational Studies in Teacher Education: A Reexamination.* (New York: Teachers College Press, "Inside the Classroom: Social Vision and Critical Pedagogy" by Bigelow, pp. 139–50.

[1] Paulo Freire and Donaldo Macedo, *Literacy: Reading the Word and the World* (South Hadley, MA: Bergin and Garvey, 1987), p. 127.

[2] See especially Ira Shor and Paulo Freire, *A Pedagogy for Liberation* (South Hadley, MA: Bergin and Garvey, 1983).

tive text"—the group portrait that emerges from the read-around.[3] Specifically, we asked them to take notes on the kinds of rights people felt they possessed; what action they took after having their rights violated; and whatever other generalizations they could draw from the collective text. Here are a few examples: Rachel wrote on wetting her pants because a teacher would not let her go to the bathroom; Christie, on a lecherous teacher at a middle school; Rebecca, on a teacher who enclosed her in a solitary confinement cell; Gina, who is black, on a theater worker not believing that her mother, who is white, actually was her mother; Maryanne, on being sexually harassed while walking to school and her subsequent mistreatment by the school administration when she reported the incident; Clayton, on the dean's treatment when Clayton wore an anarchy symbol on his jacket; Bobby, on convenience store clerks who watched him more closely because he is black. Those are fewer than a quarter of the stories we heard.

To help students study this social text more carefully, we asked them to review their notes from the read-around and write about their discoveries. We then spent over a class period interpreting our experiences. Almost half the instances of rights violations took place in school. Christie said, "I thought about the school thing. The real point [of school] is to learn one concept: to be trained and obedient. That's what high school is. A diploma says this person came every day, sat in their seat. It's like going to dog school." A number of people, myself included, expressed surprise that so many of the stories involved sexual harassment. To most of the students with experiences of harassment, it had always seemed a very private oppression, but hearing how common this kind of abuse is allowed the young women to feel a new connection among themselves—and they said so. A number of white students were surprised at the varieties of subtle racism black students experienced.

We talked about the character of students' resistance to rights violations. From the collective text we saw that most people did not resist at all. What little resistance occurred was individual; there was not a single instance of collective resistance. Christie complained to a counselor, Rebecca told her mother, many complained to friends. This provoked a discussion about what in their lives and, in particular, in the school system encouraged looking for individual solutions to problems that are shared collectively. They identified competition for grades and for positions in sought-after classes as factors. They also criticized the fake democracy of student government for discouraging activism. No one shared a single experience of schools' encouraging groups of students to confront injustice. Moreover, students also listed ways—from advertising messages to television sitcoms—through which people are conditioned by the larger society to think in terms of individual problems requiring individual solutions.

The stories students wrote were moving, sometimes poetic, and later opportunities to rewrite allowed us to help sharpen their writing skills, but we wanted to do more than just encourage students to stage a literary show-and-tell. Our larger objective was to find social meaning in individual experience—to push students to use their stories as windows not only on their lives, but on society.

There were other objectives. We hoped that through building a collective text, our students—particularly working-class and minority students—would discover that their lives are important sources of learning, no less important than the lives of the generals and presidents, the Rockefellers and Carnegies, who inhabit their textbooks. One function of the school curriculum is to celebrate the culture of the dominant and to ignore or scorn the culture of subordinate groups. The personal writing, collective texts, and discussion circles in Linda's and my classes are an attempt to challenge students not to accept these judgments. We wanted students to grasp that they can *create* knowledge, not simply absorb it from higher authorities.[4]

All of this sounds a little neater than what actually occurs in a classroom. Some students rebel at taking their own lives seriously. A student in one of my classes said to me recently, "Why do we have to do all this personal stuff? Can't you just give us a book or a worksheet and leave us

[3] See Linda Christensen, "Writing the Word and the World," *English Journal,* vol. 78, no. 2 (February 1989), pp. 14–18.

[4] See William Bigelow and Norman Diamond, *The Power in Our Hands: A Curriculum on the History of Work and Workers in the United States* (New York: Monthly Review Press, 1988), pp. 15–23.

alone?" Another student says regularly, "This isn't an English class, ya know." Part of this resistance may come from not wanting to resurface or expose painful experiences; part may come from not feeling capable as writers; but I think the biggest factor is that they simply do not feel that their lives have anything *important* to teach them. Their lives are just their lives. Abraham Lincoln and Hitler are important. Students have internalized self-contempt from years of official neglect and denigration of their culture. When for example, African-American or working-class history *is* taught, it is generally as hero worship: extolling the accomplishments of a Martin Luther King, Jr., or a John L. Lewis, while ignoring the social movements that made their work possible. The message given is that great people make change, individual high school students do not. So it is not surprising that some students wonder what in the world they have to learn from each other's stories.

Apart from drawing on students' own lives as sources of knowledge and insight, an alternative curriculum also needs to focus on the struggle of oppressed groups for social justice. In my history classes, for example, we study Shay's Rebellion, the abolition movement, and alliances between blacks and poor whites during Reconstruction. In one lesson, students role-play Industrial Workers of the World organizers in the 1912 Lawrence, Massachusetts, textile strike as they try to overcome divisions between men and women and between workers speaking over a dozen different languages.

Studying the Hidden Curriculum

In my experience as a teacher, whether students write about inequality, resistance, or collective work, school is *the* most prominent setting. Therefore, in our effort to have the curriculum respond to students' real concerns, we enlist them as social researchers, investigating their own school lives. My co-teacher and I began one unit by reading an excerpt from the novel *Radcliffe*, by David Storey.[5] In the selection, a young boy, Leonard Radcliffe, arrives at a predominantly working-class British school. The teacher prods Leonard, who is from an aristocratic background, to become her reluctant know-it-all—the better to reveal to others their own ignorance. The explicit curriculum appears to concern urban geography: "Why are roofs pointed and not flat like in the Bible?" the teacher asks. She humiliates a working-class youth, Victor, by demanding that he stand and listen to her harangue: "Well, come on then, Victor. Let us all hear." As he stands mute and helpless, she chides: "Perhaps there's no reason for Victor to think at all. We already know where he's going to end up, don't we?" She points to the factory chimneys outside. "There are places waiting for him out there already." No one says a word. She finally calls on little Leonard to give the correct answer, which he does.

Students in our class readily see that these British school children are learning much more than why roofs are pointed. They are being drilled to accept their lot at the bottom of a hierarchy with a boss on top. The teacher's successful effort to humiliate Victor, while the others sit watching, undercuts any sense the students might have of their power to act in solidarity with one another. A peer is left hanging in the wind and they do nothing about it. The teacher's tacit alliance with Leonard and her abuse of Victor legitimate class inequalities outside the classroom.[6]

We use this excerpt and the follow-up discussion as a preparatory exercise for students to research the curriculum—both explicit and "hidden"[7]—at their own school (Jefferson High

[5] David Storey, *Radcliffe* (New York: Avon, 1963), pp. 9–12. I am grateful to Doug Sherman for alerting me to this excerpt.

[6] While most students are critical of the teacher, they should always be allowed an independent judgment. Recently, a boy in one of my classes who is severely hard of hearing defended the teacher's actions. He argued that because the students laughed at Leonard when he first entered the class they deserved whatever humiliation the teacher could dish out. He said the offending students ought to be taught not to make fun of people who are different.

[7] See Henry Giroux, *Theory and Resistance in Education: A Pedagogy for the Opposition* (South Hadley, MA: Bergin and Garvey, 1983). See especially Chapter 2, "Schooling and the Politics of the Hidden Curriculum," pp. 42–71. Giroux defines the hidden curriculum as "those unstated norms, values, and beliefs embedded in and transmitted to students through the underlying rules that structure the routines and social relationships in school and classroom life" and points out that the objective of critical theory is not merely to describe aspects of the hidden curriculum, but to analyze how it "functions to provide differential forms of schooling to different classes of students" (p. 47).

School). The student body is mostly African-American and predominately working class. Linda and I assign students to observe their classes as if they were attending for the first time. We ask them to notice the design of the classroom, the teaching methodology, the class content, and the grading procedures. In their logs, we ask them to reflect on the character of thinking demanded and the classroom relationships: Does the teacher promote questioning and critique or obedience and conformity? What kind of knowledge and understandings are valued in the class? What relationships between students are encouraged?

In her log, Elan focused on sexism in the hidden curriculum:

> In both biology and government, I noticed that not only do boys get more complete explanations to questions, they get asked more questions by the teacher than girls do. In government, even though our teacher is a feminist, boys are asked to define a word or to list the different parts of the legislative branch more often than the girls are. . . . I sat in on an advanced sophomore English class that was doing research in the library. The teacher, a male, was teaching the boys how to find research on their topic, while he was finding the research himself for the girls. Now, I know chivalry isn't dead, but we are competent of finding a book.

Linda and I were pleased as we watched students begin to gain a critical distance from their own schooling experiences. Unfortunately, Elan did not speculate much on the social outcomes of the unequal treatment she encountered, or on what it is in society that produces this kind of teaching. She did offer the observation that "boys are given much more freedom in the classroom than girls, and therefore the boys are used to getting power before the girls."

Here is an excerpt from Connie's log:

> It always amazed me how teachers automatically assume that where you sit will determine your grade. It's funny how you can get an A in a class you don't even understand. As long as you follow the rules and play the game, you seem to get by . . . On this particular day we happen to be taking a test on Chapters 16 and 17. I've always liked classes such as algebra that you didn't have to think. You're given the facts, shown how to do it, and you do it. No questions, no theories, it's the solid, correct way to do it.

We asked students to reflect on who in our society they thought benefited from the methods of education to which they were subjected. Connie wrote:

> I think that not only is it the teacher, but more importantly, it's the system. They purposely teach you using the "boring method." Just accept what they tell you, learn it and go on, no questions asked. It seems to me that the rich, powerful people benefit from it, because we don't want to think, we're kept ignorant, keeping them rich.

Connie's hunch that her classes benefit the rich and powerful is obviously incomplete, but it does put her on the road to understanding that the degrading character of her education is not simply accidental. She is positioned to explore the myriad ways schooling is shaped by the imperatives of a capitalist economy. Instead of being just more of the "boring method," as Connie puts it, this social and historical study would be a personal search for her, rooted in her desire to understand the nature of her *own* school experience.

In class, students struggled through a several-page excerpt from *Schooling in Capitalist America* by Samuel Bowles and Herbert Gintis. They read the Bowles and Gintis assertion that

> major aspects of educational organization replicate the relationships of dominance and subordinancy in the economic sphere. The correspondence between the social relation of schooling and work accounts for the ability of the educational system to produce an amenable and fragmented labor force. The experience of schooling, and not merely the content of formal learning, is central to this process.[8]

If they are right, we should expect to find different hidden curricula at schools enrolling students of different social classes. We wanted our students to test this notion for themselves.[9] A friend who teaches at a suburban high school south of Portland, serving a relatively wealthy community, enlisted volunteers in her classes to host our students for a day. My students logged

---

[8] Samuel Bowles and Herbert Gintis, *Schooling in Capitalist America* (New York: Basic Books, 1976), p. 125.

[9] See Jean Anyon, "Social Class and the Hidden Curriculum of Work," *Journal of Education*, vol. 162 (Winter 1980), pp. 67–92, for a more systematic comparison of hidden curricula in schools serving students of different social classes.

comparisons of Jefferson and the elite school, which I will call Ridgewood. Trisa wrote:

> Now, we're both supposed to be publicly funded, equally funded, but not so. At Jefferson, the average class size is 20–25 students, at Ridgewood—15. Jefferson's cafeteria food is half-cooked, stale, and processed. Ridgewood—fresh food, wide variety, and no mile-long lines to wait in. Students are allowed to eat anywhere in the building as well as outside, and wear hats and listen to Walkmen [both rule violations at Jefferson].

About teachers' attitudes at Ridgewood, Trisa noted: "Someone said, 'We don't ask if you're going to college, but what college are you going to.' "

In general, I was disappointed that students' observations tended to be more on atmosphere than on classroom dynamics. Still, what they noticed seemed to confirm the fact that their own school, serving a black and working-class community, was a much more rule-governed, closely supervised environment. The experience added evidence to the Bowles and Gintis contention that my students were being trained to occupy lower positions in an occupational hierarchy.

Students were excited by this sociological detective work, but intuitively they were uneasy with the determinism of Bowles and Gintis's correspondence theory. It was not enough to discover that the relations of schooling mirrored the relations of work. They demanded to know exactly who designed a curriculum that taught them subservience. Was there a committee somewhere, sitting around plotting to keep them poor and passive? "We're always saying 'they' want us to do this, and 'they' want us to do that," one student said angrily. "Who is this 'they'?" Students wanted villains with faces and we were urging that they find systemic explanations.

Omar's anger exploded after one discussion. He picked up his desk and threw it against the wall, yelling: "How much more of this shit do I have to put up with?" "This shit" was his entire educational experience, and while the outburst was not directed at our class in particular—thank heavens—we understood our culpability in his frustration.

We had made two important and related errors in our teaching. Implicitly, our search had encouraged students to see themselves as victims—powerless little cogs in a machine daily reproducing the inequities of the larger society. Though the correspondence theory was an analytical framework with a greater power to interpret their school lives than any other they had encountered, ultimately it was a model suggesting endless oppression and hopelessness. If schooling is always responsive to the needs of capitalism, then what point did our search have? Our observations seemed merely to underscore students' powerlessness.

I think the major problem was that although our class did discuss resistance by students, it was anecdotal and unsystematic, thereby depriving students of the opportunity to question their own rules in maintaining the status quo. The effect of this omission, entirely unintentional on our part, was to deny students the chance to see schools as sites of struggle and social change—places where they could have a role in determining the character of their own education. Unwittingly, the realizations students were drawing from our study of schools fueled a world view rooted in cynicism; they might learn about the nature and causes for their subordination, but they could have no role in resisting it.

The "Organic Goodie Simulation"

Still stinging from my own pedagogical carelessness, I have made efforts this year to draw students into a dialogue about the dynamics of power and resistance. One of the most effective means to carry on this dialogue is metaphorically, through role play and simulation.[10]

In one exercise, called the "Organic Goodie Simulation," I create a three-tiered society. Half the students are workers, half are unemployed,[11]

---

[10] There is an implication in many of the theoretical discussions defining critical pedagogy that the proper role of the teacher is to initiate group reflection on students' outside-of-class experiences. Critics consistently neglect to suggest that the teacher can also be an initiator of powerful in-class experiences, which can then serve as objects of student analysis.

[11] Bigelow and Diamond, *The Power in Our Hands,* pp. 27–30 and 92–94. See also Mike Messner, "Bubblegum and Surplus Value," *The Insurgent Sociologist,* vol. 6, no. 4 (Summer 1976), pp. 51–56.

and I am the third tier—the owner of a machine that produces organic goodies. I tell students that we will be in this classroom for the rest of our lives and that the machine produces the only sustenance. Workers can buy adequate goodies with their wages, but the unemployed will slowly starve to death on their meager dole of welfare-goodies. Everything proceeds smoothly until I begin to drive wages down by offering jobs to the unemployed at slightly less than what the workers earn. It is an auction, with jobs going to the lowest bidder. Eventually, all classes organize some kind of opposition, and usually try to take away my machine. One year, a group of students arrested me, took me to a jail in the corner of the room, put a squirt gun to my head, and threatened to "kill" me if I said another word. This year, before students took over the machine, I backed off, called a meeting to which only my workers were invited, raised their wages, and stressed to them how important it was that we stick together to resist the jealous unemployed people who wanted to drag all of us into the welfare hole they are in. Some workers defected to the unemployed, some vigorously defended my right to manage the machine, but most bought my plea that we had to talk it all out and reach unanimous agreement before any changes could be made. For an hour and a half they argued among themselves, egged on by me, without taking any effective action.

The simulation provided a common metaphor from which students could examine firsthand what we had not adequately addressed the previous year: To what extent are we complicit in our own oppression? Before we began our follow-up discussion, I asked students to write on who or what was to blame for the conflict and disruption of the previous day. In the discussion some students singled me out as the culprit. Stefani said, "I thought Bill was evil. I didn't know what he wanted." Rebecca concurred: "I don't agree with people who say Bill was not the root of the problem. Bill was management, and he made workers feel insecure that the unemployed were trying to take their jobs." Others agreed with Rebecca that it was a divisive structure that had been created, but saw how their own responses to that structure perpetuated the divisions and poverty. Christie said: "We were so divided that nothing got decided. It kept going back and forth. Our discouragement was the root of the problem." A number of people saw how their own attitudes kept them from acting decisively. Mira said: "I think that there was this large fear: We have to follow the law. And Sonia kept saying we weren't supposed to take over the machine. But if the law and property hurt people why should we go along with it?" Gina said: "I think Bill looked like the problem, but underneath it all was us. Look at when Bill hired unemployed and fired some workers. I was doing it too. We can say it's a role play, but you have to look at how everything ended up feeling and learn something about ourselves, about how we handled it."

From our discussion students could see that their make-believe misery was indeed caused by the structure of the society: The number of jobs was held at an artificially low level, and workers and unemployed were pitted against each other for scarce goodies. As the owner I tried every trick I knew to drive wedges between workers and the unemployed, to encourage loyalty in my workers, and to promote uncertainty and bickering among the unemployed. However, by analyzing the experience, students could see that the system worked only because they let it work—they were much more than victims of my greed; they were my accomplices.

I should hasten to add—and emphasize—that it is not inherently empowering to understand one's own complicity in oppression. I think it is a start, because this understanding suggests that we can do something about it. A critical pedagogy, however, needs to do much more: It should highlight times, past and present, when people built alliances to challenge injustice. Students also need to encounter individuals and organizations active in working for a more egalitarian society, and students need to be encouraged to see themselves as capable of joining together with others, in and out of school, to make needed changes. I think that all of these are mandatory components of the curriculum. The danger of students' becoming terribly cynical as they come to understand the enormity of injustice in this society and in the world is just too great. They have to know that it is possible—even joyous, if I dare say so—to work toward a more humane society.

Teachers and Teacher Educators as Political Agents

At the outset I said that all teaching should be partisan. In fact, I think that all teaching *is* partisan. Whether or not we want to be, all teachers are political agents because we help shape students' understandings of the larger society. That is why it is so important for teachers to be clear about our social visions. Toward what kind of society are we aiming? Unless teachers answer this question with clarity we are reduced to performing as technicians, unwittingly participating in a political project but with no comprehension of its objectives or consequences. Hence teachers who claim "no politics" are inherently authoritarian because their pedagogical choices act on students, but students are denied a structured opportunity to critique or act on their teachers' choices. Nor are students equipped to reflect on the effectiveness of whatever resistance they may put up.

For a number of reasons, I do not think that our classrooms can ever be exact models of the kind of participatory democracy we would like to have characterize the larger society. If teachers' only power were to grade students, that would be sufficient to sabotage classroom democracy. However, as I have suggested, classrooms can offer students experiences and understandings that counter, and critique, the lack of democracy in the rest of their lives. In the character of student interactions the classroom can offer a glimpse of certain features of an egalitarian society. We can begin to encourage students to learn the analytic and strategic skills to help bring this new society into existence. As I indicated, by creating a collective text of student experience we can offer students practice in understanding personal problems in their social contexts. Instead of resorting to consumption, despair, or other forms of self-abuse, they can ask why these circumstances exist and what can they do about it. In this limited arena, students can begin to become the subjects of their lives.

When Steve Tozer of the University of Illinois asked me to prepare this article, he said I should discuss the implications of my classroom practice for people in social foundations of education programs. First, I would urge you who are teacher educators to model the participatory and exploratory pedagogy that you hope your students will employ as classroom teachers. Teachers-to-be should interrogate their own educational experiences as a basis for understanding the relationship between school and society. They need to be members of a dialogical community in which they can experience themselves as subjects and can learn the validity of critical pedagogy by doing it. If the primary aim of social foundations of education coursework is to equip teachers-to-be to understand and critically evaluate the origins of school content and processes in social context, then the foundations classroom should be a place for students to discuss how their own experiences as students are grounded in the larger society, with its assumptions, its inequities, its limits and possibilities.

As you know, a teacher's first job in a public school can be frightening. That fear mixed with the conservative pressures of the institution can overwhelm the liberatory inclinations of a new teacher. Having *experienced,* and not merely having read about, an alternative pedagogy can help new teachers preserve their democratic ideals. Part of this, I think, means inviting your students to join you in critiquing your pedagogy. You need to be a model of rigorous self-evaluation.

The kind of teaching I have been describing is demanding. The beginning teacher may be tempted to respond, "Sure, sure, I'll try all that when I've been in the classroom five or six years and when I've got a file cabinet full of lessons." I think you should encourage new teachers to overcome their isolation by linking up with colleagues to reflect on teaching problems and to share pedagogical aims and successes. I participated in a support group like this my first year as a teacher and our meetings helped maintain my courage and morale. After a long hiatus, two years ago I joined another group that meets biweekly to talk about everything from educational theory to confrontations with administrators to union organizing.[12] In groups such as this your students can

[12] My study group gave valuable feedback on this article. Thanks to Linda Christensen, Jeff Edmundson, Tom McKenna, Karen Miller, Michele Miller, Doug Sherman and Kent Spring.

come to see themselves as creators and evaluators of curriculum and not simply as executors of corporate- or administrative-packaged lesson plans.

It is also in groups like this that teachers can come to see themselves as activists in a broader struggle for social justice. The fact is that education will not be *the* engine of social change. No matter how successful we are as critical teachers in the classroom, our students' ability to use and extend the analytic skills they have acquired depends on the character of the society that confronts them. Until the economic system requires workers who are critical, cooperative, and deeply democratic, teachers' classroom efforts amount to a kind of low-intensity pedagogical war. Unfortunately, it is easy to cut ourselves off from outside movements for social change—and this is especially true for new teachers. As critical teachers, however, we depend on these movements to provide our students with living proof that fundamental change is both possible and desirable. It seems to me you cannot emphasize too strongly how teachers' attempts to teach humane and democratic values in the classroom should not be isolated from the social context in which schooling occurs.

In closing, let me return to Freire's encouragement that we live part of our dreams within our educational space. Teachers-to-be should not be ashamed or frightened of taking sides in favor of democracy and social justice. I hope your students learn to speak to *their* students in the language of possibility and hope and not of conformity and "realism." In sum, your students ought to learn that teaching is, in the best sense of the term, a subversive activity—and to be proud of it.

QUESTIONS FOR DISCUSSION AND EXAMINATION

The following questions are suggested for use as recommended in the remarks introducing questions at the end of Chapters 1 and 2. Teachers and students are encouraged to generate additional questions as well.

1. What, in your view, does the functional literacy perspective contribute to our understanding of the political economy of literacy in the United States? If these are valuable contributions, is the functional approach an adequate view of literacy on which to base educational policy? Explain.
2. E. D. Hirsch argues that his conception of cultural literacy preserves the connection between literacy and liberty found in the views of Thomas Jefferson and Martin Luther King. Do you agree? Explain.
3. To what degree do you find the critical literacy perspective consistent with John Dewey's democratic ideal, expressed in Chapter 4, of "the all-around growth of every member of society"? Explain how critical literacy theory does or does not serve this ideal.
4. What features of contemporary U.S. ideology and political economy come to light in the critical literacy perspective that do not emerge in the other literacy perspectives? In your view, should teachers try to take these features into account in their approaches to teaching? Explain.
5. What are the strengths and weaknesses of the critical literacy perspective, in your view, as illustrated in Bigelow and Christensen's classroom? If you identify any practical obstacles to such a pedagogy, to what degree are they grounded in political-economic and ideological conditions in the United States? Are these conditions insurmountable—or is critical literacy theory an inadequate foundation on which to base teaching aims and educational policy in the first place? Defend your position.
6. What kinds of learning seem to be taking place in Bigelow and Christensen's classroom that might not likely take place in other classrooms? At what expense, if any, is such learning taking place? Explain and defend your view.
7. Which of the perspectives on literacy presented in this chapter do you think is the most important for individual teachers and for schools in general to embrace in the United States today? Defend your view, taking into account relevant dimensions of political economy and ideology as you understand them.

NOTES

1. Carl F. Kaestle, "The History of Literacy and the History of Readers," in *Perspectives on Literacy*, eds. E. R. Kintgen, B. M. Kroll, and M. Rose (Carbondale: Southern Illinois University Press, 1988), p. 103. Also see Vinovskis and Bernard, in Kaestle, 1985, p. 3.
2. Kaestle, "The History of Literacy and the History of Readers," p. 109.

3. Richard D. Brown, *Knowledge Is Power: The Diffusion of Information in Early America, 1700–1865* (New York: Oxford University Press, 1989), p. 12.
4. Dale Van Every, cited in Howard Zinn, *The People's History of the United States* (New York: Harper and Row, 1980), pp. 135–36.
5. Kaestle, "The History of Literacy and the History of Readers," p. 109; Stanley Schultz, *The Culture Factory: Boston Public Schools, 1789–1860* (New York, Oxford University Press, 1973), cited in Joel Spring, *The American School, 1642–1990,* 2d ed. (New York: Longman, 1990), pp. 60–63.
6. Kaestle, "The History of Literacy and the History of Readers," p. 109.
7. U.S. Bureau of the Census, "Literacy: Current Problems and Current Research," in *Fifth Report of the National Council on Educational Research* (Washington, D.C.: National Institute of Education, 1979). See also U.S. Bureau of the Census, *The Census of the Population, 1980,* Vol. 1: The Characteristics of Population, Chapter C, General, Social and Economic Characteristics, Table 83 (Years of School Completed), Column Years 1940–1980.
8. Shirley Brice Heath, "The Functions and Uses of Literacy," *Journal of Communication,* vol. 30 (1980), pp. 123–33.
9. Ibid., p. 124.
10. Jonathan Kozol, *Illiterate America* (Garden City, N.Y.: Anchor Press/Doubleday, 1985).
11. Irwin S. Kirsch, Ann Jungeblut, Lynn Jenkins, and Andrew Kohlstad, *Adult Literacy in America* (Washington, D.C.: Educational Testing Service and National Center for Educational Statistics, 1993), p. 2.
12. N. Northcutt, *Adult Performance Level Project: Adult Functional Competency—A Report to the Office of Education Dissemination Review Panel* (Austin, TX: University of Texas, Division of Extension, 1975). The statistics released by the APL study can be potentially misleading. It will help to contextualize the statistics in order to have a better grasp of the information. Specifically, as listed, the statistics indicate that all groups are working from a shared baseline of 100. However, more correctly, the percentages should reflect more true population distributions. For example, at that time Euro-Americans composed roughly 76 to 78 percent of the population, African-Americans 12 percent, and Hispanic Americans 10 percent. It would be helpful to know the exact numbers represented by the percentage equivalents in the APL study. The numbers as stated offer a potentially false perception of the literacy rates of all groups.
13. Kirsch, et al., *Adult Literacy in America,* p. xiv.
14. Carmen St. John Hunter and David Harman, *Adult Literacy in the United States: A Report to the Ford Foundation* (New York: McGraw-Hill, 1979).
15. Ibid.
16. Ibid.
17. Northcutt, *Adult Performance Level Project;* Kirsch, et al., *Adult Literacy in America,* p. 47
18. Kozol, *Illiterate America,* p. 4.
19. *The National Assessment of Educational Progress. The Reading Report Card: Progress toward Excellence in Our Schools* (Princeton, NJ: Educational Testing Service, 1985).
20. Ibid. Also, Kirsch, et al., *Adult Literacy in America,* p. xviii.
21. Kozol, *Illiterate America,* p. 10.
22. Colin Lankshear, "Humanizing Functional Literacy: Beyond Necessity," *Educational Theory,* vol. 36 (Fall 1986), pp. 375–87.
23. Larry Rohter, "The Scourge of Adult Illiteracy," *The New York Times: Educational Life,* April 13, 1986, p. 1.
24. Stanley N. Wellborn, "A Nation of Illiterates?" *U.S. News and World Report,* May 17, 1982, p. 53.
25. Neil Postman, "The Politics of Reading," *Harvard Educational Review,* vol. 40, no. 2 (1970), p. 246.
26. Lankshear, "Humanizing Functional Literacy," p. 381.
27. Suzanne De Castell, Allan Luke, and David MacLennan, "On Defining Literacy," *Canadian Journal of Education,* vol. 6 (1981), pp. 7–18.
28. E. D. Hirsch, Jr., *Cultural Literacy: What Every American Needs to Know* (New York: Vintage Books, 1988).
29. Ibid.
30. Ibid.
31. Lynne V. Cheney, *American Memory: A Report on the Humanities in the Nation's Public Schools* (Washington, D.C.: National Endowment for the Humanities, 1987).
32. Ibid.
33. Michael Henry, "My Turn," *Newsweek* (June 22, 1987), p. 11.
34. Hirsch, *Cultural Literacy.*
35. Michael Henry, "My Turn," *Newsweek* (June 22, 1987), p. 11.
36. E. D. Hirsch, Jr., Joseph F. Kett, and James Trefil, *The Dictionary of Cultural Literacy,* 2nd ed., (Boston: Houghton Mifflin Co., 1993), p. xiv.
37. Ibid; p. xiv, xv.
38. Kwame Anthony Appiah, and Henry Louis Gates, Jr., *The Dictionary of Global Culture* (New York: Alfred A. Knopf, 1997).
39. Ibid; pp. 3–7.
40. Hirsch, Kett, and Trefil, 2nd ed. p. xv.
41. Heath, "The Functions and Uses of Literacy."

42. Quoted in Ira Shor, *Cultural Wars: School and Society in the Conservative Restoration 1969–1984.* (Boston: Routledge and Kegan Paul, 1986).
43. For example, see Paulo Freire and Donaldo Macedo, *Literacy: Reading the Word and the World* (South Hadley, MA: Bergin and Garvey, 1987).
44. Henry A. Giroux, *Theory and Resistance in Education: A Pedagogy for the Opposition* (South Hadley, MA: Bergin and Garvey, 1987).
45. Ibid.
46. Freire and Macedo, *Literacy.*
47. Stanley Aronowitz and Henry Giroux, *Education under Siege: The Conservative, Liberal, and Radical Debate over Schooling* (South Hadley, MA: Bergin and Garvey, 1985), p. 132.
48. Giroux, *Theory and Resistance.*
49. Freire and Macedo, *Literacy.*
50. See, for example, Cameron McCarthy, "After the Canon: Knowledge and Ideological Representation in the Multicultural Discourse on Curriculum Reform," in McCarthy and Crichlow, eds., *Race, Identity, and Representation in Education* (New York: Routledge, 1993), pp. 289–305.
51. Ronald Takaki, *A Different Mirror* (Boston: Little, Brown, 1993), p. 227.
52. This section is partially excerpted from Steven Tozer, "Elite Power and Democratic Ideals," in *Society as Educator in an Age of Transition,* Eighty-sixth Yearbook of the National Society for the Study of Education, eds. Kenneth D. Benne and Steven Tozer (Chicago: The Society, 1987), pp. 186–225.
53. Robert A. Dahl, *Who Governs?* (New Haven, CT: Yale University Press, 1961). President Eisenhower's address is found in Seymour Melman, *Pentagon Capitalism: The Political Economy of War* (New York: McGraw-Hill, 1970), pp. 235–39.
54. Eisenhower, in Melman, *Pentagon Capitalism,* pp. 237–38.
55. C. Wright Mills, *The Power Elite* (New York: Oxford University Press, 1956).
56. Thomas R. Dye, *Who's Running America? The Reagan Years* (Englewood Cliffs, NJ: Prentice Hall, 1983), pp. 11–20.
57. John Gaventa, *Power and Powerless* (Urbana: University of Illinois Press, 1980), p. vi.
58. T. Jackson Lear, "The Concept of Cultural Hegemony: Problems and Possibilities," *American Historical Review,* vol. 90 (June 1985), pp. 567–93.
59. See, for example, any of several recent works by Noam Chomsky, including *On Power and Ideology: The Managua Lectures* (Boston: South End Press, 1987) and *The Culture of Terrorism* (Boston: South End Press, 1988). See also Joshua Cohen and Joel Rogers, *Rules of the Game: American Politics and the Central America Movement* (Boston: South End Press, 1986). Finally, from a more conservative perspective, see *Wall Street Journal* reporter Jonathan Kwitney, *Endless Enemies: The Making of an Unfriendly World* (New York: Penguin Books, 1987).
60. Ben H. Bagdikian, *The Media Monopoly,* 3rd ed. (Boston: Beacon Press, 1990), p. 4.
61. Ibid., pp. 8–9.
62. Ibid., p. 18.
63. Ibid., p. 6.
64. Ibid., p. 175.
65. Ibid., p. 177.
66. Ibid., pp. 195–96.
67. Ibid., p. 203. UNESCO data found in Andrew L. Shapiro, *We're Number One* (New York: Vintage Books, 1992), p. 165.
68. Bagdikian, 1990, p. 23.
69. "The Media," *Harper's Magazine,* vol. 268 (April 1984), p. 28.
70. Todd Gitlin, "Television Screens: Hegemony in Transition," in *Cultural and Economic Reproduction in Education,* ed. Michael W. Apple (London: Routledge and Kegan Paul, 1982), pp. 206–46.
71. U.S. Department of Education, National Center for Education Statistics. The Condition of Education 1966. Washington DC, 1997.
72. Derek Bok, *The State of the Nation* (Cambridge: Harvard University Press, 1996), pp. 63, 66.
73. Dertouzos, Michael, *What Will Be: How the New World of Information Will Change our Lives* (New York: HarperCollins 1997), p. 10.
74. Andrew Kantor and Michael Neubarth, "How Big Is the Internet?" *Internet World,* December 1996, 7:12, pp. 44–48.
75. U.S. Department of Education, National Center for Education Statistics, Fast Response Survey System, "Advanced Telecommunications in U.S. Public Elementary and Secondary Schools, Fall 1996." Washington DC: NCES 97-944, February 1997, p. 1.
76. Ronald D. Owston, "The World Wide Web: A Technology to Enhance Teaching and Learning?" *Educational Researcher* (March 1997), 26:2, p. 33.
77. Dertouzos, p. 241.
78. Ibid., pp. 293–294.
79. Tim Jones and James Coates, "Gates Offers Hand to the Wary—and Hopeful," *Chicago Tribune,* April 30, 1997, Section 3, p. 1.
80. Michael Apple, "The New Technology: Is It Part of the Solution or Part of the Problem in Education?" in Gail E. Hawisher and Cynthia L. Selfe, eds. *Literacy, Technology, and Society* (Upper Saddle River, NJ: Prentice Hall, 1997), p. 170.

81. Jean Anyon, "Ideology and U.S. History Textbooks," *Harvard Educational Review,* vol. 49 (August 1979), pp. 361–84; "Schools as Agencies of Social Legitimation," *Journal of Curriculum Theorizing,* vol. 3 (Summer 1981), pp. 86–103; and "Social Class and Social Knowledge," *Curriculum Inquiry,* vol. 11, no. 1 (1980), pp. 3–42.
82. Anyon, "Schools as Agencies of Social Legitimation," p. 90.
83. See, for example, Richard Sennett and Jonathan Cobb, *The Hidden Injuries of Class* (New York: Random House, 1972).
84. Derek Bok, The State of the Nation (Cambridge: Harvard University Press, 1996), pp. 366–373.
85. Anyon, "Schools as Agencies of Social Legitimation," p. 94.
86. Anyon, "Ideology and U.S. History Textbooks," pp. 369–70.
87. Michael Apple, "The Political Economy of Textbook Publishing," *Educational Theory,* vol. 34 (Fall 1984), pp. 307–20.
88. John H. Faulk, "Texas Texts," *The Nation,* October 2, 1982, p. 292.
89. Prudence Cutright and Loyal Durand, Jr., *American Neighbors* (New York: Macmillan, 1980), p. 446.
90. Chomsky, *On Power and Ideology* and *The Culture of Terrorism.*
91. See, for example, Lear, "The Concept of Cultural Hegemony," p. 569.
92. Jacques Ellul, *Propaganda: The Formation of Men's Attitudes* (New York: Vintage Books, 1963), p. 11. Chomsky argues a similar point in *Media Control: The Spectacular Achievements of Propaganda* (New York: Seven Stories Press, 1997).
93. Peter Bachrach, *The Theory of Democratic Elitism: A Critique* (Boston: Little, Brown, 1967), p. 4.

Teaching in a Public Institution: The Professionalization Movement

Julius Menacher, co-author

In Chapter 3 we examined the early history of the common-school movement, which sought to reform schooling to meet what influential leaders saw as the needs of Massachusetts in the 1830s. Part of this reform movement included Horace Mann's efforts to improve the quality and quantity of teachers available to the new common schools. It led also to Mann's successful effort to centralize state control of schooling. We thus saw how an early instance of school reform produced changes in how teachers were prepared and how schools were governed.

Of particular interest was the development of *normal schools,* which were devoted to what Mann saw as teachers' educational needs. The curriculum in these normal schools included pedagogy, some psychology of learning, and the subject matter that teachers were expected to teach.

By establishing for the first time a specialized body of knowledge that all teachers were expected to master and by using this knowledge as the basis for establishing state-controlled certification standards, Mann pushed teaching in the direction of becoming a *profession.* Previously it had been a loosely organized occupation that was open to anyone regardless of training and certification. We also saw in Chapter 3 how Mann actively sought to recruit women into the normal schools for this newly professionalizing occupation, a development that would seem on its face to be good for women and good for teaching. It would appear to open professional opportunities for women and to provide a core of better-prepared practitioners for an emerging profession. Yet today, prominent school reformers are still trying to "professionalize" an occupation that, unlike other, more established professions, is predominantly female. Their efforts may have to take into account the subordination of women in American culture. If the feminization of teaching has contributed to its comparatively low status among the professions, it may also be true that teaching has not been the route to professional autonomy for women that other professions have been (though for fewer women).

Can an occupation with 2.8 million practitioners, most of whom are women, be expected to achieve professional status similar to that enjoyed by such professions as medicine, law, and architecture? Or is teaching so conditioned by its history as a gendered, publicly funded occupation that it is unsuited to certain kinds of professionalization? If so, then the efforts to improve education by professionalizing teaching may be misplaced.

Efforts to professionalize teaching are currently centered, as they were in Mann's time, around the intention to improve schooling. Just as in the 1830s and 1840s, the current professionalization movement raises questions about the funding and control of the profession of teaching, as well as questions about who should become teachers and how they should be prepared. Four of the most important issues to consider in the contemporary debate on professionalism are these:

- Preparation and licensure of practitioners for a mass profession that must serve the entire population, not just private clients who seek services.
- The consequences of public funding of the profession as compared with private funding.
- The role and status of women in the profession.
- The tension between public and professional control over teaching practice and what will be accepted as the specialized knowledge base of the profession.

Each of these issues has an impact on the status and rewards of the profession. Taken together, they define teaching as unique among the professions. They also help us understand whether the movement to professionalize teaching is likely to have an impact on the quality of schooling as we enter the 21st century.

PROFESSIONALIZATION OF TEACHING: HISTORICAL PERSPECTIVE

Common-School Reform

Each of the main periods of school reform that we have examined, from the common-school reforms through the Conant era, included as part of its reform agenda the effort to improve teaching and teachers. Horace Mann, for example, sought to make teaching more effective and respectable by treating pedagogy as a field worthy of study for all teachers. His primary purpose was not to give teaching the status of a profession, but to prepare sufficient numbers of practitioners with the skills necessary to provide high-quality education to the common schoolchildren of Massachusetts. To establish these skills, he believed, specific programs of education and training were necessary, and the normal school was born. In the normal schools, we see the beginning of one of the most critical features of any profession: the pulling together of a specialized body of knowledge that all practitioners are expected to master through extended study. Government licensure or certification is used to ensure mastery of the professional knowledge base. In fact, these two features—an identifiable body of specialized knowledge and government licensure—are identified by educational historian Joel Spring as the most important defining elements of a profession.[1]

There were other ways, too, in which Horace Mann began to confer professional status on an occupation whose practitioners varied greatly in the quality of their preparation and methods. For example, his effort to establish and enforce a moral code of behavior through both the state and local school councils can be viewed as a way to achieve something like a professional code of ethics to which practitioners could be expected to adhere. And by standardizing both the content and the conduct of schooling through the state board of education, Mann was seeking to standardize the quality of professional practice. As states gained the power to influence and even control the school day and the school curriculum, however, the decision-making autonomy of teachers became severely constrained. This tension between state control and teacher autonomy, both of which are components of professionalism, would prove to have very different consequences for teaching than for private-practice professions, such as medicine and law. In these latter fields, professional licensure did not so severely limit the control of the field by the professionals themselves.

Yet it would seem on the face of it that what resulted from Mann's ambitious reforms in Massachusetts was a solid foundation for the establishing of a true profession. But as John Goodlad has pointed out, the 20th century dawned with teaching still far short of professional status. Goodlad notes, for example, that the typical 2-year normal school curriculum provided poor professional preparation. The body of professional knowledge it presented was ill-defined, its students often did not plan to go into teaching, and its atmosphere was both unscholarly and submissive. Such characteristics do not fit well with the preparation of a professional capable of autonomous practice based on specialized expertise.[2]

Schools and teaching in early 19th-century America were more focused on moral goals than economic ones, as this picture of a female teacher being interviewed seems to suggest. This began to change late in the century with the shift to an industrial economy.

Progressive-Era Reform

These, in fact, were some of the concerns that led progressive educational reformers in the late 19th and early 20th centuries to reexamine the nature of teaching and teacher preparation. A development that came about at this time was the attachment of teacher preparation programs to 4-year baccalaureate degrees, such as law and medicine had come to require. These new 4-year programs sought to provide a greater theoretical base in the psychology of learning and in the history and philosophy of education. William R. Johnson's research suggests that normal schools had already begun extending to 4 years of study by the end of the 19th century and were increasingly emphasizing academic subject matter over pedagogy.[3] With the location of teacher education programs in 4-year state colleges and universities, the age of the 2-year normal school ended relatively early in the 20th century.

The impulse for such professionalization through more rigorous academic preparation came from the larger school reform movements of the progressive era. That era introduced the notion of the scientific management of schooling, and both the efficiency progressives and the democratic development progressives wanted teachers to have a better understanding of the newly emerging research on the psychology of learning and the principles of group management. In addition, teacher educators with a social reconstructionist orientation at Columbia Teachers College in the 1930s argued that teachers should have distinctive preparation in the history, sociology, and the philosophy of education. They could then become "educational statesmen," capable of leading the schools and their students to the forefront of democratic changes in America.[4]

An interesting tension developed here as Teachers College and other 4-year institutions began paying increasing attention to the preparation of educational administrators. On the one hand, *professional administrators* were being educated to have a greater role in school management and decision making and, on the other hand, teachers were also being given more extensive education so that they could, presumably, exercise greater autonomy in their work. By the beginning of World War II, the normal-school era had ended and teacher education was primarily a 4-year, state university enterprise. The fact that teachers were increasingly required to have a baccalaureate degree and that teaching and teacher education had come under the governance of state regulations together gave the appearance of moving teaching closer to being a profession. In truth, however, the increased control of schools and school districts by administrative experts, as described in Chapter 4, meant that teachers' autonomy was increasingly threatened.

Conant-Era Reform

Within a few years following the end of World War II, both teaching as an occupation and the education of teachers came under increasingly hostile criticism from those who considered schooling in the United States to have gone academically "soft" (see Chapter 8). In the early 1950s, books such as Arthur Bestor's *Educational Wastelands* attacked the schools' curricula. In the late 1950s, after the launching of the Soviet Sputnik, the Conant reforms called for greater academic rigor, "ability grouping," and increased emphasis on math, science, and vocational training. Then, in 1963, two books were published attacking teacher education: James D. Koerner's *The Miseducation of American Teachers* and James B. Conant's *The Education of American Teachers.* Consistent with the reform movement's increased emphasis on academic rigor for the presumably academically talented, both men disparaged teacher education courses, which they believed to be intellectually unchallenging and professionally useless, and both emphasized preparation in academic content areas.[5] In addition, Conant emphasized the importance of an intensive period of practice teaching, which was seen to be more consistent with the clinical or internship training of such professions as medicine and law. In the end, however, Conant, Koerner, and others did little during this reform period to professionalize teaching. Johnson writes:

> Teachers came to be seen as less central to the improvement of the schools during the early 1960s because, beyond a consensus among lay critics that more intensive academic training was needed, there was no agreement on how to train teachers. This was not a matter of disagreement over which models of professional training ought to be supported. There were no models. Not even imperfect ones which might, through renovation and reform, hold promise for the future.[6]

Johnson goes on to suggest that, given this skepticism concerning the preparation of teachers, the accountability movement of the 1970s and thereafter, which linked teacher evaluation to student test scores, can be understood as an effort by legislators and policymakers to control the quality of teaching from the top down. Insofar as the accountability movement emphasizes the management of teachers rather than their professional autonomy, it appears to step away from professionalism in teaching, rather than toward it. But, as Jurgen Herbst argued, professionalization in teaching has historically taken on the trappings and bureaucratic control of a *managed occupation.* This, of course, is opposed to professionalism, which emphasizes "the recognition and practice of a teacher's right and obligation to determine his or her own professional tasks in the classroom."[7] It would appear that the period following the Conant reforms produced movement away from professionalism in teaching, despite Conant's recommendations for how to achieve better schooling through reformed teacher education. And if the school reform movement of the 1980s and 1990s is any indication, educational policymakers are still not satisfied with the achievements of schools or the preparation of teachers.

PROFESSIONALISM AND CONTEMPORARY SCHOOL REFORM

The "excellence" reform movement of the 1980s has continued into the 1990s, and school performance remains a topic in the forefront of news coverage and political campaigns. A key dimension of this reform movement has been renewed attention to the education of teachers, with strong arguments made again for the professionalization of the teaching occupation. Chapter 14 will treat the origins and development of the current school reform movement in some detail. For the purposes

As the progressive era ideology of expert top-down management began to pervade schools, colleges of education began preparing professional administrators to run schools using principles of scientific management taken from business.

of this chapter, it is sufficient to note that the present reform movement has emphasized, perhaps above all else, improving the measured academic achievement of students in our schools. From the early reports in 1983, such as *A Nation at Risk,* to the most recent legislation in the 1990s, such as President Clinton's *Goals 2000: Educate America Act,* improved achievement in so-called basic academic areas has been touted as necessary for the United States to compete economically in the world marketplace. These reports have criticized our schools as having lost sight of this central academic purpose.

In the recent spate of educational reform reports, discussion of the professionalization of teaching always begins with a concern for the quality of schooling in the United States. Once it is established that education in schools is deficient, it is a simple step to hold the teachers in our schools responsible for it. If there are problems in schooling, it is asserted, these are due in part to inadequacies among the teachers. But what is inadequate about teachers? In attempting to answer this question, scholars and critics turn to professionals in other fields, such as medicine and law, for comparison. This appears at first to be appropriate, since we are accustomed to thinking of teaching as a profession that requires a college degree, claims a body of specialized knowledge, and requires a license to practice.

Comparing Teaching to Other Professions

When we look to other professions for standards of comparison, it is said, teaching as a profession fails to measure up in several ways. To use a crude production model, we might say that the quality of the raw materials (teacher education candidates), the quality of the processing (teacher education), and the quality of the final product (teachers and the organization of the profession) are all lacking—or so goes the rhetoric. In terms of the quality of the input, it is asserted that the talent or background of the candidates entering teacher training is inferior to those entering other professions. In terms of the processing, it is asserted that teacher education programs themselves are not as rigorous as the programs in medicine, law, architecture, and other professions. And in terms of the output, it is asserted that teachers, with their inferior academic talents and inadequate preparation, are often not competent to perform the complex tasks expected of them; further, they populate a profession that is structured with less autonomy, lower status, and fewer material rewards than other professions.

This three-part comparison of teachers to other professions is explicit in *Tomorrow's Teachers,* the first of three manifestos of the Holmes Group, a consortium of deans from the colleges of education of major research universities in the United States. In the midst of the school reform movement of the 1980s, the Holmes Group began its "Agenda for Improving a Profession" with the following comparison between teaching and other professions. In this comparison, the candidates, the preparation, and the structure of the profession fare poorly:

> Professional education prepares people for practical assignments: to teach, to heal, to design buildings or to manage organizations . . . Unhappily, teaching and teacher education have a long history of mutual impairment. Teacher education long has been intellectually weak; this further eroded the prestige of an already poorly esteemed profession, and it encouraged many inadequately prepared people to enter teaching. But teaching long has been an underpaid and overworked occupation, making it difficult for universities to recruit good students to teacher education or to take it as seriously as they have taken education for more prestigious professions. Teaching, after all, comes with large responsibilities but modest material rewards. Good teachers must be knowledgeable, but they have few opportunities to use that knowledge to improve their profession, or to help their colleagues improve. And, despite their considerable skill and knowledge, good teachers have few opportunities to advance within their profession.
>
> As we try to improve teaching and teacher education, then, we cannot avoid trying to improve the profession in which teachers will practice.[8]

The Holmes Report argues that teaching compares unfavorably to other professions, and it offers recommendations for how to make teaching more closely resemble those professions. Yet, if teaching is so distinctive an enterprise that it is difficult to compare with other professions, then professionalizing teaching may be the wrong solution to improving schooling. To examine whether making teaching "more professional" is best for schools, it becomes appropriate to ask, Should teaching be viewed as a profession like others, or is it so different that the differences make comparisons misleading?

After discussion of such questions, members of the Holmes Group chose to pursue the "professionalization" model for teaching, as did the Carnegie Forum's Task Force on Teaching as a Profession. These will be discussed below, because both groups made highly publicized recommendations for standardizing the teaching profession for greater professionalization and for improved schooling. Their approach to standardization, as we will see, is in some ways reminiscent of Horace Mann's, but with new ideological justification and in a different historical context.

Professionalism and Modern Liberal Ideology

All of the attempts to define professionalism presented in this chapter are grounded in modern liberalism, particularly in its commitment to specialized expertise and scientific rationality. The proponents of professionalizing teaching use as their criteria for a profession such characteristics as the existence of a scientific knowledge base that practitioners can master through prolonged study, state licensure based on demonstrated mastery of that knowledge base, and decision-making autonomy for those practitioners who demonstrate such mastery. This approach also confers elevated social status and material rewards on those who have been licensed as having acquired this specialized expertise.

Using such modern liberal criteria for a profession, it is no wonder that teaching has repeatedly been referred to as a quasi-profession. For example, some would point to the relatively low pay of teachers, as compared with physicians and lawyers, as indicative of the weak professional status of teaching. Yet other professions compare poorly to law and medicine in this respect. The clergy, for example, is one of the three original professions to be educated in American universities, yet it is typically excluded from discussions of teacher professionalization. Just as the clergy has historically been considered a profession despite its comparatively low pay, so are other occupations that require specialized training, formal certification, and adherence to occupational codes of ethics typically counted firmly among the professions. Social workers, psychologists, businessmen, and even professional musicians have rightful claim to the title "professional." The term has broader meanings than Goodlad and others would like to admit when they are arguing for improved schooling through improved teachers. The American Federation of Teachers, in contrast, places its greatest school reform emphasis on changing the funding and control structures of schooling, an approach that focuses on more fundamental political-economic issues than the professionalization of an already existing profession.[9]

To summarize, no single combination of factors such as income, status, licensure, specialized expertise, or autonomy is adequate to define all types of professions. Generally, whatever criteria are used to define the notion of a profession stem from some underlying ideological perspective. In the case of teaching, the definition used by many school-reform analysts has been based on criteria taken from the modern liberal veneration of a specialized knowledge base validated by scientific inquiry or privileged expertise. To question that modern liberal commitment to scientific rationality is not to assert that teachers do not have specialized expertise. Rather, it is to suggest that the specialized expertise of the teacher is only one part of a unique set of characteristics that define teaching as a distinctive profession.

Traditional Criteria for the Professions

Those who, like the Holmes and Carnegie commissions, look to the traditional professions as models for the occupation of teaching are taking what might be called a traditional sociological perspective. They identify several traits that characterize a profession's place in the larger society—such as autonomy grounded in certifiably expert knowledge, or social status and rewards—and then argue that if teaching adequately exhibited these traits it would clearly be a profession, and that public schooling would likely be improved.

There is, however, no full agreement on what constitutes a profession. The National Labor Relations Act attempted in 1948 to define a professional as one who is

> engaged in work predominantly intellectual ... involving the consistent exercise of discretion and judgment ... of such character that the output produced cannot be standardized ... requiring knowledge of an advanced type in a field of science or learning customarily acquired by a prolonged course of specialized intellectual instruction and study.[10]

By this definition, is a teacher a professional? Certainly the work is more "intellectual ... involving the consistent exercise of discretion and judgment" than simply physical and routine. At least among teachers we consider to be good at their craft this is true. What about the other criteria expressed above? How do teachers measure up in terms of acquiring a specialized body of knowledge through prolonged study?

While an argument could be made that teachers are professionals by the above definition, one of the most recent and comprehensive studies of professional preparation for teaching argues emphatically that teaching is "not quite" a profession. In the 1990 volume *Teachers for Our Nation's Schools,* John Goodlad writes, "The conditions necessary to a profession simply have not been a part of either teacher education or the teaching enterprise." Goodlad identifies the following as the necessary conditions for professional status:

- A reasonably coherent body of necessary knowledge and skills.
- A degree of homogeneity in groups of program candidates with respect to expectations and curricula.
- Rather clear borders demarcating qualified candidates from the unqualified, legitimate programs of preparation from the shoddy and entrepreneurial, and fads from innovation in theory and research.[11]

While Goodlad asserts that these conditions are "largely lacking," he goes on to say that teaching may be considered a profession, but a "weak" one, "not quite" the profession that others are:

> Our studies have led us to several conclusions (and related hypotheses) supporting the proposition that teaching is a weak profession ... First ... there is not a knowledge base sufficient to justify the claim that teaching warrants classification as a profession... Our second conclusion, related to the first, is that the knowledge underlying and relevant to teaching has

> been little codified. The process is just beginning... Our third conclusion is that curriculum development in teacher education is largely absent, inadequate, primitive, or all of these.[12]

Goodlad is reflecting the view, found in the Holmes and Carnegie reports, that teaching is not a profession in the sense that the major professions are, but that it could become such a profession if certain reforms in teacher education were enacted. Unlike the Holmes and Carnegie reports, he focuses only on professional *preparation* and does not go on to talk about the conditions of work (autonomy, rewards, and so on) in the occupation itself. As indicated earlier, the Holmes and Carnegie reports do make recommendations for restructuring the profession of teaching as well as preparation for it.

Professionalization and Teacher Preparation

In the mid-1980s the Holmes and Carnegie reports sought to improve the quality of schooling by upgrading the preparation of teachers and, further, by calling for new national licensing procedures. In terms of teacher preparation, for example, all of the Holmes Group's five major recommendations seek directly or indirectly to standardize and improve the quality of teacher preparation and development. Under "Our Goals" they list the following:

1. To make the education of teachers intellectually more solid.
2. To recognize differences in teachers' knowledge, skill, and commitment, in their education, certification, and work.
3. To create standards of entry to the profession—examinations and educational requirements—that are professionally relevant and intellectually defensible.
4. To connect our institutions to schools [for teacher preparation and development].
5. To make schools better places for teachers to work and to learn.[13]

Most occupations, whether identified as professions or not, are characterized by a certain degree of consensus on what constitutes good- or bad-quality work, on right and wrong ways of doing things. Thus, there is nothing inherently wrong with establishing standards for good preparation for an occupation. The centralizing of control over standards may be cause for concern, however, for such centralization, as we saw in Part 1, can foster hierarchical decision making in which individuals lose control over the decisions that affect their lives. The Holmes Group expressly recognizes "the limitations of standardized testing in predicting the future performance of teachers," but they nevertheless commit the Group "to develop and administer a series of Professional Teacher Examinations that provide a responsible basis for decisions on entry into the profession."[14] While the Holmes Group suggests a multiple set of practical and written evaluations sensitive to the various roles teachers will perform, the move toward centralization and standardization will continue to arouse objections on the part of many. In addition, their recommendation 3 seeks to standardize the restructuring of teaching into three tiers of teachers, each with different preparation, experience, status, rewards, and responsibility in the school. This restructuring recommendation will be addressed later in this chapter.

The standardization and centralization theme is more prominent in the Carnegie Report, *A Nation Prepared: Teachers for Our Nation's Schools,* than in the Holmes Report. The Carnegie Forum urges the nation, among other things, to take the following steps:

- Create a National Board for Professional Teaching Standards, organized with a regional and state membership structure, to establish high standards for what teachers need to know and be able to do, and to certify teachers who meet that standard.
- Restructure the teaching force, and introduce a new category of Lead Teachers with the proven ability to provide active leadership in the redesign of the schools and in helping their colleagues to uphold high standards of learning and teaching.
- Develop a new professional curriculum in graduate schools of education leading to a Master Teaching degree, based on systematic knowledge of teaching and including internships and residencies in the schools.[15]

As in the Holmes recommendations, the Carnegie Forum seeks to establish centralized standardization at the national rather than at the state level. Such standardization would govern preparation for the profession, entry into the profession, and the structure of the profession. The Carnegie list added, as might be expected, "Make teachers' salaries and career opportunities competitive with those in other professions."[16] In both reports, the improvement of schooling is linked to the professionalization of teaching, that is, to the selection, training, licensure, occupational hierarchy, status, and compensation of the practitioners.

Teacher Preparation and Career Ladders

Some researchers have turned their attention to professionalizing teaching through the curriculum development that Goodlad felt was "largely absent." One dimension of professional preparation in other fields is the clinical internship, in which students practice their craft for a period of 1 or more years under the guidance of practicing professionals. In *The Teaching Internship: Practical Preparation for a Licensed Profession,* Linda Darling Hammond and her co-authors look to such established professions as medicine, psychology, architecture, and engineering and observe that they "require a candidate to undergo a structured internship before being admitted to practice. Internship provides training; it safeguards the public from unskilled, unsupervised novices; and it gives guidance and support to beginning practitioners."[17]

Those who take the established professions as models, however, also recognize that differences between teaching and other professions extend beyond the nature of professional preparation and clinical experience. Again, the structure of the occupation is raised for consideration, and the concept of *career ladders* is presented by reformers as one way to restructure the occupation.

Career Ladders Those who advocate career ladders seek to establish a job differentiation within teaching that would allow teachers to move into distinctly more prestigious and responsible levels of teaching over the course of their careers—in contrast to the current system, in which all teachers perform roughly the same tasks. Reformers seek to use career ladders to improve the quality and status of teaching in two ways. First, they hope teachers themselves will feel greater rewards from and commitment to teaching as an occupation. Second, they hope to bring greater social respect to those teachers who move up the occupational ladder. This would also be a way to respond to the question, How can an occupation with 2.8 million practitioners achieve high professional status and rewards? Given the proposed job differentiation within teaching, fewer would receive the highest status and rewards.

The Holmes Report suggests at least one version of a career ladder in which there would be three levels of teaching: instructors, professional teachers, and career professionals.[18] In the Holmes model *instructors* would be certified as competent to teach within a particular subject area because of their past academic or occupational experience. Instructors could come directly from liberal arts schools, from colleges of education, or from the work force. Given new training, they would be issued a 5-year, nonrenewable certificate which would entitle them to teach under the supervision of professionals further up the career ladder. *Professional teachers* would have some advanced degree in teaching in addition to their own teaching experience. They would be viewed as competent, autonomous practitioners and would participate in running the school. However, it is the *career professionals* who would have the most advanced credentials and also the most decision-making power in schools. They would divide their time between teaching and school leadership activities such as curriculum design, the mentoring and monitoring of novice teachers, and other administrative tasks. The Carnegie Report, as we saw, also proposes a career ladder, though it differs in its details.

Those committed to the professionalization of teaching as a means of improving schooling must face two potentially serious questions regarding career differentiation. First, there is some concern that whatever decision-making power, money, and status may accrue to those at the top, the power of those at the bottom of the ladder would thereby be diminished. The Holmes Report has fueled some speculation that economic resources alone would dictate that some 50 percent of the teaching force would be instructors and therefore in no position to contribute to the professional status of the occupation. Concurrently, it is estimated that school budgets could support only 20 percent of the teaching force as career professionals. Thus, increased professional autonomy and status for a relatively few teachers would come at the expense of professional autonomy and status for most teachers.

A second problem with career ladders is their tendency not to support classroom teaching as the heart of the profession. Classroom teaching would be left primarily to those at the lower end of the career ladder, with more and more administrative functions falling to the excellent teachers at the top of the ladder. Thus career ladders do not alleviate a common complaint by teachers: that the only route to occupational advancement is leaving the classroom for administrative positions. It might be worth noting that in other professions—law and medicine, for example—professional advancement does not require leaving day-to-day practice. While there are managing partners and chiefs of staff who are lawyers and doctors respectively, they are, in fact, a very small percentage of their profession, and they answer to administrative and bureaucratic norms rather than to the norms of the medical or legal profession.

This raises the issue of what actually constitutes the heart of teaching work. In law firms, for example, part of what happens to attorneys as they scale the career ladder is that they have the opportunity to buy into a partnership. This gives them some control over the business of the firm. At the same time, when they are actually practicing they are, in fact, doing the same work. The nature of the work that senior partners do is the same as that of the first-day associate. So there is some precedent to the idea that increasing ownership and responsibility within one's practice do not necessarily mean giving up the practice itself.

Professionalization is only one of several possible approaches to improving schooling, and although it has strong supporters, it also has its critics. The professionalization approach, from Horace Mann through the Holmes and Carnegie recommendations of the 1980s, can be characterized as central to a liberal approach to school improvement, while views opposing professionalization, or least making that term subject to critical inquiry, might represent a different ideological perspective.

TEACHING AS A PUBLIC PROFESSION

Earlier we considered briefly the issue of the relatively low status of teaching among the occupations. In considering the status of school teaching as at best "a quasi-profession," educator Dee Ann Spencer presents a brief summary that identifies three factors that must be considered when assessing the prospects for professionalization of teaching. Spencer writes:

> In summary, teaching is considered a quasi-profession because of low pay and teachers' lack of control over their work place. The conditions under which teachers work are more similar to those of blue-collar workers than to those of other professionals. The way in which the organizational structure of schools has developed over time and the predominance of women in teaching have created and perpetuated these conditions.[19]

Each of these issues—low pay, lack of control over workplace decisions, and the predominance of women in teaching—interacts with the others in shaping the nature and status of teaching as a quasi-profession, and each can be examined briefly here.

In doing so, however, we will examine an alternative hypothesis: that teaching is only a "partial" or "quasi" profession if the concept of "profession" is narrowly defined. If we accept the notion that there are different kinds of professions, then teaching can be understood as a distinctive type of profession with distinctive features of its own. How one defines professions is to some degree an ideological choice. For example, to define professions by the characteristics of medicine and law, which contract private clients on a competitive basis, are male-dominated, and resist public, democratic control in favor of control of privileged expertise, is to ensure that publicly funded and controlled, female-dominated, and noncompetitive professions appear deficient. Given these defining criteria, rectifying that "deficiency" seems like a sensible thing to do. If, however, one starts from the point of view that the modern liberal emphasis on expert control of decision making might not be appropriate to all professions, different reasoning is possible.

Teaching as a Distinctive Profession

If the modern liberal view of a profession seems inconsistent with the realities of teaching, what alternative view of professionalism is available? One approach that does not compare teaching to other professions in terms of career ladders, rewards, status, and so on, was suggested by Herbst earlier in the chapter, and is worth reviewing here. Herbst contrasts *professionalization* (credentialing, career ladders, increasing specialization, more administration) with *professionalism*, which emphasizes "the recognition and practice of a teacher's right and obligation to determine his or her own professional tasks in the classroom."[20] He, like other theorists critical of the professionalization model, does not presume that teaching needs to be like other professions. He seeks instead the conditions under which teachers could determine for themselves what they want their profession to be. For the nation as a whole to move in that direction would require an ideological shift away from faith in experts as decision makers and toward a commitment to democratically shared decision making among teachers in schools.

One difficulty with that vision, however, and a potentially severe one, is that there are many stakeholders in the schools: teachers, parents, students, the business community, legislators, and others. If democratic decision-making processes require dialogue among all stakeholders, then teachers become one voice among many—and an often devalued, female voice at that. Given a commitment to democratically shared decision making, the movement toward professionalism, based on a liberal view of progress through expert autonomy, becomes suspect. A tension develops between professionalization and the special role of the teacher who seeks to serve the democratic ideals of the community.

Dealing with the tension between professional autonomy and democratic accountability to public values presents teachers with a task as complex and demanding as those in any profession. In this view, teaching is clearly a profession, but a profession of a distinctive sort, with special demands. Unlike law, medicine, or the clergy, teaching is not practiced by a relatively few practitioners serving a limited clientele. Rather, it is a publicly supported profession that serves our entire population of children and youth in a public setting. Unlike other professions, it cannot often be pursued in private practice. Moreover, its form of specialized knowledge is grounded more in public knowledge and values than in esoteric content unavailable to the public. It is not predominantly male, but more than two-thirds female in its composition. Each of these issues must be considered when one seeks to understand the nature of the teaching profession, and we shall turn to them in the next section.

To take seriously the hypothesis that teaching is already a profession, but one of a unique kind, is to undermine the professionalization movement and thus to blunt one of the weapons of the liberal school reformers. But this may be a good thing if one is interested in getting to the roots of the schools' problems. Those roots lie in dominant social structures that sustain economic inequality, unemployment, government by a powerful elite, racism, and other social ills that the professionalization movement is unlikely to address. The fact that the school reform movement has focused less on these underlying social issues than on professionalism is itself evidence of how the dominant liberal ideology of top-down decision making operates to rule some issues in and others out of the public debate.

Political-Economic Dimensions of Teaching as a Public Profession

Teaching as a Mass Public Profession The oft-cited problems of low status and rewards for teaching are not in themselves sufficient evidence that teaching is a "weak" or "quasi" profession. Although teacher pay is inevitably related to teacher status in a materialistic society, teacher pay is also related to many other factors. Among them is the need to use public funds to support 2.5 million public school teachers. This dependence on public funding (along with other factors mentioned below) has contributed to low pay for teachers relative to other professions. Teachers cannot ordinarily "hang out a shingle" as members of other professions can, that is, go into private practice, because the institutions in which they conduct their practice are primarily public institutions supported by public taxes. In private schools (where about 12 percent of teachers work), teachers are supported by tuition that often provides them with less income than the public schools. For the most part, teachers are considered public servants, who, like police and firefighters, must depend on the public for their support. In addition, teachers greatly outnumber such public servants as police and firefighters. Consequently, their salaries are often lower than other public-servant positions that do not require a college degree. There are currently over 2.8 million teachers in public and private elementary, middle, and secondary schools, and projections suggest there may be over 3 million by the year 2001.[21]

The magnitude of the support needed for a profession of this size cannot be overstated. The U.S. Bureau of Labor Statistics reports only 587,000 lawyers and 580,000 physicians practicing in the early 1990s. Furthermore, their services are selectively, not universally, available, most often on a private contractual basis as the need arises. Imagine what would happen to physicians' salaries if their numbers were quintupled and they were paid by tax dollars. Would we say that physicians were no longer professionals?

Public versus Private Funding Using 2.5 million as a conservative estimate of public school teachers, one can quickly see the enormous increase in public expenditures that would be necessary if salaries were raised even $10,000 across the occupation. An additional expenditure of $2.5 billion annually, or even half that amount, is not one that state governments or the public are likely to support (see Exhibit 10.1). Partly as a consequence of such large numbers of teachers, a rough leveling effect has operated historically to keep teachers at about the median point of all full-time occupations (the relative stability of teachers' salaries is illustrated in Exhibit 10.2). In 1929-30, teachers earned 2 percent more than the average for full-time employees working for wages or salary in all industries, *if supervisors and principals are included in these figures.* During World War II the average for teachers dropped to 15 percent less than other

EXHIBIT 10.1 **Sources of Revenue for Public Elementary and Secondary Schools; 1970–71 to 1990–91**

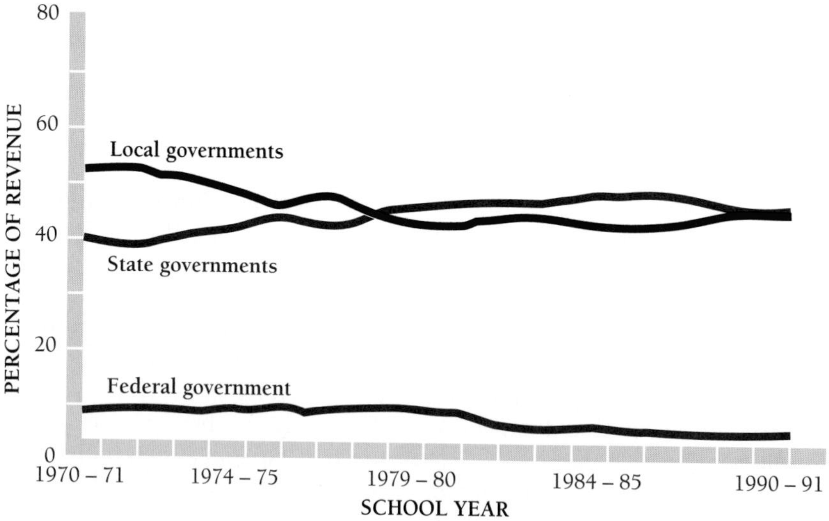

Source: Digest of Educational Statistics (Washington, D.C.: National Center for Educational Statistics, 1993), p. 50.

EXHIBIT 10.2 Salaries of Teachers

Teachers' salaries constitute a major portion of the elementary and secondary budget, and good teachers are central to a high-quality education system. Between 1980 and 1995, the average salary of all public school teachers, adjusted for inflation, increased 19 percent, rising from $31,412 to $37,436.

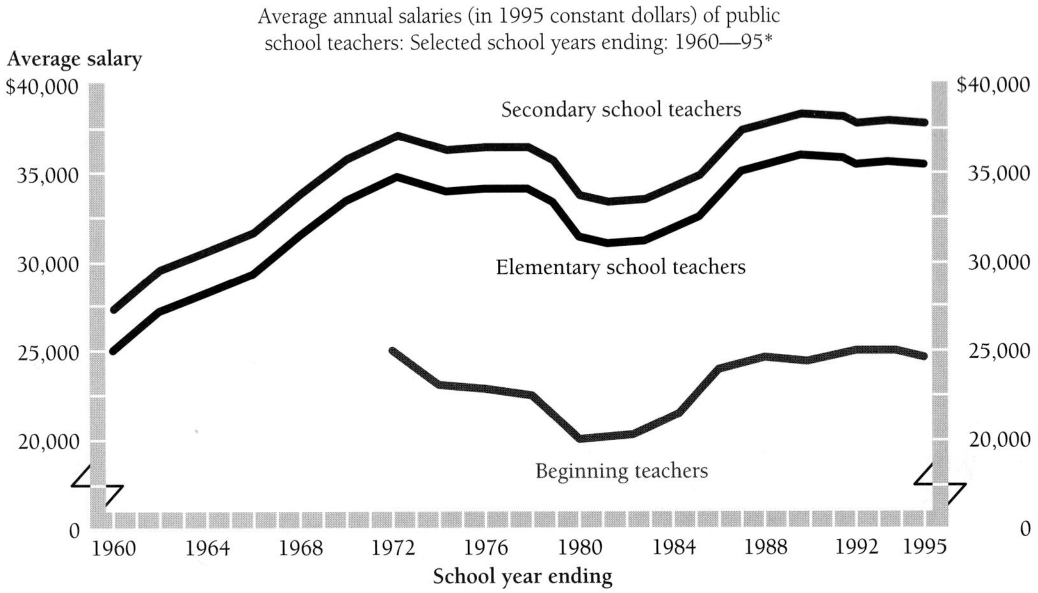

*Plotted points for average annual salaries for public school teachers are even years 1960–68 and all years 1970–95. Plotted points for average beginning salaries for public school teachers are even years 1972–88 and all years 1990–95

Source: U.S. Department of Education, National Center for Education Statistics, *Digest of Education Statistics, 1995* and Schools and Staffing Survey, 1993–94 (School, Administrator, and Teacher Questionnaires); American Federation of Teachers, *Survey and Analysis of Salary Trends 1995,* December 1995.

workers, but by 1972 it had risen to 24 percent more. Since then, the average has fluctuated between 11 percent and 22 percent more than the pay for other workers.[22] While this shows some improvement, it may well be a function of the increased numbers of higher-paid school administrators since World War II.

The fact that teacher salaries are state and locally funded is part of the nation's historical commitment to state-level control of education, and the fact that there is no national policy on teacher salaries accounts for the wide discrepancies even in the same region. In the East, for example, where average teacher salaries in 1992 were among the highest in the country, New York teachers averaged nearly $44,000 per year while Pennsylvania salaries averaged below $38,000. Per capita income in New York is nearly $3,000 higher than in Pennsylvania, making for a higher tax base. But discrepancies among average teacher salaries within a state are typically greater than between states or between regions, because in a given community, local resources can play the decisive role in funding local schools. Some towns and cities are simply much wealthier than others. Exhibit 10.1 indicates the extent to which state and local revenues have contributed most of the funding for schooling in the United States.

Whether teaching is a weak profession, not quite a profession, or a profession unique among the professions, it is clear that it is not materially rewarded as much as other professions tend to be. In 1992, when the average pay for public elementary and secondary school teachers had risen to

$34,434, this represented more than a doubling of the average salary earned in 1980 and a tripling of the average salary earned in 1972. Yet after adjustment for inflation, *the salaries had increased only $92 per year since 1972.* Federally employed general attorneys in 1990, meanwhile, averaged $57,152, while auditors and chemists employed by the Federal government earned $40,000 and $46,847, respectively. Lawyers, chemists, and accountants in private business or industry earned considerably more.[23]

This difference in salary may or may not help account for the fact that teaching seems to draw less academically skilled students into the profession than other professions do. The National Center for Education Statistics reports that in 1992, SAT scores of college-bound high school seniors intending to major in education lagged behind the scores of students intending to major in liberal arts, engineering, mathematics, and physical sciences by 35, 40, 60, and 90 points, respectively.[24]

Educational researcher Geraldine Clifford writes that teaching has been underpaid throughout history, regardless of the gender of the majority and the method of paying for teaching.[25] She asserts that this is due in part to the low social status of its clients, who are children. While the client status of children may be a factor, it seems clear that the preponderance of women in the field of teaching has also kept salaries depressed. Typically, occupations dominated by women provide earnings that are much lower than male-dominated occupations requiring similar skill levels. One report indicates that more than 80 percent of full-time working women currently have incomes less than $19,000 per year, and that full-time women workers made only 75 percent of male earnings in 1987. Even in female-dominated occupations, women on average earn significantly less than men working in the same occupations.[26]

Teaching as a Predominantly Female Profession

The question that arises, of course, is whether the movement toward professionalization of teaching will be likely to change significantly the status, rewards, and lack of control over their occupations that teachers experience. If Spencer is correct, that the predominance of women in the field is a major obstacle to teachers' obtaining professional status comparable to other professions, then there is cause to be skeptical of the professionalization approach, for teaching promises to remain predominantly female for some time to come. Further examination reveals additional relationships between gender and teaching.

As the Holmes Group notes, occupations that are female-dominated tend to earn lower income and enjoy lower status than male occupations that require comparable skills and training. And, as Spencer notes, increasing the proportion of women in a field has historically tended to expand the number of male administrative professionals who control that field.[27] Since the 1860s, women have been the majority of teachers, and this condition is not likely to change. For the last 30 years, the percentage of male public school teachers has remained fairly stable at about a third of all teachers (although the percentage of men declined in the 1980s from 33 percent to 28 percent).[28]

Historical Perspective Historically women have in several ways been thought by some to be ideally suited to the occupation of teaching. From the standpoint of town councils and local school boards, female teachers in Horace Mann's time were considered to be more malleable than men to the various demands and limitations of the job. Further, as schooling spread throughout the populace, the notion grew that teachers should be a bridge between the personal, nurturing environment of the home and the more impersonal, group-oriented environment of the school and outside world. By virtue of their experience as homemakers, as well as their nurturing instincts, women were considered ideally suited to help children cross this bridge.[29]

As the low status and salaries of 19th-century schoolmasters made the job increasingly unappealing to its traditional male candidates, there arose a simultaneous need for more teachers to staff the growing number of schools. As these new teaching positions were increasingly filled by women, any potential demands for perquisites were stifled by the fact that the only alternative occupations available, factory and domestic labor, were unappealing to many women. At the same time, as John Rury has pointed out, more rewarding management and commercial opportunities were drawing men out of teaching.[30]

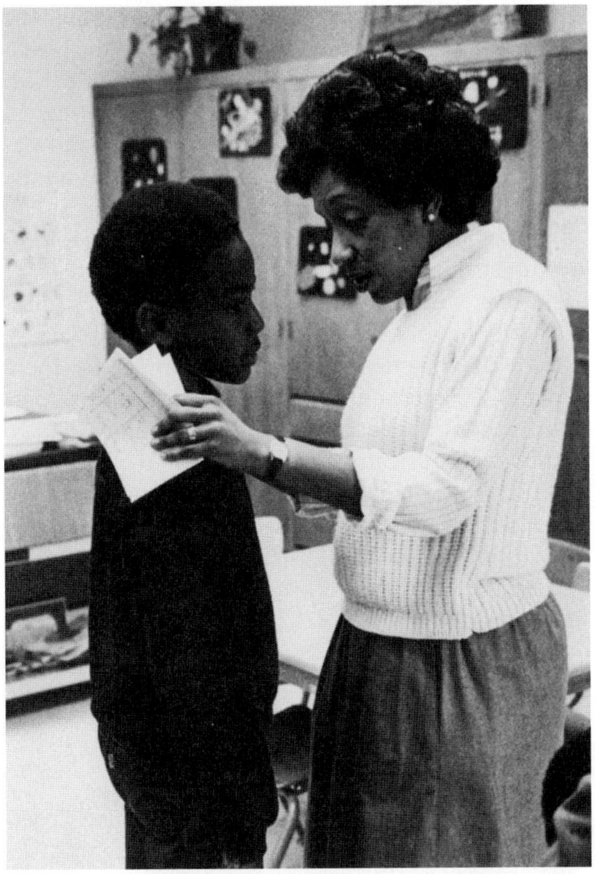

The nurturing side of teaching has been used to classify it as a "helping" profession that is more suitable to women than men. Is there any reason that a helping profession should have less status than a more impersonal one?

One reason that other occupations have historically drawn men away from teaching is the fact that teaching is a "flat" occupation. That is, good job performance does not naturally lead to a higher-paying managerial or ownership position. Except when given additional administrative chores, such as curriculum specialist or department chair, teachers at the beginnings and ends of their careers have similar responsibilities. In contrast, educational administration has a hierarchical structure that progresses from school to district to state levels. As opposed to teaching, which is female dominated, administrative jobs, which are higher-paying and more prestigious, have historically been dominated by men.

Current Reform Proposals In the liberal women's movement of the 1970s, one goal was to redress the balance of female policymakers in schools and school districts. That effort continues, although part of the focus has now shifted to addressing the empowerment of those teachers who choose not to leave the classroom for administrative posts. The choice is often made not because teachers do not value administrative tasks or desire more responsibility for policymaking and implementation, but because they do not want to leave teaching—and the choice is often either/or. Teaching remains a valued set of activities for them, and classroom life is not traded for central administration offices.

The most recent national report to emerge from the professionalization movement expressly seeks to support and reward the professionalism of teachers who remain in the classroom. This report, *What Matters Most: Teaching for America's Future,* was released in late 1996 by the National Commission for Teaching and America's Future, funded by the Rockefeller and Carnegie Foundations (see Primary Source Reading at the end of this chapter). *What Matters Most* adds substantially to the work of the earlier Carnegie Commission and Holmes Group Reports, in large part by shifting focus away from *teacher professionalization* to a focus on *student learning.* As you will read in the Primary Source Reading, the National Commission began with three fundamental premises:

1. What teachers know and can do is the most important influence on what students learn.
2. Recruiting, preparing, and retaining good teachers is the central strategy for improving our schools.
3. School reform cannot succeed unless it focuses on creating the conditions in which teachers can teach, and teach well.

By focusing on the teaching conditions necessary for optimal student learning, the issue of professionalism is framed not by seeking to make teaching look like other professions. Instead, the issue of professionalism in *What Matters Most* is grounded in how *the distinct knowledge and skills of the teaching profession* can be incorporated into the governance of teacher licensing and the nature of teacher preparation and professional development.

In addition, the report recommends the recognition and reward of teachers who have demonstrated advanced professional achievement, using rigorous standards and teacher assessments developed by the National Board for Professional Teaching Standards, which the Carnegie Commission had recommended early in the 1980s, earlier in the contemporary school reform movement. In fact, we will return to the issue of the National Board and *What Matters Most* in Chapter 14, as we assess the current state of the school reform movement in the United States.

PUBLIC CONTROL VERSUS PROFESSIONAL AUTONOMY

Spencer's earlier contention that the quasi-professional status of teaching is due in part to teachers' lack of control over their workplace is at first puzzling when we consider what appears to be considerable autonomy for teachers in the classroom. There, alone with their students, teachers can seemingly do what they wish. Spencer herself notes that "classrooms are social settings in which teachers hold the most powerful positions." She continues, however, to say that "within the context of the school or school system as an organization, teachers take a subordinate role to administrators. . ."[31]

In fact, since the progressive era, school administrators have experienced an increased role in school management. In 1920, for example, there were 21,000 principals and supervisors (3.2 percent of total instructional staff). This increased to 48,000 administrators (5.3 percent) by 1950 and 141,000 (6.1 percent) by 1980.[32] While the number (and percentage) of administrators was increasing, the number of school districts was decreasing. In 1992 there were only 15,173 local districts, while in 1923, there were 127,931.[33] This resulted, as was

Teachers appear to be in control of their classrooms; but, unlike other professions, they have little to say about the conditions of their work, such as length of the school day and year, the content of the curriculum and how it is tested, how their school is organized and governed, how school monies are budgeted, and how they are evaluated.

EXHIBIT 10.3 The Major Political Groups in Education

MAJOR GOVERNMENT ACTORS	SPECIAL INTEREST GROUPS	THE KNOWLEDGE INDUSTRY
Politicians	The Big Three	Creators
Education Policies	Foundations	Funding agencies
School Boards	Corporate sector	Researchers
Courts	Teachers' unions	Gatekeepers
	Educational interest groups	Knowledge brokers
	Single-interest groups	Testing organizations
		Distributors
		Publishing industry

Source: Joel Spring, *Conflict of Interest: The Politics of American Education* (White Plains, NY: Longman), 1988, p. 3.

described in Chapter 4, from the increasing centralization of school control during the progressive era. In that same era, the percentage of teachers who were female peaked at 86 percent in 1919, and it has dropped to around 72 percent in the 1990s.

Educational historian Joel Spring, however, describes teachers' lack of control over their workplace in terms much more elaborate than simply subordination to administrators. In *Conflict of Interest: The Politics of American Education,* Spring argues that teachers are at the focal point of a sprawling, complex array of different social, political, and economic institutions that have significant power over how schools are structured and what takes place in them. Spring organizes these various groups and institutions in three major categories (see Exhibit 10.3), some of the groups having *legal* responsibility for school regulation and control (such as the courts and school boards) and others having powerful *extralegal* (not illegal) influence over schools. Extralegal groups include research funding agencies and foundations that can influence the kind of knowledge that gets generated about schooling, testing organizations, and interest groups that influence, for example, the content of textbooks.[34] Colleges and schools of education (knowledge brokers) are also part of the control apparatus in that they are legally authorized by their respective states to prepare teachers in certain specific ways and not in others. Spring's table showing the various groups that control schooling is not completely self-explanatory, but it suggests the diversity and power of those who seek to influence schooling.[35] Spring himself devotes virtually his entire volume to explaining and supporting the organization proposed in the table.

The Limitations on Teacher Decision Making

If control over its own conditions of work is one major aspect of a profession, then Exhibit 10.3 suggests why teaching may be lacking in this condition. Fundamental decisions about the length of the school day and the school year, the content of what should be taught, how it will be tested, what counts as valid knowledge in texts, and how the school will be organized and governed are all made *primarily* by people other than teachers. Through teachers' unions and through their classroom autonomy, teachers can assert some control over their practice, but it is asserted within a complex political-economic framework controlled by others.

This is, in part, why a 1988 Gallup poll that surveyed 21,698 public school teachers for the Carnegie Foundation for the Advancement of Teaching found the following: "Except for choosing texts and shaping the curriculum, most teachers feel left out of critical decisions affecting classroom life." The poll went on to find that 10 percent or fewer "felt they had any say in issues like teacher evaluation or selection of new teachers and administrators. Just 20 percent believed they were influential in tailoring school budgets."[36] Commenting on the report, which was conducted during the education reform movement of the 1980s, National Education Association president May Hatwood Futrell said, "The report endorses what I have often said—that teachers are treated like very tall children instead of professionals."

A 1991 U.S. Department of Education survey of teachers confirms such findings in greater detail. Fewer than 20 percent of public school teachers reported having a great deal of influence over school policies related to matters such as student discipline policy, faculty training, student ability grouping, and establishing curriculum. These findings are particularly disturbing if we consider that autonomous decision making based on special training is one of the hallmarks of a profession. In fact, this same survey indicated that the majority of teachers did feel that they had complete control of a few classroom decisions: selecting teaching techniques, grading students, and determining the amount of homework to assign. Nevertheless, such decisions occur within a larger institutional framework involving curriculum, discipline, and other school policies that limit the teachers' autonomy.[37]

Who Controls the Schools?

It is not easy to determine "who controls the schools," to borrow the title of a well-known book on the subject. It is instructive to note the various agencies and constituencies that seem to be legitimate stakeholders in determining what counts as important knowledge and values in the schools and how they should be taught. In the U.S. Department of Education survey noted above, for example, two-thirds of public school teachers reported that they did not have complete control over decisions concerning classroom discipline. But, it might be argued, this is as it should be. Do we want each teacher to decide, on the basis of his or her best professional judgment, how to discipline each child—regardless of what state or local school board policy or the federal courts have ruled? It would appear that all of these constituencies have a legitimate role to play in the teacher's decision making, and the teacher's professional duty is to be influenced by these agents.

Similarly, it is difficult to hold teachers accountable to a codified body of knowledge that is influenced by so many groups. The Educational Testing Service reports that 41 states test students in order to demonstrate accountability to the taxpayers. Teachers are ill-advised to ignore the content of those tests when they are teaching. On the other hand, a recent article in the journal *School Administrator* was titled "School Reform by University Mandate" to indicate the influence that university entrance requirements have over school curricula.[38] Meanwhile, schools and colleges of education have the responsibility of preparing new teachers, but state mandates are designed to influence what schools of education can and should do in such preparation. State legislatures are in turn subject to a variety of political and economic forces exerted by various pressure groups. Among these, for example, is Citizens for Excellence in Education, based in Costa Mesa, California, a conservative Christian group that claims 120,000 members in 868 chapters in every state of the union. This group was one of several that in 1993 fought to use the courts to ban certain public school textbooks because of their "secular humanist" content.

Influence of yet a different kind comes from major foundations with the resources to sponsor research studies and policy documents. The Rockefeller Brothers Fund, for example, has weighed in on the professionalism debate with a booklet called *A Shared Vision: Policy Recommendations for Linking Teacher Education to School Reform.* Teachers are also influenced by such professional organizations as the National Council of Teachers of Mathematics and the National Council of Teachers of English, organizations that attempt to set curriculum and teaching standards for their respective fields. And, finally, those who are calling for more systematic licensure in the teaching profession seek to influence what teachers will learn by holding teacher education programs and teachers themselves accountable to specific expectations regarding what teachers should know and be able to do. The major national teachers' unions, the American Federation of Teachers and the National Education Association, have supported such recommendations.

All these organizations represent various elements of the public that the public schools are expected to serve. Who should determine the public interest if not the people themselves, through governmental bodies and special interest groups? The authority for what should be taught in schools must ultimately lie with the public as well as with professional teachers and administrators. Consequently, teachers must ultimately learn how to balance a great number of competing perspectives while focusing on the best interests of each child in every classroom. The task is truly challenging, even to the wisest and most experienced of teachers.

In order to appreciate the relationship of public control versus professional autonomy in American education, it is necessary to understand the role of the governmental structure that undergirds public education, and the various legal and extra-legal considerations that affect students, teachers, parents, and others with involvement and interest in public schools.

Legal Control Structure

An understanding of the United States' form of educational governance begins with the Tenth Amendment to the United States Constitution, which states that: "The powers not delegated to the United States by the Constitution, nor prohibited by it to the States, are reserved to the States respectively, or to the people." Since education is not mentioned anywhere in the Constitution, the individual states have plenary power over public education. However, given the early American tradition of placing government control as close to the people as possible, a form of educational government developed in which a significant portion of state control of public education was delegated to local school districts created by the state. Since government education policy is under the control of each state, there is no uniform pattern to school districts throughout America. They vary in size, number, and even in regard to whether they exist at all. For example, Illinois has about 2,000 local school districts, and the State of Hawaii has not seen fit to create any.

State Government and Local Control It is important to understand that, while most states have delegated authority for daily operations to local districts, school districts remain creatures of the state. The state legislature may create new ones or dissolve existing ones. A Michigan court decision provides a good description of this relationship: "The legislature has entire control over the schools of the state... The division ... into districts, the conduct of the school, the qualifications of teachers, the subjects to be taught therein, are all within its control."[39]

State education policy is administered through boards of education and state departments of education. State boards exercise general control over state educational policy, and recommend legislation to the state legislature. State departments advise their boards on policy and legislation, and execute policy set by state boards. State departments also promulgate rules and regulations for the conduct of public education. As a general rule, states exercise authority for establishing minimum standards, which individual school districts must meet, and may exceed if they wish. These minimum standards include teacher certification requirements, the minimum number of days public schools must be in session, compulsory student attendance rules, required subjects to be taught, graduation requirements, school health and safety standards, school finance policy, responsibilities of local boards of education, and more. Some states, e.g., California and Texas, require state approval of any textbooks used in local schools. It is important to understand that once the state has delegated specific authority to local districts, that authority cannot be arbitrarily superseded.

Local school board members, whether elected by citizens living in the school district, or appointed by the local government in which the school district is set, are representatives of state government in their communities, and generally serve without pay. School boards are empowered to set school district policy within the broad framework established by state law. Among the most important powers exercised by a local school board are appointing the school superintendent, approving the school district budget, negotiating collective bargaining agreements with teachers' unions, and acting on all district employee hiring and dismissal decisions. The role of the school superintendent has two basic components. The superintendent of schools serves as the leader of the educational staff, responsible for providing direction and supervision for all aspects of school district activity. The superintendent's other, equally important role is to advise the school board on all matters before it, recommend policy to it, and implement the policy decisions of the school board.

This structure is not without its problems, as when school boards act in such a way as to usurp the recommending and implementing authority of the superintendent, or when the superintendent assumes the policy-making function of the school board. Other problems involve conflicts between state education departments and local districts in regard to disputes over which has authority in one area or another. In such cases, state courts are called upon to interpret the law. Often, such disputes center on whether authority granted to a local district was "implied" by legislation, as opposed to an "express" grant of authority. For example, in settling such a dispute, a New York court held that:

> There can be no question that the Board of Education, by statute, has the power and responsibility to manage and administer the affairs of the school district, including the assignment of students therein. The Education Law ... specifically grants district school boards power to have in all respects the superintendence, management, and control of the educational affairs of the district and ... all the powers reasonably necessary to exercise powers granted expressly or by implication. . . .[40]

Federal Influence While constitutional authority for public education resides with state governments, the national government exercises pervasive influence over school policy. Although its authority to do so is indirect, it is nonetheless powerful. There are two major legal avenues allowing for federal involvement in education. First, there is the general welfare clause of the Constitution ("The Congress shall have Power to ... provide for the ... General Welfare of the United States") and the commerce clause, which gives Congress authority to "regulate Commerce ... among the several States." Courts have recognized the broad federal authority contained in these provisions to approve national laws that influence, but do not directly control public education. These provisions have enabled Congress to enact laws that offer money to states and school districts to establish programs that advance goals deemed important to national security and welfare.

Three of the most important national acts that have exerted enormous influence over the direction and conduct of education deserve mention. The National Defense Education Act of 1958 funded program improvements and student study grants in science, mathematics, foreign language, and guidance because the Congress deemed educational improvements in these areas necessary for the national defense during the Cold War. The Elementary and Secondary Education Act of 1965 (currently reauthorized as the Improving America's Schools Act), provides large amounts of funding to schools directed at improving the education of students whose education is limited by poverty. Finally, the Education for All Handicapped Children Act of 1975 (currently reauthorized as the Individuals with Disabilities Education Act) requires school districts to serve the needs of disabled students according to rules and regulations established by the U.S. Department of Education. While federal funding is authorized to enable school districts to meet federal guidelines for serving handicapped students, the amount of funds provided has proven inadequate, requiring schools to divert large proportions of their budgets to this purpose.[41] This last act illustrates that federal support for new mandates can be a mixed blessing for school districts.

Federal control over education extends far beyond the requirements of these and related acts. This is so because many of these acts provide that should school districts refuse to implement them, or improperly implement them, all of their federal funds may be at risk. This is a serious concern for all public school districts, since an average of about 8 percent of their budgets comes from federal funds, which most districts can ill-afford to lose.

The second source of federal influence over education comes from civil rights amendments to the Constitution, primarily the First Amendment (protections of religious freedom and freedom of expression), the Fourth Amendment (privacy protection), and the Fourteenth Amendment (rights of due process and equal protection of law). It is important to understand that public school districts are agents of state government, and therefore, subject to constitutional safeguards against government abuse of the rights of the people as set forth in civil rights amendments and statutes. Even though the language of the First and Fourth Amendments prevents only the national government from abusing civil rights, the U.S. Supreme Court has decided that state government (including public schools) is similarly forbidden from violating these fundamental rights. State and federal courts have the role of hearing complaints from students, educators, and other citizens regarding charges of civil rights abuses by public schools. Since the mid-20th century, there has been a large increase in educational litigation that affects all those involved in schooling. The extent of school-related court suits has been great enough for many to call the justices of the U.S. Supreme Court "the black-robed school board." Prospective teachers should be familiar with the major court decisions that influence school policy.

While many federal education cases focus on constitutional civil rights amendments, others are litigated on the basis of various federal civil rights acts affecting education. Chief among these is the Civil Rights Act of 1964, which forbids discrimination because of race, color, religion, sex, or national origin, by any agency receiving federal funds. Other congressional civil rights statutes that have been the source of educational litigation include Title IX of the Education Amendments of 1972, which forbids schools to discriminate in their programs on the basis of gender; the Rehabilitation Act of 1973, which forbids discrimination based on a handicap by any agency receiving federal funds; the Family Educational Rights and Privacy Act of 1974, which requires schools to allow teachers to inspect their personnel files and challenge material in it, as well as make all student records available for inspection by parents or by students aged 18 or above, and to challenge material in those records; and the Equal Access Act of 1984, which forbids schools allowing various groups to meet in the school to deny access to groups on the basis of religious, political, or philosophical views. Teachers receive specific protections against hostile actions by school boards because of pregnancy (Pregnancy Discrimination Act of 1978) or because of age (Age Discrimination in Employment Act of 1967).

Who Controls the Schools? The Role of the U.S. Supreme Court

What follows is an overview of some major decisions of the U.S. Supreme Court. These serve as examples of the way the judicial system has exerted powerful influence over the direction and control of American public education. As will be seen, these court decisions affect not only teachers, but students and their parents as well, by affecting such areas as attendance policy, parents' rights, school segregation, funding, testing, censorship, academic freedom, and religion.

Rights of Parents versus Rights of the State Before the mid-century explosion of educational litigation, two important cases were decided by the U.S. Supreme Court during the 1920s. Both resulted from the isolationist sentiments produced by American involvement in World War I. The issue in the 1922 case of *Meyer* v. *Nebraska* was a state law that forbade the teaching of a foreign language to children who had not passed the eighth grade. Meyer taught German in an elementary parochial school in violation of this act. In overturning the law as an unreasonable restriction on Meyer's liberty guaranteed by the due process clause of the Fourteenth Amendment, the Court reasoned that: "Mere knowledge of the German language cannot reasonably be regarded as harmful... His right thus to teach and the right of parents to engage him so to instruct their children, we think, are within the liberty of the amendment... No emergency has arisen which renders knowledge by a child of some language other than English so clearly harmful as to justify its inhibition with the consequent infringement on rights."[42] Even so, the Court affirmed the state responsibility for governing schools by ruling that "the authority of the state to compel attendance at some school and to make reasonable regulations for all schools is not questioned."

Two years later, the Supreme Court decided *Pierce* v. *Society of Sisters*. In this case, the state of Oregon, influenced by pressure exerted by such organizations as the Ku Klux Klan, passed a law requiring all students to attend only public schools, thereby ensuring against any interests counter to state views. The Society of Sisters appealed to the Supreme Court, as the act would put their parochial school out of business. In deciding in favor of the Society of Sisters, the Court reasoned that the act:

> unreasonably interferes with the liberty of parents and guardians to direct the upbringing and education of children under their control... The fundamental theory of liberty under which all governments in this

> Union repose excludes any general power of the state to standardize its children by forcing them to accept instruction from public teachers only. The child is not the mere creature of the state: those who nurture him and direct his destiny have the right, coupled with the high duty, to recognize and prepare him for additional obligations.[43]

Again, as in *Meyer,* the Court cautioned: "No question is raised concerning the power of the state reasonably to regulate all schools; to inspect, supervise, and examine them, their teachers, and pupils."

The conflicting rights of parents and the state reemerged in 1972, when the Supreme Court considered the case of *Wisconsin* v. *Yoder.* The issue was the refusal of the Old Order Amish community to send their children to high school up to age 16, as required by state law. The reason for Amish resistance to this law was their belief that secondary schooling, provided outside their community, encouraged values alienating their children from their religion and community. The Amish believed that their system of providing elementary education and then apprenticing youth to productive community work was better preparation for adult life than what the public high school could provide. Given the historic evidence of religious commitment and the productive, self-sufficient, law-abiding behavior of this Amish community, the Court found that the state could not provide a sufficiently compelling interest in requiring the postelementary schooling they sought. However, the Court was careful to point out that its ruling was a narrow one, and applicable only to the unique circumstances of this one particular Amish community.

These cases illustrate the role of the courts in balancing the interests of the state in providing for an educated citizenry against the rights of parents to direct the upbringing of their children. As the Supreme Court stated in *Pierce,* "the child is not the mere creature of the state." Even so, our courts are equally clear about the authority of states to require that all of its children are properly educated.

Equal Protection in Public Education The aftermath of the Civil War produced, among other legal enactments, the equal protection clause of the Fourteenth Amendment to the U.S. Constitution, for the protection of African-Americans newly released from slavery. This clause required that no state shall "deny to any person within its jurisdiction the equal protection of the laws." As with all legislation, it remained for the courts to interpret its meaning and application to a variety of circumstances. Court precedent was established in *Plessy* v. *Ferguson* in 1896, wherein the Court held that the requirements of equal protection were met by "separate-but-equal" treatment of the races by government in support of "public peace and good order." Ignoring the lone dissent by Justice Harlan that "the Constitution is color blind," this decision set the pattern for race segregation throughout the South. It took a half century for the *Plessy* precedent to be reversed. This was done in the landmark case of *Brown* v. *Board of Education* of 1954. The Court reversed *Plessy* by noting that understanding of the effects of race segregation in education had grown since *Plessy.* The Court now accepted that the enforced segregation of black children "generates a feeling of inferiority . . . that may affect their hearts and minds in a way unlikely ever to be undone." Therefore the Court concludes that "in the field of public education the doctrine of 'separate but equal' has no place. Separate educational facilities are inherently unequal."[44]

In the years following the *Brown* decision, federal courts were very active in dismantling the previously legal school race segregation in southern states. For years, such devices as forced student busing to promote integration were ordered by courts. More recently, the Supreme Court has taken a less forceful role in combating school segregation. Forced busing has been abandoned, and districts that had been under court supervision for desegregation have been released from court supervision even though serious questions remain regarding the extent and persistence of integration efforts (e.g., *Board of Oklahoma City* v. *Dowell,* 1991; *Freeman* v. *Pitts,* 1992).

Even so, some of the old aggressive antisegregation stance remains. In 1989 the Supreme Court let stand the decision in *U.S.A.* v. *Yonkers,* in which both the City of Yonkers, New York, and the Yonkers Board of Education were held liable for inhibiting integration through decisions about closing new schools and opening new schools, school attendance area boundaries, and city council siting of public housing occupied by minority residents. Then, in 1990, the Supreme Court approved a lower court order requiring the State of Missouri and City of Kansas City to raise their tax levels above state legal limits to develop highly attractive magnet schools to encourage white students to return to the predominantly black Kansas City schools. However, in 1995, the Supreme Court refused to allow the district court to order further expenditures, as the results of this voluntary approach to integration did not justify the additional tax burdens on the state and city.

Over time, equal protection was expanded from sole concentration on the rights of the black minority population who had lived under state segregation laws. In 1973, the Court addressed the less overt, but nonetheless invidious discrimination practiced in northern school districts. In *Keyes* v. *Denver,* the Supreme Court found that school board actions in this northern city promoted segregation even though there were no segregation laws. This was done by board actions (e.g., setting school attendance areas) that promoted segregation of Hispanic students from the majority student population. The Court made clear that any official government action that contributed to race or ethnic school segregation violated the equal protection clause. In the same year, the Supreme Court used the Civil Rights Act of 1964 to decide the case of *Lau* v. *Nichols.* The Court opinion held that the rights of Chinese-speaking students in San Francisco were violated because the school system did not respond to the particular language needs of these students. This decision encouraged passage of the Equal Educational Opportunity Act of 1974, which supported the development of bilingual education in public schools.

In recent years, Title IX has been used to protect teachers and students from sexual harassment. The U.S. Supreme Court allowed damages against a school district that did not adequately respond to the need to protect a student from sexual harassment by a teacher (*Franklin* v. *Gwinett County Schools,* 1992) and lower courts have found school districts liable for not adequately protecting teachers from sexual harassment, as well as not protecting students from sexual harassment by their peers. In the 1996 case of *Nabozny* v. *Podlesny,* the failure of school officials to protect a homosexual boy from harassment by other boys was held to violate his equal protection rights.

School finance was brought into the scope of the equal protection clause because the usual system of state school finance placed primary reliance on local district property tax wealth. This resulted in wide disparities among districts in the amount of money raised to support each student's education. There were, and continue to be, great disparities in local district funding, creating stark contrasts in school buildings, programs, books and supplies, and teachers' salaries between the best- and worst-funded districts. The question raised was: Since education is primarily the responsibility of the state, should the financial support for a student's education be a function of the wealth of the local school district, or should it rather be a function of the wealth of the state as a whole? The Supreme Court of California answered the question by asserting that the California Constitution's equal protection clause required equal funding of all school districts in the state (*Seranno* v. *Priest,* 1971). The same issue was brought before the U.S. Supreme Court in the case of *San Antonio* v. *Rodriquez,* 1973. The Supreme Court rejected the argument, as the Texas traditional school finance system was not technically unconstitutional. However, the Court did note that the system was "chaotic and unjust."

The *San Antonio* decision did not end the effort to equalize school funding among state school districts. Since that decision, similar suits have been filed in a majority of states, based on provisions of state constitutions, with many of these suits resulting in reforms creating more equalized funding among school districts within these states. Many of these cases continue to be litigated. Even in states where constitutional challenges have been defeated, state legislatures concern themselves with developing greater equity in school finances.

The fundamental principles of equal protection applied by the courts to education include the following:

- Government should not invidiously discriminate among classes of persons. All should be considered equal under the law.

- In education, equal protection means that all students should be provided with equal educational opportunity. In the words of the *Brown* decision: "Such an opportunity, when the state has undertaken to provide it, is a right which must be made available to all on equal terms."
- Such benign matters as school tests used for placement, state school-finance formulas, and school policies to help disadvantaged students achieve parity may fall afoul of equal protection, depending on the facts of each case.

Religious Observances in Public Schools The First Amendment's religion clauses state that "Congress [or any state agency such as a school district] shall make no law respecting an establishment of religion, or prohibiting the free exercise thereof." A comfortable relationship existed between public schools and religion since the early days of American public education. Then there were controversies in the 1930s and 1940s that proved harbingers of more serious disputes to come. In adjudicating controversies over government support of parochial schools, the Supreme Court found that the First Amendment was not violated when public schools provided textbook loans to parochial schools (*Cochran* v. *Louisiana,* 1930) and that public school districts could provide transportation to parochial school students without violating the First Amendment (*Everson v. Board,* 1947). The Supreme Court also decided cases of public school–church cooperation. It held that it was not permissible for public schools to permit clergy into the school to conduct religious instruction (*McCullom* v. *Champaign,* 1948), but then found that releasing students to attend religious instruction at local churches was permissible (*Zorach* v. *Clausen,* 1952).

A much more emotional confrontation between religion and public education emerged in 1962 when the U.S. Supreme Court decided the case of *Engle* v. *Vitale.* A New York state law requiring all public school students to be led by their teacher in reciting a state composed nondenominational prayer ("Almighty God, we acknowledge our dependence upon Thee, and we beg Thy blessings upon us, our parents, our teachers and our Country") was challenged as a violation of the First Amendment's prohibition of government establishment of religion. The Court agreed, holding that "in this country it is no part of the business of government to compose official prayers . . . as part of a religious program carried on by government."[45] This decision was reinforced the following year by the Court's judgment in the companion cases of *Abington* v. *Schempp* and *Murray* v. *Curlette.* The companion issues were public school practices requiring daily reading from the Bible and the recitation of the Lord's Prayer. Both practices were found to violate the First Amendment. The state must remain neutral in regard to religion, neither supporting or opposing it. However, the Court did indicate that the study of the Bible from the perspective of its literary and historic qualities was permissible in public schools.

These decisions gave rise to a variety of strategies developed by deeply religious groups of people, most of which were defeated by the Supreme Court. For example, the State of Arkansas barred the teaching of evolution, but the Supreme Court held that law to violate the First Amendment, since it was religiously motivated (*Epperson* v. *Arkansas,* 1982). In light of that decision, the State of Louisiana passed a law requiring that whenever the theory of evolution was taught, equal time had to be given to teaching the biblical theory of creation. The Supreme Court found that act to be similarly motivated by religion, and struck it down (*Edwards* v. *Aguillard,* 1987).

Prohibitions on religious involvement in education continued into the 1990s when the Supreme Court held that nondenominational prayers led by clergy at public school graduation exercises violated the establishment clause (*Lee* v. *Weissman,* 1992). However, some success was achieved by religious interests in the *Westside Schools* v. *Mergens* decision in 1990, which held that under the Equal Access Act, public schools could not prevent student religious extracurricular interest groups from meeting when other student groups were allowed to meet. This "open forum" principle was also invoked by the Supreme Court when it refused to allow a local school district to bar community religious groups from using school facilities when nonreligious groups were given that right (*Lamb's Chapel* v. *Center Moriches,* 1994).

The adjudication of the relationship between religious and public schools has been called an area of "consistent inconsistency." This area of controversy is likely to continue. The debate between those who believe education is not complete without religious content, and those who believe that the public education of the heterogeneous population of America is best served by what Thomas Jefferson called the "high wall" that should separate church and state. The fundamental elements of Court policy on the separation of religion and public education include the following points:

- American government is secular, but this does not require public schools to be the enemy of religion. Rather, it requires public schools to take a neutral stance toward religion.
- Laws or school policies that clearly promote religion, or unnecessarily prevent students from reasonable religious expression in extracurricular activities, are forbidden.
- In adjudicating the constitutionality of issues involving religion and education, the Court employs the following three-part test to determine constitutionality:

1. Does the law/policy have a primary religious purpose?
2. Is the law/policy neutral, neither supporting nor opposing religion?
3. Does the law/policy involve excessive church-state entanglement?

   If one or more of these questions is answered in the affirmative, the law or policy will be declared unconstitutional.

Free Expression Before the 1960s neither teachers nor students possessed much protection under the First Amendment's guarantee of free expression. This changed through the decisions of the liberal "Warren Court," named for Chief Justice Earl Warren who served from 1953 to 1969. In 1968 the Supreme Court decided the case of *Pickering* v. *Lockport.* Teacher Pickering had written a letter to the local newspaper critical of his school board's decisions on spending from new funds recently voted by the community. He was promptly dismissed, and he brought suit against the board for violating his free expression rights. The Court found in favor of Pickering, holding that teachers had the same rights as other citizens to openly criticize school board decisions that were matters of general public interest. The following year, the Court extended free expression rights to public school students in *Tinker* v. *Des Moines.* Here, students planning to wear black armbands to school in silent protest against the Vietnam War were warned not to do so, under penalty of suspension. They wore the armbands and were consequently suspended. They sued, asserting First Amendment expression rights. In finding in favor of the students, the Court wrote that: "It can hardly be argued that either students or teachers shed their constitutional rights to freedom of speech or expression at the schoolhouse gate. . . In our system, state-operated schools may not be enclaves of totalitarianism. School officials do not possess absolute authority over their students."[46]

The years following these decisions saw great expansion of teacher and student expression rights. One such area was the special type of free expression right possessed solely by educators, called "academic freedom." While the Supreme Court did not address this issue in regard to elementary and secondary school teachers, lower courts, taking their cue from related expression cases decided by the Supreme Court, made it clear that school authorities may not censure teachers for instructional approaches or written materials simply because the approaches or ideas used do not agree with the personal, idiosyncratic, political or social views held by board members or school administrators. In *Mailloux* v. *Kiley* (1971), teacher Mailloux, seeking to develop greater understanding of the use of language in his students, wrote a "taboo" word on the board to illustrate how one word for a particular human act is considered appropriate, and another "taboo." Parental complaints led to his dismissal, and he promptly sued on First Amendment grounds. In rescinding his dismissal, the court noted that school authorities had provided no guidelines to advise Mailloux that this approach was forbidden, nor had they shown that the exercise was without academic merit. This decision made clear that teachers should not have to guess about which approaches might cost them their jobs.

The case of *Parducci* v. *Rutland* (1970), involved teacher Parducci's assignment of Kurt Vonnegut,

Jr.'s satire, *Welcome to the Monkey House.* Parental objections to the controversial material in that piece led to an administration order that she withdraw that reading. Parducci refused and was dismissed, leading to the appellate court's decision to rescind her dismissal as a violation of her academic freedom. In doing so, the court wrote that:

> The Supreme Court has on numerous occasions emphasized that the right to teach, to inquire, to evaluate, and to study is fundamental to a democratic society... The right to academic freedom, however ... is not absolute, and must be balanced against the competing interests of society... In order for the state to restrict the First Amendment ... it must first demonstrate that the forbidden conduct would materially and substantially interfere with ... the operation of the school... When a teacher is forced to speculate as to what conduct is proscribed, he is apt to be overly cautious and reserved in the classroom. Such a reluctance on the part of the teacher to investigate and experiment with new and different ideas is anathema to the entire concept of academic freedom.[47]

As this decision indicates, teachers cannot say anything they please wherever and whenever they please. The Court struck a balance to these teacher rights successes in the following years, which brought decisions that indicated the limits on teacher expression. For example, in *Mt. Healthy* v. *Doyle* (1977), the Court approved the dismissal of a teacher who claimed he was fired for criticizing his school administration on a radio program in violation of his free expression rights. The dismissal was approved because the Court found that Doyle would have been fired even if the protected speech had not occurred. Then, in *Connick* v. *Myers* (1983), the Court made clear that speech by government employees which was of personal, rather than public interest, was not protected by the First Amendment.

The same balancing between the interests of the state in well-regulated schools with individual expression rights was exhibited in cases involving students. In 1986, the Court approved the disciplining of a student assembly speech that school authorities judged to contain "graphic sexual metaphor" (*Bethel* v. *Fraser*), and 2 years later rejected the free expression claims of student newspaper staff members that their rights were violated when school authorities censored articles prepared for publication in the school newspaper (*Hazelwood* v. *Kuhlmeier*). The Court reasoned that since the newspaper was an extension of the journalism class, educators had the authority to decide what was and what was not good journalism.

The guidelines for teacher and student expression that have been set by the Court include the following:

- Free expression is grounded in the American conviction that a free, democratic society cannot be maintained without full and free exchange of ideas.
- Rules restricting expression by teachers or students must be characterized by clear, reasonable guidelines. Absolute, unrestrained censorship that cannot be justified will be punished by U.S. courts.
- In deciding school free expression controversies, the court will balance the importance of restricting speech for school order and efficient functioning against the rights of individuals to express opinions on matters of public concern.

Due Process Both teachers and students possess Fourteenth Amendment due process rights. This means that they must be treated fairly when government agencies threaten their liberty or property interests. Tenured teachers may not be dismissed without fair procedures (procedural due process), nor may students be suspended or expelled without fair procedures. Further, both teachers and students have substantive due process protections against punitive actions by school authorities that are arbitrary and capricious, or result from overly broad or unnecessarily vague rules. An example of procedural due process protection for students is illustrated by the landmark case of *Goss* v. *Lopez* (1975). Several public school students were suspended for 10 days without being told the specific charges against them or afforded the opportunity to answer charges against them. The Supreme Court held that students were entitled to these protections and invalidated the suspensions, holding that, as a minimum, students "must be afforded some kind of notice and afforded some kind of hearing"[48] before suspension. Further, when the intended penalty increases to, for example, expulsion, so must the procedural due process, which would include such protections as an impartial decision maker and representation by counsel.

The teacher case of *Cleveland* v. *LaFleur* (1974) illustrates the protection afforded by substantive due process. Teacher LaFleur was pregnant, and according to board rules was required to leave her position when she entered the fifth month of pregnancy. She protested that this was an arbitrary, unreasonable rule which deprived her of her income as a teacher. The Supreme Court agreed, reasoning that teachers should not be penalized because of pregnancy, as "this court has long recognized that freedom of personal choice in matters of marriage and family life is one of the liberties protected by the Due Process Clause."[49]

The major due process guidelines for teachers to consider are:

- The Supreme Court has determined that when educators and students can establish valid liberty or property interests that are put at risk by school authorities, they are entitled to due process protections.
- Due process, as a concept, requires fairness in the treatment of individuals by government authorities. This includes fairness in procedures used to make decisions adversely affecting teachers or students (procedural due process) and substantive fairness, i.e., rules and decisions must be related to reasonable educational objectives in understandable (not unnecessarily vague) language, reasonably limited in scope (not overly broad), rational, and unbiased (free from arbitrary and capricious elements).

Privacy Public schools, as government agencies, must observe the privacy rights of people guaranteed by the Fourth Amendment. However, increased student drug abuse and violence has led the Supreme Court to expand the authority of school personnel to search students. In *New Jersey* v. *T.L.O.* (1985) the Supreme Court relaxed the traditional rule of "probable cause" justifying search of students by school authorities. Because of school order and safety problems the Court decided to "spare teachers and school administrators the necessity of schooling themselves in the niceties of probable cause and permit them to regulate their conduct according to the dictates of reason and common sense." If a search was justified at its inception, and reasonable in scope, the Fourth Amendment was not offended, because "against the child's interest in privacy must be set the substantial interests of teachers and administrators in maintaining discipline... Accordingly, we have recognized that maintaining security and order in schools requires a degree of flexibility in school disciplinary procedures."[50]

The right of educators to greater supervision of students to detect wrongdoing was further advanced in the 1995 *Vernonia* v. *Acton* case, in which the Supreme Court found that a school policy that required random urinalysis testing of students engaged in interscholastic athletic programs, as a condition of participation, did not violate the privacy rights of the students. The Court reasoned that the finding of a greater incidence of drug abuse among athletes, their status as role models, the nonpunitive result from finding illicit drug use, and the voluntary nature of participation in interscholastic athletics all combined to justify the rule.

In the area of Fourth Amendment rights, the following principles are important for teachers to understand:

- The school's interest in conducting a search will be balanced against the student or teacher's right to the Fourth Amendment's prohibition against unreasonable search and seizure.
- The intrusiveness of the search used is balanced against the severity of the problem it is designed to combat. For example, "dragnet" or "blanket" searches without particularized suspicion will generally not be allowed. Similarly, strip searches require very strong justification to meet court approval.

Who Controls the Schools? Extralegal Influences

Government legal structure, laws, and court decisions are not the only influences on school control. Government personalities, particularly the personal influence of the President, serves as a powerful extralegal influence on education policy. A prominent example of this is the influence exerted by President Reagan during the 1980s. The issuance by his administration of the "Nation at Risk" report, which criticized poor school performance as an internal threat to national security that was more serious than the external threat of Soviet communism, is a prime example of this. The result of Reagan's use of the "bully pulpit" was a wave of school reform in which almost every state in the Union participated. This has resulted in efforts to make both teachers and students more accountable for school performance.

There are a variety of nongovernmental forces that exert influence equal to that exerted by government. For example, private foundations such as Carnegie, Ford, Lilly, Kellogg, MacArthur, and others dispense millions of dollars to support higher education research directed at improving school practices, as well as to support of school programs for improving teacher ability and student programs. Foundation funds are directed to those applicants whose proposals address the issues deemed appropriate by the fundors. As a result, the boards of these private organizations exert influence over the direction of American education equal to that of the research and development funding provided by national and state governments.

Textbook publishers also exert a powerful influence on school policy (see Chapter 9). It is estimated that 75 percent of classroom time and 90 percent of homework time are spent with text materials.[51] The major textbook publishing firms exercise care in seeing to it that textbooks designed for broad national sales avoid offending any large buyers. Thus, when states with statewide adoption policies or very large districts are seen to be offended by the treatment of a particular topic, publishers may try to chart a course that produces maximum sales. The result may be harm to the intellectual integrity of their products, reducing them to a lowest common denominator of treatment designed to avoid offending any potential buyers. For example, some districts dominated by Christian fundamentalist groups complain that social studies texts fail to provide appropriate space to the contributions of Christianity to western civilization, while districts influenced by minority groups voice the same complaint regarding treatment of the contributions to civilization of their race or ethnicity.[52] Textbook publishers' attempts to please all are often the result of the profit motive, rather than a concern for scholarly rigor and pedagogical effectiveness.

A more recent pressure on the nature of textbooks has developed from the aforementioned national reform effort emphasizing school accountability. Many states now require standardized testing of students on both national and state-prepared tests. This has caused school districts to demand textbooks and related materials that emphasize the particular types of learning demanded by the state and national tests. Again, national textbook publishers attempt to respond to their largest buyers, creating problems for those schools without sufficient buying power to influence textbook development.

This influence exerted by national tests in the current reform movement is only the most recent extralegal influence of tests on school policy. For many years, schools have used nationally standardized tests to track students into various ability levels, including assignment of students into various special education categories. Those dissatisfied with the predominance of testing as a student sorting mechanism call attention to the fallibility of tests for this purpose, particularly when they serve as the only, or even primary, determinant of student classification. In California, the Association of Black Psychologists sued the California State Department of Education based on its claim that the major standardized intelligence tests, which were used to classify children as "mentally retarded," were culturally biased against black children. The resultant appellate court decision (*Larry P.* v. *Riles,* 1984) found that the tests did contain enough bias against black students to find a violation of the equal protection rights of minority students. An opposite conclusion was reached on the same issue in the Illinois federal court (*PASE* v. *Hannon,* 1980). Since the U.S. Supreme Court has never ruled on the issue, it remains a matter of controversy. The proper resolution of the problem advocated by most educators is to consider a number of sources of evidence in making decisions about the appropriate placement of students in school programs. Test results should be used, but in conjunction with evidence of school grades, teacher judgments, and other relevant information that sheds light on the educational potential of the student.

A final extralegal influence deserving attention is that of the two nationwide teacher organizations, the American Federation of Teachers (AFT) and the National Education Association (NEA). Both focus on influencing teacher welfare and educational improvement through lobbying for legislation at the national level, at the state level through state affiliates, and representing teachers in local district collective bargaining agreements. There was a time when the NEA preferred professional sanctions to teacher strikes as a way to influence school district and state education policy, and concerned itself mainly with general improvement of education rather than concentrating on teacher welfare issues, such as salary and fringe benefits. In contrast, the AFT operated more in the mold of a traditional labor union, using labor strikes as its most powerful weapon. Due to the success of the AFT at winning teacher salary increases and related teacher welfare concessions in large urban districts, thereby winning teachers from the NEA to its side, the NEA has developed a militant stance, including strikes, that rivals that of the AFT. Although the NEA is far larger than the AFT, both are very active in supporting candidates for political office who favor their positions and opposing those with contrary platforms, both publish professional journals, and both support a variety of teacher development programs for members.

As time has passed the traditional NEA-AFT rivalry has been replaced by increasing cooperation in recognition of the important political influence that can be exerted by combining forces. This has resulted in the merging of some local NEA and AFT affiliates in California and elsewhere. However, enough differences remain between the two national agencies to make earlier merger unlikely. Even while divided, the two organizations converge on a number of national issues, making their influence a powerful force on the direction of national education policy.

PROFESSIONAL SATISFACTION AND PROFESSIONAL ETHICS

Researchers are increasingly turning to teachers themselves to find out what is right, wrong, and possible in the teaching occupation. A recently instituted annual event of some interest is the Metropolitan Life survey of the American teacher. The 1993 survey showed a significant trend. Among a scientifically selected sample of 1,000 teachers, only 19 percent reported that they were very likely or fairly likely to leave teaching for another occupation in the next 5 years (a drop from 26 percent in 1988 and 1989), while 81 percent reported that this was not very likely or not at all likely for them.[53]

Studies of what teachers find most and least satisfying about their work reveal factors similar to those that operate in most occupations (see Chapter 11). Researcher Karen Seashore Louis, in studying the general literature on quality of work life, found several conditions that teachers, like other workers in various occupations, find important.[54] These include:

1. Respect and status in the larger community.
2. Participation in decision making that influences control over their work setting.
3. Frequent and stimulating professional interaction among peers within the school.
4. Opportunity to make full use of existing skills and knowledge and to acquire new ones (self-development) and the opportunity to experiment.
5. Procedures that permit teachers to obtain frequent and accurate feedback about the specific effects of their performance on student learning.
6. A pleasant physical working environment and adequate resources for carrying out the job.
7. A sense of congruence between personal goals and the school's goals, or a low degree of alienation.[55]

Louis writes that her interviews with teachers reveal that the first of these may well be the most critical factor, followed by the second, third, and fifth.

The U.S. Office of Education confirms Louis's study with regard to teachers' felt need for greater respect for their profession. While most teachers (53 percent) in a 1986 study indicated that greater respect for their profession would exert a major impact on keeping them in teaching, more involvement in decision making also received high priority. But if asked to rank factors, a plurality (26 percent) chose better pay (with more room for future increases) as the one factor that would have the greatest impact on their decision to continue or to leave teaching.[56]

One clear effect of the school reform movement of the 1980s was, in fact, the effort to increase teachers' salaries. As illustrated earlier in Exhibit 10.2, however, the average teacher salary has barely kept up with inflation over the past 25 years. And still, teachers work long hours. The average elementary school teacher, according to recent survey data, spends 47 hours per week on school duties, while the average secondary school teacher spends an average of 51. The difference may well be due to the fact that, on average, elementary school teachers have about 25 students in class, while secondary education teachers have an average of 23 students in each of five classes.[57]

Despite the importance of salary to those teachers who said better pay would affect their decision to continue or to leave teaching, recent studies remind us that other conditions are important to job satisfaction—and that job satisfaction in teaching leaves something to be desired. In 1993–94, full-time teachers in public schools earned an average base salary of $34,200, according to the U.S. Department of Education, whereas teachers in private schools averaged only $22,000 (for beginning teachers, the figures were $21,900 and $16,200, respectively). Yet 50 percent of private school teachers said they certainly would become teachers again, whereas only 40 percent of public school teachers said the same. Why would this be? The same study indicates that overall, only 11 percent of public school teachers were highly satisfied with their working conditions, compared with 36 percent of private school teachers.[58] These conditions include those that Louis identified above. Some of these, such as opportunity for frequent peer interaction and participation in decision making, are clearly conditions that school systems can address.

In fact, there are reasons to be encouraged by teachers' perceptions of their profession. In the national study cited above, in which 40 percent of public school and 50 percent of private school teachers said they would certainly become teachers again if they had the choice, each figure rises by 26 percent if we add those teachers who said they "probably" would become teachers again. Further, *USA Today* reported in a story on February 25, 1997, that teacher job satisfaction is increasing. Positive responses to such statements as "As a teacher I feel respected in today's society," have risen from 47 percent to 54 percent of those polled in recent years. Affirmative responses to whether teachers would encourage youth to enter the profession have increased from 45 percent to 67 percent. These changes may be due in part to teacher awareness of how other professions have in recent years suffered such trends as downsizing, stagnant wages, and constraints on decision making—in comparison to which teaching may be an increasingly rewarding option to those who seek to make a difference in the world around them.

Democratic Ethics and the Profession of Teaching

That teaching is situated amidst the competing values and demands of the public provides another component of its uniqueness as a profession: the professional ethics of teaching. Each profession has its own ethical codes, and teaching is no exception. The ethical codes of each profession are shaped by the activities and responsibilities unique to that profession, and since each profession has different responsibilities, the ethical codes vary accordingly. Philosopher Michael Scriven offers the following as examples of the professional ethical responsibilities of teaching:

> respecting confidentiality of student and personnel records; avoiding favoritism or harassment (sexual or otherwise) of particular students—as well as avoiding the appearance of favoritism or harassment; not presenting oneself as representing the school's viewpoint unless specifically empowered to do so; ensuring that cheating does not occur and is punished and reported when it does; avoiding all versions of "teaching to the test" and other test invalidation such as requesting that less able students stay home on test day . . . ; assisting with activities such as the development and enforcement of professional ethical standards.[59]

In this list of examples, Scriven focuses on those ethical responsibilities that derive from day-to-day activities of teaching, just as ethical codes are derived from the activities of other professions. A distinctive dimension of the ethical conduct of teaching, however, goes beyond these day-to-day activities to the underlying mission of the public school. This underlying mission is grounded in the special relationship between education and democracy: each is needed for the other to reach its full potential. No other profession takes as its fundamental goal the nurture of the knowledge, skills, and dispositions necessary for young people to take their independent places in democratic life. The teacher therefore finds that professional ethics are determined not just by the activities of the profession, not just by the need to balance fairly among competing values of the various constituencies to be served by the schools, but also by each teacher's understanding and ethical commitment to serving democratic ideals. But where does one go for guidance concerning what is meant by "democratic ideals"? Recall from Chapter 5, for example, John Dewey's belief that the moral meaning of democracy is its commitment to "the all-around growth of every member of society."[60] Among all our social institutions, only the schools have accepted such a broad mandate. Translating this ideal into classroom practice, for the "all-around growth of every member" of the class, is part of the ethical challenge that teachers may elect to meet. This challenge is thus one of the defining features of the profession of teaching.

CONCLUDING REMARKS

For the school reform movement to focus on teaching quality is a signal to teachers, school administrators, and the public that, in fact, the connections between good schooling and good teaching are strong. Efforts to improve schooling necessarily take teachers, their preparation, and their practice into account, and the professionalization effort seeks to do so. The push for professionalization could result in increased status and benefits for teachers; yet the acknowledgment and protection of teacher interests require a close examination of the ways in which professionalization could both serve and undermine them.

Teachers are a vital but not solitary component in the massive American educational system. While more power and autonomy could change the nature of teaching practice, teachers cannot be held accountable for systematic failures in the wider society which so adversely affect their work. Good teaching can open new life possibilities for young people in even the harshest living conditions, but good teaching is not likely to solve problems of drugs, violence, poverty, economic recession and the resulting unemployment, or other societal conditions that require direct solutions of their own. Yet, because the ultimate authority for what is to be taught in schools lies in the knowledge and values of the wider society, teachers tend to be held accountable by a great many different segments of the public—parents, local governments, state governments, the business community, representatives of minority groups whom the schools have not served well, and others. How to remain responsive to these various groups who have a legitimate stake in schooling, and yet continue to be autonomous professionals whose educational judgments are trusted, remains a problem for the professionalization process.

As the possibilities of improving the status of teaching are considered and implemented, the various constituencies need to take the history and particularities of teaching into account. It is possible that such a study would reveal the strengths of the qualities of an occupation that carries historically feminized values. Those values could then be integrated into the strategies that evolve for the improvement of the conditions under which teachers are educated and under which they become responsible for the education outcomes and futures of subsequent generations. We can question whether an historically feminized occupation, one with nearly 3 million practitioners, can ever expect to achieve the material rewards and status enjoyed by male-dominated professions with a fraction of as many practitioners. If this is a remote likelihood, one can further ask which dimensions of professionalization would be of benefit to teachers and their students, and how. If teaching is to have higher professional status than it now has, it will be likely nevertheless to occupy a distinct niche among the professions.

One mark of the success of the professionalization of teaching will be the degree to which teachers achieve significant influence in making the fundamental decisions that affect their working lives, while at the same time successfully engaging representatives of the many educational constituencies in dialogue over what should be taught, and to whom, and how.

Making teachers look more like other professions, however, *may* be a mistaken approach to the original question that gave rise to the professionalization discussion, which was, How can schooling be improved? Professionalization proves to be a misleading line of thought if it leads to a protracted discussion of whether teaching is really a profession or if it leads to reforms that make teaching more like other professions but that leave the quality of schooling itself little improved. If the problem to be addressed is the quality of schooling, then a better question would be, What do teachers need to *be* to accomplish their educational tasks best? The questions that follow from that would then include:

- What kinds of people make the best teachers?
- How can we select and prepare them?
- How should schools be structured for the education of the students?

Perhaps Holmes and Carnegie are correct, and the answers to those questions lead to the conclusion that teaching should be more like the other professions. But that claim needs to be persuasively argued, not just asserted through comparisons with established professions. What matters, in the end, is not the designation of "professional," but rather that teachers have a range of knowledge, skills, and dispositions to respond to distinctively educational problems effectively. Such knowledge, skills, and dispositions are not likely to be simply lay knowledge or common sense. This specialized knowledge, however, doesn't itself define a profession, for there is specializing knowledge in many crafts and occupations. But the debate whether teaching is really a profession becomes a red herring brought about by the calls to professionalize teaching. The problem at hand is to determine what teachers need to accomplish their educational tasks. One prominent answer to this question has recently been provided by the National Commission on Teaching and America's Future, which authored this chapter's Primary Source Reading.

PRIMARY SOURCE READING

Although this chapter has criticized the professionalization movement as a way to reform schooling, it does appear to endorse a view of professionalism in teaching that embraces strong professional preparation, professional commitment, and professional standards of ethics and performance. In particular, the chapter finds encouragement in the 1996 report on teaching and learning in the United States, What Matters Most: Teaching for America's Future. *Students are urged to think critically about whether the report's fundamental premises and comprehensive recommendations are likely to address what matters most in our schools. This requires some thoughtfulness, however, about the question, What does matter most?*

WHAT MATTERS MOST: TEACHING FOR AMERICA'S FUTURE

EXECUTIVE SUMMARY

This report offers what we believe is the single most important strategy for achieving America's educational goals: A blueprint for recruiting, preparing, and supporting excellent teachers in all of America's schools. The plan is aimed at ensuring that all communities have teachers with the knowledge and skills they need to teach so that all children can learn, and all school systems are organized to support teachers in this work. A caring, competent, and qualified teacher for every child is the most important ingredient in education reform.

The Commission's proposals are systemic in scope—not a recipe for more short-lived pilots and demonstration projects. They require a dramatic departure from the status quo—one that creates a new infrastructure for professional learning and an accountability system that ensures attention to standards for educators as well as students at every level—national, state, local school district, school, and classroom.

This Commission starts from three simple premises:

1. What teachers know and can do is the most important influence on what students learn.
2. Recruiting, preparing, and retaining good teachers is the central strategy for improving our schools.
3. School reform cannot succeed unless it focuses on creating the conditions in which teachers can teach, and teach well.

We propose an audacious goal for America's future. Within a decade—by the year 2006—we will provide every student in America with what should be his or her educational birthright: access to competent, caring, qualified teaching in schools organized for success. This is a challenging goal to put before the nation and its educational leaders. But if the goal is challenging and requires unprecedented effort, it does not require unprecedented new theory. Common sense suffices: American students are entitled to teachers who know their subjects, understand their students and what they need, and have developed the skills required to make learning come alive.

However, based on its two-year study, the Commission identified a number of barriers to achieving this goal. They include:

- Low expectations for student performance.
- Unenforced standards for teachers.
- Major flaws in teacher preparation.
- Painfully slipshod teacher recruitment.
- Inadequate induction for beginning teachers.
- Lack of professional development and rewards for knowledge and skill.
- Schools that are structured for failure rather than success.

We offer five major recommendations to address these concerns and accomplish our goal.

I. Get serious about standards, for both students and teachers.

- Establish professional standards boards in every state.
- Insist on accreditation for all schools of education.

What Matters Most: Teaching for America's Future (1996) National Commission for Teaching and America's Future: New York. pp. vi–vii, 62–70, 72, 74–75. (Copies of the report are available for purchase from The National Commission on Teaching and America's Future, P.O. Box 5239, Woodbridge, VA 22194-5239.)

- Close inadequate schools of education.
- License teachers based on demonstrated performance, including tests of subject matter knowledge, teaching knowledge, and teaching skill.
- Use National Board standards as the benchmark for accomplished teaching.

II. Reinvent teacher preparation and professional development.

- Organize teacher education and professional development programs around standards for students and teachers.
- Develop extended, graduate-level teacher-preparation programs that provide a yearlong internship in a professional development school.
- Create and fund mentoring programs for beginning teachers, along with evaluation of teaching skills.
- Create stable, high-quality sources of professional development.

III. Fix teacher recruitment and put qualified teachers in every classroom.

- Increase the ability of low-wealth districts to pay for qualified teachers, and insist that districts hire only qualified teachers.
- Redesign and streamline district hiring.
- Eliminate barriers to teacher mobility.
- Aggressively recruit high-need teachers and provide incentives for teaching in shortage areas.
- Develop high-quality pathways to teaching for a wide range of recruits.

IV. Encourage and reward teacher knowledge and skill.

- Develop a career continuum for teaching linked to assessments and compensation systems that reward knowledge and skill.
- Remove incompetent teachers.
- Set goals and enact incentives for National Board Certification in every state and district. Aim to certify 105,000 teachers in this decade, one for every school in the United States.

V. Create schools that are organized for student and teacher success.

- Flatten hierarchies and reallocate resources to send more dollars to the front lines of schools: Invest more in teachers and technology and less in nonteaching personnel.
- Provide venture capital in the form of challenge grants to schools for teacher learning linked to school improvement and rewards for team efforts that lead to improved practice and greater learning.
- Select, prepare, and retain principals who understand teaching and learning and who can lead high-performing schools.

Developing recommendations is easy. Implementing them is hard work. The first step is to recognize that these ideas must be pursued together—as an entire tapestry that is tightly interwoven. Pulling on a single thread will create a tangle rather than tangible progress. The second step is to build upon the substantial work that has been undertaken over the past decade. All across the country, successful programs for recruiting, educating, and mentoring new teachers have sprung up. Professional networks and teacher academies have been launched; many education school programs have been redesigned; higher standards for licensing teachers and accrediting education schools have been developed; and a National Board for Professional Teaching Standards is now fully established and beginning to define and reward accomplished teaching. All these endeavors, and those of many others, form the foundation of this crusade.

RECOMMENDATIONS: AN ACTION AGENDA FOR CHANGE

As various panaceas have been advanced in the last decade to solve the problems of learning in America, education reform has moved in fits and starts. Indeed, the "reform *du jour*" has become a problem in its own right in American schools because teachers have learned to ride out the latest fad on the well-founded assumption that it too will pass.

Reform can succeed only if it is broad and comprehensive, attacking many problems simultaneously. But it cannot succeed at all unless the conditions of teaching and teacher development change. Indeed, when this Commission's recommendations are put into place, educators will find that they end the waves of reform that crash over American schools without effect because our schools will have developed the capacity to continually renew and improve themselves.

Our proposals provide a vision and a blueprint for the development of a teaching profession for the 21st century that can make good on our nation's goals for education. They are systemic in scope—not a recipe for more short-lived pilots and demonstration projects. They require a dramatic departure from the status quo—one that creates a new infrastructure for professional learning and an accountability system that ensures attention to standards for educators as well as students at every level—national, state, local school district, school, and classroom.

If the press for higher educational standards has taught us anything, it is that congruence matters: If the actions of federal and state governments do not support the work of local school districts, and if those of school districts do not support the work of schools, very little of worth can be accomplished. What goes on in classrooms between teachers and students may be the core of education, but it is profoundly shaped by what parents and principals do and by what superintendents, school boards, and legislatures decide. When various parts of the system are working against one another, the enterprise lurches around like a carriage pulled by horses running off in different directions.

Congruence and commonality of effort in a decentralized system require that we prepare people—both educators and policymakers—to manage that system in a way that is guided by shared commitments and knowledge. Without that common knowledge base to inform practice, there can be no guideposts for responsible decision making.

What we are proposing is a set of steps to ensure the common base of knowledge and commitments upon which a truly democratic system of education can be built. We are urging a complete overhaul in the systems of teacher preparation and professional development in this country to ensure that they reflect and act upon the most current available knowledge and practice. This redesign should create a continuum of teacher learning based on compatible standards that operate from recruitment and preservice education through licensing, hiring, and induction into the profession, to advanced certification and ongoing professional development.

We also propose a comprehensive set of changes in school organization and management that will provide the conditions in which teachers can use their knowledge much more productively to support student learning. And finally, we recommend a set of measures for making sure that only those who are competent to teach or to lead schools are allowed to enter or to continue in the profession—a starting point for creating professional accountability.

For the first time, a broad-based group of policymakers and educators—including those who will have to take courageous steps to put these recommendations in place—have put forth this sweeping agenda for change and pledged to take the steps needed to implement it. We understand that these proposals are not easy to undertake and that the self-interest of various constituencies will be shaken in the process of bringing them to life. However, we believe that this comprehensive set of reforms is absolutely essential to guarantee every child a caring, competent, and qualified teacher . . . and to guarantee America a just and prosperous future.

We challenge the nation to embrace a set of turning points that will put us on the path to serious, successful, long-term improvements in teaching and learning for America. By the year 2006,

- All children will be taught by teachers who have the knowledge, skills, and commitments to teach children well.
- All teacher education programs will meet professional standards, or they will be closed.
- All teachers will have access to high-quality professional development and regular time for collegial work and planning.
- Both teachers and principals will be hired and retained based on their ability to meet professional standards of practice.
- Teachers' salaries will be based on their knowledge and skills.

- Quality teaching will be the central investment of schools. Most education dollars will be spent on classroom teaching.

We offer five recommendations to accomplish these goals:

I. Get serious about standards for both students and teachers.
II. Reinvent teacher preparation and professional development.
III. Fix teacher recruitment and put qualified teachers in every classroom.
IV. Encourage and reward teacher knowledge and skill.
V. Create schools that are organized for student and teacher success.

These recommendations are interrelated. Standards for students affect expectations of teachers and the organization of schools. Standards for teachers affect their preparation, their induction into teaching, and their continuing development as well as the roles they are capable of assuming. Experienced teachers, as well as novices and candidates, benefit from exposure to professional development schools. Changes in school structures affect everything else. However, for the sake of clarity, we treat these issues separately below. At the close, we describe how they should come together.

I. Get serious about standards for both students and teachers.

WE RECOMMEND: ***renewing the national promise to bring every American child up to world-class standards in core academic areas.***

WE RECOMMEND: ***developing and enforcing rigorous standards for teacher preparation, initial licensing, and continuing development.***

Standards for Students

The country needs to continue its work on standards defining what young people should know and be able to do. These should reflect the demands of today's society and support more challenging academic coursework and higher standards for graduation. Like those in other countries and like the much-applauded work of the National Council of Teachers of Mathematics in the United States, the standards really should be frameworks for curriculum, expressed in slim notebooks that outline a core of expectations toward which all students should strive, not a telephone book incorporating every topic under the sun. Such frameworks should be clear about common knowledge and skills while allowing for local adaptations that bring ideas to life for students in different communities and enable students to develop different interests and specialties beyond the core, especially as they move through high school. The standards and frameworks should be a central subject of ongoing conversations with parents and community members so that all those whose efforts must be mobilized on behalf of students understand what they are working toward.

States should continue to work on incorporating these standards into curriculum frameworks and assessments that provide rich information about actual student performance, enabling teachers and parents to understand what children can do and how to support their ongoing learning. In the effort to advance standards, implementation must go well beyond the platitude that "all children can learn." All children are human; by definition all of them can learn. The question is: What should they learn and how much do they need to know? And how can schools support this learning?

For standards to be meaningful, they must be accompanied by benchmarks of performance—from "acceptable" to "highly accomplished"—so that students and teachers know how to direct their efforts toward greater excellence. Clear examples of the kind and quality of work expected can motivate students and help teachers to organize their work together. They can build upon the work of their predecessors and colleagues and develop reinforcing opportunities for students to practice and develop their skills. With high-quality assessments that measure important abilities, teachers can teach more purposefully and make greater demands that students and parents can better understand and respond to. Parents can reinforce students' learning at home. And schools can better organize specific academic supports and extra study time after school, on weekends, or in the summer for students who need additional help to develop the levels of competence they need to meet.

Expectations for student achievement should shape discussions of teaching and problem solving in schools. Teachers should work collectively on curriculum that supports the standards, assess how individuals and groups of students are learning, evaluate what kinds of learning experiences they have had, and make changes in what they do. This work is a key professional activity that connects standards of learning to the building of shared standards for teaching. Evidence already exists that where school faculties are working together to translate standards into courses of study, learning tasks, and assessments, they are becoming more expert and more collective in their practice, and students are learning more.[1]

Many have voiced fears that standards and assessments will turn out to be elitist—that they will simply sort out more easily the haves from the have-nots. The Commission's vision is very different. We see standards as a starting point—not an ending point—for change. We understand that standard-setting in and of itself will not produce the changes in teaching and schooling needed to raise achievement. However, standards can create a foundation for other reforms that build the capacity of schools to help all students learn to higher levels. Ultimately, to be productive, student standards must undergird shared standards of practice that allow teachers to work more effectively together and to set expectations for themselves.

[1]Linda Darling-Hammond, Jacqueline Ancess, and Beverly Falk (eds.). *Authentic Assessment in Action: Studies of Schools and Students at Work* (New York: Teachers College Press, 1995); The Center on Organization and Restructuring of Schools, Ann Lieberman, *The Work of Restructuring Schools;* Fred M. Newmann and Gary G. Wehlage, *Successful School Restructuring: A Report to the Public and Educators by the Center on Organization and Restructuring Schools* (Madison, Wis.: Board of Regents of the University of Wisconsin System, 1995); Judith Warren Little, "Norms of Collegiality and Experimentation: Workplace Conditions of School Success," *American Educational Research Journal* 19 (Fall 1982): 215–340.

Standards for Teaching

Standards for teaching are the linchpin for transforming current systems of preparation, licensing, certification, and ongoing development so that they better support student learning. They can bring clarity and focus to a set of activities that are currently poorly connected and often badly organized. New standards and new opportunities for teacher education must be reinforced by incentives that encourage teachers to acquire ever greater knowledge and skill. These incentives can then, in turn, support the redesign of schools so that they organize themselves more effectively for student and teacher learning.

Clearly, if students are to achieve high standards, we can expect no less from their teachers and from other educators. Of greatest priority is reaching agreement on what teachers should know and be able to do in order to teach to high standards. This standard-setting task was left unaddressed for many decades, but it has recently been accomplished by the efforts of three professional bodies that have closely aligned their work to produce standards outlining a continuum of teacher development derived directly from the expectations posed by new student standards.

The new standards of the National Council for Accreditation of Teacher Education (NCATE), most recently revised in 1995, reflect the evolution of a much stronger knowledge base for teaching and require schools of education to demonstrate how they are incorporating new knowledge about the effective teaching of subject matter, various approaches to learning, and student diversity in their preparation of teachers [see Exhibit 10.4].

NCATE's standards are connected to a set of newly developed standards for beginning teacher licensing developed by a consortium of more than 30 states and professional organizations—the Interstate New Teacher Assessment and Support Consortium (INTASC)—which has tackled the question of what entering teachers must know and be able to do to teach in the ways student standards demand. The standards outline how teachers should demonstrate their knowledge of subject matter, child development and learning, classroom communication and management, planning, instruction, and assessment, and the ability to work

EXHIBIT 10.4 A Professional Continuum for Teacher Development

Recruitment to a teacher education program: Based on academic background and ability to work with children → Preservice preparation in an NCATE-accredited school of education → Initial intern license: Based on INTASC tests of subject matter and teaching knowledge → New teacher induction: 1-2 years of early career mentoring and evaluation → Continuing license: Based on INTASC performance assessments, including a portfolio of videotaped lessons, written evaluations, and student work → Ongoing professional development in and out of the classroom → Advanced certification: Based on NBPTS performance assessments and examinations

NCATE = National Council for Accreditation of Teacher Education; INTASC = Interstate New Teacher Assessment and Support Consortium; NBPTS = National Board for Professional Teaching Standards.

well with parents and colleagues as a basis for gaining a license to teach. INTASC's licensing standards are the basis for tests of subject matter and teaching knowledge for an initial license and for a performance assessment that examines teaching skills during the first year or two of supervised teaching. These tests, currently being piloted by states that belong to the consortium, will become the basis for granting a continuing professional license.

Finally, for experienced teachers, the standards for accomplished practice developed by the new National Board for Professional Teaching Standards—which are compatible with those developed by NCATE and INTASC—provide guidance for ongoing professional development. Teachers that undertake the National Board's challenging performance assessments can receive certification of accomplished practice that recognizes the high levels of expertise they have developed.

Although the work of these organizations may sound unglamorous, they offer the most powerful tools we have for reaching and rejuvenating the soul of the profession. Their standards and assessments examine and insist upon the attributes of effective teachers: subject matter expertise coupled with an understanding of how children learn and develop; skill in using a range of teaching strategies and technologies; sensitivity and effectiveness in working with students from diverse backgrounds; the ability to work well with parents and other teachers; and assessment expertise capable of discerning how well children are doing, what they are learning, and what needs to be done next to move them along. The standards reflect a teaching role in which the teacher is an instructional leader who orchestrates learning experiences in response to curriculum goals and student needs and who coaches students to high levels of independent performance.

These standards offer a cogent vision of teaching that helps to create new classroom realities. As teacher Ann Sayas noted of her experience in working for National Board Certification:

> Nothing, I repeat, nothing has forced me to examine my teaching practices as the National Board Certification process did. Nothing else has offered me a vision of what education could be like and opportunities to make the vision a reality. . . . The result is amazing to me: I am more excited about teaching than I have ever been. I no longer dream of moving up the ladder away from daily contact with my students. Not enough time exists to try all the possible ideas that examination of my own classroom has produced.[2]

In the Commission's judgment, these standards represent the new basics for accomplished practice; they include the essentials of effective teach-

[2] Ann Sayas, "To Grow a Teacher," *Basic Education* 40 (April 1996): 8–9.

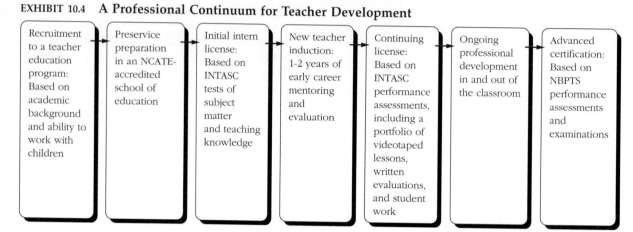

ing and focus attention on student learning. They may seem to be a tall order, but many excellent teachers are already teaching as they suggest, and some schools of education are preparing new cohorts of teachers so that they learn to do so. In the last ten years, since issues regarding the status of teaching were first brought to the public's attention,[3] a great deal of headway has been made in developing new standards for teaching, piloting and refining new assessments of teaching, and creating programs that serve as proof that substantially better education for students and teachers is possible. However, if these are to take hold and survive longer than in past eras of reform, policymakers must incorporate them into the policies that govern teaching and schooling.

To make expert teaching the rule rather than the exception, state and local policies should create a continuum of professional learning for teachers based on standards that guide teacher preparation and licensing, early induction, ongoing professional development, and advanced certification. To accomplish this, we recommend that states and local districts take the following steps:

- **Establish professional standards boards in every state.**

Developing coherent standards for teacher education, licensing, professional development, and practice requires a governing partnership between the public and the profession that is not vulnerable to constantly changing politics and priorities. Twelve states have already created boards for teaching like those that govern standard setting in other professions on the conviction that these boards are the best way to maintain rigorous standards and protect the public interest. Such boards are the conscience of each profession; they develop and enforce ethical codes as well as technical standards of practice. They should include accomplished teachers—ultimately, those who are National Board Certified—as well as teacher educators, administrators, and representatives of the public. In other professions, a national confederation of state boards develops common standards, high-quality assessments, and reciprocity agreements. Such a confederation in teaching should help develop common licensing assessments with professionally recommended cut-off scores, so that teachers command comparable skills and can move more easily from state to state.

How would a standards board help solve current problems? First, it would bring greater expertise to bear on the process of setting teaching standards and would do so in a more focused and steady fashion, as standards must be continually updated and reevaluated in light of growing professional knowledge. Second, it would allow the creation of a more coherent set of standards across teacher education, licensing, and ongoing professional development, since they would all be considered by the same body. Finally, it would create a firewall between the political system and the standard-setting process, allowing higher standards that are more connected to the professional knowledge base to be set and maintained. States with standards boards have shown that they enact and maintain more rigorous, professionally current standards than they had been able to do before the standards board was in place.

- **Insist on accreditation for all schools of education.**

States can most effectively ensure quality control over teacher education in partnership with the National Council for the Accreditation of Teacher Education, whose standards are aligned with emerging new standards for student learning as well as with those of the National Board and INTASC. NCATE's quality standards, recently revised and strengthened, are demanding, but not beyond the reach of any school of education genuinely committed to preparing excellent teachers for the classrooms of a new century. Schools that are serious about preparing teachers should take the necessary steps to become accredited. Those that are not willing and able to develop a critical mass of intellectual resources for training teachers should turn their attention to doing other things well.

[3]In 1986, seminal reports were issued by the Carnegie Forum on Education and the Economy, *A Nation Prepared: Teachers for the 21st Century* (Washington, D.C.: Carnegie Forum on Education and the Economy, 1986); The Holmes Group, *Tomorrow's Teachers;* and the National Governors' Association, *Time for Results: Task Force on Teaching* (Washington, D.C.: National Governors' Association, Center for Policy Research and Analysis, 1986).

Although teacher associations and states are increasingly willing to insist on accreditation for schools of education, the unfortunate truth is that some colleges are alarmed at the prospect of mandatory accreditation, fearing that what is in the public interest may not always coincide with institutional self-interest. It is time for states and higher education to stop playing shell games with ineffective program approval procedures and support professional accreditation by the turn of the century.

- **Close inadequate schools of education.**

The other side of the accreditation coin is that weak teacher preparation programs should be shut down. As everyone in higher education understands, accreditation amounts to a stamp of approval that a professional school is capable of delivering what it promises the public. After an initial visit, accrediting agencies provide institutions of higher education with ample time, technical assistance, and opportunity to correct shortcomings and shore up weaknesses. If schools, colleges, or departments of education are unable to do so, they should be closed to protect the public's interest in providing well-prepared teachers for all children. To those concerned about the American future, it is painful to hear that some training programs are so weak that their students belittle them, and school systems feel they must start all over again training their graduates. What is more painful is that the situation is tolerated. It should be no longer.

- **License teachers based on demonstrated performance, including tests of subject matter knowledge, teaching knowledge, and teaching skill.**

An important change in the standards we recommend is that they describe what teachers should know and be able to do rather than listing courses that teachers should take. Performance-based licensing is the norm in other professions. Rather than dictating the curriculum of professional schools, they require rigorous tests to be sure professionals have the skills they need to serve their clients well, and they allow schools to organize courses in any way that achieves the desired outcomes.

In a performance-based licensing system for teaching, all candidates should pass tests of subject matter knowledge and knowledge about teaching and learning *before* they receive an initial license and are hired. They should then pass a performance assessment of teaching skills during their first year or two of supervised practice as the basis for a continuing license. We further recommend that states use common assessments with common, professionally set cut-off scores. This will give them the benefit of reciprocity with one another, thus greatly expanding the pool of teachers upon which they can readily draw.

State partners associated with the Interstate New Teacher Assessment and Support Consortium (INTASC) are already developing high-quality performance assessments of teaching knowledge and skill that, along with improvements in existing subject matter tests, constitute the foundations of an effective licensing system. The INTASC assessments require teachers to demonstrate that they understand the fundamentals of learning and teaching and that they can teach in the way that new student standards demand. With professional accreditation in place, states should reallocate scarce resources from program approval, which is redundant with accreditation, to the administration of high-quality licensing tests that measure actual ability to teach.

In a performance-based system, teacher education programs should be accountable for enabling their graduates to meet the standards. Alternate routes to teaching, such as postgraduate programs for midcareer recruits, should meet the same standards as traditional programs: Their candidates should pass the same assessments before they enter teaching, and programs should show that they prepare candidates to do so successfully. This will allow greater innovation and diversity in teacher training without jeopardizing the welfare of students. A single standard that assesses genuine readiness to teach rather than regulating the content of courses would mean that states could stop issuing substandard teaching licenses that sanction deficiencies in preparation, and parents and students would be assured that anyone who has earned the title "teacher" has the essential skills to teach.

- **Use National Board standards as the benchmark for accomplished teaching.**

It has always been difficult to recognize and reward good teachers in ways that are credible and objective. The merit pay plans of the 1980s (like those of the 1950s and 1920s) have already disappeared because local evaluators did not have useful standards, or the time or expertise, to make reliable judgments about teacher competence. Many such plans created distrust and competition among teachers rather than supporting better practice.[4] In contrast, the careful process of National Board Certification—based on evaluation by experts according to well-developed standards and a collaborative process—provides an alternative that teachers find credible, helpful, and an extraordinary learning experience.

Analogous to the process of board certification in medicine, the National Board's standards represent a widely shared consensus about state-of-the-art practice. They are the basis for sophisticated performance assessments that allow veteran teachers to demonstrate their expertise by submitting videotapes of their teaching, lesson plans, and other samples of their own and their students' work. In assessment centers, teachers evaluate texts and teaching materials, analyze teaching situations, assess student learning and needs, and defend teaching decisions based on their knowledge of subjects, students, curriculum, and pedagogy. Teachers who have experienced the board's assessments believe the process captures good teaching and say it provides an extraordinary learning experience because it focuses all of their attention on how their decisions affect students. As states and districts begin to recognize certification as an indicator of high-level competence for purposes of hiring, evaluation, compensation, and advancement, the standards will have increasing practical effect and reach.

National Board standards should become a cornerstone for teacher development and evaluation. Some states have already decided to accept National Board Certification as fully meeting state licensing requirements for veteran teachers who cross state lines, for renewal of a license, or the award of an advanced license. Some states and districts, like Georgia, Kentucky, North Carolina, and Ohio, are acknowledging certification through financial incentives or salary bonuses; others are proposing to use certification as an indicator of qualification for roles such as mentor teacher, principal, or cooperating teacher educator. Districts like Rochester, New York, and Palo Alto, California, have incorporated National Board standards and processes, including teacher portfolios and peer coaching, as part of their teacher evaluation systems. All these strategies help to create a coherent continuum of professional learning based on common professional standards.

Standards are valuable not only in the context of formal certification systems. They can inform professional development efforts ranging from graduate school courses to local seminars and videotape groups that allow teachers to see the standards in action and reflect on their own practice. Graduate schools can organize advanced master's degree programs around the National Board standards. Within schools, vivid descriptions of good teaching can help teachers improve what they do in their daily work. It is when standards are regularly used in this way, as well as to stimulate better preparation and ongoing professional development, that they will come alive in classrooms across the nation.

[4]Richard J. Murnane and David Cohen, "Merit Pay and the Evaluation Problem: Why Most Merit Pay Plans Fail and a Few Survive," *Harvard Educational Review* 56 (February 1986): 1–17; Susan Moore Johnson, "Incentives for Teachers: What Motivates, What Matters?" *Educational Administration Quarterly* 22 (Summer 1986): 54–79; and Allen Odden, "Incentives, School Organization, and Teacher Compensation," in *Rewards and Reform: Creating Educational Incentives That Work,* edited by Susan H. Fuhrman and Jennifer A. O'Day (San Francisco, Calif.: Jossey-Bass, 1996).

THE NATIONAL BOARD'S STANDARDS

National Board Certification lets people see what teaching can be. I think that good teaching is an ability to take subject matter expertise, which is one vital component of teaching,

and actually transform that into the classroom with the students you have—to make that bridge between your subject and the students' own backgrounds. And that's no easy trick.
—BRADY KELSO, ENGLISH TEACHER

Brady Kelso, an English teacher at Scripps Ranch High School in San Diego, California, was one of the first teachers certified by the National Board for Professional Teaching Standards. A 13-year veteran, Kelso found that the process of assembling a portfolio of his teaching and students' learning "gave me an opportunity to rethink... Looking carefully at my plans and then doing the case studies to follow the kids was good... For me it was a validation of the work that I'd done."

Rick Wormeli, an English teacher at Herndon Middle School in Virginia, agrees. He credits the process of Board Certification with encouraging him to integrate other subjects into his lessons, rethink the organization of reading discussion groups, and use vocabulary words from his students' work in lieu of a book listing words out of context. Even after he'd finished the assessment, he continued to experiment with changes. "I can't turn it off," he noted.

The National Board's standards and assessments help teachers reflect on and learn from their practice. They are based on five major propositions that teachers and researchers agree are essential to accomplished teaching:

1. Teachers are committed to students and their learning. National Board-Certified teachers are dedicated to making knowledge accessible to all students. They adjust their practice based on students' interests, abilities, skills, and backgrounds. They understand how students develop and learn.
2. Teachers know the subjects they teach and how to teach those subjects to students. National Board-Certified teachers have a rich understanding of the subject(s) they teach, and they know how to reveal subject matter to students. They are aware of the knowledge and preconceptions that students typically bring. They create multiple paths to knowledge, and they can teach students how to pose and solve their own problems.
3. Teachers are responsible for managing and monitoring student learning. National Board-Certified teachers create settings that sustain the interest of their students. They command a range of instructional techniques and know when each is appropriate. They know how to motivate and engage groups of students. They use multiple methods for measuring student growth and can clearly explain student performance to parents.
4. Teachers think systematically about their practice and learn from experience. National Board-Certified teachers critically examine their practice, seek the advice of others, and draw on educational research to deepen their knowledge, sharpen their judgment, and adapt their teaching to new findings and ideas.
5. Teachers are members of learning communities. National Board-Certified teachers work collaboratively with other professionals. They use school and community resources for their students' benefit. They work creatively and collaboratively with parents, engaging them in the work of the school.

Shirley Bzdewka, a teacher at Dayton School in Dayton, New Jersey, sums up the effect of her Board Certification experience this way:

I'm a very different teacher now. I know I was a good teacher. But I also know that every teacher always has a responsibility to be better tomorrow than they were today, and I am a much more deliberate teacher now. I am much more focused. I can never, ever do anything again with my kids and not ask myself, "Why? Why am I doing this? What are the effects on my kids? What are the benefits to my kids?" It's not that I didn't care about those things before, but it's on such a conscious level now.

Sources: Adapted from Ann Bradley, "Pioneers in Professionalism," *Education Week* 13 (April 20, 1994): 18–21; "What Price Success?" *Education Week* 15 (November 22, 1995): 1. Copyright © 1994, 1995. Excerpts reprinted with the permission of *Education Week.* The National Board for Professional Teaching Standards (NBPTS), *What Teachers Should Know and Be Able to Do* (Detroit, Mich.: NBPTS, 1994).

QUESTIONS FOR DISCUSSION AND EXAMINATION

1. Jurgen Herbst was cited for arguing that *professionalization* in teaching has historically brought teaching under bureaucratic control, whereas *professionalism* in teaching emphasizes "the recognition and practice of a teacher's right and obligation to determine his or her own professional tasks in the classroom." To what degree, in your view, does the historical record support Herbst's contention? Further, has the historical trend been more positive or negative for teaching as an occupation? Defend your view on both counts.
2. This chapter noted on several occasions that the current professionalization movement stems from an expressed need to improve the quality of *schooling* in the United States. In your view, is professionalization of teaching a good way to improve schooling? Why or why not?
3. One might argue that this chapter has been unduly critical of the Holmes and Carnegie reports of 1985 in their efforts to improve the profession of teaching. In your view, what features of the Holmes and Carnegie reports are most promising for improving the quality of teaching *and* schooling? Are those features implementable, given the political, economic, and ideological realities of schooling in the United States? Defend your view.
4. This chapter lists several reasons, from the economic to the ideological to the demographic, for the relatively low professional status of teaching. In your view, are there other reasons that should be included, or do the reasons presented have adequate explanatory value? Explain.
5. Given that professional status, autonomy, and the material reward structure in teaching compare poorly to those of other professions, what do you expect to derive from teaching in terms of personal rewards? What evidence do you find in this chapter that your expectations are likely or not likely to be met? How adequate is that evidence, in your view? Explain your position.
6. This chapter has presented a skeptical viewpoint toward the value of professionalization as a response to current problems in schooling. Yet, the Primary Source Reading by the National Commission clearly supports a national teaching board to enhance professionalism in teaching. Do you find their position persuasive? Does Barringer's point of view necessarily conflict with the view expressed in this chapter? Explain.

NOTES

1. Joel Spring, *American Education: An Introduction to Social and Political Aspects*, 5th ed. (White Plains, NY: Longman, 1991), p. 44.
2. John Goodlad, *Teachers for Our Nation's Schools* (San Francisco: Jossey Bass, 1990), pp. 71–72.
3. William R. Johnson, "Teachers and Teacher Training in the Twentieth Century," in Donald Warren, ed., *American Teachers: History of a Profession at Work* (New York: Macmillan, 1989), pp. 245–47.
4. See Harold Rugg, *The Teacher of Teachers* (New York: Harper & Brothers, 1952). Also, Steven Tozer and Stuart McAninch, "Social Foundations of Education in Historical Perspective," *Educational Foundations*, Vol. 1, No. 1 (1986).
5. Johnson, "Teachers and Teacher Training," pp. 238–40.
6. Ibid, p. 239.
7. Jurgen Herbst, *And Sadly Teach: Teacher Education and Professionalization in American Culture* (Madison: University of Wisconsin Press, 1989), p. 6.
8. *Tomorrow's Teachers: A Report of the Holmes Group* (East Lansing, MI: The Holmes Group, Inc., 1986), p. 6.
9. See, for example, the AFT policy statement, "U.S. Education: The Task Before Us," *The American Education*, Winter 1992, American Federation of Teachers, pp. 19–30.
10. Louise M. Berman, "The Teacher as Decision Maker," in Frances S. Bolin and Judith McConnell Falk, eds., *Teacher Renewal: Professional Issues, Personal Choices* (New York: Teachers College Press, 1987), p. 202.
11. John I. Goodlad, *Teachers for Our Nation's Schools* (San Francisco: Jossey Bass, 1990), pp. 70–71.
12. Ibid., p. 267.
13. Holmes Group, *Tomorrow's Teachers*, p. 4.
14. Ibid., p. 65.
15. Carnegie Forum, excerpted in *Chronicle of Higher Education*, May 21, 1986, pp. 47–48.
16. Ibid., p. 48.
17. Linda Darling Hammond et al., *The Teaching Internship* (Santa Monica, CA: RAND Corporation, 1990), p. vi.
18. Holmes Group, *Tomorrow's Teachers*.
19. Dee Ann Spencer, *Contemporary Women Teachers: Balancing School and Home* (White Plains, NY: Longman, 1986), p. 5.
20. Herbst, *And Sadly Teach*, p. 6.
21. *Projections of Educational Statistics to 2001: An Update*, Washington, D.C.: National Center for Educational Statistics, 1990, p. 9; *Digest of Educational Statistics*,

Washington, D.C.: National Center for Educational Statistics, 1993, p. 13.

22. *Digest of Educational Statistics* (Washington, D.C.: U.S. Department of Education, 1988), p. 74.
23. Occupational Outlook Handbook, U.S. Department of Labor Bulletin 24000, May 1992, pp. 17, 66, 74, 94, 95, 105. Also, *The Condition of Education 1993,* p. 150.
24. *Digest of Education Statistics,* 1993, p. 128.
25. Geraldine Joncich Clifford, "Man/Woman/Teacher: Gender, Family, and Career in American Educational History," in Donald Warren, ed., *American Teachers: Histories of a Profession at Work* (New York: Macmillan, 1989), p. 316.
26. Data from U.S. Bureau of Labor Statistics and Census Bureau cited in "Nine to Five: Profile of Working Women," in *Women's Studies at Parkland College* (Champaign, IL: Summer Newsletter 1989). See also *Statistical Abstract of the United States* (Washington, D.C.: U.S. Government Printing Office, 1993), p. 426.
27. Spencer, *Contemporary Women Teachers,* p. 6, citing Grimm and Stern, 1974.
28. *Digest of Educational Statistics,* 1988, p. 70; *Digest of Educational Statistics,* 1993, p. 79.
29. Gerda Lerner, "The Lady and the Mill Girl: Change in the Status of Women in the Age of Teachers," *Journal of American Studies,* Vol. 10, No. 1, 1969, pp. 5–15.
30. John Rury, "Who Became Teachers? The Social Characteristics of Teachers in American History," in Warren, ed., *American Teachers.*
31. Spencer, *Contemporary Women Teachers,* p. 26.
32. *Digest of Educational Statistics,* 1988, p. 43.
33. "You and the System," *Teacher Magazine,* Vol. 1, No. 7 (April 1990), p. 38; *Digest of Educational Statistics,* 1993, p. 96.
34. See, for example, Michael Apple, "The Political Economy of Textbook Publishing," *Educational Theory,* Vol. 34 (Fall 1984), pp. 307–320.
35. Joel Spring, *Conflict of Interests: The Politics of American Education* (White Plains, NY: Longman, 1988), p. 3.
36. "Poll: Teachers Feel They Have Little Say in School Matters," *Champaign-Urbana News Gazette,* September 11, 1988, p. 11. Corroboration is found in *The Condition of Education 1993,* (Washington, D.C.: U.S. Department of Education, 1993), pp. 124–25, 366–67.
37. *The Condition of Education 1993,* p. 125.
38. Bill Graves, "School Reform by University Mandate," *The School Administrator,* Vol. 49, No. 10 (November 1992), pp. 8–13.
39. *Child Welfare Society of Flint* v. *Kennedy School District,* 189 N.W. 1002 (1922).
40. *Older* v. *Board of Education of District No. 1, Town of Mamaroneck,* 266 N.E. 2d 812 1971).
41. Debra Viadero, " 'Medically Fragile' Students Pose Major Dilemma for School Officials," *Education Week,* March 11, 1987, pp. 1, 14.
42. *Meyer* v. *Nebraska,* 262 U.S. 390 (1922).
43. *Pierce* v. *Society of Sisters of the Holy Name of Jesus and Mary,* 262 U.S. 510 (1925).
44. *Brown* v. *Board of Education of Topeka, Kansas,* 347 U.S. 483 (1954).
45. *Engle* v. *Vitale,* 370 U.S. 421 (1962).
46. *Tinker* v. *Des Moines School District,* 393 U.S. 503 (1969).
47. *Parducci* v. *Rutland,* 316 F. Supp. 352 (1970).
48. *Goss* v. *Lopez,* 419 U.S. 565 (1975).
49. *Cleveland Board of Education* v. *LaFleur,* 414 U.S. 632 (1974).
50. *New Jersey* v. *T.L.O.,* 469 U.S. 325 (1985).
51. Michael Apple, "Making Knowledge Legitimate: Power, Profit and the Textbook," in A. Molnar, ed., *Current Thought on Curriculum,* (Alexandria, VA: Association for Supervision and Curriculum Development, 1985).
52. Frank C. Nelson, "What Evangelical Parents Expect from Public School Administrators," *Educational Leadership* (May 1988), pp. 40–43.
53. *Digest of Educational Statistics,* 1993, p. 83.
54. Karen Seashore Louis, "Social and Community Values and the Quality of Teachers' Work Life," in Milbrey W. McLaughlin, Joan E. Talbert, and Nina Bascia, eds. *The Contexts of Teaching in Secondary Schools: Teachers' Realities* (New York: Teachers College Press, 1990), pp. 17–39.
55. Louis, "Social and Community Values and the Quality of Teachers' Work Life," pp. 18–19.
56. *Digest of Educational Statistics,* 1988, p. 5.
57. U.S. Department of Education. *Schools and Staffing in the United States: A Statistical Profile, 1993–94.* NCES 96-124 by Robin R. Henke, Susan P. Choy, Sonya Geis, and Stephen P. Broughman. Washington, D.C.: National Center for Education Statistics (1996), pp. vi–vii.
58. *Ibid.*
59. Michael Scriven, "Duties of the Teacher," unpublished manuscript, circulated as "Version Date 9/93" with support of U.S. Department of Education.
60. John Dewey, *Reconstruction in Philosophy* (Boston: Beacon Press, 1984), p. 186.

Social Diversity and Differentiated Schooling Today: Vocational and Liberal Ideals

In the 18th and 19th centuries the primary purpose of schooling was to prepare young people with academic skills. Young men and women developed workplace skills not in schools but in apprenticeships and other on-the-job training, whether for skilled crafts or for the newly developing factories. The beginning of the 20th century, however, brought with it the effort to mix job preparation with academic schooling, a mix that has remained controversial throughout the century. Just as some black educators questioned Booker T. Washington's emphasis on vocational education for African-American youth, educators from John Dewey to Mark Van Doren to contemporary curriculum theorists have criticized the class, gender, and race biases of vocational education in public schools. Despite decades of criticism of vocational education in public schooling, its advocates have continued to argue that vocational education responds to some of our most urgent economic and educational needs. The most recent example of such advocacy is the $1.3 billion Carl D. Perkins Vocational and Applied Technology Education Act Amendments of 1990, congressional legislation that will affect federal educational policy throughout the 1990s. Even long-time vocational education critic Arthur G. Wirth argues that the Perkins Amendments may bring a radically new approach to vocational education, rather than bringing old wine in new bottles.[1]

Although very few readers of this textbook will become teachers of vocational education classes, there are several reasons for all teachers to think carefully about the issues addressed in this chapter. First, it is important to note that the 1990s are a decade of renewed interest in vocational education, and that each new era of advocacy for vocational education in the schools raises perennial questions about the fundamental purposes of education and schooling. In Booker T. Washington's arguments, in the arguments of social-efficiency educators of the Progressive era, in James B. Conant's arguments in the early Cold War era, and in similar arguments presented today, the primary purpose of schooling is often defined in terms of the economic conditions and needs of the larger society, rather than in terms of what each individual needs to be a well-educated person.[2] Many teachers have not had opportunity to think carefully about the difference between the ideals of liberal education and vocational education, like Mark Van Doren did in Conant's time, for example. This chapter affords opportunity to think about those basic purposes of education in today's world.

Second, vocational education policies raise questions of fairness, as we consider that each new resurgence of interest in vocational education is stimulated in part by concern for how low-income and minority or immigrant groups will take their places in our educational and economic systems. Lester M. Salamon, coeditor of the recent volume *Human Capital and America's Future*, argues for addressing the training and educational needs of "three special target groups" that will "comprise most of the new entrants to the labor force in the years ahead." He identifies these as women, immigrants, and "minorities and the poor."[3] It seems well-established that the vocational education programs stimulated by the Smith-Hughes Act of 1917 (see Chapter 4) helped to sustain social inequalities by setting different educational goals for different groups of students, and these groups were often defined, in practice, by gender, ethnicity, and social class. Should it concern us that two supporters of the Perkins Act describe it as "the updated version of the Smith-Hughes Act"?[4]

Nearly all vocational programs in the public schools are implemented at the middle-school and secondary school levels. Yet teachers at all levels should recognize that vocational education programs in schools are a particular instance of what most teachers are asked to support in a more general form: the differentiated curriculum of ability grouping, or tracking. The assumptions underlying supposedly "homogeneous" ability groups are consistent with those underlying vocational education: that students of different skill levels have different capacities for learning; that they should be educated toward different outcomes in school; and that these outcomes correspond to different destinies in the socioeconomic order. There are those who believe, on the other hand, that whether it is called ability grouping or tracking or something else, homogenous grouping and vocational education are cousins in a family of segregationist school practices that fail to provide the best possible academic preparation to which all students are entitled. Others, however, see in the Perkins legislation the possibility of integrating vocational and liberal educational ideals in ways never before accomplished on a wide scale in schools in the United States. Such an integration might, at its best, resemble the Deweyan notion described in Chapter 4 of educating *through* vocations instead of *for* them. Alternatively, the current resurgence of vocational education may demonstrate again that the familiar vocational education arguments of the past are not what is needed for the educational future of the nation's youth.

VOCATIONAL EDUCATION IN HISTORICAL PERSPECTIVE

Chapter 4 provided an account of how vocational education developed as a prominent part of progressive schooling in the first two decades of the 20th century. In 1917, Congress passed the Smith-Hughes Act, which marked vocational education as so integral a part of American schooling that it merited federal financing. In their history of vocational education, Grubb and Lazerson write:

> The triumph of vocationalism lay less in the numbers enrolled in trade training courses than in the belief that the primary goal of schooling was to prepare youth for the job market, in the redefinition of equality of educational opportunity that accompanied the differentiated curriculum, and in growth of vocational guidance, education testing, and the junior high school to select students more effectively for educational programs on the basis of their predicted future economic roles.[5]

In fact, 1917 marked just the beginning of the federal government's involvement in funding vocational education programs, funding which increased from only $7 million per year in 1917 to $36 million per year by 1946. In the 1950s the federal government's attention to vocational education subsided somewhat, except for the National Defense Education Act of 1957, which did attend to some aspects of vocationalism.[6]

The 1960s witnessed a revival of vocational education. As we saw in Part 1, James B. Conant emphasized vocational education in his much-discussed 1959 book *The American High School Today*. Conant argued, for example, that a comprehensive high school could be regarded as successful if one of the three major things it accomplished was to offer an extensive elective program that prepared the majority of students for the workplace immediately after high school. The other two items that he identified as marking a successful comprehensive high school were the provision of a good education for all students as future citizens and an advanced curriculum aimed at the most "talented" students.[7]

Three of Conant's 21 recommendations attempted to systematize the vocational education direction established in the progressive era. Conant argued in recommendation 1, for example, that "a meaningful sequence for a majority of the students would be a series of courses leading to the development of marketable skills."[8] In recommendation 2, Conant advised that each student should choose either an academic or a vocational or commercial sequence of courses, though he cautioned that any student at any time should be able to switch from one of these sequences to another. In recommendation 7, Conant focused on diversified vocational education programs, which he believed ought to be provided in any good comprehensive high school. By these he meant secretarial and home economics courses for girls, and trade and industrial courses for boys. He argued that these programs should be geared to employment opportunities in the local community.[9]

Conant's widely publicized recommendations signaled renewed emphasis on vocational education in the late 1950s and early 1960s. One of his most significant contributions was to provide an emphatic answer to a debate which had endured since the inception of vocational education at the turn of the century. This dispute concerned whether there ought to be separate high schools for students in vocational and academic programs. Conant clearly argued that such a separation was inadvisable and that a comprehensive high school should offer different kinds of curricula under the same roof.

It is important to add that Conant also visualized the community college system as a crucial part of vocational education in the United States. His vision, in fact, helped fuel the dramatic growth of community colleges in the 1960s and the 1970s. In the 1980s and 1990s, as we will see, community colleges would grow in their significance to vocational education as high school vocational programs began to dwindle.

Although the 1960s brought more federal funding for vocational education, critics became quite strident in charging that vocational education had failed to respond to the realities of the labor market. They also charged that students in vocational education programs were stigmatized as not bright enough to take the traditional academic subjects. These were presumed to be reserved for the more "talented" students, as Conant had identified them, on the basis of school performance and test scores. Such separation was characterized as a nondemocratic educational arrangement wherein students who did not seem to have college potential were being tracked at a very early age into working-class futures.

The career education movement sought to define *all* education, college preparatory programs as well as traditional vocational education classes, in terms of career applications. By doing so, advocates hoped to defuse the stigma attached to vocational education programs.

These criticisms helped stimulate the career education movement led by the U.S. Office of Education in the 1970s, a movement which sought to frame all students' academic and vocational work in terms of career applications so there would be no distinctively different emphasis for vocational students. For a while, "career education" replaced "vocational education" as the term to use when discussing how to relate high school to the world of work. The prominent career educator Kenneth B. Hoyt argued that if career education were successful, it would be a part of every student's education in every course at every level of school, and that ultimately the term "career education" would be dropped because it would simply be taken for granted that all education was, in fact, career education. "Career education" and "education," Hoyt said, would be terms that meant basically the same thing.[10] The 1980s, however, saw a revival of the term "vocational education." For example, the influential school reform report *A Nation at Risk,* published in 1983, called for new rigor in vocational education courses. In 1984 an important report called *The Unfinished Agenda: The Role of Vocational Education in the High*

School was released by the National Commission on Secondary Vocational Education, and its language suggested that the career education movement, as supported by Hoyt and the U.S. Office of Education in the 1970s, had become a thing of the past. Yet basic components of the career education movement would reappear in the Perkins legislation of 1990.

Prior to Perkins: Vocational Education in the 1970s and 1980s

Since its early development for African-Americans in the South and for immigrant children throughout the United States during the progressive era, vocational education has been criticized on both theoretical and practical grounds. The theoretical criticism has been that in a class-divided society the vocational curriculum is class-biased, that it is undemocratic, and that it substitutes training for education. Such criticisms were leveled by John Dewey at the start of the vocational education movement.

The practical criticism involves charges that vocational education fails to prepare students adequately for the workplace. Even at the height of Booker T. Washington's influence, around 1900, concerns were raised about the degree to which the training for trades at Tuskegee adequately took account of the realities of an industrializing society that increasingly demanded either unskilled factory labor or higher education rather than skilled trades training. Nearly 100 years later, in the late 1970s, research by Grasso and Shea and others suggested that vocational education programs were not meeting their primary objectives: retaining students in school, making them more employable in the workplace, providing better knowledge of the workplace, and providing higher wage opportunities for students who were not college bound.[11] Such criticisms are cause for examining some of the data on vocational education today.

Vocational Students and Programs In 1983 Allen Weisberg's review of vocational education research indicated that approximately 17 million students were involved in vocational education at all levels in the United States and that 7.3 million of them were in programs that prepare students for specific occupations.[12] Approximately 60 percent of these occupationally specific students were in high schools, and 90 percent of these were in comprehensive high schools, much as James B. Conant recommended.[13] Well over 1,000 area vocational education schools (which take students from several different attendance districts) supplemented approximately 15,000 public comprehensive high schools or vocational high schools offering vocational education in the 1980s.[14]

The resources spent on vocational programs in this country are considerable. *Unfinished Agenda* informs us that the nation's vocational education budget in the mid-1980s was almost $9 billion per year, of which the federal government supplied only about 10 percent, the remainder coming from state and local sources. In 1994, the federal government spent $1.45 billion on vocational and adult education, about the same as it invested in school improvement programs but considerably less than the $7 billion for the "educationally disadvantaged."[15]

Of the students enrolled in vocational education programs, approximately 50 percent are female, 23 percent are minority, 12 percent are from low-income groups and are designated as "disadvantaged" students, and about 2 percent are special-education students with some kind of disability.[16] Vocational education programs are generally divided into nine different categories: agricultural education, distributive education, health education, occupational home economics, business and office education, technical trades and industrial education, vocational consumer education, homemaking education, and marketing.[17] In these many different vocational areas, however, approximately 50 percent of all students are enrolled in only two categories: business and office education, and technical trades and industrial education. The overwhelming majority of students in business and office education are female, while a similar majority of students in technical trades and industrial education are male.[18] The enrollments in these occupational programs reflect their pervasive gender typing.

Forty-two percent of all vocational education teachers in the early 1980s taught at the secondary level, a proportion that is now decreasing as vocational education programs are increasingly situated in community colleges. Of the secondary teachers, about a quarter work part-time, with most of them holding positions in the private sector. At least through the early 1980s, one out of every four high school seniors self-identified his or her high school program as vocational in nature, and the majority of all high school graduates today take at least one occupationally specific vocational course, or at least one vocational education course of some kind.[19] However, in the decade since Weisberg's 1983 research, the average number of courses in vocational-technical subjects taken by high school students has declined from 4.0 units to 3.2 units, a 20 percent decrease. This decline is due in part to the 1980s' emphasis on core academic coursework and in part to criticism of the educational value of vocational programs in secondary schools.[20]

The Decline of Enrollment in Vocational Programs

The most recent data on enrollments in vocational education programs over time were released in the *Digest of Education Statistics, 1996.* While low-income, low-achieving, and minority students are still more likely to be enrolled in vocational programs than other students, enrollments among all categories of students have declined significantly into the early 1990s. Comparisons of the years 1982 and 1992, the most recent 10-year trend available, reveal the following:

- Of all high school seniors, 35.2 percent reported they were in the general track in 1982, 45.3 percent in 1992; 37.9 percent reported they were in the college prep track in 1982, 43 percent in 1992; and *26.9 percent reported they were in the vocational track in 1982, which declined to 11.7 percent in 1992.*
- As in 1982, African-American, Hispanic, and American Indian students in 1992 were more likely to be enrolled in vocational programs than were white non-Hispanic and Asian American students. *But every group reduced its enrollment in vocational tracks by more than half, except for American Indians, which lowered its enrollment by a third.*
- Whereas in 1982, almost 40 percent of all students from the lowest SES quartile were enrolled in vocational tracks, in 1992 only 21 percent were so enrolled. It is a rare student (only 3 percent) who comes from the upper SES quartile and is enrolled in a vocational track.
- Similarly, students whose test scores place them in the upper quartile of high school seniors were rarely in vocational programs (only 2.6 percent), while 23 percent of the students from the lowest quartile of test scores were so enrolled—*compared to 45.6 percent of lowest-quartile students in 1982.*

What these figures represent is a trend away from vocational education programs in the secondary school throughout the 1980s and early 1990s. At the same time, however, support was building for the Perkins Amendments of 1990, and we have yet to see the overall impact of those amendments. It may be that a new category of enrollment will have to be developed—integrated academic/vocational, for example—before we can identify how many students are enrolled in Perkins-like programs seeking to eliminate vocational education as a separate track in the secondary school.[21]

Vocational Education Goals Historically, vocational education programs were intended to respond to different kinds of social and economic problems in the United States.[22] One major goal has been to integrate the "disadvantaged" into the economic mainstream. Since the turn of the century, vocational education programs have been aimed at those who came from specific minority or immigrant groups and from low-income backgrounds, and at those who, according to usual measures of academic ability, were not considered "college material."

A second major goal has been to help solve national economic problems: problems of unemployment, problems of mismatch between jobs and skills, and problems with respect to America's place in the world political order. Vocational education has even been supported in the effort to meet national defense needs, as in the National Defense Education Act of 1957, and to meet national economic needs, as identified in the school reform report, *A Nation at Risk,* in 1983.

A third goal has been to provide a relevant curriculum for students who are not college bound. It is important to remember that historically (and today) the majority of high school students have not been expected to obtain 4-year college degrees, and the vocational education curriculum has therefore been defended as more relevant and interesting for students destined for the world of work immediately after high school. Consequently, it is argued, vocational programs are more likely to motivate students and keep them in school longer.

A fourth goal, related to the previous one, is the historical aim of using vocational education programs to help solve such youth problems as gang activity, crime, and teenage pregnancy. As far back as Horace Mann's common school era, state-supported schooling was defended as a response to the so-called youth problem of the cities. The belief that vocational programs would be more interesting to working-class and immigrant youth suggested that such curricula would be more effective at keeping students in school and out of mischief.

Vocational Education Results The outcomes of vocational education for the first three quarters of the 20th century have been explored by Grasso and Shea in their book *Vocational Education and Training: Impact on Youth,*[23] which surveys vocational education studies prior to 1979 and analyzes the data generated by the national longitudinal Survey of Labor Market Experience. The data were generated from a sample of over 10,000 men and women between the ages of 14 and 24. It is important to note, however, that such data do not compare vocational education students with college preparatory students, who tend to have different social class backgrounds and different career aspirations.

We can examine whether vocational education programs in the past have helped to lower dropout rates. Weisberg and Grasso and Shea indicate that the evidence is somewhat conflicting. Although there is evidence that some vocational education programs do help keep students in school longer, there is also evidence that other vocational education programs do not. The National Commission for Employment Policy indicates, however, that vocational education programs are associated with a "reduced likelihood of post-secondary training," a finding that Weisberg along with Grasso and Shea also found when comparing vocational education students with those from the general education track.[24]

Are vocational education programs well matched to the needs of the labor market? Weisberg says the answer is no, that the needs of the current labor market are primarily in services, finance, and trade, positions which require strong general education skills or job-specific postsecondary training. Weisberg concludes that secondary vocational education programs are ill suited to the real needs of the labor market. He notes further that comprehensive high schools cannot stay abreast of changing workplace technologies, and therefore it is unreasonable to expect secondary schools to provide the necessary training for the labor market of today.

This conclusion leads to the important question of whether vocational education students actually do better in the labor market than general education graduates. *Unfinished Agenda* indicates that there are some positive outcomes for vocational education. It argues that among males, vocational education graduates are twice as likely as nonvocational graduates to be working in craft occupations, which tend to be better paid than occupations which require no specific skills and training. Grasso and Shea, however, note that even though "a large body of work has been completed since the passage of the Vocational Education Act of 1963, . . . it does not provide compelling evidence supporting the alleged labor market benefits of high-school-level vocational education."[25] Further, they show with their analysis of the National Labor Statistics data that only female graduates of commercial curricula reflect any such labor market benefits. In general, males do not seem to do appreciably better in the labor market as a result of their vocational education programs.

Weisberg argues that all studies seem to indicate that the number of years of school is much more significant than the type of schooling in terms of employability and income level: "Additional schooling per se, not vocational studies in particular, seems to correlate with success in the labor market."[26] Weisberg adds:

> *We know that general literacy skills are more likely than any other factor to yield success in the labor market.* Such skills facilitate further education. They qualify young people for training in the technical fields that pay well but do not require a college degree. Comprehensive high schools must make clear to youngsters the link between mastery of basic skills and expanded career opportunities.[27] (italics added)

More recently, educational researcher Ernest L. Boyer writes that "the capacity of vocational courses to help students become employed is largely disappointing . . . At graduation [vocational students] often do not have the verbal and intellectual tools to do productive work."[28]

Community Colleges and Vocational Education

A study of community colleges prepared by Harvey G. Neufeldt argues that "the true concept of the community college . . . was not realized until after World War II. It was during the decades of the 1950s and 60s that adult education, terminal education, and community service found a welcome home in the 2-year college."[29] Neufeldt goes on to argue that in many ways the community college was viewed as a democratizing institution in American society because it made higher education available to many who previously had been unable to attend college. In addition to providing an academic bridge into 4-year colleges, the community college is viewed as a major provider of vocational education. By the mid-1980s, postsecondary vocational education programs had become the fastest growing segments of higher education, and most people attending community colleges enrolled in vocational programs rather than in baccalaureate-transfer programs.[30]

Throughout the 1970s and 1980s, however, numerous studies cast doubts on the success of community colleges in two areas: vocational education and transfer to 4-year colleges. In an article entitled "False Promises of Community Colleges," Fred L. Pincus reported:

> The economic benefits of vocational education are at best modest. Although most students get jobs in the fields for which they are trained, a substantial minority does not. The employment rate of vocational education graduates (from community colleges) is no better than that of college graduates and it may be much worse.[31]

Pincus went on to argue that terminal vocational education programs that are not designed for transfer to a 4-year college

> may be part of a tracking system that reproduces and legitimates the social and economic inequalities that are endemic in a capitalist society. Working class and minority students are overrepresented in vocational programs in general, and in lower level vocational programs in particular. Women, who comprise over half of community college enrollment, have been led to believe that terminal vocational education can help overcome sex inequalities in employment but the data suggests this optimistic view is false. Vocational education and community colleges help reproduce sex inequality as well as class and racial inequality.[32]

There is some argument, therefore, that vocational education programs in community colleges are characterized by many of the same problems as vocational education programs at the secondary level.

What about the value of community college programs for transfers to 4-year colleges? The 1989 publication *Bridges to Opportunity*, produced by the College Entrance Examination Board, raises important questions on this issue. The most fundamental is reflected in its subtitle: "Are Community Colleges Meeting the Transfer Needs of Minority Students?" This volume confirms Pincus's findings regarding poor employment options and low transfer rates. What percentage of students actually do transfer from community colleges to 4-year colleges? The authors of *Bridges to Opportunity* find that "the current transfer rate is 15–25 percent of all community college students and 20–30 percent of those students who say they want to transfer." They indicate also that this transfer rate appears to have declined since the 1960s and 1970s, although the extent of the decline is not clear. Finally, they note that white and probably Asian students are more likely to transfer than black or Hispanic students, and that transfer rates are highly variable both among and within different community college systems.[33]

What about students who do transfer and then try to finish a 4-year degree? According to *Bridges to Opportunity*, not very many students succeed. In fact, *only 10 to 15 percent of all community college students ever receive a B.A., and no more than a quarter of community college students who aspire to a B.A. ever receive one.* Racial variation is again reflected: white community college students are more likely to earn a B.A. than black or Hispanic students.[34] The report also cites a study in which minority students who did graduate from college were compared with a matched set of minority students who did not graduate from college. The study found that 95 percent of the graduates held professional managerial jobs compared to less than half of the nongraduates and that the median salary for graduates was at least $10,000 more than that for nongraduates.[35]

It is precisely this kind of information, it might be argued, that vocational education programs have been least successful in delivering to students. Historically, vocational education programs have been defended on two counts: (1) they prepare students *for* the world of work, and (2) they teach students *about* the world of work. The critiques by Grasso and Shea, Weisberg, and others suggest that vocational education programs have not been very successful at preparing students *for* the world of work, and it can be argued that there is also a great deal missing with respect to teaching vocational education students *about* the world of work. In fact, Grasso and Shea present strong evidence to support the idea that graduates of vocational programs know less about the world of work than do their peers in both college preparatory and general programs.[36] Certainly the career education arguments of the 1970s as well as the vocational education arguments of the 1980s emphasized that vocational education programs should teach students about the world of work and therefore enable them to make more informed choices with respect to vocations and careers.

Some of the information cited in *Bridges to Opportunity* is not the kind that is typically presented to students in community colleges. For example, the report indicates that minority students will benefit much less from vocational programs than from a college degree. Such information might stimulate students to choose transfer programs rather than take a terminal community college degree, and this actually runs against the vocational rationale behind community colleges as developed by James B. Conant and others. There is, then, a potential conflict between two primary goals of vocational education, at both the community college and the high school level: educating *about* the workplace may actually undermine efforts to educate *for* the workplace; what students could learn about "the world of work" may discourage the pursuit of vocational education and encourage the pursuit of a baccalaureate degree.

The Perkins Act Amendments of 1990

Long-time critic of vocational education Arthur Wirth argues that four features of the Perkins Act Amendments of 1990 could benefit the education of all students by helping us rethink academic

Critics of vocational education programs point out that such programs tend to segregate students along class, race, and gender lines.

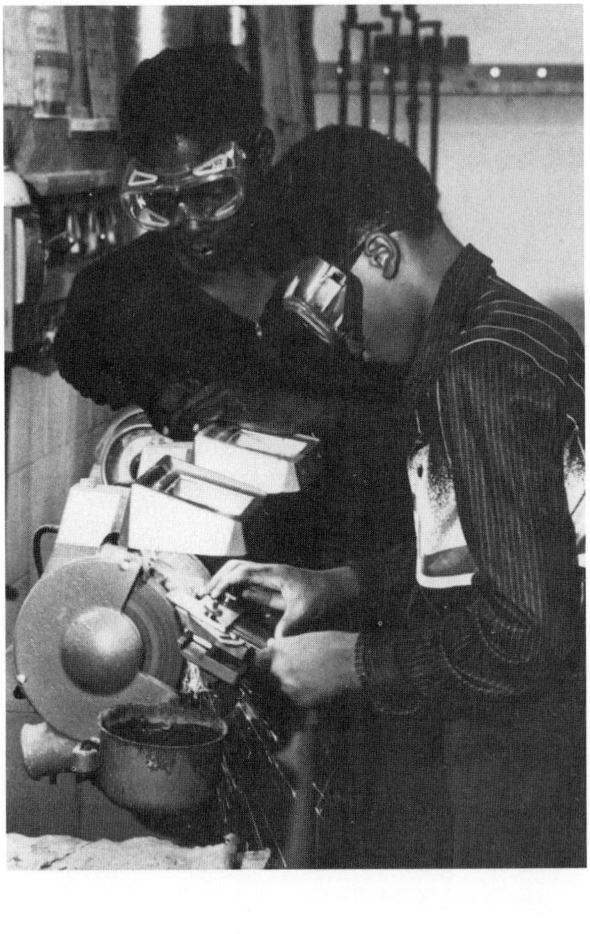

education as well as vocational education. First, he notes that the Perkins funding is by law required to be concentrated in low-income school districts. Second, the Perkins Amendments require that the vocational education initiatives must come from local school districts instead of state governments, a departure from previous vocational education policy. Third, the Perkins Amendments reject high school training for specific job skills in favor of a "tech-prep" approach that provides academic skills to prepare high school students for postsecondary technical education. Finally, Wirth believes that the most important dimension of Perkins is the new emphasis on integrating academic and vocational studies. The intention here is to use vocational activities to provide strong academic education for all students who would choose that approach.[37]

The Perkins legislation of 1990 boosted the federal funding of vocational education by 59 percent over the previous year's allocation. Of the total authorization of $41.6 billion, $1.3 billion was allocated to local school districts, area vocational-technical schools, and postsecondary institutions, of which community colleges are an important component. The history of vocational education's limited success in achieving ambitious goals, however, may lead critics once again to question whether this $1.3 billion might be better spent on development of primary academic skills rather than on expensive vocational facilities. As we shall see, there is evidence that these primary academic skills will be most in demand in the workplace of the future. Even if this were not the case, critics will continue to observe that educational goals framed in terms of the needs of the workplace, instead of in terms of the full intellectual development of students, are not educational goals at all, but are instead economic goals in which students are but means to ends that do not serve their interests well.

THE FUTURE OF THE WORKPLACE

This section examines the kinds of information that might be shared with students to help them more fully understand the realities of work in the 1990s and beyond.

Future Jobs

Wirth writes about the shift in the American workplace from manufacturing to service industries:

> In the steady trend toward a computer-driven society, there continues to be a strong shift from manufacturing to high-tech and service industries. The skills of highly paid factory workers continue to become obsolete. By the year 2000, some 75 percent of [manufacturing] employees will need to be retrained in new jobs or taught fresh skills for their old ones. On the average, workers now change jobs from four to six times in their work lives. There is a striking trend toward a requirement of more education for the fastest-growing kinds of jobs, those in technical, managerial, and professional areas. A projection of new jobs to be created between 1984 and 2000 shows that more than half will require education beyond high school, with about a third to be filled by college graduates. The median years of education required for new jobs for 2000 will be 13.5 compared with 12.8 for 1984. In absolute numbers, most new jobs will be in service occupations such as administrative support, marketing, and sales. By the year 2000, some 88 percent of the work force will hold jobs in the service sector. While the rate of growth will be greatest in higher-skill areas, the largest *number* of jobs will be for cooks, nursing aides, waiters, and janitors; for cashiers in marketing and sales; and for secretaries, clerks, and computer operators in administrative support. Other than the computer operators, most of these categories require only modest skills. But even here there will be increased expectations that these workers can read and understand directions, do arithmetic, and be able to speak and think clearly. The unskilled clearly will be the most vulnerable.[38]

Wirth is pointing out that the model of the American workplace upon which vocational education programs of the progressive period were based no longer accurately represents the American economy (see Exhibits 11.1 and 11.2). The American workplace has shifted significantly from heavy manufacturing industries to services-producing businesses, in particular small firms that require people with flexible, multiple skills.

For example, the U.S. Government reports that from 1990 to 1992, nearly a million jobs among operators, fabricators, and laborers were eliminated, while significant increases were recorded among jobs designated as managerial, professional, technical, sales, and service.[39]

EXHIBIT 11.1 Fastest-Growing Occupations (in Percentage Terms)

	Percentage Change	*Change in Total Employment*	*Percentage of Total Job Growth*
Computer service technicians	97	53,000	0.21
Legal assistants	94	43,000	0.17
Computer systems analysts	85	217,000	0.85
Computer programmers	77	205,000	0.80
Computer operators	76	160,000	0.63
Office machine repairers	72	40,000	0.16
Physical therapy assistants	68	26,000	0.09
Electrical engineers	65	209,000	0.82
Civil engineering technicians	64	23,000	0.09
Peripheral electrical operators	64	31,000	0.12

Source: Sophisticated Technology, the Workforce, and Vocational Education, Illinois State Board of Education, 1989, p. 22.

EXHIBIT 11.2 Fastest-Growing Occupations (in Absolute Terms)

	Percentage Change	*Change in Total Employment*	*Percentage of Total Job Growth*
Building custodians	27.5	779,000	3.0
Cashiers	47.5	744,000	2.9
Secretaries	29.5	719,000	2.8
General office clerks	29.6	696,000	2.7
Salesclerks	23.5	685,000	2.7
Registered nurses	48.9	642,000	2.5
Waiters and waitresses	33.8	562,000	2.2
Teachers	37.4	511,000	2.0
Truck drivers	26.5	425,000	1.7
Nursing aides and orderlies	34.5	423,000	1.7

Source: Sophisticated Technology, the Workforce, and Vocational Education, Illinois State Board of Education, 1989, p. 24.

Many of the fastest-growing occupations in the late 1980s were in fact related to high technology, as indicated in Exhibit 11.1. For example, five of the six fastest-growing jobs (in terms of *percentage* growth) were computer service technicians, computer systems analysts, computer programmers, computer operators, and office machine repairers. On the other hand, it is important to note that these high-tech positions actually constitute a very small percentage of the total job growth. That is, although such jobs are growing rapidly, relatively few of them are available. The fastest-growing job category, computer service technicians, for example, represented only 0.2 percent of the job growth in American society in the late 1980s. The same can be said for computer systems analysts, who constitute less than 1 percent of the total job growth, and so on throughout Exhibit 11.1.

For a truer picture of job growth in American society, we need to look at the growth in *numbers* of jobs in the job market. For example, although the category of computer service technician is the fastest-growing job category in terms of percentage growth, it accounts for only 53,000 new jobs. On the other hand, as Exhibit 11.2 shows, the fastest-growing job category in terms of total *number* of jobs available is building custodians, with 779,000 new jobs. In fact, by far the greatest numbers of new jobs available are service jobs that require the kinds of skills that most secondary vocational education programs are not well suited to provide. Examples include building custodians, cashiers, salesclerks, general office clerks, registered nurses, waiters and waitresses, teachers, and truck drivers. Only a few of these jobs—such as secretaries, nursing aides, and orderlies—are positions for which high school curricula are preparing students. The question arising from such data is this: Is an entire vocational education curriculum needed to prepare someone to be a secretary or a nursing aide or an orderly?

Educating for the Workplace

This question of what kind of high school education is most productive for non-college-bound workers must also be addressed when teaching students about the realities of the working world. One important question is, What do employers themselves want in a worker? What kinds of skills are most valued and sought after when businesses hire new employees? Exhibit 11.3 represents findings from a series of studies (1986 through 1988) which reflect employers' preferences in their prospective employees' skills. The five major studies conducted during this period unanimously recommend reading and comprehension skills, written and oral communication skills, thinking, problem-solving and decision-making skills, and computational skills. Such items as technical skills, flexibility, good work habits, and scientific knowledge reflect much less agreement among employers. In short, the worker characteristics upon which there is most agreement are the skills that are emphasized more in academic programs than in distinctly vocational education programs. A look at the U.S. Department of Labor projections for the year 2000 (Exhibit 11.4), for example, indicates that the overwhelming majority of new jobs are those for which either a general education at the high school level or a college degree is most suitable.

The college-degree jobs that are going to grow fastest between now and the year 2000 are registered nurses, top executives and general managers, kindergarten and elementary school teachers, and licensed practical nurses. A great many other jobs do not require occupationally specific preparation in the high school but depend instead on those kinds of skills mentioned above: the three Rs, problem solving, and critical thinking. These jobs include salespeople, food service workers, building custodians, cashiers, truck drivers, nursing aides and attendants, guards, and receptionists.

Income and Benefits

In examining work-force projections for the year 2000, the journal *American Demographics* claimed that "many of the jobs that will have the most openings in the decade ahead are service jobs that require little education and offer little hope for advancement."[40] This raises an uneasy specter. In a 1989 article in *The Nation* magazine, William Serrin reported that "half the jobs created in the U.S. between 1979 and 1987 paid wages below the poverty level for a family of four."[41] In conditions similar to those at the turn of the century, more and more family members are required to work, mothers and children included.[42]

One reason for the low wages, according to Serrin, is that most of the new jobs are not high-tech but low-tech, in services rather than in manufacturing. In 1992, for example, the median weekly wage for men in manufacturing was $406, and men in precision production earned median wages of $503 weekly. Both of these were areas of declining employment, while the expanding service jobs paid only $330 weekly. A similar situation prevailed for women, though the corresponding incomes were lower in each category. In short, as the number of manufacturing jobs declines, the jobs that are replacing them tend to have much lower wages.[43]

Another related point is that "both employed and unemployed people are experiencing a substantial erosion of benefits." Serrin argues that the number of Americans with no health insurance is growing by a million a year, and fewer than half of U.S. workers are now covered by pension plans—a significant decline from the 1970s. It is also important to note that in the new labor market only 60 percent of U.S. workers are employed full-time, all year round. Those preparing to enter the work force need to know which jobs are full-time jobs with full benefits and which are seasonal or tend toward part-time rather than full-time employment.[44]

EXHIBIT 11.3 Summary of Work Force Competency Reports: The Work Force of the Future

	WORK FORCE PROJECTION REPORT				
Desired Competency or Skill	*Michigan Employability Task Force*	*Southern Growth Policies Board*	*Workplace Basics (ASTD/DOL)*	*Building a Quality Work Force (DOL, ED, DOC)*	*Work Force 2000 (Hudson Institute)*
Reading and comprehension skills	•	•	•	•	•
Written and oral communication skills	•	•	•	•	•
Thinking, problem-solving, and decision-making skills	•	•	•	•	•
Computational skills	•	•	•	•	•
Technical skills	•	•	o	•	o
Flexibility	o	•	o	•	•
Ability to learn/adaptability	•	•	•	•	
Positive attitude, motivation, and self-direction	•	•	•	•	
Teamwork and interpersonal skills	•	o	•	•	
Creativity	•	•	•		
Understanding of the "big picture"	o	•	•		
Good work habits	o	o		•	
Multicultural skills	•			•	
Scientific knowledge	•	•			
Career and personal development	•		•		

• *Explicitly stated in the report*
o *Implied*

Source: Sophisticated Technology, the Workforce, and Vocational Education, Illinois State Board of Education, 1989, p. 33.

In examining income and benefits, students in vocational programs could also study employment and income differentials among different population groups. To examine why full-time working women only earn 72 percent of the income of men, for example, would raise opportunity for understanding gender discrimination in the workplace.[45] Similarly, study of the employment patterns of different population groups would show that African-Americans are unemployed over the decades at a rate consistently double that of the white population, despite having closed the education gaps dramatically. Thus, the effects of race on employment could be examined. Such inequities will be further addressed in Chapter 12.

Work and the Quality of Life

In addition to looking at some of the quantitative dimensions of the world of work, it is important to look at the nature of work itself. An immigrant sweatshop song from the early 20th century characterizes at least some workers' views in that era:

> I work, work, work without end.
> Why and for whom I know not.
> I care not, I ask not,
> I am a machine.[46]

One disturbing feature of contemporary work, a carryover from the scientific management move-

EXHIBIT 11.4 Employment Growth in the 1990s (in Thousands)

	EMPLOYMENT		*CHANGE IN EMPLOYMENT 1986–2000*	
	1986	*2000*	*Number*	*Percentage Change*
Salespersons, retail	3,579	4,780	1,201	33.5%
Waiters and waitresses	1,702	2,454	752	44.2
Registered nurses	1,406	2,018	612	43.6
Janitors and cleaners, including maids and housekeeping cleaners	2,676	3,280	604	22.6
General managers and top executives	2,383	2,965	582	24.4
Cashiers	2,165	2,740	575	26.5
Truck drivers, light and heavy	2,211	2,736	525	23.8
General office clerks	2,361	2,824	462	19.6
Food counter, fountain, and related workers	1,500	1,949	449	29.9
Nursing aides, orderlies, and attendants	1,224	1,658	433	35.4
Secretaries	3,234	3,658	424	13.1
Guards	794	1,177	383	48.3
Accountants and auditors	945	1,322	376	39.8
Computer programmers	479	813	335	69.9
Food preparation workers	949	1,273	324	34.2
Teachers, kindergarten and elementary	1,527	1,826	299	19.6
Receptionists and information clerks	682	964	282	41.4
Computer systems analysts, electronic data processors	331	582	251	75.6
Cooks, restaurant	520	759	240	46.2
Licensed practical nurses	631	869	238	37.7

Source: American Demographics, February 1988, p. 33.

ment of the progressive era, is the loss of decision-making power for workers. This is of particular concern when we recall Plato's definition of a slave: "one who accepts from another the purposes which control his conduct." Plato argued that slavery is grounded less in ownership than in whose purposes are controlling an activity. The immigrant sweatshop worker claimed to be a machine in part because he or she did not know (or care about) the fundamental purposes of the work.

What makes work satisfying and purposeful? In 1985, a research study by Jeylan T. Mortimer concluded that the most important determinant of job satisfaction was not income but work autonomy, the degree to which employees feel they can make their own decisions and influence what happens on the job.[47] In fact, this study found that income had little effect on job satisfaction but that people with high incomes typically had greater autonomy in the job; the autonomy itself was the significant determinant of job satisfaction.

These findings on the importance of job autonomy confirm a number of other studies that have been done over time. In 1973, a study conducted by the U.S. Department of Health, Education, and Welfare ranked income fifth in importance to workers at all levels, whether blue collar or white collar.[48] The HEW study found that interest in the work itself was the most important determinant of job satisfaction. Self-control over the quality of the output ranked second, independence ranked third, and opportunity for creativity ranked fourth. Workers considered jobs without these qualities to be frustrating, dissatisfying, and destructive with respect to relationships with others, and destructive of self-esteem.

The same HEW report investigated worker satisfaction by asking, "Would you take this occupation again if you had your life to live over?" The results were consistent with the above findings. Forty-three percent of white collar workers reported that they would choose their occupations again, compared with 24 percent of blue-collar workers.[49] An interesting note is that 93 percent of college professors answered in the affirmative. Although the pay scale for college professors is not as high as in some other professions, it is clearly the case that their autonomy is quite high.

If students are to make informed choices about their occupational future, they need to be educated about the nature of the work for which they are being prepared, including the degree to which it is alienating or injurious. Educating students in this way is a very different enterprise from simply preparing them with skills and attitudes to fit uncritically into the workplace. An alternative approach to contemporary vocational education is John Dewey's concept (introduced in Chapter 4) of educating *through* occupations rather than educating *for* occupations. Such an approach uses the activities of vocational education to achieve all kinds of literacy: functional, cultural, and critical. Thus the goals for vocational students become the same as for "college preparatory" students: development of academic skills and intellectual growth in preparation for further learning after high school. In this model, *all* secondary students seek to expand their knowledge and skills in all directions, not just in one particular direction.

VOCATIONAL EDUCATION AS A TEACHING METHOD[50]

When Dewey wrote in 1916 that "the only training *for* occupations is training *through* occupations," he was advocating an educational approach that has never been well understood.[51] Like many vocational training programs today, the vocational education Dewey advocated was activity-oriented and project-centered rather than "book-centered." Although his approach was based on activities and projects related to actual occupations, its primary objective was not preparation for a particular occupation or even a specific range of occupations, but rather "intellectual and moral growth."[52] Dewey argued that vocational education programs were not primarily aimed at such growth, and that students were instead being prepared for specific occupational futures that closed off other alternatives. As Dewey put it:

> To predetermine some future occupation for which education is to be a strict preparation is to injure the possibilities of present development and thereby to reduce the adequacy of preparation for a future right employment.
>
> When educators conceive vocational guidance as something which leads up to a definitive, irretrievable, and complete choice, both education and the chosen vocation are likely to be rigid, hampering further growth . . . If even adults have to be on the look-out to see that their calling does not shut down on them and fossilize them, educators must certainly be careful that the vocational preparation of youth is such as to engage them in a continuous reorganization of aims and methods.[53]

It appears clear that the changing nature of the workplace in the 1990s and beyond makes it very risky to train students for specific jobs. Most vocational educators recognize this fact. More difficult to articulate is an education that uses vocational activities as a means to educate students in the kind of intellectual skills and capacities that will give them maximum flexibility. If students are educated through vocations, rather than for them, they may choose to attend either 2-year or 4-year colleges, to enter the military, to pursue job-specific training, or to enter the working world. Weisberg's words are worth recalling: "We know that general literacy skills are more likely than any other factor to yield success in the labor market."[54]

The value of using vocations as a means to teach general literacy skills lies primarily in the motivational value of vocational activities and projects. Hands-on problem solving can be a powerful motivator to students alienated from conventional academic teaching methods. This is partly why, in *Democracy and Education,* Dewey saw such pedagogical potential in school shops and laboratories.[55] Many teachers in "academic" classrooms have much to learn about motivating students through activity-centered teaching, an area where vocational educators have the opportunity to provide genuine leadership. Further, vocational educators who find ways to make intellectual development come alive through concrete projects and activities may well attract a broader student clientele than they currently attract. So conceived, vocational education courses would be dramatically different from those now seen in comprehensive high schools. Their aims would not be, as they now are, very different from the aims of the academic courses. Consequently, groups of students would not be tracked into separate vocational futures; yet different teaching approaches would all seek the same academic ends.

One current program consistent with Dewey's view of vocational education is the Foxfire curriculum in cultural journalism developed in Rabun Gap, Georgia.[56] The cultural journalism curriculum centers around writing, producing, and marketing magazines, yet it is not a job-training program. Instead, it is an English curriculum aimed at developing compositional, communication, and thinking skills. Another program more familiar to most vocational educators is the rural 4-H program. For generations, it has offered young people a chance to develop a range of skills and understandings through extracurricular projects. Once again, these projects are not designed primarily to prepare youth for jobs. Instead, a wider range of educational aims is being achieved through activities that are intrinsically interesting to students.

The future of vocational education may well depend on the ability of vocational educators to develop additional programs that teach through, rather than for, vocations. As occupational skills become increasingly oriented toward computation, communications, and problem solving, it will be increasingly difficult to justify expensive programs which engage students with low academic skills in nonacademic coursework. Such students need the most effective possible instruction in reading, writing, mathematics, and critical thinking, and vocational education programs have not traditionally been the most effective means for such instruction. To counsel these students into nonacademic programs, it can be argued, is neither vocationally nor educationally sound. On the other hand, if *Unfinished Agenda* is correct in stating that "the real strength of vocational education lies in its ability to motivate students," vocational educators may have insights into methods that could prove educationally effective where traditional academic classrooms have served students poorly. Wirth is among those who believe that the Perkins Act Amendments *may* have potential to serve worthy vocational and liberal education ideals, consistent with Dewey's approach.

The authors of this volume first emphasized Dewey's notion of "education *through* vocations" in 1988 (see footnote 50) and then again in 1993, when the first edition of this textbook was published. It was therefore with considerable interest that we noted the publication in 1995 of W. Norton Grubb's two-volume edited collection of essays, *Education Through Occupations in American High Schools.*[57] Grubb, a long-time and respected critic of traditional approaches to vocational education, relies heavily on Dewey's theoretical perspective as the foundation for the two volumes. The books were written in an effort to explore the theoretical and practical potential of the notion of curriculum integration as it is described in only general terms in the Carl Perkins Amendments of 1990.

In the concluding essay of the two volumes, "Achieving the Promise of Curriculum Integration," Grubb writes, "Integrating academic and vocational education is a reform rich with possibilities precisely because there are so many purposes it can serve." These purposes include the following innovations:

1. Programs of greater intellectual sophistication for students who for various reasons have been labeled academically incompetent and presumed "manually minded," and then segregated from the high-status academic programs.
2. A new conception of vocational education—one that prepares students either for employment after high school, for postsecondary education, or for that combination of postsecondary education and employment that has become increasingly common.
3. Getting students to think about their occupational futures, about the curricular choices they make in high school, and about the relationship between school-based learning and future work life.
4. The "greatest ambition": to reshape the entire high school, for all students and all teachers . . . by replacing the aimless choice of electives with a more coherent set of academic and elective courses unified by a broadly defined occupation, an industry, or some other intrinsically important theme.

5. A way to reduce the tracking and segregation that permeates the high school by giving students genuine choice among coherent programs of study that respond to their interests.
6. Better motivation of students by engaging them in constructing their own learning and making clear how such learning is related to their own purposes.
7. A way for high schools to establish connections to institutions outside their walls, including postsecondary institutions (community colleges, 4-year colleges, technical training programs) and employers.[58]

Because the U.S. government is spending considerable sums to supplement state and local efforts to reshape vocational education in secondary education and beyond, we will see a fair amount of activity in this area in the years to come. Whether it will accomplish the goals that Grubb foresees, however, remains to be seen. As some of the selections in his two-volume book testify, there are significant obstacles to bringing about such a major change in the culture of schools, when the line between "college prep academic" and "vocational" tracks has been so sharply drawn for a century. As difficult as it is for a single school to bring about such a change in curriculum goals and teaching methods, it is still more difficult for a *school district* to bring about such changes, especially in some of the large urban centers where traditional approaches to academic and vocational education have such a poor record.

In Chicago in 1996, for example, the district administration moved to obtain a share of the $400 million in federal funds provided by the School to Work Opportunities Act to model school-to-work programs across the country. In line with the Perkins Amendment, initiatives funded under the Act must give students the academic background to qualify for postsecondary education, including 4-year colleges. Such programs are required to integrate vocational and academic curricula by, for example, including more hands-on projects and applied learning. Education writer Lorraine Forte gives examples of how this might work:

> In an automotive program, for instance, an English class might require students to write a business plan for prospective investors in a car-repair business. Science classes could cover the technology behind internal-combustion engines and newer, high-tech innovations such as electric cars. And history and social studies courses might cover the relationship between labor unions and the auto industry, the impact of a new auto plant on a community's economy and ways the industry has tackled health and safety problems.[59]

But such change is slow in coming. Chicago obtained less than $1 million per year for 5 years to bring about such change. Meanwhile, in 1996-97, Chicago is spending $67 million on vocational education, of which over 90 percent goes to traditional vocational education categories: 34 percent to industrial education, 28 percent to business education, 22 percent to computer education, and 7 percent to home economics. The grant money will go to fund five small schools and three alternative high schools that have a career focus. Illinois State Board of Education staffer Christopher Koch observes that soon Chicago will have to come up with a more comprehensive systemwide plan "that will spread to all schools within five years."[60] There really is no reason to believe at this point that the kind of systemwide change envisioned in the Perkins Amendments, or by Grubb, is on the near horizon for Chicago.

LIBERAL EDUCATION: THEORY AND PRACTICE[61]

Historical Perspectives

The Deweyan notion of educating through vocations, rather than for them, abandons the fundamental rationale for vocational education as Conant and others developed it: preparation of non-college-bound students for specific occupations. If that rationale is to be abandoned, there is no longer any reason to advocate vocational education in public schools at all. Under Dewey's approach, what is now termed "vocational education" would simply become an alternative approach to educating students for academic, intellectual, and personal growth. In other words, the traditional aims of a *liberal education* would be embraced for all students throughout their public school years, and "vocational education" would be reserved for postsecondary instruction. In fact,

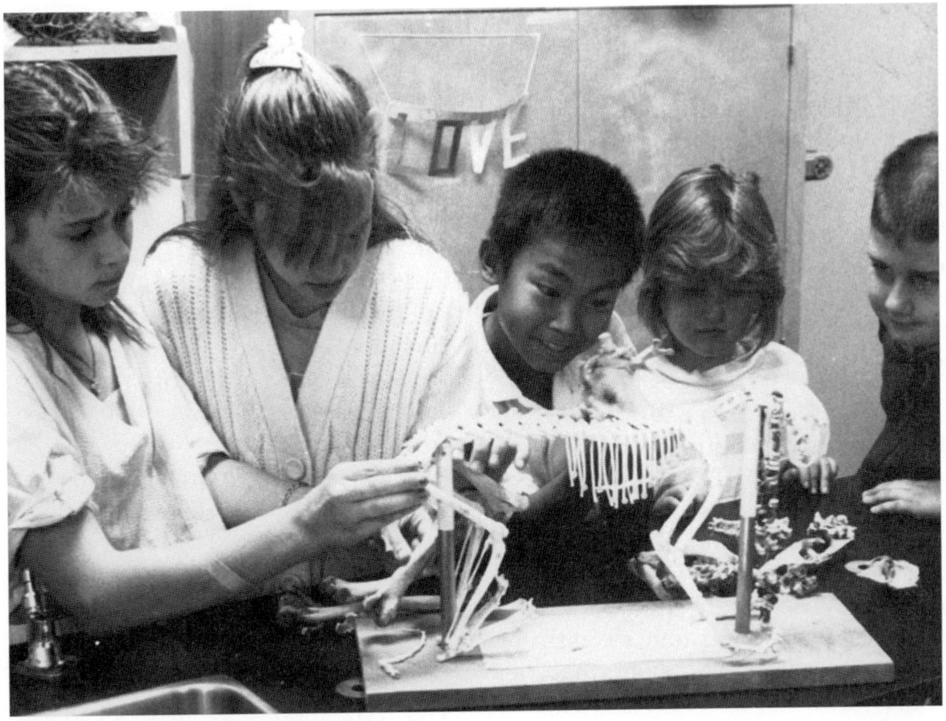

John Dewey recommended the use of vocationally oriented activities as a method of teaching traditional academic subject matter. The activity pictured here could be used to teach math and problem-solving skills as well as how to work together and how to read directions.

our nation is currently witnessing just such a shift of vocational programs from secondary schools to community colleges.

Students rarely have the opportunity to consider what the term "liberal education" means—or why anyone would advocate such an education. Most efforts to understand the term focus attention on the educational ideals of classical Athens and on ideals which informed Jefferson's thinking as described in Chapter 2. In *The Politics,* which Jefferson read, Aristotle argues that in the best kind of education, "it is the whole of excellence which ought to be cultivated, and cultivated for its own sake."[62] For Aristotle, such an education equips citizens for "a life of action and war" and other such "necessary or useful acts." Even more important is the development of those qualities that equip citizens "to lead a life of leisure and peace" and "to do good acts." How to accomplish this? For Aristotle, "The exercise of rational principle and thought is the ultimate end of man's nature," and education should be planned "with a view to the exercise of these facilities."[63] Aristotle recognizes that young people will not always choose those studies that most exercise their rational faculties, for their appetites may lead them elsewhere, "but the regulation of their appetites should be intended for the benefit of their minds."[64] For Aristotle, one of the roles of the teacher, and of good government, is to see that the appetites of the young are cultivated toward wisdom and virtue.

Aristotle's remarks might seem like a cloud of idealistic words at first, but three features of his educational thought are relevant here:

1. Educating for the "whole of human excellence" means educating for both vocational ends and for other ends that are useful "for their own sake" in the development of the good person. This is the primary reason for Aristotle's emphasis on philosophy and music, and more broadly conceived, literature and the arts.

2. Each person's education should emphasize not just "useful" and "good" acts but the qualities of mind and character needed to perform both kinds of acts. Here Aristotle argues for the development of the rational capacities, for in his view, goodness and wisdom are both grounded in reason.
3. If left to their own devices, young people may not choose their studies wisely, so they need to be guided in the cultivation of their appetites in order that their highest human capacities will be served.

It is worth noting that Aristotle accused the Greek states, as well as individuals, of choosing unwise forms of education: "The Greek states of our day which are counted as having the best constitutions . . . have fallen short of this ideal. . . . There has been a vulgar decline into the cultivation of qualities supposed to be useful and of a more profitable character."[65] Aristotle's complaint is echoed today by critics who hold that the vocational curriculum (or in higher education, professional studies) is given too much attention at the expense of liberal studies.

If Aristotle's ideal is admirable in its concern for the whole of human excellence, it is worth remembering that he did not intend his ideal for the whole of Athenian society. Only Athenian citizens were to be liberally educated, and citizens constituted a minority of that society. Women and the non-Athenian work force known as "metics" were excluded from citizenship. What is more, the citizen's opportunity for leisure and the cultivation of artistic sensibilities was made possible by the institution of slavery. Aristotle reflected classical Athenian society in promoting education for all its *citizens,* rich and poor; but classical Athens excluded the majority of its inhabitants from citizenship and failed to provide a liberal education for them. Neither women nor non-Athenians—the latter considered to be of inferior racial stock—were believed to have the rational capacities necessary for citizenship or wisdom.

This historic tendency to reserve liberal education for the social elite was also echoed by the noted Renaissance educator Vergerius:

> We call those studies liberal which are worthy of a free man; those studies by which we attain and practice virtue and wisdom; that education which calls forth, trains, and develops those highest gifts of body and of mind which ennoble men, and which are rightly judged to rank next in dignity to virtue only.[66]

Examined in its Renaissance context, the ideal of liberal education expressed here is again reserved for the few—in this case, males of courtly society. There is some temptation today to reject the vision of liberal education offered by Aristotle and Vergerius as a thoroughly elitist, sexist, and racist ideal. However, some educators read into these classic statements the possibility that *all* people might be educated in those qualities of mind and character that are most appropriate to freedom and virtue. The difficulty is to develop an educational ideal that can be embraced by all races and both genders that is conducive to the development of all of us.

Liberal Education in America

The Yale Report of 1828 One American statement for liberal education came to us in 1828 from a bastion of white male elitism, Yale University. In the 1820s, undergraduate complaints about the rigid curriculum at Yale caused the faculty to reevaluate the prescribed coursework. The result was the famed *Report on the Course of Instruction in Yale College,* released in 1828. In their report, the faculty argued that a thorough college education "must be broad, and deep, and solid."[67] Following Aristotle's notion of cultivating the mind, the Yale report went on to reflect the faculty psychology popular at that time (see Chapter 2). In doing so, it employed two metaphors of particular importance in conceptualizing liberal education. "The two great points to be gained in intellectual culture," argued the Yale report, "are the discipline and the furniture of the mind; expanding its powers, and storing it with knowledge."[68] The reference to *expanding powers* recalls the attention in Aristotle and Vergerius to the development of desired capacities of mind, while the notion of *storing the mind with knowledge* points to a concern for the knowledge that has been established as important in the disciplines up to that time.

The Yale report's call for both breadth and depth, together with its call for furnishing as well as disciplining the mind, suggests a number of things about the Yale faculty's conception of liberal education. They believed that the breadth component of the prescribed curriculum contributed to a broad range of knowledge and to the development of all the mental faculties of an educated person. "In laying the foundation of a thorough education, it is necessary that all the important mental faculties be brought into exercise," they wrote. "It is not sufficient that one or two be cultivated, while others are neglected." The purposes of cultivating these faculties are explicitly nonvocational, but are general in nature. "Our prescribed course contains those subjects only which ought to be understood, as we think, by every one who aims at a thorough education. They are not the peculiarities of any profession or art. These are to be learned in the professional or practical school."[69]

The Yale faculty embraced the historic liberal ideal of an educated person as one who is familiar with the knowledge of various disciplines and, through careful, disciplined thought, can apply that knowledge to the full range of human pursuits. A primary distinction between the notions of liberal education and vocational education, then, might be stated this way: Liberal education prepares people for the full range of public and private roles which they are expected to fulfill (in classical Athens, in Renaissance Italy, or in modern America) as opposed to preparation for a single role—namely, an occupation. Preparation for a full range of roles naturally requires development of a full range of intellectual and personal capacities, while preparation for a single role typically does not. Vocational education does not attend to the ideal of "the well-educated person" nor the qualities of mind that this ideal implies.

Following the long tradition of those who advocate a liberal education, Mark Van Doren echoed the age-old call for an education that is directed toward no social goals but, instead, seeks to liberate the mind to use all its facilities in the pursuit of a well-lived life.

Harvard's General Education in a Free Society

It is ironic that James B. Conant, later known for his advocacy of differentiated curricula and vocational education, commissioned the 20th-century's best-known endorsement of liberal education. *General Education in a Free Society,* published in 1946 after 2 years of work by a committee of Harvard faculty members, endorsed the historic aims and principles of liberal education under the rubric "general education" in an effort to avoid the elitist connotations of the older term.[70] The authors were writing not only for Harvard but also for high schools and colleges throughout the nation.

In the Harvard report, general education is seen as fundamental to an individual's life as a "responsible human being and citizen," whereas "special" (vocational) education refers to preparation for some occupation. General education seeks to form not only the good person but also the "liberated" person. To be free, the authors argue, an individual must develop the mind to "lead that self-examined life which according to Socrates is alone worthy of a free man."[71]

In contrast to the Renaissance curriculum of the trivium (grammar, logic, and rhetoric) and the quadrivium (arithmetic, geometry, astronomy, and music), the Harvard report argues for the more modern grouping of disciplines into three areas: natural science, social studies, and the humanities. However, beyond the knowledge to be acquired, the Harvard report looks to "the traits and characteristics of mind fostered by education." The report explains:

> By characteristics we mean aims so important as to prescribe how general education should be carried out and which abilities should be sought above all others in every part of it. These abilities are: to think effectively, to communicate thought, to make relevant judgments, to discriminate among values. They are not in practice separable and are not to be developed in isolation.[72]

By addressing both the disciplinary content and the qualities of mind to be developed, the Harvard report recalls the notions of the "discipline and furniture of the mind" in the Yale report over a century earlier. Following Aristotle, the Harvard faculty seeks "to limit the idea of the good citizen expressly by the ideal of a good man."[73] That is, a society's ideal for each citizen should be no less than its ideal for a human being. There should not be, for example, an ideal of citizenship which values mindlessness or drudgery in some citizens "for the good of the whole." All citizens, as Aristotle had earlier put forth, should have an education that commits them to the ideal of free inquiry and that allows them to function as both civic leaders and followers.

The notions of the good citizen and the good person have always been central to the concept of general or liberal education. The Harvard statement follows Aristotle in tying the notion of the good citizen to the ideal of the good person. Perhaps no one has better summarized the liberal education tradition than Mark Van Doren, who wrote in his classic statement *Liberal Education:*

> Liberal education is nothing less than the complete education of men as men; it is the education of persons . . . always to be understood as an end, not as means. . . . The converse [of Vergerius] is true: the free person is one who is worthy of a liberal education. There is no such thing as education for democracy. Education is either bad or good; the best education makes the best men. . . . Democracy . . . cannot afford to educate men for citizenship, for efficiency, or for use.[74]

In recasting Vergerius, Van Doren underscores the historical linkage between liberal education and the qualities of a free person: Liberal education is for people who are conceived as ends in themselves rather than as means to ends. It is this tradition, rather than that which grounds liberal education in racism, sexism, and elitism, that contemporary advocates of liberal education should bear in mind as they seek ways to answer criticisms that liberal education is an outmoded and narrow ideal.

Reconstructing the Liberal Education Ideal Although it is important to begin any consideration of liberal education with a careful examination of its historical tradition, anyone seeking to carry that tradition forward must inevitably leave parts of the past behind. In "The Study of the Past—Its Uses and Its Dangers," Alfred North Whitehead wrote:

> For each succeeding generation, the problem of Education is new. What at the beginning was enterprise, after the lapse of five and twenty years has become repetition. All the proportions belonging to a complex scheme of influences upon our students have shifted in their effectiveness. In the lecture halls of a university, as indeed in every sphere of life, the best homage which we can pay to our predecessors to whom we owe the greatness of our inheritance is to emulate their courage.[75]

Despite the stubborn resistance to ideological change that is characteristic of modern, liberal, capitalist society, our nation's history is in part a story of the reconstruction of liberal ideals. When Jefferson wrote about equality and inalienable rights, he had no intention of applying these ideals to women, for example, or to African-Americans and Native Americans. Yet, since Jefferson's time, American activists have reconstructed those ideals and used them as leverage to gain civil and political rights for women and people of color.

Likewise, if the ideals of liberal education are worth salvaging, it takes a certain amount of courage to articulate and fight for their value in an educational environment as devoted to vocationalism as ours is today. For non-college-bound students in the secondary schools, "getting a good job" is presented as the primary rationale for their staying in school, and for those who plan to go on to college, "getting a good job" is too often the fundamental rationale for a college degree. College faculty groups, educational researchers, and educational foundations are once again busy with the task of reconstructing the liberal education ideal, illustrating again Whitehead's words: "For each succeeding generation, the problem of Education is new."

These contemporary efforts have in common, first, a commitment to recognizing a distinction between learning that is an instrument in an occupation and learning that is intrinsically valuable for the way it shapes a person's understandings, character, and experience. Second, these various efforts recognize the value of both breadth of study (across areas of knowledge) and depth of study (within at least one specialized area). Finally, contemporary educators attend not only to the disciplinary content (usually expressed as required subjects or courses) of liberal education, but also to the qualities of mind that are historically associated with the educated person. But what it is to be an educated person remains a disputed and problematic concept.

Freedom, Rationality, and the Disciplines The commitment to the classical ideal of freedom through rationality, and rationality through study of the disciplines, is one that is increasingly questioned in discussions of liberal education. Prominent British philosophers Richard Peters and Paul Hirst are recent exponents of the view that locates freedom of thought in study of the academic disciplines. Hirst writes, for example, "The Greeks attained the concept of an education that was 'liberal' . . . because they saw it as freeing the mind to function according to its true nature, freeing reason from error and illusion and freeing man's conduct from wrong."[76]

Colin Lankshear is among those educators who have deeply questioned this traditional linking of rationality and freedom, arguing that the constraints which disciplinary studies impose on human thought and dispositions are not necessarily liberating, and may even be oppressive to the free character.[77] A growing feminist educational literature offers a related criticism. In an address to the women of Douglass College in 1977, Adrienne Rich argued that the disciplines themselves—those disciplines through which rationality is developed and defined—are illiberal because they are grounded in patriarchal conceptions of the world.

> What you learn here, the very texts you read, the lectures you hear, the way your studies are divided into categories and fragmented one from the other—all this reflects, to a very large degree, neither objective reality, nor an accurate picture of the past, nor a group of rigorously tested observations about human behavior. What you can learn here (and I mean not only at Douglass but any college in any university) is how men have perceived and organized their experience, their history, their ideas of social relationships, good and evil, sickness and health, etc. When you read or hear about "great issues," "major texts," "the mainstream of Western thought," you are hearing about what men, above all white men, in their male subjectivity, have decided is important. . . . Even the sciences can be sexist.[78]

More recently, in "Bringing Women into Educational Thought," educational philosopher Jane Roland Martin associates the traditional liberal arts disciplines with society's "productive processes" as opposed to its "reproductive processes." "Productive processes" typically have to do with public, income-earning activity, while the "reproductive" sphere refers to the nurturing environment of family life. In a society threatened by environmental dangers that discipline-based science and technology have helped produce, reproductive processes "have the broadest moral, social, and political significance." Martin continues:

> Care, concern, connectedness, nurturance: these are as important for carrying on society's economic, political, and social processes as its productive ones. If education is to help all of us acquire them, the ideal of the educated person and the theory of liberal education explicated by Peters and Hirst, respectively, must be redefined.[79]

Martin notes that just as society appears to place relatively low value on such supposedly feminine attributes as caring, nurturing, subjectivity, and emotional expression, so do academic disciplines appear to value rational, objective, generalizable knowledge over more "feminine" ways of knowing and experiencing the world. Martin seeks a concept of "well educated" that develops the subjective as well as the objective ways of knowing, the emotive as well as the rational ways of experiencing.

Feminist criticism of the liberally educated person provides a useful perspective in contemporary efforts to reconstruct the ideal of liberal education. The implications of this criticism for the understanding and practice of liberal education are not yet clear. In at least one important respect, feminist criticism stands inside the liberal education tradition, and that is in its commitment to inquiry, criticism, and the search for understanding. One test of liberal education's vitality will surely be its ability to respond constructively to feminist critique and revision. Jane Roland Martin, for example, does not want to abandon rationality, but to reposition it, to find where it best fits among other human capacities and values.

As institutions review and reconstruct their commitments to liberal education, it seems that one way in which the "greatness of our inheritance," in Whitehead's words, can be respected is for vigorous and open debate to prevail. The significance of liberal education lies not only in its adaptation to fit the context of each new generation, but also in how this process of adaptation is carried out. It is not yet clear that the integrative approaches recommended in Dewey's work or in the Perkins Act Amendments can work in large-scale practice in American schools.

CONCLUDING REMARKS

This chapter has examined the contemporary legacy of two conflicting educational traditions: (1) vocational education, with its roots in the era of progressive education, and (2) liberal education, with its roots in classical Athens. Examining the rationale of vocational education provided an occasion to survey findings on the nature of work in the United States today, an examination that suggests the need for including in vocational education a full range of literacy skills (computation, communication, and critical thinking) that have not been historically emphasized in vocational training. By including these general literacy skills along with a commitment to develop each student to his or her full human potential, vocational education can recast itself in line with the goals of traditional liberal education. In that event, vocational education could evolve into an activities-oriented pedagogy appropriate to learning styles that might be more effective for the academic development of a greater range of students.

Such a discussion raises questions about the fundamental aims of education for all citizens of a democratic society. Can a democracy afford to socialize major parts of its population to accept less education and intellectual development than the society is capable of offering? Or should Dewey's "all around growth of every member of society" (see Chapter 4) be the fundamental aim for all citizens? Can the limited intellectual demands of low-skill occupations define our educational aims for the millions of people who will one day fill those occupations? Or should they be educated to the limits of their capacity, on the grounds that each parent should (and usually does) want the greatest possible intellectual, emotional, and moral development of his or her children? And if human development for its own sake is our educational ideal, what kind of school experiences will help bring about such development? It should be instructive to us that the children of the upper and upper-middle classes are not typically counseled into vocational education curricula, for such curricula are not considered by members of those classes to be adequate for their children. If this is so, the belief that vocational education as it now exists is adequate for the children of the poor and working classes is one that should be questioned and resisted. If, on the other hand, we find that schools are largely unsuccessful in teaching such students using approaches found to be successful for upper- and middle-class children, then it may well be that our approaches to teaching should be expanded to fit the learning styles and dispositions of all students.

PRIMARY SOURCE READING

A fundamental assumption underlying vocational education programs, from the progressive era through the Conant reforms to today, is that millions of students in U.S. schools are ill suited for traditionally academic curricula because of their low academic skills (usually misunderstood as "abilities") and their working-class futures. For this reason, the practice of tracking students into separate vocational and academic curricula was instituted early in this century. In the Conant era of the late 1950s and early 1960s, the term "ability grouping" gained favor, and schools today, particularly middle and secondary schools, operate on the assumption that students learn better if they are grouped homogeneously with other students of similar abilities. This ability grouping, which should more accurately be termed "skill grouping," because low skills do not necessarily imply low ability to learn, is so pervasive in our school system that most teachers assume that it is the most effective way to teach students of varying skill levels. Such ability grouping promotes dividing students into one group that receives the academic education characteristic of a liberal education and another group that is urged to take vocational training for the world of work.

In the following article, John Duffy discusses how he resists the ability grouping or tracking practices of public schooling in favor of working with students at heterogeneous (varied) skill levels in the same class. Duffy teaches high school English at Proviso East High School outside of Chicago. In reporting his own experiences, Duffy challenges the assumptions underlying the division of students into vocational and liberal education curricula.

GETTING OFF TRACK: THE CHALLENGE AND POTENTIAL OF THE MIXED ABILITY CLASSROOM

John Duffy

Much has been written in the last few years about the pitfalls of tracking, or homogeneous ability grouping, as it is politely referred to in the educational establishment. Although references will be made to the research in this area, the main purpose of this article is to present curriculum guidelines/suggestions for teachers to use with curriculum after uniting students who have been kept apart to their social and educational detriment.

Even if the research evidence failed to support mixed ability grouping of children as the best way to maximize achievement, there are compelling political and social reasons to restructure the organization and instruction of students. After all, those who believe in making schools into truly democratic institutions where equity in curriculum, materials, and teacher resources is the rule, rather than the exception, know that education GNP, as measured by higher test scores, does not necessarily mean that schools have improved qualitatively or that equity prevails in the "better" schools.

The most important goal for de-tracking schools, at least for progressive or "transformative" intellectuals, as Henry Giroux (1983) calls us, is to create the conditions for true democracy and a restructuring of values in a way that leads to fuller human emancipation and freedom. Reorganizing the grouping patterns of students is one of the many steps toward these ends, but even without the institutional de-tracking of schools, truly democratic teachers need to continue to create equitable and democratic education in any and all learning situations they find themselves and their students in.

The inequities created by the reproductive features of the education system in our society are mirrored at every level of schools, right on down to the individual tracks—be they "gifted" or "basic." For this reason teachers cannot wait for institutions to change. We must, as many of us have, continue to nurture and organize a pedagogical alternative to the structures, values, social processes, knowledge, and power relations that tracking attempts to reproduce.

The most benign defense of tracking has been that separating students according to ability allows teachers to organize instruction and materials and to present them in the most efficient and effective manner. A corollary to this rationalization is the belief that students' self-esteem is best served when they are learning with peers of

Source: *Democracy and Education,* vol. 3, no. 1 (Fall 1988), pp. 11–19.

similar ability or achievement, and that, ultimately, they will best achieve under these circumstances. The overwhelming evidence supports the opposite point of view. Unfortunately, not only is achievement not enhanced, but a dual system is often created. It is the exceptional situation when there is equity in the academic isolation of students, even when equity is the intended goal. As Goodlad (1983) and Oakes (1985) have discovered through their lengthy observations of classroom instruction and interviews with students and teachers in different tracks, there is little equity in goals, expectations, or knowledge. In general, they discovered a dual status education system, despite the best intentions of planners and teachers.

At its very worst, tracking is little more than an outright attempt to reproduce in a "realistic" way the occupational structure of society. Within the hidden curriculum of tracking is the belief that, if students are ultimately going to spend their lives in the unskilled service economy, they need not examine the ethical dilemmas found in great literature or be confronted with making critical foreign policy questions with regard to Central America. Such issues in a student occupationally matched curriculum would be reserved for those students whose life situations would present them with such high level decision making (Hammer, 1983).

Instead of debating the desirability of socialism versus capitalism as the issue is raised in literature like *The Grapes of Wrath,* low tracked students would study how to prepare for a job interview, read the classified ads in the newspaper and fill out a job application. Rather than evaluating conservative, liberal and radical explanations for the Contra War against Nicaragua, low tracked students would spend class time plowing through detailed crossword puzzles on recent political history, with little understanding of the daily lexicon the mass media uses to describe America and world politics. Rather than reading a powerful firsthand account of life under apartheid in South Africa in Mark Mathubane's autobiography, *Kaffir Boy,* low tracked students would read a one paragraph explanation in an encyclopedia textbook on world history and later answer a multiple-choice test question concerning South Africa's way of life.

The shortcoming in instruction, materials and achievement for students placed in low tracks is well documented. The widespread mediocrity of instruction at all academic levels in recent years has been described by Boyer (1983), Goodlad (1983) and Oakes (1985) in their studies of secondary schools. These descriptions have told us what critics of tracking have known all along. The challenge we now face is to offer ourselves and students an alternative and to begin organizing to spread that alternative to teachers who wish to get "off track."

Critical Pedagogy: Promoting Cooperation, Dialogue and Discovery

What direction should the new path toward equitable, democratic, critical teaching take? It will be like a long trek up a great mountain—not everyone will be taking the same path. The routes will be many, the trail difficulty will vary, and the vistas will be numerous and breathtaking. Sometimes teachers will lead, but often they will follow or be alone as students explore an alpine lake or a foothills meadow. The range of mountains for exploration will be so numerous that students will have the opportunity to pick their own challenging climbs and chart their own routes. They will sometimes travel in solitude but usually face the challenge of their exploration with the variety of skills, knowledge, and camaraderie that group travel can offer. While the most difficult peaks of the most rugged and challenging mountains might be tried by fewer climbers, the skills, training and opportunity to make that climb would be open to all.

If heterogeneous curriculum is to avoid simply pouring the old curriculum into new bottles and ending up with a new concoction resembling "cherry-sevenup-coke," we have to consider major changes in our assumptions about curriculum. These changes would involve both what is taught and how it is taught. In a critical de-tracking curriculum, not only will the shape of the bottles change, but the content will also be radically different. A de-tracked curriculum will incorporate many of the features of the critical discovery model of the learning environment outlined below in "Two Models for Teaching and Learning." While the two models for teaching and learning represent polarities, too many classrooms tend to have more of the characteristics of banking educa-

Two Models for Teaching and Learning

Description	*Teacher Role*	*Student Role*
	CRITICAL EDUCATION	
Dialogical Dialectical Multisourced Grouping variety Multiple settings Values student's context Heterogeneous ability-grouped Cooperative group focus	Inquires with students Emphasizes higher-level questions Models reading and thinking skills Teaches comprehension Integrates critical thinking and content	Views knowledge base as the concomitant of higher-level thinking Becomes an active generator of own questions: • Learns and uses metacognitive strategies with teacher modeling • Learning is cooperative and focused on the group
	BANKING EDUCATION	
Lecture-oriented Linear Text-oriented Large group dominant Classroom-bound Ignores student's context Homogeneous ability-grouped Competitive individual focus	Gives knowledge to students Overemphasizes literal questions Presumes student reading and thinking skills Tests comprehension Views critical thinking as a by-product of content	Masters literal, factual knowledge base Responds to teacher questions Acquires thinking and learning strategies by trial and error Learning is competitive and focused on the individual

tion than of critical pedagogy. The best programs, tracked or heterogeneous, contain more of the qualities of the critical model. As teachers move further into constellation of critical pedagogy, they will not only incorporate more of the characteristics of the critical model, but also make major changes in how they and students function in the learning environment.

The crucial change in the dynamics of a de-tracked curriculum will involve the social relations of learning. It is here that the most fundamental differences between tracked and de-tracked education are manifest. The concept of the "banking" education model comes from Paulo Freire's (1970) description of teacher dominated classrooms. This approach, while talking of the primacy of the student, actually treats students as secondary objects in the learning process. In banking education, students become the targets for teacher's actions. Such an approach is dominated by teacher monologue and student passivity.

A critical pedagogy in a de-tracked curriculum will have the student as the key subject in the learning process, not the teacher. Student dialogue, not teacher monologue, will be the major talk of the critical classroom. Cooperative learning activities where students share their skills, knowledge and creative abilities will take the place of individualized competition, which characterizes too much of traditional banking curriculum. It is this cooperative component which will most change the social relations of the classroom. As Elizabeth Cohen (1986) so sensitively outlines in *Designing Group Work,* cooperative learning becomes the organizational foundation for mixed ability curriculum and is essential for structuring a more democratic, student-centered education.

The research of David and Roger Johnson (1987) has shown the numerous advantages for the academic, social and personal development of all students when they learn in cooperative, heterogeneous settings as opposed to homogeneous, competitive settings. Research on cooperative group learning versus individual competitive learning clearly indicates that cooperative structures are superior to individual structures in promoting a variety of quantitative improvements. Positive gains are found in student achievement, increased engagement in the learning process and an increase in the likelihood of the qualities of instruction most associated with better teaching.

Perhaps even more impressive are the improvements in the affective areas when cooperative learning approaches are utilized. One of the most striking advantages of the mixed ability classroom is its ability to promote racial, social-economic and cultural integration of students. Heterogeneous structures, however, do more than improve the achievement of the diverse student populations that may exist in the de-tracked curriculum. Students in these settings show an increase in collaborative skills and develop a more differentiated and realistic view of other students. They tend to have fewer stereotypes of students with backgrounds different than their own. Especially impressive are the findings in 72 studies of interracial and mixed ability cooperative learning groups, where only one experiment failed to find that mixed ability cooperative grouping does more to improve race relations than competitive individualistic structures.

Students in cooperative learning situations develop a more positive attitude toward their subjects and instruction and demonstrate greater willingness to learn more about their subjects. They show a greater improvement in self-esteem and a superior psychological health than those students who learn in competitive settings. In short, the research findings suggest a compelling case for the advantages of cooperative heterogeneous learning strategies. As Alfie Kohn (1986) so persuasively presents in his review of the myths of competition, there is "no contest" when comparing the advantages of cooperative over competitive learning strategies.

In many ways, a de-tracked curriculum in a social studies or English classroom will have the characteristics of a quality gifted education classroom. Yet, in this classroom, "giftedness" will not be defined by above grade level achievement or high I.Q. The de-tracked curriculum will assume that giftedness takes many different forms, which for too long have gone without notice, as Howard Gardner (1985) suggests in *Frames of Mind.* The special uniqueness that a student can contribute to a richer and more diverse learning environment will not be determined by I.Q. or G.P.A.

The very words "mixed ability" and "heterogeneous" will have a new nuance. The diversity of the academic, racial, social, and cultural composition of the community now becomes the central gift of the school. While it has always been present, in the de-tracked school it will be embraced and valued. The rich and varied fabric of human expression and potential that can be found at all achievement levels will become the guidelines for the inclusion and not the selectivity of students.

Eventually, the electric nature of the gifted classroom will permeate the curriculum of the entire school. Students will begin to be empowered in new ways in the de-tracked classroom to take more control of their learning. Finally, education will not mean being "talked" at. All students will be encouraged by opportunities to express themselves in creative and unique ways and to interact on a regular basis with their peers while learning. There will be a multitude of texts, and learning environments, as the classroom will be expanded into the community, where the people and institutions of everyday life will become key resources in education. In short, opportunities to learn in a myriad of active ways will characterize the de-tracked classroom.

Because cooperative learning involves the utilization of numerous competencies and individual perspectives found across the spectrum of student achievement levels, it is especially valuable, where possible, to utilize a multi-disciplinary approach to curriculum. In the history and English classes of most secondary schools, the subject matter and skills of each discipline provide a natural complement to each other when approached from the "critical discovery" perspective. Of course, teachers of such a curriculum will have abandoned the "banking approach" to history, which emphasizes trivial facts, rote learning and lecture. The teacher of English will be an individual who believes that language development happens best through a rich variety of practical and creative experiences, not through workbook exercises. Both teachers will share a "whole language" approach to their combined disciplines and will promote active student engagement in reading, writing and discussion and will use a variety of materials including student creations.

A de-tracked curriculum will include what Jeanne Oakes has called "high status" knowledge. Here the goal will be to offer all students the educational experience that is usually found in quality gifted programs. Just as in gifted programs based on critical discovery, the key ingredients will be the quality of the learning experience and the active engagement of students in learning and not the quantity of material covered or the speed at which it is covered. Individual group activities will be available and differentiated to meet the needs and interests of the students.

In a mixed ability history classroom, all students will be exposed to the critical thought processes of historical study. They would learn the importance of frame of reference, the value of examining conflicting evidence, and the skills for detecting bias and formulating their own interpretations of historical and contemporary issues. Individual and group problem-solving and decision-making would become a major part of each student's experience. The thinking tools for examining history and making history through informed, critical choices would become the democratic rights of all students, not just an elite minority.

Critical examination and reflection would not be limited to reading materials. Students would have experiences in writing, artistic expression, personal exploration, and interaction with real institutions and people in the world outside their classroom. The following examples of experiences in a mixed ability history course dealing with the topic of American Indians and their relationship to European and American invaders demonstrates the design in practice.

A Study of American Indians: Some Possibilities

In the last decade or so, publishers of United States history textbooks have frequently included a chapter or unit on the American Indians at the beginning of the text. The recognition that native cultures have an existence that predates the European invasion is a long overdue addition to textbooks, and provides an excellent context for introducing critical and creative activities appropriate for the de-tracked curriculum. A unit on American Indians provides many illustrations for critical lessons and student control of learning. The content focuses on the diversity and nature of Indian culture in the pre-Columbian period and an examination of the contact that developed between Europeans and native cultures. The organization of the unit provides many opportunities for students to make choices, control their own learning and finalize their own personal understanding of a given topic of study. Students have the opportunity to choose works of literature on Indian life to read and study in small groups or to work with a special interest research group and develop presentations of what they learn in a form which they have determined.

The literature base for the unit, including both fiction and non-fiction, would include variety in topics and reading difficulty. It is essential that teachers recognize the spectrum of reading ability and prior knowledge that students possess and that all students have an opportunity to develop strategic reading skills and read a variety of materials. Teachers cannot expect all students to read the same materials at all times. As often as possible text materials should be adaptable to the spectrum of reading ability. Teachers should make use of their own editing ability and begin to experiment with writing their own materials. Short selections from books, edited versions of selections, speeches, poems and legends are as meaningful as complete works. The anthologies *To Serve the Devil: America's Racial History and Why It Has Been Kept Hidden* by Jacobs and Landau (1971) and *Touch the Earth: A Self-Portrait of Indian Existence* by McLuhan (1971) are replete with short, first-hand accounts of Indian life, legend, religion and politics. Sometimes, teachers may find edited versions of books that are readily adaptable for students with comprehension difficulties. *I Heard the Owl Call My Name* by Margaret Craven (1973) appears in a full length narrative version, and a play version adapted by Gerald Di Pego (1975) is more usable for remedial readers. In short, the choice of reading materials, like the selection of student activities, should show variety and be adapted to meet the various reading skills and interest levels that children bring to the topic of study.

In a mixed ability classroom, all students would explore the critical concepts of frame of reference, bias, interpretation and ethnocentrism as the foundation tools for examining any culture. Students' notions of what happened when Columbus and the Indians first met could be tested through a creative diary writing in which students would imagine themselves to be Columbus or the Indians. They would then proceed to describe what happened when the Spanish first landed on the islands in the Caribbean. A comparison of student predictions with Columbus' real diary seldom fails to provoke a meaningful discussion of frame of reference and bias. Students can develop further critical reflection by dramatizing what might have happened when missionaries attempted to explain to Indians why they should abandon the "pagan" religion and adopt Christianity. Prepared scripts or dramatic improvisations are examined and discussed; they are then compared with authentic documents that lead to the introduction to the concept of ethnocentrism.

The use of interpretation and evidence can be taught through a critical comparison of textbook accounts of Christopher Columbus. A U.S. history text written for eighth grade students, but used with remedial eleventh graders in my high school, has an essay on the life of Columbus that gives students the traditional interpretation of Columbus as a great European explorer who died a solitary man, rejected by his kind and unaware of his own great discovery or the heroic place he would later have in the history of the Americas. Students then read all or parts of Howard Zinn's passionate detailing of the tragic and barbaric treatment of the Indians at the hands of Columbus in *A People's History of the United States.* The contrasts in interpretations are remarkable, perplexing, and upsetting. A critical discussion of historians' frame of reference and the conflicting purposes and interpretations of both texts allows students to begin to discover that texts have purposes beyond simply providing information and that what is included or left out can drastically alter the interpretation. More importantly, they begin to see that knowledge is a commodity that can be used to either promote the status quo or aid in developing a critical perspective for changing the world.

In pursuing the study of historical topics, special effort would be given to exploring the contemporary relevance of the past. The major questions of Indian culture, including self-determination, assimilation and conflicts with the larger mainstream culture, would not be overlooked. In my classrooms, students have visited the American Indian Center in Chicago to learn of Indian cultural struggle for survival in urban America. On another occasion they were completely perplexed by a classroom visit from a Crow Indian woman who lived in the community and exemplified the debate between Chief Tecumseh and Chief Pushmataha over whether to resist or accommodate American settlers in the lower Great Lakes region. Her accommodationist perspective became understandable when we discovered through further investigation that her tribe had received special favors from the U.S. government when the Crow allied themselves with the U.S. Army in the final push in the 1870's to conquer the Sioux Indians.

Students in my classes have investigated the recent struggle between the Navajo and Hopi Indians and the U.S. government at Big Mountain on the Indian land in northern Arizona. An Indian speaker from the Illinois Big Mountain Support Group and a viewing of the Academy Award-winning movie *Broken Rainbow* brought protests from conservative students interested in hearing from the power companies and accommodationist Indians. In place of those representatives, we created a congressional debate situation where students studied pro and con documents on each side of the Navajo struggle. Small group heterogeneous dialogue led to small group committee recommendations and large group debate. All students subsequently drafted letters sharing their personal critical perspective on whether the government should force the Navajo off their lands.

The above activities illustrate key aspects of a de-tracked curriculum in a social studies classroom. Obviously, they are not new. What is unusual here is the belief and action on the idea that all children, regardless of achievement level, can greatly benefit from such instruction. Quality teaching has always been grounded in the belief that all students, despite their commonality of age or grade level, have diverse talents, various learning styles, and unique interests. The best teachers have adjusted their programs to meet diversity, not to match a theoretical uniformity that has never existed in any group of 20 to 35 human beings, even when that group has single-mindedly pursued a common goal. It would be naive to assume that such an approach is simple to implement. Those of us who are willing to accept the challenge of "getting off track" are all too familiar with the energy required to create a complex, differentiated, critical classroom. As we argue the case for a de-tracked curriculum we need to rededicate ourselves to building greater collegiality in our teaching community and collectively organizing to gain those additional resources necessary to bring equity to curriculum and instruction. Just as cooperative learning is the foundation for creating a heterogeneous classroom, it is also the basis for regenerating and invigorating our professional development.

Where To? What Next?

There are some promising efforts under way around the country today that are producing encouraging results. In the last few years a number of pilot programs of de-tracked curriculum and heterogeneous grouping experiments have developed. Most of these are in the early stages, but some have already documented positive results. Thus far, the most significant outcomes have come in experimental programs in elementary schools. In California, the Program for Complex Instruction at Stanford University under the direction of Elizabeth Cohen and Rachel Lotan has been working with California school districts in implementing a math and science curriculum for heterogeneous classrooms in grades 2 through 5. The curriculum called "Finding Out/descrubrimiento," has led to significant gains in achievement, especially for low achieving students. The program emphasizes enhancing the status of low ability students, provides a well-developed training program for cooperative learning and focuses on the development of higher order thinking skills.

For the past five years, teachers at the Desert Sky Junior High in Phoenix, Arizona, have been conducting research on heterogeneous grouping. Swartzbaugh (1988) reports that heterogeneously grouped classes have scored higher than homogeneously grouped classes in 21 of 22 test comparisons in reading, math and English. In a first grade experiment in the Logansport, Indiana Schools, Kinkerk (1987) found that students who were in a heterogeneous reading class using a whole language approach to reading showed higher achievement than students in a traditional, basal-based homogeneous reading class. While the gains in skills and comprehension were slightly higher for the heterogeneous group, their scores on the tests measuring affective development showed the heterogeneous group far surpassing the control group on items such as attitudes toward reading, how students viewed themselves as learners and how well they believed they could read orally.

On the secondary level, pilot programs are in place in several schools around the country. In most cases these experiments are part of schools within schools. Three schools currently in the first years of experimentation with a de-tracked curriculum include Central Park East High School in New York, Walbrook High School in Baltimore, Maryland, and Providence High School in Providence, Rhode Island. Each of these schools is a member of the Coalition for Essential Schools under the directorship of Ted Sizer at Brown University. As coalition members, they have boldly attacked the problem of tracking in their schools by transforming classrooms to promote educational equity.

Most of this argument for a de-tracked curriculum has dealt with changing the organizational and material base for instruction. It has been based on the premise that heterogeneous grouping of children can create more equity in American schools and that the most interesting and stimulating learning environments have always incorporated a rich mixture of learning activities, a wide variety of reading materials and visual stimulation, and as much interaction among students and between students and the world beyond the school walls as possible. I believe that, in these areas, teachers who are committed to growth and change will be most willing to adapt and experiment. The greatest challenge, however, will be in changing a traditional mindset held by educators and the public that finds it perfectly rational and efficient to isolate students by ability. Those individuals among us, both in and out of schools, who are dedicated to bringing greater equity to schools will have to proceed with caution and sensitivity as we organize to change long-established patterns of tracking. The types of changes outlined above will require careful nurturing if the seeds of change are to have a chance to germinate.

As democratic educators explore strategies for creating an environment for change, we also need to develop plans for addressing several important questions that skeptics of a de-tracked curriculum will surely raise. They are the same challenging problems that teachers face today and will continue to face whether school curriculum is tracked or not. For example, how do we respond to the political realities of "gifted parents" who will argue that their children will be ill-served by a common curriculum? Will teachers in a de-tracked program be able to adequately prepare students for the cutthroat competition presented by college entrance tests? What are the limits on the academic diversity that can exist in a classroom and still meet the special needs of all children? Is it possible to mix children who are reading-disabled high school students with students reading at grade level 12 and above? How will students be evaluated in a non-competitive environment where there is a range of academic abilities? How will the low motivated and socially disruptive student fit into the de-tracked program? Finally, and perhaps most importantly, what additional material resources and time will be available for helping teachers meet the extra burdens that "getting off track" will surely require? These and many other questions require our ongoing exploration and discussion.

In the meantime, progressive teachers dedicated to struggling for equity in schools and the development of critical pedagogy need to continue to experiment with materials, activities and community-based learning opportunities that recognize the dignity of all children and nurture their individual and collective potential. Whether schools are tracked or not, transformative teachers should continue to create opportunities in their classrooms for children to become active, critical learners who will leave school with the skills, knowledge and desire to energetically participate in shaping a more democratic, just and peaceful world. The civic, social and intellectual development necessary for reaching these goals will require the critical and thoughtful involvement of all citizens. For too long, however, schools have restricted real opportunities for the development of participatory citizenship.

The development of a de-tracked curriculum organized around the principles of critical discovery pedagogy will go a long way, we hope, in finding the path to a more democratic society at peace within and with those nations and cultures we share the world with. While schools cannot change the world, in many ways they can certainly play an important role in developing those individuals and groups who might. As individual teachers who believe in this vision, we can, in the short run, recognize and encourage in a cooperative manner the diverse talents and perspectives students bring to the classroom. With other teachers, we can collectively, over time, continue to cultivate the environment for institutional change that will bring greater equity and democracy for all children.

References

Barr, Rebecca, and Dreeban, Robert (1983). *How Schools Work.* Chicago: University of Chicago Press.

Boyer, Ernest (1983). *High School.* New York: Harper.

Cohen, Elizabeth (1986). *Designing Groupwork: Strategies for the Heterogeneous Classroom.* New York: Teachers College Press.

Craven, Margaret (1973). *I Heard the Owl Call My Name.* New York: Dell.

Di Pego, Gerald (1975). *I Heard the Owl Call My Name.* In Hoopes, N., and Gordon, P. (Eds.), *Great Television Plays, Volume 2.* New York: Dell.

Freire, Paulo (1970). *Pedagogy of the Oppressed.* New York: Herder and Herder.

Gamoran, Adam, and Berends, Mark (1987). *The Effects of Stratification in Secondary Schools: Synthesis of Survey and Ethnographic Research.* Madison, WI: National Center for Effective Secondary Schools.

Gardner, Howard (1985). *Frames of Mind: The Theory of Multiple Intelligence.* New York: New Books.

Giroux, Henry (1983). *Theory and Resistance in Education: A Pedagogy for the Opposition.* South Hadley, MA: Bergin and Garvey.

Goodlad, John (1983). *A Place Called School.* New York: McGraw-Hill.

Hammer, Richard (1983). The Immorality of Ability Level Tracking. *English Journal.* 72, no. 1, 38–41.

Hierbert, Elfreda (1983). An Examination of Ability Grouping for Reading Instruction. *Reading Research Quarterly.* 18, 231–255.

Jacobs, Paul, Landau, Saul, and Pell, Eve (1971). *To Serve the Devil: America's Racial History and Why It Has Been Kept Hidden.* New York: Vintage.

Johnson, David, and Johnson, Roger (1987). *Learning Together and Learning Alone: Cooperative, Competitive, and Individualistic Learning.* Englewood Cliffs, NJ: Prentice Hall.

Johnston, S. D., Foster, W. I., Satchwell, R. (1989). *Sophisticated Technology, the Workforce, and Vocational Education,* Illinois State Board of Education, Department of Adult Vocational and Technical Education.

Kinkerk, Nedra (1987). Whole Group Language Instruction in the First Grade Classroom. Unpublished research report presented at the Great Lakes Regional Convention of the International Reading Association. October 1, 1987. Indianapolis, Indiana.

Kohn, Alfie (1986). *No Contest: The Case against Competition.* Boston: Houghton Mifflin.

Kulik, C., and Kulik, J. (1982). Effects of Ability Grouping on Secondary School Students: A Meta-Analysis of Evaluation Findings. *American Educational Research Journal.* 19, 415–428.

Mathubane, Mark (1986). *Kaffir Boy.* New York: MacMillan.

McLuhan, T.C. (1971). *Touch the Earth: A Self-Portrait of Indian Existence.* New York: Simon & Schuster.

Oakes, Jeanne (1985). *Keeping Track: How Schools Structure Inequality.* New Haven, CT: Yale University Press.

Swartzbaugh, Phil (1988). Eliminating Tracking Successfully. *Educational Leadership.* 45, no. 6, 20.

Zinn, Howard (1980). *A People's History of the United States.* New York: Harper & Row.

QUESTIONS FOR DISCUSSION AND EXAMINATION

1. This chapter contrasts the aims of vocational and liberal education. To what degree are these aims significantly different, and to what degree are they similar? Explain and defend your point of view.
2. This chapter appears to take the position that (*a*) all students are capable of benefiting from an academic, as opposed to a vocational education, and (*b*) an academic curriculum is the most appropriate one for all students. To what degree does the chapter adequately support this position, and to what degree do you agree with it? Justify your position.
3. It was remarked early in the chapter, in response to the purposes of the Carl D. Perkins Vocational and Applied Technology Education Act Amendments of 1990, that "critics will continue to observe that educational goals framed in terms of the needs of the workplace, instead of in terms of the full intellectual development of students, are not educational goals at all, but are instead economic goals in which students are but means to ends that do not serve their interests well." To what degree do you find that the historical record supports this criticism? Support your view.
4. Evaluate John Duffy's argument in favor of mixed-ability group instruction at the secondary level, and explain the degree to which his argument is relevant to critics' concerns about vocational education.
5. Duffy focuses not on the contrast between vocational education and liberal education, but instead on the idea of a "critical pedagogy." What does he mean by that term, and how similar or dissimilar is it to the aims and methods of liberal and vocational education? Support your view.
6. Critics have argued that liberal education is an outmoded ideal because it is grounded in an educational approach that is historically racist, elitist, and gender-biased. To what degree does Duffy's approach appear to be consistent with liberal education ideals and yet responsive to these criticisms? Defend your position.
7. Grubb identifies seven important purposes to be served by the new integration of vocational and liberal education. To what degree are these an improvement on the traditional goals of vocational programs, and to what degree is it likely that these goals will be successfully achieved in the new integration? Support your assessment.

NOTES

1. Arthur G. Wirth, *Education and Work for the Year 2000: Choices We Face* (San Francisco: Jossey-Bass, 1992). The actual legislation is the Carl D. Perkins Vocational and Applied Technology Education Act Amendments of 1990, Public Law 101-392 (H.R. 7), September 25, 1990.
2. See, for example, Ray Marshall and Marc Tucker, "Building a Smarter Work Force," *Technology Review,* October 1992; also in *Education 94/95,* 21st ed. (Guilford, Conn.: Dushkin Publishing Group), pp. 169–73. See also Monika Kosmahl Aring, "Word Is Costing America's Economy, *Phi Delta Kappan,* January 1993; also in *Education 94/95,* pp. 174–81.
3. Lester M. Salamon, "Overview: Why Human Capital? Why Now?" *Human Capital and America's Future,* David W. Hornbeck and Lester M. Salamon, eds. (Baltimore: Johns Hopkins University Press, 1991), pp. 17–18.
4. Marion Pines and Anthony Carnevale, "Employment and Training," in *Human Capital and America's Future,* p. 260.
5. Marvin Lazerson and W. Norton Grubb, *American Education and Vocationalism: A Documentary History,*

1870–1970 (New York: Teachers College Press, 1974), p. 32.
6. Ibid., p. 44.
7. James Bryant Conant, *The American High School Today* (New York: McGraw-Hill, 1959).
8. Ibid., p. 52.
9. Ibid., pp. 57–60.
10. Kenneth B. Hoyt, *Career Education* (Salt Lake City: Olympus Publishing, 1975).
11. J. Grasso and J. Shea, *Vocational Education and Training: Impact on Youth* (Berkeley, Cal.: Carnegie Council on Policy Studies in Higher Education, 1979).
12. Allen Weisberg, "What Research Has to Say about Vocational Education in High Schools," *Phi Delta Kappan*, Vol. 64, No. 5, p. 355. The remaining data in this paragraph are from pages 355–56.
13. Ibid., p. 356.
14. National Commission on Secondary Vocational Education, *The Unfinished Agenda: The Role of Vocational Education in the High School* (Columbus, Ohio: National Center for Research in Vocational Education, 1984), p. 29.
15. Ibid. Also see *Information Please Almanac 1994* (Boston: Houghton Mifflin, 1994), p. 864.
16. Weisberg, "What Research Has to Say," p. 355.
17. *Unfinished Agenda*, p. 30.
18. Weisberg, "What Research Has to Say," p. 356.
19. *Unfinished Agenda*, pp. 29–30.
20. *Digest of Educational Statistics 1993* (Washington, D.C.: U.S. Department of Education), p. 46.
21. U.S. Department of Education. National Center for Education Statistics. *Digest of Education Statistics 1996*, NCES 96-133, by Thomas D. Snyder. Washington, D.C.: U.S. Government Printing Office, 131.
22. Weisberg, "What Research Has to Say," p. 356
23. J. Grasso and J. Shea, *Vocational Education and Training: Impact on Youth.*
24. Ibid., pp. 80–81.
25. Ibid., pp. xxiii–xxvi and chap. 4.
26. Weisberg, p. 358.
27. Ibid., p. 359.
28. Ernest L. Boyer, "Elementary and Secondary Education," in *Human Capital and America's Future*, pp. 174–75
29. Harvey G. Neufeldt, "The Community Junior College Movement: Conflicting Images and Historical Interpretations," *Educational Studies*, Vol. 13, No. 2 (Summer 1982), pp. 172–82.
30. "Vocational Schools Get Respect," *Newsweek*, March 7, 1983, p.79.
31. Fred L. Pincus, "False Promises of Community Colleges: Class Conflict and Vocational Education," *Harvard Education Review*, Vol. 50, No. 3 (August 1980), pp. 353–54.
32. Ibid., p. 354.
33. *Bridges to Opportunity: Are Community Colleges Meeting the Transfer Needs of Minority Students?* (New York: Academy for Educational Development and the College Board, 1989), pp. 1, 13.
34. Ibid., p. 15. For more recent confirmation of the data on community college transfers and four-year degree completions, see U.S. Department of Education. National Center for Education Statistics. *The Condition of Education 1996*, NCES 96-304, by Thomas M. Smith. Washington, D.C.: U.S. Government Printing Office, pp. 23 and 57.
35. Ibid., p. 35.
36. Grasso and Shea, *Vocational Education*, p. 24. The exception to this general finding was that female graduates from the commercial program generally scored higher in knowledge of the world of work than female graduates from the general program. They scored lower, however, than females from the college preparation program.
37. Wirth, *Education and Work for the Year 2000*, pp. 166–68.
38. Ibid., p. 159.
39. *Statistical Abstract of the United States, 1993* (Washington, D.C.: U.S. Government Printing Office, 1993), p. 426.
40. Martha Farnsworth Riche, "America's New Workers," *American Demographics*, Vol. 9, No. 5 (February 1988), p. 38.
41. William Serrin, "A Great American Job Machine?" *The Nation*, September 18, 1989, p. 270.
42. Ibid.
43. *Statistical Abstract of the United States 1993*, p. 426.
44. Serrin, p. 270.
45. *Working Women: A Chartbook*, U.S. Dept. of Labor Bulletin 2385, August 1991, p. 21.
46. Paul Boller, *American Thought in Transition* (Chicago: Rand McNally, 1969), p. 99.
47. Philip M. Boffey, "Satisfaction on the Job: Autonomy Ranks First," *The New York Times*, May 28, 1985, p. 21.
48. *Work in America* (Cambridge, Mass.: MIT Press, 1973), chap. 5.
49. Ibid.
50. This section is adapted from Steven Tozer and Robert Nelson, "Implications of the Holmes Agenda for Emerging Paradigms in Vocational Education," in *Proceedings of the Rupert Evans Symposium on Vocational Education: 1988*, Mildred Griggs, ed. (Champaign: University of Illinois Press, 1989).
51. John Dewey, "Vocational Aspects of Education," *Democracy and Education* (New York: Free Press, 1966), p. 310.
52. Ibid.

53. Ibid.
54. Weisberg, "What Research Has to Say," p. 359.
55. Dewey, *Democracy and Education*, p. 162.
56. Eliot Wigginton, *Sometimes a Shining Moment* (New York: Doubleday, 1986).
57. Grubb, W. Norton, ed. (1995). *Education Through Occupations in American High Schools Volumes 1 and 2.* New York: Teachers College Press.
58. Grubb, W. Norton (1995). The Promises of Curriculum Integration. Grubb, W. Norton, ed. (1995). *Education Through Occupations in American High Schools Volume 2.* 215–219.
59. Lorraine Forte (1996). Federal Law Seeks to Retool Teaching. *Catalyst: Voices of Chicago School Reform* VII:3 (November) 6.
60. Lorraine Forte (1996). Vallas Voc-ed Plans Spark Debate. *Catalyst: Voices of Chicago School Reform* VII:3 (November) 1-4, and Lorraine Forte (1996). Chicago's Rocky Road to a Federal Grant. *Catalyst: Voices of Chicago School Reform* VII:3 (November) 8.
61. The material in this section is adapted from a portion of Steven Tozer, "The Liberal Education of Teachers: Remarks on the Holmes Agenda," *Visual Arts Research,* Vol. 14, No. 1 (Spring 1988), pp. 17–31.
62. Ernest Barker, ed., *The Politics of Aristotle* (London: Oxford University Press, 1980), p. 322.
63. Ibid., pp. 317–23.
64. Ibid., p. 323.
65. Ibid., p. 318.
66. W. H. Woodward, *Vittorino DeFeltre and Other Humanist Educators* (New York: Teachers College Press, 1963), p. 102.
67. *Report on the Course of Instruction in Yale College by a Committee of the Corporation, and the Academical Faculty* (New Haven, Conn.: Yale University Press, 1828), p. 7.
68. Ibid.
69. Ibid., pp. 8, 9.
70. Harvard Faculty Committee, *General Education in a Free Society* (Cambridge, Mass.: Harvard University Press, 1946).
71. Ibid., pp. 52–53.
72. Ibid., pp. 64–65.
73. Ibid., p. 77.
74. Mark Van Doren, *Liberal Education* (Boston: Beacon Hill, 1943), pp. 38–39.
75. Alfred North Whitehead, "The Study of the Past—Its Uses and Its Dangers," in Whitehead, *Essays in Science and Philosophy* (New York: Philosophical Library, 1948), p. 112.
76. Paul Hirst, *Knowledge and the Curriculum* (London: Routledge and Kegan Paul, 1974), p. 31.
77. Colin Lankshear, *Freedom and Education* (Auckland, NZ: Milton Brookes Publications, 1982), p. 198.
78. Adrienne Rich, "Claiming an Education," in Rich, *On Lies, Secrets, and Silence* (New York: W. W. Norton, 1977), p. 232.
79. Jane Roland Martin, "Bringing Women into Educational Thought," *Educational Theory,* Vol. 34, No. 4, p. 349.

CHAPTER 12

Diversity and Equity Today: Defining the Challenge

From its very origins, American society has struggled with questions of equity and equality. Although these terms derive from the same linguistic stem, they carry substantially different meanings. Equality denotes "equal"; equity, "fairness." Even as an ideal, democracy does not call for an identical existence for each citizen, nor does it promise to equalize outcomes. In theory, those who have the most skill and talent, work hardest, and have the best luck are expected to prosper in a free market economy. The free market is supposed to structure a system of rewards that brings out the productive best in people. In practice, however, this theory is questionable. It assumes that the starting conditions for everyone allow for fair competition or, at the very least, that social institutions treat everyone fairly. British economic historian R. H. Tawney draws the distinction in this manner:

> [To] criticize inequality and to desire equality is not, as is sometimes suggested, to cherish the romantic illusion that men are equal in character and intelligence. It is to hold that, while their natural endowments differ profoundly, it is the mark of a civilized society to aim at eliminating such inequalities as have their source, not in individual differences, but in its own organization, and that individual differences, which are the source of social energy, are more likely to ripen and find expression if social inequalities are, as far as practicable, diminished.
>
> . . . it is by softening or obliterating, not individual differences, but class gradations, that the historical movements directed towards diminishing inequality have attempted to attain their objective.[1]

LIBERAL IDEOLOGY: MERITOCRACY REEXAMINED

Social theorists and educators have long been concerned with the origins of inequality. Does inequality stem from deficiencies within certain individuals or groups or from external social and economic conditions? It is important to remember that inequalities which have their source in social organization mean that some, the socially privileged, have advantages which are denied others in the society. The privileged often find it comforting as well as expedient to interpret these socially derived inequalities as intrinsic personal qualities. Not only do they claim personal ownership of their advantages, but they often charge the socially disadvantaged with personal ownership of their deficiencies, thereby justifying the low socioeconomic benefits accruing to the disadvantaged.

In addition to frequent misuses of the terms *equity* and *equality*, much confusion has resulted from inadequately analyzing the implications of

Robert N. Carson wrote the original draft of this chapter.

inequality. What sorts of educational and social policies are needed as a result of inequality, whatever its origin? Are some individuals so unequal that they cannot benefit from the kind of education which others receive, and if so, should they be denied access to decision-making authority?

As we have seen, these equity and equality issues were settled during the first decades of the 20th century as psychologists such as E. L. Thorndike and Lewis Terman along with sociologists such as E. A. Ross and Charles H. Cooley convinced the American public that African-Americans and the "new immigrants" were innately inferior to Anglo-Saxon Americans.[2] This conclusion led to the development of different and inferior educational programs for these groups. Thus differentiated curricula soon became standard in American schools and were seen as a major component in the American system of meritocracy.[3]

The meritocracy issue reemerged during the 1960s and remained at the center of educational discussions for the next 20 years. Fueling the new debate was the *Brown* v. *Board of Education of Topeka, Kansas,* decision and the ensuing Coleman study. These, in turn, led to several "cultural deprivation" studies, which will be analyzed briefly in the next section. The cumulative effect of these works was to reestablish the idea that some individuals and groups are inherently unequal. The source of inferiority was not considered to be social or economic conditions but flaws residing within some individuals and groups. Moreover, because their inherent deficiencies were considered to be of such a magnitude, it was argued that they could not benefit from the kind of education their superiors received. Thus the 1960s debate appeared to confirm the fairness of America's meritocratic economic structure. If some children succeeded in school while others failed, it was believed, the fairness of the system ensured that children succeeded due to their own individual merit.

Social Conditions behind the New Debate

It is instructive to examine the social conditions out of which this new meritocracy debate emerged. Perhaps the first major challenge to the meritocratic conclusions reached at the beginning of this century resulted from the "GI Bill," which appeared near the end of World War II as members of the Roosevelt administration began planning for the demobilization of the American armed forces. Their primary concern was to entice GIs to enter college rather than the labor market and thus help prevent massive unemployment. Many of these GIs came from poorly educated families that earlier had been judged inferior, so they were not expected to succeed in college. In accordance with prevailing meritocratic ideas, many educators were horrified at the prospect of this horde of unprepared and ill-suited students leaving their lower-class backgrounds and crashing the citadels of learning. Educators forecast widespread failure for these new students. Much to their surprise, however, most of the GIs were very successful. As a group, they graduated at a higher rate than the regular students and achieved higher grades en route to their diplomas. This success presented a new reality, a new set of social facts which most social analysts and educators chose to ignore. Nevertheless, it represented a potential chink in the armor of the meritocratic ideology.

In 1954, immediately following the positive experience of the GI Bill, came the Supreme Court's *Brown* v. *Board of Education* ruling, which stated, "It is doubted that any child may reasonably be expected to succeed in life if he is denied the opportunity of an education . . . [and such opportunity] must be made available to all on equal terms."[4] This reopened the debate about equity in American society. Michael Harrington's 1962 best-seller, *The Other America,*[5] added fuel to the debate as he reminded the middle class that one-third of Americans were still ill-fed, ill-housed, and ill-clothed. Apparently, the umbrella of the "middle class" did not cover as much of the populace as conventional wisdom had assumed. This awareness of widespread inequality and inequity was heightened by the growing civil rights movement, led by Dr. Martin Luther King, Jr., and the urban riots which followed his murder in 1968. Meanwhile, the nation was becoming increasingly entangled in the Vietnam War and the social inequities that the war protest movement uncovered. And if the preceding events were not enough

The unexpected college success of the World War II veterans, most of whom came from working-class backgrounds, helped explode the prevailing meritocratic theories of many class-conscious educators.

to unsettle the national psyche, President Lyndon Johnson, in an attempt to secure a political coalition of urban ethnics, African-Americans, and liberal intellectuals, declared a war on poverty that found domestic foes almost as intractable as those in the rice paddies of southeast Asia. To round things out, events in the area of industrial labor relations were equally contentious, as seen in the conflict at General Motors' Vega plant, where workers demanded democratic control of the workplace.

It became clear to many that such events were causing a major reassessment of the modern liberal ideology undergirding meritocracy. Many critics questioned the "new liberal" faith in scientific expertise and scientific rationality as the best ways to organize the workplace and to plan domestic and foreign policy. Expert and elite control of social institutions did not seem to be producing the progress that modern liberalism promised. Further, the uncritical nationalism that modern liberalism had fostered in so many Americans was being questioned. And the promise of freedom for all Americans seemed to be an illusion, given the pervasive conditions of poverty that seemed to constrain millions of Americans who simply didn't have an equal chance at the American dream of a self-sufficient life.

As if these concerns were not enough, there were simultaneous attacks on the schools that were preparing children for their future roles in the meritocracy. These attacks ranged from Admiral Hyman Rickover's demand for a technological elite to defend America from the onslaught of world communism,[6] to Arthur Bestor's charge that the schools were an intellectual "wasteland"[7] which threatened the very existence of American democracy, to Nat Hentoff's assertion that the inner-city schools were so underfunded that they could not educate.[8] Thus education, the major institutional support for meritocracy, was also under severe assault.

The Coleman Report

To fulfill one of the provisions of the 1964 Civil Rights Act, the U.S. Office of Education commissioned James Coleman to conduct a survey "concerning the lack of availability of equal educational opportunity for individuals by reason of race, color, religion, or national origin." This study initiated the new debate on equity. Coleman's team of researchers gathered data on over 6,000,000 schoolchildren, 60,000 teachers, and 4,000 schools across the United States. His findings were startling. To summarize them briefly:

1. Most African-American students and white students attended different schools.
2. According to "measurable" characteristics (e.g., physical facilities, curricula, material resources, and teachers), these schools were quite similar.
3. Measured student performance on standardized tests showed considerable differences, with white students well ahead of African-American students in test results.
4. The measured differences in school resources seemed to have little or no effect on the differences in students' performance on standardized tests; that is, educational inputs (facilities, curricula, teachers) seemed to make no meaningful difference in outcomes (academic achievement).
5. The only variable which seemed to affect educational achievement ("outcomes") was "quality of peers."
6. Minority children, especially African-Americans, Latinos, and Native Americans, entered school with lower achievement scores, and this gap increased throughout their stay in school.

Although it was profoundly influential in the national discussion about schools and inequality, the Coleman study was seriously flawed. According to Samuel Bowles and Henry Levin, for example, the statistical method used to analyze the data grossly underestimated the positive effects of schooling on student achievement.[9] In other words, if the study had been conducted differently, it would have shown that schools do matter a great deal—that different levels of school input do produce very different outcomes in student learning. In addition to flaws in the statistical method used, the data collected by Coleman's team were in themselves misleading: Teacher quality, for example, was measured primarily by years of schooling and years of teaching experience.

Despite its flaws, the Coleman Report succeeded in focusing attention away from educational inputs (what schools bring to students) and toward what children bring to school. It seemed to invite the scientific investigation of unequal education achievement by looking for flaws in the children rather than in the schools or in society.

The Cultural Deprivation Studies

During the winter of 1966–67, the Carnegie Foundation sponsored a seminar at Harvard University to examine the implications of the Coleman Report. Two books were conceived during the seminar: *On Equality of Educational Opportunity,* edited by Daniel P. Moynihan and Frederick Mosteller; and *Inequality,* by Christopher Jencks and his associates. Both books reanalyzed the Coleman database; that is, they used the data collected by the Coleman researchers, rather than gathering new data. Thus both books suffered most of the same flaws as the original Coleman study.

The Moynihan-Mosteller work[10] concluded that since educational inputs are roughly the same for all children, America had achieved equal educational opportunity. The authors argued that educational expenditures were already high and, since further expenditures were not likely to raise educational achievement for minorities, such increases would be economically unwise. America, according to these writers, had already reached the point of diminishing returns regarding educational expenditures. In retrospect, it is interesting to note that the argument for a halt in rising educational expenditures did not originate with the conservative Nixon or Reagan administrations but with liberal Harvard social scientists who were supported by the Carnegie Foundation. The Moynihan-Mosteller work reinforced the Coleman Report's suggestion that the achievement problems faced by minority students rested not with the schools but with the students and their cultural backgrounds. By implication, the book also bolstered the notion that poverty stems from personal problems residing within the poor rather than from problems within the social system.[11]

Christopher Jencks's *Inequality*[12] was even more explicit, although perhaps unintentionally so, in its attempt to rescue the economic system from charges of inequity. Jencks too began by arguing that the Coleman data showed substantial equality of inputs in public schools. He also asserted that cognitive inequality was not affected by schooling but was largely dependent on the characteristics of the child upon entering school. Like Moynihan and Mosteller, he noted that unequal achievement was caused by deficiencies in the child, not the school.

Jencks's conclusions regarding economic inequality were not as predictable as his assertions about educational inequality. He argued that nothing in the Coleman data could be shown to affect future economic success. According to Jencks, family background, schooling, IQ, and cognitive skills had little or no predictive value on future economic success. He did hazard a guess, which he acknowledged lacked data support, that economic success was probably related to "luck" and special competencies, such as the ability to hit a baseball. Nevertheless, he recommended that society spend more money on schooling—even though schools do not make any difference in a person's future—because most people spend 20 to 25 percent of their lives in school and, thus, schools should be "pleasant."[13] During the following decade many educators worried, talked, and planned about making schools more "pleasant" places. The real cost of this kind of activity was to deflect attention away from questions about how to make schools more effective learning centers for children.

Henry M. Levin's review[14] of Jencks's work points out many of its major flaws. Levin notes that Jencks's conclusion that family background has little effect on future income, especially for the rich and the poor, defies the results of many studies of intergenerational mobility which show that the effect of family is quite significant. Regarding Jencks's conclusion that schooling has only a small effect on income, Levin suggests that Jencks's interpretation of what constitutes "small" may well be open to considerable interpretation. The Jencks data showed that the difference in annual income between high school graduates and elementary school graduates who were otherwise identical was 16 percent in favor of the high school graduate; between college graduates and elementary school graduates, the difference was 48 percent in favor of the college graduate. Levin notes, "Jencks apparently believes that such differences are small, but two men separated by such income disparities might not agree."[15]

In light of the massive flaws in the above studies and the fact that they nevertheless exerted, and continue to exert, considerable influence on educational and social policy, the question naturally arises, How did this happen? The most reasonable explanation seems to be that these ideas were congenial to the powerful in our society because they served to protect their advantages. Moreover, these ideas were powerful because they accorded well with the dominant ideology, modern liberalism. They reinforced and appeared to justify a meritocratic arrangement of society and schooling. They deflected arguments which questioned the validity and fairness of such arrangements. Regardless of the reasons these studies became so influential, they continue to affect the way Americans think about questions of equity and schools.

Let us now examine some of the data concerning income, race, social class, gender, and schooling. Subsequently, we shall examine theories which attempt to explain the relationships found in these data.

THE POLITICAL-ECONOMIC CONTEXT

The Demographics of Modern American Society

On the face of it, the United States is a very prosperous society. In the year 1995 the U.S. population reached 262 million. Our gross domestic product has increased almost every year since 1933 to about $7.2 trillion. In the United Nations measure of gross domestic product per capita, which measures real purchasing power per capita, the United States leads all industrialized nations.[16]

The United States is also one of the most schooled countries on earth. Spending on elementary and high school education increased since 1981 from $110 billion per year to over $240 billion in 1995. Over 85 percent of all students graduate from high school,and almost half go on to college. Over a million college students graduated in the United States in 1992 alone.[17]

These statistics give quite an encouraging picture of American society. Unfortunately, this picture is also misleading. For example, almost half of those who go on to college will drop out. And of those who drop out, a disproportionate number are from minority backgrounds. Furthermore, while the median family income stands at a reasonable $39,000, the top 5 percent of families receive more combined income than the bottom 40 percent, who Andrew L. Shapiro reports are poorer than the bottom 40 percent of any other industrialized nation. Whereas 27.5 percent of white households earn over $50,000 per year, only 12.1 percent of African-American families do. At the other end of the scale, a disproportionate number of African-American families bear the burden of poverty. Put differently, the 1994 median family income for whites was $40,884, while it was $24,698 for African-Americans and $24,318 for Hispanics, roughly the same income gaps that existed in 1970.[18]

To gain a more detailed picture of how wealth and power are distributed in society, social scientists examine data on income, educational level, childhood mortality, teenage pregnancy, substance abuse, home ownership, capital stock, and other social indices. These variables are then matched against different demographic groups organized by age, race, ethnicity, social class, gender, and so forth. The next few sections step back from this larger picture of general prosperity to examine outcomes for several different demographic groups. The intent is to reinforce with statistics what is already common knowledge—that social, economic, and political outcomes generally favor men over women, white people over people of color, and upper- and middle-class people over the urban poor and the working class.

Race, Ethnicity, and the Limits of Language

In this section we examine data for specific minority groups. Bear in mind that both *race* and *ethnicity* are socially constructed terms that are difficult to define. There is, for example, no definition of race which will stand up to scientific analysis, so it must be understood that race is not a purely biological term. For example, the distinction between white and African-American is largely determined by legal ruling, as is the case in Louisiana. There the courts have held that a person is African-American if the equivalent of one great-great-great-great-grandparent was African-American (i.e., if a person is one sixty-fourth African-American). Hispanics, on the other hand, are usually classified by virtue of a Spanish surname—clearly a cultural rather than a biological distinction. The important point is that these terms refer less to innate biological differences than to socially constructed differences in how people are perceived to be members of various groups.

There are several difficulties with trying to talk or write about these issues of race and ethnicity. One, as the *Dictionary of Race and Ethnic Relations* points out, is that every time we use the word "race," we appear to be perpetuating a concept that has no basis in science.[19] The Human Genome Diversity Project, for example, has demonstrated that the darkest-hued African and the lightest-skinned Scandinavian are 99.99 percent identical in their genetic composition.[20] Yet the concept "race" has historically operated as if the differences among large groups of people (traditionally "Caucasoid, Mongoloid, and Negroid") are so significant as to identify us as subspecies of the larger human species, a division which has no scientific basis. To continue to use the term "race" seems to perpetuate that mistaken notion. It might be better, it seems, to eliminate the term altogether from the way we refer to ourselves as humans—unless to affirm that we are all one race.

However, the term race has been historically used to differentiate us from one another, not to unite us. (For the African and the Scandinavian to say they are of the same race seems like nonsense, as if the language is being used in a way it was not meant to be used.) Therefore, focusing on race draws our attention to differences among us, rather than to the similarities. The same might be said for "ethnicity," a term which *does* have a strong basis in social science. Focus on this term, too, can make people uncomfortable, because in the midst of the effort to affirm what we have in common with one another—our essential humanness—social scientists and educators continually use a term that emphasizes our differences from one another. This may be perceived as divisive. It separates us by different languages and different cultural histories. In short, focus on ethnicity, like focus on race, seems to divide us rather than unite us, but for different reasons.

There is still another difficulty with the language of race and ethnicity: our terms of ethnic identification are disputed and often just plain inaccurate. There is not full agreement among Native Americans (or American Indians, or Indians, or indigenous peoples) about which identifying term to use. Some of these terms (Indians, Americans) are the historical legacy of conquering Europeans, and most cultures resist having their names imposed by other cultures. One's identity is in part shaped by one's name, and we resist having our own names for ourselves replaced by someone else's names for ourselves. Similarly, most Asian Americans now resist being called "Orientals," and most African-Americans resist being called "Negroes." While some African-Americans and Hispanics and Asian Americans use the term, "People of Color" to refer to non-white, non-Hispanic people in the U.S., this obscures the fact that some Hispanics in the U.S. identify strongly with their European origins, are in all outward respects "white," and do not want themselves described as "people of color." In their view, they are as "white" as any other U.S. language or ethnic group (Polish, German, Irish) of European descent. Alternatively, some Hispanics would choose to self-identify as Latino or Chicano (about which more later), terms which are chosen in part to make specific political statements about identity and self-representation.

Even when we respect the names different peoples prefer for themselves, our efforts to talk about ethnicity are stymied by the fact that broadly inclusive terms are misleading. For example, to generalize about Hispanics or Asian Americans overlooks profound cultural differences, even historical hostilities, within each of those subgroups. While Japanese and Chinese and Cambodians are very different culturally and economically in the U.S., the term "Asian American" seems to allow us to generalize about them as if they are basically similar. Similarly, Cubans, Puerto Ricans, and Mexicans have different histories and important differences in their status in the U.S. economic and educational system—but they are all Hispanics in our use of the language.

If our language is such a clumsy tool for talking about these matters, why talk about them? Why can't we all be one and stop emphasizing differences among us? (In fact, there are those who would prefer that U.S. Census Bureau and other official documents would stop requiring us to identify ourselves as African-American, Asian and Pacific Islander, American Indian, and so on.) One very important reason, as indicated in Cornel West's recent book *Race Matters*,[21] is that people in the United States are deeply affected—privileged, damaged, even killed—according to their *perceived* membership in one racial or ethnic group or another. To stop talking about race and ethnicity is to lose an important tool for understanding why some people are treated differently from others in our society. Without race and ethnicity as categories, we can't find answers to important questions about whether schools are serving all children equally well—or whether skin color or cultural background might be factors in why some children perform better than others. We would not be able to learn that Minnesota, to take one example of a state with a highly regarded school system, ranks "dead last of all the states among African-American fourth-graders," to cite a 1996 study of academic achievement. If we take away race and ethnicity as tools for analysis, we can't notice that African-American males are more likely to be killed or to go to prison in our society than they are to graduate from college. Without the tools for noticing that this is happening, we cannot begin to ask why. Without asking why, we cannot begin to do anything about it.[22]

On the one hand, then, our language about race and ethnicity is imprecise and often misleading. The very use of the term "race" seems to perpetuate a wrong-headed idea about human beings. Yet, these seem to be the best tools we have for pointing out one huge category of problems that must be addressed if a school system seeks to serve democratic ideals. Those problems exist when children experience different educational outcomes not on the basis of their individual talents and interests, but on the basis of their membership in some cultural group—whether that group is defined by race, ethnicity, family income, gender, or some other characteristic. Even when the tools of language are clumsy, they are often sufficient to help us inquire into whether all children are receiving the education they deserve in a democratic society.

Income and Wealth If race and ethnicity were of no consequence in American society, we would not expect great differences in income among different racial and ethnic groups. Where income varied among individuals, we would expect the differences to be due not to race and ethnicity but to such factors as education or individual talents or interests. Where income varied among families, we would consider such factors as the number of income earners in the household. In fact, as Sheldon Danziger points out, educational differences do not explain very much of the disparity between income earnings among non-Hispanic whites, African-Americans, and Hispanic individuals; correcting for educational differences does not eliminate most of the income differences.[23] Other differences, such as age, region, and racial bias in employment and promotion practices, are among those that must be examined. Similarly, Andrew Hacker has found that the difference between the number of two-income white households and two-income black households does not explain the large gap in household income between those two groups, especially because a higher percentage of black married women than white married women work outside the home.[24]

What is most salient for our purposes here is that the income differences are very real for different racial and ethnic groups, and these income differences lead to different life chances for children in different groups. Further, family income correlates highly with school achievement, which means that children from low socioeconomic status (SES) families will tend to perform less well in school than high-SES children. Harold Hodgkinson points out, for example, that high-SES African-American eighth-graders perform better in advanced mathematics than low-SES white or Asian American eighth-graders.[25]

Given that SES and race interact in complex ways, income disparities among different ethnic groups can have great consequences for children. And income disparities among different racial and ethnic groups are significant in the United States today. The U.S. Bureau of the Census reports, for example:

- While the median income of white and Asian/Pacific Islander families stands well above the median household income of the United States overall ($39,000 in 1994 dollars), median earnings of African-American and Hispanic families are much lower: respectively, $24,698, and $24,318.[26]
- Nearly 26 percent of all white households earned above $50,000 in 1991, and 35.6 percent of American Asian/Pacific Islander households exceeded this figure. In contrast, 15 percent of Hispanic households and 12.1 percent of African-American households earned over $50,000. Put differently, over 23 million white households have access to opportunities that such an income can provide, compared to just over 1 million black households and fewer than 0.75 million Hispanic households.[27]
- At the opposite end of the income distribution, 22 percent of all white households earned below $15,000 in 1991, while 42.4 percent of African-American and 32.8 percent of Hispanic households fell below this figure. In contrast, only 19.2 percent of Asian/Pacific Islander households (just 40,000 households) fell into this category.[28]
- When family wealth is measured, which considers not just annual income but a family's full financial assets, such as real estate and stocks, the differences are much greater. The 1992 *Federal Reserve Bulletin* reports that white families have a mean net worth of $58,500, and half of all white families have a net worth of over $203,000. In contrast, nonwhite families have a mean net worth of only $4,000, with half exceeding $45,000 in net worth.[29]
- The poverty level income in 1991 was established at $13,924, well under half the median household income for the nation. Among Asian/Pacific Islander families, 13 percent fell below poverty level, compared to 14.2 percent of white families. In contrast, 28.7 percent of Hispanics and 32.7 percent of African-Americans fell into this poverty

category. By 1994, whites in poverty had decreased to 11.7 percent, while African-Americans and Hispanics each exceeded 30 percent.[30]

In seeking explanations for such marked differences among different ethnic groups, we should avoid the simple suggestion that the higher levels of education attained by whites and Asian Americans provide the answer. It is instructive, for example, that while the education gaps between blacks and whites have steadily narrowed since the late 1960s, the poverty levels for whites have remained between 9 and 11.3 percent, while for blacks, poverty rates have remained much higher, between 21 and 30 percent.[31] When looking at individual income and educational levels in 1992, Hacker found that increased years of education for black males have not translated into increased income equality. Black male dropouts from high school earn 80 percent of white male dropouts' earnings, and black males with college degrees earn the same percentage of the earnings of white male college graduates. With five or more years of college, black male earnings actually decline to 77 percent of white male earnings. Black females (like white females) earn about 72 to 75 percent of white male earnings, when years of education are the same. While education helps an individual get ahead with respect to his or her own ethnic group, education by itself does not close the income and wealth disparities among ethnic groups.[32]

Employment Hacker shows that, for the last 30 years, unemployment rates for African-Americans have remained steadily at two to two-and-a-half times the unemployment rates for whites. Again, we are tempted to look for an explanation in educational differences. But, as Hacker tells us, African-Americans with college degrees have even worse unemployment rates, compared to college-educated whites, than African-Americans who have only a high-school diploma as compared to their white counterparts. Perhaps even more discouraging to African-Americans is the comparison of their recent unemployment rates with those 20 or 30 years ago. In the 1960s, black unemployment went above 11 percent only in one year and stayed at or below 8 percent for the last half of the decade. In the 1980s and early 1990s, despite dramatic educational increases for African-Americans, black unemployment rates have never gone below 11 percent and for most years have hovered in the 14 to 18 percent range.[33] The message is that unemployment differentials, like income disparities, are dependent upon socioeconomic conditions other than education. While additional education can create opportunities for individuals in all ethnic groups, it is not likely in itself to overcome differences among groups, as long as various forms of discrimination based on ethnicity persist.

Discrimination interacts with cultural practices and traditions differently in different ethnic groups. In the section on social theory and education in the next chapter, for example, we will see a theory suggesting a certain amount of resistance to school norms among children in some ethnic groups but not in others. A group's cultural practices, together with how groups are differently perceived by people who hire and fire in the workplace, have different consequences for different groups. The nation's unemployment rates for whites and Asian/Pacific Islanders in 1992, for example, were 6.5 percent and 6.3 percent, respectively. Regarded as the "model minority" by employers as well as by some educators, Asian/Pacific Islanders do not encounter the same sort of discrimination as that directed against African-Americans or Hispanics, the unemployment rates for whom in 1992 were 14.1 and 9.9 percent, respectively.[34]

Such data tell us some important differences *among* groups, but they obscure important differences *within* groups. For example, the relatively high household income levels cited above for Asian/Pacific Islanders hide differences among different Asian groups. While average family income for U.S.-born Chinese Americans was over $39,000 in 1990, for example, well above the median for white non-Hispanics, the average family income for U.S.-born Asian Indians and Filipinos was in the $19,000 to $21,000 range, well below the white average.[35] Similarly, in unemployment, the Cuban-American male unemployment rate for 1992 was 7.1 percent, while the Puerto Rican-American male rate was 15.6 percent, worse than the African-American unemployment rate for that year.[36] The general labels "Hispanic" and "Asian/

Pacific Islander" can cause us to overlook important cultural and economic differences among the many different groups comprised by them. Similarly, discouraging data about black poverty and unemployment can obscure the reality of the growing black middle class, which has more in common with the white middle class than with the black underclass in terms of economics, employment, and education.

Family We are learning from many quarters that changes in the American family affect all ethnic groups, but some more severely than others. The great majority of the 17.5 million children living in single-parent households, for example, are white non-Hispanic. It might seem, therefore, that information on the changing family structure in our society might better be discussed as a subtopic of economic class or gender rather than ethnicity. We are choosing to mention family characteristics here largely because of the particular significance that single-parent families have for African-American children. First, while the portion of white non-Hispanic children living with both parents has declined in the last 20 years from 85 percent to 71 percent, the decline in the black two-parent family has been more startling: from 59 to 36 percent. For Hispanic children, the change has been from 78 percent in two-parent families to 65 percent. While two-thirds or more of white and Hispanic children live with both parents, barely over a third of African-American children do so. The economic consequences hit different groups differently. Of 11 million white children living with one parent (1992 data), approximately 5 million are in families with less than $15,000 annual income, approximately poverty level. Of 5.9 million black children living with one parent, in contrast, 3.9 million live in that poverty zone.[37] As Hodgkinson notes about correlations between poverty and single-parent families, "when both parents work, family income does not double; it *triples.*"[38] Single-parent families are thus a significant reason that over 8.3 million white children, 4.6 million black children, and nearly 3 million Hispanic children were listed as living in poverty in 1991 by the U.S. Bureau of the Census. Put in percentages, 16.1 percent of white non-Hispanic children, 45.6 percent of African-American children, and 39.8 percent of Hispanic children lived in poverty in 1991. There is little doubt that these deep economic differences will contribute to different educational and life outcomes for these children.[39]

Some of these life opportunities are eliminated very early, even before birth. Hodgkinson reports that one-fourth of pregnant mothers receive no medical care during the crucial first trimester of pregnancy, when some 20 percent of handicapped children's afflictions might have been prevented by early prenatal care.[40] The United States has the highest infant mortality rate of any industrialized nation, due significantly to the effects of racism and poverty on African-Americans. African-American infants die at a rate twice that of white infants, and in some inner-city areas (such as Detroit, Chicago, and Philadelphia), infant mortality rates exceed those in Jamaica, Costa Rica, and Chile.[41]

Compared with white children, African-American children are twice as likely to be born prematurely, to suffer low birth weight, to live in poor housing, to have no parent employed, and to see a parent die. Compared with white children, African-American children are three times more likely to be poor, to live in a female-headed family, to be placed in an educable mentally handicapped (EMH) class in school, to die of known child abuse, and to have their mother die in childbirth.[42]

Housing Half the nation's African-Americans are concentrated into just 25 major metropolitan areas. Two-thirds of all African-American youth still attend segregated schools.[43] Patterns of segregation in housing nationwide have changed surprisingly little in the past 30 years, despite the rise of a highly visible African-American middle class and laws aimed at desegregating society.

The job market has changed, however, shrinking the middle class by eliminating manufacturing jobs and shifting many of the remaining jobs away from the central city to the suburbs, or overseas to sources of cheap labor. Many African-Americans in the inner city have been left behind without jobs and without opportunities for upward mobility. The breakdown of the family, the exit of African-American professionals from the inner city, the erosion of the tax base, and the increase in drug usage, violence, and crime have all served to leave the inner city a disastrous place to grow up. By the early 1990s housing and employment problems had actually worsened as the Bush administration tightened budgetary restraints on social spending.

For the purposes of illustrating socioeconomic inequalities, many of the examples presented here have contrasted African-Americans with non-Hispanic whites. This is partly because of the status of African-Americans as the largest American ethnic minority group, but also because discrimination against African-Americans is uniquely grounded in a history of enslavement and subsequent related prejudice and oppression. As Marian Wright Edelman, founder of the Children's Defense Fund, wrote in an open letter to her own children:

> It is utterly exhausting being black in America—physically, mentally, and emotionally. While many minority groups and women feel similar stress, there is no respite or escape from your badge of color. . . . It can be exhausting to be a Black student on a "white" campus or a Black employee in a "white" institution where some assume you are not as smart as comparable whites. The constant burden to "prove" that you are as smart, as honest, as interesting, as wide-gauging and motivated as any other individual tires you out.[44]

While the African-American experience in the United States has been distinctively oppressive, the fastest-growing minority groups in the nation are Asian Americans and Hispanic Americans, groups with great internal variation that are affected by different kinds of discrimination. More will be said about Asian Americans and Hispanics as we move later to the issues of education and ethnicity.

Gender

Originally, political representation in America excluded women. The family rather than the individual was assumed to be the political unit, and men represented the family unit. Remaining single for men and for women was discouraged by social censure and, at times, by political and economic means as well. As documented in Chapter 5, paternalistic social arrangements drawn from European society dated back through medieval times to the classical formulations of Greece and Rome. *Paternalism* refers to a male-dominated social arrangement embedded in traditional family, state, and church structures. When the purpose of education is seen as preparing individuals for places in society, there are clear implications for the education of females in a male-controlled society. Although the proportion of women completing high school and college and ascending to positions of responsibility, power, and wealth has increased dramatically since the days when women were legally subordinate to men, significant differences still exist between the conditions and experiences of modern men and women. A closer look at some of these differences will establish a foundation for later discussions of gender issues in American education.

Employment Most people, men and women, feel that an occupation is important to their well-being. In a survey conducted by the U.S. Department of Education, 84 percent of males and 77 percent of females indicated that being successful in work was far more meaningful to them than having high income. Furthermore, most of those surveyed felt that a woman could successfully balance career aspirations and family obligations. And an impressive 98 percent of the respondents felt that a woman should have exactly the same educational opportunities as a man.[45] Almost as many felt that women should have the same pay for equal work, as well as the same opportunity for management and other positions of responsibility. In attitude, at least, the public seems to have adjusted to the notion that women are entitled to equality in the workplace. Most women felt that the equal rights movement had made their lives better.

Although attitudes seem to test well, reality is less accommodating. Women who are in the upper ranks of the socioeconomic scale are closer to men in status and opportunity than are women in the bottom ranks. Variables of race and social class further compound the issues. Poor African-American women, for example, present an especially dismal economic picture: African-American women headed 56 percent of all African-American households in 1990, and, as we have seen, their incomes average near the poverty level. Only 12 percent of African-American females over age 25 have completed college, and another 56 percent have completed high school.[46]

There seems to be a "glass ceiling" which prevents women from reaching the top positions in the economic world, although it does not prevent women from *seeing* the top echelon. Most commentators agree that this barrier has been constructed by the materials of gender discrimination rather than by any inherent deficiency in women. Nevertheless, some gains are clearly visible. Women have entered into the ranks of lawyers, doctors, and other professionals in numbers unparalleled in previous generations. Between 1972 and 1990, the proportion of lawyers who were women rose from 4 percent to 21 percent. In the same time period, the proportion of women physicians nearly doubled, to 19 percent, according to the U.S. Department of Labor Bureau of Labor Statistics.

Despite these gains, many occupations remain predominantly female. Dental hygienists, preschool and elementary teachers, secretaries, receptionists, practical nurses, day care workers, domestic servants, typists, dressmakers, registered nurses, dietitians, speech therapists, teacher's aides, and bank tellers are still over 93 percent female, and some of these jobs are nearly 100 percent female. Some 59 percent of all female workers are employed in sales, clerical, and service work. Conversely, some jobs remain over 95 percent male: loggers, auto mechanics, tool-and-die makers, skilled building tradesmen, millwrights, engineers, mechanical engineers, aircraft mechanics, carpenters, civil engineers, industrial engineers, welders and cutters, machinists, and sheet metal workers.

Income In some of the jobs sampled, women earned as little as 35 percent of what men earned in the same fields, and overall women tend to earn about 74 percent of what men earn for comparable work. The U.S. Bureau of the Census reports the following profile of median annual income in 1991 for male and female full-time workers at various levels of education:

- While in 1980 female year-round full-time workers earned 60 percent of male earnings for year-round full-time work, that figure improved to 70 percent in 1991. Overall, full-time female workers earn $21,245, compared to the male workers' $30,332.
- Black and Hispanic women full-time workers earn significantly less than their white female counterparts: $19,134 and $16,548, respectively.
- African-American women thus earn 85 percent as much as black male full-time workers and 61.8 percent as much as white male full-time workers, illustrating the effects of race and gender together on group income levels.
- Similarly, Hispanic women working full-time earn 83 percent of their Hispanic male counterparts' earnings, and only 53.5 percent of white male earnings.
- When education is accounted for, women still earn consistently less than men with the same educational background in terms of years of schooling. In fact, women with a high school degree and some college work earn less than male high school dropouts, on average. Similarly, women with a bachelor's degree or better make less than male college dropouts, and only 65 percent of what male college graduates make: $33,144 for women and $50,747 for men.[47]

Living Situation The 56.5 million working women in America represent 45 percent of the entire labor force over age 16, and over 10 million of the women are heads of households. Having children can be economically dangerous for working women, since the United States is the only western democracy that fails to protect the careers of young working mothers. *Family Circle Magazine* (Aug. 1, 1986) reported:

- Swedish working women get a nine-month maternity leave at 90 percent of pay.
- Italian working women get a five-month maternity leave at 80 percent of pay.
- Hungarian working women get 20 weeks' leave at 100 percent of pay.
- Most American women get nothing for maternity leave, and some lose their jobs.

In 1992, Shapiro reported that the United States is the only industrialized nation without a mandated maternity leave policy; paid leave at 60 to 100 percent of salary is the norm in most of the other nations. U.S. employers also resist paying for advanced education and additional training for female employees on the grounds that they may subsequently have children and quit. This flaunts the fact that male employees also quit: men change jobs every 7 years on average, and are encouraged to do so to keep from stagnating.[48]

Socioeconomic Class

Socioeconomic class is an arbitrary designation intended to group people whose social interests coincide by virtue of similar levels of wealth, income, power, occupational responsibility, social prestige, and cultural identity. Although it is difficult to establish criteria separating one class from another, the notion of class is still useful for noting group differences. As we saw in Chapter 4, the dominant ideology of American society derives from an essentially middle-class, enlightenment vision of progress, which holds that rational people can control their own destiny and get what they deserve. Some social critics now charge that this vision is deeply flawed. The world is not as rational as was once believed, nor is human society so easily perfected. These critics also maintain that modern liberalism cannot protect the interests of certain groups in society. The values and worldview of one class do not necessarily apply to people situated elsewhere in the social structure.

The myth that virtually all Americans are middle class obscures what the numbers say. It neatly hides the fact that a small percentage at the top is fabulously wealthy, and it obscures the reasons why a disproportionate number of people at the bottom are truly distressed. Finally, our long-cherished faith in social mobility is not very well supported by the evidence. Class structure tends to be more rigid than most of us realize or care to admit. This rigidity has been maintained partly in the interests of social stability.[49]

The news media do depict a poverty class, but all too often as a problem of minority populations. Although African-American poverty rates are three times white poverty rates, white non-Hispanics still account for 23.7 million of the more than 40 million people living in poverty in the United States. And though 32.7 percent of African-Americans and 28.7 percent of Hispanics live in poverty, most members of both groups do not. Still, poverty is a problem that hits ethnic minorities and women, as well as the young, at disproportionate rates.[50]

These poverty rates are particularly disturbing on two counts: their stability over time and their resistance to the increasing educational attainment of all groups involved. Since 1969, for example, white poverty rates have increased from 9.5 percent to 11.3 percent in 1991. During that same period African-American poverty rates have remained essentially stable: in 1969, poverty among blacks stood at 32.2 percent, and in 1991 it was 32.7 percent. Since 1975, when the government began keeping records on Hispanics, the Hispanic poverty rate has remained relatively stable at about 27 to 29 percent, with some slightly better years in the late 1970s. It would appear that in economic periods, good and bad, poverty is a fact of life for large segments of American society, particularly minority populations. Yet for all three of these broad population groups, the educational levels have improved considerably since 1969–1970. White non-Hispanic high school graduation rates since then have increased from 54 percent to 81 percent, while white poverty has increased. Black high school graduation rates have increased from 31 percent to over 67 percent, while poverty has not abated. And Hispanic graduation rates have increased from 37 percent to 52 percent, while poverty among Hispanics has slightly deepened.[51]

Income If the middle class is defined by income level, it is shrinking. However, if it is defined according to the percentage of white-collar jobs, it has grown overall, since many well-paid manufacturing jobs are being replaced with white-collar jobs at or near the minimum wage. Perhaps the simplest and most common way to designate class is by income bracket. Many economists define the middle class by income levels between $20,000 and $60,000, which includes about 60 percent of the American population, according to the January 14, 1992, *New York Times*.

Philip Mattera reports that income distribution across the nation has remained very stable since the end of World War II, with the top fifth of income earners making about nine times the earnings of the bottom fifth in 1987 as well as in 1947.

Although women have made impressive educational and employment gains over the past two decades, overall, women still earn less than three-fourths of what men do for comparable work.

In fact, the top fifth earns a bigger portion of the national income pie now (43.7 percent) than it did in 1957 or 1967, for example (40.4 percent in each of those years), and the poorest fifth earns a smaller share than at any other time in the last 40 years. In fact, the bottom three-fifths of the population earns less than a third of the income of income earners nationwide, while the top two-fifths are paid more than two-thirds of the available pie. While more and more people are increasing their education, the gap between rich and poor grows greater over time.[52]

Power Social class is significant in part because different classes wield more political and economic power than others. Thomas Dye's research, examined in Chapter 9, is worth summarizing here.

The 7,000 leadership positions Dye selected represent key positions of control in the 100 largest industrial corporations, the 50 largest utilities, the 50 largest banks, the 50 largest insurance companies, and the 15 largest investment groups in the United States. The positions also include the most influential people in mass media, education, foundations, law, civic and cultural organizations, the three branches of the federal government, and the military. Since some people fill more than one of these roles, the actual number involved is only 6,000. Dye makes the point that it is not the individual who is powerful, but the leadership role in a large and powerful organization. These organizations hold over 50 percent of the nation's industrial assets, 50 percent of the nation's banking assets, 50 percent of all utilities and transportation, 66 percent of all insurance assets, over 50 percent of all private endowments in higher education, over 90 percent of all broadcast TV news, and 33 percent of the daily newspapers in America.

One of Dye's objectives was to find out how socially open these positions had been. Of the top 7,000 positions, only 4.3 percent were filled by females and only 0.3 percent were filled by African-Americans. Over 90 percent came from the upper 20 percent of the socioeconomic ladder.[53]

The pattern that emerges from these figures had led some scholars to suggest that there is a sort of ruling caste in American society. C. Wright Mills called it the "power elite" and tried to show that there is a high correlation of ideological, cultural, social, political, and economic interests in this group.[54] Although individuals occupying positions of power compete with one another, they tend not to question the rules of the game or to take measures that might upset the basic inequalities of the social system over which they preside.[55] This enormous concentration of wealth and power in the hands of a very few people simply cannot be explained on the basis of talent and ability. So we must look for additional mechanisms to explain how society can function so neatly in the interests of these privileged few.

How can we account for these very unequal results? Are there special qualities that are inherent in males, white Americans, the upper classes? Are females, minorities, and lower-class children somehow inherently "deficient"? Or are these differences largely societal—a result of inequality? If so, what processes are at work to yield such inequality? Do schools play a role in supporting or reproducing such inequalities?

EDUCATION: ETHNICITY, GENDER, AND CLASS

We now turn to the issue of social equity in schooling. Do schools promote the success of some members of society while hampering the success of others? Do the schools uniformly serve the needs of all children, or do they contain mechanisms that subtly and systematically discriminate against some students? We do know, contrary to the conclusions of the Coleman Report, that schools in poor areas where academic achievement is low tend to be poorly staffed, overcrowded, underfunded, undersupplied, and wrought with physical and emotional dangers. These conditions represent one form of social inequity. Are there others, perhaps more subtle and even more effective in maintaining the status quo? Are there fundamental differences in the way African-American, white, Indian, Latino, or Asian children experience the institution of schooling? Are there fundamental differences between the experiences of male and female, rich or poor? And do schools provide equitable treatment to students who are judged to have physical or psychological disabilities or handicapping conditions? Let us begin this portion of our inquiry by returning to the general demographic categories described earlier to examine the outcomes of schooling for children according to racial and ethnic characteristics, gender, and class differences.

Race, Ethnicity, and Education

In examining the data on schooling, bear in mind the distinction between equality of results and equity of social conditions. Inherited talents and dispositions may well vary from student to student, so different outcomes can be expected for different students. What intrigues and disturbs social scientists is the situation in which whole groups of people systematically perform below the levels of other groups. We must question the institutional arrangements which produce unequal results for certain groups.

We should also bear in mind that much progress has been made in spreading formal education to broader segments of society. This tells us that reform is not futile, and problems can in fact be addressed. In 1900, for example, only about 10 percent of the population graduated from high school. In 1940, 24.5 percent graduated from high school and 4.6 percent completed college. By 1991, 86 percent of the population had completed high school and 19 percent had at least 4 years of college.[56] This represents progress. It also reflects the need for more formal education in an increasingly complex society. Today, most if not all educators believe that a high school graduation rate of 86 percent is no longer satisfactory.

As the data are subdivided, differences in the success rates of racial and ethnic groups become evident. Although 90 percent of white students graduate from high school, only 81 percent of African-American students and 61 percent of Chicanos, Puerto Ricans, and Native Americans do. With each successive stage of formal schooling, the pool of minority students eligible for the next stage gets further reduced. About 38 percent of white students enter and 23 percent complete college; 29 percent of African-American students enter and only 12 percent complete college. Chicanos, Puerto Ricans, and Native Americans complete college at the rate of roughly 9 percent of the population. Completion of graduate or professional school is 8 percent for white Americans, 4 percent for African-Americans, and 2 percent each for Chicanos, Puerto Ricans, and Native Americans.[57]

Admission to higher education depends upon standardized tests such as the SAT and the ACT.[58] These tests do not measure intelligence. They measure the acquisition of ideas, information, and patterns of thought which are representative of the dominant culture and, as such, are used as predictors of first-year success in college. What they correlate with most strongly is the economic background of the student, with some differences also attributable to gender and ethnicity.[59] This economic variable helps account for the fact that the average SAT score of African-American students is 200 points less than that of white and Asian students on a scale ranging from 400 to 1600. Desegregation has not succeeded in bringing minority students into sufficient contact with the white majority—that is, with the culture that the system rewards. Both neighborhood and school segregation result in isolation from a cultural norm whose values and icons are often different, for example, from those of the African-American culture. The following details are illustrative:

- About 63 percent of African-American students attend predominantly minority schools.[60]
- Only 13 percent of teachers are African-American or Hispanic, a proportion that has levelled off in recent years.[61]
- In many supposedly desegregated schools, the upper-level courses enroll almost all white students, while the lower-level and vocational courses enroll mostly African-American students. Thus segregation continues within supposedly desegregated institutions.
- Most advances in desegregation occurred between 1968 and 1972; desegregation efforts have effectively stalled since 1976, and in much of the Northeast minority students are finding themselves increasingly isolated. In Illinois, New York, Michigan, California, and Mississippi, over 75 percent of black students attend schools in which they are the majority population in the school.[62]

Given the significance of cultural differences and economic deprivation for school performance, it is not surprising that so many African-American children encounter difficulty in schools and on standardized tests. But other ethnic groups also lag behind the performance of the non-Hispanic white majority, in ways that must be attributed to socioeconomic factors rather than to native learning ability.

Since the *Brown* v. *Board of Education* decision in 1954, national concern about educational equity has focused largely on the education of African-Americans, the largest American minority group. Currently, 76 percent of the U.S. population is white non-Hispanic, 12 percent is African-American, 9 percent is Hispanic, and 3 percent is Asian American or Pacific Islander. These proportions are projected to change dramatically, however, so that by the year 2000, white non-Hispanics will represent only 52 percent of the national

Scholastic Achievement Tests do not measure intelligence. They measure the acquisition of the ideas, information, and thought patterns of the dominant culture and, as such, are used as predictors of first-year college success.

population, African-Americans 16 percent, Hispanics 16 percent, and Asians 10 percent.[63] Because the track record of American schools in dealing with some minority groups has not been good, the challenge to educators in the next 10 years is considerable.

Already, according to the U.S. Census Bureau, 2.9 million U.S. households, or 3.2 percent of the nation's total, are linguistically isolated, meaning that "no person above age 14 speaks English fluently." Of these households, 1.6 million speak Spanish and 0.5 million speak an Asian language. The greatest growth since 1980 has been in Asian languages, which are now four of the top ten spoken. Chinese has doubled, and Korean and Vietnamese have more than doubled; with the addition of Tagalog (spoken in the Philippines), they represent over 3 million people. Nationwide, 13.8 percent of all residents speak a language other than English at home.[64]

The Model Minority Historian Ronald Takaki writes that "today, Asian Americans are celebrated as America's 'model minority.' " Takaki cites feature stories in *Fortune* and the *New Republic* applauding Asian Americans as "America's Super Minority," and "America's greatest success story." Takaki objects to this characterization as inaccurate, however. "In their celebration of this 'model minority,' the pundits and the politicians have exaggerated Asian American 'success' and have created a new myth . . . Actually, in terms of personal incomes, Asian Americans have not reached equality . . ." Income inequalities among Asian American men were evident in Takaki's data: Korean men earned only 82 percent of the income of white men, Chinese men 69 percent, and Filipino men 62 percent.[65] Takaki explains:

> The patterns of income inequality for Asian men reflect a structural problem: Asians tend to be located in the labor market's secondary sector, where wages are low and promotional prospects minimal. Asian men are clustered as janitors, machinists, postal clerks, technicians, waiters, cooks, gardeners, and computer programmers; they can also be found in the primary sector, but here they are found mostly in the lower-tier levels.[66]

Takaki notes that although they are highly educated, Asian Americans are generally not represented in positions of executive leadership and decision making. A comment that appeared in *The Wall Street Journal* is telling: "Many Asian Americans hoping to climb the corporate ladder face an arduous ascent. Ironically, the same companies that pursue them for technical jobs often shun them when filling managerial and executive positions."[67]

Counter to the view that Asian Americans are uniformly successful in school, a recent Seattle study showed that one-fifth of the school population was Asian American, and that as a whole over 39 percent of this group scored in the "at risk" category on the district's standardized reading test, about the same as the Hispanic students. Some Asian American subgroups, notably the Vietnamese, Samoan, and Southeast Asian students, did appreciably worse than the Hispanic students in reading and language skills together, while other groups, such as the Japanese and Chinese, did nearly as well as or better than the white American students.[68] The effects of economic, cultural, and linguistic differences are further revealed in the 1993 study cited in Chapter 9, *Adult Literacy in America.* This massive inquiry shows white non-Hispanic adults to be significantly more proficient, in all three literacy areas under investigation, than all other population groups, including African-Americans, Asian/Pacific Islanders, American Indians, and five different groupings of Hispanic origins.[69]

As we have seen, a term such as "Asian American" can usefully draw our attention to a general classification of people, even if there are significant differences among cultural histories within that larger classification. Those cultural histories need further attention. Historian Sucheng Chan notes that almost a million people from China, Japan, Korea, the Philippines, and India came to the U.S. and Hawaii from the mid-1800s to the early 1900s (in contrast to 35 million European immigrants from 1850 to 1930). Of those Asian and Pacific immigrants, the Chinese (about 370,000) came first, pushed out by poverty and strife in China and attracted by California gold and jobs in Canada and the American West. Next, in the late 1800s and early 1900s, about 400,000 Japanese came, followed by 180,000 Filipinos and less than 10,000 Koreans. They were recruited by

TABLE 12–1

Asian Pacific Americans: Population by Ethnicity: 1980 and 1990

	1980	1990	Percent Growth
Total Asian/Pacific	3,726,440*	7,273,662	95%
Chinese	806,040	1,645,472	104
Filipino	774,652	1,406,770	82
Japanese	700,974	847,562	21
Asian Indian	361,531	815,447	125
Korean	354,593	798,849	125
Vietnamese	261,729	614,547	135
Hawaiian	166,814	211,014	26
Samoan	41,948	62,964	50
Guamanian	32,158	49,345	53
Other Asian/Pacific	226,001	821,692	264%

**The 1980 number for Asian/Pacific Americans in this table is slightly higher than that used in other published reports because it includes the count for "other" Asian/Pacific American groups. Other published census reports include only nine specific Asian/Pacific American groups for the 1980 count. Therefore, our calculation of percent growth is 95%, which is lower than the published 108% growth.*

Source: The State of Asian Pacific America: Policy Issues of the Year 2020. (Los Angeles: LEAP Asian Pacific Public Policy Institute and the UCLA Asian American Studies Center, 1993) p. 12.

Hawaiian sugar plantation owners who needed thousands of workers, and these workers and their families often migrated east to the United States, which soon created an independent flow of immigration from the Asian and Pacific countries.[70] These immigrants, like immigrants from Europe, took jobs, started businesses, sent their children to school, and over time began to assimilate into the mainstream culture, language, and values, while still retaining some cultural values and practices from their home countries.

After a sharp reduction in Chinese and Japanese immigration brought about by the world wars and the subsequent Cold War, Europeans, Canadians, and Mexicans constituted the great majority of new immigrants to the U.S. Then a new source of Asian-American immigration developed during and after the war in Vietnam. The 1965 Immigration Act and its amendments, the 1975 Indochina Migration and Refugee Assistance Act, the 1980 Refugee Act, and the 1987 Amerasian Homecoming Act, have facilitated increased immigration from Southeast Asia. Since 1965, Asian-Pacific immigration has increased to the point that it now constitutes half of all immigration into the United States.[71]

Today, the fastest-growing minority group in the nation is Asian and Pacific Americans, more than doubling in size since 1980. It is projected to more than double again by 2020, resulting in an Asian/Pacific population of nearly 20 million in the United States. By the early 1990s, there were nearly 2 million Asian American children and youth between the ages of 5 and 19 in school in the U.S., with heavy concentrations of that population in major cities, where Asian languages are spoken in the home and in the community. Interestingly, it was the 1970 class action suit brought by Kinney Lau and 11 other Chinese-American students against Alan Nichols and the San Francisco Board of Education that led to the historic Supreme Court case *Lau* v. *Nichols*. The Court's ruling provided the basis for the nation's bilingual education mandates, which in turn have had a profound effect on the education of Hispanic Americans. The Court unanimously ruled:

> there is no equality of treatment merely by providing students with the same facilities, textbooks, teachers, and curriculum; for students who do not understand English are effectively foreclosed from any meaningful education.[72]

The public at large, and perhaps some educators as well, perceive Asian Americans to be high-achievers in school, students who don't need the support of the courts. We have seen, however, that different Asian American groups perform differently in school, and language can be an element of the problem for some students. It will be important for educators not to make assumptions about the growing number of Asian American students in their schools and classrooms, other than that all children will need our best educational support. The Asian American experience has been a difficult one, even when success is apparent for some families. As Chan writes:

> Thus the acculturation process experienced by Asians in America has run along two tracks: even as they acquired the values and behavior of Euro-Americans, they simultaneously had to learn to accept their standing as racial minorities—people who, because of their skin color and physiognomy, were not allowed to enjoy the rights and privileges given acculturated European immigrants and native-born Americans. In short, if they wished to remain and to survive in the United States, they had to learn how to "stay in their place" and to act with deference toward those of higher racial status . . . Asian Americans, more so than black or Latino Americans, live in a state of ambivalence—lauded as a "successful" or "model minority" on the one hand, but subject to continuing unfair treatment, including occasional outbursts of racially motivated violence, on the other.[73]

Hispanic American Diversity Just as it is an error to generalize about the experience of all 17 different Asian immigrant groups now part of the American culture, so it is a mistake to think of "Hispanic" as describing a single people. As Holli and Jones write:

> Hispanic, is an umbrella term encompassing Spanish-speaking people of different races and twenty separate nationalities. Hispanics come from as far as Uruguay, at the edge of South America, or as near as Texas, once a part of Mexico. Some have been here since the First World War, while others arrived only yesterday. They include high skilled professionals, political refugees trying to regain what they have lost, and peasants who never had much to lose. They share a language and a culture.[74]

These regional differences remind us of the very different cultural histories of different Hispanic groups. While Cubans began making their presence felt in the 20th century, for example, most heavily immigrating after the communist revolution in Cuba in 1959, Mexican Americans had a long history in the Southwest before it became the southwest United States. Thousands from Texas to California did not immigrate to the U.S. at all, but found themselves inside this nation's borders when their lands were conquered. It has sometimes been said of that historically Mexican population that they did not cross the border, but the border crossed them instead. Yet people readily assume that most Mexican Americans and other Hispanics are immigrants, if not "illegal aliens." However, three-fourths of the Hispanic population in this country was born in the United States.[75]

Different Hispanic groups have very different migration histories. They have come from different parts of the hemisphere—North America (Mexico), Central America, the Carribean (Puerto Rico and Cuba), and South America—and they have tended to concentrate in different parts of the U.S. Carrasquillo writes:

> In general, Mexicans settled in the southwest, the Puerto Ricans and Dominicans in the northeast, the Cubans in the southeast and northeast, and South and Central Americans have spread out in the United States with large numbers found in the west and south (Nicaraguans) and in the northeast (Colombians, Peruvians and Ecuadorians) of the United States.[76]

Astonishingly, by 1990, these migration patterns added up to over 17 million Spanish-speaking people residing in the United States. The next most numerous group of speakers of English as a second language in 1990 was designated "other," a group of several languages including Native American tongues, totaling 4.3 million speakers.[77]

Despite their common language and some shared cultural practices, and despite their grouping under the designation "Hispanic" for political purposes, differences among these cultures are significant. Referring to the Hispanic experience in Chicago, where half a million Hispanics reside, Holli and Jones write:

> As a result of migration history, each Hispanic group holds deeply felt concerns and attitudes not shared by others. For example, many Cubans share a strong anticommunist sentiment reflected in several organizations formed to oppose Cuban leader Fidel Castro . . . Cubans, therefore, are suspicious of communist influences in the community-based develop-

> ment efforts that are prevalent in Mexican and Puerto Rican areas . . . Immigrants from Cuba and South America, because many are affluent, are dismissed by some Mexicans and Puerto Ricans as not really Hispanic.[78]

Such social class differences can influence the experiences of Hispanic children in schools. Those from the lower economic rungs are, all too often, struggling academically, even if they are born in this country.

As Laura E. Perez points out in quoting the National Council of La Raza,

> *Hispanic undereducation has reached crisis proportions.* By any standard, Hispanics are the least educated major population in the United States; Hispanic students are more likely to be enrolled below grade level, more likely to drop out, less likely to be enrolled in college, and less likely to receive a college degree than any other group.[79]

Yet Perez notes different experiences of different subgroups within the Hispanic population, and that the largest group, Chicanas and Chicanos (Americans of Mexican descent) have the lowest educational attainment. Cubans, in contrast, have the highest, with Puerto Ricans falling closer to the Mexican Americans. The low educational attainment is paralleled by low socioeconomic measures for the Mexican American community. The per capita income cited by Perez for Mexican Americans is about 60 percent that of whites, and about 38 percent of Mexican American children live in poverty. Perez cites research showing that "Chicana/o primary and secondary students are in significant disproportion held back grades and tracked into programs for slow learners or the mentally retarded or 'special' inferior academic or vocational tracks."[80]

Not only economic class differences, but language differences as well, influence the school experiences of Hispanic young people. Limited English Proficiency (LEP) refers to a level of listening/speaking and/or reading/writing in English that is not at or near native-level proficiency, and by far the largest group of these in the U.S. is Spanish-speaking. Cisneros and Leone report that of the 2.2 million LEP students in U.S. schools, federal bilingual program funds are provided only for 251,000 of them, or about 11 percent. These authors believe that bilingual programs would assist LEP students' success in schools, and that the problem of developing a sound bilingual educational policy will increase as numbers of LEP students rise in the coming years. If the data cited by Cisneros and Leone are reliable, as much as 20 percent of the population of the U.S. will be Hispanic by the year 2040, though it is not yet clear how many of these will be LEP. Table 12–2 indicates the 10 states with the highest LEP enrollments today. Chapter 13 will address the question of whether we are prepared to meet the challenge of educating these young people in our schools.

Socioeconomic Class and Education

Thomas Toch has observed that the links between family economic status and school labeling are significant:

> By far, the nation's economically disadvantaged students pay the highest price for the pervasiveness of tracking in public education . . . In other words, disadvantaged students [as measured by an index that includes parental income and education, parental occupation, and the presence of consumer goods in a household] are three times less likely to be in the academic track than affluent students are, but three times *more* likely than affluent students to be in the vocational track.[81]

Social class may prove to be a more effective predictor of future opportunities than either race or gender. With the breakdown of housing segregation, minority families who succeed financially can now move into the suburbs, where their children will experience life very much as the children of white middle-class families do. And girls born into middle- and upper-class families now tend to experience a climate more supportive of personal autonomy and professional aspirations than did their mothers and grandmothers. In the case of poor and working-class children, however, the evidence strongly indicates that neither the processes nor the outcomes of schooling are the same as they are for children of the upper classes. Social scientists are now exploring several evident patterns.

Children who are poor tend to go to schools with other children who are poor. Minority stu-

TABLE 12–2

States With Highest LEP Enrollments

California	986,462
Texas	313,234
New York	168,208
Florida	83,937
Illinois	79,291
New Mexico	73,505
Arizona	65,727
New Jersey	47,560
Massachusetts	42,606
Michigan	37,112
TOTAL	1,897,642

Source: From OBEMLA, 1992. Cisneros and Leone, Editors Introduction, *The Bilingual Research Journal* (Summer, Fall 19:3 and 4), p. 363.

dents attend school with other minority students of similar socio-economic background. The suburbs, where the wealth tends to be located, are not part of the general tax base which supports inner-city schools, so there is little or no cross-fertilization of resources or equalization of conditions. The "better" schools get more qualified teachers and the best science labs, computer systems, reading materials, and other resources. Poor children are not expected to be as smart or to work as hard as middle- and upper-class children. They are not expected to know as much or to learn as much. They are not expected to do as well in life.[82] These lower expectations lead to differential treatment by teachers.

Parents of upper- and middle-class standing are more likely to become involved in the process of their children's education. They tend to feel welcome in the school environment, and to feel that they are equipped to make a contribution.[83] Conversely, the parents of lower-class children tend to feel alienated from their children's school and education. The cultural patterns and icons of poor and working-class children are different from those of the dominant class, are not a part of the school's culture, are not rewarded, and are not generally understood by teachers whose own background differs from that of the students. Disputes over bilingual education further illustrate the separation of culture between schools and their minority students.[84] Chapter 13 will revisit bilingual education as a response to the needs of limited-English-proficient students.

Equity, Education, and Handicapping Conditions

We have seen how membership in an ethnic or economic group can influence how individuals in that group perform and are evaluated and rewarded in schools and in the larger society. Questions of equity arise, as noted early in the chapter, when individuals' standing in school or society seems to be influenced by their group membership rather than by their own individual merits. Such questions apply to children and adults with physically or psychologically handicapping conditions. It is not always clear whether such individuals are allowed to succeed on the basis of their own merits, especially when they are labeled and treated as a group for whom expectations of success are lower than for others who have not been so labeled and grouped.

In 1975, Congress sought to address such equity questions with the Education for All Handicapped Children Act (EHA). As Judith Singer and John Butler write:

> Hailed as a "Bill of Rights" for children with handicaps, the law outlined a process whereby all children, regardless of the severity of their handicap, were assured the same educational rights and privileges accorded their nonhandicapped peers: "a free appropriate public education." EHA was to transform special education practice across the nation by bringing all states up to the standard that some states, prompted by court action and advocacy by handicapped rights groups, already had adopted.[85]

One result of this act, for reasons soon to be mentioned, has been to increase the number of students designated by the schools as disabled or handicapped. Currently, 4.3 million students, out of a total K–12 public school population of over 41 million students, have been designated as special needs students in some way. The largest and fastest-growing of these categories throughout the 1980s was "learning disabled," which grew from 32 percent of the special education population in 1980 to 49.2 percent by 1991. "Speech impaired" was the next largest group, with 22.8 percent of special needs students in 1991, followed by "mentally retarded" (12.4 percent), "emotionally disturbed" (9.0 percent), and then several categories each with no more than 2.2 percent of the population of students designated with disabilities: hard of hearing and deaf, orthopedically handicapped, other health impaired, visually handicapped, multihandicapped, and deaf-blind.[86]

Education analyst Thomas Toch explains part of the reason that learning disabled has become the largest of these categories. First, it "has proven particularly hard to define." Toch elaborates:

> The U.S. Department of Education's definition of the term, "a disorder in one or more basic psychological processes involved in understanding or in using language spoken or written . . . ," is broad. And it is only one of approximately fifty official but often vague and overlapping definitions of the term in use in public education today. As a result, in many school systems "learning disabled" has become a catchall category, and an increasing number of disadvantaged but otherwise "normal" students are being relegated to it, even though P.L. [Public Law] 94-142 prohibits inclusion in the category of students whose learning problems stem from "environmental, cultural or economic disadvantages."[87]

Even Madeleine C. Will, the U.S. Department of Education's official in charge of special education between 1983 and 1989, acknowledged that the "misclassification" of learning-disabled students has become a "great problem."[88] Toch also cites Alan Gartner, a former director of special education in the New York City school system, who wrote, "The students in such programs are not held to common standards of achievement or behavior." Toch elaborates, noting that "only rudimentary skills and topics are taught in classes for the learning disabled, homework is rarely if ever assigned, and the instructors for the learning disabled typically have little or no background in the academic subjects they teach."[89]

The issue of labeling is a critical one in the delivery of services to children with handicapping conditions, real or perceived. Certainly some children have such obvious physical challenges—sightlessness, cerebral palsy, or some other multihandicapping condition—but the growth of the learning-disabled category suggests that some students are being labeled as handicapped who in another social environment might not be perceived as different from other children at all. Yet, with extra funding tied to the identification of students as handicapped, there is incentive for well-meaning educators to label students in ways that might prove damaging. Toch addresses both the labeling and the incentive issues as follows:

> There is a powerful stigma attached to "special education" in the school culture; to be labeled a learning disabled student in a public school is to suffer the disparagement of peers and teachers alike. And rarely do students who have been labeled learning disabled return to the mainstream of school life. Indeed, since schools receive additional funding for learning-disabled students, . . . they have an incentive to continue classifying a student as "LD."[90]

Another incentive for schools to identify more students as learning-disabled is that the performance scores of these students will then not be averaged into those of the school district when standards of accountability are implemented as part of the educational reform movement. Even the U.S. Education Department has issued a warning that raised standards may be "exaggerating the tendency to refer difficult children to special education."[91]

Gender and Education[92]

We have discussed how race, ethnicity, economic class, and handicapping conditions may influence the experience of schooling of different groups of students. The largest of all "minority" groups (often a majority) is females. In studying the relationship between gender and education, we need to ask, (1) Are the processes of education different for girls than for boys? and (2) Are the outcomes of schooling different for women than for men? The answer appears to be yes on both counts.

During most of western history, as we saw in Part 1, women were characterized differently from men and these characterizations were used to certify their inferior and subordinate status. Generally women were characterized as emotional, affectionate, empathetic, and more prone to sensual behavior. Men were characterized as rational, just, more directly in the "image of God," and susceptible to seduction by women's sensual intrigues. Thus men were seen as naturally more fit for social and family leadership roles. Educational institutions and ideals usually reflected these male-female characterizations. Consequently, women were often relegated to education at their mother's side rather than in schools.

Societal Definitions of Gender

Chapter 6 presented an historical account of exclusions and limitations on the education of girls and women in American schools and colleges. The central issue of female education in the last quarter of the 20th century is not *de jure* equal access to educational institutions and curricula. Girls and women are no longer denied equal access to education by law; indeed, since Congress enacted Title IX in 1972 and the subsequent Women's Educational Equity Act in 1974, sex bias in school access, services, and programs has been illegal. However, women are still in practice excluded from educational opportunities, through processes more subtle and complex than prior to Title IX. This *de facto* exclusion of some women from educational opportunities revolves around gender definitions. The central issue in female education today is therefore the problems related to gender and the way those problems affect women's self-concept and academic performance.

Sex refers to the biological characteristics of males and females; gender refers to societal expectations, roles, and limitations placed on a person simply because he or she is male or female. It is the *socially* sanctioned expectations and limitations, not the fact of biological sex differences, that cause the greatest difficulties for females in contemporary educational settings. Gender definitions compose a complex and sometimes subtle set of problems. The powerful impact of gender definitions may be more easily understood when one considers that gender definitions result in learned or socialized "roles."

Most of our social behavior stems from learned roles. There are roles associated with race, social class, occupations, and religion as well as gender. All humans begin to learn some of these roles almost at birth. Other roles are learned at various other life stages. It is important to understand that individuals are not entirely passive recipients in this socialization process. Each brings somewhat different experiences to the process. Thus, different individuals will learn slightly, or even vastly, different roles when exposed to the same socializing conditions.

It is also vital to understand that the socialized roles and the resulting expectations become "reality" for individuals, groups, and society. For example, many 19th-century white southerners believed the role assignment to African-American slaves which designated them as happy, passive, shiftless, lacking rationality, and needing direction. The fact that society or some group in society assigns a role to a particular group and believes the reality of that role does not make the role assignment natural, fair, or moral. Nevertheless, it does make it very difficult for anyone to renounce or reject it because one seems to be contradicting reality. The process of role socialization reflects what social theorists call "social construction of reality." One of the factors which contributes to the strength of this social construction of reality regarding roles is that the content of a role always serves some social function. The role content assigned to African-American slaves provided the structure of justification for slavery and for the labor system of the antebellum south. The fact that the role assignment serves some social function should not lead one to assume that it is therefore desirable or fair. This assumption is made especially often in the case of gender roles.

Early in the 20th century George Herbert Mead and other social psychologists explained how an individual develops her or his sense of self primarily through interaction with groups. It is the way that others react to the individual which helps to define that person's identity. On a simpler level, the nursery story of the "Ugly Duckling" demonstrates the process. As long as the baby swan was in the company of ducks who responded to her as if she were ugly, she believed and acted as if she were indeed ugly. Only when she grew into a swan and was confronted with other swans who reacted to her as if she were truly beautiful did she change her understanding of herself. Unfortunately, for most humans, it is much more difficult to move from the society of ducks to that of swans.

Sex Roles in Infancy It is very instructive to examine the messages contemporary American society provides for girls at every stage of their maturation. Barbara Sinclair Deckard provides a revealing account of social interactions which confront girls and from which girls must construct their self-identification.

> Before a newborn baby leaves the delivery room, a bracelet with its family name is put around its wrist. If the baby is a girl, the bracelet is pink; if a boy, the bracelet is blue. These different colored bracelets indicate the importance our society places on sex differences, and this branding is the first act in a sex role socialization process that will result in adult men and women being almost as different as we think they "naturally" are. . . . Perhaps because sex is such an obvious differentiating characteristic, almost all societies have sex roles. Women are expected to think and behave differently. The societal expectation and belief that women and men are very different tends to become a *self-fulfilling prophecy.*[93]

These societal expectations strongly influence the way parents react to children. Deckard reports on one study where parents described their girl babies "as significantly softer, finer featured, smaller, and less attentive than boy babies, even though there actually was no difference in the size or weight of the two sexes." Another clinical study of college students' descriptions of babies found that the students described the babies as "littler," "weaker," or "cuddlier" when informed that the baby was a girl.[94] Thus, even at birth our evaluations of a baby are directed by social expectations of gender.

Babies are brought home to a gender-directed color-coded world. It is not that blue is better than pink; rather that all girls are seen as different from boys. This difference continues, according to Deckard, into early infancy as the child begins play activities. Parents encourage boys to take chances and develop independence, while girls are protected and shepherded toward dependence. Boys are praised for aggressiveness and girls for willingness to take direction. Boys are counseled to be like Dad; girls like Mom. Parents buy cowboy outfits and dump trucks for their sons and Barbie dolls for their daughters.

Research indicates that these gender lessons are learned by children. At age 2 or 3 children use the terms *boy* and *girl* as "simple labels rather than the conceptual categories." A year or so later they begin to view the sexes as opposite and distinguish between girls' things and boys' things. And by age 6 both girls and boys begin to enforce sex roles. "Boys more consistently choose and prefer sex-typed toys and activities, and these preferences accelerate with age throughout early childhood."[95] This seems to be the natural outcome of the fact that society generally values male roles and denigrates female roles. Children learn these gender values early. Lawrence Kohlberg found that among 5- and 6-year-old children, "Fathers are perceived as more powerful, punitive, aggressive, fearless, instrumentally competent and less nurturing than females. . . . Thus, power and prestige appear as one major attribute of children's sex-role stereotypes."[96] Observers should find little surprise that one of the most hurtful epithets to be hurled at a boy is to call him a girl. Gender lessons are among the earliest and most powerful lessons of infancy and early childhood.

Sex Roles in Early Education Sex roles continue to play a significant part in early education. When children enter preschool they are confronted with constant reminders of gender differences. Kirsten Amundsen's study found that teachers encouraged boys to be aggressive, assertive, and independent. Girls, on the other hand, were discouraged when they exhibited daring or aggressiveness and were encouraged to be timid, cooperative, and quiet.[97] Preschool classroom research shows that girls receive less instructional time, less affection, and less teacher attention than boys.[98]

This pattern continues in primary schools. Studies have found that primary school teachers talk more to boys. They talk to boys even when the boys are in remote classroom locations, but they talk to girls only when they are close to the teacher. Boys are asked higher-order questions more often than girls. Teachers tend to give boys instructions about projects, while they often show girls how to complete the work. Boys are praised more frequently for the intellectual quality of their work, while girls tend to be praised for neatness and following directions.[99] The lessons are clear: boys are important and expected to be competent, and girls are unimportant and expected to need help. One study of elementary and middle-school students showed that boys shouted answers eight times more often than girls. Moreover, when boys called out answers, teachers tended to listen, but when girls responded in a like manner, they were most often told to raise their hand if they wished to speak.[100] Moreover, teachers are more apt to ask questions of boys when they do not volunteer.[101] Such teacher behavior reinforces the subtle messages which girls receive from home and society.

One study asked groups to evaluate a variety of items ranging from paintings to resumes. When the subjects were led to believe that the author of the item was male, they consistently valued it more highly. When a second group was asked to evaluate the same items with the supposed authors' sexes reversed, they consistently evaluated the item lower when they believed its author was a woman.[102] A similar study asked college students to evaluate scholarly articles. In this study both women and men rated the articles higher when they believed they were written by men.[103] Societal messages reinforce school gender lessons. Women are viewed as less capable, and their work is devalued. The result is to emphasize to girls that they are not expected to be independent, creative, intellectually competent, or aggressive. Surely these messages must contribute to the general lack of self-confidence which researchers find in girls at the secondary school level and beyond.[104]

Unfortunately, instructional materials communicate many of the same messages to students. During the past two decades several studies analyzing sex bias in instructional materials have been published.[105] The seminal work was *Dick and Jane as Victims: Sex Stereotyping in Children's Readers.* It analyzed almost 2,800 stories in 134 elementary school readers used in three New Jersey suburbs during the 1970s. Most of the stories were about males: there were two and one-half times as many stories about boys as there were about girls, three times as many stories about men as about women, six times as many male biographies as female biographies, and even twice as many male animal stories as female animal stories. In the stories boys and men were portrayed as brave, creative, smart, diligent, and independent. Girls were most often timid, passive, adventureless, and dependent on boys to help them. Men were shown in 147 different occupations; women were shown in 26, mostly traditional female occupations.[106]

Gender Bias in Secondary Schools The problem persists in secondary school curriculum materials. A 1971 study of popular secondary U.S. history texts found that women were almost totally absent, and the little material devoted to women tended to be less than complimentary.[107] The 1992 study by the American Association of University Women, *How Schools Shortchange Girls,* concluded:

> Studies from the late 1980s reveal that although sexism has decreased in some elementary school texts and basal readers, the problem persists, especially at the secondary school level, in terms of what is considered important enough to study.
>
> A 1989 study of book-length works taught in high school English courses reports that, in a national sample of public, independent, and Catholic schools, the ten books assigned most frequently included only one written by a woman and none by members of minority groups. This research, which used studies from 1963 and 1907 as a base line, concludes that, "the lists of most frequently required books and authors are dominated by white males, with little change in overall balance from similar lists 25 or 80 years ago."[108]

The report noted that research during the 1980s and 1990s in other secondary school subject areas, such as social studies and foreign languages, showed similar developments. Research on social studies texts indicated that "while women were more often included, they are likely to be the usual 'famous women,' or women in protest movements. Rarely is there dual and balanced treatment of women and men, and seldom are women's perspectives and cultures presented on their own terms."[109] In instructional material for foreign languages the research commonly found "exclusion of girls, stereotyping of members of both sexes, subordination or degradation of girls, isolation of materials on women, superficiality of attention to contemporary issues or social problems, and cultural inaccuracy."[110]

Linda K. Christian-Smith's "Voices of Resistance: Young Women Readers of Romance Fiction" highlights an important curriculum issue with respect to young women with low reading ability in secondary schools.[111] Since the early 1980s teen romance novels have become the third most widely read young adult books. They are now a

$500-million-a-year industry.[112] The teen romance novels are designed for "reluctant readers" and are sold through school book clubs to students. Often students are allowed to substitute these works for more traditional English readings which they see as too difficult or too boring. The books are gender-differentiated, with mystery and adventure books for males and romance, dating, and problem-solving novels for females. Christian-Smith investigated the use of these romance novels in a midwestern city and intensively studied the reactions of about 30 young women to this literature. Not surprisingly, teachers were reluctant to allow their students to abandon traditional literature, but quickly acquiesced to pressure from both the students and educational authorities who demanded improvement in reading scores. The young women reported that the romance novels offered "escape, a way to get away from problems at home and school," "better reading than dreary textbooks," "enjoyment and pleasure," and "a way to learn about romance and dating."[113] Christian-Smith found that the young women often developed their own interpretations for the social situations portrayed in the novels. However, because teachers did not require discussion of these readings, the young women seldom had any opportunity to understand the novels in a way that would help them "to locate the contradictions between popular fiction's version of social relations and their own lives as well as help them to develop the critical tools necessary to make deconstructive readings that unearth political interests that shape the form as well as content of popular fiction."[114] Thus, "when young women read teen romance novels similar to Quin-Harkins *California Girl,* they become parts of a fictional world where men give meaning and completeness to women's lives and women's destinies are to tend the heart and hearth."[115]

The teen romance novel issue points to two problems faced by teenaged women in American schools. The first is the double burden of gender and class. Working-class and lower-class young women are faced with many curricular choices. Usually they are without guidance. Their families often do not have the experience, information, or knowledge necessary to provide useful guidance. The schools normally abrogate their responsibility to provide the essential guidance. Christian-Smith indicated that teachers did not long insist on providing reading guidance, and when students chose romance novels, teachers did not follow with discussions of the materials which might have provided an educationally sound experience. Carl A. Grant and Christine E. Sleeter note that schools generally provide resources for students but tend to take a *laissez-faire* attitude toward students, especially working-class students.[116] These students often then follow the "path of least resistance," taking the courses or completing the readings that are easiest or require the least amount of time and work. Often the students do not realize what is at stake when they make these decisions. Schools do not help make the issues clear.

The second problem highlighted by the teen romance novel issue is related to puberty, dating, and romance. As young women enter puberty they are presented gender roles by parents, television, movies, magazines, romance novels, and commercials. Most of these sources emphasize the importance of popularity. In order to be popular in contemporary American society, a young woman must cultivate the interest of young men. This requires both socially conditioned beauty and socially sanctioned demeanor. One of the young women in Christian-Smith's study put the issue succinctly: "The prettiest and most popular girls have their pick of the boys."[117] Girls are constantly bombarded by television and other mass media with models of beauty. Few, indeed, are the young women who can fit the conventional mold for beauty: slim, long slender legs, large—but not too large—breasts, blond, full-bodied hair, clear and fair complexion, between five feet two inches and five feet nine inches tall, fashionable clothes, and the latest cosmetics. It is little wonder that most young women spend a large amount of money, time, and energy on their physical appearance. And the results do not lead to self-satisfaction. A 1990 national survey discovered that only 29 percent of high school girls were "happy the way I am."[118] One should not be surprised that many young women are often depressed or that eating disorders are a problem among teenage girls.

If appearance concerns are not sufficient to distract many young women from academic matters, the demands of demeanor certainly do not contribute to their academic success. By the time young women reach the teen years they have learned the appropriate demeanor for a "popular" girl. Deference to male pride is essential. Girls must never "show up" boys. It is an unusual young woman who does not know that she is not supposed to seem smarter than the boys if she is to be popular. Deckard states, "The really popular, successful high school girl is not a 'brain' or even an athlete; she is a cheerleader. She embodies the supportive and admiring role assigned to girls. She is defined in terms of her relationship to boys."[119] It is relatively certain that this aspect of gender roles does not contribute to the academic success of young women. How much it detracts is a complex and difficult question. Unfortunately little research has been devoted to it.

Gender and Academic Achievement There is an enormous amount of research data on academic achievement and participation. Much of it is discussed in the AAUW report. Summarizing some significant recent studies, the report states:

> Despite a narrowing of the "gender gaps" in verbal and mathematical performance, girls are not doing as well as boys in our nation's schools. The physical sciences is one critical area in which girls continue to trail behind. More discouraging still, even the girls who take the same mathematics and science courses as boys and perform equally well in tests are much less apt to pursue scientific or technical careers than their male classmates. This is a "gender gap" our nation can no longer afford to ignore.[120]

It is well documented that as young women advance in high school and college they increasingly lower their estimation of their academic abilities and lower their goals.[121] Although the process leading to this condition is complex, it is difficult to ignore the central role of gender in the decline of self-confidence by young women. This decline in self-confidence results in many missed academic and career choices.

Evidence of Concern for Gender Equity

It would be comforting to believe that since the passage of Title IX in 1972, which mandates equal educational opportunity for girls and boys, there has been an increased awareness and marshaling of resources to eliminate gender inequality in American education. Indeed, there have been some encouraging signs. Female participation in high school athletics has increased from 4 percent to 26 percent and the success of U.S. women in team sports in the 1996 Olympics has been directly attributed to the success of Title IX.[122] There has been a narrowing of the achievement gap between males and females as measured by standardized tests. In some areas curriculum materials are less gender-biased. Some important research on gender equity and education has been published. On the whole, however, it is fair to say that the effort has been poorly financed and its results are less than sterling.

Researchers Myra and David Sadker have made Herculean efforts to bring gender equity to the attention of teacher educators. Nevertheless, in 1980 they conducted a study of what they considered the 24 most influential textbooks in the core areas of teacher education.[123] They believed it "likely that if teacher-education texts included the materials on sexism in schools and its possible impact on children, future teachers might be more likely to alleviate sex bias in the classroom."[124] What they found 8 years after the passage of Title IX was quite disappointing. Most of the texts simply ignored the issues of gender equity, a few made passing or vague mention of the problems, and none contained a full airing of the educational impact of sex bias. One is left with the impression that teacher education has yet to address the problems associated with gender and education. If future teachers do not learn about the effects of gender bias in education and how to combat those effects, it is unlikely that we will see major changes in classroom practices.

Since 1983, when the U.S. Department of Education issued its report *A Nation at Risk,* there have been at least 35 reports by major educational task forces. Only one addressed the question of gender equity.[125] At least part of the problem may be the fact that few women were members of the 35 groups issuing the reports. One had no woman. In only two did women comprise at least 50 percent of the membership. The 35 groups had a total of 834 male and only 171 female members.[126] Perhaps it should not be a surprise that there was very little mention and almost no discussion of gender issues as part of the problems facing American education.

Lack of adequate female representation in leadership positions is a continuing problem in American education. In 1991 only 9 of the 50 chief state school officers were women. Female representation on American local school boards increased from 10 percent in 1927 to only 33 percent in 1990. Also in 1990, 72 percent of all school teachers were women; however, 72 percent of school principals and 95 percent of superintendents were men.[127] These numbers represent only a slight improvement in the percentage of females in administrative posts in the past 20 years: in 1971, 99 percent of superintendents were men and 72 percent of principals were men.[128]

This disparity does not exist because there are many fewer qualified women available for administrative positions or because men are better educational administrators. One study in the mid-1970s showed that about the same number of male and female teachers had the necessary credentials, the major difference being that the median number of years of teaching experience before appointment to the principalship was only 5 for men while it was 15 for women.[129] There is no evidence to suggest that women are less effective than men as educational administrators. Indeed, a 1960s study by Neal Gross and Anne Trask showed that "professional performance of teachers and the amount of student learning were higher on the average in schools with women principals. Further, the morale of the staff did not depend on the gender of the principal."[130]

Remaining Barriers Many of the obstacles which colonial American women faced have been removed. The *de jure* barriers which kept women from educational institutions and professions in the early eras have been dismantled. Women can now enter primary and secondary schools and institutions of higher education. It is illegal to bar a woman from any educational setting simply because she is a woman. Unfortunately, we have discovered that admission to a school does not necessarily mean equal access to an education. Most of the current barriers hindering women from equal access to education involve societal definitions of gender and resulting social and educational practices.

Until American society begins to believe that all *persons* are equal and treats everyone as an individual rather than typing people according to group membership, we will continue to experience problems of equal educational opportunity. As long as we believe that women are different from men, with qualitatively different characteristics and abilities, we will continue to believe that certain occupations are for males and certain others are for females. The corresponding denigration of women's gender roles will continue to contribute to the vast inequality of income between women and men. The inevitable result is a lowering of self-esteem and a closure of opportunity for women.

The fact that societal attitudes and behaviors are central to the problem of equal educational opportunity for women is not an excuse for inaction on the part of schools or teachers. If we believe that every child has the right to the best education she or he can absorb, we must act to counter the damaging educational effects of gender bias. As teachers we have an obligation to understand the causes of any problem which inhibits the learning of any group of children. While this is much more easily said than done, schools in several communities throughout the country are showing us ways to teach all groups of children more successfully. We turn to this challenge in Chapter 13.

CONCLUDING REMARKS

This chapter has challenged a basic assumption underlying 20th-century schooling in the United States. The belief that in our educational system, a person's success in school and in economic life is based only on his or her own learning ability has been shown to be unfounded. This challenge was grounded in a critical examination of social science theories which purport to explain why some racial, ethnic, and social class groups consistently perform more poorly than others in schools and in the economy. In addition, gender differences in school and society were examined briefly for their contribution to understanding inequality and inequity in schooling.

Liberal ideology locates the source of school success and failure in individuals, and some educators are fond of the maxim that treating all students as individuals will ensure equitable educational experiences. Yet research indicates that the group differences in school performance cannot be attributed simply to individual talent and motivation without taking account of the cultural contexts that shape individuals. If individuals are importantly influenced by their cultures, and if students in American schools come from identifiably different cultural backgrounds, then treating all students as individuals requires attention to the cultural differences among them.

There is significant evidence that the content and processes of American schools have been relatively hospitable to the achievement of white, middle-class students, and it has been especially hospitable to white, middle-class male students. Certainly, females succeed in schools, too, as do a great many children from African-American, Hispanic, Native American, Asian, and other racial and ethnic backgrounds. But if members of any of those groups perform disproportionately poorly in schools, educators should become alerted to a possible mismatch between the school culture and the home culture of the student. All too often such an observation leads to two destructive misunderstandings. The first is that students from such mismatched cultural backgrounds are culturally (and, it is often thought, linguistically) deficient, and therefore the schools have to correct these deficiencies; the second is that any Native American, African-American, or Hispanic child necessarily has cultural barriers to surmount in school.

The cultural deficiency misunderstanding is grounded in the failure to recognize that students from different racial and ethnic backgrounds are already living in full and rich cultures with customs, histories, and linguistic systems that don't need correcting. Educators have no sufficient reason to believe that such students are not capable of learning rigorous academic material, and, to the contrary, there are shining examples of how schools can respond to such students to support their academic success. What needs to be recognized is that the American school's content and processes reflect the values and practices of a dominant culture that devalues the language, values, and practices of many minority cultures. Moreover, such students are too easily judged deficient by inadequate standards that are class- or race-biased. It would be more educationally sound for educators to examine the interaction of the school and the child, rather than just the performance of the child as measured by dominant standards. Some educators have developed an analysis of school experience which suggests that schools can indeed respond in ways that secure the success of students from subordinated cultures. Such responses demand a conception of cultural pluralism which respects diversity among peoples and among students' different ways of encountering the school culture.

Gender theory suggests a way to avoid the second misunderstanding: that an individual possesses certain characteristics just by virtue of belonging to a racial, ethnic, or gender group. To make such an assumption conforms to the definition of bias, and this is something which most educators wish to avoid. Yet to ignore ethnic or gender differences—to be "gender-neutral" or "race-neutral" in treatment of students, for example—may overlook a variable that is crucial to understanding a student's experience of the world and of school. If students come to school with very different preparations for success in the distinctively white middle-class school culture, then to ignore important differences in the effort to achieve "equal treatment" may lead to very inequitable results. It seems we are caught on the horns of a dilemma: to take account of students' group differences may be biased, but *not* to take account of them is to treat different learners as if they were the same, which will benefit some learners at the expense of others.

To treat students as individuals is, at its best, to try to take account of and respond to differences among students. If gender or cultural background is significant in making a student the individual he or she is, then there are times when that factor needs to be taken into account. Yet to assume that an African-American student should be treated differently simply because he is African-American, or that a girl needs special treatment because she is a girl, is to risk racial or gender bias. Jane Roland Martin's contribution to the solution of this dilemma has been the notion of "gender sensitivity," in which the teacher seeks to recognize when gender is a significant variable in student learning and when it is not. In addition, part of gender sensitivity is learning to celebrate and reward certain socialized feminine characteristics, such as caring, cooperation, and nurturance—which are not well-rewarded in society or in schooling—while at the same time helping female students develop the skills and self-confidence to succeed in traditionally male domains such as mathematics, science, and community leadership. Similarly, the contributions of all minority groups can be celebrated and affirmed while students from African-American, Native American, Asian, and Hispanic cultures are helped to succeed in the linguistic and academic skills that the dominant culture rewards. Culture sensitivity, however, is not just recognizing African-American History Month; it is learning to recognize when the subordinating forces of the dominant culture are interfering with a student's learning potential, and then seeking to equip students to respond to those forces. Not all African-American students, or all American students, experience such interference, and those who do may not experience it all the time. Being culturally sensitive and pluralistic requires one to learn to recognize when race or ethnicity, just as gender or social class, is a significant variable in a student's learning experience.

PRIMARY SOURCE READING

Robert Lake (Medicine Grizzlybear), a member of the Seneca and Cherokee Indian tribes, is an associate professor at Gonzaga University's School of Education in Spokane, Washington. His son, Wind-Wolf, knows the names and migration patterns of more than 40 birds. He knows there are 13 tail feathers on a perfectly balanced eagle. What Wind-Wolf needs is a teacher who can take his full measure.

AN INDIAN FATHER'S PLEA

Robert Lake (Medicine Grizzlybear)

Dear Teacher:

I would like to introduce you to my son, Wind-Wolf. He is probably what you would consider a typical Indian kid. He was born and raised on the reservation. He has black hair, dark brown eyes, and an olive complexion. And like so many Indian children his age, he is shy and quiet in the classroom. He is 5 years old, in kindergarten, and I can't understand why you have already labeled him a "slow learner."

At the age of 5, he has already been through quite an education compared with his peers in Western society. As his first introduction into this world, he was bonded to his mother and to the Mother Earth in a traditional native childbirth ceremony. And he has been continuously cared for by his mother, father, sisters, cousins, aunts, uncles, grandparents, and extended tribal family since this ceremony.

From his mother's warm and loving arms, Wind-Wolf was placed in a secure and specially designed Indian baby basket. His father and the medicine elders conducted another ceremony with him that served to bond him with the essence of his genetic father, the Great Spirit, the Grandfather Sun, and the Grandmother Moon. This was all done in order to introduce him properly into the new and natural world, not the world of artificiality, and to protect his sensitive and delicate soul. It is our people's way of showing the newborn respect, ensuring that he starts his life on the path of spirituality.

The traditional Indian baby basket became his "turtle's shell" and served as the first seat for his classroom. He was strapped in for safety, protected from injury by the willow roots and hazel wood construction. The basket was made by a tribal elder who had gathered her materials with prayer and in a ceremonial way. It is the same kind of basket that our people have used for thousands of years. It is specially designed to provide the child with the kind of knowledge and experience he will need in order to survive in his culture and environment.

Wind-Wolf was strapped in snugly with a deliberate restriction upon his arms and legs. Although you in Western society may argue that such a method serves to hinder motor-skill development and abstract reasoning, we believe it forces the child to first develop his intuitive faculties, rational intellect, symbolic thinking, and five senses. Wind-Wolf was with his mother constantly, closely bonded physically, as she carried him on her back or held him in front while breast-feeding. She carried him everywhere she went, and every night he slept with both parents. Because of this, Wind-Wolf's educational setting was not only a "secure" environment, but it was also very colorful, complicated, sensitive, and diverse. He has been with his mother at the ocean at daybreak when she made her prayers and gathered fresh seaweed from the rocks, he has sat with his uncles in a rowboat on the river while they fished with gill nets, and he has watched and listened to elders as they told creation stories and animal legends and sang songs around the campfires.

He has attended the sacred and ancient White Deerskin Dance of his people and is well acquainted with the cultures and languages of other tribes. He has been with his mother when she gathered herbs for healing and watched his tribal aunts and grandmothers gather and prepare traditional foods such as acorn, smoked salmon, eel, and deer meat. He has played with abalone shells,

Source: Teacher Magazine, September 1990, pp. 48–53.

pine nuts, iris grass string, and leather while watching the women make beaded jewelry and traditional native regalia. He has had many opportunities to watch his father, uncles, and ceremonial leaders use different kinds of colorful feathers and sing different kinds of songs while preparing for the sacred dances and rituals.

As he grew older, Wind-Wolf began to crawl out of the baby basket, develop his motor skills, and explore the world around him. When frightened or sleepy, he could always return to the basket, as a turtle withdraws into its shell. Such an inward journey allows one to reflect in privacy on what he has learned and to carry the new knowledge deeply into the unconscious and the soul. Shapes, sizes, colors, texture, sound, smell, feeling, taste, and the learning process are therefore functionally integrated—the physical and spiritual, matter and energy, conscious and unconscious, individual and social.

This kind of learning goes beyond the basics of distinguishing the difference between rough and smooth, square and round, hard and soft, black and white, similarities and extremes. For example, Wind-Wolf was with his mother in South Dakota while she danced for seven days straight in the hot sun, fasting, and piercing herself in the sacred Sun Dance Ceremony of a distant tribe. He has been doctored in a number of different healing ceremonies by medicine men and women from diverse places ranging from Alaska and Arizona to New York and California. He has been in more than 20 different sacred sweat-lodge rituals—used by native tribes to purify mind, body, and soul—since he was 3 years old, and he has already been exposed to many different religions of his racial brothers: Protestant, Catholic, Asian Buddhist, and Tibetan Lamaist.

It takes a long time to absorb and reflect on these kinds of experiences, so maybe that is why you think my Indian child is a slow learner. His aunts and grandmothers taught him to count and know his numbers while they sorted out the complex materials used to make the abstract designs in the native baskets. He listened to his mother count each and every bead and sort out numerically according to color while she painstakingly made complex beaded belts and necklaces. He learned his basic numbers by helping his father count and sort the rocks to be used in the sweat lodge—seven rocks for a medicine sweat, say, or 13 for the summer solstice ceremony. (The rocks are later heated and doused with water to create purifying steam.) And he was taught to learn mathematics by counting the sticks we use in our traditional native hand game. So I realize he may be slow in grasping the methods and tools that you are now using in your classroom, ones quite familiar to his white peers, but I hope you will be patient with him. It takes time to adjust to a new cultural system and learn new things.

He is not culturally "disadvantaged," but he is culturally "different." If you ask him how many months there are in a year, he will probably tell you 13. He will respond this way not because he doesn't know how to count properly, but because he has been taught by our traditional people that there are 13 full moons in a year according to the native tribal calendar and that there are really 13 planets in our solar system and 13 tail feathers on a perfectly balanced eagle, the most powerful kind of bird to use in ceremony and healing.

But he also knows that some eagles may only have 12 tail feathers, or seven, that they do not all have the same number. He knows that the flicker has exactly 10 tail feathers; that they are red and black, representing the directions of east and west, life and death; and that this bird is considered a "fire" bird, a power used in native doctoring and healing. He can probably count more than 40 different kinds of birds, tell you and his peers what kind of bird each is and where it lives, the seasons in which it appears, and how it is used in a sacred ceremony. He may have trouble writing his name on a piece of paper, but he knows how to say it and many other things in several different Indian languages. He is not fluent yet because he is only 5 years old and required by law to attend your educational system, learn your language, your values, your ways of thinking, and your methods of teaching and learning.

So you see, all of these influences together make him somewhat shy and quiet—and perhaps "slow" according to your standards. But if Wind-Wolf was not prepared for his first tentative foray into your world, neither were you appreciative of his culture. On the first day of class, you had difficulty with his name. You wanted to call him

Wind, insisting that Wolf somehow must be his middle name. The students in the class laughed at him, causing him further embarrassment.

While you are trying to teach him new methods, helping him learn new tools for self-discovery and adapt to his new learning environment, he may be looking out the window as if daydreaming. Why? Because he has been taught to watch and study the changes in nature. It is hard for him to make the appropriate psychic switch from the right to the left hemisphere of the brain when he sees the leaves turning bright colors, the geese heading south, and the squirrels scurrying around for nuts to get ready for a harsh winter. In his heart, in his young mind, and almost by instinct, he knows that this is the time of year he is supposed to be with his people gathering and preparing fish, deer meat, and native plants and herbs, and learning his assigned tasks in his role. He is caught between two worlds, torn by two distinct cultural systems.

Yesterday, for the third time in two weeks, he came home crying and said he wanted to have his hair cut. He said he doesn't have any friends at school because they make fun of his long hair. I tried to explain to him that in our culture, long hair is a sign of masculinity and balance and is a source of power. But he remained adamant in his position.

To make matters worse, he recently encountered his first harsh case of racism. Wind-Wolf had managed to adopt at least one good school friend. On the way home from school one day, he asked his new pal if he wanted to come home to play with him until supper. That was OK with Wind-Wolf's mother, who was walking with them. When they all got to the little friend's house, the two boys ran inside to ask permission while Wind-Wolf's mother waited. But the other boy's mother lashed out: "It is OK if you have to play with him at school, but we don't allow those kind of people in our house!" When my wife asked why not, the other boy's mother answered, "Because you are Indians and we are white, and I don't want my kids growing up with your kind of people."

So now my young Indian child does not want to go to school anymore (even though we cut his hair). He feels that he does not belong. He is the only Indian child in your class, and he is well aware of this fact. Instead of being proud of his race, heritage, and culture, he feels ashamed. When he watches television, he asks why the white people hate us so much and always kill our people in the movies and why they take everything away from us. He asks why the other kids in school are not taught about the power, beauty, and essence of nature or provided with an opportunity to experience the world around them firsthand. He says he hates living in the city and that he misses his Indian cousins and friends. He asks why one young white girl at school who is his friend always tells him, "I like you, Wind-Wolf, because you are a good Indian."

Now he refuses to sing his native songs, play with his Indian artifacts, learn his language, or participate in his sacred ceremonies. When I ask him to go to an urban powwow or help me with a sacred sweat-lodge ritual, he says no because "that's weird" and he doesn't want his friends at school to think he doesn't believe in God.

So, dear teacher, I want to introduce you to my son, Wind-Wolf, who is not really a "typical" little Indian kid after all. He stems from a long line of hereditary chiefs, medicine men and women, and ceremonial leaders whose accomplishments and unique forms of knowledge are still being studied and recorded in contemporary books. He has seven different tribal systems flowing through his blood; he is even part white. I want my child to succeed in school and in life. I don't want him to be a dropout or juvenile delinquent or to end up on drugs and alcohol because he is made to feel inferior or because of discrimination. I want him to be proud of his rich heritage and culture, and I would like him to develop the necessary capabilities to adapt to, and succeed in, both cultures. But I need your help.

What you say and what you do in the classroom, what you teach and how you teach it, and what you don't say and don't teach will have a significant effect on the potential success or failure of my child. Please remember that this is the primary year of his education and development. All I ask is that you work with me, not against me, to help educate my child in the best way. If you don't have the knowledge, preparation, experience, or training to effectively deal with culturally different children, I am willing to help you with the few resources I have available or direct you to such resources.

Millions of dollars have been appropriated by Congress and are being spent each year for "Indian Education." All you have to do is take advantage of it and encourage your school to make an effort to use it in the name of "equal education." My Indian child has a constitutional right to learn, retain, and maintain his heritage and culture. By the same token, I strongly believe that non-Indian children also have a constitutional right to learn about our Native American heritage and culture, because Indians play a significant part in the history of Western society. Until this reality is equally understood and applied in education as a whole, there will be a lot more schoolchildren in grades K–12 identified as "slow learners."

My son, Wind-Wolf, is not an empty glass coming into your class to be filled. He is a full basket coming into a different environment and society with something special to share. Please let him share his knowledge, heritage, and culture with you and his peers.

Lake reports that Wind-Wolf, now 8, is doing better in school, but the boy's struggle for cultural identity continues.

QUESTIONS FOR DISCUSSION AND EXAMINATION

1. As you consider the prospects of academic success for Wind-Wolf in the reading for this chapter, how do you assess his potential as a learner in American schools? What characteristics in Wind-Wolf, in the school, and in the interaction between the student and the school need to be addressed to answer this question thoroughly? Finally, how can teachers best respond to Wind-Wolf to make his academic success as well as his cultural self-respect more likely? Support your position.
2. We often think of "motivation" as a highly individualistic character trait. Individuals within any racial or ethnic group may be highly motivated to achieve or apparently lacking in motivation altogether. Yet some authors argue that ethnicity is important in shaping motivation to learn and other attitudes toward schooling. Evaluate this argument.
3. This chapter focuses on gender as well as on race, ethnicity, and social class in considering the issue of educational and social equity as it concerns different groups of students. To what degree do you find that considering all these different variables in one treatment obscures important differences among them, and to what degree does it illuminate similarities that are profitably considered together? Defend your view.

NOTES

1. R. H. Tawney, *Equality,* 4th ed. (London: George Allen and Unwin, 1952), pp. 49–50.
2. See Clarence J. Karier et al., *The Roots of Crisis* (Chicago: Rand McNally, 1973), esp. chaps. 3, 5, and 6.
3. See Paul C. Violas, *The Training of the Urban Working-Class* (Chicago: Rand McNally, 1978).
4. "Brown et al. v. Board of Education at Topeka et al." August 1952, 1953, 1954. 347 US 483(1954). U.S. Supreme Court decision written by Chief Justice Earl Warren.
5. Michael Harrington, *The Other America: Poverty in the United States* (New York: MacMillan, 1962).
6. Hyman Rickover, *Education and Freedom* (New York: Dutton, 1959).
7. Arthur Bestor, *Educational Wastelands: The Retreat from Learning in Our Public Schools* (Urbana: University of Illinois Press, 1953).
8. Nat Hentoff, *Our Children Are Dying* (New York: Viking Press, 1966).
9. Samuel Bowles and Henry Levin, "The Determinants of Scholastic Achievement," *Journal of Human Resources,* Vol. 2 (Winter 1968), pp. 3–25.
10. Fredrick Mosteller and Daniel P. Moynihan, *On Equality of Educational Opportunity: Papers Deriving from the Harvard University Faculty Seminar on the Coleman Report* (New York: Random House, 1972).
11. It is not without interest that Daniel Moynihan had 5 years earlier paved the way for such an argument with his work *The Negro Family* (Cambridge: 1967). In it he argued that a major reason for African-American inequality was structural defects in the black family. This conclusion was soundly criticized by historians Herbert G. Gutman, *The Black Family in Slavery and Freedom, 1750–1925* (New York: 1976); and James D. Anderson, "Black Conjugations," *The American Scholar,* Vol. 46, No. 3 (Summer 1977), pp. 384–93.
12. C. Jencks et al., *Inequality: A Reassessment of the Effect of Family and Schooling in America* (New York: Harper & Row, 1973). A summary of the conclusions of *Inequality* was published under the title "The Schools and Equal Opportunity," *Saturday Review/Education,* Vol. 55, No. 38 (October 1972), pp. 37–42.

13. Jencks also suggested that, since schools could not improve economic inequality, the government should institute a guaranteed-income program to ensure everyone an income equal to one-half the national average. In assuming that economic inequality is both natural and functional, Jencks again showed his modern liberal moorings. The concern of modern liberal reform has always been simply to reduce the gap between the extremes of wealth and poverty.
14. H. M. Levin, "Schooling and Inequality: The Social Science Objectivity Gap," *Saturday Review/Education* (December 1972), pp. 49–51.
15. Ibid., p. 2.
16. *The American Almanac, 1996–97: Statistical Abstract of the United States* (Austin, Texas: Hoover's, Inc. 1966) 16, 443. Also, Andrew L. Shapiro, *We're Number One* (New York: Vintage Books, 1992), pp. 75–76.
17. From *The American Almanac 1996–97,* p. 170; *The Condition of Education,* Vol. 1 (Elementary and Secondary Education) (Washington, D.C.: U.S. Department of Education, 1988). Also, *1994 Information Please Almanac,* pp. 863, 864.
18. *Statistical Abstract of the United States 1993,* p. 457. Also, Shapiro, *We're Number One,* p. 77; *The American Almanac 1996–97,* p. 466.
19. Cashmore, Ellis (1996). *Dictionary of Race and Ethnic Relations, 4th ed.* (London and New York: Routledge).
20. Salopek, Paul (1997). We Are All the Same. *Chicago Tribune* (April 27) p. 1.
21. West, Cornel. *Race Matters* (Boston: Beacon Press, 1993).
22. Herard, Vladimire (1996). Schools Failing Minorities. *The Chicago Defender* (December 4) p. 1; and *The American Alamanac 1996–97: Statistical Abstract of the United States.* (Austin, TX: Hoover's, Inc., 1997) pp. 159, 204, 219.
23. Sheldon Danzinger, "The Poor," in David W. Hornbeck and Lester M. Salamon, eds., *Human Capital and America's Future* (Baltimore: Johns Hopkins Press, 1991), p. 153.
24. Andrew Hacker, *Two Nations: Separate, Hostile, Unequal* (New York: Charles Scribner's Sons, 1992), p. 94.
25. Harold Hodgkinson, "Reform versus Reality," in Fred Schultz, ed., *Education 93/94* (Guilford, CT: Dushkin Publishing Group, 1993), p. 39.
26. Economics and Statistics Administration, U.S. Department of Commerce, *The American Almanac 1996–97: Statistical Abstract of the United States* (Austin: Hoover's, Inc. 1996), p. 466.
27. Economics and Statistics Administration, *The American Almanac,* p. 460.
28. Ibid.
29. Ibid., p. 477.
30. Ibid., p. 469; *The American Almanac 1996–97, p. 473.*
31. Ibid.
32. Hacker, *Two Nations,* p. 95.
33. Ibid., pp. 103–104.
34. *The American Almanac,* pp. 46–50.
35. *Asian American Handbook* (Chicago: National Conference of Christians and Jews, Asian American Journalists Association, and Association of Asian Pacific American Artists, 1991), pp. 9, 73.
36. *The American Almanac,* p. 367.
37. Ibid., pp. 63–64.
38. Hodgkinson, "Reform versus Reality," p. 37.
39. *The American Almanac,* p. 469.
40. Hodgkinson, "Reform versus Reality," p. 36.
41. Shapiro, *We're Number One,* pp. 17–18.
42. These comparisons are found in Marian Wright Edelman, *Families in Peril—An Agenda for Social Change* (Cambridge, MA: Harvard University Press, 1987).
43. Gary Orfield, "Separate Societies: Have the Kerner Warnings Come True?" in F. R. Harris and R. W. Wilkins, eds., *Quiet Riots—Race and Poverty in the United States* (New York: Pantheon, 1988), pp. 106–10. Hacker, *Two Nations,* p. 162.
44. Marian Wright Edelman, *The Measure of Our Success: A Letter to My Children and Yours* (Boston: Beacon Press, 1992), pp. 23, 24.
45. All statistics in this paragraph are from *Digest of Education Statistics 1988* (Washington, D.C.: U.S. Department of Education, Office of Educational Research and Improvement, September 1988).
46. Statistics for African-American households are from Hacker, *Two Nations,* pp. 68, 94: and *The American Almanac,* p. 153.
47. *The American Almanac,* p. 465.
48. *1992 Information Please Almanac,* pp. 54, 56; Shapiro, *We're Number One,* pp. 10–11.
49. Clarence Karier, "Testing for Order and Control in the Corporate Liberal State," *Educational Theory* 22 (Spring 1972), pp. 154–80. Also see Paul Violas, "Progressive Social Philosophy: Charles Horton Cooley and Edward Alsworth Ross," in Karier et al., *The Roots of Crisis,* pp. 40–65.
50. *The American Almanac,* p. 470.
51. Ibid., p. 153.
52. Philip Mattera, *Prosperity Lost* (Reading, MA: Addison-Wesley, 1990), p. 15.
53. Figures are taken from a recap of Dye's work in Steven Tozer, "Elite Power and Democratic Ideals," in *Society as Educator in an Age of Transition,* Eighty-sixth Yearbook of the National Society for the Study

of Education, ed. Kenneth D. Benne and Steven Tozer (Chicago: University of Chicago Press, 1987).
54. C. Wright Mills, *The Power Elite* (New York: Oxford University Press, 1956).
55. This argument is presented in summary form in Tozer, "Elite Power and Democratic Ideals."
56. Figures in this paragraph come from *New York Times*, September 22, 1988, and the National Center for Education Statistics, Announcement 92-129a, October 1992.
57. R. Wilson and S. C. Melendez, *Second Annual Report on the Status of Minorities in Higher Education* (Washington, D.C.: Office of Minority Concerns, American Council on Education, 1983). Also, *Statistical Abstract of the United States 1993*, p. 153.
58. Robert Pool, "Who Will Do Science in the 1990s?" *News & Comment*, April 27, 1990, pp. 433–35.
59. David Owen, *None of the Above* (Boston: Houghton Mifflin, 1985); Myra Sadker and David Sadker, *Failing at Fairness: How America's Schools Cheat Girls* (New York: Charles Scribner's Sons, 1994).
60. National Coalition of Advocates for Students, *Barriers to Excellence: Our Children at Risk* (Boston, MA: The Coalition, 1985).
61. *The American Almanac*, p. 160.
62. Jennifer Hochschild, *Thirty Years after Brown* (Washington, D.C.: Joint Center for Policy Studies, 1985), p. 3. Hacker, *Two Nations*, pp. 162–63.
63. "The Numbers Game," *Time*, Vol. 142, No. 21 (Fall 1993), p. 15.
64. "Linguistic Diversity in the USA," *USA Today*, December 15, 1993, 9A.
65. Ronald Takaki, *Strangers from a Different Shore* (New York: Penguin Books, 1989), p. 475.
66. Ibid., p. 49.
67. Ibid.
68. Valerie Ooka Pang, "Asian-American Children: A Diverse Population," *Educational Forum*, Vol. 55, No. 1, pp. 49–66.
69. Irwin S. Kirsch, Ann Jungeblut, Lynn Jenkins, and Andrew Kolstad, *Adult Literacy in America* (Washington, D.C.: Educational Testing Service, 1993), p. 33.
70. Chan, Sucheng (1991). *Asian Americans: An Interpretive History.* (New York: Twayne Publishers) p. 3.
71. Chan (1991), p. 145.
72. *The State of Asian Pacific America: Policy Issues of the Year 2020* (1993). (Los Angeles: LEAP Asian Pacific American Public Policy Institute and UCLA Asian American Studies Center). p. 26.
73. Chan (1991), p. 187–88.
74. Holli, Melvin G. and Peter d' A. Jones (eds). *Ethnic Chicago: A Multicultural Portrait* (Grand Rapids: William B. Eerdmans Publishing Co. 1995) p. 346.
75. Carasquillo, Angela L. (1991), *Hispanic Children and Youth in the U.S.* (New York: Garland). p. 24.
76. *Ibid.*, p. 4.
77. Cisneros and Leone, (1995), Editors Introduction. *The Bilingual Research Journal* (Summer, Fall, 19:3 and 4), p. 361.
78. Holli and Jones (1995), p. 346.
79. Laura E. Perez, "Opposition and the Education of Chicana/os," in Cameron McCarthy and Warren Crichlow, eds., *Race Identity and Representation in Education* (New York: Routledge, 1993), p. 276.
80. Ibid., p. 276.
81. Thomas Toch, *In the Name of Excellence* (New York: Oxford University Press, 1991), p. 127.
82. These conclusions are drawn from a study by Jean Anyon, "Social Class and School Knowledge," in *Curriculum Inquiry*, Vol. 2, No. 1 (1981), pp. 3–42.
83. This issue is explored in a nicely detailed account by Annette Lareau of Southern Illinois University in "Social Class Differences in Family-School Relationships: The Importance of Cultural Capital," *Sociology of Education*, Vol. 60 (April 1987), pp. 73–85.
84. The last conclusion relates to the field of sociolinguistics. Exemplars include the works of William Labov, Basil Bernstein, and Michael Stubbs. See also the Primary Source Reading of this chapter.
85. Judith D. Singer and John A. Butler, "The Education for All Handicapped Children Act: Schools as Agents of Social Reform," *Harvard Educational Review*, Vol. 57, No. 2 (May 1987), p. 125.
86. *The American Almanac*, p. 166.
87. Toch, *In The Name of Excellence*, p. 125.
88. Ibid., p. 126.
89. Ibid., pp. 126–27.
90. Ibid., p. 127.
91. Ibid.
92. Peggy Orenstein, *School Girls: Young Women, Self Esteem, and the Confidence Gap* (New York: Doubleday, 1994), and Myra Sadker and David Sadker, *Failing at Fairness: How America's Schools Cheat Girls* (New York: Charles Scribner's Sons, 1994).
93. Barbara Sinclair Deckard, "The Self-Fulfilling Prophecy: Sex Role Socialization," in Barbara Sinclair Deckard, ed., *The Women's Movement: Political, Socioeconomic and Psychological Issues*, 2d ed. (New York: Harper & Row, 1979), p. 29.
94. Ibid., p. 30.
95. AAUW report, *How Schools Shortchange Girls* (Wellesley, MA: American Association of University Women Educational Foundation and National Education Association, 1992), p. 10.
96. Lawrence Kohlberg, "A Cognitive-Developmental Analysis of Children's Sex-Role Concepts and Attitudes," quoted in Deckard, p. 32.

97. Kristen Amundsen, *The Silenced Majority* (Englewood Cliffs, NJ: Prentice Hall, 1971), pp. 116–17.
98. L. Serbin et al., "A Comparison of Teacher Responses to Pre-Academic and Problem Behavior of Boys and Girls," *Child Development,* Vol. 44 (1973), pp. 796–804; M. Ebbeck, "Equity for Boys and Girls: Some Important Issues," *Early Child Development and Care,* Vol. 18 (1984), pp. 119–31.
99. Myra P. Sadker and David M. Sadker, *Sex Equity Handbook for Schools* (New York: Longman, 1982), pp. 107–9; Carol S. Dweck et al., "Sex Differences in Learned Helplessness, II: The Contingencies of Evaluative Feedback in the Classroom" and "III: An Experimental Analysis," *Development Psychology,* Vol. 14, No. 3 (1978), pp. 268–76; Judith M. Bardwick, *Psychology of Women* (New York: Harper & Row, 1971), p. 113.
100. M. Sadker and D. Sadker, "Sex Equity and Special Education," *The Pointer,* Vol. 26 (1981), pp. 33–38.
101. D. Sadker and M. Sadker, "Is the Classroom OK?," *Phi Delta Kappan,* Vol. 55 (1985), pp. 358–67.
102. Veronica F. Nieva and Barbara A. Gutek, "Sex Effects on Evaluation," *Academy of Management Review,* Vol. 5, No. 2 (1980), pp. 267–76.
103. Phillip Goldberg, "Are Women Prejudiced against Women?" *Trans-Action,* Vol. 5 (1968), pp. 28–30.
104. Angele M. Parker, "Sex Differences in Classroom Intellectual Argumentation," unpublished M.S. Thesis, Pennsylvania State University, 1973; R. Simmons and D. Blyth, *Moving into Adolescence: The Impact of Pubertal Change and the School Context* (New York: Aldine de Gruyter Press, 1978), p. 227.
105. P. Arnow and C. Froschl, "Textbook Analysis," in F. Howe, ed., *High School Feminists Studies* (Old Westbury, N.Y.: Feminist Press, 1976); Kathryn P. Scott and Candace Garrett Shau, "Sex Equity and Sex Bias in Instructional Materials," in S. Klien, ed., *Handbook for Achieving Sex Equity through Education* (Baltimore: Johns Hopkins Press, 1985), pp. 218–36; G. Britton and M. Lumpkin, *A Consumer's Guide to Sex, Race, and Career Bias in Public School Textbooks* (Corvallis, OR: Britton Associates, 1977); M. Hulme, "Mirror, Mirror on the Wall: Biased Reflections in Textbooks and Instructional Materials," in A. Carelli, ed., *Sex Equity in Education: Readings and Strategies* (Springfield, IL: Charles C. Thompson, 1988), pp. 187–208; Marjorie B. U'Ren, "The Image of Women in Textbooks," in Vivian Gornick and Barbara K. Morgan, eds., *Women in Sexist Society* (New York: Signet, 1971); L. Weitzman and D. Russi, *Biased Textbooks and Images in Elementary School Textbooks* (Washington, D.C.: Resource Center on Sex Roles in Education, 1976).
106. *Dick and Jane as Victims* (Princeton, NJ: Women on Words and Images, 1972), pp. 6–27.
107. J. Trecker, "Women in U.S. History High School Textbooks," *Social Education,* Vol. 35, No. 3 (1971), pp. 249–60, 338.
108. AAUW report, *How Schools Shortchange Girls,* p. 62.
109. Ibid., p. 62.
110. Ibid., p. 63.
111. In Lois Weis and Michelle Fine, eds., *Beyond Silenced Voices: Race, Class, and Gender in United States Schools* (Albany: State University of New York Press, 1993), pp. 169–90.
112. Ibid., pp. 170–71.
113. Ibid., p. 176.
114. Ibid., p. 187.
115. Ibid., pp. 169–70.
116. Carl A. Grant and Christine E. Sleeter, "Race, Class and Gender and Abandoned Dreams," *Teachers College Record,* Vol. 90, No. 1 (Fall 1988), pp. 19–40.
117. Linda K. Christian-Smith. "Voices of Resistance: Young Women Readers of Romance Fiction," in Lois Weis and Michelle Fine, eds., *Beyond Silenced Voices,* pp. 183–184.
118. AAUW report, p. 12.
119. Barbara Sinclair Deckard, p. 43.
120. AAUW report, p. 16.
121. AAUW report, pp. 48, 67, 70; Sumru Erkit, "Expectancy, Attribution, and Academic Achievement: Exploring Implications of Sex-Role Orientation," Working Paper No. 27, Wellesley College Center for Research on Women, 1979.
122. Ibid., p. 45. This still represents only one-half of the male participation.
123. M. Sadker and D. Sadker, "Sexism in Teacher Education Texts," *Harvard Educational Review,* Vol. 50, No. 1 (February 1980), pp. 36–46.
124. Ibid., p. 37.
125. AAUW report, pp. 6–8.
126. Ibid., pp. 6, 90–91.
127. Ibid., p. 7.
128. Kathleen D. Lyman and Jeanne J. Spieler, "Advancing in School Administration," *Harvard Educational Review,* Vol. 50, No. 1 (February 1980), p. 25.
129. Suzanne E. Estler, "Women as Leaders in Public Education," *Signs,* Vol. 1 (1975), pp. 363–85, cited in Lyman and Spieler, p. 27.
130. Ibid., p. 29.

CHAPTER 13

Diversity and Equity Today: Meeting the Challenge

Chapter 12 explored how such variables as race, ethnicity, gender, and economic class can affect different groups' experiences in school and in the wider society. It seems clear that many people experience social institutions differently, according to their group memberships. Further, these differences seem regularly to advantage those whose group membership is white, economically middle-class or better, and male. This is not to claim that people of color, people from low-income backgrounds, and females never succeed in this country's educational and social institutions; virtually anyone reading this book knows of such successes. Rather, we tried to show that trends or patterns of inequality often influence an individual's life chances not simply on the basis of that individual's native abilities and applied efforts, but also on the basis of that individual's membership in one or more ethnic, gender, or economic groups.

Institutional biases along lines of class, ethnicity, and gender are, as Chapter 12 demonstrated, alive and persistent in the 1990s. Simply watching the newspapers carefully can reveal dimensions of the challenge to educators, as research studies are often reported in the press. For three decades, for example, girls have scored substantially lower than boys on the SAT exam, thus receiving only 40 percent of the National Merit Scholarships despite outnumbering boys 56 percent to 44 percent in taking the PSAT, the first step of that scholarship competition.[1] Turning to the performance of Hispanic and African-American students on standardized measures of academic proficiency, recent comparisons to white, non-Hispanic students show that the gaps between minority and majority students are once again growing.[2] Meanwhile, despite a booming national economy, the poverty rates for African-Americans and Hispanics are more than double, almost triple, the poverty rate of white non-Hispanics, which bodes ill for future educational attainment for large numbers of people from those ethnic groups.[3]

These inequalities take place in two (among many) problematic institutional contexts: the first is the wider United States society, in which countless acts of overt racism (including prosecutable hate crimes) are committed every single day, while institutional racism is thoroughly embedded in the socioeconomic system.[4] The second context is school, in which taken-for-granted approaches to testing, grouping, and tracking students work against the success of low-income and minority students, while at the same time appearing to many educators and the public to be consistent with good educational and democratic practice.[5]

It is important to engage in critical study of the nature and consequences of racism and sexism in this country's social institutions, especially in schools, which influence young people's perceptions of themselves and others in important ways. But critique is not enough; it is also important to examine ways in which schools and teachers can serve the interests of all children equally well, rather than contributing unequally to the position of advantaged groups. Although we can certainly locate the sources of school inequities outside the schools, in the larger socioeconomic system, this wider system does not necessarily *determine* what goes on in schools and classrooms. It would be more accurate to say that the wider society *influences* the classroom. Just as individuals from disadvantaged groups can succeed against the statistical odds, so can individual schools and classrooms chart independent courses against prevailing patterns of inequality. But how? What do we know about schools and teachers that might help us see what must be done so that children from low-income groups, for example, will be allowed to succeed on the basis of their talents rather than on the basis of whether they were born into the "right" demographic category? The purpose of this chapter is to examine what we know about meeting the challenges of diversity and equity in contemporary schools.

JANE ELLIOTT'S EXPERIMENT

It is enlightening to reflect on the following experiment conducted by an elementary school teacher. She was initially motivated toward the experiment in April 1968 while watching the television coverage following the murder of Martin Luther King, Jr. The death of a national figure was sad enough, but Jane Elliott was stunned by the insensitivity of newscasters interviewing African-American leaders: "Who is going to hold your people together now? What will they do? Who will control their anger?"[6]

Jane Elliott was a third-grade teacher in Riceville, Iowa, an all-white, all-Christian farming community, population 898. When she arrived at class the next day, her children had already heard the news. And Elliott had already made up her mind to teach them what prejudice and discrimination were really about. The experiment she conducted that day and repeated in subsequent years would eventually make national news. It would also project Elliott to national prominence following a documentary special by ABC News titled "The Eye of the Storm."[7]

Most of the children had had little contact with African-American people. What they knew of African-Americans would have come from their parents and from television. So Elliott started there. As the children described their impressions, a pattern began to emerge: African-American people were poor; they did not manage as well as white people; they were not as smart, not as honest, not as civilized, not as moral; they fought a lot and were prone to riot; they smelled bad. The children were not being mean or vindictive. They were saying matter of factly what they had picked up here and there regarding the nature of African-American people. Elliott pressed further. Are African-Americans discriminated against? Yes. Do they deserve it? Well, maybe not. How would you feel if you were discriminated against? Not very good. These were all nice, appropriate responses. But Elliott knew from experience and observation that these are the common sentiments of a nation that is, in the opinion of many, fundamentally racist.[8]

How would it feel to be an African-American boy or girl? Would you like to find out what discrimination feels like? she asked. Her students said they would. The children were lumped into two status groups. The 17 children in her class who had blue eyes became one group. The other group, called the "brown eyes," consisted of the 11 children whose eyes actually were brown and the 3 children who had green eyes.

"Today, the blue-eyed people will be on the bottom and the brown-eyed people on the top," Elliott explained. To their questioning looks she added, "What I mean is that brown-eyed people are better than blue-eyed people. They are more civilized than blue-eyed people. And they are smarter than blue-eyed people."

Because of these traits, Elliott continued, different rules would have to apply, depending upon whether a child had blue eyes or brown eyes. Brown-eyed children could use the drinking fountain, but blue-eyed children had to use a paper cup. Brown-eyed children would have five extra minutes of recess. But inferior, blue-eyed children were not allowed to play with them, unless specifically invited to do so. Nor could blue-eyed children use the big playground equipment.

Brown-eyed children got to go to lunch first, could go back for seconds, and could choose their lunch-line partners. None of the blue-eyed children were allowed those special privileges. When asked why these various rules should apply, the brown-eyed children eagerly supplied reasons. Jane Elliott nodded her approval.

The children caught on very quickly, and they assumed their various roles with chilling realism. Once the sense of it was clear, the roles became real and the children entered into the constructed reality. Elliott continued to play her role. Every time a blue-eyed child made a mistake, she identified it as evidence of inferiority. Every time a blue-eyed child had difficulty reading, she shook her head and asked a brown-eyed student to take over. She said later:

> By the lunch hour, there was no need to think before identifying a child as blue- or brown-eyed. I could tell simply by looking at him. The brown-eyed children were happy, alert, having the time of their lives. And they were doing far better work than they had ever done before. The blue-eyed children were miserable. Their posture, their expressions, their entire attitudes were those of defeat. Their classroom work regressed sharply from that of the day before. Inside of an hour or so, they looked and acted as though they were, in fact, inferior. It was shocking.

The following Monday she reversed the scheme: "I lied to you on Friday. I told you brown-eyed people were better than blue-eyed people. That's not true. The truth is that blue-eyed people are better than brown-eyed people. They are smarter than brown-eyed people. They are more civilized. They are . . ."

As easily as that she reversed the roles, and once again the children entered into their assigned identities. Those children who had been discriminated against on Friday were gleeful, and many of them were bent on revenge. Those brown-eyed children who had felt like "hot shots," who had felt "smarter, bigger, better, and stronger," quickly learned how demoralizing it is to be categorized and treated as inferior.

Later, Jane Elliott would write:

> All of the children enjoyed being considered superior. . . . But some of them took a savage delight in keeping the members of the "inferior" group in their place, in asserting their superiority in particularly nasty ways. . . Nor had I realized until I saw it how destructive a feeling of inferiority really is, how it can literally change a personality, how it can drag down efficiency, destroy motivation.[9]

Jane Elliott's Discrimination Day exercises were repeated for many years, and at the request of business and government she has subjected adult audiences to the same experience, with strikingly similar results. With few exceptions, members of a group identified as superior tend to act and feel superior. Curiously, Elliott discovered that members of the "superior" group gained new confidence in their schoolwork, glimpsed new capabilities in themselves, and actually shot ahead academically. Those identified as inferior tended to accept the constraint, lost confidence in themselves, could not concentrate, and suffered a measurable decline in academic performance. When the experiments were over, Jane Elliott conducted a skillful debriefing, restored shattered friendships and crushed egos, and helped her students draw from the experience the important lessons it contains.

THEORIES OF SOCIAL INEQUALITY

Jane Elliott's experiment can help us develop a theory, or at least hypotheses, about factors that lead to school success or failure. If we are to understand how to respond to social and educational inequalities, we need to understand them. In this section, we will examine three different theoretical approaches to explaining inequality in society and in school performance. These theories differ significantly in where they locate the source of inequality. A theory of genetic inferiority locates it in the individual; a theory of cultural deprivation, also recognizable as cultural or linguistic deficit theory, locates it in the individual's home culture; finally, a theory of cultural subordination locates it in the structural relationships of power differences between different social groups. These labels themselves suggest which theory Jane Elliott may have found most compatible with her own view.

The first two theories, genetic inferiority and cultural deficit, are taken from liberal social and intellectual traditions, which assume that individuals craft their own destinies. The theories often lead to the conclusion that society and the law should leave individuals alone to rise or sink according to their own merit. Most important, these theories tend to embrace a particular view of the world that we have previously identified as a middle-class, scientific worldview, a cultural orientation that Henry Giroux refers to as technocratic rationality.[10] As we shall see, theories of genetic or cultural inferiority stem from modern liberalism because they leave the existing social order essentially intact, they vindicate the liberal resistance to a government role in individual (but not corporate) economic success and failure, and they locate the source of social inequalities in the victims themselves.

The third type of theory derives from that branch of thought called critical theory, which is characterized by a willingness to question the existing rules of society and to locate the source of inequalities in social structural arrangements rather than in individuals or groups. Critical theorists see inequitable power relations in society as the fundamental source of social, economic, and educational inequality among social groups.

Genetic Inferiority Theory

Long ago, Plato wrote that one social group could subordinate another social group only if it were able to tell convincingly a certain "necessary lie." The full account is in the *Republic,* Book III (414A–415E). Here is the essential passage:

> "[You] are all brothers in the city," we shall tell them in our fable, "but while God molded you, he mingled gold in the generation of some, and those are the ones fit to rule, who are therefore the most precious; he mingled silver in the assistants; and iron and brass in farmers and the other craftsmen."

This necessary lie is known as the "myth of the metals." It is the classic statement of that imagined, God-given superiority that justifies social inequalities in the minds of those whose chances for success have been greatly enhanced by inclusion in the dominant social group. Later, during medieval times, the nobility was sanctioned by church authorities as having been ordained by God to rule over commoners. The myth of the metals persists even to the present. Here, in a passage written in 1923 by educational psychologist Lewis Terman, is its modern equivalent dressed in scientific terminology:

> Preliminary investigations indicate that an I.Q. below 70 rarely permits anything better than unskilled labor; that the range from 70 to 80 is preeminently that of semi-skilled labor, from 80 to 100 that of the skilled or ordinary clerical labor, from 100 to 110 or 115 that of the semi-professional pursuits; and that above all these are the grades of intelligence which permit one to enter the professions or the larger fields of business.[11]

The myth of the metals has thus been transformed into the myth of the IQ score, whose scientific appearance makes it seem even more convincing and potent. Terman's passage offers an explanation of social classes in terms of genetic intelligence. The same criteria can easily be adapted to racial and ethnic inequalities. Here is a sample from a passage written during the early part of this century by Henry Garret, in a pamphlet entitled *Breeding Down:*

> You can no more mix the two races and maintain the standards of White civilization than you can add 80 (the average I.Q. of Negroes) and 100 (average I.Q. of Whites), divide by two and get 100. What you would get would be a race of 90s, and it is that 10 percent differential that spells the difference between a spire and a mud hut.[12]

Garret does not specify to which aspects of white civilization he is referring—certainly not the period of the Thirty Years' War in Europe, when ignorance, disease, poverty, filth, and sheer animal savagery prevailed. Nor does he specify which standards of African civilization he has in mind, though he probably does not mean the ancient dynasties of Egypt, in which all modern European civilizations are ultimately grounded.

Theories of genetic inferiority are tenacious in part because they appeal to the self-images of those judged to be superior. Jane Elliott's Discrimination Day exercise demonstrates how vigorous that particular reflex is. The theories are also tenacious, as Plato suggests, because they are so useful to those in power: Nothing can be done, or should be done, to compensate inferior human stock; unequal outcomes should be expected and are clearly justified. In this view, crumbs from the master's table are given as charity, a gesture that elevates the moral worth of the giver. No changes are called for in the social order, and any efforts to control and regulate the activities of the inferior group are accepted as necessary and benevolent. Likewise, efforts to locate inferior groups socially, politically, and economically are justified, lest such groups corrupt civilization's fragile growth.

The genetic, or biological, argument has been repeatedly used to rationalize the suppression of racial minorities, females, and people from lower socioeconomic classes. It has been particularly evident in white discrimination against African-American people, in part because of its continuity with the racist beliefs that once sustained slavery. Its modern, pseudo-scientific defense is exemplified by Arthur Jensen, William Shockley, and Richard Herrnstein, each of whom has used interpretations of IQ and standardized test scores as part of the effort to explain the "findings" of the Coleman, Moynihan-Mosteller, and Jencks studies.[13]

The Jensen and Herrnstein studies, conducted in the late 1960s, were built on the following assumptions: (1) that IQ tests are valid measures of intelligence, (2) that intelligence is mainly inherited, (3) that lower IQ test scores indicate that African-Americans are less intelligent and therefore less educable than whites, (4) that occupational level and income are dependent on intelligence and resulting academic achievement, and (5) that poverty therefore results from inherited deficiencies in the poor, not from unequal school and employment opportunities.

Critics of the Jensen-Herrnstein thesis quickly replied that IQ test scores measure the cultural knowledge of children from middle- and upper-class families, not intelligence. They also pointed out that Jensen and Herrnstein offered no evidence linking intelligence with heredity and that their database was a patchwork accumulation of old, flawed data that had been compiled over sixty years by various researchers under varying conditions and for various purposes. It is ironic that, as a result of the Jensen-Herrnstein episode, IQ tests have lost much of their credibility, although they continue to reinforce racial stereotypes of "deficient" minority groups.

The breakdown of genetic inferiority theory began as a result of the Army Alpha test administered to 1,750,000 draftees during the 1917 call-up for World War I. The test purported to show the mental age of white recruits as several years higher than that of African-Americans. In fact, 89 percent of the African-American men tested were ranked as "morons," and thousands of men who had recently immigrated from Europe scored as "feeble-minded." In 1945 Harvard anthropologist Ashley Montague made a more detailed analysis of the data. He pointed out that the gap between white and African-American test scores was greatest in the deep South, smallest in the North. Furthermore, African-Americans in the northern states had scored better than whites in the southern states. The claim that the test measured "intelligence" was finally called into question, as was the conclusion that African-Americans were less intelligent than whites. Since scores varied by location, it was clearly not the case that genetic endowment was being measured.

Theories of genetic inferiority break down any time social and educational programs successfully close the gap between test scores for different groups—a phenomenon that is happening with increasing frequency as educational practice becomes better adapted to cultural differences. Finally, genetic theories of inequality have lost favor because they deal with only a small amount of evidence and because the conclusions drawn from them do not lead in any useful direction. They neither stimulate strong research nor contribute to the resolution of social and educational inequalities. Nonetheless, in 1994 Herrnstein drew national attention with publication of *The Bell Curve,* in which he and his co-author C. Murray again claimed to have found genetic origins of intelligence differences among different groups. Again their research was widely disputed.[14]

Cultural Deficit Theory

After modern theories of genetic inferiority lost favor in the early 1970s, liberal social scientists began searching for another model that would help organize the data and explain the persistence of low achievement rates in minority youth. They began to reason that these children were not biologically inferior but came from an inferior home environment. Poor and minority children did not have the same social, cultural, and intellectual opportunities as middle-class white children; they did not travel, visit libraries and art museums, go to zoos, or participate on a daily basis in sophisticated adult conversations. Their poorer, less-educated parents were unable to prepare them for school. So went the cultural deficit argument.

The language of the "ghetto" was brought into question and attacked as an inadequate linguistic vehicle. Poor children, especially poor African-American children, did not grow up in circumstances that would teach them to think, to reason, and to speak in the manner generally approved by the dominant social order. Thus, it was reasoned, they were victims of linguistic or cultural deficiencies. When these children entered the formal stages of their public education, many of them could not compete with white children whose preschool experience had prepared them for the cultural environment and the social structure of the school.[15] This preparation gap served as the pretext for grouping poor and minority children into vocational and nonacademic curricula and placing them into educable mentally handicapped (EMH) classes at a rate three times that of their white peers. The penalty for not coming to school equipped with the approved social and cultural graces was relegation to an education devoid of challenging intellectual content. In short, poor and minority students were expected to fail, and they were put into programs that encouraged failure.

Since some children entering school could not read or count, did not know the letters of the alphabet, and could not name the colors, claims of cultural deficiency were not entirely groundless. Poverty does take its toll on children. Thus there was enough evidence supporting the theory of cultural deficiency that it gained widespread acceptance.

Theories of cultural and linguistic deficiency guided the whole compensatory education movement during the 1960s and 1970s. These programs were attractive because they left existing social and cultural arrangements intact, located the problem of low achievement in the student's home culture, and seemed to point the way toward a solution. If children were growing up with an inadequate grounding in the basics, society merely

Programs such as Project Head Start were designed to equip minority and poor children from "under-privileged backgrounds" with the same school-readiness abilities as their better-off peers from the mainstream culture.

needed to provide remedial education to older students and compensatory or preventive schooling for young children. Programs such as Project Head Start were designed to equip minority and poor children from low-income backgrounds with the same abilities and knowledge as their better-off peers.

These programs did show results. Follow-up on Project Head Start and similar programs revealed positive effects for children on standardized tests, dropout rates, and so forth. But despite these encouraging results in the area of schooling, inequalities persist. One major problem is the fact that cultural deficit theory takes for granted the legitimacy of the dominant culture, and does not call into question its privileged status as the cultural norm. Since children from minority cultures are tested and evaluated using the language and social knowledge of the dominant culture, they are operating at an obvious disadvantage. Standardized testing procedures do not test for the competencies developed in other cultural and linguistic systems.

Critics argue that there is not a single American culture but numerous cultures competing, intermingling, and informing one another. And in each culture, or subculture, ways of behaving and relating to others, ways of knowing, ways of thinking, modes of expression, shades of meaning, icons and symbols, memories and history—the thousands upon thousands of subtle associations upon which a cultural system is built—are different. What was needed, some scholars argued, was a theory to help investigate the relationships among these several cultures in order to understand social, economic, and political patterns of dominance and subordination.

Critical Theory

Liberal theories are characterized by the tendency to take for granted the existing social, economic, and political organization that has come down from classical and Enlightenment conceptions of humanity and society (see Chapter 2). In the two liberal social theories we have examined so far, middle-class, Anglo-American, Protestant culture serves as the conceptual frame of reference from which all other groups are considered. This cultural hegemony has been allowed to happen, critics charge, because the dominant social group has accumulated sufficient power to make its standards prevail.

Whereas liberal theories derive from the entrenched position of the dominant culture, critical theory is characterized by a willingness to call into question the whole social order and to use various viewpoints in discussing a given problem. In the critical theories we are about to examine, the point of view of each party or group involved is legitimated and their relationships are considered. Critical theories rely on multiple frames of reference, as the following examples illustrate.

If a child from a minority family is having trouble in school, the quality of any assessment of the conflict depends greatly upon what is taken for granted. School authorities may point to the child as the source of the problem. The child acts bored, seems uncommitted, uninterested; the child fantasizes, skips school, gets into fights. Since Anglo children do well at the same school, how can the problem lie with the school? School officials blame the child. Yet the parents know that the child does well at home, relates appropriately to family and peers, and is curious and generally cheerful. So how can the problem lie with the child? The parents suspect the school of discriminatory practices toward their child. Although the authority of the school will likely prevail in a situation like this, there is clearly a problem here that cannot be resolved merely by recourse to hierarchical superiority.

Critical theory asks that we look not so much at the child or at the school, both of which function well in certain contexts, but at the *relationship* between the child and the school as the primary unit of analysis. Specifically, critical theory looks at the relationship between the child's culture and the culture of the school in an effort to assess conflicts. Instead of assuming the greater legitimacy of one culture over another, it merely asks, What is the relationship among these cultures? When a conflict between child and school is identified, it is treated not as a problem residing in the student, but as a mismatch between the culture of the student and the culture of the school. A search for solutions to these mismatches is then conducted in such a way that both the needs of the student and the legitimate interests of the larger society are respected.[16]

Cultural deficit theorists view bilingual education as an attempt to overcome cultural "deficiencies," while cultural difference theorists view it as the school's attempt to help students from different but equal cultures adjust to the mainstream culture.

Cultural Difference Theory Perhaps nothing has so clarified the inadequacy of traditional social science scholarship as the advance of minority interests in this century. As minority groups have gained power, their self-assertion has compelled the dominant culture to recognize alternative frames of reference. The historical bondage to a single, monolithic cultural perspective runs counter to the dimension of the classical-liberal view of education that values understanding and adaptation of multiple perspectives as the key to a fuller and more mature intellect. And it cherishes a diverse and many-sided understanding of perennial issues as the very key to human liberty. But modern liberalism has privileged another strain of classical liberalism, in which the cultural products of classical societies have become canonized as "culture."

The transition from cultural deficit theories to cultural difference theories marks a significant passage in the social sciences. It represents a transition from a fixed frame of reference to multiple frames of reference. Anthropologists and linguists, disgraced by their willing endorsement of imperialism, nationalism, and cultural jingoism leading up to the world wars, have since acquired a respect for human culture in all its splendid variety. This view allows for a richer, more appreciative sense of the human cultural panorama. Other social scientists have followed suit.

Cultural difference theory, then, respects the variety of human cultures and assesses the relationships among various cultural groups. Within education, one of the first tasks of cultural difference theory has been to investigate how the experience of schooling differs for children who grow up in different cultural settings. In the past, educators and others have tended to undervalue the fact that children generally do well when schooled and evaluated within their own culture. It is when children of one culture are schooled by the institutions of another that cultural mismatches result. This is what happens to countless minority children in American society.

Cultural mismatches can occur with respect to subject matter, learning styles, ways of knowing

Summary of Differences between Various Theories of Inequality

	Genetic Inferiority	*Cultural Deficit*	*Cultural Subordination*
Causes of inequality	Inherited	The inferior cultural background of the poor, and the superior cultural background of the rich.	Power differences, imbedded in the socioeconomic structure between the rich and poor
Remedy	None	Force poor to acculturate to the culture of the advantaged class	Change power relationships in the socioeconomic structure
Implications for schooling	Tracking poor into less rigorous or vocational programs	Compensatory classes to eliminate the cultural commitments of the poor and provide them with superior culture of the advantaged class; tracking	Critical teaching about power relationships to arm the poor to demand changes and inform the rich that some of their advantages are socially derived and not personal traits

and demonstrating knowledge, attitudes toward authority, modes of behavior, and socialization patterns, among other factors. For example, Native Americans, who as scholars have mastered the dominant culture in addition to their own, point to many discontinuities between the Indian culture and the dominant Anglo culture of the United States. For the most part, Indians are not a competitive people in the ways that the larger society sanctions. Tribal life tends to encourage social cohesion and cooperation rather than competitive individualism. Also, the Indian worldview does not separate mind and body, as western civilizations have done since the time of Plato. Indians cherish a tribal life quite different from the acquisitive, self-assertive materialism of cosmopolitan westerners, who have largely tried to subdue nature rather than live in harmony with it.

Learning styles also differ between Anglo and Indian cultures. Whereas white children are accustomed to trying things, to learning new tasks by trial and error, Indian children are often taught to learn by observation (see the reading at the end of Chapter 12). They are taught not to make mistakes, but to acquire new skills by watching them being performed.[17] In school, Native American students resist being pushed into public learning tasks they have not yet mastered. Interpreted through Anglo criteria, the hesitant Indian youth seems to lack initiative.

There are other differences between Anglo and Indian culture: the interpretation of history, for example, and the criteria for what constitutes excellence in art, literature, and music. And there are extreme differences in how best to interpret and to understand nature, human society, and the relation of humanity to nature. American Indians have never fully accepted the notion that the land itself can be parceled out and sold to the highest bidder. European science and technology, for all its pragmatic success, has had a devastating impact on cultures around the globe through the imperialism, cultural hegemony, and environmental damage it has produced. American Indians have good reasons not to be enamored of the consequences.

The Native American example is simply an illustration. Other cultural groups, too, differ in important ways from the dominant group. Traditional definitions of culture have centered around the formal expressions of a people's common existence—language, art, music, and so forth. If culture is more broadly defined to include such things as ways of knowing, ways of relating to others, ways of negotiating rights and privileges, and modes of conduct, thought, and expression, then the term culture applies not only to ethnic groups but to people grouped on the basis of gender and social class. Gender identity, then, entails cultural as well as physiological dimensions. And class is characterized by differences of culture as well as differences of socioeconomic status. By expanding the idea of culture to include gender and social class distinctions along with race and ethnicity, we can analyze how different groups experience the world and express themselves and how patterns of dominance and subordination arise between groups.

That schools participate in the subordination of certain social groups is something scholars have tended to resist examining. The traditional view has held that schools are neutral places where common learning experiences prepare everyone equally well for life in an equitable society. However, critical and radical scholarship of recent decades shows how schools serve as instruments of social policy in which the interests of the dominant group are served at the expense of other groups.

Mechanisms of subordination do not depend upon physical duress. Far more effective is the subtle yet systematic reduction of self-confidence—the crippling of personal and group identity that this chapter describes. Castelike minority groups have regularly and deliberately resisted assimilation for the express reason that it would destroy the last vestiges of their group identity and solidarity. And the schools, when faced with such resistance, have tended toward punishment and the withholding of opportunities for status and mobility. Failure to conform to Anglo standards of culture and civility is treated as evidence of an inferior intellect. Our current task, then, is to assess how cultural differences become the basis of cultural subordination.

A common retort is, "If the Irish made it, the Germans made it, and the Asians are making it, then why can't the African-Americans, why can't the Indians, and why can't the Mexicans and Puerto Ricans?" The answer is that many of them are making it, but for those who are not, it is necessary to recognize that group status depends upon historical circumstances. John Ogbu suggests differentiating among minorities according to whether they have autonomous, voluntary immigrant, or castelike backgrounds.[18] Autonomous minorities, such as the Amish, Jews, and Mormons, are insulated from some of the more devastating jolts of cultural differences because they form self-protective social enclaves. Members of these groups sustain one another emotionally, culturally, and even economically, so that they are able to control the degree of contact between themselves and the larger society.

Voluntary immigrant minorities, such as the Irish and the Germans, avoid the psychologic effects of discrimination by bringing with them a sense of self rooted in their parent culture. Ogbu writes: "As strangers they can operate psychologically outside established definitions of social status and relations." Ogbu cites the Chinese as an example, since traditional Chinese culture equips people with a culturally intact sense of self.

Finally, castelike minorities, writes Ogbu, are groups that have been relegated to a subordinate status by legal and extralegal means. As in the traditional caste system of India, the rules of structured inequality are well defined and fairly rigid. African-Americans, Mexican Americans, Native Americans, and Puerto Ricans are cited as examples of castelike minority groups that experience forms of institutional racism and bias not generally directed at other minority groups.[19]

Cultural Subordination Theory Cultural subordination theory examines the social processes that lead to lower status for minority groups. It also examines the inequalities that appear to be structured into the social system. Subordination theory followed difference theory when scholars finally realized that discrimination was not an accidental or inevitable consequence of cultural differences. Cultural subordination theory has application not only to relations between dominant and subordinate racial and ethnic groups but to gender relations and social class relations as well.

To see what role schools might play in perpetuating social inequalities, Jean Anyon studied five modern elementary schools in New Jersey. In the study, schools serving working-class children were found to be relatively indifferent to academic content beyond "the basics." Teachers rated their students as "lazy" and as not knowing anything. Instruction was by rote and repetition, intended to inculcate basic facts and procedures. Teachers insisted that students follow set ways of doing things. Upon interviewing students, Anyon concluded that most had not developed a very clear sense of how knowledge is created. When asked where knowledge came from they said it came from "books," "the dictionary," even "The Board of Ed."[20] Anyon documented how students resisted and sabotaged teachers' efforts, and, in turn, how teachers resented students.

Anyon then investigated conditions in a school serving "middle class" students, a school serving children of "affluent professionals," and finally a school in which the children's parents were described as the "executive elite." Throughout this progression up the socioeconomic ladder, the quality of education improves and the nature of instruction changes. The teachers no longer emphasize "the basics" but concentrate on helping students develop advanced intellectual skills. "My goal is to have the children learn from experience. I want them to think for themselves," said one teacher from the affluent professional school.[21] In such schools, students are urged to make decisions, to think things through, to take risks and test hypotheses. Individualism is emphasized, and students understand that knowledge is something people construct from their interaction with the world. They have a good sense of how science operates.

Finally, in the "executive elite" school, teachers frankly confessed that these children of privilege would "go to the best schools, and we have to prepare them." High expectations have been set by parents who are accustomed to having their phone calls answered and their instructions followed. These are educated parents who know how to demand an education for their children. Students in such a school might be asked to debate whether the Athenians were wrong in condemning Socrates for his beliefs.[22] They have a conservative view of knowledge and see it as a store of traditional information that must be mastered. However, most also understand that the knower plays a significant role in knowing. These students are competitive, confident, and relatively sophisticated in their mastery of the school environment.

If the schools Anyon describes are representative, it must be conceded that the processes and outcomes of schooling are not the same for all children in American society. Far from serving as the great equalizer in our society, the schools tend to prepare students for destinies that generally correspond to their social class background. Nor is it any secret how this occurs.

In modern public schools, selection into a given track starts as early as the first grade, when assignments are made to reading groups.[23] Longitudinal studies show very little movement up or down once a student has been assigned to an ability group. But on what basis is this initial selection made? The Coleman Report (1966) showed a high correlation between "achievement" and social class. It also showed that this correlation was not significantly affected by elementary education.[24]

Modern schooling includes testing, tracking, and counseling children into separate destinies. Ability grouping has been criticized as undemocratic because it tends to restrict the entry of many students into opportunities for stimulating, higher-order thinking, and because it perpetuates the social class structure of the larger society. John Duffy cites research showing "the numerous advantages for the academic, personal and social development of all students when they learn in cooperative, heterogeneous settings as opposed to homogeneous, competitive settings."[25]

Boards of education, school administrations, and teaching staff are all comprised primarily of white, middle-class professionals with a heavy ideological commitment to the status quo. By the end of this century, it is estimated, minority enrollments in public schools could top 40 percent, yet the percentage of minority college students preparing for roles in education has actually declined in the past 10 years.[26] This cultural imbalance between teachers and students will further perpetuate the status quo.

The curriculum also reflects a largely white, male, middle-class worldview. It emphasizes mathematics and science and favors intellectual skills and knowledge over social skills. The literature studied sends a message to minority children that culture is a largely European attainment. The civics, history, and sociology studied tend to vindicate the European experience while devaluing the experience of African-Americans, Native Americans, women, Asians, and Latinos.

The structural arrangements of schools and classrooms can also affect how students fare. Large classes may favor socially assertive people. Female and Native American students may, more frequently than their classmates, find a competitive, urgent, and noisy classroom climate uncongenial.

And the minority student sitting among self-confident members of the dominant group may feel continuously threatened by the lack of reinforcement for his or her own cultural background. The climate of learning is important because confidence is so necessary to a person's growth, and yet so fragile during the years of childhood and adolescence. As Jane Elliott's Discrimination Day exercise demonstrated to dozens of well-off students, it takes very little to shatter that confidence and so turn a potential winner into a second-class citizen.

Resistance Theory One corollary to cultural subordination theory is resistance theory. Researchers have found that students experiencing discriminatory practices soon retreat into a posture of resistance in which they stop working with the school and its agents. Adolescent girls, for example, have been found to act dumb, to curtail their efforts, and to refrain from demonstrating intellectual prowess because of social pressure and the assumption that, as females, they will eventually assume a role subordinate to males in society. Although this is less true of upper- and middle-class girls, some female high school valedictorians lose confidence when they get into college. This rarely happens to male valedictorians, however, since society expects them to continue doing well.

Some African-American students, too, exhibit resistance strategies. Cooperation with the schools means capitulation to an alien culture that has long held African-Americans in bondage. To take on the cultural attributes of white people is to enter into a client relation with the dominant culture, to engage in "Uncle Tomming." But that is exactly what is required in order to succeed. And so young African-Americans, caught between cultures, tend to drop out of school at disproportionate rates and to engage in otherwise self-destructive patterns of resistance. Students of lower socioeconomic backgrounds also engage in resistance strategies. And when they do so, an unsophisticated teaching staff can conclude that they simply have no interest and no talent for learning.

In order to better understand how cultural differences can set up patterns of interference with learning, let us examine a topic that has received a great deal of attention in recent decades: the English dialect characteristic of inner-city African-American children. The misunderstandings on this topic run deep, and the consequences are severe when a teacher misinterprets why the language of African-American children differs from that of the dominant culture. The study of African-American English is representative of cultural differences in general and of the consequences that are obtained when subordinate cultural patterns conflict with those of the dominant group. Let us look first at the basic ideas that most linguists who have studied this problem generally agree upon.[27]

First, all of the thousands of languages and dialects that currently exist in the world are capable of supporting complex cognitive processes, and all can adequately express human problems, dreams, and scientific, aesthetic, historical, philosophical, and religious impulses. All of these languages can and do generate or borrow new words to express new ideas or relationships. All have a complex grammatical structure. In short, it is not true that one of these languages or dialects is superior or inferior, as a means of communication within a culture. "Cockney" is as good as BBC English, African-American vernacular is as good as standard American speech, and Spanish is as good as French, English, or German.

Second, the prestige attached to a language or dialect depends not on its intrinsic linguistic characteristics but on the economic and military power of the group that uses it as a primary language. Thus English is granted higher value than French in Canada. Sometimes a ruling class will decree its language as the official language of the state in order to entrench its own power while making access more difficult for those speaking other languages. For example, after the Norman conquest, French became the official language of England. In Greece the ruling class even created an artificial language in order to exclude lower-class individuals, who could not afford tutors, from full participation in the civil process.

Third, all people, including children, learn better if they can better comprehend the language of instruction. Thus instruction in the mother tongue is most effective. *It is necessary, however, for nonstandard speakers eventually to learn to negotiate the standard language if they wish to experience success where that language is dominant.*

Fourth, not all nonstandard speakers have developed their primary language to the same degree. Those who are less proficient in their own native language may need ongoing work in that language in order to acquire the new language. Thus a bilingual program whose goal of a speedy transition to standard English leads to elimination of instruction in the primary tongue may be less efficient with many students than a program in which primary language instruction is continually developed.

Fifth, the way a child's primary language is valued, especially by teachers and peers, strongly affects the student's self-concept. A positive self-concept is important for effective learning. Thus, when teachers continually tell students that the usage of their primary language is wrong or incorrect, the effect is to diminish the students' confidence as learners and potentially reduce their ability to learn.

Sixth, every language has a variety of linguistic styles. For example, a professor's standard English speech will vary according to whether he or she is lecturing to a class, delivering a paper before professional colleagues, or rehashing the "good old days" with high school friends. It is important to remember that a person's total linguistic capacity cannot be measured through a single linguistic environment. Unfortunately, we frequently make such linguistic generalizations about schoolchildren.

Seventh, a major cause of reading failure is the cultural conflict that occurs between standard-English speaking teachers and children from nonstandard language backgrounds. The problem is not the difference in cultural or linguistic values but the teacher's ability to recognize and address those differences.

A Useful Digression: Bilingual and ESL Instruction as Bridges to English Proficiency

Language and culture are intertwined in complex ways. Since the 1974 *Lau* v. *Nichols* decision, which affirmed the right of language minority students to receive instruction tailored to their needs, the United States has struggled with different approaches to supporting the academic success of Limited English Proficient (LEP) students, who are more likely to perform poorly in school and to drop out of school than English proficient students. LEP students are defined by the 1978 Amendments to the Bilingual Education Act as "individuals who come from environments where a language other than English is dominant," or "where a language other than English has had a significant impact on their language proficiency," and who therefore "have sufficient difficult speaking, reading, writing, or understanding the English language to deny such individuals the opportunity to learn successfully in classrooms where the language of instruction is English or to participate fully in our society."[28] A 1997 report from the U.S. Department of Education identifies over 2.1 million public school students in the U.S. as LEP, about 5 percent of all public school students. These students comprise, however, nearly a third of all Hispanic, Asian/Pacific Islander, and Indian/Alaskan Native students. The number of students who speak a language other than English at home is even greater—perhaps as many as 6.3 million.[29]

Because these students are widely distributed throughout the nation, 42 percent of all public school teachers have at least one LEP student in their classes. Only 7 percent of these teachers have classes with over 50 percent LEP students. Of all schools with LEP students, 76 percent provide programs in English as a Second Language (ESL), while 36 percent offer bilingual education programs.[30] These are very different approaches to instruction for LEP students. Because there are more than 10 times as many Spanish-speaking students in the U.S. as the next highest language (French), Spanish-speaking students are those most likely to receive bilingual instruction (academic instruction in two languages, intended to progress to proficiency in English) though bilingual education may be offered in other languages, too, when the concentration of students is high enough (as it is, for example, in a Polish neighborhood in Chicago). Given the hundreds of thousands of students who speak French, Chinese languages, Korean, Arabic, Portuguese, German, Cambodian, Greek, Italian, Yiddish, Farsi, Russian, and scores of other languages, however, it is not possible to offer instruction to those students in their home language and in English, as bilingual programs do. Therefore, ESL programs are offered so those students can spend concentrated school time making a transition from their language to English. This chapter offers primary-source readings that go into some depth on the distinctions between ESL and bilingual programs.

What might be said at this point is that such programs have been devised for LEP students as a bridge from where they are, linguistically, to where they need to be to partake fully of the educational and economic benefits of the dominant culture. It was apparently this kind of reasoning that led the Oakland, California, School District to pass a new policy that stirred national controversy, although the basic idea was an admirable one: that many African-American students are entitled to a linguistic bridge from their "Black English Vernacular"—or "Ebonics," as the Oakland Board of Education termed it (from ebony phonics)—to standard English. Unfortunately, the policy was unclear enough, and the public (including some African-American leaders) hostile enough to the policy, that a great national stir was created, obscuring some of the more interesting educational issues at stake for African-American youth who speak a nonstandard form of English.[31] Eventually, the Oakland Board revised their policy to make clear that they were not trying to teach Ebonics on an equal footing with Standard English, but were trying to honor the richness of students' language and culture as a foundation on which to build academic success, including proficiency in Standard English.

BEV: Language and Cultural Subordination

Although the Oakland Board did not cite this passage from author James Baldwin in their policy, it offers a telling comment on the relations between language and culture. It was written nearly 20 years ago in an essay titled, "If Black English Isn't a Language, Then Tell Me What Is?" Baldwin writes:

> The brutal truth is that the bulk of the white people in America never had any interest in educating black people, except as this could serve white purposes. It is not the black child's language that is despised. It is his experience. A child cannot be taught by anyone who despises him, and a child cannot afford to be fooled. A child cannot be taught by anyone whose demand, essentially, is that the child repudiate his experiences, and all that gives him sustenance, and enter a limbo in which he will no longer be black, and in which he knows he can never become white. Black people have lost too many black children that way.[32]

Baldwin concludes that Black English, with its own cultural history and purposes unique to its origins in slavery, is clearly a language. This thought bears further examination.

One of the first difficulties an African-American child (not all, but some) might encounter in public school is the well-meaning teacher who tries to correct his or her speech patterns. A child who says, "They be mine," or "I ain't got none" is speaking a dialect of American English sometimes known as Black English Vernacular (BEV). Bolinger and Sears explain:

> According to one theory, the historical basis for Black English is the African pidgin used in the slave trade, the only language available to blacks sometimes thrown together from different language backgrounds to keep them from communicating effectively with one another. As with all pidgins . . . the nuisance irregularities of morphology were discarded and syntax was simplified. The result was that as blacks gradually rebuilt a speech community in the lands to which they were transported, they had to reconstitute the grammar, which retained certain features of the pidgin even while it was being "relexified" with words taken in constantly from the standard.[33]

The authors quote a passage from Fickett,[34] describing verb tenses in BEV: "I do see him." "I did see him." "I done seen him." "I been seen him." These passages lead progressively into the past tense. In the opposite direction, future tenses leading away from the present include these: "I'm a-do it." "I'm a-gonna do it." "I gonna do it."

BEV systematically drops the copula (connective link) "to be" when it is actually superfluous in Standard American English (SAE). "He going" instead of "He *is* going," and "It mine" instead of "It *is* mine" lose nothing in precision or meaning if the convention of usage is understood. Other examples of linguistic differences include "I ask *did he do it*" in place of the "if" construction in SAE: "I asked *if* he did it." The expression "John moves" in SAE becomes a double-subject "John, he move" in BEV. Third-person possessives in BEV drop the "s": "John cousin" instead of "John's cousin." In BEV the present tense of the verb "to be" is rendered "be": "He *be* here." This is a durative (continuing) form of the present tense to indicate ongoing action as distinguished from a fleeting condition in the present. Last in this incomplete list of features is the use of negative concord (double negatives) such as "I don't want none" and "He ain't got none."[35]

Related to the linguistic issue are patterns of thought, ways of knowing the world, that are embedded in the language of African-American students. When these ways of knowing and of expression encounter scholastic challenges phrased in standard English, patterns of interference can be set up that result in confusion and nonlearning. In mathematics classes, for example, conflicting ways of employing English prepositions can make word problems difficult for some African-American students to understand and to solve.[36]

At issue here is neither the inadequacy of African-American intellects (genetic inferiority) nor the inadequacy of African-American culture as a preparation for school (cultural deprivation), but rather a mismatch between African-American culture and the dominant Anglo culture of America. Aware of the long history of racial antipathy, African-American students tend to resist assimilationist policies designed to "whiten them up" to Anglo standards. The teacher's understanding of cultural differences largely determines whether the uniqueness of African-American culture becomes a cause of celebration or a source of discrimination. William Labov writes:

> When the everyday language of black children is stigmatized as "not a language at all" and "not possessing the means for logical thought," the effect of such labelling is repeated many times each day of the school year. Every time that a child uses a form of the BEV without the copula or with negative concord, he will be labelling himself for the teacher's benefit as "illogical," as a "nonconceptual thinker." This notion gives teachers a ready-made, theoretical basis for the prejudice they may already feel against the lower-class black child and his language. When they hear him say *I don't want none* or *They mine,* they will be hearing, through the bias provided by the verbal deprivation theory, not an English dialect different from theirs, but the primitive mentality of the savage mind.[37]

Of course, it must be emphasized that the term "black English" should not be taken to mean that all African-American children speak in that linguistic system. The language one speaks is not biologically determined but is a function of one's cultural background. A great many African-Americans grow up in the dominant Anglo culture, speaking standard English. Millions of African-American children, however, especially those from poorer families that tend to live in neighborhoods segregated from white communities, speak a language different from that of the larger society and the school because that is the dominant language of their neighborhood and of their home. Theories of cultural subordination show that traits valued in the larger society are those that are also valued and rewarded in the schools. Cultural traits subjected to discrimination in the larger society become the target of subordination in the schools. The question arises, then, of what to do with students whose cultural background is not legitimated by the dominant society.

Benign neglect is not the answer. Critical theorists point out that when cultural differences are simply ignored or overlooked by well-meaning teachers, students suffer in the long run because they wind up unequipped to function in the larger society. To leave students as they are is not to empower them to function in the larger society. Characteristics of racial and ethnic minorities, females, and people of lower socioeconomic backgrounds should not be subjected to patterns of censure. But if differences are to be accepted and celebrated, new approaches to education must be found.

PEDAGOGICAL APPROACHES TO PLURALISM

There appear to be three general strategies for teachers to use with respect to cultural and social-group differences. These terms are being used here in the broadest sense to include differences grounded in race and ethnicity, social class, and gender. The three approaches are (1) to ignore differences and to teach to a single standard, (2) to seek to eliminate differences by having all students conform to a single standard, and (3) to teach in a manner sensitive to differences *without* being biased by group differences—that is, without attributing characteristics to individuals by virtue of their membership in groups. The first two ways tend to be a denial of differences or of the significance of differences. The third approach, based upon sensitivity toward differences, rejects the stigma associated with such differences and chooses instead to use these cultural resources as a bridge to the kinds of learning valued by the dominant culture.

Gender Theory: An Illustration of Sensitivity to Differences

Feminist theory has explored these three possibilities with respect to gender issues. In the early phases of modern feminist thinking, scholars asked that girls not be socialized differently from boys or treated in a different manner. While this "gender-free" approach to education overcame some of the grosser policies of sex discrimination, it did not serve to equalize educational results. By ignoring gender-based differences in favor of gender "neutrality," teachers allowed those differences to create a subtle form of social dominance as boys proved more gregarious and forceful in their classroom tactics.

In the second phase of feminist theory, scholars recommended strategies to compensate or equalize the effects of gender differences within the classroom as it was traditionally arranged. This "bias" approach proved less than satisfactory because it still retained a male-oriented framework. It assumed that standards of male performance should be the norm, and that by active compensatory measures females could be brought into line with those standards.

In a third phase of thinking, feminist scholars have begun to reconsider all the operational premises of education and society. Instead of looking for ways of overcoming the differences between males and females, they have begun a quest to ensure that these differences are recognized, respected, and incorporated into the mainstream of American society and education.

Current research is exploring the extent to which female traits are grounded in socialization and the extent to which they are grounded in biology. The assessment may never be completed, and at present the preference is to see biological determinism as a relatively weak component of genderization. What is significant to the current discussion is not whether nature or nurture is most responsible for gender differences, but how those differences are treated by society. When women are relegated to a subordinate status, traits of personality and intellect thought of as female also become devalued. In American society these traits include nurturance, feeling, caring, empathy, social interest, and the capacity to cultivate meaningful and long-range social relationships. Education, designed initially to serve in the preparation of males, emphasizes qualities deemed essentially masculine: rationality, individualism, detachment, commercial productivity, competitiveness, and aggressiveness.

Jane Roland Martin has pointed out that traditional theories of education took no account of gender and seldom even mentioned females.[38] When females were mentioned, as in Rousseau's *Émile,* the objective was to cultivate a companion for the male, not an interesting, autonomous being. Or in the case of Plato's *Republic,* women were trained as if they were men, without recognition of gender differences. Martin describes the traditional American education as one based upon attributes generally associated with males and devoted primarily to the "productive" aspects of society: aspects valued for their production of material well-being. She urges adaptation of a "gender-sensitive" approach that gives equal value to such "reproductive" virtues as caring and nurturance and intimate social connections and, in the process, helps to reconstruct society along more cooperative and humane lines.

A gender-sensitive approach to education requires that schooling be conducted so that traits deemed to be feminine are not stigmatized but are recognized, respected, and cultivated by everyone. In this broadened view, by freeing both men and women from gender stereotypes, everyone stands a better chance of developing in accordance with his or her unique nature, rather than in accordance with restrictive stereotypes. Martin writes: "Care, concern, connectedness, nurturance: these are as important for carrying on society's economic, political, and social processes as its reproductive ones. If education is to help all of us acquire them, the ideal of the educated person and the theory of liberal education . . . must be redefined."[39]

Martin's call for a gender-sensitive education has a great deal in common with the general pluralistic trend currently emerging in educational theory and practice. This trend does not assume that all performance differences in schools are due to gender, ethnic, or social-class differences. Rather, it recognizes that group differences often *can* be important in explaining the relative performance of individuals, and that teachers can teach more effectively if they are sensitive to such cultural origins of individual performance. Sophisticated classroom approaches to cultural pluralism, which include consideration of gender and social class, may well become the next major educational reform, one in which teachers will be asked to teach in a way that is "culturally responsive" to their students' diversity. Gordon Berry has suggested that "the secondary school pupil has a moral responsibility to learn, understand, and respect values inherent in other races and religions, and to practice behaviors that will ensure dignity and civil rights to males and females of cultural groups different from [his or her] own."[40]

Multicultural Education and Democratic Pluralism

The convergence of these several concerns is made explicit in a work by Christine Sleeter and Carl Grant[41] that describes five approaches to achieving a pluralistic education. Sleeter and Grant's categories recall the distinction made between "assimilationist" and "pluralist" approaches to cultural differences described in connection with Native Americans in Chapter 7. Roughly summarized, the assimilationist educational approach seeks to obliterate cultural differences among minority groups so that those groups will have the same cultural knowledge and values as the dominant culture. The pluralist approach seeks ways to preserve and celebrate distinctive cultural heritages as valuable contributions to the vitality and diversity of the wider culture. Applying that distinction to Sleeter and Grant's five approaches to multicultural education reveals some of them to be more assimilationist and others to be more pluralist in orientation.

Teaching the Exceptional and Culturally Different In the teaching-the-exceptional approach, the goals are to "fit people into the existing social structure and culture." This is done by use of "bilingual education, ESL, remedial classes and special education, all of which are seen as temporary and intensive aids to fill gaps in knowledge." The general strategy is to create bridges between the student's present knowledge and the traditional curricular aims of the school. Because the student must conform to the dominant culture, this approach is favored mainly by "white, middle class teachers who take their own background and culture for granted and are searching for a way to incorporate or deal with those they view as different."[42]

Human Relations In the human relations approach, the primary goals are to "promote feelings of unity, tolerance, and acceptance within [the] existing social structure" and to "promote positive feelings among students, reduce stereotyping, [and] promote students' self-concepts."[43] These goals are to be met by teaching lessons about stereotyping and name calling, and to counter such tendencies by teaching positive images of minority groups and by teaching about individual differences. This approach, designed to make people feel good about themselves and each other, is criticized on the grounds that the fundamental sources of discrimination and poverty which lead to feelings of inferiority do not reside in human relations, but in institutional arrangements that promote inequality.

Single-Group Studies The goals of single-group studies are to foster social equality, acceptance, and recognition of the identified group and to "promote willingness and knowledge among students to work toward social change that would benefit the identified group."[44] These goals would be addressed by teaching specific units about the identified group, including that group's own perspective, how it has been victimized, and the issues it currently faces. Ethnic studies courses (women's studies, Indian studies, African-American studies) are examples. This approach serves a purpose, but it also suffers limitations. It does not effectively alter the main curriculum, which in the view of many critics only reinforces the very problems a multicultural education attempts to correct. The traditional curriculum derives from the experience of white, middle-class males. Single-group studies convey a sort of add-on approach which lacks incorporation or serious challenge to the status quo.

Multicultural Education The goals of multicultural education include promotion of "social structural equality and cultural pluralism (the United States as a 'tossed salad')" and promotion of "equal opportunity in the school, cultural pluralism and alternative life styles, respect for those who differ, and support for power equity among groups."[45] Ideas and concepts should be represented as the product of many peoples' contributions; critical thinking and analysis of alternative viewpoints should be taught; and instruction should be allowed to proceed in more than one language. Some critics have argued that an emphasis on different cultures soon decays into a sort of balkanization of culture, in which different groups are allowed to develop according to their own ethos and as a result become further disfranchised from participation in the main society. Other critics have argued that in trying to teach a little about every special-interest group, no in-depth learning occurs. Advocates of particular groups are likely to feel slighted when their group gets less attention than they feel it deserves.[46] Finally, critics argue that merely teaching about diversity does little to empower change.

A culturally sensitive teacher learns to recognize when a variable such as race, ethnicity, gender, or handicapping condition is playing a significant role in a student's learning experience.

Education That Is Multicultural and Social Reconstructionist Proponents of the reconstructionist approach desire an education that is multicultural, but they also want it to equip students for life "in the real world." The real world, they argue, is not devoted to feel-good pedagogy and to the benevolent compensation of inequalities. Instead, the real world is fundamentally sexist, racist, and class-biased. In response to this grim scenario, the goal of multiculturalism is combined with the goal of social reconstructionism—a pedagogy which equips students not only to understand the world, but to criticize it effectively, and to change it.

Advocates of this approach do not loudly and clearly articulate one particular vision of the ideal society. They begin by assuming that resources should be distributed much more equally than they are now and that people should not have to adhere to one model of what is considered "normal" or "right" to enjoy their fair share of wealth, power, or happiness. But advocates believe that it would be another form of elitism for a small group of educators to tell other people what the "right" vision of the better society is. Rather, young people—particularly those who are members of oppressed groups—should understand the nature of oppression in modern society and develop the power and skills to articulate their own goals and vision and to work constructively toward that.[47]

Advocates of multicultural and social reconstructionist education argue for (1) practicing democracy, (2) analyzing the circumstances of one's own life, (3) developing social action skills, and (4) forming social coalitions across the boundaries of race, ethnicity, social class, and gender.

Practicing democracy entails a kind of active engagement in the decisions that affect one's own life. Unfortunately, schools often do not encourage such engagement. Relationships in schools are structured hierarchically, and the traditional lecture format from grade school to graduate school encourages passivity and boredom. Practicing democracy means taking active command of one's own life and education, "learning to articulate one's interests, openly debate issues with one's peers, organize and work collectively with others, acquire power, exercise power, and so forth."[48]

Analyzing the circumstances of one's own life means learning to see reality as it is, stripped of the myths which often mask it. Students have to unravel the discrepancies between their common-sense understanding of the world and the ideological explanations they have internalized as truth. Brazilian educator Paulo Freire has long used this approach.

Developing social action skills is a goal incorporated by critical theorists as they watched the repeated failure of earlier protest movements and individual forms of resistance which often proved self-destructive. Stanley Aronowitz and Henry Giroux, for example, argued that "if students are to be empowered by school experiences, one of the key elements of their education must be that they acquire mastery of language as well as the capacity to think conceptually and critically."[49]

Forming social coalitions requires that relatively disempowered social groups, whether defined by race, ethnicity, gender, income, or some other shared characteristic, must seek collective influence by working together toward common goals. The question arises, of course, How might schools provide experiences that would help prepare students for such coalition-building?

Programs That Work

The view that schools operate as autonomous centers of learning, independent of environing cultural conditions, has proved to be dangerously naive. Schools are institutions embedded in the elaborate context of a society's social, economic, and political structures. What is taught in the schools of any given society and how it is taught, depend upon the values and views of that society's dominant social group—including that society's values concerning cultural diversity.

Social relations in the larger society tend to be replicated in the schools. For teachers concerned with the fate of disenfranchised children, and concerned generally with the future of democracy, the outlook can be discouraging. In the 1960s the language of critique ripened into a language of anger and despair as social critics began to understand the extent to which power and cunning have contributed to social inequalities. These critics lost faith in the axioms that society is fair and that the underprivileged are deserving of their fate.

From the far left came calls for violent overthrow of the corporate capitalist state. Although revolutions are messy and the results are seldom gratifying, there are good moral and ethical as well as social reasons to work for a more equitable society. Even for individuals whose relative prosperity is guaranteed by current social arrangements, there are good reasons to want to see changes made. Moreover, there are strategies which each teacher can employ to promote equity without waiting until someone organizes the revolution. This brings us to the language of possibility. What can be done?

Many critical theorists now view gradual and localized change as the most reasonable goal, especially for educators, who are among educated society's least empowered people. There are discernible practices that work both to educate students and to empower teachers.

For example, math educator Uri Treisman succeeded in turning around the dismal failure rate of minority students entering freshman calculus courses at the University of California at Berkeley, where the "minority" population now accounts for two-thirds of the total enrollment. The mathematics workshop Treisman established cut the dropout rate among African-Americans and Hispanics in calculus classes from 60 percent to just 4 percent—an achievement that has been sustained for several years.[50] The goal was accomplished not by babying students but by challenging them, not by driving them to compete harder, but by structuring effective group study sessions that resulted in a professional community of devoted young scholars.

Treisman began by studying the success patterns of another minority group, Asian Americans, who were excelling in calculus. What Treisman found was that Asian students had set up a support network. They studied together, helped one another, maintained a dialogue by which conceptual understanding was constantly monitored and corrected. African-American students, on the other hand, were accustomed to a sort of rugged individualism. They socialized together, but they studied alone, and they seldom asked for help or acknowledged difficulties. This independent approach had stood them in good stead in high school, where peer influences often were resisted in favor of individual academic success.

Treisman set up a workshop in which African-American students were invited to study together. A math department staff member was on hand during study sessions to lend support. The workshop was neither billed nor run as a remedial program for losers, but as a professional support group, an honor society having high expectations. Study became a social activity, an accepted and ongoing part of these students' lives.

The success of Treisman's approach has since been replicated at several universities, including the University of Illinois by Merit Workshop Program director Paul McCreary. Minority students in McCreary's workshop cut the rate of unsatisfactory performance from 44.5 percent to 23.8 percent, outscoring all other sections on the final exam. Again, this success has been sustained over each semester of the workshop's existence.

Public schools also may benefit from this sort of commitment to high standards and strategies that work. An article in the *Journal of Negro Education*[51] describes the success of a high school set up by the New York City public school system on the campus of the City College of New York. In a city where the dropout rate runs to 30.7 percent and where an estimated 60 percent of African-American students never finish high school, the A. Phillip Randolph High School graduates all but 1.8 percent and sees from 92 percent to 97 percent of its students accepted into four-year colleges. In this same school, 44 percent of the students receive some form of public assistance; 76 percent are African-American, and 23 percent are Hispanic.

The school succeeds in part because high standards have been set, a clear sense of direction has been provided, curriculum development is ongoing, teachers are directly involved in all stages of planning, and parents, students, staff, and the community are all drawn into the process. Nationwide, these seem to be the characteristics of schools that work. The attitude of the Randolph School is that "every child can learn, must learn, and will learn."[52] The curriculum is rigorous. It emphasizes math and science, as well as a mastery of written English and speech. Students are required to devote 80 hours to community service to instill values of civil and social responsibility. Students undergo frequent testing and evaluation to ascertain current academic levels, ensuring correct placement in courses and upward movement when warranted. They are also coached in the skill of test taking so that they will score well when it comes time to take the SAT. Because of concerted, well-managed effort by all involved, Randolph High School has placed in the top 5 percent of all secondary schools in the nation and has sent over 45 percent of its students on to Ivy League schools, including Harvard, Yale, Brown, and Columbia.[53]

These few examples reflect some of the principles of a multicultural, reconstructionist education described in the following passage by Sleeter and Grant, leaders in the research on cultural pluralism. They call for an educational approach

> that advocates making the school and classroom reflect and celebrate diversity. [The] curriculum, including materials, visual displays, films, guest speakers, and content taught orally, should regularly represent experiences, perspectives, and contributions of diverse groups and should do so in a conceptual rather than a fragmented manner. This should be done all the time, in all subject areas. Nonsexist language should be used, and bilingualism or multilingualism should be endorsed. The curriculum should be equally accessible to all student groups; grouping practices or teaching procedures that enable only certain groups of students access to high-status knowledge or better teaching should be avoided. Teachers should build on students' learning styles rather than assuming that all learn best in the same way, and they should maintain high expectations for all students. Cooperative learning should be

> used to develop skills and attitudes of cooperation. Sexist teacher behavior should be avoided, and teachers should develop positive self-concepts in all students. Biased evaluation procedures should be avoided; evaluation should be used for improving instruction, not for sorting and ranking students. Home/community-school relations should be developed, and parents should be actively involved, particularly if they are lower-class and/or minority. Staffing patterns should reflect cultural diversity and offer a variety of role models for males and females of different race and class backgrounds. Finally, extracurricular activities should not perpetuate race and sex stereotypes.[54]

Such a vision may be rejected by some as utopian, but there are too many instances to ignore in which American schools serve as successful environments for low-income, African-American, and Hispanic students. The late educator Ron Edmonds reminded us that resistance to belief in the academic abilities of students from different cultural backgrounds lies more in prejudice than it does in the students' abilities to learn. Edmonds wrote in 1979:

> How many effective schools would you have to see to be persuaded of the educability of poor children? If your answer is more than one, then I suspect that you have reasons of your own for preferring to believe that basic pupil performance derives from family background instead of the school's response to family background.[55]

Like critical theorists, gender theorists, and cultural pluralism theorists, Edmonds urged that the analysis focus not primarily on the characteristics of the student, not primarily on the characteristics of the school, but on the interaction between the school and the child. Only by examining such relationships can we see how the school culture interacts with the culture and characteristics of the child to support or discourage learning and human development. Edmonds believes that students from all social groups are equally capable of learning, and that the duty of the educator is to help create an environment that responds to each child's needs—needs that are importantly conditioned in our culture by social variables such as race, ethnicity, gender, and social class.

It is important to observe at this point that this discussion of approaches that succeed with low-income and minority students is not a discussion about self-esteem. Although strong self-esteem is something valuable to each of us, it is not a substitute for learning. Educator Lilian Katz drew national media attention in 1993 when she pointed out how many educational programs were focusing on self-esteem as if good feelings were the same as good academic development.[56] Then in February 1997, an article written by AFT President Albert Shanker was published the day after his death making a similar argument in response to a recent report suggesting that some students, teachers, and the public are still being hoodwinked by a "self-esteem movement" that substitutes big doses of praise for effective instruction. Self-esteem should not be a product of praise, he argued, but of the satisfaction that comes with successful learning.[57]

A recent volume by Michael S. Knapp and associates presents a major, nationwide research study of teachers who succeed with children in high-poverty classrooms. As you would expect, these classrooms are disproportionately populated by children of color. Knapp found that teachers who succeed in bringing about measurably strong academic learning with high-poverty children are those who do three things well: maintain classroom order, respond effectively to diverse cultural backgrounds, and *teach for meaning*. By "teaching for meaning," Knapp means that teachers reject a traditional focus on student deficiencies and the traditional emphasis on learning discrete skills ordered from "basic" to "advanced." Instead, he writes, those who teach for meaning use a number of alternative approaches designed to engage students in using higher-order thinking skills to make connections between academic learning and their own life experiences. Specifically, teaching for meaning helps students make greater meaning of their studies by maximizing the following:

- First, where they [students] are actively engaged in the attempt to make sense of things they experience in school, they are encouraged to be meaning makers.
- Second, they derive meaning from seeing the relationship of parts to a whole, rather than being left with only parts. Opportunities to connect one concept or one skill to another increase

their conceptual grasp of what they are doing, whether it involves communication, problem solving, appreciation of artwork, or carrying out projects.

- Third, they find meaning by connecting new learning experiences to their existing body of knowledge, assumptions, and meanings, many of which are rooted in their upbringing and cultural roots.[58]

This study by Knapp and his associates is particularly meaningful because of its scale: 140 classrooms were studied in diverse school settings in the West, Midwest, and eastern United States. The findings serve to remind us that the intellectual capacities of low-income children demand our respect and our most challenging—not our most "dumbed down"—instructional strategies.

DIVERSITY, EQUITY, AND SPECIAL EDUCATION

In Chapter 12 we briefly visited the relationship between the growing number of students identified as "learning disabled" and the low academic performance of students from low-income backgrounds. The special education debates that have been ongoing at least since the 1960s have tried to address questions of equity for special-needs students. The very act of labeling students as "special needs" or "handicapped" has itself raised equity issues. Recently, Thomas Skrtic argued that the educational and equity needs of students with weak academic skills, many of whom are now labeled learning disabled, cannot be addressed without significant school reforms that place greater decision-making power in the hands of well-trained and educated teachers.[59]

Multicultural education specialist James Banks has offered a definition of multicultural education that is intended to place questions of equity and school reform at the heart of the meaning of multicultural education:

> There is an emerging consensus among specialists that multicultural education is a reform movement designed to bring about educational equity for all students, including those from different races, ethnic groups, social classes, exceptionality, and sexual orientations.[60]

Banks's definition is intended to draw attention to his view that multicultural education is the most equitable way to address the educational needs of all students, and that for schools to provide the necessary structure and resources to do so will require reforms in the way schools conduct their business. Banks's definition draws attention to another issue, as well: there are many kinds of student diversity, and it might serve students well if we would resist partitioning off some kinds of differences as "special" needs—especially when the educational needs of most children identified as special are the same as the needs of all children. Special educational programs, even under the Education for All Handicapped Students Act of 1975 and in the recent Regular Education Initiative, which is intended to improve on the negative consequences of that Act, become another form of tracking. Skrtic writes, "The restructuring debate does not recognize special education as a form of tracking." However, he continues:

> Students whose needs fall on the margins or outside of these standard programs must be either squeezed into them or squeezed out of the classroom. Given the inevitability of human diversity, a professional bureaucracy can do nothing but create students who do not fit the system. In a professional bureaucracy, all forms of tracking—curriculum tracking and in-class ability grouping in general education, as well as self-contained and resource classrooms in special, compensatory, remedial and gifted education—are organizational pathologies. . . . Students are subjected to—and subjugated by—these practices because, given their structural and cultural contingencies, traditional school organizations cannot accommodate diversity and so must screen it out.[61]

This is not to say that students with severe and obvious physical disabilities should not receive special educational attention. Rather, it reminds us of what Toch pointed out in Chapter 12: The labels on most students may say more about the system than about the students. Skrtic reports that the leading special education advocates of the Regular Education Initiative in special education all agree that "the EHA and mainstreaming are fundamentally flawed, particularly for students who are classified as mildly to moderately handicapped (hereafter mildly handicapped); that is, students classified as learning disabled, emotionally disturbed, or mentally retarded, who make up over two-thirds of the 4.5 million students served under the law."[62]

The challenge to the teacher, then, is to devise an environment that will support learning for students with very different skill levels and interests—so different that some of these students have been traditionally excluded from regular classrooms. Banks and other multicultural education advocates believe that multicultural perspectives are at bottom a way to respond to the learning needs of the widest array of students.

CONCLUDING REMARKS

In contrast to Chapter 12, which described some of the dimensions of inequality in contemporary schooling and society, Chapter 13 has focused on how teachers and schools can respond equitably to differences among students. Jane Elliott's classroom experiment with her elementary school students, first conducted over 25 years ago, reminds us that even children can understand that qualities judged as inferior or superior among people are not inherent and permanent, but are socially constructed. We see as well that whatever social group is most powerful has the opportunity to define superiority and inferiority in ways that are advantageous to that group.

How human differences are defined and valued in our culture is deeply rooted in ideology. Despite its history-changing positive emphasis on liberty and equality, the history of liberal ideology is marked by racist and sexist assumptions. These assumptions play a role in attempts to explain why one group performs better or is more highly rewarded than another in schooling and in society more generally. Efforts to understand these group differences often become theories of social and educational inequality. Differences among these theories are extremely important because they have very different implications for how to respond to differences among individual students and among groups of students in schools. For example, a theory of genetic inferiority was used in the pre-Civil War era to justify slavery and the exclusion of African-Americans from schooling. Later, genetic inferiority theory was used to justify the tracking of different groups of students into different school experiences and consequently different places in the socioeconomic order.

As the explanation of differences in group performance shifted from genetic deficit theory to cultural deficit theory, a new way of blaming the victim was introduced. In this approach, the problem of low school performance was attributed no longer to the genetic inheritance of the individual but to the individual's home life, or cultural inheritance. Such thinking led to efforts to place low-achieving students into remedial programs that would address their supposed cultural deficiencies, thus protecting the assumption that the performance problem lay with the student, not with the school.

While a great many citizens, including educators, most likely still adhere to a cultural deficit explanation of group and individual differences in school performance, recent years have seen increased attention to cultural difference theory. This approach portrays minority subcultures not as deficient but instead as different from the dominant school culture, leading to a mismatch that advantages students whose home lives most closely resemble the school culture's in language, values, and nonverbal communication. Such thinking has led to a questioning of why some cultures' practices are rewarded and honored in the school environment, while others' are devalued. The resulting explanation, which recognizes that schools institutionalize the power and ideology of the dominant social group, has led to a cultural subordination theory. The example of black English vernacular illustrates how a perfectly complete linguistic system can be devalued in the school culture, and how that devaluing can play a role in teachers' expectations of student achievement, thereby advantaging students whose primary language matches the school's.

How to respond to such differences of language and culture so that the needs of every child are served? Is it sensible to assume that the learning needs of all African-American children are different from their Hispanic and white non-Hispanic counterparts? Or that the learning needs of all boys are different from the needs of all girls? To make such assumptions is to define individuals only according to their group membership, which is clearly a bias to be avoided. Here the differences among bias, neutrality, and sensitivity become important. Treating students neutrally, as if the differences between them did not exist, risks disadvantage to those students whose starting points lag behind, so neutrality along lines of gender, ethnicity, or social class does not present a solution. The stance of gender sensitivity, or ethnic sensitivity, or class sensitivity, however, allows teachers to keep before them the question, When is race or gender or class a relevant variable in this student's or group of students' performance, and when is it not? When performance differences originate in group membership, as in the case of language or the different socialization of girls and boys, then a teacher's response might well be different than if the origins are idiosyncratic to the child.

To be sensitive to, and to respect, such differences is a major component of a multicultural approach to teaching. There are several different varieties of multiculturalism, as this chapter has shown, with perhaps the most promising one focusing on James Banks's notion of educational equity for all students. Such an approach honors the importance of group differences, including those identified as physical and mental handicaps, and seeks a pluralistic approach to teaching that benefits all students. Our two end-of-chapter readings, one addressing "anti-racist" education and the other addressing bilingualism, show two different approaches to multiculturalism in classroom teaching. Other examples given in the chapter include the Randolph School in New York City and Uri Treisman's successes with college calculus. All these approaches are grounded in the belief that all students can learn, and that we must continue to learn how to optimize their learning opportunities.

PRIMARY SOURCE READING

It is difficult to find a single primary source that effectively discusses how to meet the challenge of optimally educating all children, regardless of gender, race, ethnicity, income class, or physical or mental exceptionality. Perhaps there is no such source. Yet, when Enid Lee, in our first reading, remarks that "you need to look at how the dominant culture and biases affect your view of non-dominant groups in society," she is articulating a principle that can apply to any teacher's work with all students. For Lee, issues of power, of domination and subordination, are critical to a multiculturalism that will actually make a difference in the lives and futures of children. To distinguish this approach to multiculturalism from other approaches that do not look at discrimination, she uses the term "anti-racist education." It calls for teachers to be sensitive and responsive to how the school culture might be serving some cultural groups of children better than it serves others and to confront that reality in their teaching.

The second reading, a group of selections on English as a second language and on bilingual education, reminds us that culturally responsive teaching requires different approaches for different groups of students. While it is not reasonable to provide bilingual instruction for the dozens of different language groups that may attend a single school in large cities and their suburbs, the extraordinarily large number of children from one second-language group, Spanish, may require a singular response: bilingual instruction. There has been much opposition to this special treatment for Spanish-speaking children, and this opposition is as vocal now as it was when Lau *v.* Nicholls *was ruled in 1974 These arguments remain entirely relevant to today's "English-only" efforts, which would disallow the official use of any language but English in public settings, including schools. How compelling, or not so compelling, do you find the argument that children who speak English as a second language should have access to bilingual education so they may make a transition into fully competent speakers of English in contemporary society? This grouping of ESL and bilingual resources was published together in The* Bilingual Research Journal, *Summer/Fall 1995.*

TAKING MULTICULTURAL, ANTI-RACIST EDUCATION SERIOUSLY: AN INTERVIEW WITH EDUCATOR ENID LEE

The following is condensed from an interview with Enid Lee, a consultant in anti-racist education and organizational change, and author of Letters to Marcia: a Teachers' Guide to Anti-Racist Education. *Based in Toronto, Lee is the former supervisor of race/ethnic relations for the North York Board of Education in metropolitan Toronto. She was born and raised in the Caribbean, and has been working in the field of language, culture, and race for more than 15 years in Canada and the United States. She was interviewed by Barbara Miner of* Rethinking Schools.

What do you mean by a multicultural education?

The term "multicultural education" has a lot of different meanings. The term I use most often is "anti-racist education."

Multicultural or anti-racist education is fundamentally a perspective. It's a point of view that cuts across all subject areas, and addresses the histories and experiences of people who have been left out of the curriculum. Its purpose is to help us deal equitably with all the cultural and racial differences that you find in the human family. It's also a perspective that allows us to get at explanations for why things are the way they are in terms of power relationships, in terms of equality issues.

So when I say multicultural or anti-racist education, I am talking about equipping students, parents, and teachers with the tools needed to combat racism and ethnic discrimination, and to find ways to build a society that includes all people on an equal footing.

It also has to do with how the school is run in terms of who gets to be involved with decisions. It

Source: Barbara Miner, "Taking Multicultural, Anti-Racist Education Seriously: An Interview with Educator Enid Lee," *Rethinking Our Classrooms: Teaching for Equity and Justice* (Milwaukee: Rethinking Schools, 1994), pp. 19–22.

has to do with parents and how their voices are heard or not heard. It has to do with who gets hired in the school.

If you don't take multicultural education or anti-racist education seriously, you are actually promoting a monocultural or racist education. There is no neutral ground on this issue.

Why do you use the term "anti-racist education" instead of "multicultural education"?

Partly because, in Canada, multicultural education often has come to mean something that is quite superficial: the dances, the dress, the dialect, the dinners. And it does so without focusing on what those expressions of culture mean: the values, the power relationships that shape the culture.

I also use the term anti-racist education because a lot of multicultural education hasn't looked at discrimination. It has the view, "People are different and isn't that nice," as opposed to looking at how some people's differences are looked upon as deficits and disadvantages. In anti-racist education, we attempt to look at—and change—those things in school and society that prevent some differences from being valued.

Oftentimes, whatever is white is treated as normal. So when teachers choose literature that they say will deal with a universal theme or story, like childhood, all the people in the stories are of European origin; it's basically white culture and civilization. That culture is different from others, but it doesn't get named as different. It gets named as normal.

Anti-racist education helps us move that European perspective over to the side to make room for other cultural perspectives that must be included.

What are some ways your perspective might manifest itself in a kindergarten classroom, for example?

It might manifest itself in something as basic as the kinds of toys and games that you select. If all the toys and games reflect the dominant culture and race and language, then that's what I call a monocultural classroom even if you have kids of different backgrounds in the class.

I have met some teachers who think that just because they have kids from different races and backgrounds, they have a multicultural classroom. Bodies of kids are not enough.

It also gets into issues such as what kinds of pictures are up on the wall? What kinds of festivals are celebrated? What are the rules and expectations in the classroom in terms of what kinds of language are acceptable? What kinds of interactions are encouraged? How are the kids grouped? These are just some of the concrete ways in which a multicultural perspective affects a classroom.

How does one implement a multicultural or anti-racist education?

It usually happens in stages. Because there's a lot of resistance to change in schools, I don't think it's reasonable to expect to move straight from a monocultural school to a multiracial school.

First there is this surface stage in which people change a few expressions of culture in the school. They make welcome signs in several languages, and have a variety of foods and festivals. My problem is not that they start there. My concern is that they often stop there. Instead, what they have to do is move very quickly and steadily to transform the entire curriculum. For example, when we say classical music, whose classical music are we talking about? European? Japanese? And what items are on the tests? Whose culture do they reflect? Who is getting equal access to knowledge in the school? Whose perspective is heard, whose is ignored?

The second stage is transitional and involves creating units of study. Teachers might develop a unit on Native Americans, or Native Canadians, or people of African background. And they have a whole unit that they study from one period to the next. But it's a separate unit and what remains intact is the main curriculum, the main menu. One of the ways to assess multicultural education in your school is to look at the school organization. Look at how much time you spend on which subjects. When you are in the second stage you usually have a two- or three-week unit on a group of people or an area that's been omitted in the main curriculum.

You're moving into the next stage of structural change when you have elements of that unit integrated into existing units. Ultimately, what is at the center of the curriculum gets changed in its prominence. For example, civilizations. Instead of just talking about Western civilization, you begin to draw on what we need to know about India, Africa, China. We also begin to ask different questions about why and what we are doing. Whose interest is it in that we study what we study? Why is it that certain kinds of knowledge get hidden? In mathematics, instead of studying statistics with sports and weather numbers, why not look at employment in light of ethnicity?

Then there is the social change stage, when the curriculum helps lead to changes outside of the school. We actually go out and change the nature of the community we live in. For example, kids might become involved in how the media portray people, and start a letter-writing campaign about news that is negatively biased. Kids begin to see this as a responsibility that they have to change the world.

I think about a group of elementary school kids who wrote to the manager of the store about the kinds of games and dolls that they had. That's a long way from having some dinner and dances that represent an "exotic" form of life.

In essence, in anti-racist education we use knowledge to empower people and to change their lives.

Teachers have limited money to buy new materials. How can they begin to incorporate a multicultural education even if they don't have a lot of money?

We do need money and it is a pattern to underfund anti-racist initiatives so that they fail. We must push for funding for new resources because some of the information we have is downright inaccurate. But if you have a perspective, which is really a set of questions that you ask about your life, and you have the kids ask, then you can begin to fill in the gaps.

Columbus is a good example. It turns the whole story on its head when you have the children try to find out what the people who were on this continent might have been thinking and doing and feeling when they were being "discovered," tricked, robbed and murdered. You might not have that information on hand, because that kind of knowledge is deliberately suppressed. But if nothing else happens, at least you shift your teaching, to recognize the native peoples as human beings, to look at things from their view.

There are other things you can do without new resources. You can include, in a sensitive way, children's backgrounds and life experiences. One way is through interviews with parents and with community people, in which they can recount their own stories, especially their interactions with institutions like schools, hospitals and employment agencies. These are things that often don't get heard.

I've seen schools inviting grandparents who can tell stories about their own lives, and these stories get to be part of the curriculum later in the year. It allows excluded people, it allows humanity, back into the schools. One of the ways that discrimination works is that it treats some people's experiences, lives, and points of view as though they don't count, as though they are less valuable than other people's.

I know we need to look at materials. But we can also take some of the existing curriculum and ask kids questions about what is missing, and whose interest is being served when things are written in the way they are. Both teachers and students must alter that material.

How can a teacher who knows little about multiculturalism be expected to teach multiculturally?

I think the teachers need to have the time and encouragement to do some reading, and to see the necessity to do so. A lot has been written about multiculturalism. It's not like there's no information. If you want to get specific, a good place to start is back issues of the *Bulletin* of the Council on Interracial Books for Children.

You also have to look around at what people of color are saying about their lives, and draw from those sources. You can't truly teach this until you reeducate yourself from a multicultural perspective. But you can begin. It's an ongoing process.

Most of all, you have to get in touch with the fact that your current education has a cultural bias, that it is an exclusionary, racist bias, and that it needs to be purged. A lot of times people say, "I just need to learn more about those other groups." And I say, "No, you need to look at how the dominant culture and biases affect your view of non-dominant groups in society." You don't have to fill your head with little details about what other cultural groups eat and dance. You need to take a look at your culture, what your idea of normal is, and realize it is quite limited and is in fact just reflecting a particular experience. You have to realize that what you recognize as universal is, quite often, exclusionary. To be really universal, you must begin to learn what Africans, Asians, Latin Americans, the aboriginal peoples and all silenced groups of Americans have had to say about the topic.

How can one teach multiculturally without making white children feel guilty or threatened?

Perhaps a sense of being threatened or feeling guilty will occur. But I think it is possible to have kids move beyond that.

First of all, recognize that there have always been white people who have fought against racism and social injustice. White children can proudly identify with these people and join in that tradition of fighting for social justice.

Second, it is in their interest to be opening their minds and finding out how things really are. Otherwise, they will constantly have an incomplete picture of the human family.

The other thing is, if we don't make it clear that some people benefit from racism, then we are being dishonest. What we have to do is talk about how young people can use that from which they benefit to change the order of things so that more people will benefit.

If we say that we are all equally discriminated against on the basis of racism or sexism, that's not accurate. We don't need to be caught up in the guilt of our benefit, but should use our privilege to help change things.

I remember a teacher telling me last summer that after she listened to me on the issue of racism, she felt ashamed of who she was. And I remember wondering if her sense of self was founded on a sense of superiority. Because if that's true, then she is going to feel shaken. But if her sense of self is founded on working with people of different colors to change things, then there is no need to feel guilt or shame.

What are some things to look for in choosing good literature and resources?

I encourage people to look for the voice of people who are frequently silenced, people we haven't heard from: people of color, women, poor people, working-class people, people with disabilities, and gays and lesbians.

I also think that you look for materials that invite kids to seek explanations beyond the information that is before them, materials that give back to people the ideas they have developed, the music they have composed, and all those things which have been stolen from them and attributed to other folks. Jazz and rap music are two examples that come to mind.

I encourage teachers to select materials that reflect people who are trying and have tried to change things to bring dignity to their lives, for example Africans helping other Africans in the face of famine and war. This gives students a sense of empowerment and some strategies for making a difference in their lives. I encourage them to select materials that visually give a sense of the variety in the world.

Teachers also need to avoid materials that blame the victims of racism and other "isms."

In particular, I encourage them to look for materials that are relevant. And relevance has two points: not only where you are, but also where you want to go. In all of this we need to ask what's the purpose, what are we trying to teach, what are we trying to develop?

What can school districts do to further multicultural education?

Many teachers will not change curriculum if they have no administrative support. Sometimes, making these changes can be scary. You have parents on your back and kids who can be resentful. You can be told you are making the curriculum too political.

What we are talking about here is pretty radical; multicultural education is about challenging the status quo and the basis of power. You need administrative support to do that.

In the final analysis, multicultural or anti-racist education is about allowing educators to do the things they have wanted to do in the name of their profession: to broaden the horizons of the young people they teach, to give them skills to change a world in which the color of a person's skin defines their opportunities, where some human beings are treated as if they are just junior children.

Maybe teachers don't have this big vision all the time. But I think those are the things that a democratic society is supposed to be about.

When you look at the state of things in the United States and Canada, it's almost as if many parts of the society have given up on decency, doing the right thing and democracy in any serious way. I think that anti-racist education gives us an opportunity to try again.

Unfortunately, I feel that this educational movement is going to face a serious challenge. The 1980s were marked by very conservative attitudes, and some of the gains of the social change movements in the 1960s and 1970s were rolled back.

A major struggle is taking place in the 1990s to regain those victories of the 1960s and 1970s. I think that anti-racist education can help us do that. But the conservative forces are certainly not going to allow this to happen without a battle. We'd better get ready to fight.

PRIMARY SOURCE READING: THREE RESOURCES IN BILINGUAL AND ESL INSTRUCTION

1. Bilingual Education Program Models: A Framework For Understanding

Cheryl A. Roberts
University of Northern Iowa

Source: The Bilingual Research Journal, Summer/Fall 1995, Vol. 19, Nos. 3 & 4, pp. 369–378

ABSTRACT

Bilingual education remains a controversial topic of discussion in the United States locally and nationally. Issues of educational benefits need to be kept separate from political issues; both must be informed by understanding of the larger society. In this paper I describe different possible bilingual education models and comment on the educational costs and benefits associated with each.

INTRODUCTION

Bilingual education continues to fuel debate in the national as well as local arenas. Some believe passionately that use of any language other than English in the U.S. creates divisiveness; others believe that freedom to speak whatever language one chooses is a fundamental human right. Yet others feel that other languages in education are a luxury that cannot be afforded in difficult economic times. As recent demographic projections show (see editors' introduction), the number of children classified as limited English proficient (LEP) will continue to grow; thus, bilingual education is likely to continue to be a topic of debate.

In order to understand the contentiousness of this issue, it may be helpful to briefly consider assumptions and questions underlying some of the more commonly articulated arguments related to bilingual education. First, many appeal to national unity as a prime reason to reject bilingual education. An equally passionate view relates to language rights, and notes that as the Constitution does not endorse one religion, neither does it proclaim one language. A third perspective is that bilingual education is a generous attempt to help less fortunate non-native English speakers that simply is not affordable in difficult economic times.

Common to all three of these divergent views is the assumption that bilingual education is intended to promote bilingualism, and that it does in fact produce students who are either bilingual or whose English is less developed than that of their native English-speaking peers. Both assumptions can be challenged; bilingual programs are so diverse that it is problematical to make generalizations. In fact, efforts to review the efficacy of bilingual education programs, the most famous example of which is the AIR report (Hakuta,

1986), are criticized for failure to take into account the significant variations in programs. Labeling a program as transitional bilingual education, for example, does not ensure that the program is transitional nor that it is bilingual. The students served, languages spoken, grades and ages involved, number of teachers, their specializations and languages, subject matter taught, hours in the program, and so on are all variables that make each program distinct. The program descriptions in this issue demonstrate this very well.

Yet it is possible to provide a framework for systematically investigating bilingual educational programs, and it is the intent of this paper, along with the collection of papers following, to provide a framework for investigation and discussion. In order to provide this framework, I will briefly discuss a range of societal, linguistic, and educational goals and outcomes of bilingual education programs. Next, I will identify and comment on specific program models, with their typical goals and outcomes. Finally, I will review the importance of considering bilingual education programs as specific responses to local conditions, in a national context. The programs described in the rest of the papers may then be seen as variations on a particular model.

BILINGUAL EDUCATION GOALS AND OUTCOMES

Goals

Goals can be examined with respect to national or societal goals, linguistic goals, and educational goals. In general, national goals are of two types: assimilationist and pluralistic (Baker, 1993). Assimilationist goals seek to assimilate minority language speakers into the majority language and culture; in doing so, the minority language would become less important or even disappear. These goals characterize images of a "melting pot" culture and suggest that failure to assimilate may lead to separatism. Pluralistic goals typically affirm individual and group language rights, and are seen as support for group autonomy, which may or may not be viewed as a threat to larger group unity.

Assimilationist and pluralistic goals reflect ideological and philosophical differences; however, it must be noted that many, more specific goals, might not be identifiably either. For example, an individual's desire to learn more than one language may be related to improved job opportunities, to reinforcement of religious beliefs (Hebrew or Arabic, for example), personal travel, maintenance of historical family connections, personal enrichment, and so on. In the case of bilingual education, an important educational goal of using a minority language is to promote ability in the majority language (through transfer of skills and knowledge, improved emotional support, and so on). Thus, while considering the goals of the program type, we must keep in mind what groups and individuals, both majority language speakers and minority language speakers, will bring to the discussion group and individual goals.

Outcomes

Outcomes are typically categorized as that which results from bilingual education programs, or even from bilingualism as a result of societal forces. Wallace Lambert (1975) first identified two possible outcomes: additive bilingualism and subtractive bilingualism. Additive bilingualism is what results from a program in which students maintain their first language and acquire their second language. Subtractive bilingualism characterizes the situation in which students lose their first language in the process of acquiring their second language. According to Cummins (1981), students who experience additive bilingualism will show cognitive benefits. These might include greater metacognitive ability and greater mental flexibility. Subtractive bilingualism typically has a negative effect on students' educational experience.

It should be noted that programs may have the stated goal of additive bilingualism, but for a variety of reasons may not achieve that goal. Furthermore, the community's support and resources may be inadequate to support additive bilingualism. For these reasons, goals and outcomes should be looked at independently as well as together.

PROGRAM MODELS

Submersion

The submersion model, sometimes mistakenly identified as the immersion model in the U.S., mainstreams non-native English speaking students into regular English-speaking classrooms.

The goals of this model are assimilationist; that is, the goal is to have the non-native speaker learn English and assimilate to North American society. Since the first language is not supported, it is frequently lost and so the model is also considered subtractive. Cummins (1981) asserts that subtractive bilingualism leads to negative cognitive effects, and experience shows that learners who receive neither L1 support nor ESL have a difficult time succeeding in school. Such students frequently feel marginalized and drop out before finishing high school.

Submersion is not a legal option for schools with non-native English speakers; however, oversight and enforcement are lax, and many smaller schools with low populations of NNS students are simply unaware that they are required to provide some sort of services to these students. Parents of these children, for cultural and other reasons, tend not to demand the services their children are entitled to; thus it is not uncommon to find submersion in U.S. public schools.

ESL Pullout

In this model, students are "pulled out" of some other classes in order to receive English as a second language class. They are mainstreamed into other classes. ESL pullout is also assimilationist in its goals, and subtractive bilingualism is the usual outcome. Students in this model may receive as little as twenty minutes or as much as several hours or more (often these programs are called language intensive) but students may still fall behind in content areas as they struggle to learn English.

ESL pullout is commonly found in areas with students of a variety of language backgrounds, making it difficult to find enough bilingual teachers and aides, and in areas where resources, particularly financial, are limited. It is also not uncommon to find pullout programs in somewhat homogeneous communities where assimilationist attitudes prevail, although it is certainly not limited to those types of communities.

The issue of which class to release children from should be thoughtfully considered; generally, it makes sense to release children from English Language Arts for native speakers. It is less appropriate to take children from content classes or from classes in which they can form friendships with native speakers of English, such as P.E., music, or art.

A related program type is the sheltered model, in which ESL and content area classes are combined, and taught either by an ESL-trained subject area teacher or by a team. These classes are designed to deliver content area instruction in a form more accessible than the mainstream. They may use additional materials, bilingual aides, adapted texts and so on to help students of diverse language backgrounds acquire the content as well as the language. Sheltered programs, or classes, are also assimilationist.

Transitional Bilingual Education

Transitional bilingual education provides content area support in the native language while teaching the student English. Initially, the learner is taught content classes in the native language, is taught English as a Second Language, and may also take music, P.E., art, and similar classes in English, partly because these classes require less language proficiency and also because it is important that the learner know English speaking students (for language and social development).

The transitional model serves as a bridge for students, helping them move from their native language to English, and any given program may do so more quickly or more slowly. Federal guidelines now suggest that 3 years is the target amount of time for learners to receive L1 support, in spite of studies showing that 5–7 years is a more realistic time frame for learners to reach levels comparable to their native English speaking peers (See Collier, 1989; Krashen et al., 1982).

The goals of transitional bilingual education are still assimilationist, and the outcome is generally subtractive bilingualism. Still, it is hoped that these programs will provide the content area support which will enable these students to remain in school.

These programs are often found in communities with significant populations of non-native English speakers, particularly of one or two language backgrounds. This makes it easier and more desirable in terms of community attitudes to find bilingual teachers. The U.S. government, through Title VII grants, funds transitional programs.

Maintenance Bilingual Education

Maintenance bilingual programs differ significantly from the previous models in both goals and outcomes. In maintenance programs, the learners are transitioned into English content classes, and are given support in their first language, as in transitional programs. However, they also receive language arts in their native language, enabling them to become literate in that language, and they continue to receive content area classes in their first language as well, so that they become literate in both languages.

The goal of maintenance bilingual programs is to promote bilingualism and biliteracy; rather than an assimilationist goal, this model promotes pluralism. Languages other than English are seen as resources. Because it promotes the development of two languages, the outcome is additive bilingualism, which is associated with positive cognitive benefits (Cummins, 1981).

Maintenance programs exist where there are sufficiently large numbers of students on one language background to make it possible to hire bilingual teachers and where there is interest and support in the community for having a bilingually educated population. While the financial investment may not be much more than for a transitional program, it is essential that the community and school staff, both speakers of majority and minority languages, support a maintenance program. It may be possible for a maintenance program to succeed with limited support on the part of the minority language community as long as the majority language speakers do not actively object. However, without support from the minority language community, such a program is unlikely to exist. There are minority language speakers who object strongly to the use of languages other than English in the public school system, and again care must be taken to address parent and community goals as an important determinant of educational goals.

Enrichment, Two-way, or Developmental Bilingual

Enrichment bilingual education in the U.S. involves not only non-native speakers of English but also native English speakers. (Enrichment programs in Canada can be immersion programs, discussed below. These do not include both minority and majority language speakers in the same classes in the early grades.) While the non-native English speakers are essentially in a maintenance program, the native English speakers are in a similar maintenance program in the second language. From the start and continuing throughout, the learners serve as resources for each other. While there are segregated ESL or L1 content classes initially, the goal is to have the students of both language backgrounds studying content classes in both languages.

Like maintenance bilingual education, the goal of enrichment bilingual education is pluralistic: the development of biliterate and bilingual individuals. Both (or several) languages are valued. Outcomes of enrichment bilingual programs are additive bilingualism, not just for one ethnic group but for majority and minority speakers.

In order to ensure a balance of languages, several alternatives are possible. For example, classes taught in the morning might be taught in one language, while classes taught in the afternoon might be taught in the other. It is recommended that the languages switch slots periodically, as students are said to be more alert in the morning. Another possibility is to teach one content class such as math in one language, and then teach the next math class in the other language the following semester. These two possibilities are identified as alternate because languages are alternated by time or by subject matter.

A second approach is known as concurrent, in which classes are simultaneously taught in both languages in a team teaching approach, where one teacher represents English and the other represents another language. In the preview-review technique of concurrent language teaching, one teacher previews the lesson in his/her language, the other teaches the lesson in the other language, and the first reviews the lesson in the first language. Unfortunately, team teaching can have several drawbacks. First, though the goal is to provide a balance of input in both languages, it has been found that English tends to dominate (Ovando & Collier, 1985, p 83). In addition, there can be a great deal of repetition, which may waste time. Finally, students who know they will hear the material in both languages may simply not pay attention until the teacher begins using their preferred language. (Wong-Fillmore, 1980; cited in Ovando & Collier, 1985). These obstacles can be overcome when there is a commitment to the goals of the program.

Enrichment bilingual education programs require a high level of community support and involvement, both financial and human, by both majority and minority speakers. They are more complicated to set up, and the scheduling of students, teachers, and classes requires more effort. However, the results are highly promising for those who feel that the non-English languages spoken in the U.S. and Canada are valuable resources for the future.

Immersion (Canadian Model)

The immersion model was originally developed in Canada, and was and is used successfully with English speakers learning French as well as with growing numbers of minority language children (Taylor, 1992). Though nothing in the definition of immersion bilingual education excludes minority language children, it may happen in practice.

When immersion is used with majority English speakers learning French, immersion bilingual education is generally pluralistic and promotes additive bilingualism. Learners become biliterate and bilingual in two languages. However, when minority language speakers are immersed in the majority language, the goal is frequently assimilationist and results in subtractive bilingualism.

A variety of immersion models are used with majority English speakers in Canada, from early to late total immersion and from partial to full immersion; differences in outcomes between these models seem to be relatively minor (Swain, 1978).

Again, due to confusion in the usage of the terms, it is critical to differentiate between submersion for minority students in English-speaking classrooms and French immersion for minority students in French-speaking classrooms: the difference relates to L1 or L2 oriented pedagogy. That is, "minority language students in an English-medium class with mother tongue speakers of English experience pedagogy intended for L1 speakers; hence, English is not presented as an L2, neither is pedagogy necessarily appropriate for L2 learners. In an L1 classroom, on the other hand, minority and majority children alike are not expected to speak French as an L1; hence, the program is entirely geared to L2 learning and the pedagogy is geared to L2 learners" (Taylor, 1995, personal communication).

CONCLUSION

Although each program is unique, it is generally possible to identify an underlying basic program model. Variations can and should occur, as a program is adjusted to suit the characteristics of a particular school and community. As the following papers show, there are as many designs as there are programs. In looking at possible models, and in reading about actual programs, the reader should be aware of the goals and outcomes of different programs, as well as the details of implementation.

REFERENCES

Baker, C. (1993). *Foundations of bilingual education and bilingualism.* Philadelphia: Multilingual Matters.

Collier, V. P. (1989). How long? A synthesis of research on academic achievement in a second language. *TESOL Quarterly, 23*(3), 509–531.

Cummins, J. (1981). The role of primary language development in promoting educational success for language minority students. In California State Department of Education (Ed.), *Schooling and language minority students: A theoretical framework* (pp. 3–49). Los Angeles: Evaluation, Dissemination and Assessment Center, California State University.

Ferguson, C. A., Hougton, C., & Wells, M. H. (1977). Bilingual education: An international perspective. In B. Spolsky & R. Cooper (Eds.), *Frontiers of bilingual education* (pp. 159–194). Rowley, MA: Newbury House.

Krashen, S., Long, M., & Scarcella, R. (1979). Age, rate, and eventual attainment in second language acquisition. *TESOL Quarterly 13*(4), 573–582.

Lambert, W. E. (1975). Culture and language as factors in learning and education. In A. Wolfgang (Ed.). *Education of Immigrant Students.* Toronto: O.I.S.E.

Ovando, C. J. & Collier, V. P. (1985). *Bilingual and ESL classrooms: Teaching in multicultural contexts.* New York: McGraw-Hill.

Swain, M. (1978). Bilingual education for the English-speaking Canadian. In J. E. Alatis (Ed.), *International Dimensions of Bilingual Education.* Washington, D.C.: Georgetown University Press.

Taylor, S. (1992). Victor: A case study of a Cantonese child in early French immersion. *Canadian Modern Language Review, 48*(4), 736–759.

2. Tesol Statement on the Role of Bilingual Education in the Education of Children in the United States

What is TESOL?

Teachers of English to Speakers of Other Languages, Inc. (TESOL) is an international professional organization whose mission is to strengthen the effective teaching and learning of English around the world while respecting individuals' language rights. In its policies, programs, and publications, TESOL supports native language rights and bilingual education. Thus, TESOL:

- endorses the goal of bilingualism for all students and
- encourages both students from linguistically and culturally diverse communities and students who speak only English to learn from each other in integrated classrooms.

What is bilingual education?

In the U.S., bilingual education is an approach to schooling that, while fully recognizing the importance of English in the world community, also recognizes that the home language of many students is a language other than English and that for monolingual English-speaking children, it is of great benefit to learn a second language.

Students who come from homes where a language other than English is used will be at different stages of development in their home and second languages. Bilingual education enables these children to use their home language initially as a tool for learning new concepts, while at the same time developing proficiency in their second language so that they will have both languages as tools for future learning and for use in their lives beyond their families and immediate community.

Source: The Bilingual Research Journal, Summer/Fall 1995, Vol. 19, Nos. 3 & 4, pp. 661–669.

For students who come from homes where only English is used, bilingual education means the opportunity to add another language to their repertoire so that they, too, will have alternate means of learning and communicating beyond their families and immediate community. Thus, bilingual education in the U.S.:

- uses students' primary languages as vehicles to learn a second language,
- recognizes that students' language proficiencies are at different stages of development,
- uses linguistic, academic, and sociocultural resources of students' home communities as tools to teach academic knowledge and skills, and,
- focuses on students' linguistic, cognitive/academic, and sociocultural development.

How are bilingual education and English-as-a-second-language (ESL) programs interrelated?

For children who enter U.S. schools using languages other than English, school systems sometimes provide an ESL program, sometimes a bilingual education program, and sometimes nothing. In an ESL program, which is often provided where children of diverse language backgrounds attend school together, typically the home languages of the children are not used in class. In a bilingual education program, where children of the same home language background can be grouped together, that home language is used in class and, in addition, the program includes an English-language-teaching component. English-language proficiency is a common objective of both program types.

ESL instruction consists of:

- monolingual English instruction, using ESL methods to teach oral and written English,
- often, sheltered instruction (that is, classes taught in simplified English with many visual aids) in the subject areas using ESL techniques.

Exemplary ESL programs incorporate cultural aspects of students' backgrounds into meaningful language learning experiences and apply ESL techniques to content areas taught through English. In

English-as-subject classes, for example, vocabulary and grammatical structures are taught not in isolation but in meaningful contexts, relevant to students' learning experiences and to their lives as members of linguistically and culturally diverse communities. Sometimes native-language support is available in an ESL program.

Bilingual education consists of:

- primary/native language instruction in areas such as science, mathematics, and social studies to develop cognitive/academic concepts,
- ESL instruction to develop oral and written English, and often,
- sheltered English to reduce language barriers to subject matter in English.

In exemplary bilingual education programs in the U.S., students learn through two languages—their native language and English. These exemplary programs encompass both the mainstream curriculum and the history and culture associated with the native language and develop and maintain students' self-esteem and pride in both cultures, without disruption of their cognitive/academic development. These programs also recognize that the stronger the students' cognitive and academic proficiency in the first language, the stronger their proficiency in a second language. In other words, native language literacy skills—whether in English or another language—are necessary for successful second language development.

What types of bilingual programs are there?

While bilingual education takes many different forms, in the U.S. there are three major types:

- A transitional bilingual program provides instruction and cognitive development through students' dominant language only until students have acquired sufficient proficiency in English to function effectively in a monolingual English setting.

The goal is to develop proficiency in English, using two languages to get there. However, this model often fails to recognize how long it takes to develop both cognitive and academic literacy in a second language. Thus, the period of instruction is generally long enough (one to two years) for young learners to acquire basic social language skills in English, but it is often not long enough to develop the cognitive and academic language proficiency needed for school success—typically a matter of five to nine years. These programs usually do not reflect the research finding that most long-term bilingual instruction is more efficient and cost-effective than most short-term instruction.

- A maintenance bilingual program uses content-subject instruction in both the home language and English to achieve the goal of bilingual and bicultural [literacy. Although it] takes many years, this model views the development of bilingual proficiency as an asset that more than justifies the investment of time.
- A two-way bilingual program is an integrated model that enables learners from linguistically and culturally diverse communities, as well as learners who come from homes where only English is used, to learn each other's languages and cultures.

In the transitional bilingual model, the goal is to replace a student's first language with English, at least for academic purposes. In both maintenance and two-way programs, the ultimate goal is to enrich the student's linguistic repertoire by adding a second language as an alternate means of learning and communicating. None of these three program types is considered remedial.

Which bilingual programs are the most effective?

TESOL strongly endorses maintenance and two-way programs because their designs:

- recognize that a strong first language (oral and written) leads to a strong second language;
- assure sufficient time to acquire the strong classroom language and academic concepts needed for successful academic-language learning, going beyond the acquisition of social language skills;
- have a strong, carefully integrated ESL component;
- promote bilingualism and biculturalism as assets, while showing respect and appreciation for students' language rights.

Unfortunately, a monolingual English-only classroom, with no ESL or home language support, is the only program available for many linguistically and culturally diverse students. Because this setting offers no support in ESL or bilingual education, it has none of the advantages of the other programs.

What are the parents' roles in bilingual education and ESL programs?

All parents of children in bilingual education and ESL programs, including those who come from language backgrounds other than English, have much to contribute to the school community and have the same rights as any other parents regarding the education of their children. In the U.S., these rights include:

- communicating with school teachers, administrators, and staff;
- receiving communications from the school in their stronger language, which may not be English;
- volunteering and assisting at school;
- participating in their children's learning activities at home; and
- participating in governance and advocacy activities—for example, parent-teacher organizations, school management teams, and school board meetings—through interpreters, if necessary.

Research shows that greater parental participation results in more successful students, parents, and schools.

What preparation do teachers need to function in a culturally diverse school?

All teachers and administrators who come into contact with culturally and linguistically diverse populations need to be familiar with the theory and methodology of ESL, second language acquisition, and bilingual education. Teachers, administrators, and support staff should become familiar with ways to support the students' home languages, even when these people do not themselves speak the students' home languages and cannot provide services in the students' home languages.

In exemplary schools, the bilingual education, ESL, and mainstream teachers work together as a professional team to reach the same long-range goal—the development of bilingual proficiency—for the same student population, fostering their students' development of first and second languages so that their bilingualism becomes an asset.

Teachers in mainstream classrooms have much to contribute to the education of bilingual students, because these students ultimately spend much more time in mainstream classrooms than in bilingual or ESL classes. To ensure the integration of linguistically and culturally diverse students in the classroom, mainstream teachers need to provide comprehensible lessons that are culturally relevant and cognitively demanding, to use cooperative learning methods, peer support across the curriculum, and two-way sharing of languages and cultures, and to include bilingual students in all curricular and extra-curricular school activities.

What does TESOL recommend for K-12 educational programs in the U.S.?

So that all students will have an opportunity to realize their full potential and will be able to make choices within the societies in which they live, TESOL endorses the following principles:

For students from linguistically and culturally diverse communities (communities that use English and another language or languages):

- teachers who are professionally prepared in the theory and methodology of ESL, second language acquisition, and bilingual education and who are themselves proficient in both the home and second languages of their students;
- age-appropriate and grade-appropriate subject matter in students' dominant language, as far as that is possible, to minimize disruption of students' cognitive and academic development;
- assessment appropriate to a student's age, grade, and culture, in the student's dominant language;
- opportunities to learn English through a sheltered approach to subject matter, in a curriculum that clearly distinguishes between English

as a subject and English as a medium of instruction;
- opportunities to develop and maintain self-esteem and pride in their home language and culture;
- opportunities for their parents to actively participate in school affairs, through oral and written communication in the parents' dominant language;
- opportunities for interaction with peers whose first language is English in an integrated total school program; and
- ESL or bilingual education instruction, or both, as required by state and federal laws and monitored by the U.S. Department of Education, Office of Civil Rights.

For students who come from homes where only English is used:

- teachers who understand and communicate the benefits of having a culturally and linguistically diverse classroom—and larger community—and who set an example by themselves being proficient in more than one language; and
- opportunities to learn the language and culture of their linguistically and culturally diverse peers in an integrated total school program.

What resources are available to teachers and schools in the U.S.?

- The National Clearinghouse for Bilingual Education (NCBE), in Washington, D.C., can provide information about free or low cost assistance with implementation, training, evaluation, and parental involvement in bilingual education and ESL programs, as well as legal requirements for bilingual education and ESL programs in various communities: 1-800-321-NCBE.
- Teachers of English to Speakers of Other Languages, Inc. (TESOL) in Arlington, VA: 1-703-836-0774. Individual and institutional TESOL members may participate in the activities and receive a newsletter of the Bilingual Education Interest Section.
- The National Association for Bilingual Education (NABE) in Washington, D.C.: 1-202-898-1829.
- TESOL and NABE state affiliates. Call the TESOL or NABE central offices in Virginia or Washington, D.C. for the appropriate names and phone numbers.
- The U.S. Department of Education, Office for Civil Rights (OCR). Contact OCR for their latest policy statements on the legal responsibilities of educational agencies serving language minority students, and call NCBE for the locations and phone numbers of the ten Desegregation Assistance Centers (DACs).
- The Office of Bilingual Education and Minority Language Affairs (OBEMLA) has 16 federally-funded resource centers (MRCs). Call NCBE for appropriate names and phone numbers.
- State education agencies. Call your state Department of Education or NCBE for appropriate names and phone numbers.

Approved and adopted by the TESOL Executive Board, October 24, 1992.

Prepared by the TESOL Bilingual Education Interest Section Task Force, Beti Leone, chair. The following persons acted as contributors and discussants in the development of this paper: Mark Arias, Lisa Baldonado, George Blanco, Angela Carrasquillo, Robert Carlisle, Ida Carrillo, René Cisneros, Virginia Collier, Yvonne Freeman, Else Hamayan, Jean Handscombe, Michelle Hewlett-Gómez, Cheryl Huffman, Beti Leone, Leona Marsh, Jean McConochie, Suzanne Medina, Diamond Navarro, Roger E. Winn-Bell Olsen, Cecilio Orozco, Carlos Ovando, Joyce Penfield, Albar Pena, Lorraine Valdez Pierce, Cheryl Roberts, José Torres, Richard Tucker, Lillian Vega Castañeda, Dorthy Waggoner, and Joan Wink.

3. The Tesol Standards: Ensuring Access to Quality Educational Experiences for Language Minority Students

Languages minority students are those students who learned a language other than English as their first language. These students may be immigrants, refugees, or native born Americans. They may come to school with extensive formal education or they may be academically delayed or illiterate in their first language. Such students arrive at school with varying degrees of English proficiency. Some may not speak English at all; others may speak English, but need assistance in reading or writing English.

Whatever the case, it is clear that schools that hope to help these students meet the National Education Goals must provide special assistance to them. While the type of special assistance may vary from one district or school to another, all special assistance programs must give language minority students full access to the learning environment, the curriculum, special services and assessment in a meaningful way. Teachers of English to Speakers of Other Languages (TESOL) offers the following standards of access to help schools judge the degree to which programs of special assistance are helping language minority students to meet the National Education Goals. The standards have been developed by the TESOL Task Force on the Education of Language Minority Students, K-12, in the US. They are based on the most current research on language learning in academic settings.

Access to a Positive Learning Environment

1. Are the schools attended by language minority students safe, attractive, and free of prejudice?
2. Is there evidence of a positive whole-school environment whose administrative and instructional policies and practices create a climate that is characterized by high expectations as well as linguistically and culturally appropriate learning experiences for language minority students?
3. Are teachers, administrators, and other staff specifically prepared to tailor instructional and other services to the needs of language minority students?
4. Does the school environment welcome and encourage parents of language minority students as at-home primary teachers of their children and as partners in the life of the school? Does the school inform and educate parents and others concerned with the education of language minority students? Does the school systematically and regularly seek input from parents on information and decisions that affect all critical aspects of the education of language minority students, their schools and school districts?

Access to Appropriate Curriculum

5. Do language minority students have access to special instructional programs that support the second language development necessary to participate in the full range of instructional services offered to majority students?
6. Does the core curriculum designed for all students include those aspects that promote (a) the sharing, valuing, and development of both first and second languages and cultures among all students and (b) the higher order thinking skills required for learning across the curriculum?
7. Do language minority students have access to the instructional programs and related services that identify, conduct and support programs for special populations in a district? Such programs include, but are not limited to, early childhood programs, special education programs, and gifted and talented programs, as well as programs for students with handicapping conditions or disabilities, migrant education programs, programs for recent immigrants, and programs designed for students with low levels of literacy or mathematical skills, such as Chapter 1.

Access to Full Delivery of Services

8. Are the teaching strategies and instructional practices used with language minority students developmentally appropriate, attuned to students' language proficiencies and cognitive levels, and culturally supportive and relevant?
9. Do students have opportunities to develop and use their first language to promote academic and social development?

Source: The Bilingual Research Journal, Summer/Fall 1995, Vol. 19, Nos. 3 & 4, pp. 671–674

10. Are nonclassroom services and support services (such as counseling, career guidance, and transportation) available to language minority students?
11. Do language minority students have equal access to computers, computer classes and other technologically advanced instructional assistance?
12. Does the school have institutional policies and procedures that are linguistically and culturally sensitive to the particular needs of language minority students and their communities?
13. Does the school offer regular, nonstereotypical opportunities for native English-speaking students and language minority students to share and value one another's languages and cultures?

Access to Equitable Assessment

14. Do language minority students have access to broadly based methods of assessing language and academic achievement in the content areas that are appropriate to students' developmental level, age, and level of oral and written language proficiency in the first and second languages? Are these measures nonbiased and relevant? Are the results of such assessments explained to the community from which the student comes in the language which that community uses?
15. Do language minority students have access to broadly based methods of assessing special needs? Again, access is further defined by using measures that are nonbiased and relevant, the results of which are explained to the community from which the student comes and in the language which that community uses.

Tesol Resource Packet Available

TESOL has developed a resource packet to help schools implement quality educational programs for language minority students. The packet includes reprints of articles by outstanding authors such as Scott Enright, Sarah Hudelson, Mary Lou McCloskey, and Pat Rigg.

The packet sells for $17.95 and may be obtained by contacting:

TESOL Central Office
1600 Cameron St., Suite 300
Alexandria, VA 22314-2751
703-836-0774

QUESTIONS FOR DISCUSSION AND EXAMINATION

1. While there is a clear contrast between cultural deficit theory and cultural difference theory, cultural subordination theory is presented as flowing conceptually from cultural difference theory. What are the conceptual connections between these latter two theories, in your view, and what difference might these connections make to the classroom teacher?
2. Enid Lee says there is "no neutral ground" regarding taking multicultural education seriously. What does she mean by this, and do you agree? Explain.
3. Lee writes, "What we are talking about here is pretty radical; multicultural education is about challenging the status quo and the basis of power. You need administrative support to do that." This seems like a contradiction: can teachers really expect administrators, who hold the greatest power in the school building and in the school district, to support a challenge to the basis of their power? How might Lee be interpreted so that her argument is valid? How might she be interpreted so that her position is faulty? Explain.
4. Several different views of multicultural education were presented in the chapter: not just the five taken from Grant and Sleeter, but also James Banks's view and the authors' implicit position as well. Are any of these viewpoints consistent with Enid Lee's concept of anti-racist education? Are any inconsistent? Explain how closely her perspective is reflected in selected perspectives from the chapter.
5. In what regard might it be said that bilingual education is a form of multicultural education? To what degree is bilingual education consistent or inconsistent with Enid Lee's conception of anti-racist education? Explain your position on both questions.
6. If you do not speak Spanish and therefore cannot offer bilingual instruction, how can you best support the learning of children whose first language is Spanish and who are limited in their English proficiency? How does this relate to the approach you will use with speakers of English as a second language from other language backgrounds, such as those of Asia or Eastern Europe? finally, is any aspect of your approach relevant to supporting student learning for speakers of black English vernacular? Explain your position on all three issues.

NOTES

1. Katharine Q. Seelye, "Group Seeks to Alter S.A.T. to Raise Girls' Scores," *New York Times* (March 14, 1997), A25.
2. Peter Applebome, "Minorities Falling Behind in Student Achievement," *New York Times* (December 29, 1996), Y9.
3. Steven A. Holmes, "For Hispanic Poor, No Silver Lining," *New York Times* (October 13, 1996), E5.
4. Cornel West, *Race Matters* (Boston: Beacon Press, 1993). Michelle Campbell, "Hate Crimes in Illinois: 1.4 per Day," *Chicago Sun Times* (November 24, 1996).
5. Jeannie Oakes, Amy Stuart Wells, Makeba Jones, and Amanda Datnow, "Detracking: the Social Construction of Ability, Cultural Politics, and Resistance to Reform," *Teachers College Record,* 98:3 (Spring 1997), pp. 482–510.
6. The following account, and all quotes, are taken from William Peters, *A Class Divided—Then and Now* (New Haven, CT: Yale University Press, 1987).
7. Video cassettes and 16mm print films of this documentary are available from Guidance Associates, The Center for Humanities, Communications Park, Box 3000, Mount Kisco, NY, 10549. The follow-up documentary is available from PBS Video.
8. In an August 1988 poll taken by Media General-Associated Press, 53 percent of white Americans and 68 percent of African-Americans surveyed said the society is racist.
9. Peters, *A Class Divided,* pp. 37–38.
10. The topic is covered extensively in Henry Giroux, *Teachers as Intellectuals* (Granby, MA: Bergin and Garvey, 1988).
11. Lewis M. Terman, *Intelligence Tests and School Reorganization* (New York: World, 1923). We have taken this quote from Clarence Karier, "Testing for Order and Control in the Corporate Liberal State," *Educational Theory* 22 (Spring 1972), pp. 154–80.
12. Quoted in Karier, "Testing for Order and Control."
13. See, for example, Arthur R. Jensen, *Bias in Mental Testing* (New York: Free Press, 1980).
14. R. Herrnstein and C. Murray, *The Bell Curve* (New York: The Free Pres, 1994).
15. See, for example, William Deutsch (ed.), *The Child's Construction of Language Behavioral Development* (San Diego: Academic Press, 1982); Basil Bernstein, *Class Codes and Control,* 2d revised ed. (London: Routledge and K. Paul, 1974).
16. Lisa Delpit, *Other People's Children* (New York: New Press, 1995).
17. Longstreet conducted a study of learning styles among Navajo children. Mentioned by Karen Swisher, "Styles of Learning and Learning of Styles: Educational Conflicts for American Indian/Alaskan Native Youth," *Multilingual and Multicultural Development,* Vol. 8, No. 4 (1987), p. 348.
18. John U. Ogbu, "Minority Status and Schooling in Plural Societies," *Comparative Educational Review,* Vol. 27, No. 2, pp. 168–90.
19. John U. Ogbu, "Understanding Diversity," *Education and Urban Society* 22(4) Aeylon 1990), 425–29.
20. Anyon, "Social Class and School Knowledge," *Curriculum Inquiry,* Vol. 2, No. 1 (1987), pp. 3–42.
21. Ibid, p. 17.
22. Ibid., p. 26. This was one of the questions found in a text used by the executive elite school.
23. In recent decades, the competition for elite preschools has grown.
24. Ray C. Rist, "Student Social Class and Teacher Expectations," *Harvard Review,* Vol. 40, No. 3 (August 1970).
25. John Duffy, "Getting Off Track: The Challenge and Potential of the Mixed Ability Classroom," *Democracy and Education,* Fall 1988, pp. 11–19. Duffy is citing the 1987 research by David and Roger Johnson.
26. P. A. Graham, "Black Teachers: A Drastically Scarce Resource," *Phi Delta Kappan,* April 1987.
27. William Labov, *Sociolinguistic Patterns* (Philadelphia: University of Pennsylvania Press, 1972); Michael Stubbs, *Language Schools and Classrooms,* 2d ed. (London and New York: Methuen, 1983); Peter Trudgill, *Sociolinguistics* (New York: Penguin Books, 1983); J. B. Pride and J. Holmes (eds.), *Sociolinguistics: Selected Readings* (Harmondsworth, England: Penguin Modern Linguistics Readings, 1972).
28. Ursula Casanova and M. Beatriz Arias, "Contextualizing Bilingual Education," in *Bilingual Education: Politics, Practice, and Research; Ninety-second Yearbook of the National Society for the Study of Education Part II* (Chicago: NSSE, 1993), p. 13.
29. *A Profile of Policies and Practices for Limited English Proficient Students: Screening Methods, Program Support, and Teacher Training* (SASS 1993–94). U.S. Department of Education Office of Educational Research and Improvement NCES 97–472. Washington, DC (January 1977), p. 5.
30. Ibid.
31. Lynn Schnaiberg, "Ebonics Vote Puts Oakland in Maelstrom," *Education Week* XVI: 16 (January 15, 1997), pp. 1, 32. The story was carried by all major national and big-city news outlets, as well.
32. James Baldwin, "If Black English Isn't a Language, Then Tell Me What Is?" *The Price of the Ticket: Collected Nonfiction 1948–1985* (New York: St. Martin's Press, 1985), p. 652.

33. D. Bolinger and D. A. Sears, *Aspects of Language* (New York: Harcourt, Brace, Jovanovich, 1981), p. 198.
34. Joan G. Fickett, "Tense and Aspect in Black English," *Journal of English Linguistics*, Vol. 6 (1972), p. 19. The quote referred to appears in Bolinger and Sears, *Aspects of Language*, p. 198.
35. Most of these examples are taken from Bolinger and Sears, *Aspects of Language*, Table 9–1, p. 199.
36. Eleanor Wilson Orr, *Twice As Less* (New York: W. W. Norton, 1987).
37. William Labov, "Academic Ignorance and Black Intelligence," *The Atlantic*, Vol. 229, No. 6 (June 1972), pp. 59–67.
38. Jane Roland Martin, *Reclaiming a Conversation* (New Haven, CT: Yale University Press, 1985).
39. Jane Roland Martin, "Bringing Women into Educational Thought," *Educational Theory*, Vol. 34, No. 4 (Fall 1984), p. 349.
40. Gordon L. Berry, "The Multicultural Principle: Missing from the Seven Cardinal Principles of 1918 and 1978," *Phi Delta Kappan*, June 1978, p. 745. For an extended account of one approach to culturally responsive teaching, see C. A. Bowers and David J. Flinders, *Responsive Teaching* (New York: Teachers College Press, 1990).
41. Christine Sleeter and Carl A. Grant, *Making Choices for Multicultural Education: Five Approaches to Race, Class, and Gender* (Columbus, OH: Merrill, 1988).
42. Ibid., p. 66.
43. Ibid., p. 100.
44. Ibid., p. 131.
45. Ibid., p. 168.
46. Ibid., p. 166.
47. Ibid., p. 166.
48. Ibid., p. 187.
49. Ibid., p. 190.
50. Cited in Allyn Jackson, "Minorities in Mathematics: A Focus on Excellence, Not Remediation," *American Educator*, (Spring 1989).
51. Lottie L. Taylor and Joan R. Pinard, "Success Against the Odds: Effective Education of Inner-City Youth in a New York City Public High School," *Journal of Negro Education*, Vol. 57, No. 3 (1988), pp. 347–61.
52. Ibid., p. 351.
53. Ibid., p. 361.
54. Sleeter and Grant, *Making Choices*, pp. 193–94.
55. Quoted in The Committee on Policy for Racial Justice, *Visions of a Better Way: A Black Appraisal of Public Schooling* (Washington, DC: Joint Center for Political Studies Press, 1989), p. 1.
56. "Lilian Katz, "All About Me," *American Educator* (Summer 1993), pp. 18–23.
57. Albert Shanker, "Love Ya!" *New York Times* (February 23, 1997), E7.
58. Michael S. Knapp and Associates, *Teaching for Meaning in High Poverty Classrooms* (New York: Teachers College Press, 1995), pp. 3, 7–8.
59. Thomas M. Skrtic, "The Special Education Paradox: Equity as the Way to Excellence," *Harvard Educational Review*, Vol. 61, No. 2 (May, 1991), pp. 148–206.
60. James Banks "It's Up to Us," *Teaching Tolerance*, (Fall 1992), p. 21.
61. Skrtic, p. 177.
62. Ibid., p. 154.

Contemporary School Reform: The Post–Cold War Era

It is possible to view the evolution of American society through periodic efforts to reform its educational system. Large-scale social changes inevitably produce corresponding changes in our schools. For example, we saw in Chapter 1 how Jefferson and the other colonial leaders committed themselves to the notion of a statewide community school network through which all potential voters could acquire the knowledge and literacy skills needed to function effectively in a democratic society. The ideals of literacy and political freedom were inextricably intertwined in the minds of those colonial leaders. Thus America's great experiment in political democracy brought an equally radical experiment in mass education. As the right to vote gradually spread throughout the population, so too did access to some form of community or state-sponsored education.

In Chapters 3, 4, and 6 we saw how wave after wave of late-19th-century immigration and migration not only radically increased America's overall population but radically changed its racial and ethnic composition. Northern cities were increasingly populated with ethnically diverse people looking for work, and America's newly emerging factory system had much work to offer. It is no accident that common school improvement, which sought to socialize these diverse masses to American values and language and to a factory-oriented work ethic, arose during this period. The schools were seen as a panacea for handling the massive urbanization and industrial problems of the 19th century.

Just prior to this period of industrialization came the emancipation of four million black Americans following the Civil War. Once again the schools were expected to solve the attendant problems of social, political, and economic integration into mainstream American life. During this period, an educational revolution took place in the South as African-Americans swarmed to various kinds of schools in an attempt to achieve the education that was rightfully theirs under a system that was supposed to guarantee political and economic equality.

School reform took another major turn in the first half of the 20th century with the emergence of progressive education. Driven by the belief in progress through scientific management, leaders in American government, industry, and education all began supporting larger, more centrally controlled institutions under the direction of scientifically trained experts. Schools broadened their curricula to include extensive vocational educational programs and infused into their academic programs the practice of classroom democracy and student-centered learning. School reform was driven by the idea that classrooms should reflect the reformers' view of the "real world" of work and citizenship. Once again, schools were seen as primary for socializing a diverse population into a culturally homogeneous one with appropriate vocational and political skills and attitudes.

Whereas citizenship goals dominated the discourse of colonial school reform, socialization and economic goals dominated school reform agendas during the late 19th and early 20th centuries. Then, following World War II, America experienced yet another wave of school reform. This time, however, it was motivated largely by fear of an external military and political threat. The Soviet Union had successfully launched Sputnik, the world's first artificial satellite. This scientific achievement, coupled with the Soviets' aggressive program of political expansion, caused American leaders to launch a massive investment in defense-oriented school reform. As we saw in Chapter 8, defense-related subjects such as math, science, and foreign languages became the focus of the new "core" curricula that sprang up around the country. Simultaneously, comprehensive high schools sponsoring new, advanced curricula for students scoring high on standardized achievement tests began appearing. Reform leaders were clearly concerned with the development of elite students capable of shoring up our national defense.

This brief historical account of past school reform efforts is offered as a prelude to the following discussion of the present school reform movement. We will begin with a general examination of reform activity during the past decade, and then look at the three stages that have characterized this and other reform movements. We will then conclude, as we began, by looking briefly at the political-economic and ideological context of the current reform effort.

SCHOOL REFORM IN THE 1980s AND 1990s

In April 1991, President George Bush announced the report *America 2000: An Education Strategy*[1] with the words, "There will be no renaissance without revolution." The plan was presented by Educational Secretary Lamar Alexander as "a bold, comprehensive, and long-range plan to move every community in America toward the National Education goals adopted by the President and Governors" in 1990. Such strong talk suggested, of course, strong action for reform of the nation's schools.

Upon release of the *America 2000* report, observers of the nation's schools immediately recalled another presidential school reform initiative, *A Nation at Risk,* released in 1983. This document, too, had used persuasive language in an attempt to mobilize national support for changes in the nation's schools. Although a number of states had begun school reform legislation before the publication of *A Nation at Risk,* that report is generally recognized as the beginning of the national school reform movement of the 1980s. "Our nation is at risk," proclaimed the Reagan-appointed National Commission on Excellence in Education, which authored the report. "[The] educational foundations of our society are presently being eroded by a rising tide of mediocrity that threatens our very future as a nation and a people."[2]

By using the national print and broadcast media to focus public attention on the nation's schools, the Reagan administration clearly contributed toward a decade of sustained efforts to reform America's schools according to the *Nation at Risk* vision. As the 1990s began, *America 2000* sought to continue, in different language and with somewhat altered methods, what the Reagan administration began. Shortly after the plan's release, Professor Gary Orfield asserted, "*America 2000* is not a plan for American education but a plan for re-electing the President."[3] Ironically, President Bush was not reelected, but his plan lived on in the Clinton administration. On March 31, 1994, President Clinton signed into law the Goals 2000: Educate America Act. This Act, P.L. 103-227 (see Exhibit 14.1) remains consistent with several of the central themes of the school reform movement begun in the 1980s, and it is useful to consider as school reform continues in the 1990s.

Contemporary School Reform: Its Language and Themes

So many educational buzzwords have entered the language of contemporary school reform that the dust jacket of one book on the subject was covered with line upon line of them: equity, excellence,

EXHIBIT 14.1 **The National Education Goals of P.L. 103-227: Goals 2000 (1994)**

1. By the year 2000, all children in America will start school ready to learn.
2. By the year 2000, the high school graduation rate will increase to at least 90 percent.
3. By the year 2000, all students will leave grades 4, 8, and 12 having demonstrated competency over challenging subject matter including English, mathematics, science, foreign languages, civics and government, economics, arts, history, and geography, and every school in America will ensure that all students learn to use their minds well, so they may be prepared for responsible citizenship, further learning, and productive employment in our Nation's modern economy.
4. By the year 2000, the Nation's teaching force will have access to programs for the continued improvement of their professional skills and the opportunity to acquire the knowledge and skills needed to instruct and prepare all American students for the next century.
5. By the year 2000, U.S. students will be first in the world in mathematics and science achievement.
6. By the year 2000, every adult American will be literate and will possess the knowledge and skills necessary to compete in a global economy and exercise the rights and responsibilities of citizenship.
7. By the year 2000, every school in the United States will be free of drugs, violence, and the unauthorized presence of firearms and alcohol and will offer a disciplined environment conducive to learning.
8. By the year 2000, every school will promote partnerships that will increase parental involvement and participation in promoting the social, emotional, and academic growth of children.

restructuring, back to basics, school site management, merit pay, career ladder, accountability, professionalization, parental involvement, standardization, achievement, teacher empowerment, local control, values. The list goes on. The volume *Education Reform: Making Sense of It All* is aptly titled. How does one make sense of all these terms? Which are most central to understanding the essence of contemporary school reform, and how do these disparate terms relate to one another?[4]

There are various ways of organizing the many components of contemporary school reform. For example, Harry Passow, Michael Kirst, and others organize them chronologically, speaking of a "first wave" and a "second wave" of school reform.[5] The first wave, in this view, focused on the "centralization of goal-setting authority."[6] That is, political and education leaders sought to achieve a national consensus on the reforms they thought necessary. The second wave was (and is) a "decentralization of implementation authority."[7] That is, once the national goals for education contained in *A Nation At Risk* were adopted by states, it became the business of local agencies to determine how best to implement them. This is an interesting way of analyzing the last decade of school reform, particularly in view of President Clinton's adoption of President Bush's *America 2000* strategy, which explicitly argues for national goals, national consensus on curriculum, and even national standards of achievement, while simultaneously urging locally designed methods for implementing these national goals. This tension between federal, state, and local decision making is, as we shall later see, a major source of criticism of the *Goals 2000* plan.

Although the two-wave description of recent school reform is a useful one, it is limited for two reasons. First, the simple division into earlier and later stages does not tell us anything about the character of the reforms being proposed or enacted, and therefore does not provide a very clear conceptual organizer. Second, the two-wave account obscures the fact that a fair amount of state and local activity was already in progress before the centralized first wave appeared. Also, the two stages really overlap considerably, since political and educational leaders continue to debate national educational goals well into the decentralized second wave. Nonetheless, there are important differences in emphasis between the earlier and later reform efforts, as we will see.

A different way of analyzing current school reform is by considering its similarities to and differences from earlier school reform movements.

Not since the progressive era, with its tremendous influx of immigrants, has cultural pluralism been such a central concern of our schools.

Readers will recognize that most, if not all, of the central themes of contemporary school reform have appeared during earlier historical contexts. For example, the issues of professionalization and standardization in teaching were central to Horace Mann's efforts to establish a consensus of moral and educational values in the common schools of Massachusetts in the 1830s and 1840s. In the late 19th and earlier 20th centuries, tensions involving local and centralized control of schools, efforts at curricular reform, and debate over which values were most appropriate to a changing economic and social order were at the heart of the progressive movement. More recently, during and immediately following the "Conant reforms" of the late 1950s and 1960s, issues of excellence, equity, and the restructuring of school governance and curriculum in an era of global tension became prominent.

When we consider the reform movements of the common school era, the progressive era, and the cold war era, we realize that, first, in each case dramatically new social and economic conditions caused business and professional leaders to reexamine our schools in an effort to respond to these new conditions. Next, a new consensus was consciously promoted to win support for change in our schools' educational values and curriculum goals. Finally, an effort was made to formally restructure the governance, organization, and curriculum of schooling. These three interlocking ideas—schooling as a response to new social and economic conditions; achieving a new consensus on educational goals and values; and school restructuring—can be thought of as stages of school reform and can be used to study virtually any school reform movement, whether historical or contemporary. In using these three concepts to make sense of the current school reform movement, we will again rely on illustrations from the three earlier reform movements mentioned above.

Schooling as a Response to New Social and Economic Conditions

During the progressive era, urbanization, new immigration, and the emerging corporate-capital industrial system convinced a coalition of business, political, and professional leaders that the classical approach to schooling was inadequate. Partly as a result, progressive reformers introduced compulsory public schooling to instill necessary skills and industrial values in all citizens, a differentiated curriculum for students with different skill levels, vocational education to prepare students for the world of work, and extracurricular activities to further socialize students with values appropriate to the new industrial order.

In strikingly similar fashion, contemporary political and business leaders have begun pointing to changing social and economic conditions that they feel necessitate school reform. The three new economic and social realities most frequently cited are (1) the decline of manufacturing as the economic base of the United States and the concurrent rise of information processing, service industries, and high technology; (2) our declining ability to compete in world markets, with the result that the United States has gone from being a major lending nation to perhaps the world's leading debtor nation; and (3) the apparent decline in the academic skills of American students, whether measured against past American performance or against that of students from other industrialized nations. An often-cited demographic factor in this declining academic picture is the rising proportion of Latino and African-American students in the nation's schools, with attendant problems of poverty and cultural and language difficulties. Not since the new immigration of the progressive era has cultural pluralism been such a central concern of our nation's schools.

These economic and demographic changes have led business and government leaders to the view that our schools should respond to an economy "at risk" by elevating the academic performances of all students at all levels of achievement. These better-educated students would then be able to perform well in an information-processing economy and thereby help the United States become more competitive in the world marketplace. The argument of the policymakers was helped considerably by data showing what appeared to be genuinely dismal academic performance by U.S. students. SAT and ACT scores had been declining steadily since the early 1960s; approximately 700,000 students were dropping out of school each year, and of those who remained in school, fewer than 40 percent of 17-year-olds could analyze moderately complicated reading passages about topics studied in high school; finally, our 13-year-olds ranked behind such nations as Korea, Spain, and Ireland, and several Canadian provinces in mathematics performance.[8] (See Exhibits 14.2 and 14.3.)

EXHIBIT 14.2 Trends in SAT College Entrance Examination Scores

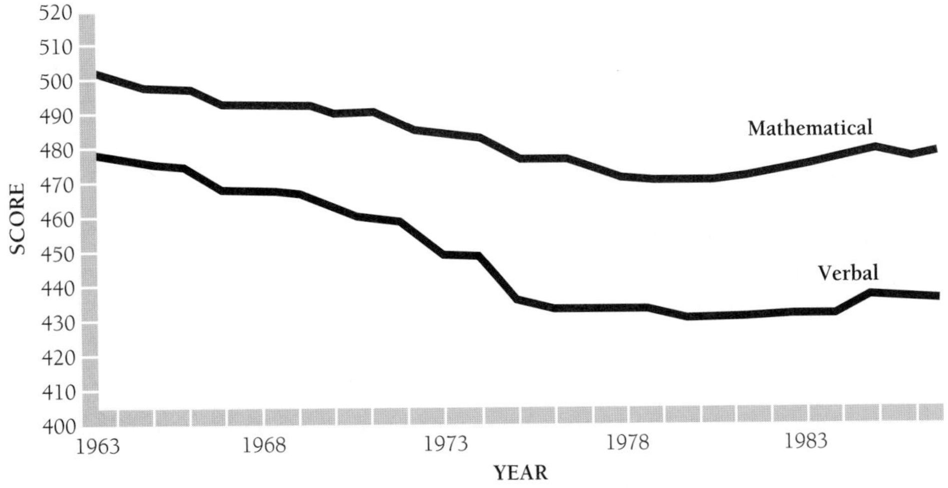

Source: National Center for Education Statistics, U.S. Department of Education, *The Condition of Education—Volume 1* (Washington, D.C.: U.S. Government Printing Office, 1988).

EXHIBIT 14.3 Trends in ACT Composite Entrance Examination Records

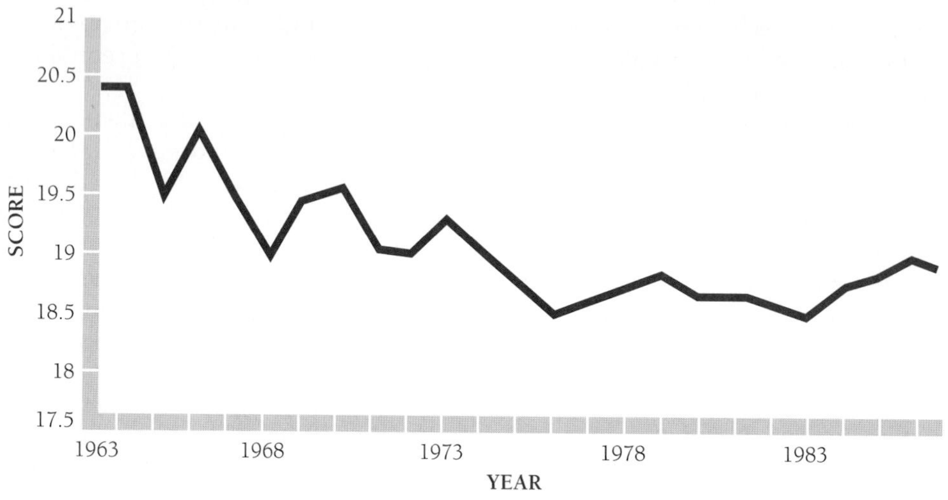

Source: National Center for Education Statistics, U.S. Department of Education, *The Condition of Education—Volume 1* (Washington, D.C.: U.S. Government Printing Office, 1988).

EXHIBIT 14.4 Percentage of In-School 17-Year-Olds at or above Various Reading Levels

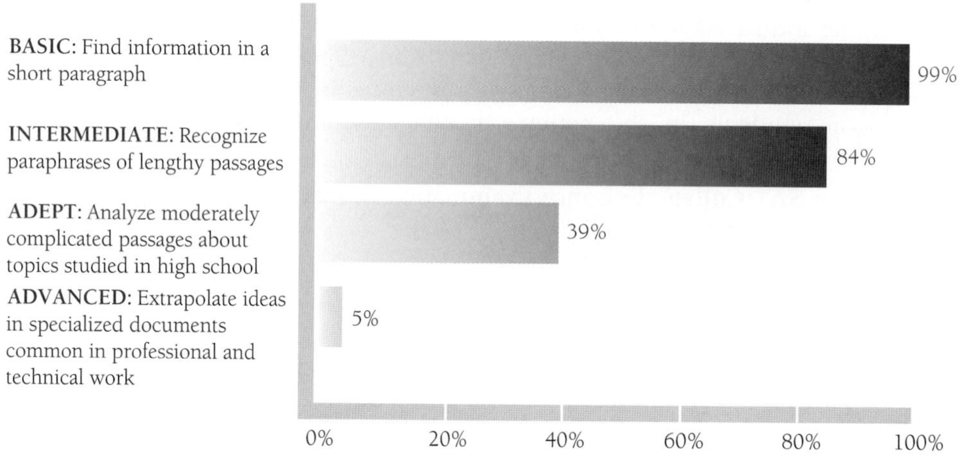

Source: National Assessment of Education Progress, *The Reading Report Card* (Princeton, N.J.: Educational Testing Service, 1986).

The data for African-American and Latino students was even more discouraging, with dropout rates in some Chicago and New York schools ranging from 63 to 68 percent. Further, "disadvantaged urban 17-year-olds" lagged 22 points behind the national average in a 1984 national reading assessment.[9] (See Exhibit 14.4.) Members of the business community were quick to translate such educational problems into financial costs to the nation. The dropout rate, for example, was estimated to cost the nation some $240 billion annually.[10] (See Exhibits 14.5 and 14.6.)

EXHIBIT 14.5 **High School Completion Rates among 18- and 19-Year-Olds by Race and Hispanic Origin**

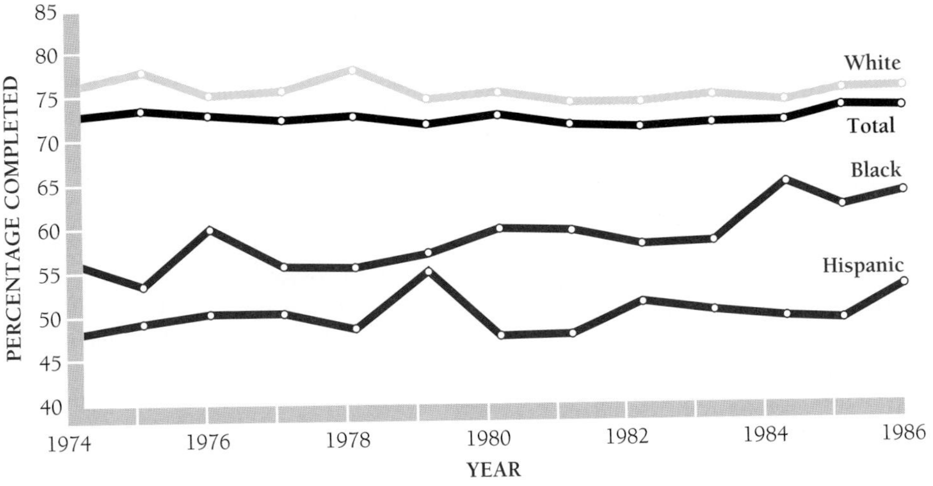

Source: National Center for Education Statistics, U.S. Department of Education, *The Condition of Education—Volume 1* (Washington, D.C.: U.S. Government Printing Office, 1988).

EXHIBIT 14.6 **High School Completion Rates among Adults Aged 25-29, by Race and Hispanic Origin**

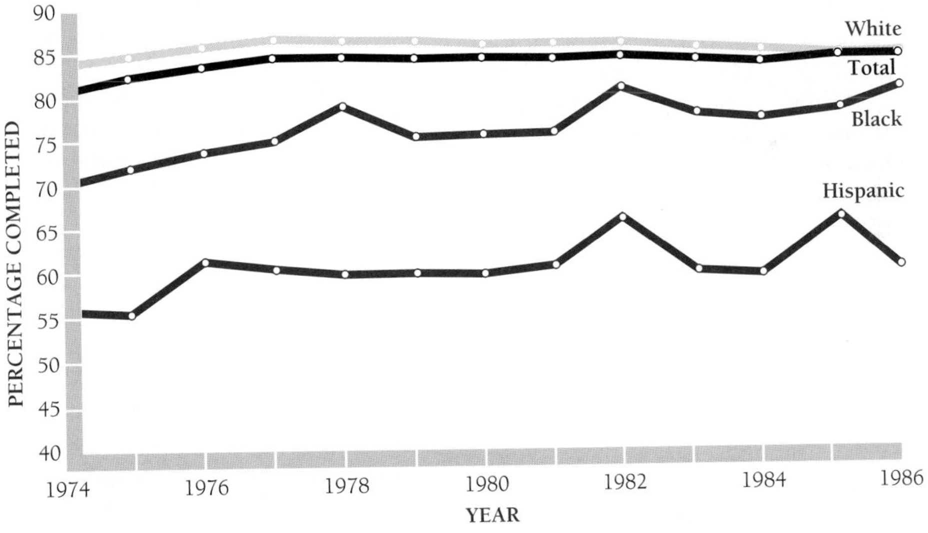

Source: National Center for Education Statistics, U.S. Department of Education, *The Condition of Education—Volume 1* (Washington, D.C.: U.S. Government Printing Office, 1988).

The New Consensus on Excellence in Education

In order for there to be widespread agreement that these were indeed the economic and social conditions to which schools should respond, and for there to be agreement on *how* the schools should respond, consensus had to be consciously built among government, business, and educational leaders at the state and national levels. Mark G. Yudof wrote early in the reform movement:

> Perhaps the most noteworthy aspect of the new era in educational policy, the one that partially explains

> the popular appeal of the many recent reports on the status of education, is the attempt to generate, locate and reinforce a consensus on U.S. public schooling. *A Nation at Risk* helped to serve that consensus-building role, proclaiming that "the Federal Government has *the primary responsibility* to identify the national interest in education."[11]

The specific issue of national interest will be discussed later in the chapter. What is notable here is the early-1980s perception among policymakers that one of the ills affecting American education was precisely the *lack* of consensus about what schools should achieve and why. In 1986, Secretary of Education William J. Bennett urged just such a consensus when he argued for the "three Cs: character, content and choice." In calling for schools to teach a common culture of "common values, common knowledge, and a common language," Bennett recalled Horace Mann's efforts to build universal values and a uniform curriculum into the common school movement in Massachusetts.[12] As we shall see, the tensions between common content and choice would later create serious problems in the *America 2000* proposal for school reform.

This effort to establish common cultural values, knowledge, and language has met with great resistance from those who hold what they regard as democratic commitments to diversity of values, knowledge, and language. This close connection between diversity and democracy, however, is not viewed by the consensus builders as part of the "common political vision" they feel to be the national interest.[13] In their consensus-building campaign, several major themes have emerged, and all of these themes, with some shifts in emphasis, have been sustained within the second wave of reform efforts. The four major themes running through the last 9 years of reform (as well as from early reports) may be identified as follows:

1. **An academic-achievement definition of "educational excellence."** *A Nation at Risk* sought to define excellence primarily in terms of measurable results in standardized achievement tests targeted at traditional academic curricula. Bennett's concern for a common content is reflected in the Reagan and Bush administration reports, each of which argues for a common core of five academic subjects similar to Horace Mann's "five Rs." The "five new basics" for secondary school graduation articulated in *A Nation at Risk* are English, mathematics, science, social studies, and computer science. *America 2000* replaces these five with a slightly different list: English, mathematics, science, history, and geography. Both reports call for greater rigor in academic standards, assignments, homework, and time on task for all students, not just for those considered college bound. (See Exhibit 14.7.)

   The call for higher standards was accompanied by a call for greater "accountability." School report cards, state report cards, and national achievement testing, for example, are all ideas that have been proposed or implemented since *A Nation at Risk.* These are seen as measurable ways to hold schools and districts accountable for their "products," the students. In addition, the early reports called for lengthening the school day and the school year as a means to achieve the new vision of excellence. Finally, a number of reports identified the need for better trained and more talented teachers as a necessary component of this new excellence. More will be said on this topic in item 4.
2. **A tension between concerns for "excellence" and concerns for diversity and equity.** Distinctly at odds with some aspects of the purported new consensus is the view that democratic schooling will suffer if the various forms of diversity—racial, ethnic, gender, and handicapping conditions—are not adequately understood and respected in the teaching-learning processes of schools. To focus on a narrow core of common values and content stemming almost entirely from a male-dominated European tradition may well exclude or disadvantage children with backgrounds that are not white, male, and middle-class; on the whole, the schools have not served those children well in the 20th century. Further, it is argued, the standardized tests, which have historically been used as accountability measures, will further disadvantage students from cultures that are unaccustomed to the language and codes of such tests.

   Concerns such as these, however, did not come into clear focus until the second wave of

EXHIBIT 14.7 Recommendations from *A Nation at Risk*

I. Content

A. Raise high school graduation requirements; institute the five New Basics:
  1. Four years of English, to include extended reading and writing skills and knowledge of our literary heritage
  2. Three years of math:
     a. Higher-level mathematics, such as geometry, algebra, and statistics
     b. Estimation, approximation, measurement, and accuracy testing
     c. A curriculum for those not planning college immediately
  3. Three years of science:
     a. Higher-level sciences, scientific reasoning, and inquiry
     b. Application of scientific knowledge and technology
  4. Three years of social studies:
     a. Historical and cultural studies of ourselves and others
     b. Social, economic, and political systems
  5. One-half year of computer science:
     a. Basic computer literacy and use of computers in other subjects
     b. Comprehension of electronics and related technologies

B. Provide foreign language, art, and vocational education for college–bound students

C. Upgrade elementary curriculum—foreign language, English development in writing, problem-solving skills, science, social studies, and the arts

D. Involve outside experts in order to improve and disseminate quality curricular materials, including evidence of text quality and currency from publishers

II. Standards and Expectations

A. All educational institutions to adopt more rigorous academic standards

B. Grades to be indicators of achievement

C. Standardized tests of achievement at transition points

III. Time

More learning time: efficient time use, longer day, or longer year
  1. More homework and instruction for study skills
  2. Districts to consider seven-hour days and 200- to 220-day school years
  3. Efficient management of the school day and class organization
  4. The strengthening of attendance incentives and sanctions
  5. Reduction of teachers' administrative and discipline burdens

IV. Teaching

Improve preparation for and desirability of teaching
  1. Higher standards for incoming teachers; judge programs by quality of graduates
  2. Competitive, market-sensitive, and performance-based salaries; career decisions based on evaluation
  3. Career ladders and 11-month contract
  4. Alternative credentialing, grants, and loans to attract teachers
  5. Master teachers plan programs for and supervise probationary teachers

V. Citizen and Federal Involvement and Fiscal Support

A. Citizens oversee reform and provide financial support

B. Adminstrative and legislative officials provide stability and finance for reforms

C. Federal government identifies national interest, provides leadership, supports state and local district efforts to meet student needs

Source: William A. Firestone, Susan H. Fuhrman and Michael W. Kirst, *The Progress of Reform: An Appraisal of State Education Initiatives* (Palo Alto: Center for Policy Research in Education, 1990), p. 9.

reform reports began to deal with the narrow cultural consciousness reflected in the first wave. Just as Horace Mann had difficulty winning the battle for a consensus of cultural values, so contemporary resistance arose against the imposition of a cultural consensus that appears inadequately to value diversity of knowledge and values. After nearly 10 years of school reform, however, the *America 2000* proposal gives scant notice to the multicultural perspective.

3. **Choice in schooling.** Bennett's reference to "school choice" reflects a theme that has run steadily through the school reform movement since the beginning—weakly at first but strongly and explicitly advocated in *America 2000.* According to this concept, parents and students should be allowed to select any school of their choice, whether or not it is in their neighborhood, on the basis of its perceived quality and its compatibility with their personal educational goals. Some schools might be very traditional, and others very innovative, but parents and students should be able to "vote with their feet," in this view. The schools would be supported by a "voucher" system, in which each family would receive a voucher for the tuition of each child, and the school that the child attended would be paid by the state on the basis of the number of vouchers it received. The system would thus be designed so that the better schools would flourish because of high state revenues derived from high attendance, and poor schools would have to improve or perish. The philosophy here is very grounded in the notion of laissez-faire, free market economy. More will be said on this as we examine the ideology of reform.
4. **Restructuring school governance, school processes, and the teaching profession.** In *A Nation at Risk,* specific proposals were made for establishing career ladders, higher salaries (including "merit pay"), and new ways of structuring the teaching profession to enable experienced teachers to take a greater role in inducting new teachers into the profession. In addition, higher standards for entering the profession were recommended. Soon after, national reform reports such as the Holmes Group's *Tomorrow's Teachers* and the Carnegie Commission's *A Nation Prepared: Teachers for the 21st Century* similarly recommended major changes in the structure of the teaching profession.[14] One of the major streams of these recommendations for restructuring was the view that teachers should have much more decision-making autonomy in schools, so they could decide themselves what content and methods are best for their students. More will be said on these reports later.

At the same time, however, *A Nation at Risk* and other reports recommended an increased role for citizens, especially for the business community, in school governance and leadership. Despite the tension between greater teacher autonomy and greater community and business input into school decision making, the thrust toward restructuring the teaching profession and school governance grew in importance throughout the 1980s and became for some analysts synonymous with the second wave of school reform.[15] For some, the restructuring movement meant primarily the movement to decentralize school governance, while for others, as we shall see, restructuring referred to new approaches to school curriculum. Although restructuring in one form or another has been central to every major school reform movement in U.S. history, the particular character of the current restructuring movement merits its own discussion.[16]

Restructuring

Historian David Tyack observes that the concept of restructuring "has become a magic incantation" that "is now gaining the popularity of *excellence* in the early 1980s or *equality* in the 1960s."[17] Tyack notes, however, that school "restructuring" has come to mean very different things to different people. In general he agrees with Passow, Kirst, and others that restructuring is partly a response to the failures of the early "excellence" movement of the 1980s to produce the reforms envisioned in *A Nation at Risk.* In reading Tyack's characterization of what restructuring has come to mean in the second wave of reform, we can see distinct elements of the first wave still contained within it:

> People regard restructuring as a synonym for the market mechanism of choice, or teacher professionalization and empowerment, or decentralization and school site management or involving parents more in their children's education, or national standards in curriculum with tests to match, or deregulation, or new forms of accountability, or basic changes in curriculum and instruction, or some or all of these in combination. Slogans suitable for bumper stickers proclaim the new dogmas: Choice is the answer; small is beautiful; blame the bureaucrats.[18]

Certainly one major stream of the restructuring effort has to do with the processes of decision making in schools and school districts. Perhaps the most ambitious example of this kind of restructuring is found in Chicago, which in 1989 elected 542 local school councils, or local boards of education, one at each of Chicago's public schools. Each council consists of six parents, two teachers, two community representatives, and the principal. Thus nearly 6,000 citizens now exercise genuine authority in Chicago schools, including the power to hire principals, draft local school improvement plans, and control the school budget to accomplish their aims.[19]

A second example of school restructuring seeks to improve education by reshaping the teaching profession and entry into it. The work of the Holmes Group, a consortium of about 100 deans of the nation's leading colleges of education, clearly illustrates this effort. This 1986 report *Tomorrow's Teachers: A Report to the Holmes Group* set five goals for the teaching profession:

1. Teacher education curricula should have stronger liberal arts requirements so that teachers will be more generally educated.
2. Standards of entry into the teaching profession should be raised.
3. Career ladders should be established for teachers so that those with greater experience and formal education can receive status and financial rewards commensurate with other professions.
4. New relations should be established between public schools and colleges of education so that prospective teachers can receive greater "clinical" training.
5. Public schools should be transformed into sites where experienced teachers have greater professional autonomy in their decision making.

The Carnegie Forum on Education and the Economy produced its own report on restructuring teaching *(A Nation Prepared: Teachers for the 21st Century)* at about the same time as the Holmes Group. Although the general thrust is similar to that of the Holmes Group, one notable difference is the Carnegie group's recommendation that a National Board of Professional Teaching Standards be created so that all teachers can be certified according to a national standard for teaching knowledge and skills. This recommendation illustrates how some "restructuring" proposals for the teaching profession flow against the sentiment characterized by Tyack as "small is beautiful; blame the bureaucrats." Such a national teaching board is a step toward centralization of control, not decentralization.

A prominent example of the third stream of restructuring, that which seeks to significantly alter the aims and conduct of teaching and learning in schools, is the Coalition for Essential Schools. Founded by Brown University professor Theodore Sizer, the coalition seeks to operate on a "less is more" principle of education. The principle asserts that the *amount* of material covered in a school year is much less important than the depth of thought stimulated by the material studied. The nine basic tenets of the Essential Schools Coalition emphasize critical thinking in academic subjects for all students, small student-teacher ratios at the secondary level to allow guided practice of all students' work, and noncompetitive teaching and evaluation processes for heterogeneous groups of students. This restructuring effort is especially interesting in that the coalition is a voluntary network of schools whose membership is determined by the vote of each school's teachers, an arrangement that stands in contrast to the mandated reforms implemented by virtually every state in the 1980s.

Despite the existence of these three examples of restructuring, Tyack concludes that there is historical reason not to be optimistic that schools will change dramatically along such lines. He argues that the contemporary school reform effort remains basically a "top-down" reform movement and that such movements have historically failed because teachers, who are ultimately responsible for the conduct of classrooms, were not full partners in the process.[20] Whether teachers are likely to become such partners in the current reforms will be considered below.

Changes Brought by the Early Stages of the Contemporary Reform Movement

In May 1984, a little over a year after *A Nation at Risk* was published, the U.S. Department of Education released another education report intended to capture public attention, this one titled *A Nation Responds: Recent Efforts to Improve Education.* It reported that a new national consensus over educational goals had developed and that business leaders, professional educators, and state governors and legislatures had mobilized for educational reform. Although the Department of Education's assessment of its own initiatives may have been optimistic, Passow reports that the first year following *A Nation at Risk* did indeed see "over 300 state-level task forces working toward some aspect of school reform." In addition, there were numerous new initiatives on the part of national educational organizations, such as the National Education Association and the American Federation of Teachers, as well as new efforts on the part of local school districts, corporations, and businesses.[21]

Two years later, in December 1986, the educational reform movement appeared to be losing none of its steam. The Education Commission of the States (ECS) noted in that year that "more rigorous academic standards for students and more recognition and higher standards for teachers" were the most prominent results of the first wave of reform.[22] The ECS study found that "most states have been actively reassessing the structure of the teaching profession, including such matters as the requirements for certifying teachers, ways of recognizing and compensating good teachers, and ways of introducing the concept of career ladders into the teaching profession."[23] With regard to the efforts made toward raising student standards, the ECS study found among other new developments:

- Forty-five states and the District of Columbia increased their reported course requirements for earning a standard high school diploma.
- Mathematics requirements were increased in 42 states.
- Thirty-four states increased their science requirements, and from 18 to 26 states changed requirements in language arts and social studies.
- The school attendance age increased in 15 states, and 6 states increased the length of the school year (while 7 others decreased it). The length of the school day, however, did not undergo a major shift.[24]

Such quantitative increases, of course, do not necessarily indicate that the quality of learning has improved. Kirst's research on the results of the mid-1980s reform movement confirms the finding that "quantities of education increased substantially."[25] For example, Kirst finds:

- Educational expenditures after inflation increased by 25 percent in 3 years, although this growth was in part independent of the reform movement and reflected the growth in the national economy.
- Entry-level teacher salaries similarly increased.
- High school course enrollment patterns changed to reflect more emphasis on math, science, foreign languages, and world history and much less on vocational education and on other electives such as geography.
- Despite increased academic requirements, there was no measurable increase in the number of dropouts, but this may in part be due to the difficulty of measuring dropout rates reliably.
- A few states instituted career ladders for teachers with significantly higher pay at the upper end.
- Many state achievement test scores increased slightly, but it is not clear whether this increase was due to reform or to other variables.

By 1990, the trends noted above had begun to deepen in some instances and to shift in others. In *The Progress of Reform: An Appraisal of State Education Initiatives,* William Firestone, Susan Fuhrman, and Michael Kirst found that (among other things) the first 7 years of reform had produced the following results:

1. As suggested by the earlier findings, the *states* concentrated most of their reform activities in the strengthening of academic requirements, including implementation or expansion of mandatory achievement testing programs. California took the additional step of coordinating

statewide tests with statewide textbook adoption and curriculum standards.

2. A second widespread initiative of the states was an attempt to upgrade the teaching force through increased certification requirements and salaries. Forty-six states now require a state teacher certification test, and over 20 states have developed an alternative certification route that allows liberal arts graduates to enter teaching without going through traditional teacher education programs.
3. Although some states increased monitoring of "at risk" students, concerns for equity were overshadowed by emphasis on implementing "higher standards." The researchers report, however, that interest in broader equity concerns "remained high as the decade drew to an end. Nowhere was this better illustrated than in the restructuring movement, with its emphasis on improving teaching and learning for all students, enhancing the role of parents in their children's education, and transforming schools into collegial communities." As the national economy flagged, however, and state budgets shrank, resources for equity initiatives lagged significantly behind resources allocated to the "excellence" initiatives. In general, efforts to redistribute resources more equitably, including "moving money, status, or authority from those in more advantaged positions to those in more disadvantaged positions," did not fare well.
4. School restructuring has been very slow and erratic. If the second wave of restructuring reform can be characterized by calls for better instruction and deeper learning involving higher-order thinking—as opposed to greater amounts of content, greater school site autonomy, shared decision making among school staff, enhanced roles for teachers and parents, and regulatory simplicity—then the second wave is not nearly as successful as the first wave. In contrast to restructuring, the first wave of reforms was more focused and relatively easy to implement, did not cost a great deal, and did not cause significant reorganization of schooling.
5. *Local school districts* responded well to, and in some cases exceeded, state-level initiatives to increase academic content. Further, any successful efforts at restructuring, especially in school-based management and teacher autonomy, usually took place at the district level.[26]

One group of researchers identifies three areas in which state-level activity has been concentrated in the first decade of the current reform movement: student standards (translating into student testing), teaching, and governance.[27] The following trends were evident in these areas in the early 1990s.

1. Criticism of the mass increase during the 1980s in state testing of minimum student competencies has led to a new emphasis on testing higher-order thinking skills. Arizona, for example, has moved away from exclusively multiple-choice tests to "more open-ended formats that require more complex cognitive processes." Other states have at least reduced their emphasis on minimum-competency standardized tests.[28]
2. The massive rush toward state level teacher certification testing has now come under criticism for testing very little about prospective teachers' higher-order thinking skills or pedagogical skills. While it was generally conceded that the tests primarily screen out "fundamentally unprepared candidates rather than ensuring that teachers know how to teach the curriculum for which they are responsible," confusion about whether teacher professionalism requires more or less state level control led to a virtual standstill in state initiatives for reform of the profession early in the decade.[29] (A new national reform report in 1996, however, would rekindle the teacher professionalization movement at state levels, as Chapter 10 detailed.)
3. The tension between first-level stage centralization and second-stage decentralization in school reform has led to a dramatic slowdown in state-level school governance reform. If anything, there is a tendency toward moderation, with states that favored marked centralization early in the decade now allowing greater district control, and states that earlier favored greater local control now instituting more state-level initiatives.[30]

CONTEMPORARY SCHOOL REFORM: A CRITICAL VIEW

We began this chapter with a discussion of how changing social conditions inevitably lead to school reform efforts. We then examined the three stages of school reform that seem typical of school reform movements: how perceived changes in social conditions are followed by consensus building and then by restructuring efforts of various kinds. Following this we briefly examined four major themes of the contemporary reform movement: academic achievement, balancing "excellence" and "equity," school choice, and restructuring. Finally, we reviewed the major results of the school reform movement to date. These results show a concentration of state-level activity regarding the first-wave goal of academic achievement but little progress regarding "equity" considerations, choice, or school restructuring. However, some local districts—those in Chicago and those involved in the Essential Schools Coalition, among many others—seem to be making progress in terms of school restructuring.

At this point it is useful to return to our analytical framework and use the notions of political economy and ideology to think critically about how the contemporary school reform movement began.

The Political-Economic Origins of the Contemporary School Reform Movement

Basing his analysis on work by economists critical of the policies of corporate capitalism and an education reform report, *Action for Excellence,* that was published within two months of *A Nation at Risk,* educator Frank Margonis offers an alternative perspective on the political economy of school reform.[31] *Action for Excellence* was published in 1983 by the Education Commission of the States Task Force on Education for Economic Growth. It was supported by liberal as well as conservative governors and other leaders at the state level because it suggested a national economic and educational strategy for helping economies of the states, which were enduring the worst recession since the Depression of the 1930s. Rather than accepting the standard argument that American industry was failing in world markets because American schools were doing their jobs poorly, Margonis argues that the poor performance of the American economy was due to economic factors apart from the schools. The growing inability of the United States to dominate world markets through military might since the Vietnam War, the rise of union participation at home, and federal regulation of corporate activity had led many businesses to reinvest in nonunion states and in foreign countries. Margonis cites one study estimating that 38 million jobs were lost to these processes in the 1970s, losses that severely damaged the economies of many states. Holding these events responsible for the economic plight of the United States is very different from holding schools responsible, so Margonis's analysis is important to consider.

One notable exception to the states that were suffering economically in the early 1980s was Massachusetts, which had been very successful in attracting high-technology firms into and around the highly educated Boston area. This highly publicized feat eventually provided much of the political leverage for catapulting Governor Michael Dukakis into the Democratic party's presidential nomination for the 1988 election, but before that, it had sent a message to other states about what was needed for economic recovery: high-tech industry, which requires a strong educational environment.

Other states naturally sought to duplicate Massachusetts's success in attracting high-tech firms. However, lacking equivalent educational resources, they turned to the federal government for support in upgrading their educational facilities. The resulting coalition between corporate America, the states, and the federal government produced what came to be known as the "excellence" movement in education. As previously noted, the goal was to upgrade the academic skills of all students, both the gifted and those who were "at risk," for the workplace of the future.

This brief scenario explains how, in the early 1980s, deteriorating economic conditions together with an increasingly international economy led to a new era of educational reform in America. The movement was economically motivated. The cause of our economic problem was seen largely as a failure of our educational system to provide an

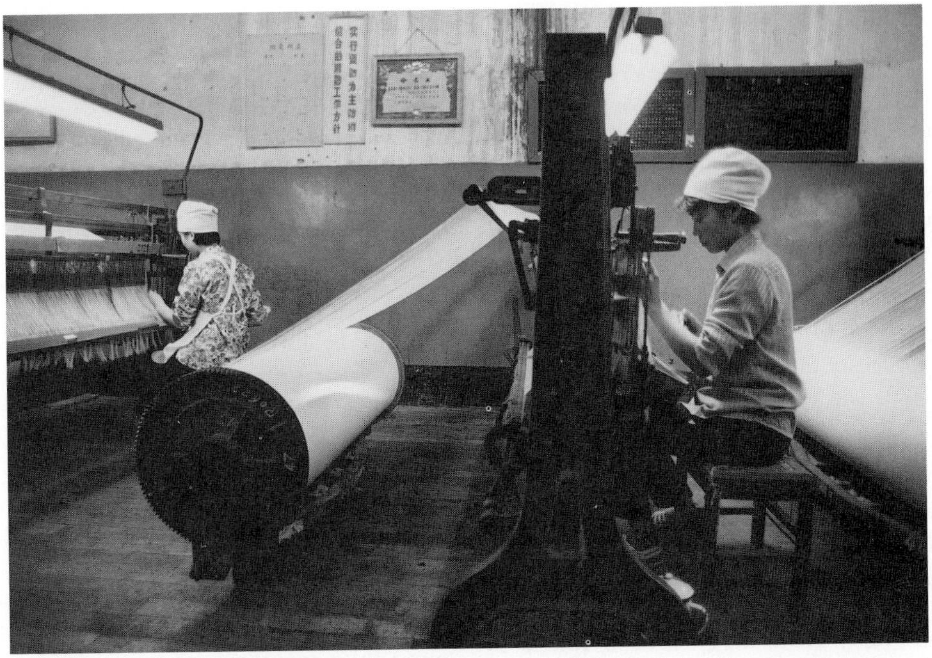

Deteriorating economic conditions in the United States combined with an increasingly global economy that requires a competive labor force are behind the current reform movement in education.

internationally competitive labor force, and the way to correct this failure was to form a new educational coalition between state and federal governments and corporate America. At this point it is worth taking a look at each of these underlying assumptions.

The first assumption, that the motivating force behind the current reform movement lay in a deteriorating economy, is proclaimed in the language of the early reform documents themselves. It is also evident in the organizations that sponsored these educational reform documents: the Business Higher Education Forum, the Economic Commission of the States, the Carnegie Forum on Education and the Economy, and so on.

The second proposition, that the failure of our educational system was the principal cause of our depressed economy, deserves the sort of detailed analysis that Margonis, among others, has offered. Rather than accepting the standard argument that American schools were doing their jobs poorly, Margonis argues that this poor performance of the American economy was due to economic factors apart from the schools, as noted above. Citing economists Carnoy, Shearer, and Rumberger, Margonis sums up his analysis in the following dense but revealing paragraph:

> By systematically directing investment away from factories located in the U.S. major corporations struck back at labor and citizen groups which had infringed upon business control of production [through minimum wage laws, fair labor standards, occupational health and safety provisions, equal employment opportunity, extended unemployment benefits, and improvements in worker compensation]. The devastation of regional economies resulting from such disinvestment set the conditions for many businesses to gain greater public subsidization for corporate research, favorable tax laws, a weakening of anti-trust legislation and environmental regulation, and a new educational policy. More than anything else, the educational reforms of 1983 testify to the indirect power capital can exercise over political processes by constantly shopping for desirable plant locations.[32]

This loyalty to the free market rather than to the public good, argues Margonis, should warn us of the dangers of the states' strategy of trying to attract business through educational upgrades.

> While high-technology industries are likely to locate research facilities near educational centers, nationalistic rhetoric should not lead us to expect loyalty from them. Such firms, because of their high labor intensity, are particularly mobile and have played states off against one another, abandoned plants, and located much of their production in low-cost labor markets. An educational program designed to serve these industries does not amount to a unified national mobilization; rather, it is a part of a corporatist movement in which greater public resources are expected, in [Senator Paul] Tsongas's words, to "reflect the priorities of the private sector."[33]

If Margonis is right that corporate policy rather than educational failure was the principal cause of our economic woes, what can be said regarding the third proposition underlying current reform efforts? That proposition, you might recall, maintained that a new educational coalition between state and local governments and corporate America was the way to upgrade the nation's educational system and thereby upgrade its labor force. According to Margonis, such a coalition is suspect, since the analysis of the origin of the nation's economic problems is mistaken: it is not education that lies at the heart of the problem, but economic policy itself, and economic policy is not being addressed in the school reform movement.

This view is echoed by educational historian Christine Shea, who agrees with Margonis that the educational strategy of the reform movement was designed to benefit business first and the citizenry second. She argues that a basic claim of the reform consensus builders, that a new education for all students is needed for the labor demands of high technology, simply misrepresents the reality of the high-technology industry. Shea, like Margonis, cites *Action for Excellence,* noting that the education most emphasized in this document is the development of "learning to learn" skills for the new technological labor market. "Most factory and service industry jobs in America today," says the report, "fall into this category." *Action for Excellence* then goes on to describe the minimal communication and computation skills it designates as "learning to learn" skills. This leads Shea to conclude that the liberal reform agenda

> has been designed for an increasingly small sector of American youth. For the vast majority of noncollege-bound/minimal-competency students, the end of formal schooling is expected to occur as soon as they demonstrate acquisition of "learning to learn" minimal-competency skills. As such, the school reform proposals are intended to do little more than to prepare minority children for a series of dead-end, low-paying jobs in the secondary labor market . . . [*Action for Excellence*] admits that highly skilled labor will not likely be in great demand in America's high tech future, but it "sugar coats" this bitter reality in the soothing rhetoric of "advancing technology, upward mobility, and increasing opportunity."[34]

Shea goes on to cite data similar to those presented in Chapter 11, showing that most of the jobs in the new service economy are not going to require high-technology knowledge. Yet this reality is obscured by the corporate liberal ideology behind the reform proposals.

Understanding the political economy of the origins of the contemporary school reform movement thus requires recognition of several factors. First, the sources of the nation's economic problems resided primarily in economic and political policies, not in schooling policies. Even though the educational achievement of the nation's youth in the early 1980s was deficient, and the economy too was in serious trouble, the former did not cause the latter; therefore, improving educational achievement was not likely to cure the nation's economic woes. In fact, the nation's economy has improved tremendously since the 1980s, leading to President Clinton's reelection, *without* a corresponding improvement in student learning in schools.

Second, it appears clear that the emerging technological and service workplace does not require a great many highly educated people, because *most* new jobs do not require advanced understanding of math, science, and technology. Insofar as the state governments are increasing requirements in those areas, and insofar as business is intervening to help fund advanced learning, it appears that the "high tech" rationale for school improvement can justify concentration of resources only in a relatively small minority of skilled students. It would take a rationale different from the economic argument—for example, a rationale emphasizing the right of each citizen in a democratic society to be educated to participate fully in the political processes of that society—to justify school reform that would benefit all citizens, regardless of skill level, social class background, or ethnicity. Third, if the contemporary school reform movement reflects "the priorities of the private sector," it can be expected to remain limited in its impact on the educational lives of most students in most schools throughout the country. In a later section, we will examine that thought a bit more thoroughly.

The Ideology of Contemporary School Reform

Just what is the corporate liberal philosophy behind the current school reform movement? Perhaps the best way to understand this term is to contrast it against the laissez-faire ideology of the late 19th century and the progressive philosophy of the early 20th century.

You will recall from Chapter 4 that in the late 19th century a laissez-faire, or "hands off," philosophy characterized the relationship of government to business. The Jeffersonian dictum, "That government governs best which governs least," remained the prevailing business ideology for a time, as industrialization swept the United States. In the late 19th century unregulated American capitalists gradually destabilized the economy and caused a series of recessions, depressions, and business failures. Eventually, a succession of gigantic corporations began to overwhelm their respective industries. But rather than prospering, these industrial giants began to falter as they lost their innovative spirit, antagonized labor, and became mired in massive overhead costs and inefficient bureaucracy. Soon they began shedding their cherished laissez-faire philosophy in favor of government intervention—on their own behalf. Thus came into being the start of the progressive era, with its efficiency experts practicing top-down management of both business and government.

What has been referred to as the corporate liberal ideology that guides the current school reform movement is really an uneasy marriage of the laissez-faire and progressive ideologies. On the one hand, corporate and government leaders seek a "national plan" for education that will establish national standards for satisfactory school performance. This idea is consistent with the top-down management approach, which corporate liberals have sought to implement since the efficiency involvement of the early progressive era. It is an approach that liberal democrats would like to see applied to the economy as well, on the view that a well-regulated economy is necessary to avoid the devastation wrought in so many states by corporate flight and deregulation of the economy.

Powerful business interests can successfully resist such top-down management of the economy, except as they wish to invite it in the interest of profits or to "bail out" a failing business, a bank, or a whole dimension of business, like the savings and loans industry bail-outs of the early 1990s. Schools, however, are unable to resist so easily. Consequently, a national plan for education is emerging but not, in contrast to France, Japan, and other industrialized nations, a national plan for the economy. Yet both types of planning were recommended in the *Action for Excellence* report in 1983.

Both the Reagan and early Bush administrations supported the development of a national education program, but they did so with some ideological misgivings. President Reagan, in particular, with his strong laissez-faire ideology, was, according to Margonis, an "unwilling heir" to the excellence movement.[35] His hesitancy stemmed from the fact that he was not fundamentally in support of federal assistance to the states. Still, it was a public relations victory to appear to launch a national education reform effort for the good of all. Furthermore, the federal government did not actually have to commit funds for education as the states were requesting. In fact, Margonis notes, the Reagan administration came under fire for not following through with federal support as the reform movement progressed, the same charge that was later leveled at the Bush administration for its lack of fiscal support for the agenda in *America 2000.* While the Clinton administration has been able to generate fiscal support for *Goals 2000,* it has lost much of its focus, as we shall see.

An increasingly visible collaboration between business and education was celebrated and promoted in *America 2000.* Teacher and political commentator Stan Karp writes:

> In most accounts of this growing collaboration, there is a largely unchallenged assumption that those who

> own and manage our economy hold answers to what's wrong with our schools and, likewise, that the job of educators is to prepare students for the world these interests own and operate. Sometimes this pro-business bias is out in the open, as when school officials welcome with open arms direct corporate sponsorship of their activities. At other times it's slightly more subtle, as when reforms are proposed to introduce the "discipline" of the workplace and the market into schools. At any rate, corporate influence is growing over the country's most inclusive public institution—the public schools.[36]

Karp goes on to cite Department of Education figures showing that school "adoptions," usually by corporate sponsors, rose from about 40,000 in 1983 to 140,000 in 1988. "Nine million students and about 40 percent of all schools are involved in some sort of business partnership," ranging from "slices of pizza for kids with good attendance" to "management training for central office personnel and development of entirely new schools and curriculums." What is more, this increased presence in and influence over the schools is being achieved, writes Karp, with negligible increases in corporate donations to schools.

The results of the top-down management of school reform were described in 1988 by curriculum theorist Henry Giroux:

> The ideological shift that characterizes the current reform period is also evident in the ways in which teacher preparation and classroom pedagogy are currently being defined. With few exceptions, the major reform proposals exacerbate conditions that erode the authority and intellectual integrity of teachers . . . At both the local and federal levels the new educational discourse has influenced a number of policy recommendations, such as competency-based testing for teachers, a lockstep sequencing of materials, mastery learning techniques, systemized evaluation schemes, standardized curricula, and the implementation of mandated basics.[37]

While promoting a national plan for schooling in *America 2000,* the Bush administration sought at the same time to embrace laissez-faire, free market principles by advocating schools of choice. Yet a problem exists here. If a national system of testing is being explicitly proposed to hold students, teachers, and school districts "accountable" for their use of tax dollars, to what degree is genuine choice going to be available? Because of criticism, the five basics of the narrowly defined curriculum of the *America 2000* proposal have been expanded to nine subject areas (item 3 of Exhibit 14.1). These were intended to constitute the substance of the national tests and therefore were to become the curriculum of schools that wished to succeed on such tests. Just as the "free market economy" in truth has no free markets, so schools of choice would be very limited in the freedom of choice they would offer within a national program of education. This tension between top-down management of school policy and local funding and control of schools has been a problem for the school reform movement since the outset. Further examination reveals other problems as well. The ideological tensions that lie beneath the current school reform movement may be illustrated by some of the concerns that have been raised about its real effectiveness at improving schooling in the United States. Some of these specific concerns follow.

CURRENT CONCERNS ABOUT SCHOOL REFORM

In his book on contemporary school reform based on research in 60 schools across the United States, Thomas Toch titles the concluding chapter, "Conant Was Wrong: The Human Side of Schools."[38] Toch argues that Conant's attention to the bureaucratic management of schools overlooked the quality of human relationships that must be nurtured if education is to succeed. As an example, Toch points to Conant's central mission to eliminate small high schools in favor of large, comprehensive high schools as a means to facilitate such reforms as ability grouping, vocational coursework and guidance, enhanced science curricula, and advanced placement programs. "I can sum up my conclusions in a few statements," wrote Conant in *American High School Today.* "The number of small high schools must be drastically reduced through district reorganization. . . . Aside from this important change, I believe no radical alteration in the basic pattern of American education is necessary in order to improve our public high schools."[39]

Concerning Conant's considerable influence, described in Chapter 8 of this text, Toch offers two important additional insights. First, not only did the number of American school districts decline from over 40,000 to under 18,000 within a decade after Conant's report was issued, but the trend continues today in a number of states. Already over half the secondary school students in the nation attend secondary schools enrolling over 1,000 students (including junior high schools beginning with grade seven).[40] Second, as Toch puts it, "Conant was wrong."[41] If Toch is correct, Conant was wrong because he did not understand the genuine ills of the American High School in post-war America and his solutions further exacerbated those ills: inequitable treatment of different groups of students, the fostering of alienation and apathy among students and teachers, and, in short, the schools' failure to provide an environment for tapping the intellectual potential of most students in the schools.

It could be argued that Conant failed adequately to analyze the emerging needs of the schools in post-war America and that his solutions consequently missed the mark, contributing to the serious deterioration of schools in the decades that immediately followed, in which schools seemed unable to respond to demographic changes in the cities especially. As we examine the prescriptions for school reform today, again there is evidence of missing the mark. Teacher alienation from the reform agenda and the persistent failure of reformers to meet the needs of the students whose futures are most threatened with school failure and economic dependency give us reasons to be skeptical about the current reforms.

Teachers' Voices

In August 1984, approximately a year after the release of *A Nation at Risk,* a massive survey of American teachers conducted by Metropolitan Life revealed that 72 percent of the survey participants felt that "teachers' opinions in general have not been given an adequate hearing in the current debate on education."[42] Yet the survey indicated that teachers strongly supported several different dimensions of the reforms proposed up to that point. In particular:

- 87 percent favored career ladders providing greater responsibility and higher pay for teachers.
- 90 percent favored requiring teacher certification candidates to serve in apprenticeships.
- 75 percent favored some form of merit pay if an "objective standard" could be established, while 70 percent opposed merit pay under current evaluation systems.
- 91 percent supported strengthening high school graduation requirements with more academic work.
- 74 percent approved increasing the amount of homework assigned.
- 92 percent supported increasing instruction in foreign language and computer use.[43]

However, teacher support for the major components of the reform movement did not last long. By 1986 Adam Urbanski, president of the Rochester (New York) Teachers Association and former social studies teacher, wrote: "Although teachers have been the focus of the attention, there has been little attention to their concerns as they see them from the front lines. Those who know best have been consulted the least."[44] This perception, that teachers' voices had been left out of the reform movement, was partly responsible for that trend in the second wave of reform that sought to empower teachers by giving them greater decision-making authority in schools and school districts. Yet the overall trend of the reform movement is not encouraging in this regard, as indicated by the *America 2000* insistence on establishing national standards, independent of local teachers' concerns, for schooling. The ideology of management and control is clearly superseding an ideology of democratic problem solving and participation: teachers' voices still are not being adequately heard at the highest levels of government. However, as we shall see, national and state efforts to control the schools are proving to be much less effective than legislators might have expected.

Stan Karp, English and journalism teacher at John F. Kennedy High School in Patterson, New Jersey, illustrates the resentment teachers feel at finding themselves to be members of a profession over which they appear to have little control. Karp writes:

> *America 2000* frames education issues in terms that reflect the need corporate planners see for better elite technical training and for a moderate overall increase in the number of high school graduates prepared for middle and entry level jobs. . . . But an education policy driven by the logic of economic efficiency does not necessarily lead to universally effective schooling for all.[45]

Karp goes on to note that the plan is primarily ideological in its force because the federal government foresees appropriating so little money for the reforms proposed:

> The most crucial battle in education today is probably the struggle between rich and poor school districts over inequitable funding systems, which are currently being challenged in more than 20 state courts. Fiscal inequity and growing social polarization have helped create a dual school system nearly as separate and unequal as the one declared illegal by the Supreme Court in 1954. But Bush proposes investing less money in his "educational renaissance" than he spent in half a day of the Gulf War.[46]

In 1989, David Hill wrote in *Teacher Magazine* that many teachers have come to doubt the achievements of the school reform movement. In an article titled "What Has the 1980s School Reform Movement Accomplished?" he concluded:

> There is no shortage of skeptics—including some teachers. According to a survey of 13,500 teachers conducted last year by Ernest Boyer and the Carnegie Foundation for the Advancement of Teaching, the school reform movement deserved a C. One in five teachers gave it a D or F, and nearly half the teachers believed the morale within the profession had substantially declined since 1983.[47]

The fact that teachers have come to feel alienated from the reform movement, even after being at first receptive to its basic thrust, suggests a serious problem for educational reform. If the people who will ultimately be most responsible for executing the reform agenda do not feel ownership of that agenda, if they do not feel that it expresses their own aims and aspirations for education, there is little hope that the agenda will be executed successfully. Perhaps, if the reform movement itself is seriously lacking in its analysis of the source of and solutions to educational problems, the teachers' resistance to this particular set of reforms is a blessing. At the very least, the reform movement appears to fail the test posed by the following criterion for democracy: that people should have a significant role in shaping the decisions that affect their lives. But corporate liberal ideology, in its liberal and conservative variants, has historically failed that test in business, industry, and schooling.

Whose Needs Are Being Met?

Raising the question of whether the reforms address the real problems of education, Linda Darling-Hammond writes:

> All students are affected by teacher shortages, but those who reside in districts that can offer fewer inducements to teachers suffer most. Shortages are three times higher in central-city schools than elsewhere. Of the tens of thousands of uncertified teachers hired on emergency credentials in recent years, the great majority teach in central cities. This means that districts with the greatest concentrations of poor children, minority children, and children of immigrants are also those where incoming teachers are least likely to have training in up-to-date teaching methods or to have had courses on how children grow, learn, and develop. In New York City alone, 4,600 uncertified teachers were hired last year. Of these, more than three-fourths had little or no training, and only about 20 percent received any mentoring or similar assistance on the job. Many of these teachers left before their first year was over.[48]

Rather than speak about revolutions in education that do not provide resources to address such fundamental issues, Darling-Hammond suggests that federal initiatives should seek to:

- Recruit new teachers, especially in fields and in locations marked by shortages, through scholarships and forgivable loans for high-quality teacher education;
- Strengthen and improve teachers' preparation through incentive grants to schools of education;
- Improve teacher retention and effectiveness by improving clinical training and support during the beginning teaching stage, when 30 percent to 50 percent of teachers leave the field.[49]

Like teacher Stan Karp, researcher Darling-Hammond believes that "major change does not come easily, and it does not come cheap."[50]

Perhaps the greatest limitation of the school reform movement of the 1980s and early 1990s has been its failure to recognize the realities of the "third world" nature of the experience of millions of American children—and the effects of poverty and oppression on learning and development. In this as in other respects, the latest of the reform reports, *Goals 2000*, is representative. One observer, reviewing a collection of appraisals of the Bush plan, which spawned the Clinton plan, notes, "The most critical comments about *America 2000* focus on the fact that it ignores the rising level of poverty among children and the continuing inequities in access to high-quality education."[51] This observation becomes most salient when it is viewed in the context of the demographic realities that seem to have been largely ignored by the contemporary school reform movement. Demographics researcher Harold Hodgkinson writes that "America's children are truly an 'endangered species.' And second, educators alone cannot 'fix' the problems of education, because dealing with the root causes of poverty must involve healthcare, housing, transportation, job-training, and social welfare bureaucracies." Hodgkinson argues that since the beginning of the reform movement, "there has been no change in graduation rates, in most test scores, or in other indicators of quality." He compares the school reform movement to a house in which the owners try to stop deterioration by fixing the wiring, the floors, the windows, and everything except the *cause* of the deterioration—namely, a leaky roof. Hodgkinson points out the following data for consideration for those who think education can be reformed by making teachers and students work harder:

- Since 1987, one-fourth of all pre-school children in the U.S. have been in poverty (the highest rate of any industrialized nation).
- Every year, about 350,000 children are born to mothers who were addicted to cocaine during pregnancy. Those who survive birth often become children with strikingly short attention spans, poor coordination, and serious learning difficulties.
- Today, 15 million children are being reared by single mothers, whose family income averages about $11,400 in 1988 dollars (within $1000 of the poverty line). The *average* family income for a married couple with children is [in contrast] slightly over $34,000.
- At least two million school-age children have no adult supervision at all after school. Two million more are being reared by *neither* parent.
- On any given night, between 50,000 and 200,000 children have no home.
- While the schools have been least effective at educating the nonwhite students in U.S. schools, the proportion of nonwhite students will rise from 30 percent in 1990 to 38 percent in 2010. In at least 8 states, nonwhite students will constitute a majority of school-age students.
- More than 80 percent of America's one million prisoners in jails are high-school dropouts. Each prisoner costs taxpayers upwards of $20,000 per year. A college student costs taxpayers, in contrast, about $3,300 of tax money per year. While on the one hand, every dollar spent on Head Start saves taxpayers $7 in later services the child will not need, *America's prison population doubled in the 1980s, making the U.S. incarceration rate the highest in the world.*[52]

The question with which Hodgkinson confronts us is simply this: Do we really think that the school reforms proposed by the Reagan, Bush, and Clinton administrations and by corporate leaders will significantly affect the social conditions underlying our educational problems? The answer, for Hodgkinson, is an unequivocal no:

> It is clear that many nations invest a larger share of their wealth in their children's education than we do. In addition, the per-pupil expenditures *within* the U.S. are unmatched by any nation with a centralized education system. In many states in the U.S., the amount spent on *some* children is three or four times the amount spent on other children in the same state.[53]

Like high school teacher Stan Karp and educational researcher Linda Darling-Hammond, Hodgkinson believes that the problems to be faced in education cannot be addressed without taking seriously the resources needed to educate all our children. If, however, Karp and Christine Shea are correct, the school reform movement was never intended to address the learning needs of all children, for the economic agenda of the reformers did not require that all children's needs be taken into account. In the reformers' view, the economic needs of corporate America can be met quite well with greater attention to the marketable achievement levels of those students who will have the greatest impact on corporate productivity.

SCHOOL REFORM AT CENTURY'S END

What we have been calling the "contemporary period of school reform" is now nearly 15 years old, yet educational reform continues to be a live issue in elections, in state and federal lawmaking, and in the news media. Education critic Stanley Pogrow writes that "governmental and foundation elites" are responsible for a series of reforms that were doomed from the start by a poor analysis of what is needed, and poorly thought-out remedies. "These reforms include," he writes, "whole language, full inclusion, heterogeneous grouping, schoolwide models, teacher empowerment, the middle school movement, authentic assessment, learning communities, school restructuring, multidisciplinary curricula, overreliance on staff development, and many others."[54]

Pogrow's point is that a great many different things have been tried in the name of school reform, and opinions diverge regarding the nature and extent of the problems that need remedying. Some observers argue that early 1980s claims about a "crisis" in education were inflated, and that students in the U.S. were then, and are now, performing about like their peers in other industrialized nations. Researcher Lawrence Stedman, however, replies that although there never was good evidence of steep decline in U.S. achievement levels, those levels were not very good in the first place. In fact, compared to other nations, he assesses the performance of students in the U.S. as "reason to be concerned":

> Consistently poor achievement for over 50 years is disturbing news. It calls into question traditional teaching practices and our historical, bureaucratic school structures . . . There is extensive, compelling evidence that our schooling and learning are seriously deficient. Fundamental reform is warranted.[55]

Other observers, as we near the century's end, agree that while we have seen some progress in measured student learning, there is little room for celebration. One of the most trusted measures of student learning was summarized as follows in a special supplement to *Education Week* in January 1997:

> Results from the National Assessment of Educational Progress [the only ongoing national survey of students' educational achievement] are cause for genuine concern. In every participating state, a majority of 4th and 8th graders perform at the "basic" level or below in reading and mathematics. This means that they have only partially mastered the knowledge and skills that are fundamental for proficient work at their grade levels.
>
> There is no state in which at least half the students perform at the "proficient level" or above ["well prepared for the next level of schooling"].
>
> Every state still has a large percentage of students who perform at a "below basic" level.[56]

Although it may be true, as Berliner and Biddle point out in *The Manufactured Crisis: Myths, Fraud, and the Attack on America's Public Schools,* that the NAEP scores have not declined in the last two decades, this does not say very much for the success of nearly 15 years of school reform.[57]

Education professor Martin Haberman offers an explanation for why school reform has accomplished so little. He believes that the public and the "experts" are at odds in their perceptions of what the schools need.

> The public wants to improve a system that it believes in while most of the experts want to take the whole thing apart and start over. The people are interested in efficiency: they want more learning and greater cost control. The movers and shakers in education are concerned with some ideal state that can be attained if only the schools are reconceptualized and reconstructed . . . The basic condition preventing significant school change is that the public doesn't want it.[58]

The ongoing school reform movement is too complex to be measured in terms of student achievement alone, and Haberman's assessment might be a bit too casual. Who are "the people" or "the public" here? Certainly parents in low-income neighborhoods who are worried about their children's future want to see changes in the schools. But they rarely have the economic or political clout to bring real change about.

A more complex assessment than Haberman's reveals that we have learned more from recent school reform than the questionable claim, "the public doesn't want it." One recent research report suggests the following findings from school reform research:

- Schools in the United States have demonstrated important, positive changes in practice, attitude, and student achievement in recent years.
- Most states and many districts have adopted standard-based reforms, in an effort to forge a more coherent policy.
- Education policy has not yet provided coherent, effective guidance on how to improve instruction in the United States.
- Reforms are not always realistic, or based on understanding of what will actually work.
- Reformers often put too much emphasis on structural changes, such as lengthened class periods or common teachers' planning time, and pay inadequate attention to high-quality instruction, because they wrongly assume that structural changes will automatically boost achievement.
- Policymakers do not pay enough attention to the role that students could play in raising their achievement levels (e.g., effort).
- Funding is a key element of education reform and reform policy. Current school-funding systems create too many inequities among schools, deny critical resources to schools that serve disadvantaged students, and are not well-suited to dynamic, school-based reform.[59]

Although we have learned much about the obstacles to successful school reform, we have learned something of what is required for school reform to succeed. These 1996 findings from the U.S. Office of Educational Research and Development provide insight into what is needed:

- Leadership: Strong leadership enhances the prospect of successful reform.
- Goals: Reform goals should be based on a shared vision and have the active support of a wide range of stakeholders who participate in achieving them.
- Timing: School reform takes time and involves risk.
- Training: Participants must have training before they implement reform.
- Flexibility: Reform strategies should be flexible to accommodate multiple solutions to a given problem.
- Infrastructure: Reform may require redesigning organizational infrastructure.
- Managing resources: Reform prospects improve if there is a means to redirect or reallocate resources in ways that meet the needs of the new, emerging system. Reform is not cost free.
- Self-assessment: Reform is an ongoing process.[60]

Late 1990s School Reform: New and Continuing Initiatives

We have seen how different themes were emphasized at different points in the course of the last 15 years of school reform, and that these different points of emphasis—first on centralizing standard setting, then on "restructuring" and having site-based decision making, for example—led to different efforts at change. Some areas of emphasis in the late 1990s were not emphasized at all in the early 1980s (computer technology, for example) and others can be traced right back to the beginning—not just the beginning of this reform era but to the beginning of common schools. Teacher professionalization would be a prime example. These are two of five areas of prominent school reform activity as we near the year 2000. The others are school choice, parent involvement in schools and in school decision making, and school-to-work reforms.

Computer Technology Desktop computers did not become widely available until the late 1980s, and now, a decade later, schools are rarely without them. Computers are part of a wider information revolution in society, rather than simply a component of school reform. We have already noted that funding from *Goals 2000*, however, is being used by states to support growth of computer technology in schools. We have also discussed, in Chapter 9, the already rapid growth of the World Wide Web in educational settings and homes, and recent research suggesting that the Web can, if used appropriately, enhance teaching and learning. We have also raised cautions about whether the Web might, as educational innovations and reforms often do, serve economically privileged youth and children better than lower-income youth who have less access to the equipment and less access to well-prepared teachers.

The President of the United States proclaimed in his 1996 State of the Union Address that "every classroom in America must be connected to the information highway." This is an enormously expensive goal, one that must necessarily compete with other approaches to improving student learning. Larry Cuban argues that the "techno-reformers" are part of a significant problem in introducing computer technology to schools, in that the techno-reformers do not understand the social organization of classrooms and schools, tend to make inflated claims for what computers can accomplish, help cause administrators to invest massive sums in a technology that is not being used productively, and end up blaming the teachers for the waste.[61]

Given the pace of technological change, it is very difficult to predict the eventual impact of the Web on schools and school reform. It might serve to bring teachers and administrators into more immediate contact, for example, with "best practices" and successful reforms in schools and districts. The federally funded North Central Regional Educational Laboratory in Oak Brook, Illinois, for example, has an internet server, Pathways to School Improvement, that any teacher in the nation can use to investigate a wide range of innovations in areas such as curriculum, school organization, or student assessment. The URL is http://www.ncrel.org/ncrel/sdrs/pathways.htm. Communication of the best ideas in schooling is more readily available than ever before, though the distance from an idea to its successful implementation still requires complex professional and personal qualities from those who would want to accomplish change.

Community and Parent Involvement in Schools Increased awareness of the importance of a home environment that supports academic success has caused educators to look more closely at the relationship between school and home, teachers and parents. Part of that examination has resulted in a call to involve parents more significantly in school and school district decision making, including making decisions about school reform. National PTA officers Joan Dykstra and Arnold Fege recently expressed concern about the way in which school reform efforts have regularly excluded parents from the process. They caution:

> Don't use the development of educational standards as a ruse for control. Many parents are skeptical about who will write the standards, for whoever does will ultimately control the educational program for that state. Every effort should be made to employ the democratic process . . . The public must be a full partner to the dreams and visions educational policy makers have for America's children.[62]

Site-based decision making at the school level often includes parents and community members. A very recent national study indicated that all states reported having some site-based decision-making bodies in local schools, from a high of 86 percent of schools in Virginia to a low of 22 percent in Nebraska; and the U.S. average for site-based governance is 56 percent of all schools. The majority of these reported bodies included principals, teachers, and parents. Although principals and teachers were included about 95 percent of the time, parents were represented on 79 percent of the governing bodies and students 28 percent. Site-based decision-making bodies typically consider parent and community input on curriculum and student discipline issues; only a third confer on school personnel issues, however. Parental activism in schools, and efforts to involve parents in schools, may well become a lasting legacy of current school reform.

Secondary Schools and School-to-Work Educational researcher Gerald W. Bracey writes, "by far the most common buzz-phrase I hear these days is 'school-to-work-transition.'"[63] As we saw in Chapter 11, federal and state governments are actively interested in the preparation of secondary school students for a productive transition to the workplace. We also saw that this has historically been a contentious issue that raises questions about the fundamental purposes of a public school in a democratic society. Bracey is clear in his opposition to the school-to-work emphasis:

> The old saying, 'the business of America is business,' has lately been rendered as, 'The business of schools

is business.' What has been lost in all the rhetoric is that schools have no business with business. They should not be preparing students for the world of work.[64]

Samuel Halperin, citing current practices in Europe and Israel, defends the school-to-work model:

There, as we are beginning to see in the United States, enlightened businesses and supportive government policies are enabling young people to experience the best of both worlds: high-quality academic learning and practical experience in the workplace that reinforces classroom study.[65]

Bracey, however, sides with a viewpoint that by now should be familiar to readers of this volume: Asking: "What kind of education ought we to offer to all children?" Bracey quotes a contemporary philosopher of education:

Israel Scheffler defines education as 'the formation of habits of judgment and the development of character, the elevation of standards, the facilitation of understanding, the development of taste and discrimination, the stimulation of curiosity and wondering, the fostering of style and a sense of beauty, the growth of a thirst for new ideas and visions of the yet unknown.'

Bracey concludes, "That sounds good to me—a liberal education, one that liberates. Schools should prepare children to live rich, generous lives in the hours that they are freed from work."[66] As Chapter 11 discusses, the school-to-work initiative has deep historical roots, and the consequences of this most recent reform effort remain to be seen.

School Choice, Vouchers, and Charters

The "choice movement" in public schooling has its roots in the alternative school or "free school" movement of the 1970s. Early in the 1980s, school reformers such as Hofstra University's Mary Anne Raywid saw that some parents wished to send their children to nearby public schools rather than the one to which their children were assigned by the district. Research found that parents and children who were able to choose which public school to attend tended to have greater investment in the school and had higher morale as a result. As Berliner and Biddle write:

Thus, if larger school districts really want to promote higher morale and greater involvement among parents, one simple thing they might consider is to allow parents to choose among schools in the district. Some urban districts fear that this would cause chaos, unwanted competition among local schools, and increased ethnic or racial segregation, but the evidence so far available does not support such fears.[67]

So far so good. But soon, the call for "public schools of choice" underwent what seemed to be a logical transformation: a movement to provide every school-age child or youth with a tax voucher—a kind of coupon in the amount the district would ordinarily spend on that child's education—to be "spent" at whatever school the family wanted, public or private. The argument was (and is) that in a free market system, private schools should have as much right as public schools to be supported by the government, and the best schools would attract the most students, thereby thriving and multiplying, while inadequate schools would simply die or have to improve due to lack of "customers." School-choice advocate Raywid objected strongly:

In the cities, vouchers would quickly solidify a two-tiered educational system consisting of nonpublic schools and pauper schools. That development would impoverish us all, because it would represent an abandonment of efforts to improve education for disadvantaged youngsters, who are already a majority in most U.S. cities.[68]

By examining the inequitable and inefficient voucher system currently used in Australia, and then comparing it with the much more successful and equitable public school system in France, Berliner and Biddle concur that Raywid's concerns are well founded.[69]

Not only would vouchers for private schools be likely to serve those with money at the expense of the poor, but another problem quickly becomes evident: using tax money for funding religious education, or religious schools, violates the First Amendment separation of church and state. But some school reformers are happy to use the choice movement to move to a voucher movement, with something called "charter schools" as a transition between the two. National Education Association's President Bob Chase quotes one such school reformer:

> 'What is called for is an incremental strategy that helps acclimatize the public to school choice, readying them for phase two, vouchers,' said voucher activist Roxane Premont, in a speech at the Christian Coalition's annual conference in September [1996]. 'Christians can enjoy the control they exercise in charter schools even as they push for vouchers.'[70]

The future doesn't look good for such a strategy. In 1997 a court decision declared the Cleveland, Ohio voucher system unconstitutional after nearly a year of operation. The issue was church-state separation, because most of the 1900 students using the voucher plan were doing so for religious institutions. The state had been providing for low-income students to attend religious schools at state expense.[71]

But what is this "charter school" to which Premont refers? A charter school is one for which the school district grants a group of people, which could include parents, community members, and teachers, a charter, or authorization, to open a school that reflects their shared educational philosophy. The district then funds that school like any public school. NEA President Chase concedes that charter schools have become laboratories for innovation, helping to strengthen public schools, but he is concerned that they have also attracted privatization abuses. "In states such as Massachusetts, Michigan, and Arizona, these groups have succeeded in passing laws that grant charter status not just to legitimate public schools, but also existing private schools, to home-schoolers, and even to individuals and for-profit companies with no track record in education." [72] Chase is seeking to protect what he perceives as the public, democratic mission of the tax-supported school system, which he believes is threatened when tax dollars are used to support private beliefs, interests, and even profits. Despite such objections, new plans for "privatizing" schooling continue to be developed and acted on. One of the most recent is the idea of "contract schools," which would extend the charter school approach to all public schools by having each one set up a contract with the local school board for its funding, its mission, and its accountability. The board would then have the right to terminate weak schools and fund promising ones—much like the practice of firing employees who don't perform well and giving raises to those who do.[73] But should this principle be applied to schooling in a democratic society?

Critics of vouchers and their variants say that they are incapable of having any major reform impact on the massive public school system, and that at best they will amount to "tinkering on the fringe of reform," as Gerald Tirozzi says.[74] He argues that with 46 million public school students, the private school capacity of 6 million students will never expand sufficiently to address the needs of the great majority. Political scientist John Witte agrees. He has written that the choice movement is like a pack of terriers nipping at the heels of the public school system. The terriers will not go away, but they won't have the power to change the system in fundamental ways.[75]

Standards-Based Professional Preparation and Development of Teachers

The final major thrust of current school reform to be mentioned here has been discussed in some detail in Chapter 10: the standards-based professional preparation and development of teachers. After years of trying to restructure the system—school governance, the school year, the school day, the "system" of schooling—many are now arguing that teachers and school administrators are the key ingredient in changing what students experience in schools. As Michael Fullan writes:

> 'Systems' have a better track record of maintaining the status quo than they have of changing themselves. This is why attempting to change the system directly, through regulation and structural reform, does not work. It is people who change systems, through the development of new critical masses. Once a critical mass becomes a majority, we begin to see the system change. The lesson of systemic reform is to look for those strategies that are most likely to mobilize large numbers of people in new directions. Evaluation should focus on this development, not because it will always result in clear measures, but because such a focus will propel the very changes essential for system breakthroughs.[76]

This is the kind of thinking that lies beneath *What Matters Most: Teaching for America's Future,* the 1996 Report of the National Commission on Teaching and America's Future, an excerpt from which is the primary source reading at the end of Chapter 10.[77]

As promising as this new direction for reform might be, researcher Dee Ann Spencer argues that the Commission report is just another effort to "professionalize" teaching, that it is "malevolent" in tone, and that it is guilty of "teacher bashing." The standards-based model of reform presented there, in which national standards would guide the assessment of what each teacher knows and is able to do in the classroom, is too monolithic and top-down, she argues:

> Instead, a more fluid and dynamic model would reveal the complexities of classroom interaction and allow the diversity and variability of teachers' multiple voices to be heard . . . This constancy of variability is what must be captured in recommendations for educational reform."[78]

While we find such a recommendation vague, it is important to recognize that not everyone is satisfied with the National Commission report.

Certainly, the call for standards—standards for student achievement, standards for curriculum, standards for teaching quality—has been central to the current reform movement from the 1980s until now. But the power to regulate education and schooling has always resided first and foremost with the states, not with the federal government, so when national standards have been proposed, resistance has followed close behind. David Hoff writes that this resistance has weakened President Clinton's *Goals 2000* initiative.

> *Goals 2000* has lost its original focus on standards bit by bit since President Clinton first proposed the plan in the early days of his presidency. Fears that the program would lead to federal control over local curriculum decisions have driven Congress, governors, and school administrators to move *Goals 2000* away from its standards emphasis toward a loosely affiliated series of projects and computer purchases . . . 'There are a number of states where the money may be put to good general use, but it's not being spent on thoughtful and integrated reform,' U.S. Undersecretary of Education Marshall S. Smith, one of the program's architects, said [79]

In the current fiscal year, $340 million have been allocated for *Goals 2000* participating states, and next year this amount will increase to $476 million. After 2 years as the only state to reject these funds as too constraining on local control, Virginia will now apply for about $15 million, which the governor reports they want to use on technology purchases, allowable under the terms of the legislation.

George Bush wanted to be known as "the Education President," But there is no evidence that this will be his legacy. Similarly, unless President Clinton changes course, educational reform will not be identified with his 8 years in office. Berliner and Biddle write:

> The most serious charge that can and should be laid against the Clinton education agenda, however, is that it continues to ignore or downplay soaring social problems that directly afflict American schools. For example, we can detect little concern for and less action with regard to the huge, and growing, level of poverty among America's children; the enormous differences in levels of support given to America's schools; or the low average salaries of America's teachers. Absent initiatives to improve these conditions, it is difficult to understand how the Clinton administration can hope to have a significant impact on American education.[80]

As an illustration, this is the President who ended "welfare as we know it." If Berliner and Biddle are correct, then that legislative/executive action may have a greater impact on the quality of children's development than any feature of *Goals 2000*. The impact of the change in welfare laws, however, is yet to be clearly seen.

CONCLUDING REMARKS

Citizens of the United States, perhaps more than any other people, seem to have a deep-seated, even exaggerated faith in the ability of their schools to solve major social problems. Certainly this is true of those businesspeople, professionals, and other reform leaders who have expressed that faith throughout the nation's history. Yet the particular nature of school reform in any historical period varies with the perceptions, shared by those most in power, of the problems to be solved.

We have seen, for example, how at least early American political leaders were primarily concerned with freedom from despotic, centralized political control and how this perception framed their vision of schools dedicated to democratic values and central literacy. Then, during the late

19th century, school reform was driven by the realization of the socialization problems that accompanied the massive immigration of ethnically diverse Europeans and the emancipation of 4 million African-Americans. Again, during the cold war era, perceptions of an external military threat from communist Russia sparked school reforms intended to strengthen the national defense by identifying America's most academically able students and developing their intellectual abilities. Finally, the current reform movement, although multidimensional, received its initial motivation from a growing sense of insecurity in the face of international economic competition.

The above sketch of major school reform movements deals only with what classical-liberal and then modern-liberal reformers (including those who are popularly called conservatives, because of their shared commitment to principles of corporate liberalism) perceived to be the dominant problem of each historical period. Also, embedded in most reform movements are perceptions of other, lesser problems. For example, the current reform movement, although primarily focused on economic rehabilitation, also contains a host of issues related to the education of an increasingly multicultural population and to the empowerment of teachers and parents. Likewise, such national problems as the AIDS epidemic and drug abuse seem to find their way into the reform agenda.

This discussion of the relationship between perceived social problems and school reform leads us back to such perennial education questions as these:

- Have we perceived our social problem(s) correctly?
- *Who* should have a voice in deciding what the problems are and how schools should go about solving them?
- Does our school reform agenda address too many social problems and too few distinctly educational problems?
- How amenable are these social problems to an educational solution?
- Once problems are defined and goals agreed upon, what restructuring strategies seem most compatible with the goals?
- What are the political-economic and ideological barriers to investing the kinds of fiscal and human resources necessary to really address the social and educational problems that confront us as educators?

This last question will be addressed in the concluding chapter.

PRIMARY SOURCE READING

In 1985, the first wave of the contemporary school reform movement was well under way and the second wave was about to emerge. Writing in Harper's Magazine, *education critic Walter Karp called into question the very purposes of the school reform movement, arguing that the schools are* not *failing to accomplish what they were designed to do, but that schools are succeeding at their historical task of socializing people to be compliant, poorly informed about democratic ideals and practices, and ill prepared to think critically. While Karp's language tends toward inflammatory rhetoric, his critical perspective is worth applying to the progress of school reform today, a decade later.*

WHY JOHNNY CAN'T THINK

Walter Karp

Until very recently, remarkably little was known about what actually goes on in America's public schools. There were no reliable answers to even the most obvious questions. How many children are taught to read in overcrowded classrooms? How prevalent is rote learning and how common are classroom discussions? Do most schools set off gongs to mark the change of "periods"? Is it a common practice to bark commands over public address systems in the manner of army camps, prisons, and banana republics? Public schooling provides the only intense experience of a public realm that most Americans will ever know. Are school buildings designed with the dignity appropriate to a great republican institution, or are most of them as crummy looking as one's own?

The darkness enveloping America's public schools is truly extraordinary considering that 38.9 million students attend them, that we spend nearly $134 billion a year on them, and that foundations ladle out generous sums for the study of everything about schooling—except what really occurs in the schools. John I. Goodlad's eight-year investigation of a mere thirty-eight of America's 80,000 public schools—the result of which, *A Place Called School,* was published last year—is the most comprehensive such study ever undertaken. Hailed as a "landmark in American educational research," it was financed with great difficulty. The darkness, it seems, has its guardians.

Happily, the example of Goodlad, a former dean of UCLA's Graduate School of Education, has proven contagious. A flurry of new books sheds considerable light on the practice of public education in America. In *The Good High School,* Sara Lawrence Lightfoot offers vivid "portraits" of six distinctive American secondary schools. In *Horace's Compromise,* Theodore R. Sizer, a former dean of Harvard's Graduate School of Education, reports on his two-year odyssey through public high schools around the country. Even *High School,* a white paper issued by Ernest L. Boyer and the Carnegie Foundation for the Advancement of Teaching, is supported by a close investigation of the institutional life of a number of schools. Of the books under review, only *A Nation at Risk,* the report of the Reagan Administration's National Commission on Excellence in Education, adheres to the established practice of crass special pleading in the dark.

Thanks to Goodlad et al., it is now clear what the great educational darkness has so long concealed: the depth and pervasiveness of political hypocrisy in the common schools of the country. The great ambition professed by public school managers is, of course, education for citizenship and self-government, which harks back to Jefferson's historic call for "general education to enable every man to judge for himself what will secure or endanger his freedom." What the public schools practice with remorseless proficiency, however, is the prevention of citizenship and the stifling of self-government. When 58 percent of the thirteen-year-olds tested by the National Assessment for Educational Progress think it is against the Law to start a third party in America, we are dealing not with a sad educational failure but with a remarkably subtle success.

Consider how effectively America's future citizens are trained not to judge for themselves about anything. From the first grade to the twelfth, from one coast to the other, instruction in America's classrooms is almost entirely dogmatic. Answers are "right" and answers are "wrong," but mostly answers are short. "At all levels, [teacher-made] tests called almost exclusively for short answers and recall of information," reports Goodlad. In more than 1,000 classrooms visited by his researchers, "only *rarely*" was there "evidence to suggest instruction likely to go much beyond mere possession of information to a level of understanding its implications." Goodlad goes on to note that "the intellectual terrain is laid out by the teacher. The paths for walking through it are largely predetermined by the teacher." The give-and-take of genuine discussion is conspicuously absent. "Not even 1 percent" of instructional time, he found, was devoted to discussions that "required some kind of open response involving reasoning or perhaps an opinion from students. . . . The extraordinary degree of student passivity stands out."

Sizer's research substantiates Goodlad's. "No more important finding has emerged from the inquiries of our study than that the American high school student, *as student,* is all too often docile, compliant, and without initiative." There is good reason for this. On the one hand, notes Sizer, "there are too few rewards for being inquisitive." On the other, the heavy emphasis on "the right answer . . . smothers the student's efforts to become an effective intuitive thinker."

Yet smothered minds are looked on with the utmost complacency by the educational establishment—by the Reagan Department of Education, state boards of regents, university education departments, local administrators, and even many so-called educational reformers. Teachers are neither urged to combat the tyranny of the short right answer nor trained to do so. "Most teachers simply do not know how to teach for higher levels of thinking," says Goodlad. Indeed, they are actively discouraged from trying to do so.

The discouragement can be quite subtle. In their orientation talks to new, inexperienced teachers, for example, school administrators often indicate that they do not much care what happens in class so long as no noise can be heard in the hallway. This thinly veiled threat virtually ensures the prevalence of short-answer drills, workbook exercises, and the copying of long extracts from the blackboard. These may smother young minds, but they keep the classroom quiet.

Discouragement even calls itself reform. Consider the current cry for greater use of standardized tests to judge the "merit" of teachers and raise "academic standards." If this fake reform is foisted on the schools, dogma and docility will become even more prevalent. This point is well made by Linda Darling-Hammond of the Rand Corporation in an essay in *The Great School Debate.* Where "important decisions are based on test scores," she notes, "teachers are more likely to teach to the tests" and less likely to bother with "nontested activities, such as writing, speaking, problem-solving or real reading of real books." The most influential promoter of standardized tests is the "excellence" brigade in the Department of Education; so clearly one important meaning of "educational excellence" is greater proficiency in smothering students' efforts to think for themselves.

Probably the greatest single discouragement to better instruction is the overcrowded classroom. The Carnegie report points out that English teachers cannot teach their students how to write when they must read and criticize the papers of as many as 175 students. As Sizer observes, genuine discussion is possible only in small seminars. In crowded classrooms, teachers have difficulty imparting even the most basic intellectual skills, since they have no time to give students personal attention. The overcrowded classroom inevitably debases instruction, yet it is the rule in America's public schools. In the first three grades of elementary school, Goodlad notes, the average class has twenty-seven students. High school classes range from twenty-five to forty students, according to the Carnegie report.

What makes these conditions appalling is that they are quite unnecessary. The public schools are top-heavy with administrators and rife with sinecures. Large numbers of teachers scarcely ever set foot in a classroom, being occupied instead as grade advisers, career counselors, "coordinators," and supervisors. "Schools, if simply organized," Sizer writes, "can have well-paid faculty and fewer than eighty students per teacher [16 per class] without increasing current per-pupil expenditure." Yet no serious effort is being made to reduce class size. As Sizer notes, "Reducing teacher load is, when all the negotiating is over, a low agenda item for the unions and school boards." Overcrowded classrooms virtually guarantee smothered minds, yet the subject is not even mentioned in *A Nation at Risk,* for all its well-published braying about a "rising tide of mediocrity."

Do the nation's educators really want to teach almost 40 million students how to "think critically," in the Carnegie report's phrase, and "how to judge for themselves," in Jefferson's? The answer is, if you can believe that you will believe anything. The educational establishment is not even content to produce passive minds. It seeks passive spirits as well. One effective agency for producing these is the overly populous school. The larger schools are, the more prison-like they tend to be. In such schools, guards man the stairwells and exits. ID cards and "passes" are examined at checkpoints. Bells set off spasms of anarchy and bells quell the student mob. PA systems interrupt regularly with trivial fiats and frivolous announcements. This "malevolent intruder," in Sizer's apt phrase, is truly ill willed, for the PA system is actually an educational tool. It teaches the huge student mass to respect the authority of disembodied voices and the rule of remote and invisible agencies. Sixty-three percent of all high school students in America attend schools with enrollments of 5,000 or more. The common excuse for these mobbed schools is economy, but in fact they cannot be shown to save taxpayers a penny. Larger schools "tend to create passive and compliant students," notes Robert B. Hawkins Jr. in an essay in *The Challenge to American Schools.* That is their chief reason for being.

"How can the relatively passive and docile roles of students prepare them to participate as informed, active and questioning citizens?" asks the Carnegie report, in discussing the "hidden curriculum" of passivity in the schools. The answer is, they were not meant to. Public schools introduce future citizens to the public world, but no introduction could be more disheartening. Architecturally, public school buildings range from drab to repellent. They are often disfigured by demoralizing neglect—"cracked sidewalks, a shabby lawn, and peeling paint on every window sash," to quote the Carnegie report. Many big-city elementary schools have numbers instead of names, making them as coldly dispiriting as possible.

Public schools stamp out republican sentiment by habituating their students to unfairness, inequality, and special privilege. These arise inevitably from the educational establishment's longstanding policy (well described by Diane Ravitch in *The Troubled Crusade*) of maintaining "the correlation between social class and educational achievement." In order to preserve that factitious "correlation," public schooling is rigged to favor middle-class students and to ensure that working-class students do poorly enough to convince them that they fully merit the lowly station that will one day be theirs. "Our goal is to get these kids to be like their parents," one teacher, more candid than most, remarked to a Carnegie researcher.

For more than three decades, elementary schools across the country practiced a "progressive," non-phonetic method of teaching reading that had nothing much to recommend it save its inherent social bias. According to Ravitch, this method favored "children who were already motivated and prepared to begin reading" before entering school, while making learning to read more difficult for precisely those children whose parents were ill read or ignorant. The advantages enjoyed by the well-bred were thus artificially multiplied tenfold, and 23 million adult Americans are today "functional illiterates." America's educators, notes Ravitch, have "never actually accepted full responsibility for making all children literate."

That describes a malicious intent a trifle too mildly. Reading is the key to everything else in school. Children who struggle with it in the first grade will be "grouped" with the slow readers in the second grade and will fall hopelessly behind in all subjects by the sixth. The schools hasten this process of falling behind, report Goodlad and others, by giving the best students the best teachers and struggling students the worst ones. "It is ironic," observes the Carnegie report, "that those who need the most help get the least." Such students are commonly diagnosed as "culturally deprived" and so are blamed for their failures inflicted on them. Thus, they are taught to despise themselves even as they are inured to their inferior station.

The whole system of unfairness, inequality, and privilege comes to fruition in high school. There, some 15.7 million youngsters are formally divided into the favored few and the ill-favored many by the practice of "tracking." About 35 percent of America's public secondary school students are enrolled in academic programs (often subdivided into "gifted" and "non-gifted" tracks); the rest are relegated to some variety of non-academic schooling. Thus the tracking system, as intended, reproduces the divisions of the class system. "The honors programs," notes Sizer, "serve the wealthier youngsters, and the general tracks (whatever their titles) serve the working class. Vocational programs are often a cruel social dumping ground." The bottom-dogs are trained for jobs as auto mechanics, cosmeticians, and institutional cooks, but they rarely get the jobs they are trained for. Pumping gasoline, according to the Carnegie report, is as close as an auto-mechanics major is likely to get to repairing a car. "Vocational education in the schools is virtually irrelevant to job fate," asserts Goodlad. It is merely the final hoax that the school bureaucracy plays on the neediest, one that the federal government has been promoting for seventy years.

The tracking system makes privilege and inequality blatantly visible to everyone. It creates under one roof "two worlds of schooling," to quote Goodlad. Students in academic programs read Shakespeare's plays. The commonality, notes the Carnegie report, are allowed virtually no contact with serious literature. In their English classes they practice filling out job applications. "Gifted" students alone are encouraged to think for themselves. The rest are subjected to sanctimonious wind, chiefly about "work habits" and "career opportunities."

"If you are the child of low-income parents," reports Sizer, "the chances are good that you will receive limited and often careless attention from adults in your high school. If you are the child of upper-middle-income parents, the chances are good that you will receive substantial and careful attention." In Brookline High School in Massachusetts, one of Lightfoot's "good" schools, a few fortunate students enjoy special treatment in their Advanced Placement classes. Meanwhile, students tracked into "career education" learn about "institutional cooking and clean-up" in a four-term Food Service course that requires them to mop up after their betters in the school cafeteria.

This wretched arrangement expresses the true spirit of public education in America and discloses the real aim of its hidden curriculum. A favored few, pampered and smiled upon, are taught to cherish privilege and despise the disfavored. The favorless many, who have majored in failure for years, are taught to think ill of themselves. Youthful spirits are broken to the world and every impulse of citizenship is effectively stifled. John Goodlad's judgment is severe but just: "There is in the gap between our highly idealistic goals for schooling in our society and the differentiated opportunities condoned and supported in schools a monstrous hypocrisy."

The public schools of America have not been corrupted for trivial reasons. Much would be different in a republic composed of citizens who could judge for themselves what secured or endangered their freedom. Every wielder of illicit or undemocratic power, every possessor of undue influence, every beneficiary of corrupt special privilege would find his position and tenure at hazard. Republican education is a menace to powerful, privileged, and influential people, and they in turn are a menace to republican education. That is why the generation that founded the public schools took care to place them under the suffrage of local communities, and that is why the corrupters of public education have virtually destroyed that suffrage. In 1932 there were 127,531 school districts in America. Today there are approximately 15,840 and they are virtually impotent, their proper role having been usurped by state and federal authorities. Curriculum and textbooks, methods of instruction, the procedures of the classroom, the organization of the school day, the cant, the pettifogging, and the corruption are almost uniform from coast to coast. To put down the menace of republican education its shield of local self-government had to be smashed, and smashed it was.

The public schools we have today are what the powerful and the considerable have made of them. They will not be redeemed by trifling reforms. Merit pay, a longer school year, more homework, special schools for "the gifted," and more standardized tests will not even begin to turn our public schools into nurseries of "informed, active and questioning citizens." They are not meant to. When the authors of *A Nation at Risk* call upon the schools to create an "educated work force," they are merely sanctioning the prevailing corruption, which consists precisely in the reduction of citizens to credulous workers. The education of a free people will not come from federal bureaucrats crying up "excellence" for "economic growth," any more than it came from their predecessors who cried up schooling as a means to "get a better job."

Only ordinary citizens can rescue the schools from their stifling corruption, for nobody else wants ordinary children to become questioning citizens at all. If we wait for the mighty to teach America's youth what secures or endangers their freedom, we will wait until the crack of doom.

PRIMARY SOURCE READING

Twelve years after the publication of "Why Johnny Can't Think," the editors of Education Week *compiled a 238-page analysis of the state of schooling in the United States. They introduced their analysis with the overview reprinted here.*

THE STATE OF THE STATES

(Editors, *Education Week,* January 22, 1997)

Public education systems in the 50 states are riddled with excellence but rife with mediocrity. Despite 15 years of earnest efforts to improve public schools and raise student achievement, states haven't made much progress.

As the new millennium approaches, there is growing concern that if public education doesn't soon improve, one of two outcomes is almost inevitable:

- Our democratic system and our economic strength, both of which depend on an educated citizenry, will steadily erode; or,
- Alternative forms of education will emerge to replace public schools as we have known them.

This will not happen next year or perhaps even in the next 10 years. But in time, if our education systems remain mediocre, we will see one of those two results. Either would be a sad loss for America.

The nation's governors realize this. Last March, they met at the National Education Summit to reaffirm their commitment to school reform. They invited the voters to hold them accountable and called for "an external, independent, nongovernmental effort to measure and report each state's annual progress."

We agree that Americans should hold their representatives—and themselves—accountable for the quality of their public schools. To help them do that, *Education Week,* with support from the Pew Charitable Trusts, is publishing this report.

Education Week's editors spent the better part of the past year studying the condition of public education in the states. We reviewed thousands of pages of data from a variety of government and private sources, surveyed policymakers and business leaders in every state, and polled educators.

We then compiled statistics on more than 75 specific indicators and graded states on their policies and performance in four major categories—academic standards, quality of teaching, school climate, and funding. We also ranked the states on their students' scores on the National Assessment of Educational Progress.

We relied on research and experience in choosing the most useful indicators to evaluate public education in the states. Our goal was to focus on policies that really matter, that research tells us are most likely to result in better schools and more learning.

In addition, staff writers have summarized the progress and problems in each state. They searched 15 years of *Education Week's* archives, pored over numerous reports and reviewed hundreds of experts.

In a nutshell, here is what we found:

1. **Standards and assessments.** What do we expect students to know and be able to do and how do we judge their performance? That

question goes straight to the purpose and nature of public schooling. It is being discussed in every state, and it is one that every parent and taxpayer should be involved in.

High standards for student performance lay the foundation for the significant changes that must follow. And the work in this area appears to be paying off. This is where the states earned their highest overall grade—a solid B. Encouraging as that is, we must note that the B, at this point, is more for effort than results. In most states, the standards haven't found their way into classrooms. Teachers, by and large, are not prepared to teach to them. We don't know how rigorous they are. The tests aren't yet in place to measure student progress. And few states are ready to hold either schools or students accountable for meeting the new standards.

- Overall grade for the states: B.
- 22 states earn A's.
- 13 get B's.
- 2 states get F's, mainly because they have not decided to develop statewide standards and assessments.

2. **Quality of teaching.** How are teachers prepared and supported? The system can only be as good as its teachers. Research shows that a good teacher in every classroom is the most effective way of improving student performance. Great strides have been made at the policy level to turn teaching into a real profession with higher standards for training and more rigorous licensing requirements. At the national level, the crucial pieces of a system are falling into place, but there is much work to be done. On average, four out of 10 secondary teachers do not have a degree in the subject they teach. Too many unlicensed teachers are in classrooms. Not enough prospective teachers receive the high-quality education they need. On-the-job education for teachers is still more of a goal than a reality.

- Overall grade for the states: C.
- 8 states get B's.
- 3 get D's.
- The rest receive C's.

3. **School climate.** How should a school be organized and run to be effective?

We know a lot about what makes good schools. They should be small enough for teachers to know their students and work effectively with their colleagues. They should have a clear, shared sense of mission and be focused on student learning. They should capitalize on what we know about how children learn. And they should be safe and orderly. That is the goal. The reality is that nearly half of our elementary teachers have classes of 25 or more pupils; more than half of high school English teachers teach 80 or more students a day. There is not enough parent and community involvement.

Strong traditions of local control dilute the effectiveness of state policy in changing the way schools are organized and operated. And ultimately, it is in the school and the classroom where we win or lose. In school climate, states get their lowest scores.

- Overall, the states earn a C–.
- No states get A's.
- 4 states receive B's.
- 19 get D's, and the rest get C's.

4. **Resources.**

• Are states allocating enough money to do the job? Most states are spending more money for education than they did 10 years ago, and the increases generally have outpaced inflation. But too few of the additional dollars have reached classrooms. Most of the increased funding has been spent on the approximately 12 percent of students in special education, on trying to keep up with enrollment growth, and on rising salaries for an aging teaching force.

- Overall, states get a C+ on whether they spend enough.
- 5 states get A's, and 20 get B's.
- 17 states get C's, and 7 states get D's.
- 1 state gets an F.

• Do states make sure that everyone gets a fair share? After more than three decades of lawsuits and legislative haggling, the system has become somewhat more equitable. But progress notwithstanding, intolerable disparities persist between rich schools and poor schools within states and across states, and the extent of that inequity is not revealed in the letter grades. The fact is that the quality of a child's education depends greatly on skin color, family income, and where he or she lives. The problem is most severe in inner cities and poor rural areas.

- Overall, the states get a low B– on equity.
- 5 states get A's.
- 6 states get D's.
- The rest earn B's and C's.

• **Do states spend their money on the right things?** How money is spent is as important as how much is spent. States do not concentrate enough funding in the classroom—on teaching and learning. Technology has great potential to increase productivity in a labor-intensive endeavor. Schools have made remarkable gains in acquiring computer equipment, but there is little evidence that it is being effectively used to help all children. Finally, states have failed to make sure that school buildings are sound and safe. Districts have deferred maintenance to the point where millions of children attend schools that need to be replaced or substantially repaired.

- States get a C– in the allocation of dollars.
- 6 states get B's
- 28 states get C's.
- 16 states either barely passed or failed.

5. **Student achievement.** This is the bottom line. The question of student achievement can't be answered as fully and accurately as it should be because the states don't collect the necessary information to permit comparisons—data such as course-taking, dropout rates, and attendance rates. The only comparable measures of student performance are the NAEP scores, and they are discouraging.

- Maine has the best score in the nation on the 1994 NAEP 4th-grade reading test, and 59 percent of its 4th graders could not read at a proficient level.
- Iowa led the nation on the 1992 NAEP math exam, and 69 percent of its 8th graders were below the proficient level.
- 85 percent of Louisiana's 4th graders read below the proficient level.
- 94 percent of Mississippi's 8th graders score below proficient in math.

The public education systems in the 50 states have been a century or more in the making. They cannot be transformed quickly, but they can be significantly improved. In every state, there are examples of successful, effective schools. Their success does not permit us to tolerated mediocrity any longer or anywhere.

QUESTIONS FOR DISCUSSION AND EXAMINATION

1. In one of the primary readings for this chapter, Walter Karp writes, "What the public schools practice with remorseless proficiency . . . is the prevention of citizenship and the stifling of self-government." How adequately does he support this claim in the article? Give examples of evidence and arguments he marshals to support his view, and identify from your own knowledge any evidence and arguments he omits which might strengthen or weaken his case.
2. Karp says that schools provide a system of unfairness, inequality, and privilege not by accident but by intent. Relying on your knowledge of current and past school reform as well as on Karp's arguments, to what extent do you agree with him? Defend your view.
3. Karp attacks the first wave of school reform reports as "merely sanctioning the prevailing corruption, which consists precisely in the reduction of citizens to credulous workers." To what degree do you see the second wave of reform—which emphasizes restructuring of curriculum, decision making, and teacher education—achieving different outcomes? Use evidence and arguments from this chapter to defend your view.
4. Today's college students, for the most part, attended the nation's schools during the contemporary school reform movement. To what degree has your education been influenced by such school reform? Explain.

NOTES

1. *America 2000: An Education Strategy* (Washington, D.C.: U.S. Department of Education, 1991).
2. National Commission on Excellence in Education, *A Nation at Risk: The Imperative for Educational Reform* (Washington, D.C.: Government Printing Office, 1983), pp. 12, 16.
3. Gary Orfield, "Choice, Testing, and the Re-election of a President," in *Voices from the Field: 30 Expert Opinions on America 2000, the Bush Administration Strategy to "Reinvent" America's Schools* (Washington, D.C.: William T. Grant Foundation Commission on Work, Family and Citizenship and Institute for Educational Leadership, 1991), p. 3.
4. Samuel B. Bacharach, ed., *Education Reform: Making Sense of It All* (Boston: Allyn and Bacon, 1990).

5. Michael W. Kirst, "Recent State Education Reform in the United States: Looking Backward and Forward," *Educational Administration Quarterly* 24 (August 3, 1988), pp. 319–28; and A. Harry Passow, "Whither (or Wither?) School Reform," in Bacharach, *Education Reform,* pp. 10–19.
6. Bacharach, *Education Reform,* p. 9.
7. Ibid.
8. Ernest L. Boyer, "Elementary and Secondary Education," in *Human Capital and America's Future,* Hornbeck and Salamon, eds. (Baltimore: Johns Hopkins University Press, 1991), pp. 172–75.
9. Ibid., 176–77.
10. Ibid., p. 173.
11. Mark G. Yudof, "Educational Policy Research and the New Consensus of the 1980s," *Phi Delta Kappan,* March 1984, pp. 456–59.
12. Christine M. Shea, "Pentagon vs. Multinational Capitalism: The Political Economy of the 1980s School Reform Movement," in *The New Servants of Power: A Critique of the 1980s School Reform Movement,* Christine M. Shea, Ernest Kahane, and Peter Sola, eds. (New York: Praeger, 1989), p. 20.
13. Ibid.
14. Holmes Group, *Tomorrow's Teachers: A Report of the Holmes Group* (East Lansing, MI: Holmes Group, 1986); Carnegie Forum Task Force on Teaching as a Profession, *A Nation Prepared: Teachers for the 21st Century* (New York: Carnegie Forum on Education and the Economy, 1986).
15. William A. Firestone, Susan H. Fuhrman, and Michael W. Kirst, *The Progress of Reform: An Appraisal of State Education Initiatives* (Palo Alto: Center for Policy Research in Education, 1990), p. 13.
16. David Tyack, "Restructuring in Historical Perspective: Tinkering toward Utopia," *Teachers College Record,* Vol. 92 (Winter 1990), pp. 170–91.
17. Ibid., p. 170.
18. Ibid., p. 171.
19. William Ayers, "Perestroika in Chicago Schools," *Educational Leadership* 48 (May 1991), p. 71.
20. Tyack, p. 187.
21. A. Harry Passow, "Present and Future Directions in School Reform," in *Schooling for Tomorrow: Directing Reforms to Issues That Count,* Thomas J. Sergiovanni and John H. Moore, eds. (Boston: Allyn and Bacon, 1989), p. 15.
22. Ibid., p. 17.
23. Cited in ibid.
24. Ibid.
25. Michael W. Kirst, "Recent State Education Reform in the United States," p. 321.
26. Firestone, Fuhrman and Kirst, *The Progress of Reform,* 1990.
27. William A. Firestone, Sheila Rosenblum, Beth D. Bader, and Dianne Massell, "Recent Trends in State Educational Reform: Assessment and Prospects," *Teachers College Record,* Vol. 94, No. 2 (Winter 1992), pp. 254–78.
28. Firestone et al., "Recent Trends in State Educational Reform," p. 260.
29. Ibid., p. 262.
30. Ibid., p. 263–66.
31. Frank Margonis, "What Is the Meaning of Contemporary Educational Nationalism?" in *Philosophy of Education 1988* (Normal, IL: Philosophy of Education Society), pp. 343–52.
32. Ibid., pp. 349–50.
33. Ibid., p. 351.
34. Shea, "Pentagon vs. Multinational Capitalism," pp. 32–33.
35. Margonis, "Contemporary Educational Nationalism."
36. Stan Karp, 1989, p. 95.
37. Henry Giroux, "Education Reform in the Age of Reagan: Schooling for Less," *Democratic Left,* Vol. 16, No. 2 (March–April 1988), p. 8.
38. Thomas Toch, *In the Name of Excellence: The Struggle to Reform Our Nation's Schools, Why It's Failing, and What Should be Done* (New York: Oxford University Press, 1991).
39. Ibid., p. 263.
40. Ibid., p. 235.
41. Ibid., p. 264.
42. Linda Chion-Kenney, "Most Teachers Support School Reforms, Survey Finds," *Education Week,* August 22, 1984, p. 27.
43. Ibid., p. 14
44. Adam Urbanski, "Forces that Undermine Reform: A Teacher's Perspective," *American Educator,* Spring 1986, p. 18.
45. Stan Karp, "Bush Plan Abandons Schools," *Rethinking Schools,* Vol. 6, No. 1 (October–November 1991), p. 4.
46. Ibid.
47. David Hill, "What Has the 1980s School Reform Movement Accomplished?" *Teacher Magazine,* Vol. 1 (September–October 1989), pp. 50–55.
48. Linda Darling-Hammond, "Achieving Our Goals: Superficial or Structural Reforms?" *Phi Delta Kappan* 72, No. 4 (December 1990), p. 291.
49. Ibid., p. 292.
50. Ibid., p. 294.
51. Anne C. Lewis, "Voices of the Loyal Opposition," *Phi Delta Kappan,* Vol. 73, No. 1 (September 1991), p. 5.
52. Harold Hodgkinson, "Reform versus Reality," *Phi Delta Kappan,* Vol. 73, No. 1 (September 1991), pp. 9–16.

53. Ibid., p. 14.
54. Stanley Pogrow, "On Scripting the Classroom," *Education Week,* Vol. 16, No. 4 (September 25, 1996), p. 52.
55. Lawrence C. Stedman, "Deep Achievement Problems: The Case for Reform Still Stands," *Educational Researcher,* Vol. 26, No. 9 (April 1997), p. 27.
56. *Quality Counts: A Report Card on the Condition of Public Education in the 50 States.* A Supplement to *Education Week,* Vol. 16 (January 22, 1997), p. 26.
57. David C. Berliner and Bruce J. Biddle, *The Manufactured Crisis: Myths, Fraud, and the Attack on America's Public Schools* (White Plains, NY: Longman, 1997), p. 26.
58. Martin Haberman, "The Top Ten Fantasies of School Reformers," *Phi Delta Kappan* Vol. 75, No. 9 (May 1994), pp. 689, 690, 692.
59. *Public Policy and School Reform: A Research Summary* Consortium for Policy Research in Education. Report #36 (Philadelphia: University of Pennsylvania, 1996), p. 1.
60. *Fitting the Pieces: Education Reform That Works* (1996). Washington, DC: U.S. Department of Education, Office of Educational Research and Improvement, p. iii.
61. Larry Cuban, "Techno-Reformers and Classroom Teachers," *Education Week,* Vol. 16, No. 6 (October 9, 1996), p. 39.
62. Joan Dykstra and Arnold F. Fege, "Not Without Parents," *Education Week,* Vol. 16, No. 25 (March 19, 1997), p. 44. The data in the following paragraph are found in "How Widespread Is Site-Based Decision-making in the Public Schools?" (1996), *Issue Brief,* U.S. Department of Education Office of Educational Research and Improvement (December 1996), IB-8-96.
63. Gerald W. Bracey, "Schools Should Not Prepare Students for Work," *The Council Chronicle,* (November 1996), p. 10.
64. Ibid.
65. Salmuel Halperin, "School-to-Work, Employers, and Personal Values," *Education Week,* Vol. 16, No. 24 (March 12, 1997), p. 52.
66. Bracey (1966), p. 10.
67. Berliner and Biddle, p. 333.
68. Quoted in Berliner and Biddle, p. 173.
69. Ibid, p. 179.
70. Bob Chase, "Which Charters Are Smarter?" *Education Week,* Vol. 16, No. 14 (December 14, 1996), p. 52.
71. Mark Walsh, "Voucher Plan in Cleveland Is Overturned," *Education Week,* Vol. 16, No. 32 (May 7, 1997), p. 1.
72. Chase, p. 52.
73. Paul T. Hill, Lawrence C. Pierce, and James W. Guthrie. "How Contracting Can Transform America's Schools," *Education Week,* Vol. 16, No. 33 (May 14, 1997), p. 60.
74. Gerald Tirozzi, "Vouchers: A Questionable Answer to and Unasked Question," *Education Week,* Vol. 16, No. 30 (April 23, 1997), p. 64.
75. John F. Witte, "Politics, Markets, or Money? The Political-Economy of School Choice." Presented at American Political Science Association Annual Meeting, San Francisco, August 29–September 1, 1996, p. 27.
76. Michael G. Fullan, "Turning Systemic Thinking on Its Head," *Phi Delta Kappan,* Vol. 77, No. 6 (February 1996), p. 423.
77. *What Matters Most: Teaching for America's Future,* Report of the National Commission on Teaching and America's Future (New York: Teachers College, Columbia University, 1996).
78. Dee Ann Spencer, "Teachers and Educational Reform," *Educational Researcher,* Vol. 25, No. 9 (December 1996), p. 17.
79. David J. Hoff (1997) "Goals 2000 Loses Its Way on Standards." *Education Week,* Vol. 16, No. 17 (January 22, 1997), p. 16.
80. Berliner and Biddle, p. 214.

Conclusion: School and Contemporary Society

In large part, the purpose of this book has been to engage teachers and other educators in developing new concepts and perspectives. With these tools, together with their own experiences and ideas, students can think more critically about the relationships between schools in the United States and the social fabric in which those schools are an important thread. The book suggests that our schools express much about the larger society's dominant beliefs, ideals, and economic and political institutions. The extent, for example, to which our schools admit all students through their doors regardless of ethnicity, gender, or social class; the extent to which these variables influence how different children and youth experience schooling; the extent to which schools are hierarchical in their governance; the extent to which they expect and support far greater achievement for some students than for others; and the extent to which the economic resources provided for different schools differ dramatically: all of these, when further investigated, reveal something about what the larger society finds acceptable and useful in its political, economic, and social institutions and in the prevailing beliefs and values that support the social order.

Special thanks to Lillie R. Albert and Tammie L. Swopes for assistance on this chapter.

All of this may be interesting to the sociologist or the historian, but why is it useful to the teacher? The answer to this important question resides in an undeniable fact: teachers are required to make a great many decisions about complex problems that have social dimensions. First, for example, the practice of classroom teaching is heavily decision-laden. Teachers must make countless moment-by-moment decisions in the classroom, and they must make these decisions on the basis of immediate interpretations of complex situations involving student characteristics, environmental conditions, and educational aims. Second, teachers are increasingly called upon to participate in making educational decisions outside the classroom—decisions about texts, curricula, school organization, and school policies. A recent study of over 21,000 teachers indicated that 79 percent reported involvement in choosing textbooks and other instructional materials, and 63 percent reported involvement in shaping the curriculum. Again, a great many variables must be taken into account when making such decisions.[1] Third, something greater than common sense or lay (nonspecialized) understanding is necessary if teachers are to make the best possible judgments in these decision-making situations. This is because the problems they face have multiple dimensions: historical, sociological, economic, psychological, philosophical, and so on. To study such dimensions of educational practice can equip the teacher with a richer framework of professional understanding within which to interpret problems of professional practice. If common sense or lay understanding were enough, there would be no need to have teacher education programs at all.

In short, educational problems are many-sided, and in order to be professionally effective problem solvers who can achieve their own aims in the classroom, teachers must first become adept at recognizing the various dimensions of a problem. Ultimately, almost all problems of classroom practice and student learning have some connection to larger social, cultural, economic, and political forces outside the classroom. To understand these forces and how their invisible tentacles penetrate the textbooks, curriculum guides, organizational arrangements, and codes of behavior that constitute classroom life is to have a solid foundation for teaching all students well.

THE 1990s: ENTERING THE 21st CENTURY

Applying the orientation of this volume to our contemporary educational situation, it is necessary to look briefly at the political-economic and ideological conditions of the 1990s. If we focus on the persistent poverty and economic inequality, the decreasing political participation, and the strengthening of a business-oriented ideology in educational policies, the picture is a grim one. Yet it must be examined if we are to understand the society that is the "great educator" within which schools work. Such an understanding is necessary if teachers are to decide intelligently what it is possible for them to do, and what they *ought* to do. The following discussion will first examine our current economic and political difficulties, then the dominant ideology that masks the nature of these problems. This will be followed by an examination of how these conditions affect the educational prospects of millions of young people and, finally, what teachers can do to influence the lives of their students, even those whom the schools typically serve most poorly.

Political-Economic Conditions of the 1990s

It is not clear which is the most significant economic legacy of the 1980s: the negative position of the United States in world markets, or the deepening domestic economic inequalities and the related social crises such as poverty and homelessness. Economist James K. Galbraith suggested in 1991 that these two legacies of the 1980s are closely connected:

> America's economic problems are real. We have seen the collapse of certain heavy industries (steel), severe erosion in others (autos), a sharp decline in high-wage, blue-collar employment, a flood of low-wage imports, and a decline in the trade balance at high employment, an increase in wages and income inequality, rising poverty, and a deepening of fundamental social problems—all within the last decade.[2]

Why are these conditions important to teachers? One reason, as W. Davis and E. McCaul point out, is that teachers should recognize that one out of five children in the United States lives in poverty. They continue: "Children represent the single largest and fastest growing poverty group in the United States," and "of all the major indicators which are commonly associated with educational disadvantage, poverty is the most significant indicator."[3] Further, teachers need to recognize the importance of literacy and problem-solving skills in the changing workplace in which their students will be employed, as well as the need for a citizenry that can think critically about growing social problems that resist top-down solutions.

In part because of the decline of the industrial economy and in part because of the increasing share of tax dollars being used to finance the national debt and such 1980s debacles as the multibillion-dollar collapse of the savings and loan industry, it is not only the poor who are affected: the working and middle classes in the United States are suffering as well. The U.S. Census Bureau recently reported that the number of full-time workers earning only poverty wages has increased by 50 percent since 1979 to approximately one in five workers, or a total of 14.4 million full-time employees. As might be predicted, the workers most adversely affected are those without a high school degree, African-Americans and Latinos as the hardest hit within that group.[4] Middle-class buying power has actually declined nearly 20 percent in the past two decades, and families are maintaining their economic level only because so many wives and mothers have gone to work. The number of women working full time rose from 21 million in 1970 to 36 million in 1992.[5] Economist Robert Reich, Secretary of Labor in the first Clinton Administration, sums up the middle-class plight as follows:

> In most families, two wage-earners are necessary to make ends meet, whereas years ago one would do. Average family size is shrinking. Young people are having difficulty affording houses nearly as nice as the homes they grew up in. For the first time since the 1930s, the percentage of Americans who own their own homes is declining. . . . The average American family is no better off today than it was 15 years ago, even though America is now living off borrowed funds. Were the borrowing to stop, our standard of living would fall precipitously.[6]

Throughout most of the 20th century, American citizens have been accustomed to believing that theirs is the highest standard of living in the world. This has had ideological and political significance because it has allowed American leaders to argue that although the political system might be flawed, it is still the best in the world. Consequently, citizens should be tolerant of its flaws rather than seeking to change the system in significant ways. The claim "We're number one" rose to prominence again in 1991 when the United States led a United Nations military intervention in the Persian Gulf region. During this period President Bush assured the American people that the United States was "the undisputed leader of the world."[7]

Reich's remarks about the precarious standard of living in this country, however, raise the question, In what ways does the United States lead the world? In his recent book, *We're Number One*, Andrew L. Shapiro examines this question and finds that the United States leads all industrialized nations in the following categories:

- Defense spending.
- Percentage of children and elderly living in poverty.
- Unequal distribution of wealth.
- Homelessness.
- Military aid to developing countries (but last in humanitarian aid to developing countries).
- Foreign debt and domestic budget deficit.
- Infant mortality and percentage of infants with low birth weight.
- Percentage of population without health insurance.
- Percentage of people who have been crime victims.
- Percentage of people who commit murder.
- Murder of children.
- Death by capital punishment.
- Percentage of population imprisoned (well ahead of even South Africa and the former Soviet Union).[8]

This selective and intentionally sobering list is a reminder that a great proportion of Americans live in grim conditions. While the proportion of wealth and income accumulated by the wealthy in U.S. society increased throughout the 1980s, the proportion of wealth and income decreased for the poorest two-fifths of the population. A higher standard of living for the few at the top has been purchased at the expense of the many.[9] It is important for the educator to realize that a great many of our students are growing up in an intensely violent and unhealthy society. By recognizing the conditions of that society, educators can better understand the conditions they are fighting against and the possibilities for success that still exist.

As we examine these signs that the economic conditions of the United States have resulted in a standard of living that, in comparison with other industrialized nations, is shocking for its inequalities and its depravities, four points about schooling are worth making here. One is that the children who are victimized by deep social and economic inequities are the most likely to be poorly educated in schools, as Jonathan Kozol's recent book *Savage Inequalities* so dramatically illustrates.[10] Second, failure to educate these children adequately creates a cycle of poverty in which they are likely to be victimized by the social structure that penalizes nonstandard literacy and communications skills. Third, poverty and racism are not insurmountable obstacles to a quality education, and a handful of well-known schools throughout the country have found ways to educate these children successfully.[11] Fourth, while education clearly can make a difference in the life prospects of individuals, the temptation to believe that school improvement and educational reform movements can correct basic social and economic ills should be resisted. James K. Galbraith remarks:

> As an examination of the industries where the United States is most successful reveals, the well-springs of competitive success simply are not to be found in the public schools. Rather, they lie in blunter and more sweeping instruments: development of agricultural and energy resources, technology forcing mechanisms, and wholesale subsidy of industrial research and development. . . . [T]here is no strong reason to believe that better education in the U.S. can do much to offset the wage gap and no compelling reason to subordinate education policy to the pursuit of economical wills-o'-the-wisp.[12]

In other words, economic ills require direct economic remedies, not indirect and historically futile efforts to correct economic problems through the schools. As this volume has suggested before, teachers should be wary of efforts to use the schools to correct social and economic problems that did not originate in the schools. Unfortunately, the American voter is still being told by politicians, with news media as willing participants, that better education will lead directly to national economic success. This is a promise made on behalf of teachers but one which teachers are not likely to be able to keep, as Galbraith points out, because there are more direct influences on the economy than schools. The promise that teachers *can* keep is that, given necessary support and resources, children from all ethnic and economic backgrounds can learn to read and write and compute and think well. *Teachers can keep educational promises they are willing to make much better than they can keep economic promises that have been made for them.*

Not only is the American voter ill informed about the relations between the economy, social problems, and schooling, but fewer voters are participating in elections. In contrast to recent voter participation increases among the wealthy, voting has declined among the majority of Americans. Uninformed even about that decline, American voters are last among industrialized nations in voter participation, while we are number one in people who claim to have an active interest in politics. When 55 percent of eligible voters, for example, voted in the 1992 presidential election, it was the highest percentage in 20 years. Yet the President was elected by less than a third of the American electorate.[13] In 1996, the voter turnout declined to the lowest percentage in modern history: under 50 percent. What are we to believe about this level of voter participation? That people are not voting because they are satisfied with their standard of living? If so, then why are the wealthy not satisfied enough to relax their voting as well? Or is it that an increasing proportion of Americans don't believe their vote makes a difference in how their lives will be conducted? A number of recent opinion polls illustrate conclusively that most Americans realize that the 1980s resulted in a triumph for the nation's wealthy at the expense of the majority. However, it is also clear that they do not know what to do about it.[14] This lack of perceived options recalls the account of ideological hegemony discussed in Chapter 9.

The Dominant Ideology Today

We have argued that 20th-century corporate liberalism, in both its "liberal" and "conservative" manifestations, is the offspring of classical liberalism. The political "left" (liberal) and "right" (conservative) wings among modern liberals are not that different from each other in their commitments to a business ethic and to a close working relationship between business and government—as Chapter 9 details. Further, both the liberal and conservative wings of corporate liberalism fail to examine our social ills in terms that show how these problems are the predictable result of our political and economic structures. Rather than beginning their analysis by looking at the entire *system* and its effects on individuals, both groups begin their examination of social ills by focusing directly on individuals themselves. This individualistic point of view is illustrated in the remark of a psychologist in the economically troubled middle-class community of Bethesda, Maryland, who said recently, "The people I see are more likely to blame themselves."[15]

The hegemony of this dominant ideology is further illustrated in a 1991 U.S. Census report on the political thinking of college students surveyed in 1989. When asked how they classify themselves, over 50 percent of the students classified themselves as "middle of the road," while the remaining students were divided about equally between "liberal" and "conservative" in their own estimations. Part of what is interesting is that nearly all students find themselves comfortably within the relatively narrow ideological boundaries described by these three categories of corporate liberalism. Even more significant is the fact that the Census Bureau offered only three choices of political viewpoint—choices not very different from one another. Certainly in many European nations, including those that rank ahead of the United States in overall standard of living, there are many more choices on both ends of the ideological spectrum, choices that receive public debate and strong support from students, voters, and candidates. These include strong environmental parties that place ecological preservation ahead of individual freedoms, socialist parties that support centralized distribution of public services such as utilities and medicine, and others. Returning to the discussion of American college students, in 1992 a study of over 200,000 freshmen was conducted to identify college students whose political views lie outside the central mainstream. It found that 96.4 percent of first-year college students identified their political views as liberal, middle-of-the-road, or conservative, while the remaining 3.6 percent were far left (2.3 percent) or far right (1.3 percent).[16]

Although liberals and conservatives are not far apart in the corporate liberal mainstream, their differences on social policy issues are sometimes significant, as the 1980s setbacks for the poor and for minority rights demonstrated. In *Prosperity Lost,* Philip Mattera reports that

> what emerged in the early 1980s was an unprecedented alliance of business, the federal government, and the right, all dedicated to a radical restructuring of the U.S. political economy. . . . As in New York, business interests stepped in to exercise much more direct control over public affairs. But what made things worse at the federal level was that the power now resided not with corporate liberals . . . who still saw the need to maintain some degree of social equilibrium, but with right-wing crusaders who were prepared to pursue their agenda regardless of consequences.[17]

What was this agenda? Mattera believes it can be summed up in one word, "greed." Others more charitably argue that the conservative agenda is grounded in the belief that modern liberalism has abandoned the classical liberal commitment to individual freedom in favor of too much government regulation, and that the social welfare will be better realized if business is left to pursue its ends unfettered, thus resulting in a wealthier society for all. Regardless of one's interpretation of the conservative agenda, its consequences in the early 1990s appear to have benefited the rich at the expense of the poor and the middle class, and there has been an ideological shift in favor of business at the expense, says educator Henry Giroux, of democracy itself.

> At all levels of national and daily life, the breadth and depth of democratic relations are being rolled back. This is seen in the rising apathy expressed in the refusal of eligible voters to participate in national elections, the systematic transfer of wealth from the poor to the rich, the ongoing attacks by the government and courts on civil rights and the welfare system, and the proliferating incidents of racist harassment and violence on college and public school sites. The eclipse of the discourse of public life can be seen in a growing sentiment that 'dismisses morality and human rights as a leftover of bygone days'. . . The retreat from democracy is also evident in the absence of serious talk about how as a nation we might educate future generations in the language and practice of moral compassion, critical agency, and the utopian horizons of social imagination.[18]

In large part, President Clinton based his campaign on a rejection of the politics of greed and a return to the language of compassionate democracy, but, in 1994, the "Conservative Revolution" swept Republicans into majority control of both the House and Senate. As "revolutions" go, however, this one was tame. By shifting his own positions, on welfare and the economy, for example, toward the conservatives slightly, President Clinton was able to hand conservative Republican candidate Bob Dole a resounding defeat in 1996. Again, the distance from the liberal to the conservative side of corporate liberalism just wasn't very far to travel.

What we continue to see in our educational policymaking is an apparent agreement among liberals and conservatives that our primary educational concerns should be business-driven, as if the success record of American business, which leads the world in bank failures and indebtedness, is one the schools should emulate. As pointed out in Chapter 14, business has taken a strongly activist role in school reform in the 1980s and 1990s. Like their conservative counterparts, leading liberal-Democrat economists such as former Clinton cabinet member Robert Reich easily fall into the mistake of representing schools as largely economically oriented institutions:

> Whatever the cause, raising the lowest achievers to minimal levels of productive competence is a large part of the challenge of American education in the next economy. Not only do we need a larger population of productive people to help pay off our international debt, but we also need them to support a growing population of retirees.[19]

The corporate liberal ideology, in both its conservative and liberal dimensions, is a powerful one that influences political and educational policy makers. If it is true, as a recently published poll illustrates, that "public school teachers are . . . excluded from most critical decisions on school policy," we are left to wonder how teachers themselves might shape schools if they had the opportunity.[20]

Schooling and Teaching in the 1990s

If educational policy continues to be more grounded in corporate liberalism than in a developmental ideal of democracy that seeks, as Dewey said, "the all around growth of every member of society," perhaps it is not surprising that a decade of school reform has produced discouraging results. Shapiro reports in 1992 that the United States is last among industrialized nations in math and science achievement.[21] In 1990, U.S. Secretary of Education Lauro Cavazos declared that "nearly a decade of school reform efforts has produced virtually no improvement in the reading and writing skills of the nation's schoolchildren." Only African-American students showed improvement, and these were primarily at more rudimentary levels. Among all 17-year-old students, a significant decline took place in advanced reading abilities.[22]

Understanding why the current school reform movement has not achieved its very limited aims—academic achievement as measured on standardized tests—requires recognizing the poverty of top-down school reform efforts in a society as diverse and economically unequal as our own. Davis and McCaul warn that our current approaches are inadequate to the realities that our schools are facing:

> The United States public school population in the year 2000 will be more ethnically and linguistically diverse than ever before. It will represent a population that is poorer, more precariously housed, and more vulnerable to the pressures of socioeconomic disadvantage. It will include the large and growing numbers of "crack-cocaine babies," which are now being born at an alarming rate. We could be talking about the majority of our nation's youth [at socioeconomic disadvantage]—not the minority—by early 2010. it is critical, therefore, that educational equity be once again considered a priority.[23]

Davis and McCaul argue that what is at stake is *not* that we do not know how to address the educational problems of low-income youth (see Chapters 12 and 13), but that these problems are not matters of high priority in today's political-economic and ideological climate. They contrast the national response to our current educational challenges with President Bush's response to the multibillion dollar war effort in the Middle East: "Cost cannot be an issue—whatever it costs, we will have to pay for it—our future American lifestyle is being threatened."[24] In contrast, we are reminded, teachers in the United States are the lowest paid among eight comparable industrialized nations, and spending on public education is next to last.[25]

EDUCATIONAL GOALS FOR THE 1990s AND BEYOND

While teachers can be politically active in their communities and, through their professional organizations, can help bring about a greater national and local commitment to education, it is clear they cannot wait for dramatic social changes before setting their individual teaching goals. Nor can they defer decisions on how best to serve the interests of each and every student, no matter what their race, gender, physical challenges, or economic circumstances—especially in a complex and conflicted society.

Teachers who wish to reflect on how they can best serve their students' interests might begin with consideration of this simple formulation by educators Leonard Waks and Rustum Roy:

> The stated goals of education in modern democratic societies remain constant: the development of each person as (*a*) a worker, (*b*) a citizen, and (*c*) an individual. Basic democratic education thus has a vocational, a political, and a personal dimension. However, as the . . . context changes, the specific interpretations of these goals and the means for attaining them must be reassessed.[26]

For the teacher who earnestly asks how he or she can help each student develop as fully as possible in all three of those directions—vocationally, politically, and personally—the classroom can be a challenging and rewarding place.

Thinking about these three educational goals underscores the importance of understanding the society into which young people are being educated. If the society is becoming increasingly dependent on jobs that require advanced literacy, computational, and problem-solving skills, and if students can be expected to change occupations several times in their lifetime, then their education should reflect these realities. To train them for a narrow job description or to settle for anything less than well-developed literacy, mathematics, and collaborative problem-solving skills represents a failure of educational commitment. Such high expectations of all of our students can open doors for them that might otherwise not be opened. At the same time, however, when hundreds of thousands of new jobs are service-level jobs that do not require advanced skills, we cannot let the workplace alone determine our educational aspirations for our students. The concepts of "citizen" and "person" (or individual) remind us that the educational challenge is not met merely by preparing a student for employment, important as that may be.

When we think about our students as citizens, for example, we do well to ask what they should be taught to expect as members of a democratic society. Should they understand democracy as a system in which each person has the opportunity to vote for elected officials? Or should they acquire a more demanding understanding of democracy, in which all citizens should expect to influence the decisions that affect their lives? In this latter formulation, students would aspire to something that was referred to in Chapter 9 as "critical literacy." Here each student aspires to think critically about political and social institutions. Such an approach was exhibited in Bill Bigelow's account of his own classroom (see the Primary Source Reading of Chapter 9), in which students learn to think critically about their own degree of influence in the institutions that affect them. If the teacher believes that common citizens should have such influence, the question arises, What skills, understandings, and dispositions are necessary for such participatory citizenship, and how can I foster these in my classes, no matter what the subject matter at hand?

Finally, a teacher's notion of what it means to be a fully developed person or individual is even more fundamental than a student's future as a citizen or worker. Curriculum theorist Bill Schubert believes that all curriculum planning must ultimately rest on the philosophical question, "*What does it mean to live a good and fulfilling life?*" Schubert goes on to say that the resultant curriculum question is, "*What kind and quality of knowledge and experience enable a person to live a good and fulfilling life?*"[27] It isn't fair to expect teachers to have a definitive answer for these questions for all students from all different backgrounds. But the second question suggests that teachers should provide students with the wherewithal to ask and answer that first question for themselves.

We might follow Schubert's lead and put a question inside a question as follows: What would it take to provide each student with the knowledge, skills, and dispositions to ask and answer intelligently the question, What does it mean to lead a good and fulfilling life as a worker, a citizen, and a person? Certainly one of the things it would take would be the ability to see as clearly as possible the nature of the society around us, its strengths and weaknesses together, that gives the roles of worker, citizen, and person their meanings. And if teachers wish their students to understand that society, they must themselves continually strive for such understanding. This book is intended to be a step in that direction.

If the federal or state governments truly controlled all major curricular decisions, teachers would simply execute the plans and ideas of others. But even in the states with the greatest top-down curriculum control, state influence on what goes on in the classroom is very limited, as Alexander K. Tyree's recent research shows.[28] Local control and teacher decision making have the greatest impact on what students experience.

A teacher, as it is often said, does not just teach subjects; a teacher teaches people. Our social institutions, processes, and ideals create the context within which people learn, for better or for worse, and they thus create the context in which teachers and students must function. As society changes, so change the dimensions of the teacher's task—in some ways preparing students to fit into society, but in some ways preparing students to *resist* elements of society. Throughout history, strong teachers have carried with them a vision of what students need "to live a good and fulfilling life." Today's teachers can apply such a vision to all of their students, regardless of gender, social class, race, ethnicity, or physical challenge. We conclude this volume (see the Primary Source Reading) with the words of one such teacher, later a principal, whose daily work reminds us that students can, indeed, rise to the greatest of our expectations.

PRIMARY SOURCE READING

Deborah Meier, a former teacher and later the founder of the Central Park East Schools in New York City, has brought national attention to her schools because of their great success in departing from "business as usual" in teaching and learning. Educating children from a wide range of economic and ethnic backgrounds, the Central Park East Schools are public schools, serving both elementary and secondary school students. George Wood, in Schools That Work *(see note 11), writes that Central Park East Secondary School is thought by many to be "one of the best secondary schools in New York or perhaps the entire United States" (p. 42). Its predominantly low-income, African-American, and Latino student body appears to make it "a prototype for schools that fail" (ibid.). Yet at CPESS the dropout rate is very low, the students compete with those in the best New York City schools on standardized tests, and the students are enthusiastic about learning. CPESS, like the other Central Park East Schools, is a success story that owes its achievements in no small part to the educational approach of its founder, who empowers teachers and students to make a great many of their own teaching and learning decisions. Deborah Meier writes about her life's work in* The Power of Their Ideas, *published by Beacon Press in 1995.*

The following excerpt, "Reinventing Teaching," is condensed from an earlier attempt by Deborah Meier to articulate the educational approach that has attracted nationwide attention over the past several years, an attempt that clearly remains an exception, rather than the rule. But it is one of many such exceptions that remind us of what can be achieved by all of us.

REINVENTING TEACHING

Deborah Meier

Since I began teaching, some twenty-five years ago, I have changed the way I think about what it means to be a good teacher. Today it is clear that since we need a new kind of school to do a new kind of job, we need a new kind of teacher, too.

The schools we need require different habits of work and habits of mind on the part of teachers—a kind of professionalism within the classroom few teachers were expected to exhibit before. In addition, to get from where we are now to where we need to be will require teachers to play a substantially different role within their schools as well as in public discourse. Teachers need to relearn what it means to be good in-school practitioners, while also becoming more articulate and self-confident spokespeople for the difficult and often anxiety-producing changes schools are expected to undertake. If teachers are not able to join in leading such changes, the changes will not take place. Politicians and policymakers at all levels may institute vast new legislated reforms; but without the understanding, support, and input of teachers, they will end up in the same dead end as such past reforms as "new math" or "open ed." For all the big brave talk, they will be rhetorical and cosmetic, and after a time they will wither away. . .

The lessons drawn from sixteen or more years of school experience as a student remain largely intact and dictate the way most people handle their role as teachers. This is hardly surprising. Many of those who enter teaching hope to do unto others what the teachers they knew and loved did unto them. In a few cases—and I tend to have a fondness, however short-lived, for these exceptions—teaching as a career attracts young people who did not like their schooling or were not naturally successful at it. They hope that as teachers they might be able to do unto others what they wished their teachers had done for them. They have come into teaching to change practice, not perpetuate it—to break a tradition, not carry it on. But such teachers often leave teaching quickly when they discover that their students do not love them for being different, less authoritarian, more genial, smarter. They often leave with new ideas about what is wrong with "these" kids or the evils and stupidities of their fellow teachers—the ones who stayed. Some people, fortunately, enter teaching at a later age, not fresh out of school. They bring to their jobs a wider range of experience, and are accustomed to different kinds of institutional arrangements and ways of relating to colleagues.

Source: Deborah Meier, "Reinventing Teaching," *Teachers College Record 93,* No. 4 (Summer 1992), pp. 594–609. A version of this article was presented as the DeGarmo Lecture for the Society of Professors of Education at the annual meeting of the American Education Research Association, April 4, 1991, in Chicago.

Sometimes they even come to teaching after they have had children, and if they are lucky, at least one of their children has not found school so easy. They are not quite so quick to judge parents at fault, and may have a special personal empathy for school losers. But in most cases the constraints of the job, plus old habits and a kind of societal nostalgia for what school "used to be like," make teachers part of the broader inertia that makes fundamental change hard to implement.

In short: The habits of schooling are deep, powerful, and hard to budge. No public institution is more deeply entrenched in habitual behavior than schools—and for good reason. Aside from our many years of direct experience as students, we have books, movies, television shows, advertisements, and myriad other activities, games, and symbols that reinforce our view of what school is "supposed" to be. Our everyday language and metaphors are built on a kind of prototype of schoolhouse and classroom, with all its authoritarian, filling-up-the-empty-vessel, rote-learning assumptions.

For example, the other night I watched a semidocumentary entitled "Yearbook." It purported to depict the life of a school by following a group of seniors during their last year in high school. We watch, with a kind of false nostalgia, the senior year so few of us truly had but believe we should have had: the selection of cheerleaders and homecoming queens in the fall, the pains of dating, the sports fields, the trivia of home economics classes, and so forth. There is not even a momentary bow to the intellectual purposes of high school. At Central Park East schools, we laugh sometimes about how our own students (and even our own children), many of whom have never attended any school but ours, still play "pretend school" in a traditional way—lining up the desks, and yelling at the children. Our Central Park East School (CPESS) high school students complain about not having lockers—that is where true high school life takes place, the absence of bells, passing time, proms, and so forth. They view these as essential rites of passage. My four-year-old granddaughter loves playing school with me—but I am required to be the mean principal who does awful things to bad children. She cannot wait until she gets to such a real school.

It is no easier to change such habits, built around age-old metaphors about teaching and learning, about getting ahead, than it is to change our personal habits (like giving up smoking), or our seemingly ingrained primitive ideas about the physical universe. It is current wisdom to recognize that despite all the correct information offered in physics and astronomy courses, including laboratory experiences and visits to the planetarium, the average citizen's real-life view of the universe remains amazingly heliocentric at best (and geocentric, if not New York–centric, at worst). We pile new theories on top of old conceptions rooted in childhood experience, language, and symbols, and they are absorbed in some odd commonsensical way. The sky remains up, as does the North Pole; we imagine looking up at the moon and therefore assume that the men on the moon must look down to see the Earth; we know that the moon is very far away—about halfway to Mars or Venus. This is now old-hat theory, yet few schools are successful in getting their students to see the world in post-Copernican terms. Habit and everyday common sense rule. So why should it be any different when it comes to teaching adults how to teach?

Until we are ready to engage students in a far different form of pedagogy, with far greater in-depth exploration, such commonsense habits will not be overcome in physics classes. Our graduates may be able to recite more modern ideas, but their understanding will remain paper-thin and school-bound. That may suffice for physics, because few have to base their future practices on a different view of the universe. In everyday life, in fact, the old pre-Copernican view works quite well.

So too with education courses, and pedagogical theories. As in physics, our habitual view of teaching as telling and learning as remembering is hard to dislodge. The difference is, of course, that we expect would-be teachers to overcome such views and then act on the basis of their new wisdom. We pretend that this can be so, despite the fact that we know that teaching, more than virtually any field (aside from parenting, perhaps), depends on quick, instinctive habits, behaviors, and deeply held ways of seeing and valuing. Teachers are confronted with literally hundreds of decisions and unmonitored responses every hour they work, which cannot be mediated by cool calculation. Nothing is more unsettling in the presence of real-live students in real-live classrooms than an uncertain teacher, searching for the right response. A doctor can examine patients slowly and carefully, and look up the answers in books before being required to commit to action. Not so a teacher.

In short, we come to be teachers knowing all about teaching. We have been exposed to more teaching and teachers than to any other single phenomenon. Most of us have spent more time with teachers than with our parents. To make matters worse, what we learn from our parents in a more informal pedagogy is rarely even thought of as having been taught. In fact, the more "naturally" and "readily" we learn something, the less credit we give to those who taught us. Furthermore, our first exposure to teaching is done under the frequently scornful eye of experienced teachers who are quick to put down the green ambitions of innovators, whose early innovations are likely to be dismal failures.

If teaching and schooling are so entrenched, if our habits are so deeply rooted and so hard to change, is there no hope for school reform? The answer will depend on how serious we are about the need to change, and how long we are willing to stick with the effort to effect it. . .

If it were possible to escape the issue by somehow inculcating the next generation with a different set of habits, thus bypassing both teachers and their parents, it would be an attractive idea. Otherwise, this is a kind of pulling-oneself-up-by-the-bootstraps problem. Every revolutionary ideology comes up against this same conundrum and, historically, most revolutionaries think they can resolve it only by totalitarian measures. Some try removing children from their families, sowing suspicion between generations, forcing prescriptive ideological training from infancy on up, or creating a network of "big brothers." They hope thus to breed a new generation that leaps over the weaknesses of the present misguided and corrupted generation. In a milder form, most school reform efforts are not so different in conception. It is the familiar design that rest on hopes for teacher-proof curriculum, reform by testing and monitoring, by penalties and threats. They will have no more luck.

One cannot impose such change—not because it is immoral or unpleasant, but because it does not work. And the price paid for trying to wipe out the past by fiat is enormous. Benign schemes for trying to do the same thing fail just as the obviously malign ones do. This is not surprising. It is illogical to imagine that we can produce thoughtful and critical thinkers by rote imposition or that we can build strong intellectual understanding through required amnesia. If the logic of it fails to impress, years and years of failed efforts to do so ought to. It is, at the very least, a great waste of time, a diversion of energy and resources that we can ill afford. We cannot pass on to a new generation that which we do not ourselves possess. That is the conundrum, the seemingly impossible paradox.

How might we approach such a riddle? We can change the schools so as to promote thoughtful and critical practices on the part of teacher practitioners, and in ways that undercut any need for teachers themselves to become lobbyists against change. Teachers must lead the way toward their own liberation.

Teachers were force-marched to the promised land of "new math," and the results should be a warning. Impatience for rapid improvement in math education following *Sputnik* produced a dud—and today, thirty years later, we are once again trying to introduce just such a math education. Had we been more patient thirty years ago we would be thirty years ahead of the game now.

The only route possible requires involving all parties to education in the process of reinventing schooling. Not, please note, revolution or reform, but reinvention is required. It is our mind set that needs changing, and the institutional arrangements that either support or impede the new mind set. However, you do not and should not fool with people's minds loosely. It requires the utmost respect, a stance that is not easy for us to assume. The changes needed are not changes in the solo acts teachers perform inside their classrooms, hard as that might be to accomplish. We are talking about creating a very different school culture, a new set of relationships and ideas. We are talking about changes that will affect not just teachers (although without them it is pointless), but also their constituents—parents and children. Given enough time—if we are not in too much of a hurry; if we allow for lapses and half-measures, and do not give up—we might begin to see changes. It is through collective co-ownership of new designs for schooling, in an atmosphere that allows for reflective examination and reshaping based on experience, that something new might emerge.

We can change teachers only by changing the environment in which teaching takes place. Teaching can be changed only by reinventing the institutions within which teaching takes place—schools. Reinvention has to be done by those who will be stuck in the reinvented schools. It cannot be force-fed—not to teachers, nor to parents and children. All three constituents can sabotage the best-laid plans. While parents and children will put up with some dissonance and anxiety, the mismatch between what they expect and what they experience cannot be ignored or evaded. Their willingness to participate in change is critical. While such willingness can be encouraged by various public policies, a thoroughly "converted" and committed faculty is a must.

When school people visit CPESS they often dismiss our achievements—which I believe to be modest compared with the achievements that lie ahead of us—on the basis that we, after all, had the opportunity to start from scratch, whereas they must reform an existing huge, sluggish institution, only some of whose members want to change. If we had your freedom, they suggest, we too could produce Central Park East's successes. I think they are right, so I suggest they be given precisely the same freedom we have had. That is what public policy can create.

Our visitors argue that we have the advantage of having a student and parent body who chose to come to our school. I propose that all schools be given precisely the same freedom: a student and parent body of those who choose to come to their school. (Note that by "school" I do not necessarily mean a building. A single building can contain many such reinvented schools of choice.) Visitors argue that we had a chance to select our staff, from among those who agree with us. It is much easier to carry out a collective policy when people agree on the policy, they complain. We propose that all schools should have this same freedom. Professionals should work in a school that they want to work in because they share its assumptions. Visitors complain that our work is not replicable because we have been given the freedom to organize our day, select our curriculum, and design our forms of assessment in the way we think best—and to change them whenever we find they do not work. We propose that all other schools be offered the same freedom, along with the same responsibilities we have accepted.

If these are the four freedoms that you envy, we tell our visitors, why not demand the same for yourselves? But you have to want such freedom and you have to accept the responsibility that goes with it. It will be exhausting, even at times frustrating. The thing we keep telling our colleagues in other schools is that it surely will not lead to "burnout"—because people burn out when they are treated like appliances. This kind of teaching and schooling is, in contrast, never dehumanizing. It rests on intense human interaction and involvement.

You can only change people's habits, at best, when they have strong reasons to want to change and an environment conducive to it. That is the first requirement. For teachers, this means sufficient support from those they depend on—school boards, administrators, parents—to take some risky first steps. They need, furthermore, the luxury of being able to waste money on ideas that will not work, rather than feeling obliged to pretend that everything they do is successful. They need access to expertise without promising to follow expert advice. They need time. They need more time in a daily, weekly, monthly sense—to reflect, examine, redo. They also need recognition of the other kind of time—the years it will take to see it through. These are the conditions we know work whenever we are really in a hurry to do something difficult: cure cancer, go to the moon, invent new technologies, or win a war.

The greater the desire for change on the part of teachers, parents, and children, the less it will cost. Unpaid volunteer armies can defend their homeland better than highly trained and equipped mercenary troops. Very eager and driven reformers are ready to exploit themselves, putting in endless hours and sleepless nights—although they often also exhaust themselves too soon. But the more timid, the less eager, the less confident and self-motivated the reformers, the more ideal the circumstances must be before we get the necessary sustained effort. Money (for extra personnel, financial incentives, paid time, equipment) compensates for zeal. We will not get large-scale school reform in the United States if we count only on zealots, but we would be foolish indeed not to promote such zeal, and give such ardent reformers the room and space to work their hearts out as we build up credibility for more ambitious national efforts.

The job of those in policymaking positions who want to improve the quality of teachers must be to change the conditions of teaching. They must offer incentives for change, and above all the resources (in this case the key is well-designed staff development time) to enable teachers to learn from their changed conditions. Unlike most industries, we cannot retool by closing down the factories and sending all the workers back to school. We need to do everything at once. It is driving while changing the tires, not to mention the transmission system.

Our schools must be labs for learning about learning. Only such labs can teach both children and their teachers simultaneously. They must create a passion for learning, not only among children, but also among their teachers. Both have become "passion-impaired." In the words of Ginny Stiles, a kindergarten teacher at Reek Elementary School in Wisconsin, "It's my job to find the passion, to open eyes and weave a web of intrigue and surprise." Indeed, she notes, too many teachers have themselves become what she calls passion-impaired. The motivator par excellence is our heart's desire, our taste for "the having of wonderful ideas," as Eleanor Duckworth calls it.[1] How better to impart such ideas than by engaging in the having of wonderful ideas oneself?

If I could choose five qualities to look for in prospective teachers they would be: (1) a self-conscious reflectiveness about how they themselves learn and, maybe even more, how and when they do not learn; (2) a sympathy toward others, an appreciation of their differences, an ability to imagine their "otherness"; (3) a willingness to engage in, better yet a taste for, collaborative work; (4) a desire to have others to share some of one's own interests; and (5) a lot of perseverance, energy, and devotion to getting things right.

Since we cannot count on finding enough teachers who already possess all five qualities, we need to create the kind of schools that will draw out these qualities. Of course, when I say we need schools that will encourage such characteristics, I include liberal arts colleges and schools of education as well as schools for children and adolescents. Nothing we have discovered lately about how the brain works is uniquely true for children versus adults, or would-be teachers versus would-be anything else. The kind of education that is best for teachers is one that is best for learners in all subjects and domains.

We will change American education only insofar as we make all our schools educationally inspiring and intellectually challenging for teachers, not just students. It is not enough to worry about some decontextualized quality called teacher "morale" or "job satisfaction." Those words, like "self-esteem," are not stand-alones. Neither happy teachers nor happy students are our goal. What we need is a particular kind of job satisfaction that has as its anchor intellectual growth. The school itself must be intellectually stimulating—organized to make it hard for teachers to remain unthoughtful. High teacher (or student) morale needs to be viewed as a by-product of the wonderful ideas that are being examined under the most challenging circumstances. During our first year at CPESS we went around muttering under our breath that our job was not to make the children happy but to make them strong. That goes for teacher education too.

Mindlessness as a habit may drive employers crazy, but it is a habit we have too often fostered in schools. The habit of falling back on excuses—"I had to," "that's the way it's supposed to be"—can be rooted out only by major surgery. It will be painful, and it will not all come out at once. Expecting teachers to take responsibility for the success of the whole school requires that they begin to accept responsibility for their own as well as their colleagues' teaching—surely no overnight task. At the very least, one must imagine schools in which teachers are in frequent conversation with each other about their work, have easy and necessary access to each other's classrooms, take it

[1] Eleanor Duckworth, *"The Having of Wonderful Ideas" and Other Essays on Teaching and Learning* (New York: Teachers College Press, 1987).

for granted that they should comment on each other's work, and have the time to develop common standards for student work. They need frequent and easy access to the kind of give-and-take with professionals from allied fields that is the mark of a true professional. They need opportunities to speak and write publicly about their work, attend conferences, read professional journals, and discuss something besides what they are going to do on Monday. There must be some kind of combination of discomfiture and support—focused always on what does and does not have an impact on children's learning.

What would be the role in such schools of administration and supervision? I do not think the answer is yet in regarding the nature of school governance best suited to faculty growth. Insofar as the faculty are prevented from blaming others for their problems, they are more likely to look to their own practice. So some form of work-place democracy is essential, but there are numerous possible candidates for the form and style that best frees teachers to work together on professional matters. What is certain is that this kind of collegiality works best in settings that are sufficiently small and intimate so that self-governance and staff-development schemes do not exhaust teachers' energies or divert them from their central task. . . .

The Central Park East schools were created, invented if you will, with all these considerations, plus a few more, in mind. They were efforts to imagine the kind of collegial setting in which adults could and would learn side by side with their students. We sought to create an intellectually transformative environment, a culture of mutual respect for others, a set of habits of mind that foster inquiry as well as responsibility. We based our work on some simple principles, familiar enough to those who work with young children, but less familiar to those who work with adolescents or adults. We started with the premise that there is far more in common between a five-year-old, a fifteen-year-old, and a fifty-year-old than there are differences. Our common humanity means we learn in much the same way. That was, in fact, our first principle. Good kindergarten practice is probably on target at any age, including the age of teachers.

For example, we knew that five-year-olds learn best when they feel relatively safe—physically as well as psychically. (Young children need to feel comfortable about going to the bathroom, for example. How about teenagers? How about teachers?) Feeling safe includes trusting at least some of those "in charge," not to mention being able to predict with some degree of accuracy how the place works. The same is true for adults. For young children we know it also means that parents need to see the school as safe so that they can reassure their children that "those people are okay," "you can trust them to care for you," "they are not our enemies." It turns out that this is also critical for the development of fifteen-year-olds. They too suffer if they come to school carrying wary or hostile warnings from their families. The appropriate rebellion of adolescence cannot be carried out successfully in a setting in which the adults may truly be seen as dangerous. Healthy "testing out" rests on a basic trust that there are adults prepared to set limits. Is it so different at fifty? Do we not need a work place that is safe, predictable, and on our side, if we expect to do our best work?

A second principle, one at the heart of the Coalition of Essential Schools' "Nine Basic Principles," can be put succinctly: You cannot teach well if you do not know your students well. That means size and scale are critical. Even prisons, or army units, are not as huge, impersonal, and anonymous as many schools for young children, not to mention the average American high school. It is not just children who suffer from this depersonalization of work; adults do too. All but a few stars become lookers-on, admirers, or wallflowers, not active participants.

Our third principle is an old familiar one: You cannot use the coach or expert well if he or she is also judge and high executioner. As my son explained to me one day when I was trying to convince him to ask his teacher to explain something to him, "Mom, you don't understand. The last person in the world who I'd let know what I don't understand is my teacher." Schooling becomes a vast game in which teachers try to trick students into revealing their ignorance while students try to trick teachers into thinking they are not ignorant. Getting a good grade, after all, is getting the teacher to think you know more than you do. Is it so different for teachers, whose only source of help and support is precisely the person who rates and rules them? The metaphor "teacher as coach" is full of possibilities not only for the relationship between adults and children, but in all teaching/learning settings.

A fourth principle for an efficient learning environment is that we learn best when we are in a position to make sense of things—especially to make sense of things we are interested in. Human beings are by nature meaning-makers, trying to put the puzzle together. From the moment of birth until our death this is our preeminent mode. Schools rarely capitalize on it. A nursery school teacher uses the room itself to create interest and curiosity. She carefully sets up the environment so that it invites questions; and she spends her time moving about the room, prodding, inquiring, changing materials and tools so that curiosity is kept lively and current. She creates dissonances as well as harmonies; she creates confusion as well as serenity. Contradictions are accepted as natural. By the time students reach high school we have stripped the environment bare, and lessons are dry and "clear cut." No high school teacher (and surely not a college professor) worthy of her salt assumes the actual physical setting of the classroom is a relevant part of her job. The typical explanation for why we teach what we do is that it is required at the next grade level—or, at best, that it is required on a state-mandated exam. Teaching becomes simplified, focusing more and more on test-taking skill. Nor do teachers view the courses they are required to take to get a license or upgrade their status much differently. Teachers' own interests are often irrelevant, or sneaked into a high school schedule. A teacher with a love for physics and expertise in the field may teach biology because that is what is "needed." No wonder that the phrase "It's academic" means it is irrelevant.

Fifth, human beings by nature are social, interactive learners. We check out our ideas, argue with authors, bounce issues back and forth, ask friends to read our early drafts, talk together after seeing a movie, pass on books we have loved, attend meetings and argue out our ideas, share stories and gossip that extends our understanding of ourselves and others. Talk lies at the heart of our lives. This kind of exchange is never allowed in school, nor modeled there—not between children, nor between adults. Monthly faculty meetings are no better imitations of true discussion than the average so-called classroom discussion. The most powerful motivation for becoming learned—that we might influence others—is purposely removed from students and their teachers. No one among the powerful policymakers wonders, as they imagine the perfect curriculum, what it means to teach a subject year after year, based on someone else's design. We organize schools as though the ideal were an institution impervious to human touch.

If we intend dramatically to improve the education of American children we need to invent very different environments for them. Teachers must be challenged to invent schools they would like to teach in, organized around the principles of learning that we know matter. That is the simple idea we put into practice at Central Park East.

What did we do? First, children stay with teachers for two years, so it is worth getting to know each other well—students, their families, and the teacher. Even high school students do not move around every forty-five minutes, do not change courses in midyear, and stay with the same faculty for two years. There are no pull-outs, and no seven-period days. In the high school most students see no more than two to three different teachers a day, including an advisor who spends an hour a day with a small group of his or her own fifteen advisees. Furthermore, each teacher teaches an interdisciplinary course: literature and history or math and science, for example.

A typical class is long enough (often two hours) to include whole-class seminars, small-group work, independent study, and one-on-one coaching by teachers and fellow students. Students do their writing and reading in school, not just as homework, so they can get feedback and insight into how to read and write more effectively. Teachers, furthermore, teach in collaborative settings; four to five teachers work in physically contiguous rooms and with the same set of students so that they can easily make decisions, alter plans, rearrange schedules, regroup students, share ideas, and observe each other at work.

Decisions are made as close to each teacher's own classroom setting as possible, although all decisions are ultimately the responsibility of the whole staff. The decisions are not merely on minor matters—length of classes or the number of field trips. The teachers collectively decide on content, pedagogy, and assessment as well. They teach what they think matters. The "whole staff" is not enormous—none of our Central Park East schools is larger than about 450 students, most are 200 to 300. That means a faculty that can sit in a circle in one room and get a chance to hear each other. Governance is simple. There are virtually no permanent standing committees. Finally, we work together to develop assessment systems for our students, their families, ourselves, and the broader public—systems that represent our values and beliefs in as direct a manner as possible. When we are asked "Does it work?" we have had a voice in deciding what "work" means. Our forms of assessment are constantly open to public review and what is open is direct evidence: Observers may visit our classrooms, read our students' work, examine our scoring grids, look at samples of graduation-level portfolios. We even invite experts to review our work and our students' performances, as a way to sharpen our insights and check our potentially overgenerous hearts.

The result: Our students succeed in far greater measure than their socioeconomic, ethnic, and racial background and prior academic skills would predict. We have not closed the gap between rich and poor, we have not sent all our graduates to prestigious colleges, nor made enough difference to ensure that none will fall through the cracks of the larger society. But in a city in which nearly half of all students fail to complete high school, about 90 percent of those who attend Central Park East schools do complete high school, even after only four to six years in our elementary schools. While the fact that half of those who graduate from our elementary schools go on to college is a promising piece of data, the numbers are much higher for those who attend our secondary school. We hope, over time, to prove that their capacity to stick it out in college and hold good jobs and be strong citizens will be even more convincing. Whether they leave us at twelve or eighteen, they are far better able to join society as productive and socially useful citizens than are their counterparts.

It is not enough. It never will be. But the fact that schools cannot do the job alone is a far cry from claiming that schools cannot do their job better if they take seriously what they know about teaching and learning and practice it at every age and grade level. Period.

Just as our student body is not exceptional, but reflects the general population of New York City schools, our faculty are by no means exceptionally well educated, more learned than the average teacher in New York City, and certainly no more experienced. Many had virtually no prior experience as teachers and some had taken no courses in teaching. Many started as interns with us, spending their first year in low-paid assistant teaching roles. Some came from other schools where they had been good but not exceptional teachers (the most exceptional often build comfortable niches for themselves and are hard to woo away). But they all came with a willingness to learn from each other, although often vulnerable, prickly, and defensive, and they have all grown incredibly in the process of becoming better teachers. Today many speak about our work all over the country, something we consciously committed ourselves as a faculty to help each other learn to do. Others write about our work, again something we have helped each other learn to do. They see themselves first as the teachers of a particular group of youngsters, but they also see themselves as the governing body of a school and the carriers of an idea.

My colleague Ann Bussis claims that teaching is not so complex as to verge on the impossible or to defy conception at an abstract level, but it does defy concrete prescriptions for action—there is neither a prescription for action nor a checklist for observation to assure intelligent and responsive teaching. All that can be offered is a guiding theory and abundant examples.

That is what schools must help us develop—guiding ideas and abundant examples, and then the opportunity to put such guiding ideas into practice and to learn from our abundant examples. It is hoped that someday, not too far in the future, we will have abundant enough examples of what such reinvented schools might be like for them to become the norm.

In summary, if we want schools for the twenty-first century to resemble schools of the twentieth century, we can afford to tinker a little and leave the structure pretty much intact. Then teacher-training institutions need only follow suit, tinkering too. But if we want the least of our citizens to know and be able to do the kinds of things that only those lucky few at the top of the ladder have ever achieved before, then we need to begin a slow and steady revolution in how and what teachers must know and know how to do. To do this means we have to learn how to drive while changing not only the tire but the whole mechanism! Impossible? No, but very, very hard. The place it will happen is in the schools themselves—not the schools as we now know them, but reinvented schools created by school people and their communities. And it does not come with guarantees.

QUESTIONS FOR DISCUSSION AND EXAMINATION

1. In this chapter Davis and McCaul are cited as saying that the solutions to successfully educating low-income and minority youth are not beyond our professional expertise but beyond our social and political commitment. Given your knowledge, derived from this text and elsewhere, of how to educate economically disadvantaged youth, do you believe that Davis and McCaul are correct in their assessment? Explain.
2. This chapter argues, roughly, that teachers cannot be expected to change the political and economic structure of society, but they can be expected to change the life chances of their students. Do you fully agree with this view? Defend your position with evidence from the text and from your own experience.
3. Deborah Meier writes early in her article that "we expect would-be teachers to overcome such [habitual] views and then act on the basis of their new wisdom." What in this text or in your college education has potential for developing in you new skills, understanding, or dispositions to act in ways other than what the habits of schooling have taught you about being a teacher? If you can identify such an influence, explain what difference it might make to how you teach, and why. If you cannot identify anything, explain whether you think the habits of schooling you have learned are adequate to the challenges of teaching today and why.
4. Meier claims that "teachers must lead the way toward their own liberation." What does she mean by this, and is this a realistic aspiration for educational change in this country? Explain your answer.
5. Meier describes "four freedoms" that are characteristic of her schools. Since it is not perfectly clear what these four freedoms are, try to identify them. Second, assume for the purposes of this question that each of these freedoms is not equally important. Given that assumption, which of them is most important for educational success, and which is least important? Explain.
6. Soon after describing the four freedoms, Meier identifies five qualities she looks for in prospective teachers. Which among these qualities is your greatest strength, and which is your greatest weakness? Assuming that Meier is correct in naming these as important qualities for the teacher, what might you do to strengthen the relative weakness you have identified?
7. In the last one-third of the article, Meier identifies five principles underlying the success of Central Park East Schools. Putting aside the first one (that people learn best when they feel physically and psychically safe), which of the remaining four seems to you to be most necessary for successful schooling? What concrete steps could you take to implement this principle in your own teaching?

NOTES

1. "Study Shows Teachers Still Feel Left Out on Policy," *New York Times*, Education Section, September 14, 1988, p. 27.
2. James K. Galbraith, "A New Picture of the American Economy," *The American Prospect*, Fall 1991, p. 30.
3. W. Davis and E. McCaul, "The Emerging Crisis: Current and Projected Status of Children in the United States," Monograph (Orono: University of Maine, 1993), p. 3.
4. "Census Says 1 in 5 Earns Poverty Wage," *Chicago Tribune*, May 12, 1992, p. 12.
5. Peter T. Kilborn, "The Middle Class Feels Betrayed, but Maybe Not Enough to Rebel," *New York Times*, January 12, 1992, Section 4, p. 1. "Has Our Living Standard Stalled?" *Consumer Reports*, June 1992, p. 392.
6. Robert B. Reich, "Must New Economic Vigor Mean Making Do with Less?" *National Education Association Today*, Vol. 7, No. 6 (January 1989), p. 14.
7. Andrew L. Shapiro, *We're Number One* (New York: Vintage Books, 1992), p. xiii.
8. Ibid., especially chaps. 1, 4, and 6. These findings are confirmed by Derek Bok, *The State of the Nation* (Cambridge: Harvard University Press, 1996).
9. Kilborn, *New York Times*, p. 1; Philip Mattera, *Prosperity Lost* (New York: Addison-Wesley, 1991), p. 59; *The State of American Children Yearbook 1996 (Washington DC: Children's Defense Fund), p. 3.*
10. Jonathan Kozol, *Savage Inequalities* (New York: Crown Publishers, 1991).

11. See, for example, George H. Wood, *Schools That Work* (New York: Dutton, 1992).
12. James K. Galbraith, "A New Picture of the American Economy," p. 35.
13. Shapiro, *We're Number One,* p. 105; Economics and Statistics Administration, *The American Almanac: Statistical Abstract of the United States 1993–1994* (Austin, TX: The Reference Press, 1994), p. 284.
14. Kevin Phillips, *The Politics of Rich and Poor* (New York: Random House, 1990), p. 243.
15. Kilborn, *New York Times,* p. 2.
16. *The Chronicle of Higher Education Almanac Issue,* Vol. 40, No. 1 (August 25, 1993), p. 15.
17. Philip Mattera, *Prosperity Lost,* pp. 42–43.
18. Henry A Giroux, "Educational Leadership and the Crisis of Democratic Government," *Educational Researcher* 21, No. 4 (May, 1992), p. 4. Citing R. Kearney, "Ethics and the Postmodern Imagination," *Thought* 62, No. 24, pp. 39–58.
19. Robert Reich, "Must New Economic Vigor Mean Making Do with Less?" p. 16. In this same article, Reich cautions against shaping schools only or even mainly around economic aims. Yet such cautions are easily lost amid specific recommendations such as the one cited here.
20. "Study Shows Teachers Still Feel Left Out on Policy," September 14, 1988, p. 27.
21. Shapiro, *We're Number One,* pp. 64, 66. Students will recall the preceding Dewey quote from Chapter 4 of this text, where it is quoted from *Reconstruction in Philosophy.*
22. "Now, the Results," *Teacher Magazine,* Vol. 1, No. 6 (March 1990), pp. 18–19.
23. Davis and McCaul, p. 9.
24. Ibid., p. 11.
25. Shapiro, *We're Number One,* pp. 54, 63.
26. Leonard Waks and Rustum Roy, "Learning from Technology," in Kenneth D. Benne and Steven Tozer (eds.), *Society as Educator in an Age of Transition: Eighty-Sixth Yearbook of the National Society for the Study of Education* (Chicago: NSSE, 1987), p. 24.
27. William H. Schubert, *Curriculum: Perspective, Paradigm, and Possibility* (New York: Macmillan, 1986), p. viii (emphasis added to both questions).
28. Alexander K. Tyree, Jr., "Examining the Evidence: Have States Reduced Local Control of Curriculum?" *Educational Evaluation and Policy Analysis,* Vol. 15, No. 1 (Spring 1993), pp. 34–50.

Selected Sources for Further Reading

These sources are suggested for those students who wish to do further reading on their own. Each chapter's sources are a select few from among those available. Students are encouraged to expand this selected bibliography further by consulting the chapter endnotes, where additional sources may be found.

CHAPTER 1

Andrews, Antony. *The Greeks* (New York: W. W. Norton and Co., 1967).

Apple, Michael. *Ideology and Curriculum* (London and Boston: Routledge and Kegan Paul, 1979).

Benne, Kenneth, and Steven Tozer (eds.). *Society as Educator in an Age of Transition: Eighty-Sixth Yearbook of the National Society for the Study of Education,* Part II (Chicago: National Society for the Study of Education, 1987).

Curti, Merle. *The Social Ideas of American Educators* (Totowa, N.J.: Littlefield, Adams, and Co., 1966).

Educational Foundations: A Journal of the American Educational Studies Association, special issue on Social Foundations of Education, Vol. 7, No. 4 (Fall 1993).

Freeman, Kenneth. *Schools of Hellas* (New York: Teachers College Press, 1969).

Giroux, Henry. *Ideology, Culture, and the Process of Schooling* (Philadelphia: Temple University Press, 1981).

Johanningmeier, Erwin V. "Through the Disarray of Social Foundations: Some Notes toward a New Social Foundation," *Educational Foundations,* Vol. 5, No. 4 (Fall 1991), pp. 5–39.

Levi, Albert William. *Philosophy as Social Expression* (Chicago and London: University of Chicago Press, 1974).

Lord, Carnes. *Education and Culture in the Political Thought of Aristotle* (Ithaca: Cornell University Press, 1982).

Stanley, William O. *Education and Social Integration* (New York: Teachers College Press, 1953).

Stanley, William O., B. Othanel Smith, Kenneth D. Benne, and Archibald W. Anderson. *Social Foundations of Education* (New York: Holt, Rinehart and Winston, 1956).

Tozer, Steven, and Stuart McAninch. "Social Foundations of Education in Historical Perspective," *Educational Foundations,* Vol. 1, No. 1 (1986).

CHAPTER 2

Bailyn, Bernard. *Education in the Forming of American Society* (Chapel Hill: University of North Carolina Press, 1960).

Cott, Nancy F. *The Bonds of Womanhood: "Woman's Sphere" in New England 1780–1835* (New Haven: Yale University Press, 1977).

Cremin, Lawrence. *American Education: The National Experience* (New York: Harper and Row, 1980).

Curti, Merle. *The Social Ideas of American Educators* (Totowa, N.J.: Littlefield, Adams, and Co., 1966).

Ekirch, Arthur A. *The Decline of American Liberalism* (New York: Atheneum Books, 1967).

Hobhouse, L. T. *Liberalism* (New York: Oxford University Press, 1964).

Hofstadter, Richard. *America at 1750* (New York: Knopf, 1971).
Honeywell, Roy J. *The Educational Work of Thomas Jefferson* (Cambridge, Mass.: Harvard University Press, 1931).
Kaestle, Carl. *Pillars of the Republic* (New York: Hill & Wang, 1983).
Karier, Clarence J. *The Individual, Society, and Education* (Champaign: University of Illinois Press, 1986).
Kerber, Linda K. *Women of the Republic: Intellect and Ideology in Revolutionary America* (Chapel Hill: University of North Carolina Press, 1980).
Koch, Adrienne, and William Peden. *The Life and Selected Writings of Thomas Jefferson* (New York: The Modern Library, 1944).
Lee, Gordon. *Crusade against Ignorance: Thomas Jefferson on Education* (New York: Teachers College Press, 1967).
Miller, Perry. *The New England Mind: From Colony to Province* (Cambridge, Mass.: Harvard University Press, 1953).
Nye, Russell B. *The Cultural Life of the New Nation* (New York: Harper and Bros., 1960).
Nye, Russell B., and Norman Grabo. *American Thought and Writing: The Colonial Period* (Boston: Houghton Mifflin, 1965).
Peterson, Merill. *Thomas Jefferson and the New Nation: A Biography* (New York: Oxford University Press, 1970).
Takaki, Ronald. *Iron Cages: Race and Culture in 19th Century America* (Oxford, England: Oxford University Press, 1979).
Tyack, David. *Turning Points in American Educational History* (Waltham, Mass.: Blaisdell Publishing Co., 1967).
Woodson, Carter G. *The Education of the Negro prior to 1861* (New York: Arno Press, 1968).

CHAPTER 3

Bartlett, Irving H. *The American Mind in the Mid-Nineteenth Century* (New York: Thomas Y. Crowell, 1967).
Butts, Freeman, and Lawrence Cremin. *A History of Education in American Culture* (New York: Henry Holt, 1953).
Cremin, Lawrence (ed.). *The Republic and the School: Horace Mann on the Education of Free Men* (New York: Teachers College Press, 1957).
Finkelstein, Barbara. *Governing the Young: Teacher Behavior in Popular Primary Schools in 19th Century United States* (London: Falmer Press, 1989).
———. "Perfecting Childhood: Horace Mann and the Origins of Public Education in the United States," *Biography*, Vol. 13, No. 1, pp. 6–21.
Gutman, Herbert G. "Work, Culture, and Society in Industrializing America, 1815–1919" *The American Historical Review*, Vol. 78, No. 3 (June 1973), pp. 531–88.
Kaestle, Carl F. *Pillars of the Republic* (New York: Hill & Wang, 1983).
Kaestle, Carl F., and Maris A. Vinovskis. *Education and Social Change in Nineteenth Century Massachusetts* (Cambridge: Cambridge University Press, 1980).
Mann, Horace. *Lectures on Education* (Boston: Ide & Dutton, 1855).
Messerli, Jonathan. *Horace Mann: A Biography* (New York: Alfred A. Knopf, 1972).
Montgomery, David. "The Working Classes of the Pre-Industrial American City, 1780–1830," *Labor History*, Vol. 9 (Winter 1968), pp. 3–22.
Nasaw, David. *Schooled to Order: A Social History of Public Schooling in the United States* (New York: Oxford University Press, 1980).
Schultz, Stanley K. *The Culture Factory* (New York: Oxford, 1973).
Tyack, David. *The One Best System: A History of American Urban Education* (Cambridge, Mass.: Harvard University Press, 1974).

CHAPTER 4

Barrett, James R. *Work and Community in the Jungle* (Champaign: University of Illinois Press, 1987).
Bowles, Samuel, and Herbert Gintis. *Schooling in Capitalist America* (New York: Basic Books, 1976).
Brody, David. "The American Worker in the Progressive Age," in *The Worker in Industrial America: Essays on the Twentieth Century Struggle* (London: Oxford University Press, 1980).
Braverman, Harry. *Labor and Monopoly Capital* (New York: Monthly Review Press, 1974).
Callahan, Raymond E. *Education and the Cult of Efficiency* (Chicago: University of Chicago Press, 1962).
Cremin, Lawrence A. *The Transformation of the School* (New York: Vintage Books, 1961).
Dewey, John. *The Child and the Curriculum/The School and Society* (Chicago: The University of Chicago Press, 1968).
———. *Democracy and Education* (New York: Macmillan, 1916).
———. *Reconstruction in Philosophy* (Boston: Beacon Press, 1920, 1948).
Dinnerstein, Leonard, and David M. Reimers. *Ethnic Americans: A History of Immigration*, 3d ed. (New York: Harper and Row, 1988).
Eliot, Charles W. "The Function of Education in a Democratic Society," *Educational Reform* (New York: Century, 1898), pp. 401–18.
———, 1908. "Equality of Educational Opportunity," in Marvin Lazerson and W. Norton Grubb (eds.), *Ameri-*

can Education and Vocationalism (New York: Teachers College Press, 1974).

Graham, Patricia Albjerg. *Progressive Education: From Arcady to Academe* (New York: Teachers College Press, 1967).

Karier, Clarence J. "Psychological Conceptions of Man and Society," in C. J. Karier (ed.), *The Individual, Society, and Education* (Champaign: University of Illinois Press, 1986) pp. 150–83.

Karier, Clarence J., Paul C. Violas, and Joel Spring. *Roots of Crisis* (Chicago: Rand McNally, 1973).

Kessler-Harris, Alice. *Out of Work: A History of Wage-Earning Women in the United States* (New York: Oxford University Press, 1982).

Kolko, Gabriel. *The Triumph of Conservatism* (New York: Free Press, 1963).

Krug, Edward A. *The Shaping of the American High School: 1880–1929* (Madison: University of Wisconsin Press, 1969).

Pollack, Norman. *The Populist Response to Industrial America* (Cambridge, Mass.: Harvard University Press, 1962).

Raybeck, Joseph G. *A History of American Labor* (New York: Free Press, 1966).

Rury, John. *Education and Women's Work: Female Schooling and the Division of Labor in Urban America, 1870–1930* (Albany: State University of New York Press, 1991).

Stave, Bruce M. (ed.). *Urban Bosses, Machines, and Progressive Reformers* (Lexington, Mass.: D. C. Heath, 1972).

Tyack, David. *The One Best System: A History of American Urban Education* (Cambridge, Mass.: Harvard University Press, 1974).

______. "City Schools: Centralization of Control at the Turn of the Century," in Jerome Karabel and A. H. Halsey (eds.), *Power and Ideology in Education* (New York: Oxford University Press, 1977).

Violas, Paul. *The Training of the Urban Working Class* (Chicago: Rand McNally, 1978).

______. "Progressive Social Philosophy: Charles Horton Cooley and Edward Alsworth Ross," in Clarence Karier, Paul C. Violas, and Joel Spring (eds.), *Roots of Crisis* (Chicago: Rand McNally, 1973).

Weinstein, James. *The Decline of Socialism in America* (New York: Monthly Review Press, 1967).

Westbrook, Robert. *John Dewey and American Democracy* (Ithaca: Cornell University Press, 1991).

Wiebe, Robert. *The Search for Order* (New York: Hill and Wang, 1967).

CHAPTER 5

Cott, Nancy F. *The Bonds of Womanhood: "Woman's Sphere" in New England 1780–1835* (New Haven: Yale University Press, 1977).

Cott, Nancy F., and Elizabeth H. Pleck (eds.). *A Heritage of Her Own: Toward a New Social History of American Women* (New York: Simon and Schuster, 1979).

Gilman, Charlotte Perkins. *Herland* (New York: Pantheon Books, 1979). Originally published in serial form in 1915.

Maclear, Martha. *A History of the Education of Girls in New York and New England 1800–1870* (Washington, D.C.: Howard University Press, 1926).

McClellan, B. Edward, and William J. Reese. *The Social History of American Education* (Champaign: University of Illinois Press, 1988).

Nicholson, Linda J. *Gender and History: The Limits of Social Theory and the Age of the Family* (New York: Columbia University Press, 1986).

Pagels, Elaine. *Adam, Eve, and the Serpent* (New York: Random House, 1988).

Rowbotham, Sheila. *Hidden from History: Rediscovering Women in History from the 17th Century to the Present* (New York: Vintage Books, 1976).

Schneir, Miriam (ed.). *Feminism: The Essential Historical Writings* (New York: Vintage Books, 1972).

Sochen, June. *Herstory: A Woman's View of American History* (New York: Alfred Publishing, 1974).

Wertheimer, Barbara Mayer. *We Were There: The Story of Working Women in America* (New York: Pantheon Books, 1977).

Woody, Thomas. *A History of Women's Education in the United States,* Vol. 1 (New York: Science Press, 1929).

CHAPTER 6

Anderson, James D. *The Education of Blacks in the South 1860–1935* (Chapel Hill: University of North Carolina Press, 1988).

Bond, Horace Mann. *Negro Education in Alabama: A Study in Cotton and Steel* (New York: Atheneum, 1939).

Brawley, Benjamin G. *A Social History of the American Negro* (New York: Macmillan, 1921).

Curti, Merle. *The Social Ideas of American Educators* (New York: Charles Scribner's Sons, 1935).

Du Bois, W. E. B. *The Autobiography of W. E. B. Du Bois* (New York: International Publishers Co., 1968).

Foner, Eric. *Reconstruction: America's Unfinished Revolution, 1863–1877* (New York: Harper and Row, 1988).

Franklin, John Hope (ed.). *Three Negro Classics* (New York: Avon Books, 1965). (Contains *Up From Slavery,* the autobiography of Booker T. Washington, as well as Du Bois's *The Souls of Black Folk.*)

Harlan, Louis R. *Booker T. Washington: The Making of a Black Leader 1856–1901* (New York: Oxford University Press, 1972).

______. *Booker T. Washington: The Wizard of Tuskegee, 1901–1915* (New York: Oxford University Press, 1983).

———. *Separate and Unequal: Public School Campaigns and Racism in the Southern Seaboard States 1901–1915* (first published, 1958; reprint, New York: Atheneum, 1968).
Harlan, Louis R., Pete Daniel, Stuart B. Kaufman, Raymond W. Smock, and William M. Welty. *The Booker T. Washington Papers, Vol. 2, 1860–1889* (Champaign: University of Illinois Press, 1972).
Lewis, David L. *W. E. B. Du Bois 1868–1919: Biography of a Race* (New York: Holt, 1993).
Margo, Robert A. *Disenfranchisement, School Finance, and the Economics of Segregated Schools in the United States South, 1890–1910* (New York: Garland Publishing, 1985).
Norrell, Robert J. *Reaping the Whirlwind: The Civil Rights Movement in Tuskegee* (New York: Alfred A. Knopf, 1985).
Stampp, Kenneth M. *The Era of Reconstruction, 1865–1877* (New York: Vintage Books, 1965).
Tyack, David, Thomas James, and Aaron Benavot. *Law and the Shaping of Public Education 1785–1954* (Madison: University of Wisconsin Press, 1987).
Washington, Booker T. *My Larger Education: Being Chapters from My Experience* (Garden City, N.Y.: Doubleday and Page, 1911).
Wiener, Jonathan M. *Social Origins of the New South: Alabama, 1860–1885* (Baton Rouge: Louisiana State University Press, 1978), pp. 93–111.
Wolters, Raymond. *The New Negro on Campus: Black College Rebellions of the 1920s* (Princeton, N.J.: Princeton University Press, 1975).

CHAPTER 7

Beatty, Willard W. *Education for Action: Selected Articles from Indian Education 1936–43* (Washington, D.C.: U.S. Indian Service, 1944).
———. *Education for Cultural Change: Selected Articles from* Indian Education *1944–51* (Washington, D.C.: U.S. Indian Service, 1953).
Deloria, Vine, Jr. *God Is Red* (New York: Grosset and Dunlap, 1973).
———. *Behind the Trail of Broken Treaties* (New York: Dell, 1974).
Dippie, Brian W. *The Vanishing American: White Attitudes and U.S. Indian Policy* (Middletown, Conn.: Weslyan University Press, 1982).
Forbes, Jack. *Native Americans and Nixon* (Los Angeles: Native American Studies Center, 1983).
Hauptman, Laurence M. *The Iroquois and the New Deal* (Syracuse: Syracuse University Press, 1981).
Jennings, Francis. *The Invasion of America: Indians, Colonialism and the Cant of Conquest* (Chapel Hill: University of North Carolina Press, 1975).
Kehoe, Alice B. *North American Indians: A Comprehensive Account* (Englewood Cliffs, N.J.: Prentice Hall, 1981).
Levitan, Sar, and Barbara Hetrick. *Big-Brother's Indian Programs: With Reservations* (New York: McGraw-Hill, 1971).
McNickle, D'Arcy. *Native American Tribalism* (New York: Alfred A. Knopf, 1973).
McQuiston, John B., and Rodney Brod. "The Status, Educational Attainment, and Performance of Adult American Indian and Alaska Natives" (Philadelphia, Mich.: National Indian Management Service of America, Inc., 1981; ERIC, ED 237 249).
Philp, Kenneth R. *John Collier's Crusade for Indian Reform, 1920–1954* (Tucson: University of Arizona Press, 1977).
Prucha, Francis Paul. *The Great Father: The U.S. Government and the American Indians* (Lincoln: University of Nebraska Press, 1984).
Senese, Guy B. *Self Determination and the Social Education of Native Americans* (New York: Praeger Press, 1991).
Szasz, Margaret. *Education and the American Indian: The Road to Self-Determination since 1928* (Albuquerque: University of New Mexico Press, 1977).
Talbot, Steve. *Roots of Oppression: The American Indian Question* (New York: International Publishers, 1981).
Thompson, Laura, and Alice Joseph. *The Hopi Way* (Chicago: University of Chicago Press, 1944).
U.S. Commission on Civil Rights. *The Navajo Nation: An American Colony* (Washington, D.C.: U.S. Government Printing Office, 1975).
Vogel, Virgil (ed.). *This Country Was Ours: A Documentary History of the American Indian* (New York: Harper and Row, 1972).

In addition, an important source for Native-American perspective on contemporary social questions is contained in such tribal and pan-Indian publications as *Akwasasne Notes*, *Wassaja*, and the newspapers published by individual tribes.

CHAPTER 8

Bestor, Arthur, *Educational Wastelands* (Champaign: University of Illinois Press, 1953).
Conant, James B. *The Child, the Parent, and the State* (New York: McGraw-Hill, 1959).
———. *Education and Liberty* (Cambridge, Mass.: Harvard University Press, 1953).
———. *Education for a Classless Society* (Cambridge, Mass.: Harvard University Press, 1940).
———. *Education in a Divided World* (Cambridge, Mass.: Harvard University Press, 1948).

______. *My Several Lives* (New York: Harper and Row, 1970).

______. *Public Education and the Structure of American Society* (New York: Teachers College Press, 1945).

______. *Slums and Suburbs* (New York: McGraw-Hill, 1961).

______. *Thomas Jefferson and the Development of American Public Education* (Charlottesville: University of Virginia Press, 1963).

Cremin, Lawrence. *The Transformation of the School* (New York: Vintage Books, 1961).

Douglass, Paul. *Six upon the World* (Boston: Little, Brown, 1954).

General Education in a Free Society (Cambridge, Mass.: Harvard University Press, 1945).

Grissom, Thomas. "Education and the Cold War: James B. Conant," in Clarence Karier, Paul Violas, and Joel Spring (eds.), *Roots of Crisis* (Chicago: Rand McNally, 1973).

Lipset, Seymour Martin, and David Riesman. *Education and Politics at Harvard* (New York: McGraw-Hill, 1975).

McClellan, James. *Toward an Effective Critique of American Education* (Philadelphia: J. B. Lippincott, 1968).

Nairn, Allan. *The Reign of ETS* (Washington, D.C.: Ralph Nader Report on the Educational Testing Service, 1980).

Perkinson, Henry. *200 Years of American Educational Thought* (New York: Longman, 1976).

Ravitch, Diane. *The Troubled Crusade* (New York: Basic Books, 1983).

Scott, C. Winfield, and Clyde M. Hill. *Public Education under Criticism* (New York: Prentice Hall, 1954).

Zeran, Franklin (ed.). *Life Adjustment Education in Action* (New York: Chartwell House, 1953).

CHAPTER 9

Appiah, Kwame Anthony, and Henry Louis Gates, Jr. *The Dictionary of Global Culture.* (New York: Alfred A. Knopf, 1997).

Aronowitz, Stanley, and Henry Giroux. *Education under Siege: The Conservative, Liberal and Radical Debate over Schooling* (South Hadley, Mass.: Bergin & Garvey, 1985).

Bok, Derek. *The State of the Nation.* Cambridge: Harvard University Press, 1996).

Booth, Wayne. "Cultural History and Liberal Learning: An Open Letter to E. D. Hirsch," *Change,* Vol. 20, No. 4 (November 1984), pp. 16–21.

Brown, Richard D. *Knowledge is Power: The Diffusion of Information in Early America, 1700–1783* (Oxford, Eng.: Oxford University Press, 1989).

Cheney, Lynne E. *American Memory: A Report on the Humanities in the Nation's Schools* (Washington, D.C.: National Endowment for the Humanities Office of Publications, 1987).

Chomsky, Noam. *On Power and Ideology: The Managua Lectures* (Boston: South End, 1987).

De Castell, Suzanne, Allan Luke, and Kieran Egan (eds.). *Literacy, Society, and Schooling: A Reader* (Cambridge, Mass.: Cambridge University Press, 1986).

Dertouzos, Michael. *What Will Be: How the New World of Information Will Change Our Lives.* (New York: HarperCollins, 1997).

Ellul, Jacques. *Propaganda: The Formation of Men's Attitudes* (New York: Vintage Books, 1973).

Freire, Paulo. *Pedagogy of the Oppressed* (New York: Herder and Herder, 1972).

______. *The Politics of Education: Culture, Power, and Liberation* (South Hadley, Mass.: Bergin & Garvey, 1985).

Freire, Paulo, and Donaldo Macedo. *Literacy: Reading the Word and the World* (South Hadley, Mass.: Bergin & Garvey, 1987).

Giroux, Henry A. *Theory and Resistance in Education: A Pedagogy for the Opposition* (South Hadley, Mass.: Bergin & Garvey, 1983).

______. *Schooling and the Struggle for Public Life: Critical Pedagogy in the Modern Age* (Minneapolis: University of Minnesota Press, 1988).

______. *Teachers as Intellectuals: Toward a Critical Pedagogy of Learning* (South Hadley, Mass.: Bergin & Garvey, 1988).

Graff, Harvey J. *The Literacy Myth: Literacy and Social Structure in the Nineteenth-Century Cities* (New York: Academic Press, 1979).

______. *The Legacies of Literacy: Continuities and Contradictions in Western Culture and Society* (Bloomington: Indiana University Press, 1987).

Henry, Michael. "A True Test or a Trivia Game?" *Newsweek,* June 22, 1987, p. 11.

Hirsch, E.D., Jr., Joseph F. Kett, and James Trefil. *The Dictionary of Cultural Literacy, 2nd Ed.* (Boston: Houghton Mifflin, 1993).

Judy, Stephen N. *The ABCs of Literacy: A Guide for Parents and Educators* (New York: Oxford University Press, 1980).

Kirsch, Erwin S., Ann Jungeblut, Lynn Jenkins, and Andrew Kohlstad. *Adult Literacy in America* (Washington, D.C.: Educational Testing Service and National Center for Educational Statistics, 1993).

Kozol, Jonathan. *Illiterate America* (New York: Anchor Press/Doubleday, 1985).

Lankshear, Colin. "Humanizing Functional Literacy: Beyond Utilitarian Necessity," *Educational Theory,* Vol. 36 (Fall 1986), pp. 375–87.

National Coalition of Advocates for Students. *Barriers to Excellence: Our Children at Risk* (Boston: The National Coalition of Advocates for Students, 1985).

Shor, Ira. *Culture Wars: School and Society in the Conservative Restoration 1969–1984* (Boston: Routledge & Kegan Paul, 1986).

Takaki, Ronald. *A Different Mirror* (Boston: Little, Brown, 1993).

CHAPTER 10

Apple, M. *Teachers and Texts: A Political Economy of Class and Gender Relations in Education* (New York: Routledge and Kegan Paul, 1987).

Berman, Louise M. "The Teacher as Decision Maker," in Frances S. Bolin and Judith McConnell Falk (eds.), *Teacher Renewal: Professional Issues, Personal Choices* (New York: Teachers College Press, 1987).

Beyer, Landon, Walter Feinberg, Jo Anne Pagano, and James Anthony Whitson. *Preparing Teachers as Professionals: The Role of Educational Studies and Other Liberal Disciplines* (New York: Teachers College Press, 1989).

Biklen, S. K. "Confiding Woman: A Nineteenth-Century Teacher's Diary," *History of Education Review,* Vol. 19, No. 2 (1990), pp. 19–35.

Casey, Kathleen, and Michael W. Apple. "Gender and the Conditions of Teachers' Work: The Development of Understanding in America," in Sandra Acker (ed.), *Teachers, Gender, and Careers* (Philadelphia: Falmer Press, 1989), pp. 173–74.

Clifford, Geraldine Joncich. "Man/Woman/Teacher: Gender, Family and Career in American Educational History," in Donald Warren (ed.), *American Teachers: Histories of a Working Profession, AERA* (New York: Macmillan, 1989).

Goodlad, John. *Teachers for Our Nation's Schools* (San Francisco: Jossey-Bass, 1990).

Herbst, Jurgen. *And Sadly Teach: Teacher Education and Professionalization in American Culture* (Madison: University of Wisconsin Press, 1989).

Jackson, Philip W. *The Practice of Teaching* (New York: Teachers College Press, 1986).

Jackson, Philip W., Robert E. Boostrom, and David T. Hansen, *The Moral Life of Schools* (San Francisco: Jossey-Bass, 1993).

Johnson, William R. "Teachers and Teacher Training in the Twentieth Century," in Donald Warren (ed.), *American Teachers: History of a Profession at Work* (New York: Macmillan, 1989).

Laird, Susan. "Reforming 'Woman's True Profession': A Case of 'Feminist Pedagogy' in Teacher Education?" *Harvard Education Review,* Vol. 58, No. 4 (November 1988), pp. 449–63.

Langford, G. *Teaching as a Profession* (Manchester, Eng.: University Press, 1978).

Lortie, Dan. *Schoolteacher* (Chicago: University of Chicago Press, 1975).

Louis, Karen Seashore. "Social and Community Values and the Quality of Teachers' Work Life," in Milbrey W. McLaughlin, Joan E. Talbert, and Nina Bascia (eds.), *The Contexts of Teaching in Secondary Schools: Teacher's Realities* (New York: Teachers College Press, 1990), pp. 17–39.

Noddings, Nel. *Caring: A Feminine Approach to Ethics* (Berkeley: University of California Press, 1984).

Rubin, Louis J. *Artistry in Teaching* (New York: Random House, 1985).

Rury, John. "Who Became Teachers? The Social Characteristics of Teachers in American History," in Donald Warren (ed.), *American Teachers: Histories of a Working Profession, AERA* (New York: Macmillan, 1989).

Simon, Roger I. *Teaching against the Grain: Texts for a Pedagogy of Possibility* (New York: Bergin & Garvey, 1992).

Spencer, Dee Ann. *Contemporary Women Teachers: Balancing School and Home* (White Plains, N.Y.: Longman, 1986), p. 5.

Spring, Joel, *Conflict of Interests: The Politics of American Education* (White Plains, N.Y.: Longman, 1988).

______. *American Education: An Introduction to Social and Political Aspects,* 5th ed. (White Plains, N.Y.: Longman, 1991).

Tomorrow's Teachers. A Report of the Holmes Group (East Lansing: The Holmes Group, 1986).

Tozer, Steven, and Stuart McAninch. "Social Foundations of Education in Historical Perspective," *Educational Foundations,* Vol. 1, No. 1 (1986).

What Matters Most: Teaching for America's Future. (New York: National Commission for Teaching and America's Future, 1996). (Copies available from The National Commission on Teaching and America's Future, P.O. Box 5239, Woodbridge, Virginia, 22194-5239.)

Zeichner, Kenneth M. "Contradictions and Tensions in the Professionalization of Teaching and the Democratization of Schools," *Teachers College Record,* Vol. 92, No. 3 (Spring 1991).

CHAPTER 11

Bridges to Opportunity: Are Community Colleges Meeting the Transfer Needs of Minority Students? (New York: Academy for Educational Development and the College Board, 1989).

Dewey, John. "Vocational Aspects of Education," in *Democracy and Education* (New York: Free Press, 1966).

Grasso, John, and J. Shea. *Vocational Education and Training: Impact on Youth* (Berkeley: Carnegie Council on Policy Studies in Higher Education, 1979).

Grubb, W. Norton, ed. *Education Through Occupations in American High Schools, Volumes 1 and 2.* (New York: Teachers College Press, 1995).

Harvard Faculty Committee. *General Education in a Free Society* (Cambridge, Mass.: Harvard University Press, 1946).

Hirst, Paul. *Knowledge and the Curriculum* (London: Routledge and Kegan Paul, 1974).

Hoyt, Kenneth B. *Career Education* (Salt Lake City: Olympus, 1975).

Lankshear, Colin. *Freedom and Education* (Auckland: Milton Brookes Publications, 1982).

Lazerson, Marvin, and W. Norton Grubb. *American Education and Vocationalism: A Documentary History, 1870–1970* (New York: Teachers College Press, 1974).

Martin, Jane Roland. "Bringing Women into Educational Thought," *Educational Theory,* Vol. 34, No. 4 (1984).

National Academy of Sciences. *High Schools and the Changing Workplace: Employers' View* (Washington, D.C.: National Academy Press, 1984).

National Alliance of Business. *A Nation at Work: Education and the Private Sector* (Washington, D.C.: National Advisory Council on Vocational Education and National Alliance on Business, 1984).

______. *Employment Policies: Looking to the Year 2000* (Washington, D.C.: National Alliance on Business, 1986).

National Commission on Secondary Vocational Education. *The Unfinished Agenda: The Role of Vocational Education in the High School* (Columbus: National Center for Research in Vocational Education, 1984).

Neufeldt, Harvey G. "The Community Junior College Movement: Conflicting Images and Historical Interpretations," *Educational Studies,* Vol. 13, No. 2 (Summer 1982), pp. 172–82.

Pincus, Fred L. "False Promises of Community Colleges: Class Conflict and Vocational Education," *Harvard Education Review,* Vol. 50, No. 3 (August 1980).

Rodriguez, Ester M. and Sandra S. Ruppert *Postsecondary Education and the New Workforce.* (State Higher Education Executive Officers. U.S. Department of Education Office of Educational Research and Improvement: Washington, D. C. 1996).

Reports on the Course of Instruction in Yale College, by a Committee of the Corporation, and the Academical Faculty (New Haven: Yale University Press, 1828).

Rich, Adrienne. "Claiming an Education," in Adrienne Rich, *On Lies, Secrets and Silence* (New York: Norton, 1977).

Serrin, William. "A Great American Job Machine?" *The Nation,* September 18, 1989, pp. 270–71.

Shapiro, Svi. "Schools, Work and Consumption: Education and the Cultural Contradictions of Capitalism," *Journal of Educational Thought,* Vol. 17, No. 3 (December 1983).

Tozer, Steven, and Robert Nelson. "Implications of the Holmes Agenda for Emerging Paradigms in Vocational Education," in Mildred Griggs (ed.), *Proceedings of the Rupert Evans Symposium on Vocational Education: 1988* (Champaign: University of Illinois, 1989).

Van Doren, Mark. *Liberal Education* (Boston: Beacon Hill, 1943).

Violas, Paul C. "Reflecting on Human Capital Theories, Skill Training, and Vocational Education," *Educational Theory,* Vol. 31, No. 2 (Spring 1981).

Wigginton, Eliot. *Sometimes a Shining Moment* (New York: Doubleday, 1986).

Wirth, Arthur. "Contemporary Work and the Quality of Life," in Kenneth D. Benne and Steven Tozer (eds.), *Society as Educator in an Age of Transition: Eighty-Sixth Yearbook of the National Society for the Study of Education* (Chicago: National Society for the Study of Education, 1987).

______. *Education and Work for the Year 2000: Choices We Face* (San Francisco: Jossey-Bass, 1992).

Woodward, W. H. *Vittorino DeFeltre and Other Humanist Educators* (New York: Teachers College Press, 1963).

Work in America: A Report by the U.S. Department of Health, Education and Welfare (Cambridge, Mass.: MIT Press, 1973).

CHAPTERS 12 and 13

The American Almanac 1996-97: Statistical Abstract of the United States. (Austin, Texas: Hoover's, Inc., 1997).

American Association of University Women. *How Schools Shortchange Girls* (Wellesley, Mass.: American Association of University Women Educational Foundation and National Education Association, 1992).

Anyon, Jean. "Social Class and School Knowledge," in *Curriculum Inquiry* (Ontario: John Wiley & Sons, 1981).

Asian American Handbook (Chicago: National Conference of Christians and Jews, Asian American Journalists Association, and Association of Asian Pacific American Artists, 1991), pp. 9–73.

Baldwin, James. "If Black English Isn't a Language, Then Tell Me What Is?" *The Price of the Ticket: Collected Nonfiction 1948–1985* (New York: St. Martin's Press, 1985).

Banks, James. "It's Up to Us," *Teaching Tolerance,* Fall 1992, p. 21.

Bastion, Ann, et al. *Choosing Equality* (New York: New World Foundation, 1985).

Bolinger, D., and D. A. Sears. *Aspects of Language* (New York: Harcourt Brace Jovanovich, 1981).

Bowles, Samuel, and Henry Levin. "The Determinants of Scholastic Achievement," *Journal of Human Resources,* Vol. 2 (Winter 1968), pp. 3–25.

Casanova, Ursula and M. Beatriz Arias, "Contextualizing Bilingual Education" in *Bilingual Education: Politics, Practice, and Research;* Ninety-second Yearbook of the National Society for the Study of Education Part II. (Chicago: NSSE, 1993).

Cashmore, Ellis (1996). *Dictionary of Race and Ethnic Relations, Fourth Edition.* (London and New York: Routledge).

Chan, Sucheng. *Asian Americans: An Interpretive History.* (New York: Twayne Publishers, 1991).

Committee on Policy for Racial Justice. *Visions of a Better Way: A Black Appraisal of Public Schooling* (Washington, D.C.: Joint Center for Political Studies Press, 1989).

Daniels, Roger. *Asian America: Chinese and Japanese in the United States since 1850* (Seattle: University of Washington Press, 1988).

Deloria, Vine. "Education and Imperialism," *Integrateducation,* Vol. 19, Nos. 1–2 (1981), p. 59.

Duffy, John. "Getting Off Track: The Challenge and Potential of the Mixed Ability Classroom," *Democracy and Education* (Fall 1988).

Edelman, Marian Wright. *Families in Peril—An Agenda for Social Change* (Cambridge, Mass.: Harvard University Press, 1987).

Fickett, Joan G. "Tense and Aspect in Black English," *Journal of English Linguistics,* Vol. 6, Nos. 17–19 (1972), p. 19. The quote referred to appears in Bolinger and Sears, p. 198.

Giroux, Henry A. *Teachers as Intellectuals* (Granby, Mass.: Bergin & Garvey, 1988).

Hochschild, Jennifer. *Thirty Years after Brown* (Washington, D.C.: Joint Center for Policy Studies, 1985), p. 3.

Hornbeck, David W., and Lester M. Salamon (eds.). *Human Capital and American's Future* (Baltimore: Johns Hopkins Press, 1991).

Jackson, Allyn. "Minorities in Mathematics: A Focus on Excellence, Not Remediation," *American Educator,* Spring 1989.

Jencks, Christopher, et al. *Inequality: A Reassessment of the Effect of Family and Schooling in America* (New York: Harper and Row, 1973).

Jensen, Arthur. "How Much Can We Boost Scholastic Achievement and I.Q.?" *Harvard Educational Review,* Vol. 39, No. 1 (1969).

———. "Political Ideologies and Educational Research," *Phi Delta Kappan,* Vol. 65, No. 7 (March 1984), pp. 460–62.

Karier, Clarence. "Testing for Order and Control in the Corporate Capitalist State," *Educational Theory,* Vol. 22 (Spring 1972), pp. 154–80.

Michael S. Knapp and Associates, *Teaching for Meaning in High Poverty Classrooms* (New York: Teachers College Press, 1995).

Labov, William. "Academic Ignorance and Black Intelligence," *The Atlantic,* Vol. 229, No. 6 (June 1972), pp. 59–67.

Lee, Joann Faung Jean. *Asian Americans: Oral Histories of First to Fourth Generation Americans from China, the Philippines, Japan, India, the Pacific Islands, Vietnam and Cambodia* (New York: The New Press, 1992).

Little, Judith Warren, and Milbrey Wallin McLaughlin (eds.). *Teachers' Work: Individuals, Colleagues, and Contexts* (New York: Teachers College Press, 1993).

Martin, Jane Roland. *Reclaiming a Conversation* (New Haven: Yale University Press, 1985).

Martin, Jane Roland. "Bringing Women into Educational Thought," *Educational Theory,* Vol. 34, No. 4 (Fall 1984), p. 349.

National Coalition of Advocates for Students. *Barriers to Excellence: Our Children At Risk* (Boston: National Coalition of Advocates for Students, 1985).

Oakes, Jeanne. *Keeping Track: How Schools Structure Inequality* (New Haven: Yale University Press, 1985).

Oakes, Jeannie, Amy Stuart Wells, Makeba Jones, and Amanda Datnow, "Detracking: the Social Construction of Ability, Cultural Politics, and Resistance to Reform." *Teachers College Record.* 98:3 Spring 1997. 482–510.

Ogbu, John U. "Minority Status and Schooling in Plural Societies," *Comparative Education Review,* Vol. 27, No. 2, pp. 168–90.

Okihiro, Gary Y. *Margins and Mainstream: Asians in American History and Culture* (Seattle: University of Washington Press, 1994).

Orfield, Gary Y. "Separate Societies: Have the Kerner Warnings Come True?" in F. R. Harris and R. W. Wilkins (eds.), *Quiet Riots—Race and Poverty in the United States* (New York: Pantheon Books, 1988), pp. 106–110.

Orr, Eleanor Wilson. *Twice As Less* (New York: W. W. Norton, 1987).

Owen, David. *None of the Above* (New York: Houghton-Mifflin, 1985).

Peters, William. *A Class Divided—Then and Now* (New Haven: Yale University Press, 1987).

Riley, Patricia. *Growing Up Native American: An Anthology* (New York: William Morrow, 1993).

Rist, Ray C. "Student Social Class and Teacher Expectations," *Harvard Review,* Vol. 40, No. 3 (August 1970).

Rose, Stephen J. *The American Profile* (New York: Pantheon, 1986).

Schlesinger, Arthur M., Jr. *The Disuniting of America: Reflections on a Multicultural Society* (New York: W. W. Norton, 1992).

Skrtic, Thomas M. "The Special Education Paradox: Equity as the Way to Excellence," *Harvard Educational Review*, Vol. 61, No. 2 (May 1991), pp. 148–206.

Sleeter, Christine, and Carl A. Grant. *Making Choices for Multicultural Education: Five Approaches to Race, Class, and Gender* (Columbus: Merrill, 1988).

The State of Asian Pacific America: Policy Issues of the Year 2020 (1993). (Los Angeles: LEAP Asian Pacific American Public Policy Institute and UCLA Asian American Studies Center).

Taylor, Lottie L., and Joan R. Pinard. "Success against the Odds: Effective Education of Inner-City Youth in a New York City Public High School," *Journal of Negro Education*, Vol. 57, No. 3 (1988), pp. 347–61.

Terman, Lewis M. *Intelligence Tests and School Reorganization* (New York: World Book, 1923).

Tozer, Steven. "Elite Power and Democratic Ideals," in Kenneth D. Benne and Steven Tozer (eds.), *Society as Educator in an Age of Transition: Eighty-Sixth Yearbook of the National Society for the Study of Education* (Chicago: National Society for the Study of Education, 1987).

Weiner, Lois. *Preparing Teachers for Urban Schools: Lessons from Thirty Years of School Reform* (New York: Teachers College Press, 1993).

Weis, Lois. *Class, Race and Gender in American Education* (Albany: State University of New York Press, 1988).

Weis, Lois, and Michelle Fine (eds.). *Beyond Silenced Voices: Class, Race, and Gender in United States Schools* (Albany: State University of New York Press, 1993).

West, Cornel. *Race Matters.* Boston: Beacon Press, 1993.

Wilson, R., and S. E. Melendez. *Second Annual Report on the Status of Minorities in Higher Education* (Washington, D.C.: Office of Minority Concerns, American Council on Education, 1991).

CHAPTER 14

America 2000: An Education Strategy (Washington, D.C.: U.S. Department of Education, 1991).

Association for Supervision and Curriculum Development. *School Reform Policy: A Call for Reason* (Alexandria, Va.: ASCD, 1986).

Bacharach, Samuel B. (ed). *Education Reform: Making Sense of It All* (Boston: Allyn and Bacon, 1990).

Boyer, Ernest L. "Elementary and Secondary Education," in D. W. Hornbeck and L. M. Salamon (eds.), *Human Capital and America's Future* (Baltimore: Johns Hopkins University Press, 1991), pp. 171–92.

Business–Higher Education Forum. *America's Competitive Challenge: The Need for a National Response* (Washington, D.C., 1983).

Darling-Hammond, Linda. "Achieving Our Goals: Superficial or Structural Reforms?" *Phi Delta Kappan*, December 1990.

Firestone, William A., Susan H. Fuhrman, and Michael W. Kirst. *The Progress of Reform: An Appraisal of State Education Initiatives* (Center for Policy Research in Education, 1990), pp. 7–16.

Fullan, Michael G. Turning Systemic Thinking On Its Head. *Phi Delta Kappan*, 77:6 (February 1996), pp. 420–23.

Goodlad, John I. *A Place Called School: Prospects for the Future* (New York: McGraw-Hill, 1983).

Haberman, Martin. The Top Ten Fantasies of School Reformers. *Phi Delta Kappan*, 75:9 (May 1994), pp. 689–692.

Hill, David. "What Has the 1980s School Reform Movement Accomplished?" *Teacher Magazine*, Vol. 1 (September–October 1989), pp. 50–55.

Hodgkinson, Harold. "Reform versus Reality," *Phi Delta Kappan*, Vol. 73, No. 1 (September 1991), pp. 9–16.

Karp, Stan. "Bush Plan Abandons School," *Rethinking Schools*, Vol. 6, No. 1 (October–November, 1991).

Kirst, Michael W. "Recent State Education Reform in the United States: Looking Backward and Forward," *Educational Administration Quarterly*, Vol. 24 (August 3, 1988), pp. 319–28.

______. "Recent State Education Reform in the United States: Looking Backward and Forward," in S. B. Bacharach (ed.), *Education Reform: Making Sense of It All* (Boston: Allyn and Bacon, 1990).

Lightfoot, Sara Lawrence. *The Good High School: Portraits of Character and Culture* (New York: Basic Books, 1983).

Margonis, Frank. "What Is the Meaning of Contemporary Educational Nationalism?" in James M. Giarelli (ed.), *Philosophy of Education 1988: Proceedings of the Forty-Fourth Annual Meeting of the Philosophy of Education Society* (Normal, Ill.: Philosophy of Education Society, 1989), pp. 343–52.

National Coalition of Advocates for Children. *Barriers to Excellence: Our Children at Risk* (Boston, 1985).

National Commission on Excellence in Education. *A Nation at Risk: The Imperative for Educational Reform* (Washington, D.C.: Government Printing Office, 1983).

Passow, A. Harry. "Present and Future Directions in School Reform," in Thomas J. Sergiovanni and John H. Moore (eds.), *Schooling for Tomorrow: Directing Reforms to Issues That Count* (Boston: Allyn and Bacon, 1989), pp. 13–39.

———. "Whither (or Wither?) School Reform?" in Samuel B. Bacharach (ed.), *Education Reform: Making Sense of It All* (Boston: Allyn and Bacon, 1990).

Public Policy and School Reform: A Research Summary. Consortium for Policy Research in Education. Report #36 (Philadelphia: University of Pennsylvania, 1996).

Raywid, Mary Anne, Charles Tesconi, and Donald Warren. *Pride and Promise: Schools of Excellence for All the People* (Wesburg, N.Y.: American Educational Studies Association, 1984).

Shea, Christine M. "Pentagon vs. Multinational Capitalism: The Political Economy of the 1980s School Reform Movement," in Christine M. Shea, Ernest Kahane, and Peter Sola (eds.), *The New Servants of Power: A Critique of the 1980s School Reform Movement* (New York: Praeger, 1989), pp. 3–36.

Shea, Christine M., Ernest Kahane, and Peter Sola. *The New Servants of Power: A Critique of the 1980s School Reform Movement* (New York: Praeger, 1989).

Sizer, Theodore R. *Horace's Compromise: The Dilemma of the American High School* (Boston: Houghton Mifflin, 1984).

Stedman, Lawrence C. "Deep Achievement Problems: The Case for Reform Still Stands." *Educational Researcher* (April 1997), pp. 27–29.

Task Force on Education for Economic Growth. *Action for Excellence: A Comprehensive Plan to Improve our Nation's Schools* (Denver: Education Commission of the States, 1983).

Toch, Thomas. *In the Name of Excellence* (New York: Oxford University Press, 1991).

Tyack, David. " 'Restructuring' in Historical Perspective: Tinkering toward Utopia," *Teachers College Record,* Vol. 92, No. 2 (Winter 1990), pp. 170–91.

Urbanski, Adam. "Forces That Undermine Reform: A Teacher's Perspective," *American Educator,* Spring 1986, p. 18.

Voices from the Field: 30 Expert Opinions on America 2000, The Bush Administration Strategy to "Reinvent" America's Schools (Washington, D.C.: William T. Grant Foundation Commission on Work, Family and Citizenship and Institute for Educational Leadership, 1991), pp. 7–8.

Yudof, Mark G. "Educational Policy Research and the New Consensus of the 1980s," *Phi Delta Kappan* (March 1984), pp. 456–59.

CHAPTER 15

Central Park East Secondary School. *The Promise* (New York: Author, 1988).

Davis, W., and E. McCaul, "The Emerging Crisis: Current and Projected Status of Children in the United States." Monograph (Orono: University of Maine, 1991).

Democracy and Education. A journal for teachers, published quarterly by the Institute for Democracy and Education (McCracken Hall, Ohio University, Athens, OH 45701).

Ellsworth, Elizabeth. "Why Doesn't This Feel Empowering? Working through the Repressive Myths of Critical Pedagogy," *Harvard Educational Review,* Vol. 59 (1989), pp. 297–324.

Fairtest Examiner. A newsletter on alternatives to standardized testing (National Center for Fair and Open Testing, Box 1272, Harvard Square Station, Cambridge, MA 02238).

Ginsburg, Mark. *Contradictions in Teacher Education and Society: A Critical Analysis* (Lewes, England: Falmer Press, 1988).

Giroux, Henry A. "Educational Leadership and the Crisis of Democratic Government," *Educational Researcher,* Vol. 21, No. 4 (May 1992).

———. *Teachers as Intellectuals: Toward a Critical Pedagogy of Learning* (South Hadley, Mass.: Bergin & Garvey, 1988).

Hands On. A journal for teachers, published quarterly by the Foxfire Teachers Outreach (c/o Hilton Smith, Rabun Gap, GA 30568).

Kozol, Jonathan. *Savage Inequalities* (New York: Crown Publishers, 1991).

Mattera, Philip. *Prosperity Lost* (New York: Addison-Wesley, 1991).

Newman, Fred, and Don Archibald. *Beyond Standardized Testing* (Reston, Virginia: National Association of Secondary School Principals, 1988).

Rethinking Schools. A newsformat journal for teachers (1001 East Keefe Avenue, Milwaukee, WI 53212).

Schubert, William H. *Curriculum: Perspective, Paradigm, and Possibility* (New York: Macmillan, 1986).

Shapiro, Andrew L. *We're Number One* (New York: Vintage Books, 1992).

Waks, Leonard, and Rustum Roy. "Learning from Technology," in Kenneth D. Benne and Steven Tozer (eds.), *Society as Educator in an Age of Transition: Eighty-Sixth Yearbook of the National Society for the Study of Education* (Chicago: National Society for the Study of Education, 1987).

Wiggenton, Eliot. *Foxfire: 25 Years* (Garden City, N.Y.: Doubleday, 1991).

Wood, George H. *Schools That Work* (New York: Dutton, 1992).

Photo Credits

Chapter 1

4: Robert Finken/The Picture Cube

Chapter 2

19: North Wind Picture Archives. **22:** Library of Congress. **26:** The Granger Collection. **36:** Culver Pictures.

Chapter 3

49: Culver Pictures. **54:** National Portrait Gallery/Smithsonian Institution. **64:** Culver Pictures. **66:** Culver Pictures. **68:** The Bettmann Archive. **68:** The Bettmann Archive.

Chapter 4

84: Lewis W. Hine/Collection, International Museum of Photography at George Eastman House. **90:** Metropolitan Life Insurance. **93:** AP/Wide World Photos. **101:** The Granger Collection. **106:** Office of Public Information, Columbia University.

Chapter 5

124: UPI/Bettmann. **126:** The Bettmann Archive. **129:** The Bettmann Archive. **131:** The Bettmann Archive. **131:** The Bettmann Archive. **137:** The Granger Collection. **141:** Corbis Bettmann.

Chapter 6

155: The Bettmann Archive. **161:** The Bettmann Archive. **168:** National Portrait Gallery, London. **170:** North Wind Picture Archives. **173:** Library of Congress.

Chapter 7

194: (left) Courtesy of the American Museum of Natural History. **194: (right)** Culver Pictures. **196:** The Bettmann Archive. **200:** Culver Pictures. **204:** The Bettmann Archive.

Chapter 8

221: Tom McHugh/Photo Archive. **223:** The Bettmann Archive. **225:** UPI/Bettmann. **229:** Arthur Grace/Stock, Boston.

Chapter 9

247: Elizabeth Crews/Stock, Boston. **252:** The Bettmann Archive. **261:** Eric A. Roth/The Picture Cube. **265:** Spencer Grant/The Picture Cube.

Chapter 10

289: North Wind Picture Archives. **291:** Doug Plummer/Photo Researchers. **301:** Elizabeth Crews. **302:** Kathy Sloane/Photo Researchers.

Chapter 11

333: Nita Winter/The Image Works. **338:** Rick Freidman/The Picture Cube. **347:** Robert Finken/The Picture Cube. **349:** AP/Wide World Photos.

Chapter 12

367: UPI/Bettmann. **378:** Joel Gordon. **380:** Alan Carey/The Image Works.

Chapter 13

408: Sybil Shelton/Monkmeyer. **410:** Elizabeth Crews. **420:** Elizabeth Crews.

Chapter 14

448: Elizabeth Crews/Stock, Boston. **459:** The Bettmann Archive.

Index